clinical psychiatry for medical students

J.B. LIPPINCOTT COMPANY
Philadelphia

Grand Rapids   *New York*   *St. Louis*   *San Francisco*
London   *Sydney*   *Tokyo*

clinical psychiatry for medical students

Edited by

alan stoudemire, m.d.

Associate Professor
Director, Medical Student Education in Psychiatry
Department of Psychiatry
Emory University School of Medicine
Atlanta, Georgia

47 CONTRIBUTORS

Acquisitions Editor: Lisa McAllister
Sponsoring Editor: Paula Callaghan
Project Editor: Tracy Resnik
Art Director: Susan Hess Blaker
Designer: Doug Smock
Indexer: Ruth Elwell
Copyeditors: Patrick O'Kane, Gail Turner, Wendy Walker
Production Manager: Helen Ewan
Production Coordinator: Kathryn Rule
Compositor: Circle Graphics
Printer/Binder: R.R. Donnelley and Sons Company
Cover Printer: New England Book Components, Inc.

6   5   4   3   2   1

Library of Congress Cataloging in Publication Data
Clinical psychiatry for medical students/edited by Alan Stoudemire;
  45 contributors.
      p.   cm.
  Includes bibliographical references.
  ISBN 0-397-50972-3
  1. Psychiatry.   I. Stoudemire, Alan.
  [DNLM: 1. Mental Disorders. 2. Psychophysiologic Disorders.   WM
100 C641]
RC454.C539   1990
616.89—dc20
DNLM/DLC
for Library of Congress   89–13619
                                                          CIP

The authors and publisher have exerted every effort to ensure that drug selection and dosage set forth in this text are in accord with current recommendations and practice at the time of publication. However, in view of ongoing research, changes in government regulations, and the constant flow of information relating to drug therapy and drug reactions, the reader is urged to check the package insert for each drug for any change in indications and dosage and for added warnings and precautions. This is particularly important when the recommended agent is a new or infrequently employed drug.

Accompanying text:

Human Behavior: An Introduction for Medical Students
Edited by Alan Stoudemire, M.D.

This book is dedicated to Susan, Anna, and Will

Disease in man is never exactly the same as disease in an experimental animal, for in man the disease at once affects and is affected by what we call the emotional life. Thus, the physician who attempts to take care of a patient while he neglects this factor is as unscientific as the investigator who neglects to control all the conditions that may affect his experiment. The good physician knows his patients through and through, and his knowledge is bought dearly. Time, sympathy, and understanding must be lavishly dispensed, but the reward is to be found in that personal bond which forms the greatest satisfaction of the practice of medicine. One of the essential qualities of the clinician is interest in humanity, for the secret of the care of the patient is in caring for the patient.

Francis Peabody, *The Care of the Patient*
Journal of the American Medical Association 88:882, 1927

CONTRIBUTORS

David Abrams, *Ph.D.*

Associate Professor of Psychiatry and Human Behavior, Brown University, Director, Division of Behavioral Medicine, The Miriam Hospital, Providence, Rhode Island

Jerry Carter, *M.D.*

Assistant Professor of Psychiatry and Internal Medicine, Medical College of Pennsylvania; Staff Psychiatrist, Allegheny Neuropsychiatric Institute, Pittsburgh, Pennsylvania

Dennis S. Charney, *M.D.*

Associate Professor of Psychiatry, Yale University School of Medicine, West Haven, Connecticut

CDR Alberto Diaz, Jr., MC, *USNR*

Assistant Professor in Psychiatry, Uniformed Services University of the Health Sciences, Department of Psychiatry, Naval Hospital, 29 Palms, California

William R. Dubin, *M.D.*

Deputy Medical Director, Philadelphia Psychiatric Center, Professor of Psychiatry, Temple University School of Medicine, Philadelphia, Pennsylvania

Mina K. Dulcan, *M.D.*

Associate Professor of Psychiatry, Chief, Child and Adolescent Psychiatry, Emory University School of Medicine, Atlanta, Georgia

Peter J. Fagan, *Ph.D.*

Assistant Professor of Medical Psychology, Department of Psychiatry and Behavioral Sciences, Johns Hopkins University School of Medicine, Baltimore, Maryland

Donald C. Fidler, *M.D.*

Associate Professor of Psychiatry, West Virginia University School of Medicine, Morgantown, West Virginia

David G. Folks, *M.D.*

Associate Professor of Psychiatry, University of Alabama School of Medicine, Birmingham, Alabama

Charles V. Ford, *M.D.*

Professor of Psychiatry, University of Arkansas for Medical Sciences, Little Rock, Arkansas

Allan J. Frances, *M.D.*

Professor of Psychiatry, Cornell University Medical College, New York, New York

Mark G. Fuller, *M.D.*

Assistant Professor of Psychiatry, West Virginia University School of Medicine, Morgantown, West Virginia

Richard J. Goldberg, *M.D.*

Associate Professor, Departments of Psychiatry and Medicine, Brown University, Psychiatrist in Chief, Rhode Island Hospital and Women & Infants Hospital, Providence, Rhode Island

Michael G. Goldstein, *M.D.*

Assistant Professor of Psychiatry and Human Behavior, Brown University Program in Medicine, Providence, Rhode Island

Barrie J. Guise, *Ph.D.*

Clinical Assistant Professor of Psychiatry and Human Behavior, Brown University Program in Medicine, Providence, Rhode Island

Robert Hales, *M.D.*

Clinical Professor, Psychiatry, University of California, San Francisco; Chair, Department of Psychiatry, Pacific Presbyterian Medical Center, San Francisco, California

Carl A. Houck, M.D.

Assistant Professor of Psychiatry, Division of Consultation-Liaison Psychiatry, University of Alabama-Birmingham, Birmingham, Alabama

Mark E. James, M.D.

Assistant Professor of Psychiatry, Emory University School of Medicine, Atlanta, Georgia

Roger G. Kathol, M.D.

Associate Professor of Psychiatry and Internal Medicine, University of Iowa, Iowa City, Iowa

Wayne J. Katon, M.D.

Associate Professor and Chief, Division of Consultation Liaison Psychiatry, Department of Psychiatry and Behavior Sciences, University of Washington Medical School, Seattle, Washington

John H. Krystal, M.D.

Director of Clinical Research, Psychiatry Service, West Haven Veterans Administration Medical Center, Assistant Professor, Department of Psychiatry, Yale University School of Medicine, West Haven, Connecticut

James L. Levenson, M.D.

Associate Professor of Psychiatry and Medicine and Chairman, Division of Consultant Liason Psychiatry, Medical College of Virginia, Commonwealth University, Richmond, Virginia

Steven T. Levy, M.D.

Professor, Emory University School of Medicine and Chief of Psychiatry, Grady Memorial Hospital, Atlanta, Georgia

Rosalind M. Mance, M.B.B.S.

Assistant Professor, Grady Department of Psychiatry, Emory University Medical School, Atlanta, Georgia

Deborah B. Marin, M.D.

Readers Digest Fellow and Instructor of Psychiatry, Cornell University Medical College, New York, New York

Michael G. Moran, M.D.

Assistant Professor of Psychiatry and Medicine, University of Colorado School of Medicine, Denver, Colorado

William D. Murphy, Ph.D.

Associate Professor, Department of Psychiatry, University of Tennessee/Memphis—The Health Science Center, Memphis, Tennessee

Linda M. Nagy, M.D.

Assistant Professor of Psychiatry, Yale University, Chief, Anxiety and Post Traumatic Stress Disorder Clinic, West Haven Veterans Administration Hospital, West Haven, Connecticut

Philip T. Ninan, M.D.

Associate Professor of Psychiatry, Emory University School of Medicine, Atlanta, Georgia

Michael A. Raciti, Ph.D.

Clinical Assistant Professor, Department of Psychiatry and Human Behavior, Brown University Program in Medicine, Providence, Rhode Island

Quentin R. Regestein, M.D.

Director, Sleep Clinic, Brigham and Women's Hospital, Boston, Massachusetts, Associate Professor of Psychiatry, Harvard Medical School, Boston, Massachusetts

S. Craig Risch, M.D.

Professor, Department of Psychiatry, Emory University School of Medicine, Atlanta, Georgia

Emile D. Risby, M.D.

Assistant Professor, Department of Psychiatry, Emory University School of Medicine, Atlanta, Georgia

Laurie Ruggiero, Ph.D.

Assistant Professor of Psychiatry (Research), Brown University Program in Medicine, Rhode Island Hospital, Providence, Rhode Island

Chester W. Schmidt, Jr., M.D.

Associate Professor of Psychiatry, The Johns Hopkins School of Medicine, Baltimore, Maryland

Elizabeth D. Schwarz, *M.D.*

Director of Residency Training, University of Tennessee, Memphis, Tennessee

Edward K. Silberman, *M.D.*

Associate Professor and Director at Residency Training in Psychiatry, Medical College of Pennsylvania, Philadelphia, Pennsylvania

Jonathan M. Silver, *M.D.*

Assistant Professor of Clinical Psychiatry, College of Physicians and Surgeons of Columbia University, Director of Neuropsychiatry, Presbyterian Hospital, New York, New York

Robert M. Swift, *M.D., Ph.D.*

Assistant Professor of Psychiatry and Human Behavior, Brown University, Providence, Rhode Island

Robert J. Ursano, *M.D.*

Professor, Associate Chairman, Uniformed Services University of Health Sciences, Bethesda, Maryland

Edward A. Walker, *M.D.*

Assistant Professor, Department of Psychiatry, Adjunct Assistant Professor, Department of Family Medicine, University of Washington, Seattle, Washington

Thomas A. Widiger, *Ph.D.*

Associate Professor of Psychology, University of Kentucky, Lexington, Kentucky

Joel Yager, *M.D.*

Professor, Department of Psychiatry and Biobehavior Sciences, University of California at Los Angeles, Los Angeles, California

William R. Yates, *M.D.*

Assistant Professor of Psychiatry, University of Iowa College of Medicine, Iowa City, Iowa

Stuart C. Yudofsky, *M.D.*

Professor and Chairman, Department of Psychiatry, University of Chicago School of Medicine, Chicago, Illinois

FOREWORD

Why should medical students study psychiatry? One may give several cogent answers to this question.

Firstly, psychological factors play a significant contributory role in the etiology, course, response to and compliance with treatment, and outcome of every physical illness. The American Board of Internal Medicine has formulated the criteria for clinical competence, one of which is the ability to "Recognize and be attentive to the patients' emotional needs and recognize their potential influence on the symptoms and course of the illness." An understanding of the psychosocial aspects of physical illness has been a major contribution of the behavioral sciences, including psychiatry, to the practice of clinical medicine. Awareness of how patients respond to such illness—cognitively, emotionally, and behaviorally—and how such responses modify its course and outcome, constitutes an indispensable aspect of a competent physician's knowledge and attitude.

Secondly, epidemiologic studies have amply documented the positive statistical association between medical and psychiatric morbidity. The term *comorbidity* has come into use in recent years and refers to the coexistence of a physical and psychiatric illness. Such comorbidity is common, notably in elderly patients, and calls for proper medical and psychiatric diagnosis as well as treatment of both of the associated conditions.

Thirdly, studies have shown that a substantial proportion of patients who seek general medical care do so for emotional rather than medical reasons, and the majority of those given a psychiatric diagnosis present with somatic symptoms that lack a relevant pathologic basis. This tendency to complain of somatic rather than psychologic symptoms, or somatization, constitutes a common problem in all medical practice settings. Patients who display this tendency most often suffer from a depressive or an anxiety disorder or both, and it is essential for the physician to be able to recognize and treat the psychiatric disorder appropriately.

And fourthly, some patients who suffer from a physical, say cerebral, disease may present to the physician with what may appear to be a purely mental disorder. It is thus important for a physician to be familiar with psychiatric modes of presentation of physical illness. For example, an elderly patient may initially present with delirium as the only manifestation of myocardial infarction or pneumonia. It follows that every physician needs to be able to diagnose delirium, an organic mental syndrome, and start investigations at once to determine its underlying organic cause.

The above four major reasons provide ample justification for the study of psychiatry and familiarity with a whole range of psycho-pathological syndromes as well as with the psychosocial reactions to physical illness and injury. This textbook of clinical psychiatry fulfills admirably its intended purpose of providing a medical student and future physician with the basic knowledge of this subject. Its comprehensive coverage of the psychiatric syndromes and of the principles of psychiatric treatments, both biological and psychological, helps prepare the student to diagnose and treat conditions that will comprise a major portion of his or her future clinical practice.

Z.J. Lipowski, M.D., F.R.C.P.(C), Dr. Med. (HON)
Professor of Consultation-Liaison Psychiatry
University of Toronto, Toronto, Ontario, Canada

PREFACE

It is the fundamental premise of this text that psychiatric illness must be understood, evaluated, and treated in a multidimensional manner. Hence, biological, psychological, and sociological factors are all considered to be potentially important in evaluating and treating psychiatric illness. While it will be noted in the introductory chapter on assessment that the amount of attention given to any particular area will vary depending on the clinical situation, the complexity of psychiatric illness requires that a comprehensive assessment of the patient be performed to facilitate accurate diagnosis and effective treatment.

Recent developments in descriptive and biological psychiatry have provided physicians with more exact methods of diagnosis as well as psychopharmacologic treatments that are often dramatically effective. Some psychiatrists, while acknowledging the importance of recent developments in the classification of psychiatric disorders and biologic treatments, have been concerned that the importance of understanding developmental and experiential aspects of the patient's life and the role of psychotherapy in treatment may be being neglected in the process. A fundamental premise that has guided the development of this text is that multiple perspectives (biological, psychological, sociological) must be simultaneously invoked in research and clinical practice to fully understand and effectively treat psychiatric disorders. While controversy still reigns as to which *forms* of treatment are most effective for certain disorders and to what the relative contribution of psychological and biological factors is in determining disease vulnerability, there is no excuse for clinicians to fail to understand patients and their illnesses in the context of their developmental life experiences and their current interpersonal relationships. Those who still argue the "nature vs. nurture" issue are fundamentally missing the point: Elements of both almost always influence vulnerability to emotional illness and need to be considered in treatment. It appears that a new generation of psychiatrists is emerging who will be able to fully integrate both the perspectives of developmental psychology and biologic understanding of the etiology and treatment of psychiatric disorders. It is this integrated approach in research and clinical practice which forms the future for psychiatry. While the complete scientific integration of psychoanalytic, behavioral, sociologic, and biologic theories is not yet possible, the inability to do so is primarily the result of our insufficient understanding of the etiology of psychiatric illness.

As will be noted in the first chapter, this text will advocate a structured approach to psychiatric diagnosis within the matrix of the biopsychosocial model. In addition, as will be discussed in Chapter 2, the importance of understanding the patient's developmental life experiences and quality of their interpersonal relationships is considered to be of crucial importance in personality formation, vulnerability or resistance to stress, as well as susceptibility and adaptability to both medical and psychiatric illness. Comprehensive patient care must be based on examining each aspect of the patient's life development and current situation from the biological, psychological, and social perspectives.

This text is unique in that it deals with the major clinical psychopathological syndromes from this perspective as well as specifically addressing, in the second half of the text, the management of the common psychiatric disorders encountered in medical and surgical practice. These latter chapters are all written by clinicians and researchers who have extensive experience in working with physicians in medical settings, so readers should find them both precise and practical. In addition, Chapter 15 addresses the major childhood psychiatric disorders that are likely to be encountered in family and pediatric practice and emphasizes their diagnosis and treatment.

Finally, it should be noted that this text provides only an overview and covers the essential aspects of clinical psychiatry that are most pertinent for students of medicine. Each chapter is followed by an annotated bibliography of recommended references that students are referred to for more extensive reading, and a general reading list is provided. It should also be noted that this text is best used when it is preceded by reading the companion volume to this series, *Human Behavior: An Introduction for Medical Students,* which covers the fundamental principles of human behavior in health and illness using the biopsychosocial model and a psychobiological perspective.

It is hoped that in using and studying this text students will gain some appreciation of the exciting developments that have evolved in psychiatry and will be able to use this knowledge in providing excellent integrated medical and psychiatric care to their patients.

Alan Stoudemire, M.D.

ACKNOWLEDGMENTS

This text could not have been completed without the tireless dedication, hard work, and loyalty of my administrative assistant, Ms. Lynda Mathews, to whom I am deeply appreciative. In addition, I would like to thank Dr. Jeffrey Houpt, Chair of the Department of Psychiatry and Dean of Emory University School of Medicine, for his ongoing support and encouragement in my career development that made this text a reality.

The contributors to this textbook are all dedicated clinicians and researchers that represent the very best in academic psychiatry. It has been a pleasure and a privilege to work with them. Their dedication to patient care and medical education will be evident in the quality of the chapters contained herein.

RECOMMENDED TEXTBOOKS

Diagnostic and Statistical Manual of Mental Disorders, 3rd ed rev. Washington, DC. American Psychiatric Association, 1987

> This is the "bible" of descriptive psychiatry. It contains epidemiological and descriptive data of the major psychiatric disorders.

Hales RE, Yudofsky SC (eds): Textbook of Neuropsychiatry. Washington, DC. American Psychiatric Press, 1987

> This is a clearly written and practical guide to neuropsychiatric disorders.

Kaplan HI, Sadock BJ (eds): Comprehensive Textbook of Psychiatry, 5th ed, Vols 1 and 2. Baltimore, Williams & Wilkins, 1989

> This is an encyclopedic textbook that covers all areas of psychiatry. Detailed and comprehensive, it should be primarily used as a reference source.

Michels R (ed): Psychiatry, Vols I–III. Philadelphia, JB Lippincott, 1987

> This is an excellent and comprehensive textbook of clinical psychiatry. Published in three volumes, the chapters are lucid, well edited, and are kept fresh by a subscription process that periodically updates the material.

Nicholi AM Jr (ed): New Harvard Guide to Psychiatry, 2nd ed. Cambridge, MA, Belknap Press of Harvard University Press, 1988

> This is an excellent overview of clinical psychiatry that is very readable and practical for a medical student audience. Chapters that are especially strong are those on the biological aspects of depression, the genetic aspects of schizophrenia, and the chapters on psychodynamic and psychoanalytic theory by Meissner, Vaillant, and Nemiah.

Stoudemire A, Fogel BS (eds): Principles of Medical Psychiatry. Orlando, Grune & Stratton, 1987

> This textbook is a detailed reference on the psychiatric disorders as encountered in medically ill patients. It contains detailed information regarding diagnosis, psychotherapy, and psychopharmacologic modifications that are required in treating psychiatric disorders in the medically ill.

Talbott J, Hales RE, Yudofsky S (eds): Textbook of Psychiatry. Washington, DC, American Psychiatric Press, 1988

> This is an excellent textbook of clinical psychiatry that is eminently readable and practical. The chapters will provide a somewhat more expanded discussion of the psychopathological syndromes contained in this text.

Winokur G, Clayton P: The Medical Basis of Psychiatry. Philadelphia, WB Saunders, 1986

> For students interested in basic descriptive, epidemiological, and genetic data relative to psychiatric disorders, this text provides a state-of-the-art review.

CONTENTS

clinical psychiatry for medical students

1

Psychiatric Assessment, DSM-III-R, and Differential Diagnosis

Roger G. Kathol, Jerry Carter,
and William R. Yates

During the past 20 years, advances in psychiatric research have led to a better understanding of mental and emotional difficulties. This improved knowledge has modified the approach to evaluating and treating patients with psychiatric conditions. This chapter focuses on how to perform a basic and practical evaluation of psychiatric problems. It provides a method of psychiatric evaluation, useful in both the psychiatric and medical setting, that increases the likelihood that the most effective treatment of psychiatric disorders will be given.

The *biopsychosocial* approach currently is advocated as the best paradigm of psychiatric assessment (Fink, 1988). Using a model of assessment based on general systems theory, this approach encourages that equal emphasis be given to the evaluation of the psychological, social, and biological factors impacting on the patient's clinical presentation. In the clinical setting, however, the importance of each of these areas of assessment varies depending on the emotional or behavioral difficulty with which the patient presents. For example, in a patient experiencing marital problems where neither spouse has interfering medical difficulties, the psychological assessment (the patient's view of his or her role in the relationship, the patient's expectations of the marriage, the patient's ultimate life goals) and social assessment (the relationship with the spouse, the causes of conflicts, family member influences, economic constraints) would receive greater attention than the biological assessment. Thus, therapeutic intervention directed toward the psychological and social realms would receive the most emphasis, unless a concurrent medical illness in one of the family members was a primary cause of the crisis. Alternatively, if a patient is delirious, biological factors (underlying medical differential diagnosis, likelihood of improvement, or complications with various interventions) become paramount.

As in all areas of medicine, students learn to balance their evaluations to best explore the complaints and needs of the patient. The astute clinician develops skills in each area of assessment and incorporates them when the clinical situation dictates.

In this introductory chapter, a biopsychosocial approach using a structured system of psychiatric diagnosis will be presented for patient assessment. In addition, the importance of understanding patients in light of both their present and past experiences will be emphasized.

VALUE OF A DIAGNOSIS

Although many psychiatrists spend a good deal of their time assisting *normal* patients in their adjustment to *normal* life experiences, the main reason for psychiatric evaluation is the identification of mental and emotional disorders. To do this effectively, clinicians must develop a basic understanding of what constitutes "abnormal" behavior.

During medical training, students and residents learn to differentiate the normal human condition from the abnormal. When is the liver enlarged? When is a cardiac murmur clinically significant? How high does the alkaline phosphatase level have to go before further diagnostic testing is needed? Implicit in the answers to these questions is an understanding of what is "normal." In most medical disciplines, the distinction between normal and abnormal has been quantified. Laboratory tests list a "normal range," which indicates an acceptable deviation from the mean for a control population. Alternatively, the presence of certain findings indicates abnormality. Examples would include fungating skin lesions or rales in the chest, which are uniformly absent in normal individuals.

One of the most perplexing but seldom asked questions in psychiatry is, "What constitutes normal emotions and behavior?". Without an answer to this question, is it possible to define the "abnormal?" In one experimental study, Rosenhan (1979) reported that nonpsychiatrically ill "pseudopatients," who faked having heard the words "hollow," "thud," and "empty" for several days, presented themselves for psychiatric evaluation. The pseudopatients were diagnosed as having schizophrenia, in remission, during 11 of 12 inpatient encounters at independent hospitals. One must question if so few symptoms, which cause no incapacity and resolve spontaneously and immediately after the initial evaluation, are sufficient to label a person schizophrenic with its attendant personal, social, legal, and economic repercussions.

Although there are diverse opinions on what constitutes psychiatric normalcy, most consider it to be defined by behavior that falls within a commonly recognized cultural standard. Aberrant behavior can be identified by this method, although the reliability of such an approach, especially in mild conditions, is limited by the United States's cultural diversity (ethnic—white, black, Asian; religious—Hari Krishna, Jehovah's Witness, fundamentalist; organizational—Ku Klux Klan, motorcycle gangs) and by the cultural background and norms of the person performing the examination. Essentially, what is deemed "normal" ends up being that which is not too different from the accepted cultural and behavioral norms of the evaluator.

Mere recognition of those with "abnormal" behavior is insufficient for diagnosing a psychiatric illness. That would be equivalent to calling a jockey who races horses and a person who plays center on a basketball team medically ill because they fall at the extremes of the bell-shaped curve for height. Yet doctors often consider those who do not conform to their concept of appropriate behavior psychologically unstable.

Despite the difficulty in specifying abnormal emotions and behavior, there are clearly individuals who are *functionally impaired* as a result of emotion, thought, or behavior. Few would argue that a delirious or profoundly depressed patient represents a variant of normal behavior. *It is, in fact, impairment of function that distinguishes "eccentric behavior" from psychiatric illness.* As with all other medical disorders, psychiatric *disease* includes conditions associated with pain, disability, death, or an increased liability to these states (Robins and Guze, 1970).

A disease is more than a *descriptor* of conditions causing human suffering. Perhaps more importantly, it is a *predictor.* Consistent and reliable identification of syndromes with specific symptoms and signs allows documentation of the condition's cause, the mode of transmission, family involvement, the age of onset, the natural course of the symptoms, and the treatments that might alter the ultimate outcome. One of the primary objectives of the rapidly changing editions of the *Diagnostic and Statistical Manual of Mental Disorders-III-Revised* (DSM-III-R) (American Psychiatric Association, 1987) is categorization of incapacitating aberrant behavior (see Chapter 1 Appendix). Reliable identification using this "cookbook" approach can improve our ability to study these predictive factors. This nomenclature system has been a major advance in psychiatric diagnosis during the past 20 years.

The following case study will be presented and then used throughout the chapter as a teaching example of the correct way to perform a medical/neurological assessment (which includes the mental status examination) in a patient with psychiatric symptoms and an example of use of the DSM-III-R classification scheme. Readers should study it carefully, because reference to this case will be made throughout the first part of this chapter. Reasons for the therapeutic intervention will be provided at the conclusion of the chapter.

A CASE STUDY

Patient Identification
RH is a 57-year-old alcoholic man admitted to the emergency room drowsy and somewhat combative after being brought from a boarding house by the police.

Chief Complaint
"Bugs crawling on my skin and the mob is after me."

History of Present Illness
The patient was marginally responsive and was unable to say why he was brought to the hospital. He had been drinking his usual fifth of whiskey until 2 days before admission when "the mob stole" his social security check and he had no money for liquor. Since then he had "holed up" in his room and "nearly starved to death." He refused to give more history for fear that it might have "repercussions."

After the patient gave reluctant permission, the family was contacted. They stated that the patient had been drinking since the age of 13 and had been hospitalized on numerous occasions for alcohol-related problems. Volumes of hospital charts on the patient confirmed this information. He had binged since age 16 and had been drunk nearly every day, except when in treatment, since his mid-30s. His first blackout occurred at age 22, "the shakes" had predictably come on with abstinence of greater than 18 hours for many years, and he had had several episodes of "the DTs." There was no history of withdrawal seizures, however. Short periods of enforced sobriety occurred when the patient was hospitalized for hemorrhaging gastric ulcers. Numerous alcohol rehabilitation programs failed to change his drinking habits.

The family kept track of the patient because "he was a good man when he wasn't drinking," but they didn't want him home because he was abusive during periods of inebriation and was arrested frequently for public intoxication. He had not had a job for many years and had a strong family history for alcoholism. When he was feeling remorseful about his effect on his family, he became despondent and talked of killing himself, but he had never attempted suicide. His suicidal tendencies did not occur during periods of abstinence.

Medical and Psychiatric History
The patient had a 120-pack-a-year smoking history and had been treated unsuccessfully for hypertension due to noncompliance. He had been given benzodiazepines in an apparent attempt to help curb his drinking, but he denied nervousness or panic attacks in the absence of alcohol intoxication or during withdrawal. He had numerous alcohol-related injuries and sequelae. His history did not include abuse of controlled substances or over-the-counter medication. He was prone to fighting while under the influence but had no difficulty with the law when sober.

Developmental/Social History
The patient was the only son in a family of four. There were no known problems with gestation, delivery, or reaching developmental milestones. His childhood was disturbed by frequent fights between his parents, mainly over his father's drinking. He was raised largely by his mother, who was nurturing and attentive to his needs until he was in high school, when he began getting into trouble with authorities. He was suspended and eventually expelled for drinking on school premises, when he had "run-ins" with his teachers. While in school he had a close group of friends, was reasonably successful in organized sports, and participated in extracurricular activities. After holding numerous small jobs, he spent 3 years in military service and received a general discharge. He was married at age 23, when he was working as a laborer in a steel mill, and had two daughters. After 14 years of marriage, the patient's wife divorced him because "it was apparent that nothing was going to change." Since then, the patient had lived in numerous places on social security and provided little in the way of child support.

Family History
The patient's father, paternal uncle, and paternal and maternal grandfathers were alcoholics. One paternal aunt saw doctors nearly all the time for health problems. Deaths in the family were mainly due to liver

and heart problems. There were no other family medical or psychiatric illnesses.

Review of Systems
Unable to be obtained.

Physical Examination
The patient was disheveled, cachectic, and had poor hygiene. Blood pressure was 160/94. Pulse was 98 and regular. Respirations were 20 and unlabored. Temperature was 36.2°C. The skin revealed profuse sweating, several ecchymoses, palmar erythema, and numerous spider angiomata, but no jaundice. There was a recent bruise on the patient's forehead. Poor compliance prevented observation of the patient's fundi. The heart examination revealed normal sounds without murmurs or rubs, and there were diffuse pulmonary rhonchi. The liver was enlarged and tender. No ascites could be demonstrated. Stool was brown and positive for occult blood. Cranial nerves were "grossly intact," and the patient could move all extremities. There was no strabismus. The patient was tremulous and responsive to pinching in all extremities. Deep tendon reflexes were 1 + and symmetrical, while the plantar response was downgoing bilaterally. Gait was unsteady, and the patient refused to tandem walk.

The mental status examination revealed the patient to be drowsy, uncooperative, and intermittently agitated. His speech was slurred and coherent but his responses to questions were appropriate only occasionally. He remained silent and lying flat with eyes closed when not pressed to respond but lashed out when shaken. His mood was angry and distrustful. Affect was exaggerated but appropriate to the stimulus. He denied thoughts of harming himself or others but stated that he sure would protect himself if anyone "came at him." The patient's statements were understandable but laced with concerns about being imprisoned and tortured (by the mob). He had difficulty maintaining a coherent train of thought. Complaints of the floor crawling with snakes or other repulsive animals and feeling bugs under his skin were frequent. The patient could not maintain attention long enough for full assessment of cognitive function with the Mini–Mental State Examination.

Screening Laboratory
The patient's sodium, magnesium, and calcium levels were low, and his liver enzymes and amylase levels were elevated. B_{12} was normal, but folate was low. There was a macrocytic anemia and thrombocytopenia; however, bleeding parameters were normal. Blood alcohol level was 2 mg/dl (intoxicated 50–100 mg/dl). Urine screen for other drug abuse was negative. Chest x-ray and electrocardiogram were normal.

Hospital Course
The patient initially required large doses of chlordiazepoxide for alcohol withdrawal. This was tapered during the first 9 days of his hospital stay

with gradual resolution of the changes in mental state. Sodium, magnesium, and calcium levels returned to normal with replacement and adequate nutrition. Thiamine and multivitamins were given. When the patient became less paranoid and confused, he scored 29/30 on the Mini–Mental State Examination. Elevated amylase levels returned toward normal spontaneously, and blood in the stool disappeared after treatment of alcoholic gastritis documented by endoscopy.

The patient expressed remorse for his drinking behavior and promised to attend Alcoholics Anonymous (AA) meetings when released from the hospital. Contact was made with AA during his hospitalization. He demonstrated no evidence of depression when his withdrawal symptoms had resolved. After 3.5 weeks of treatment, he was preparing for discharge when he had a grand mal seizure. Electroencephalogram demonstrated diffuse slowing with increased prominence on the right. Computed tomography of the head revealed a large right frontoparietal subdural hematoma. The hematoma was surgically evacuated, and the patient was discharged to his boarding house 6 weeks later with the intent to initiate alcohol outpatient treatment. An AA sponsor was contacted to ensure the patient's participation in outpatient treatment.

HISTORY, PHYSICAL EXAMINATION, AND LABORATORY ASSESSMENT IN THE PSYCHIATRIC EVALUATION

Psychiatric evaluations can be conveniently divided into those that take place in the psychiatric setting (inpatient psychiatric hospital, outpatient psychiatry clinic, psychiatry consultation service, or other situations in which the patient expects to see a psychiatrist for possible psychiatric problems) and those that take place in the medical (nonpsychiatric) setting. In the first situation, patients are referred or are being treated specifically for psychiatric problems. In the second instance, the patient's principal problem probably is nonpsychiatric in nature, but psychiatric factors could be involved. Because misconceptions exist about what constitutes an appropriate psychiatric evaluation in these two situations, they will be addressed separately.

Psychiatric Evaluation in a Psychiatric Setting

The principal features of the psychiatric evaluation are the *psychiatric history* and the *mental status examination*. These establish the presence of a psychiatric syndrome. A medical history, physical examination, and laboratory assessment also are included in psychiatric evaluations, although little emphasis is placed on their role during medical training when patients are assumed to have "primarily psychiatric problems." *Because 30–50% of psychiatric inpatients and outpatients have medical disease concurrent with their psychiatric symptoms (LaBruzza, 1981), 5–30% of which either actually cause or exacerbate the psychiatric problem, it is inappropriate for psychiatrists or medical students to neglect the medical part of the evaluation in patients with psychiatric symptoms.*

It is not reasonable to expect psychiatrists to complete a medical history and a physical examination every time they see a patient, just as it is not logical for primary care physicians to perform complete psychiatric examinations on all the patients they see. In two studies, medical findings in 45% of psychiatric patients led to reconsideration of the psychiatric diagnosis, and in 6–9% they led to a *major* alteration in the approach to treatment (Hoffman, 1982; Chandler and Gerndt, 1988). *It is therefore essential to include the physical examination as an integral part of the psychiatric evaluation in all first-time inpatients and outpatients being appraised for a psychiatric disease.* This point is particularly true when the risk for an organic component is high, such as in patients over 50 years old, in those with atypical psychiatric presentations or adverse (or no) responses to treatment for disorders in which improvement should be expected, or in patients with known or suspected underlying medical conditions that could contribute to their symptoms.

Psychiatric Evaluation in the Medical Setting

Medical students are usually taught psychiatric evaluation in *psychiatric* settings. In most medical centers, little or no instruction is given for initiating psychiatric questions in patients seen in primarily medical settings, despite the fact that 80% of patients with psychiatric conditions are seen by primary care specialists (Regier et al., 1978). Medical students frequently are indoctrinated with the idea that "nonpsychiatric patients shouldn't be asked embarrassing psychiatric questions." The end result of this advice is that, in their future practices, psychiatric problems in many if not most of their primary care patients are overlooked.

Psychiatrists have little difficulty asking patients referred for psychiatric evaluation personal and confidential questions. That, after all, is what psychiatrists are trained to do. Medical patients, however, come to see nonpsychiatric physicians for "physical" problems. To embark on a series of psychological questions usually is unexpected and may be viewed initially by the patient as an invasion of privacy unless the reasons for the questions are explained or the patient can be led to see a possible connection to the presenting complaint or general condition. The patient also may be both relieved and reassured that the physician is interested in him or her "as a person" and may use the opportunity to express worries and emotional and psychological distress.

Because psychiatric questions are not asked routinely in the medical setting, psychiatric illness frequently remains undetected, or, alternatively, a psychiatric illness may be presumptively diagnosed without just cause. The prevalence of mental illness, the availability of effective treatments for many psychiatric disorders, and the harm of inappropriate diagnosis make it imperative that all physicians develop the skills for initiating psychiatric evaluations. Nothing can replace specific psychiatric questions in documenting the presence or absence of a psychiatric disorder.

Psychiatric Interviewing

The psychiatric interview is an interaction between patient and physician designed to assess psychiatric status or to provide treatment of an emotional or behavioral problem. During the first interview, patients typically describe their perception of the difficulty. The physician clarifies the chief complaint and enhances the patient's history by observing the patient's behavior during the interaction *(infra vide)* and listening to the patient's responses to open-ended questions. During this encounter, the physician should establish a rapport, if possible, by being honest and straightforward during the interview, by showing empathy for the patient's condition or situation, and by demonstrating his or her willingness and ability to improve the patient's problem.

Ideally, when the patient is coherent, the patient and physician arrive at a general understanding of the nature of the problem and agree on the form and duration of treatment. This approach clearly and unambiguously defines the limits of the relationship, the goals, and the expectations of each party. Such an approach is particularly important when working with patients with certain psychiatric disorders. For instance, patients with psychotic disorders or borderline/antisocial personality disorders often distort, misinterpret, or manipulate what is said; thus, initial clarification and guidelines are necessary (see Chapter 4).

Certain critical ingredients are important during the initial interview. First, *adequate time* should be set aside for the interview. This entails not only time to obtain the necessary information to make a diagnosis but also time to initiate the interview on a personal note. Patients can then feel that you are seeing and treating them as individuals. Second, if possible, steps should be taken to ensure that there are no interruptions. Third, the patient should be put at ease. Such details as providing adequate space for patient movement, equal eye level of the examiner and patient, the presence or absence of other support personnel or the patient's acquaintances, and limiting noise can make significant differences in the patient's willingness to share pertinent information about problems. Fourth, note-taking should be limited, especially if it makes the patient feel uncomfortable. These simple, seemingly inconsequential details can affect not only the type of behavior demonstrated and information obtained during the initial interview but also the course of treatment. Finally, if the situation permits, the physician should usually *sit down* when speaking to the patient and avoid standing over and shifting around him or her when standing at their bedside.

There are some who consider the psychiatric interview to be different and distinct from the interview performed in primary care. In fact, considerable importance is given to observing behavior and obtaining data related to psychiatric issues during the general medical history-taking process (Bates and Hoekelman, 1983). The primary care physician, however, is usually dealing with signs and symptoms of medical conditions in the absence of psychiatric involvement. Therefore, observations such as the color of the patient's skin, the rapidity of his or her breathing, and the coarseness of a tremor take on greater clinical importance. When complaints in the primary care setting point to a psychiatric problem, nonpsychiatric physicians, like psychiatrists, merely need to extend their observations to include mood, behavior, and thought processes. Additional questions to confirm or deny the presence of a psychiatric syndrome complete the history. There is no magic in this as long as the basics about psychiatric syndromes and symptoms are known.

A good deal of emphasis in psychiatry is placed on the interpretation of answers to questions or manifest behaviors. When a patient who obviously looks depressed because of poor eye contact, tearfulness, apparent fatigue, latency of response, or stooped posture says he or she does not feel sad (essentially denying being depressed), how should this be handled? It is best to take what the patient says at face value initially and try to make sense of it in relation to the remainder of the clinical picture before suggesting that the patient is unable to identify emotions, is unable to report accurately, is lying, or is massively denying. It is just as possible that the patient with the symptoms described above is suffering from anemia or cancer.

Psychiatric interviews are designed to be predominantly diagnostic or therapeutic, but elements of both are often contained in initial evaluations. Primarily diagnostic interviews detect and characterize psychiatric illness. Interviews arranged to follow the course of psychiatric illness or response to therapy might also be considered partly diagnostic because they provide a steady flow of information that allows for ongoing assessment of the patient's condition. Therapeutic interviews involve the use of psychotherapeutic techniques. These are primarily intended to provide treatment in the form of support, reassurance, and exploration of the patient's past history and current stresses to facilitate expression of painful feelings and to provide insight.

The form of psychotherapy employed may influence the nature of patient questioning beyond that required to make a DSM-III-R diagnosis. For example, the cognitive therapist might pursue details regarding the manner in which one deals with current life problems, whereas the psychoanalyst or psychodynamically oriented psychotherapist might be interested in details regarding one's perceptions of, and emotional reactions to, historical life events. These forms of therapy and special interview techniques will be covered in other chapters in this text (see Chapters 16 and 18).

In addition to gathering historical data narrated by the patient, the physician derives diagnostic data by observing and assessing the patient's appearance, behavior, and various aspects of mental functioning during the interview process. Thus, in addition to assessing the *content* of the patient's history, the psychiatrist routinely looks beyond the narrative to assess the patient's mental apparatus that perceives, formulates, and elaborates the history and the behavior that emanates from it. This will provide objective data in a manner analogous to the physical examination of the internist. For example, patients with major depression frequently demonstrate poor eye contact, stooped posture, latency of response, and psychomotor retardation. When a patient presents with a history that corresponds with the clinical picture, an initial diagnosis can be made with more confidence.

The importance of documenting information from both the history (including history provided by the patient's family) and direct observation of the patient is essential because signs and symptoms during the interview may be limited. For instance, there are medical conditions that show no evidence of disease on physical examination (e.g., migraine headache), just as there are patients with certain psychiatric conditions who may demonstrate completely normal mental function and behavior during the examination (e.g., alcohol dependence, eating disorders, sexual disorders, and so forth). The reverse is also true for patients with dementia, who may have no idea that problems exist, although their behavior may demonstrate the opposite.

One means of acquiring more accurate information as well as a better understanding of the mental and emotional state is to perform the interview using open-ended, unstructured questions. Many medical and psychiatric interviews resemble interrogations, with rapid-fire questions that require "yes" or "no" answers and leave almost no chance for the patient to elaborate on his or her own perception of the problem, much less express painful emotions or experiences. Avoiding leading questions allows patients to provide an unbiased account of their perception of the problem. Contextually accurate information is obtained by following the patient's lead with questions directed at clarifying or enlarging on historical items. As the interview progresses, it may become increasingly structured and specific to fill in details and to complete the history, as detailed in following sections.

Many physicians are afraid of open-ended, unstructured questions because time constraints do not allow the luxury that questioning during numerous hour-long psychotherapy sessions provides. For this reason, psychiatric questions are often avoided altogether. Nonetheless, a limited amount of time devoted to this type of questioning is essential for a more accurate diagnostic impression, regardless of time constraints. The accomplished physician develops skill in providing a balance between the open-ended, person-to-person questions and the single-answer questions that are required to make a diagnosis. In this way, critical information from and about the patient can be obtained while controlling interviewing time and maintaining a more predictable schedule.

Factors Affecting the Interview

Patients present to psychiatrists in a variety of situations that greatly influence the form of the interview, nature of patient–physician interaction, and overall goals. These situations range from the highly functioning patient presenting for an outpatient evaluation of a moderate depression to the emergency evaluation of a hostile, psychotic patient taken to the emergency room in restraints by police officers, as in the case presented at the beginning of this chapter. In the first situation (moderate depression in an outpatient), one might obtain a meticulous psychiatric and medical history, physical and mental status examination, and screening laboratory evaluation. Such interviews facilitate therapeutic decision-making. In the situation of an agitated, medically ill alcoholic, the evaluation would initially include documenting the presence of delirium, performing the physical examination, and admitting the patient for inpatient care. Only later, when information can be obtained from charts, relatives, and the patient, when he or she becomes better controlled, will a comprehensive, accurate understanding of the case become possible.

Other factors also may influence the ability to conduct a thorough psychiatric interview. For instance, some patients may be so fatigued from medical illness that they require a concise interview. Alternatively, some patients refuse to cooperate. Often this can be a clue to their diagnosis, as in the case of a patient with borderline personality or paranoid disorder. In such cases, additional information from the patient's doctor, nursing personnel, or descriptions in the chart can provide valuable insight into the nature and cause of the patient's difficulties and lead perhaps to more effective management. Thus, the skilled interviewer must be flexible and ever mindful of not only the details of a patient's psychiatric condition but also the interwoven social, legal, and medical factors that complicate psychiatric assessment and intervention.

Specific Interview Situations

Although each patient is unique, necessitating a flexible and individualized interview style, many psychiatric disorders influence aspects of the interview in a manner that is predictable and characteristic of that disorder. Thus, the following comments are not intended to offer a "cookbook" approach to these patients but rather offer suggestions in the interpretation and planning of specific interview situations.

The Depressed Patient

A prominent feature of severe depression is the tendency for all perceptions to be colored by bleakness and pessimism. When the history is taken, therefore, it is essential to keep in mind that many descriptions presented by the patient in a negative light by way of his depressed state may actually be more positive or at least neutral. For example, it is common for depressed patients to think that they are going bankrupt or doing terrible things to family and friends. Information from other sources may reveal that the situation is not nearly so dismal.

Depressed patients are often in desperate need of hope and reassurance. They may repeatedly ask whether they are a bad person or if they can be helped. Nonetheless, when reassurance is provided, it may be received with quiet skepticism and generally results in only temporary relief.

Depressed persons often have their own ways of accounting for suffering. For example, they may be convinced that they are being justly punished by God for transgressions. Such beliefs may become delusional in psychotic depressions, such as when patients think they have committed the "unforgivable" sin; think they, or the world, no longer exists (nihilism); or think they are riddled with cancer (somatic). Explaining that such ideas are the result of depression and will go away with treatment offers momentary hope but is unlikely to alter their opinion until improvement occurs.

The Psychotic Patient

The term "psychosis" includes a broad range of clinical presentations unified by loss of contact with reality and the presence of delusions or hallucinations. Such presentations range from the patient who appears to function normally (with the exception of a well-circumscribed paranoid delusional system) to the acutely disorganized, agitated, vividly hallucinating patient. The severity of the patient's thought disorder and degree of departure from reality will determine the structure of the interview. The former patient may be able to provide a history that is complete and reliable with the exception of issues relating to the delusional system. When the patient discusses these beliefs, details should be sought regarding the nature and extent of the delusions and how the patient makes sense of them. These details, as well as the degree of conviction in the delusional beliefs, can be followed to assess the course of and response to treatment. When delusions are persecutory in nature, the patient may be reluctant or unwilling to provide information or even consent to be interviewed for fear that the interviewer is an agent of the persecutory process. Such was the situation in the case presented earlier.

When a patient is floridly psychotic, the interview may involve little more than observing the patient as findings are noted. Interacting with such patients often provides stimulation that may make evidence of psychosis more apparent. In addition to grossly distorting reality, acutely psychotic patients are often very frightened. Both of these factors can result in unpredictable and, rarely, even violent behavior. While such patients should be treated with kindness and understanding, necessary precautions must be taken. *Florid psychosis should not deter the physician from performing the physical examination or laboratory assessment, although special care and techniques may be required. These are essential to rule out an organic cause for the psychosis.* (See also Chapters 3 and 18.)

The Hostile Patient

When assessing a hostile patient, interviewers must take whatever precautions are necessary to ensure their safety. The initial step is identification of the potentially violent patient. Clues include a previous history of violent behavior, such as that often seen in patients with antisocial personality disorder, alcoholism, and substance abuse; a paranoid psychosis; and a person who is angry and threatening violence, even in the absence of a psychiatric disorder.

One sensitive indicator of whether the situation is becoming dangerous is your emotional response to the patient's behavior, that is, your "gut level" reaction. If the interviewer feels uncomfortable or fearful of the patient, precautions should be taken *immediately* to ensure safety. If concern is minimal, precaution may involve nothing more than sitting between the patient and an open door or making sure other personnel are nearby. When the index of concern is higher, one or several security officers—without guns—may be stationed in the interview area or be used to restrain the patient if needed during the interview. Such precautions are often a relief to confused, psychotic, or agitated patients because they provide the situation with structure and absolve patients of the necessity of making decisions at a time when they may not be in control of their actions. Chapter 18 on emergency psychiatry also discusses special considerations in interviewing violent and hostile patients.

The Somatic Patient

Many psychiatric disorders manifest somatic symptoms in which a precipitating organic disease is not readily found. These include conversion disorder, hypochondriasis, somatization disorder, a somatic delusional syndrome, and nonspecific complaints associated with anxiety or depression. Such complaints, however, may just as likely be the result of medical disease too early in onset to diagnose due to insensitivity of the physical examination and laboratory tests; a medical problem more benign than the evaluation needed to diagnose it; or merely the patient's attempt to receive attention. Care must be taken, therefore, in diagnosing somatoform disorders (see Chapter 8).

A convenient way to categorize patients with unexplained somatic complaints is to determine whether the complaints are *single or multiple.* If the somatic complaint is single, the evaluation should proceed until a physical cause has been reasonably excluded *and* a psychiatric cause is deemed possible. This may entail no more than a careful history with a brief physical examination, but occasionally it requires more extensive testing.

If the complaints are multiple and somatization disorder is a possibility, then symptoms must be *seriously listened to,* but only objective evidence of disease on basic evaluation should lead to further work-up. At the first evaluation, time should be taken to obtain a directed history about the main complaint and each complaint with a potentially dangerous cause. A complete physical examination and basic laboratory evaluation (if not already done) are required. Records from prior physicians and hospitals are particularly helpful and should be obtained before further work-up unless eminent problems are evident. Any objective finding on the physical examination or laboratory evaluation should prompt further investigation or treatment after the nature and extent of previous evaluations have been delineated.

In patients with multiple somatic complaints, the physician should place particular emphasis on the terms of agreement regarding specific responsibilities of physician and patient. The physician should agree to evaluate symptoms when deemed appropriate and to follow the patient at regular intervals to assess change. The patient should allow the physician adequate time to complete the evaluation and should seek no other medical evaluations unless consent is first obtained from the physician. This approach will not guarantee ease in caring for such patients but may result in the development of rapport and trust, which are essential if the patient's suffering is to be eased and the pursuit of evaluations slowed. The diagnosis and management of patients with chronic somatic complaints is further discussed in Chapter 8.

The Psychiatric History

Many psychiatric patients make the process of obtaining an accurate history a challenge for a variety of reasons. First, they may have illnesses, such as dementia or delirium, that prevent them from revealing details related to the onset and type of symptoms that brought them to the physician's attention. Second, they may wish to hide salient facts related to their difficulties because of embarrassment, mistrust, or outright deception. Third, they may present with symptoms that follow a variable pattern or are difficult to describe. It is for these reasons that *obtaining additional information from a second or, preferably, a third and fourth source, such as family members, friends, or police,* as well as scrutinizing available information in the patient's records, is *critical* to assure that the correct diagnosis is made and appropriate treatment is given. Table 1-1 outlines the main sections of the psychiatric

Table 1–1 **The Psychiatric History**

Chief complaint
Medical history
Personal and family history of psychiatric
   disorders and treatment
Personal development
Social history
     Interpersonal relationships
     Sexual history
     Alcohol and substance abuse
Review of systems

history. Important factors related to each part of the psychiatric history are enumerated below.

Chief Complaint

Often the patient's chief complaint differs from the examining physician's perception of the problem. In this situation the primary problem that the patient perceives should be addressed first while the "real" problem waits. In this way the patient is indirectly told that his or her complaint is important, thus creating an alliance in trying to clarify and relieve both the perceived and the "real" problem.

As with any medical evaluation, clarification of the chief psychiatric complaint lies at the heart of the psychiatric history. Pertinent information includes an accurate description of the difficulty, the mode of onset and duration, the course of the symptoms (steady, intermittent, progressively worse), exacerbating and alleviating factors (medication, position, time of day), and factors such as recent deaths or illnesses in the family, marital or family relationship problems, financial or legal problems, medical illness, problems at work, or intractable social problems where the patient feels unable to cope, possibly associated with the onset and continuation of the symptoms. These details relevant to the chief complaint are supplemented with pertinent features from the past medical and psychiatric history, past personal history, family history, sexual history, and review of systems. The objective in obtaining this information is to typify the difficulty that the patient is experiencing, to establish whether it warrants psychiatric diagnosis, and to consider ways in which the problem might be alleviated, whether or not a psychiatric disease is present.

Information obtained in this data-gathering section of the interview is coupled with observations made during the interaction with the patient that constitutes part of the mental status examination. It is important that the patient's history and clinical presentation be consistent with the psychiatric condition under consideration; otherwise, alternative explanations should be explored. As might be recalled in the study by Rosenhan using "fake" patients presenting with complaints of hearing "hollow," "thud," and "empty" (auditory hallucinations?), there was neither a syndrome picture (early age of onset, chronic deteriorating clinical course, and so forth) nor other past or present clinical signs (thought disorder, blunted affect, ambivalence, anhedonia) that suggested schizophrenia as a primary diagnostic entity.

Medical History

Any medical history pertinent to the chief complaint is included in the history of present illness. Such information usually becomes evident during the careful questioning used in delineating the chief complaint. Thus, current medical illnesses, which might be contributing to the symptoms and medications, and familial medical illnesses that are known to be associated with the development of psychiatric symptoms would be enumerated in the history of present illness and their possible association with the current psychiatric condition suggested.

In addition to the review of pertinent organic factors in the history of present illness, other seemingly less relevant medical or surgical difficulties, allergies, and medications should also be recorded. Even though they may not be helpful in understanding the patient's reason for seeking psychiatric assistance, they frequently become important when assessing the need for additional information concerning the patient's case when deciding on the type of treatment to be given. For instance, in the case of RH, if it had been known that he had a bleeding disorder, then the bruise on his head might have precipitated a more extensive neurologic investigation before the development of the seizure.

Personal and Family History of Psychiatric Disorders and Treatment

As with the past medical history, pertinent past psychiatric history related to the chief complaint should be included in the history of present illness. *The longitudinal course of psychiatric symptoms and responses to treatment is one of the most important ingredients in making a psychiatric diagnosis.* It is known, for instance, that alcoholism often begins in the teenage years to the 20s, has a fluctuating but progressive course unless the individual maintains prolonged abstinence, and often leads to chronic disability. Had patient RH had a good premorbid history and only started drinking weeks to months before his admission, then the primary diagnosis of alcoholism with alcohol withdrawal delirium (delirium tremens) would have become suspect. Alternative explanations for the drinking behavior and delirium would have been required.

Other factors related to the psychiatric history should be reported under a separate heading. Even though no apparent relation to the current presentation can be shown, they can sometimes provide additional insight into the patient's problem and may alter the course of treatment or investigation. Past suicide attempts should be carefully documented.

Specific questions that delineate the past psychiatric history include the following: First, the patient can be asked, using colloquial terms, if he or she has ever had difficulties with nerves or emotions or whether or not he or she has ever had a "nervous breakdown." Often patients will not remember or do not think they should reply in the affirmative unless they were hospitalized for the problem. Therefore, the patient should be asked whether he or she has been given medication by a primary physician for "nerves" or emotional problems or whether he or she has seen a counselor, pastor, psychologist, social worker, or physician for counseling.

Second, the patient should be asked if there has ever been a time when they felt they needed help but did not get it. Hence, the history should involve both untreated and formally treated bouts of psychiatric illness. If the patient did get treatment, where did he or she get it and for how long were they treated? Were they ever hospitalized for a psychiatric problem? If they did get treatment, including medications, what drugs were given and what was his or her response? Were there any side effects that caused problems?

Third, and perhaps most important, the same questions should be asked of someone who knows the patient well enough to confirm or deny the patient's answers.

A family history of psychiatric illness is crucial, because certain psychiatric disorders have a genetic component (schizophrenia, mood disorders, alcoholism, Alzheimer's disease). In fact, a strong family history of affective disorder can be used to reinforce a diagnostic impression in a patient with an otherwise confusing presentation. It is important to ask about the nature of symptoms, type of treatment (medication or electroconvulsive treatment), response to treatment, complications, and hospitalizations for involved family members. A family history of suicide and violence should also be elicited.

Personal Development

The personal history includes information about the patient's relationships, schooling, employment, personal achievements and failings, and goals. As might be expected, each of these areas can impact in a major way on the course and duration of psychiatric symptoms.

A person's prenatal history and development through the various stages of infancy, childhood, and adolescence are the principal areas of interest in the personal development section of the examination. Items such as birth trauma, developmental physical and emotional milestones, illnesses, parental and sibling relationships, important memories, rewards and punishments, exposure to abuse, and the establishment of independence are addressed. Major milestones, frustrations, and problems in childhood and adolescence should be identified, when appropriate, along with the quality of family and peer relationships during each phase of development. Except in those undergoing psychodynamic/psychoanalytic psychotherapy which is beyond the scope of this chapter, information obtained in this section of the psychiatric history has limited value regarding the diagnosis and treatment selection.

One frequently *unasked* question is whether or not sexual molestation occurred as a child. Patients should be asked about sexual molestation in a frank and straightforward manner, although some tact may be required. For example, one might ask, "Were you every sexually molested or attacked as a child by anyone—including members of your family?" Most patients harbor severe shame and guilt about incest in particular, requiring special sensitivity to this issue in the session.

When pursuing a psychodynamic understanding of the patient's problems, a chronological picture of the patient's developmental history—including his adult history—should be reconstructed, and events or experiences that may have been psychologically or emotionally traumatic should be noted. Past life experiences that appear to correlate with current life events or stresses should be noted by the examiner and explored with the patient. Since current psychiatric diagnostic nomenclature no longer requires a psychodynamic formulation, medical students and physicians should not be deterred from asking psychiatric questions listed in other parts of the history if time does not allow thorough evaluation in this area.

Social History

This part of the psychiatric history recounts the patient's educational background and functioning in the school system; encounters with the law; lawsuits or criminal connections; premarital, postmarital, marital, and extramarital relationships; relationships and problems with children; employment (types, frequency of change, reasons for job changes, compensation issues) and fiscal responsibility; military history (assignment and nature of discharge, history of combat experience); and personal goals and expectations. Criminal charges, arrests, convictions, or time served in prison should be carefully addressed, as should the circumstances leading up to the encounter with the law. During the process of gathering this information, the physician can identify areas in the patient's life that might serve as precipitating stresses or recurrent patterns of problematic social relationships. *All social factors of importance to the presenting complaint should be included in the history of present illness, while the remainder are recorded under the personal or social history section of the examination.*

When considering those areas of the social history that may be stresses involved in precipitating the patient's presenting complaint, it should be remembered that life is literally a "series of crises." It is always possible to point to a flat tire, fight with a relative or friend, failed test, or unpaid bill as a potential stressor for the development of symptoms. A means of placing social factors in proper perspective is to establish whether current stressors in relation to other stressors the patient has previously experienced are of sufficient magnitude to influence the patient's ability to cope.

Interpersonal relationships. Of major importance in the patient's social history is the nature, pattern, and stability of his or her interpersonal relationships, whether they relate to romantic involvements, friendships, occupational relationships, or relationships with authorities. For example, is the patient capable of forming stable relationships based on trust? Is the patient capable of forming close friendships? What is the pattern of the patient's romantic and sexual involvements? How successful have they been in working with peers and for those in authority? Problematic patterns in interpersonal and social relationships often indicate the presence of a personality disorder. One of the cardinal symptoms of a personality disorder is the tendency of the individual to "repeat mistakes" in their interpersonal and social relationships, to fail to learn from experience, and to assign fault to others rather than examine their own contributions to their life difficulties.

The sexual history. There are occasional situations in which the sexual history is of significant importance in understanding the patient's problem. Certainly basic questions concerning sexual function, such as whether the patient is sexually active, what the sexual preference is, and whether there is concern about a venereal disease, should always be asked, because most persons cannot be expected to volunteer such information. When the problem involves potential difficulty within relationships, sexual deviancy, or other problems that may influence sexual function, then more detailed information may be necessary. Because this area of questioning is highly personal, the physician may encounter more resistance than in other areas of the examination. As the doctor–patient relationship becomes better established, however, patients will often become more willing to talk about such matters. Details of a comprehensive sexual history are listed in Table 1-2 and are also discussed in Chapter 13. Physicians should focus on various parts of the history as the clinical situation dictates.

Alcohol and substance abuse. Obtaining a substance-abuse history should be of paramount importance in the history given the prevalence of alcoholism and drug abuse in our society. Use of alcohol, cocaine, marijuana, stimulants, sedative-hypnotics, analgesic opiates, and sleeping pills should be rigorously investigated, including age at first use, frequency of use, amount, and complications in the interpersonal,

Table 1–2 **Basic Sexual History**
(Modified to Age of Patient and Clinical Circumstances)

Introductory comments about why the interview is being conducted and its routine or special
  nature given the clinical situation at hand; reassurance about confidentiality
Open-ended question to give the patient an opportunity to voice any areas of special worry or
  concern regarding the part of the interview or sexual concerns in general
Source of information about sex in growing up
Attitudes of the parents toward sex
Age of onset of puberty
Age of menarche and menstrual history in women
Age of first intense romantic or sexually oriented relationship
History of childhood molestation or incest
History of venereal diseases
Attitudes about masturbation and frequency of masturbation
Age of first intercourse; number of partners
General pattern of attraction to person of the opposite or same sex; general patterns of
  heterosexuality or homosexuality
Abortions, miscarriages, pregnancies
Method(s) of birth control
Frequency of current sexual activity and its nature
Physical discomfort with sexual activity:
  Men: Problem with arousal or achieving/maintaining erection, ejaculation control
  Women: Problems with arousal, lubrication, achieving orgasm, physical comfort with intercourse
Conflicts in relationship or marriage over sexual matters: frequency, methods of birth control,
  sexual dysfunction
Medications or illness that seem to negatively affect sexual desire or functioning
Issues regarding decision to avoid or achieve conception and have children
Risk factors for AIDS or other concerns regarding this disease

(From Becker J: Sexual development. In Stoudemire A (ed): Human Behavior: An Introduction for Medical Students.
Philadelphia, JB Lippincott, 1990)

---

occupational, medical, and legal spheres that may have resulted. A history of the
results of intoxication, withdrawal, and "bad trips" should be explored. The use of
caffeine (coffee, tea, soft drinks, chocolates) is almost always overlooked by exam-
iners, even though caffeine may be addicting and is associated with a withdrawal
syndrome. The use of tobacco products—perhaps the most lethal substance abused
in our society—should also be documented. Pertinent aspects of the substance use
history are also discussed in Chapter 9.

Review of Systems

One of the principal ways in which unexplained somatic complaints are identified is through a review of the symptoms the patient has experienced. The review of
systems also serves as a means of reviewing potential organic causes for the principal
complaint of the patient. Frequently it will uncover a problem that has a direct and
pertinent relation to the chief complaint. Each positive finding on the review of
systems should be understood well enough to know whether further investigation is
needed. Such investigation may include anything from a spot physical examination to
an invasive x-ray procedure.

In medical settings, most patients with psychiatric problems initially present with *physical* symptoms (such as in depression). Physical symptoms of anxiety and depression may be mixed with symptoms of concurrent underlying medical illness as well, thus further complicating the clinical assessment. For example, somatic symptoms associated with depression include sleep fragmentation (usually early morning awakening with an inability to get back to sleep), headaches, constipation, physical fatigue, decreased appetite, weight loss, and gastrointestinal distress.

Psychophysiological symptoms of anxiety include palpitations, tachycardia, diaphoresis, hyperventilation, diarrhea, urinary urgency and frequency, restlessness, chronic fatigue, insomnia, dry mouth, blurred vision, nausea, vomiting, chest pain, dizziness, choking, difficulty swallowing, headaches, muscle aches, and pain. Patients with schizophrenia will occasionally have bizarre physical sensations such as their brain dissolving or body parts feeling disconnected. Patients with somatoform disorders such as hypochondriasis are preoccupied with physical complaints to an excessive, unrealistic degree. Hence, while somatic complaints are nonspecific, they often constitute a predominant component of the signs and symptoms of psychiatric disorders. Care must, however, be taken since it is all too easy to ascribe a physical complaint to a psychiatric condition when, in fact, it is caused by an underlying medical illness.

Assimilation of the Psychiatric History

When a psychiatric syndrome is suggested by the information gathered during the psychiatric history, only the beginning of the diagnostic process has been completed. Depressive symptoms, anxiety symptoms, psychosis, and symptoms from most other psychiatric syndromes can, after all, be caused by a spectrum of psychiatric and medical diseases and also can be seen in some normal individuals. For instance, some clinicians automatically think that patients who meet criteria for major depression develop their symptoms in response to a primary psychiatric illness. Medical conditions such as hypothyroidism and cancer are frequently responsible for the production or exacerbation of depression or symptoms that mimic depression. Even patients with other psychiatric conditions, such as somatization disorder or alcoholism, can have a depressive symptom complicating their primary psychiatric condition. It is for these reasons that the psychiatric history should not be limited to the identification of symptom complexes themselves but should incorporate pertinent medical, personal, and social information to complete the assessment. This additional information can have a substantial impact on the approach taken in the patient's treatment.

Preparing Medical Patients for Psychiatric Evaluation

How can a physician lead into psychiatric screening questions without antagonizing the patient? First, it cannot be done in every case. Regardless of how tactful you are, some may be offended at first. Table 1-3 outlines a way to decrease the likelihood of offending medical patients. This approach will often "break the ice" and allow the patients to describe areas in their lives that have been troubling but that they find difficult to discuss. Occasionally these questions will lead to the most dreaded reaction of all, "What! Do you think I'm putting this on?" or "Do you think this is all in my head?" or "Do you think I'm crazy?" In response to this, the patient might be told, "Emotional factors and stress can influence physical symptoms (some people get headaches, some ulcers from stress—the medical problem is real but can be triggered by stress). I routinely ask these and other questions of all my patients so that I can give the best and most appropriate treatment and don't miss anything important." Thereafter, additional psychiatric screening questions (Table 1-4) can be asked if circumstances warrant. If screening questions are positive, a more detailed psychiatric history can be obtained.

Table 1–3 **Initiating Psychiatric Questions in Patients with Nonpsychiatric Complaints**

Discuss and define the nonpsychiatric problem with the patient first (it may be related to the emotional problem).
If there is some question about whether the nonpsychiatric complaint is "real," do not challenge the patient with this possibility. You don't have to state that you feel the complaint is or isn't real, but you can acknowledge the patient's perception of its presence.
Ask, "Do you think your symptom(s) is (are) affected by nerves or emotions?" "Do you think that your symptom(s) is (are) related to stress?"

Table 1–4 **Psychiatric Screening Questions for Patients in the Primary Care Setting**

Depression

"Have you been feeling sad or depressed? Is this accompanied by trouble with sleep or appetite, low energy, or decreased interest in doing things? Do you have feelings of guilt or thoughts of harming yourself?"

Mania

"Do you feel on top of the world? Is this out of proportion to your usual self such that you talk more, don't need as much sleep, your thoughts race, or your enthusiasm gets you into trouble?"

Psychosis

"Have you heard or seen things that others didn't? Do you feel that you have special powers? Have you felt that others were watching or following you? Have you received peculiar or special messages or felt that others knew or controlled your thoughts?"

Alcoholism

"Have others thought you had a drinking problem? Has drinking alcohol caused problems with friends or relatives, caused you to miss work or lose a job, resulted in arrest, or caused health problems? Do you use recreational drugs?"

Anxiety disorder

"Have you had trouble with nervousness, anxiety, or feeling panicky?"

Anorexia nervosa

"Do you take special measures to keep your weight at its current level?"

When Is It Appropriate to Ask Medical Patients Psychiatric Questions?

In many patients, psychiatric illness with or without concurrent medical illness is readily apparent. Presence of a persistent and pervasive depressed mood, frank psychosis, or an agitated confusional state are clear indications to pursue further psychiatric evaluation. Unfortunately, psychiatric illness is often not so apparent. The following indicators are helpful in detecting patients with psychiatric disorders presenting in a subtle or ambiguous manner: (1) nonresponse to treatment in situations in which it is usually effective (particularly true when litigation is pending); (2) multiple somatic complaints not accounted for by known medical conditions or symptoms not conforming to the bounds of anatomy or physiology; (3) a chaotic lifestyle (e.g., unstable relationships, frequent job changes, substance abuse, frequent legal problems, and so forth); (4) a history of "hopping" from one physician to another; (5) symptoms related to stress, anxiety, or depression; (6) a personal or family history of psychiatric illness; (7) a degree of disability or resultant lifestyle changes out of proportion to symptoms; and (8) suspected alcohol and substance abuse. Although none of these indicators is pathognomonic, they suggest the possibility of psychiatric illness.

Perhaps of equal importance are factors indicating that psychiatric illness should be viewed with a relatively *lower* index of suspicion than other possible causes of the patient's symptoms. This is particularly important because inappropriately labeling a patient's symptoms as "psychiatric" can lead to delay in identifying the correct primary diagnosis. Items in this category include (1) any *objective* finding on physical examination or laboratory evaluation that appears directly related to the symptom; (2) previous emotional *stability* as reflected by work responsibilities, family relationships, and personal endeavors, in a person with questionable "psychiatric" symptoms; (3) an atypical psychiatric presentation of the characteristics of the possible psychiatric syndrome under consideration; and (4) the lack of any acute or chronic stressors in the patient's life. It is in these patients that there is a high risk of labeling the symptoms "psychiatric" when there actually is an underlying organic disease. This brings us to the importance of the physical assessment as part of the evaluation process.

Physical Examination

The physical examination is currently included in 0–11% of outpatient psychiatric evaluations and in 4–40% of inpatient evaluations (Krummel and Kathol, 1987). Ideally, all psychiatric patients should receive a physical examination. Unfortunately, many psychiatrists, like other medical specialists, logically focus their examination on areas related to their specialty. Few "primary" psychiatric diagnoses can be confirmed by positive findings on the physical examination; thus, it is often bypassed altogether.

Of what importance, then, is the physical examination in the evaluation of psychiatric patients? Unlike many subspecialties in medicine, psychiatry deals with clinical presentations that frequently have as their origin a primary medical disorder that causes the patient's symptoms. The list for major depression alone includes diseases from most organ systems (Hall, 1980). To exclude an underlying medical disorder as a cause of the patient's symptoms, a systematic evaluation is required that traditionally has included a physical examination.

The next obvious question is whether clinical tradition is correct in requiring the performance of a physical examination as a part of the assessment, because most medical diagnoses are made from historical information alone. Hampton, Harrison, Mitchell et al. (1975) answered this question when they found that the physical examination confirmed, denied, or narrowed the differential diagnosis arrived at from historical information in 30% of patients in a primary medical setting. In 7.5% it uncovered unexpected yet important findings that led to the diagnosis of a disease that was not necessarily related to the chief complaint. Considering that Chandler and Gerndt (1988) showed similar findings in 224 consecutively examined psychiatric inpatients, the need for a physical examination to confirm or deny organic factors is evident. It is for these reasons that psychiatrists should include a physical examination in psychiatric patients at risk for medical illness co-morbidity. This would include (1) any new patient with a psychiatric disorder, (2) patients older than 50 years of age, (3) patients with an atypical psychiatric presentation or response to treatment, (4) patients with medical conditions known to cause or exacerbate psychiatric symptoms, and (5) patients with significant complaints from the review of systems.

There are some clinicians who think that adding a neurological examination to the psychiatric interview is sufficient to exclude most underlying medical causes of psychiatric symptoms. Although there are certainly a number of neurologic conditions that can cause behavioral or emotional problems (Taylor, Sierles, and Abrams, 1987), medical illness frequently mimics psychiatric disorders (Chandler and Gerndt, 1988). For this reason, it is important to perform a complete physical examination. Hall, Gardiner, Stickney et al. (1980) showed that a cursory physical examination was unreliable in identifying physical changes when they were present; thus, a complete physical is required. When findings are identified, they should be explained and treated along with the psychiatric manifestations accompanying them.

The scope of this chapter does not allow individual treatment of the different sections of the physical examination. These can be reviewed in Bates' (1983) *A Guide to Physical Examination.* A word can be said, however, about the difficulties that are encountered in performing the physical examination in the psychiatric setting. This portion of the psychiatric evaluation is often neglected, only partially because it is not patently pertinent to the presenting complaint. Other factors are also involved. These include (1) worry about missing abnormalities due to lack of experience, (2) no examination facilities, (3) no assistant (or chaperone) for the examination, (4) no reimbursement for the "extra effort," (5) concern that the examination might influence the therapeutic relationship, and (6) dislike for doing physical examinations.

The student should know that, with a little effort in setting up an office or hospital practice, examination facilities and support personnel can be made available. This will enable more frequent physical examinations and thus reduce concern about the quality of the examination. Payment schedules can often be set up to provide fair reimbursement for time used in adding this essential aspect to the remainder of the psychiatric assessment.

Koranyi (1980) showed that physical examination did not adversely affect the therapeutic relationship in over 2000 psychiatric outpatient evaluations. Those who claim transference and countertransference problems due to the physical examination are creating imaginary dragons, because the psychoanalytic/psychodynamic process involves working through these and other psychological conflicts. More likely, those who suggest this reason for avoiding the physical examination are merely rationalizing their dislike of doing them. In some outpatient settings, however, it may be more realistic for the psychiatrist to insist that a physical examination be performed by a family physician or internist as part of the overall evaluation before formal psychiatric treatment proceeds.

Laboratory Assessment

Laboratory assessment, like the physical examination, should be performed in patients at risk for medical co-morbidity (*supra vida*). Screening tests included in an initial evaluation are a complete blood count, electrolytes, blood chemistry screen, and urinalysis. Medication blood levels and urine screen for drug abuse should be included when indicated. In patients over 50 years old, an electrocardiogram and chest x-ray may be added. Depressed and anxious patients should have a thyroid-stimulating hormone (TSH) level drawn, even in the absence of clinical symptoms or signs.

Although there is a great deal of interest in the measurement of other hormones and neurotransmitters in patients with psychiatric disorders, none of these have been found to be useful in diagnostic or therapeutic decision-making. Even the dexamethasone suspension test (DST), widely researched in patients with mood disorders, has value only in predicting who is likely to relapse when it remains positive after successful treatment.

The basic evaluation listed above provides a screen for organic factors that might be contributing to the psychiatric presentation. This does not replace the need to perform specific laboratory tests when the clinical history dictates. For instance, a chronic schizophrenic patient from a state hospital who presents with a documented 2-month history of weight loss and low-grade fevers even in the absence of "basic" laboratory abnormalities requires further work-up to explain the presenting complaints. Just such a case was diagnosed as having tuberculous meningitis on a recent admission to our institution.

Although all diagnostic testing procedures, regardless of complexity and invasiveness, should be considered when the clinical assessment dictates, computed tomography (CT) of the head, magnetic resonance imaging (MRI) of the head, and electroencephalography (EEG) deserve special attention, because they are frequently considered in the evaluation of patients presenting with psychiatric symptomatology. Head CT is a specialized, noninvasive x-ray technique that allows visualization of the anatomy of the head in slices of various thickness. MRI, using an entirely different imaging technique, provides similar slices; however, it has an advantage in that radiation is not involved, the images are not interfered with by bony structures, the images can be obtained in multiple planes, and the differentiation between gray and white matter is better delineated. EEG is the measurement of electrical activity on the surface of the brain. (Use of these techniques in neuropsychiatric assessment is also discussed in Chapter 3.)

There is no simple formula to cover all the indications for these procedures.

Simply stated, MRI is the most expensive but the most sensitive test to pick up anatomic pathology. Because the images using this technique are not altered by bony structures and can be obtained in multiple projections, posterior fossa and brain stem abnormalities are better seen with MRI. For these reasons, some authorities consider it the noninvasive test of choice. Some types of pathology can be seen on MRI that cannot be seen on CT. Examples would include strokes within the first 3 to 7 days of occurrence and multiple sclerosis lesions. Basically, all that can be seen on head CT can be seen on MRI, but the cost, accessibility, limits in interpretation, and problems with patient cooperation in lying still during a relatively lengthy period make it unlikely that it will replace head CT completely.

EEG complements MRI and CT but does not replace them. EEG is not a tool that separates normal from abnormal anatomy; rather, it separates normal and abnormal electrical physiology. In some situations, the two can correspond, as is seen with some brain tumors. In others, the EEG may identify changes (epilepsy) while the imaging procedures remain normal, or vice versa.

MRI, CT, and EEG should all be used to differentiate organic causes of psychiatric behavior from those originating from primary psychiatric disease. Clinical clues about when the EEG, CT, and MRI are more likely to be abnormal are: (1) if there are focal neurological deficits; (2) if there has been a recent and marked change in mental status; (3) if there is a history of substance abuse/alcoholism, head trauma, or other central nervous system (CNS) pathology; (4) if the patient is elderly; and (5) if the patient presents in an atypical fashion and has a history that does not suggest psychiatric involvement. It should be remembered that medicine is based on probability. A certain number of normal tests are necessary to ensure that abnormal tests aren't missed.

The Mental Status Examination

The term mental status examination is somewhat misleading, because it suggests a circumscribed period of assessment that takes its turn, as would auscultation of the heart or inspection of the fundi. To the contrary, the skilled interviewer gathers data regarding the multiple facets of mental functioning as they are observed and elicited during the psychiatric interview. For example, performing tests of recent memory imparts little information not already apparent in a patient who provides an accurate, detailed history. In fact, such exercises may convey a sense of rote mechanical detachment rather than empathy and positive regard for the patient. Furthermore, some aspects of the mental status examination, such as judgment, can be better assessed by what brought the patient to your attention than by asking the patient artificial questions.

Not all areas of the mental status examination are adequately covered during the psychiatric interview. These must be addressed more directly with questions specifically formulated to assess mental function or emotional state. In developing a technique that is both thorough and personalized, it is essential to have a clear understanding of each of the mental status parameters.

A rational method of organizing the mental status examination is to follow the order in which findings are apparent during the interview. Appearance, level of consciousness, psychomotor activity, behavior, and general mood state are observed before and also throughout the interview. Speech, thought content and form, orientation, and memory are appraised throughout the interview. Insight and judgment are usually determined at the conclusion of the interview.

This overview of the basic aspects of the mental status examination is intended to provide a guide to the many areas of inquiry that should be evaluated and recorded in the process of patient assessment. Assignment of a formal psychiatric diagnosis requires completely integrating the patient's psychiatric and medical history and laboratory assessment with the findings on mental status examination. Knowledge of how certain signs and symptoms "fit" into certain categories in the current psychiatric nomenclature system determines the diagnosis.

The mental status examination is a systematic method to gather behavioral and psychological data with the understanding that such data is then processed, analyzed, and integrated to determine whether or not a diagnosis of a formal psychiatric disease should be made. The principal features can be found in Table 1-5. Even if the degree and severity of the patient's symptoms do not warrant formal DSM-III-R diagnosis, one may nevertheless assess the possible relationship between the symptoms and current stresses to identify a point of therapeutic intervention.

Appearance and Behavior

Any clues regarding the patient's mental functioning and emotional state should be noted. A slovenly appearance, tattered and dirty clothes, pungent body odor, unkempt hair, and dirty hands are often seen in patients with undifferentiated schizophrenia, alcoholism, or dementia. Stooped posture, poor eye contact, tearing, and slow response to questions in a person with an otherwise normal appearance, on the other hand, are more likely to be seen in patients with depression. Other facets of a

---

Table 1–5 **Mental Status Examination Outline**

Appearance and behavior
Speech
Mood and affect
    Anxiety
    Suicidal and homicidal ideation
Language and thought (language and thought
  disorders, delusions)
Perceptions (hallucinations, illusions,
  depersonalization)
Cognitive functioning
    Level of consciousness
    Orientation
    Concentration and attention
    Calculations
    Memory (short, intermediate, and long-term)
    Intelligence
Insight and judgment

patient's appearance and behavior include the patient's apparent health (well developed, bed-ridden), nutritional state (well nourished, emaciated), posture (catatonic, vigilant), mannerisms (tics, hand-wringing), and actions (compulsions, apparent response to hallucinations, random acts). Behavioral and neurological signs and symptoms of intoxication or medication side effects should be noted here as well.

Another aspect of observing behavior is noting the attitude toward the interviewer. For instance, patients who are unusually guarded and suspicious suggest paranoia. Patients who are flattering and ingratiating but then demand special privileges or request disability compensation suggest the manipulative behavior of antisocial, histrionic, or borderline personality disorders. Other descriptors of attitudes toward the interviewer include friendly, cooperative, hostile, threatening, seductive, challenging, and competitive. Each provides a clue to normal and abnormal function when coupled with other aspects of the patient's presentation.

Speech

Tone, rate, and volume of speech should be noted. Depressed patients may speak slowly and quietly with effort, whereas the speech of the manic patient is often rapid, pressured, and resists interruption. The speech of an anxious patient may be both rapid and frantically expressive. Intoxicated patients often speak with loud, slurred speech and are disinhibited in *what* they say.

Mood and Affect

Mood describes the *prevailing* affective state, whereas "affect" generally addresses the degree of appropriateness and variability within that state. The mood may be euthymic (normal mood state), happy, sad, euphoric, suicidal, guilty, bored, anxious, irritable, agitated, panicky, terrified, angry, enraged, or sensual. If affect varies appropriately with the content of the patient's thoughts (becomes bright and warm when discussing close relatives or sad when discussing the death of a friend), the patient is demonstrating a *full* and *appropriate* affect. When the patient is depressed or in a manic euphoria, the affect is characteristically *confined* to that particular range of mood. In some patients with depression or schizophrenia, the affect may be described as *blunted* or *flat* when it is uniform, regardless of the environmental stimuli. Patients with schizophrenia, and occasionally other conditions, may also demonstrate *inappropriate* affect by laughing or grinning while describing an unfortunate or tragic event. Other descriptors of affect are *superficial, shallow, or labile*.

Depressed mood is characterized by general hopelessness, passivity, lifelessness, dysphoria, demoralization, and pessimism. Patients are often irritable, labile, and querulous. Some patients may be profoundly agitated and anxious, whereas others may be quietly apathetic and vegetative. Crying spells may be frequent and uncontrollable. Anhedonia, the inability to experience pleasure and interest in life, is a cardinal symptom of depression. Physical symptoms may also be prominent in depression. In psychotic depression, paranoia and somatic delusions of parasitic infestation or venereal infection may be present. Other symptoms of depression include low self-esteem, feelings of inadequacy, helplessness, guilt, unloveability, worthlessness, excessive self-criticism, and suicidal thoughts.

In mania, the mood is inappropriately euphoric, giddy, silly, disinhibited, or extremely irritable. Grandiose ideas and schemes as well as an inflated self-image may be observed. Emotional expansiveness and excessive and intrusive gregariousness may be observed with the patient's manic mood.

Anxiety. Components of acute or chronic anxiety are often reported by way of the expression of psychophysiologic symptoms. Subjectively, patients may complain of being tense, nervous, fearful, frightened, anxious, worried, fretful, or unable to relax or sleep. Phobic symptoms may be present, such as circumscribed simple phobias (of snakes or spiders, for example), social phobia, or agoraphobia (fear of being alone or being in open or crowded spaces). Anxiety, as part of an obsessive–compulsive disorder, can lead to severe crippling anxiety usually centered around intrusive thoughts or fears. Patients with posttraumatic stress disorders are often chronically anxious and plagued by nightmares and startle responses and are hypervigilant. Symptoms of anxiety are often mixed with those of depression.

Suicidal and homicidal ideation. Detailed questions should be asked about present and past suicidal behavior. Patients should be asked directly if they have had any thoughts of hurting or killing themselves. If such thoughts have occurred, the patient should be asked about his or her plan, the exact methods considered, and how far he or she got with the thoughts or plans. If previous suicide attempts have occurred, their nature, severity, and precipitating cause should be documented, as well as any family history of suicide (assessment of the suicidal patient is further discussed in Chapter 18).

The patient also should be asked if they have had thoughts of hurting others, and if so, what the thoughts have been and how far the planning has progressed. Have they been violent before? Toward whom? And what were the circumstances and consequences? Do they have weapons in their possession, or do they have access to them? Have they ever been arrested or incarcerated for violence? Were drugs or alcohol involved? Do they feel in control of their impulses at the current time?

Language and Thought

An impairment in the ability to translate thoughts into symbols or to use symbols in communication *(language disorder)* differs from a *thought disorder* in that the latter implies a compromised ability to organize, coherently associate, and effectively use information and ideas. Both problems are identified during the process of human interaction and usually require the production of speech. Examples of language disorders include aphasias, alexias, and agraphias and are by definition the result of focal brain dysfunction. A screening examination for language disorders includes the evaluation of spontaneous speech, repetition of words and sentences, comprehension of spoken and written language, the ability to produce names of objects on confrontation, and the ability to write. These are all found on the Mini–Mental State Examination discussed at some length in Chapter 3.

Thought is subdivided into *production of thought, form of thought* (thought process), and *content of thought* and can be disordered in several ways.

Disorders of the production of thought. This refers to the abundance of thought as evidenced by a person's interactional capabilities. In most situations this is assessed by observation of the patient's verbal communication; however, those with speech impediments or congenital mutism can also demonstrate difficulties in this area through other modalities of communication. *Poverty of thought* is characterized by a decrease in the apparent ability or interest in interacting with the environment and other people. This is seen most frequently in schizophrenia and major depression. In some situations, one's thoughts race ahead of one's ability to communicate them *(flight of ideas)*; this is usually seen in mania. *Thought blocking* is characterized by an abrupt cessation of communication before the topic of discussion is completed. The delay that follows may be prolonged, following which patients are often unable to recall the topic. Patients sometimes explain this by stating that their "mind went blank."

Disorders of the form of thought. Form of thought or *thought process* refers to the manner in which thoughts are connected or associated. Normal thinking is goal-directed, with sequential thoughts having logical connections. The "train of thought" can be easily followed, and the communicant reaches the intended goal. Conditions characterized by abnormalities in thought processing, such as psychotic disorders, may be manifested in several ways (see Table 1-6).

Disorders of thought content. Disorders of thought content are often divided into two broad categories—preoccupation and delusions. Preoccupations include phobias, obsessions, and compulsions. A *phobia* is an irrational, pathologic dread of a specific type of stimulus or situation that results in marked anxiety and avoidance of the situation. An *obsession* is a disturbing persistent thought, feeling, or impulse that cannot be eliminated from consciousness. Common obsessions include fear of con-

Table 1-6 **Disorders of Thought Processing**

Circumstantiality
Marked by tedious and unnecessary details but eventually reaches the point.

Tangentiality
Marked by skirting the question rather than answering it. Connections between subsequent thoughts are apparent, but a goal is never reached.

Loosening of associations
A jumping from subject to subject without apparent connection.

Verbigeration
Conveys little information despite adequate volume of speech due to vagueness, empty repetitions, or obscure phrases.

Word salad
An incoherent collection of words and phrases.

Neologisms
Made-up words that have meaning only for the patient.

Clang associations
Words or phrases connected due to characteristics of the words themselves (rhyming, punning) rather than the meaning they convey.

Echolalia
Repetitive, often playful repetition of the words of others.

tamination or losing control and harming others. Obsessions may involve fear of self-harm or suicide, even though the patient may deny feeling depressed or wishing to die. Such suicidal thoughts would be properly included in this portion of the mental status examination. *Compulsions* are irresistible urges to perform meaningless, often ritualistic motor acts.

Delusions are fixed, false beliefs that have no basis in reality, are not held by one's culture, and from which the patient will not be dissuaded despite evidence to the contrary. Delusions can be mood-congruent with the psychiatric state, such as those of *nihilism* (life or world is ending), *poverty* (all life possessions have been lost), *somatic* distress (a serious illness [cancer] has invaded the body), or *sin* (heinous sins have been committed for which punishment is necessary), as is sometimes seen in depression. Delusions of *grandeur*, in which special powers are claimed, are characteristically found in mania. Delusions also can be incongruent with the prevailing mood, such as delusions of reference (unrelated events apply to oneself) or control (outside force controlling actions). These usually are more characteristic of schizophrenia. Karl Schneider described a group of delusions characterized by externally imposed influences concerning thought, feelings, and somatic function. These are referred to as the "first-rank symptoms of schizophrenia," although they are known to occur in affective and organic psychoses as well (see Table 1-7). These symptoms also are reviewed in the chapter on schizophrenia (Chapter 4).

Perception

Perceptual disturbance involves disordered processing of sensory information. Hallucinations are perceptions that occur in the absence of actual stimuli. Illusions are

Table 1–7 **Schneider's First-Rank Symptoms of Schizophrenia**

	BELIEF
Thought insertion	An external agency is inserting thoughts into the passive mind.
Thought withdrawal	An external agency is removing thoughts from the passive mind.
Thought broadcasting	Thoughts are audible to others.
Made feelings (passivity feelings)	Feelings being experienced are imposed by an external source.
Made drives (passivity feelings)	Powerful drives (to which the patient usually responds) are being imposed by an external agency.
Made volitional acts (passivity feelings)	Actions are completely under the control of an external influence.
Somatic passivity (passivity feelings)	Bodily sensations are being imposed by an external agency against the will.
Delusional perception	A two-stage phenomenon in which a normally perceived stimulus is followed by a delusional belief regarding the meaning of the stimulus.

Other first-rank symptoms involve specific types of auditory hallucinations.

misinterpretations of existing stimuli. Auditory hallucinations occur most frequently in the psychoses of schizophrenia, mania, or other "functional" disorders. Visual hallucinations occur more frequently than auditory hallucinations in organic psychotic episodes (such as those due to substance abuse, toxins, and intrinsic brain disease), although visual hallucinations are often associated with primary psychiatric disease. Olfactory and gustatory hallucinations often occur as prodromal symptoms of complex partial seizures. Haptic hallucinations, especially the sensation of bugs crawling on one's skin (formication), frequently occur in delirium induced by sedative withdrawal. There is considerable overlap in these symptoms, however, and none is specific to, or pathognomonic of, the disorders noted.

Paranoid delusions may be highly systematized (such as elaborate systems of observations by the FBI or CIA, plots) or bizarre (Martians peering at one from outer space). Paranoia as an isolated symptom is not specifically diagnostic. It is the nature, duration, *and* severity of the paranoia in the context of the patient's history that relates it to one particular diagnosis or the other. For example, the isolated delusion that one's wife is having an affair in the absence of other signs or symptoms would be diagnosed as delusional disorder. A severely depressed patient who had paranoid delusions of being persecuted would most likely have a major depression with psychotic features; a woman with paranoid delusions of being watched and followed by the CIA, with a longtitudinal course and other more pervasive symptoms of a thought disorder, might be diagnosed as having paranoid schizophrenia; a man with paranoid ideation in the context of amphetamines might be considered to have an organic delusional disorder. Somatic delusions such as feelings of rotting inside, being infected with a venereal disease, or having AIDS may be seen in psychotic depression. Alternatively, general suspiciousness, mistrust, cynicism, and querulousness of others that does not reach overtly delusional proportions may be seen as a trait of a paranoid personality.

Depersonalization refers to feelings that one is falling apart, fragmenting, "not the same," not one's self, becoming unreal, or detached and may be seen in a number of psychiatric disorders—principally anxiety disorders, but also organic mental disorders, including those that are substance induced. Symptoms of *derealization* include the feeling that the world is not real, people are not real, or things are becoming distant, alien, or strange. Both types of symptoms are variations on the same theme and may be seen in CNS disease, such as complex partial seizures.

Cognitive Functioning

Level of consciousness. It is best to describe a patient's level of consciousness by his or her ability to respond to the environmental stimuli. Extremes include hyperalertness and coma. *Hyperalertness* is characterized by hypervigilance, often with agitation or tremulousness, and is seen most often in mania or delirium. *Alert* describes normal wakefulness and awareness of the environment. *Lethargic* indicates the patient has a tendency to drift into unresponsiveness if left alone but is easily roused to verbal stimulus. *Stupor* reflects the need for continual stimulation to maintain consciousness, and *coma* is characterized by unconsciousness and the absence of response to any stimuli.

Orientation. Orientation assesses awareness of identity, time (day of week, month, exact day of month, year, time of day), place, and situation. Awareness of person usually indicates that a person can remember his or her name. Awareness of time and place involves the ability to provide the correct date and current location, while awareness of situation suggests a grasp of the circumstances surrounding the patient's current plight. In confusional states, the first manifestation of disorientation normally involves time and situation, and these are usually the last to normalize with recovery.

Concentration (attention). Concentration refers to the ability to direct and sustain attention. Patients with impaired attention require repetition of questions and may be distracted by seemingly inconsequential stimuli. Concentration is formally tested by performance of serial 7s or 3s (counting backward from 100 by 7s or 3s). Alternatively, the patient can be asked to repeat strings of random numbers forward (average normal—seven digits) or in reverse (average normal—five digits). Failure is identified by two unsuccessful attempts at the same number. Gross impairment of concentration (attention) is characteristic of delirium and is usually recognized by the patient's inability to respond to your requests consistently and coherently.

Memory. Tests of memory assess the ability to retrieve and recite information previously stored (retrograde memory) and to form new memories (anterograde memory). Remote memory (usually retrograde) involves remembering events that occurred many years ago, such as the name of a school attended, the nature of previous jobs, and so forth. With disorders of declining intellectual function, this is usually one of the last to be affected. Recent past memory (retrograde and/or anterograde) involves remembering events occurring months ago and may be assessed as the patient provides believable and/or confirmed details of the present illness or events leading up to the assessment.

Inability to form new memories (anterograde) is clinically identified when patients are unable to recall events that have just occurred or people they have just met. Less obvious forms of anterograde memory dysfunction can be assessed by providing the names of three unrelated objects that the patient immediately repeats (immediate recall) and then recalls after 5 minutes (short-term memory). Impairment of immediate recall, especially with repeated attempts, suggests an attention deficit that precludes further anterograde memory testing. Intact immediate recall with impaired recall after 5 minutes suggests impairment of short-term memory.

Isolated deficits in cognitive function are diagnostically nonspecific because they can occur with intellectual decline of varied cause. If identified by the screening tests performed on the mental status examination, they should be further characterized by more formal neuropsychological testing (*infra vide*). Use of the Mini–Mental State Examination, a structured approach to assessing memory, is discussed in Chapter 3. Further discussion of cognitive assessment is deferred to that discussion.

Intelligence. Some observations may be made about the patient's general education level and the ability to learn, integrate, and process new information. Formal education level does not necessarily indicate intelligence, because intelligence, most basically, is an assessment of the individual's ability to learn new information, process that information, and solve problems. Individuals with relatively little or no formal education can be quite intelligent. On the other hand, a person who has completed his or her doctorate would not be expected to function in the range of those with borderline intellectual function. Formal psychological testing may be needed, especially in children or where mental retardation is expected, to assess the patient's intelligence level accurately.

Insight and Judgment

Insight refers to awareness of factors influencing one's situation. When a patient has a psychiatric illness, insight refers to the appreciation that an illness or psychiatric difficulty is occurring, recognition of its impact on the ability to function, and awareness of the need to take steps to correct it. The most meaningful method of assessing insight is to gather data about these factors throughout the history. The presence or absence of insight has profound impact on adjustment to illness, compliance with treatment, and consequent level of function. Thus, an estimation of a patient's insight is helpful in planning an effective treatment strategy.

The patient's capacity for self-observation and demonstration of empathy are also measures of insight that are helpful in assessing the presence of a personality disorder. Patients with a personality disorder are often egocentric, tend to blame others for their problems, and resist self-examination to determine their personal contribution to their difficulties in life.

Empathy refers to the ability to identify with the feelings of others and to "feel with them." It is also a measure of consideration for the feelings, welfare, and rights of others. Patients with some personality disorders (antisocial, paranoid, narcissistic, and borderline personality disorders) often show a lack of empathy for others and exploit other people for their own gratification. Traits found in personality disorder and details about their diagnosis are discussed in Chapter 5.

Judgment refers to a person's ability to handle finances; manage day-to-day activities; and avoid danger, including exposure to heat, cold, malnutrition, and crime. Insight into factors influencing a person's well-being must be present before options and priorities can be weighed and judgment exercised. Standardized methods of assessment, such as asking what a person would do if he or she found a stamped, addressed envelope on the sidewalk, are inadequate for most purposes. It is more helpful to rely on an understanding of the circumstances that led to the patient's seeking psychiatric attention in assessing judgment. For instance, a person walking in the snow with shorts and no shoes would, in the absence of extenuating circumstances, be exhibiting poor judgment. Despite the subjective nature of the assessment, impaired judgment resulting from mental illness or substance dependence that directly or indirectly places the patient or others in danger is a prerequisite for involuntary commitment in many states.

PSYCHOLOGICAL AND NEUROPSYCHOLOGICAL TESTING

Tests of psychological and neuropsychological function complement, but do not replace, the psychiatric history and mental status examination, just as laboratory and radiologic procedures complement but do not replace the medical history and physical examination. This is a particularly important point, because no standardized test used in clinical practice provides an assessment that allows a psychiatric diagnosis to be made, with the possible exception of dementia. There is a tendency among nonpsychiatrists to use psychological tests, such as the Minnesota Multiphasic Personality Inventory (MMPI) or the General Health Questionnaire (GHQ), to establish whether a psychiatric disorder may be involved in a patient's symptom picture. As will be discussed later, this can lead to inappropriate labeling and ineffective treatment. When correctly used, however, psychological and neuropsychological tests provide an important adjunct to the psychiatric evaluation and treatment plan.

Neuropsychological tests assess cognitive abilities and require the expertise of a psychologist who has received specialized training in their administration and interpretation (a neuropsychologist). *Psychological tests* were developed to identify the presence and frequency of psychological symptoms in various populations. Some psychological tests are easily administered or self-administered and can be readily scored merely by reading a short description of the test. Others are more complex and require skills in the interpretation and quantification of the behaviors being tested. Those with master's degrees or doctorates in psychology usually possess the skills necessary to perform these tests if they choose to emphasize this area in their work. Not all psychologists, however, specialize in giving and interpreting psychological tests, so care should be taken to assure that the person doing the testing has an adequate background and interest.

Psychological and neuropsychological tests are best used to clarify specific important questions during patient assessment and management. Although the multitude of standardized tests cannot be covered in this chapter, four common clinical questions in which psychological and neuropsychological tests can help with clinical decision making will be addressed. These include (1) Are psychiatric factors involved in the patient's clinical presentation? (2) Can the severity of the patient's psychiatric symptoms be reproducibly assessed and used to monitor improvement? (3) Does the patient's personality assessment give a clue about psychiatric involvement? and (4) Does the patient have impaired brain function? Because it is impossible to review all the tests that could potentially assist in answering these questions, only a few widely used and well-standardized tests will be discussed. More extensive discussion of these and other tests can be found in the book by van Riezen and Segal (1988). Psychological tests are used to address the first three questions, whereas neuropsychological tests are used in the last.

Screening Tests for Psychiatric Involvement

Are there screening tests that detect the presence of specific psychiatric disorders? *No!* There are, however, self-administered screening questionnaires that can be used before a psychiatric assessment that identify those at risk for psychiatric difficulties. These instruments are best used in primary care outpatient and inpatient settings. Because these tests are often exquisitely sensitive but have limited specificity, it is necessary to be aware of the need for more formalized psychiatric assessment before a diagnosis is considered and treatment for a "psychiatric" condition is instituted.

The General Health Questionnaire (GHQ) is a widely studied self-report instrument validated primarily in nonpsychiatric outpatient populations. A low score on this test predicts that a psychiatric disorder is unlikely and that psychiatric factors are probably not involved in the symptom presentation. High scores suggest the need for further questioning if the presentation of the patient suggests that psychiatric factors may be playing a role. The GHQ can save valuable time in screening new outpatients attending a primary care clinic by alerting the clinician to patients who might require more careful psychiatric evaluation in addition to the medical work-up.

Depression is one of the most common psychiatric disorders seen in primary care medical populations. The Center for Epidemiologic Studies–Depression Scale (CES-D) is a self-report questionnaire that has been standardized to identify those at risk for depression in the general population. It lists the presence of a number of depressive symptoms but does not, even when the score is elevated, suggest that a pathological depression is present or that treatment should be administered. The CES-D is a sensitive screen for depression in clinical samples requiring confirmation through clinical evaluation.

The Mini–Mental State Examination (MMSE) screens for deteriorating *cognitive* function and is not a comprehensive psychiatric assessment instrument. This exam is administered by the physician at the bedside and covers a variety of cognitive skills. Unlike the GHQ and screening tests for depression, impaired function (scores of less than 24 or 25 out of 30 in an alert subject) on the MMSE is highly suggestive of cognitive difficulties. More specific neuropsychiatric testing should be done in these patients. The use of the MMSE is addressed in detail in Chapter 3.

Screening for Severity of Illness

One of the most important tasks of the clinician is to establish a baseline level of symptoms and to confirm that the treatment being given results in their reduction. Although the patient interview is the principal means of accomplishing this purpose, several tests that reliably document psychiatric symptoms can improve consistency. Depression severity and change can be monitored with the Beck Depression Inventory (self-report) or the Hamilton Rating Scale for Depression (interviewer-rated). The Hamilton Rating Scale for Anxiety (interviewer-rated) is available to quantitate symptoms of anxiety. General psychiatric severity can be assessed with the Hopkins Symptoms Checklist 90 (HCL-90) (self-report), whereas psychotic symptoms can be enumerated with the Brief Psychiatric Rating Scale (interviewer-rated). Because the HCL-90 is divided into subscales pertaining to specific areas of psychiatric symptoms, the questions pertinent only to that area can be repeatedly administered during treatment.

Screening with Personality Questionnaires

Although personality disorders have received relatively little rigorous, systematic research attention, there is growing evidence that the presence of personality disorder in patients with other major psychiatric disorders is associated with increased severity and poorer outcome. Additionally, personality disorder may increase the likelihood of contact with health professionals for medical conditions (Reich, 1987).

The Minnesota Multiphasic Personality Inventory (MMPI) is perhaps the most commonly used personality assessment instrument. It has nine clinical scales from which profiles of behavioral patterns are derived and, when originally formulated (1939), was well standardized in a large control population. Two problems arise with the use of the MMPI in current practice. First, the MMPI was standardized when cultural mores were considerably different from today and well before the psychiatric diagnostic system in current use. The importance of this problem is emphasized by the fact that restandardization of the MMPI in a contemporary population showed that there was a 20–30% difference in the identification of dysfunction between the old and new standards (Colligan, Osborne, Swenson, Offord, 1983). Despite these findings, which suggest that many patients are being misclassified, few testing centers have switched to the new standards, and the revised MMPI is just beginning to be implemented at the level of the general community practice setting.

Not only are there problems with the use of a dated population standard, but there are also difficulties in the interpretations made based on test results. In the 1940s, interpretation was based on a conceptualization of psychiatric disease very different from that espoused today. The relevance of "standard" (often computer-generated) personality profiles from the MMPI to current psychiatric disorders is uncertain, because they are based on different theoretical constructs. Significant differences can therefore occur between the MMPI results and a diagnosis revealed through clinical interview.

The second major problem with the MMPI is that it is commonly used to assess patients with medical illness. Because the test was standardized in a nonmedically ill control group, using this instrument to determine whether psychiatric factors may be involved in the complaints of patients with real or potential medical illness is inappropriate (Osborne, 1987). Such patients will routinely rate high on the hypochondriacal and depressive scales because a number of the questions in these scales reflect the presence of physical symptoms (real or imagined). Unfortunately, those evaluating patients in whom a functional cause is in the differential are frequently enamored by the fact that the MMPI gives real and reproducible numbers to quantitate psychiatric disturbances while forgetting that the results are of questionable validity. *For this and the reasons listed above, the MMPI is not recommended as a routine adjunct to the clinical interview,* and its use should be limited to special situations.

Because the MMPI is not useful for DSM-III-R personality disorder diagnosis, new interviews to assess DSM-III and DSM-III-R personality disorder have been created (see Chapter 5). The Personality Diagnostic Questionnaire (PDQ) (self-report) and the Structured Interview for the Diagnosis of Personality (SIDP) (interviewer-rated) are examples of such instruments. These new instruments are currently used mainly in research but, when better standardized, may find wider clinical use.

Screening for Impaired Brain Function

The principal aims of neuropsychological testing are to provide an estimate of the severity of cognitive deficit, to localize the areas of the brain that are impaired, and to assess the degree and estimated duration of functional limitations. The Halstead–Reitan Battery and the Luria–Nebraska Inventory are two extensive test batteries that help answer questions related to the areas above. Unfortunately, the length of testing makes these tests unsuitable in severely ill psychiatric patients. The Wechsler Adult Intelligence Scale—Revised and other briefer screens (Berg, Franzen, Wedding, 1987) of cognitive function now frequently replace the more comprehensive batteries (see Table 1-8). These tests require the assistance of a neuropsychologist for administration and interpretation. Additionally, the comprehensive neuropsychological batteries can be expensive. Nevertheless, complete neuropsychological batteries may be helpful in defining subtle cognitive deficits and are indicated in some clinical situations, such as in evaluating patients who have sustained severe head injuries or occupational exposure to potential neurologic toxins, patients who may have temporal lobe seizures, or patients with cerebrovascular disease. Comprehensive neuropsychological inventories also can be helpful when legal compensation issues are important or for planning rehabilitation programs.

CLASSIFICATION OF PSYCHIATRIC DISEASE: DSM-III-R

As in all medical disciplines, the nature of the information obtained during the diagnostic interview conforms to the classification of illness used. The classification, in turn, should be derived from the ability to consistently identify complexes of signs and

Table 1-8 **Comprehensive Neuropsychologic Batteries and Specific Function Tests**

NEUROPSYCHOLOGIC BATTERIES	NUMBER OF SECTIONS	COMMENTS
Halstead–Reitan Battery (HRB)	10	Includes MMPI & WAIS. Full test may take several days
Luria–Nebraska Inventory	11	Provides score on 14 measures of cognitive function with *t* scores

Tests of Specific Function	**Function Tested**	
Wechsler Adult Intelligence Screen-R (WAIS)	Verbal and nonverbal skills	Provides verbal and performance intelligence scores as well as a full-scale IQ
Token Test	Speech	Can be used as a screening test for aphasia
Wechsler Memory Scale	Memory	Seven subtests; provides memory quotient similar to IQ
Wisconsin Card Sort	Abstraction—conceptual shifting	Considered a test of frontal lobe function
Trail-Making Test	Visuomotor tracking	Contains parts A and B; performance decreases with age
Seashore Rhythm Test	Nonverbal auditory	Part of HRB; tests ability to discriminate between two tone groups
Finger-Tapping Test	Motor	Cortical damage slows tapping speed

symptoms that predict etiology, natural course, family involvement, outcome, and response to treatment of a condition that causes or leads to impairment. DSM-III-R reflects the state of the art in classifying psychiatric disease in the United States and, at least in part, stems from two previous classification systems used since the mid-1970s in psychiatric research (the "Feighner criteria" [Feighner et al., 1972] and Research Diagnostic Criteria [Spitzer, Endicott, Robins, 1978]).

DSM-III-R uses a signs-and-symptoms, criterion-based approach to psychiatric diagnosis. If certain symptoms are present in sufficient degree and for sufficient duration, then the diagnosis can be made. Those meeting "criteria" are thus more likely to conform to the predictive factors known about the disease being diagnosed. As might be expected, some conditions have greater validity than others. For instance, depression, mania, schizophrenia, panic disorder, alcohol and substance abuse, and somatization disorder can be reproducibly identified. As a result, definite statements can be made regarding the likely age of onset, sex distribution, familial involvement, course if untreated, and probability of response to certain interventions in those carrying these diagnoses. Other diagnoses, however, such as personality disorder (with the exception of antisocial personality disorder), adjustment disorders, and psychosexual disorders, currently have less predictive value. As more research is performed, these will be further refined or deleted, depending on the findings.

Those who do not meet criteria for diagnosis according to DSM-III-R can be diagnosed with "no psychiatric disorder" or the possible/probable distinction for a certain condition. This occurs commonly when DSM-III-R is correctly used and does not preclude that such patients be treated. What such diagnoses say is that these patients do not warrant a label with its positive and negative connotations, although a clinical trial may be attempted to see whether symptoms improve.

In an attempt to ensure that information of value in planning treatment and predicting outcome is recorded, DSM-III-R uses a multiaxial system of evaluation. Axes I and II comprise mental disorders; Axis III, physical disorders and conditions; and Axes IV and V, severity of psychosocial stressors and global assessment of functioning, respectively.

Axis I diagnoses include clinical syndromes that represent a deterioration from a previous level of functioning, such as schizophrenia, major depression, and substance-abuse disorders. Axis II includes developmental disorders and personality disorders. Patients with Axis II diagnoses, in contrast to Axis I, usually have symptoms extending back into the early developmental years. Axis I and II disorders frequently coexist, requiring careful evaluation of Axis I disorders in patients with personality disorder. Physical disorders (Axis III) exacerbate or cause Axis I and II disorders in up to 50% of patients with psychiatric conditions (LaBruzza, 1981). It is therefore very important to document the medical conditions present and assess whether they may be impacting on the psychiatric symptoms.

Although DSM-III-R does not identify stress as a major cause of psychiatric disorders, the importance of psychosocial stressors is noted in Axis IV. Acute and chronic stressors are listed and rated as 1 to 6 (none to extreme). Axis V rates the current global assessment of function (GAF) and the highest functioning of the patient in the past year in terms of social, occupational, or academic activity. Ratings of impairment are made on a 0 (most) to 90 (least) scale. An example of the multiaxial patient assessment as it relates to RH is listed in Table 1-9.

Table 1–9 **DSM-III-R Multiaxial Evaluation for Patient RH**

Axis I: 293.00 Delirium
291.00 Alcohol withdrawal delirium (provisional)
303.90 Alcohol dependence
Axis II: 799.90 Diagnosis deferred on Axis II
Axis III: Status post–head trauma
Subdural hematoma
Alcoholic cirrhosis of liver
Alcoholic gastritis
Pancreatitis
Hyponatremia
Hypomagnesemia
Hypocalcemia
Macrocytic anemia
Thrombocytopenia
Essential hypertension
Axis IV: Psychosocial stressors
Acute events—none
Severity: 1—none
Enduring circumstances—divorce, unemployment, few friends
Severity: 4—severe
Axis V: Current GAF: 10 (on admission)
Highest GAF past year: 60

GAF, global assessment of function.

"V" (the letter) codes constitute emotional situations not attributable to a mental disorder. Examples include marital problems, uncomplicated bereavement, and so forth, and were described previously as "problems in living." When a patient does not have a psychiatric condition yet seeks emotional support, these are used to describe the circumstances in either Axis I or II. V codes allow description of the presenting problem without assigning the patient a psychiatric diagnosis with its negative implications.

Important Diagnostic Issues

Two medical problem-solving principles are important in identifying psychiatric illness (Elstein, Shulman, Sprafka, 1978). First, common diseases are the most likely to be seen and should not be overlooked. Table 1-10 shows that mood disorders, anxiety disorders, alcohol and substance abuse, and adjustment disorders are seen often in several clinical settings. They therefore deserve special attention and consideration. Second, uncommon problems have increased importance when effective treatment is available. Missing an uncommon problem in this situation can be catastrophic. This frequently happens in patients with reversible organic causes of psychiatric syndromes.

Finally, diagnosis of psychiatric disorders that may be complicated by suicidal or homicidal ideation should not be overlooked. Depression, schizophrenia, substance

Table 1–10 **Rank Order of Psychiatric Diagnoses by Site of Encounter**

SURVEY OF OUTPATIENT PHYSICIANS	GENERAL HOSPITAL PSYCHIATRIC CONSULTATION	INPATIENT PSYCHIATRIC SERVICE	COMMUNITY SURVEY
Anxiety disorders	Mood disorders	Mood disorders	Substance abuse
Mood disorders	Adjustment disorders	Schizophrenia	Anxiety disorders
Substance abuse	No psychiatric diagnosis	Substance abuse	Mood disorders
Psychophysiologic disorders	Substance abuse	Organic mental disorders	Antisocial personality
Adjustment disorders	Organic mental disorders	Adjustment disorders	Schizophrenia

abuse, and antisocial personality deserve serious attention, because all may endanger the patient or others.

Differential Diagnosis

Identifying the underlying psychiatric problem(s) and the variables that might be impacting on it (them) involves a stepwise process. Initially, the chief complaint and associated symptoms related in the history of present illness will suggest the major DSM-III-R diagnostic category (for students they help identify the appropriate diagnostic decision tree in DSM-III-R [1987]). (See also Fig. 1-1.) Once the principal symptoms or problems are identified, then refinements (first differential) are made during the history-taking process to help establish which diagnostic category best describes the clinical situation. Because the end product of this process will influence the treatment or assistance given to the patient, thoroughness is very important.

The decision trees for primary psychiatric disease in DSM-III-R suggest that organic factors should be identified at the onset of the evaluation. If they are, then the clinician steps into the decision tree for organic mental disorders. In some cases this is possible, for such conditions as steroid psychosis or lupus cerebritis are often readily identifiable at the onset, thus facilitating the recognition of the organic nature of the mental symptoms.

Much more often, the patient will present with no evidence or limited evidence of organic conditions that might be related to the psychiatric symptoms. In these circumstances, decisions about the psychiatric syndromes in question are made based on the assumption that symptoms are unrelated to medical illness. For instance, a patient with undiagnosed hypothyroidism who has many symptoms in common with depression (Table 1-11) presents to a primary physician or psychiatrist with complaints of weakness, constipation, crying spells, difficulty sleeping, and weight gain. Because the patient appears depressed and, in fact, has many symptoms of depression, the differential for mood disturbance is entertained. Sure enough, the patient meets all the criteria for a severe single major depressive episode, and yet the underlying problem is hypothyroidism.

This suggests that even after a presumed psychiatric condition is diagnosed, it is often necessary to run through another differential (the second) of conditions that

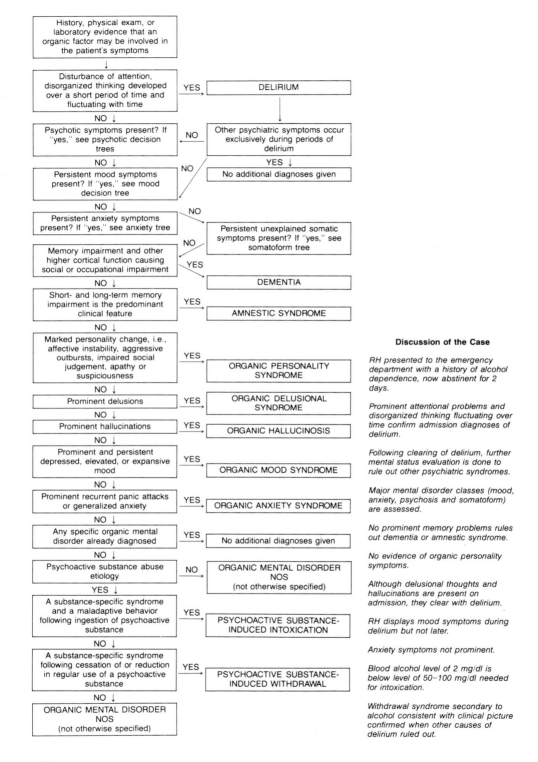

Discussion of the Case

RH presented to the emergency department with a history of alcohol dependence, now abstinent for 2 days.

Prominent attentional problems and disorganized thinking fluctuating over time confirm admission diagnoses of delirium.

Following clearing of delirium, further mental status evaluation is done to rule out other psychiatric syndromes.

Major mental disorder classes (mood, anxiety, psychosis and somatoform) are assessed.

No prominent memory problems rules out dementia or amnestic syndrome.

No evidence of organic personality symptoms.

Although delusional thoughts and hallucinations are present on admission, they clear with delirium.

RH displays mood symptoms during delirium but not later.

Anxiety symptoms not prominent.

Blood alcohol level of 2 mg/dl is below level of 50–100 mg/dl needed for intoxication.

Withdrawal syndrome secondary to alcohol consistent with clinical picture confirmed when other causes of delirium ruled out.

Table 1–11 **Comparison of Psychological Symptoms in Hypothyroidism and Depression**

HYPOTHYROIDISM (%)	DEPRESSION
Loss of energy (25–98)	Loss of energy
Weakness (25–95)	Weakness
Poor concentration	Poor concentration
Memory loss (48–66)	Memory loss
Slowed actions (48–91)	Motor retardation
Decreased sex drive	Decreased libido
Constipation (38–61)	Constipation
Insomnia (25–98)	Insomnia
Nervousness (13–58)	Agitation

may be causally or casually related to the syndrome. In the case of major depression, for instance, symptoms could be the result of underlying medical conditions, such as endocrine disease, cancer, anemia, hypoxemia, medication reaction, epilepsy, and so forth. It could be the result of stress, such as the death of a loved one. It could be secondary to a preexisting psychiatric condition, such as antisocial personality disorder, alcoholism, and so forth. Or it could be feigned by someone who wants compensation, attention, and so forth.

The reason that this second differential is important in the care of patients is that, depending on the complicating circumstances, major differences may occur in the way the patient is handled. This is illustrated in Table 1-12. *This second differential is not presented nor discussed in DSM-III-R yet represents an essential part of the differential diagnosis process.*

The psychiatric evaluation as outlined in this chapter helps to perform this function in a time-efficient yet thorough manner. The chief complaint and history of present illness are used to identify the principal difficulty of the patient. The history of present illness helps determine whether a syndrome of behavior is present and how typical it is. It also documents the presence of variables that may directly influence the production or continuation of symptoms.

The past medical and psychiatric history, personal and social history, and review of systems uncover information and discrepancies that could have a bearing on the presenting complaints but do not, at first glance, appear to have a relationship. And the physical examination and laboratory assessment confirm or deny suspicions derived from the history about possible organic involvement and check for signs of diseases not entertained.

One help in differentiating primary psychiatric disorders from those related to the secondary conditions noted is to have a good understanding of the primary psychiatric disorders. Such knowledge includes symptom presentation, age of onset, sex ratio, natural course, family involvement, and likelihood of response to treatment. For example, major depression is more frequent in women, has its onset during the 20s to 40s, runs a recurrent course, has a higher incidence in other members of the family,

◄ **Figure 1–1.** *Differential diagnosis of organic mental syndromes. (Adapted from Diagnostic and Statistical Manual of Mental Disorders, 3rd ed rev.)*

Table 1–12 **Sample Treatment Strategies in the Treatment of Patients with Depression**

CLINICAL SITUATION	TREATMENT
Primary major depression	Antidepressant medication
	Cognitive psychotherapy
	Social support
Depression secondary to hypothyroidism	No antidepressant medication
	Supportive psychotherapy
	Reassurance and social support
	Thyroid replacement
	Education about when symptoms will resolve
Adjustment disorder with depression in histrionic personality disorder and somatization	No antidepressant medication
	Supportive psychotherapy
	Social support
Depression in a patient caught faking the symptoms	Empathic confrontation
	No antidepressant medication
	Supportive psychotherapy
Depression two weeks after mother's death	Supportive psychotherapy
	Social support

has few or no residual symptoms between episodes, and has a good likelihood of response to cyclic antidepressants or other antidepressant therapies. Therefore, if a patient presents for the first time in his or her 70s, has no history of emotional problems, other family members have had no difficulty with affective problems, and the symptoms are cluttered with unusual complaints, then causes for the psychiatric presentation other than primary depression should be given greater consideration.

DSM-III-R Case Formulation

Refer to, or reread, the case of RH presented at the beginning of this chapter. This case presentation describes a middle-aged man with a life-long history of alcohol abuse that progressed to the point that he abstained only when sleep, unconsciousness, illness, or the inability to procure more intervened. He was admitted agitated and incoherent with paranoid thoughts and physical signs and symptoms suggesting alcohol withdrawal. Other causes of delirium were possible, because the patient had liver enzyme and electrolyte disturbances, pancreatitis, a gastrointestinal bleed, and cerebral trauma. Nonetheless, because the clinical history from the patient, the police, and the family was most compatible with alcohol withdrawal delirium (delirium tremens), it was considered the most likely Axis I diagnosis (Table 1-9). Despite this working diagnosis, other possible causes of the patient's mental state were being considered or corrected while the patient was treated for alcohol withdrawal.

During the years before admission, he demonstrated dependence and tolerance to alcohol. His education was shortened, marriage broken, job lost, and health impaired because of alcohol consumption. Despite attempts at in- and outpatient treatment, he persisted in nearly continuous intoxication. He showed drinking behavior consistent with that of other first- and second-degree family members. This tight history of mental and emotional problems related to alcohol ingestion supports the Axis I diagnosis of alcohol dependence (see DSM-III-R for criteria). The differential diagnosis decision tree for organic mental disorders allowed the diagnoses of delirium and alcohol dependence to be made in the case of RH (Fig. 1-1). The diagnoses, however, did not reflect the complicated nature of his case. Although the diagnosis of delirium was apparent, the differential for the potential causes is not listed. This is particularly important, because the cause usually dictates the treatment. Furthermore, it was necessary to modify the decision tree after the treatment of the delirium had been successful to once again exclude the possibility of primary psychiatric disease. The decision trees in DSM-III-R are not made for complicated cases.

Other psychiatric syndromes are seen frequently in men with alcohol dependence. These include depression, other forms of substance abuse, antisocial personality disorder, anxiety, and dementia. RH had a history of antisocial traits, but these were insufficient to make the diagnosis of antisocial personality disorder. Furthermore, the antisocial traits that were present (school expulsion, difficulties with teachers, frequent fights, arrests) always occurred under the influence of alcohol. RH denied abuse of other substances, and this was confirmed, at least at the time of admission, by the absence of other substances of abuse in his urine. The family also confirmed that he didn't use "pills."

RH had a history of depressed affect during intoxication or withdrawal accompanied by suicidal ideation on several occasions. During periods of abstinence, depression had never been a problem. Both during and after treatment of the patient's withdrawal delirium, there was no evidence of depression, despite an apparently dismal life situation. Despite treatment with antianxiety medications, he showed no evidence for current or past anxiety disorder.

It was impossible to assess cognitive function of the patient during the delirious state. After adequate treatment, however, he was able to score 29 of 30 on the MMSE (see screening tests section and Chapter 3). Although this does not exclude the possibility that more subtle evidence for cognitive impairment is present in this high-risk patient, it does suggest that dementia is not a major problem. More specialized cognitive testing was not performed in RH for reasons that will be discussed later. As in many patients with alcohol dependence, the patient exhibits some traits of avoidant, dependent, schizoid, and passive aggressive personality disorders. There is insufficient evidence to make the diagnosis of any one of these or to make a diagnosis of mixed personality disorder because the influence that alcohol has on these traits cannot be parceled out, even when the chart is reviewed thoroughly. The Axis II diagnosis is therefore deferred. As previously mentioned, antisocial personality disorder, which has greater validity and reliability than other personality disorders, has been excluded.

The Axis III diagnoses for RH are listed in Table 1-9 and are primarily related to complications of alcohol abuse. The patient, however, had a seizure 3 weeks into his hospital stay. Although alcohol withdrawal seizure is a logical choice in the differential, it occurred outside the expected period (3 to 14 days) for this complication to happen. The EEG and CT, documenting a subdural hematoma, were done not only because the presentation was atypical (although this would have been enough) but also because RH was at high risk for an alternative cause of new seizure onset because of his history of alcohol abuse and thrombocytopenia. In addition, it may be recalled that the patient had a head bruise on physical examination, and the fundoscopic examination had not been performed because of poor patient compliance.

The subdural hematoma could have been identified earlier had a more aggressive central nervous system work-up for delirium been done at the outset. This is where systematic and thorough examination and informed clinical judgment become so important. The patient is at a high risk for other causes of central nervous system pathology because of the unreliable alcoholic state, and a fundoscopic examination was not initially possible during the delirium. Delirium alone should be sufficient to warrant further evaluation in such a case. Decisions such as these have important implications regarding patient care.

Before the onset of this admission, the patient experienced no acute stressors (Axis IV, Code 1) that would have predisposed him to admission. Although not receiving his disability check could have been considered an acute stressor, it is more likely that the lack of alcohol was a major factor in his presentation. However, he was unemployed, had no social support system, and suffered from intermittent medical problems related to his alcohol abuse, which qualify as severe, enduring stressful circumstances (Axis IV, Code 4). The patient's global assessment of function during the delirious state suggests that he wouldn't have been able to maintain his personal care on his own (Axis V, Code 10). Highest function during the past year would, at best, be moderate impairment (Axis V, Code 60), because he had limited friends, no job, and few productive activities.

RH responded well to high-dose benzodiazepines for withdrawal within a few days of initial hospitalization. Other medical factors were evaluated and treated during the initial hospital stay. As the patient's delirium resolved, further information was obtained from the patient, and his behavior was observed to confirm the initial impression and determine whether other psychiatric conditions might be present, especially those with a high frequency in alcohol dependence. Particular emphasis was placed on observing the patient's ability to identify familiar personnel, locate his room, and perform activities of daily living. He did these without trouble after the delirium cleared, suggesting that he would be able to function satisfactorily outside a structured environment. Furthermore, documenting these behaviors obviated the need to perform more formalized and expensive neuropsychological testing.

RH had participated in several alcohol treatment programs without lasting benefit. For this reason, legal commitment to an inpatient treatment center was deemed unlikely to benefit him. This particular admission was occasioned by a serious threat to the patient's life. It is at times like these that some alcoholics become sufficiently frightened that they enter and follow through on their resolve to stay sober. Because he expressed an interest in reinitiating contact with Alcoholics Anonymous, this was encouraged during his hospital stay. Such a program, if adhered to, effectively uses group support, confrontation, religious motivation, and behavior modification to modify the long-term behavior of alcoholics. Because it is run by former alcoholics, rationalizations and ploys are much more difficult to get away with than when mental health professionals administer treatment.

Social factors also often play a role in when and how much alcoholics drink. One thing that has not been done is to have the patient live in a more structured environment, such as a nursing home, in the hope that opportunities to imbibe would not be as frequent. The patient would have to agree to this and be willing to cooperate with the personnel in abiding by rules at the facility.

When the clinical situation warrants, a systematic psychiatric assessment is important for appropriate patient care, regardless of the setting. It requires an understanding of current psychiatric nomenclature (DSM-III-R) and predictive value of the disorders being diagnosed. Because psychiatric conditions are no longer diagnosed merely by excluding other illnesses that can cause similar complaints, it is important to know what questions to ask and how to ask them, as well as to accurately observe the behaviors that lead to making a psychiatric diagnosis. The skilled use of the mental status examination, psychological and neuropsychological tests, and laboratory evaluations will help differentiate medical from psychiatric problems or identify the relationship between the two. DSM-III-R provides a framework, albeit not perfect, for considering psychiatric diagnosis in the differential diagnosis of many patient problems. Chapter 2 discusses basic aspects of psychodynamic assessment, and other chapters will discuss the major psychiatric diagnostic categories in more detail, including specific issues relevant to clinical diagnosis and treatment.

ANNOTATED BIBLIOGRAPHY

American Psychiatric Association: Diagnostic and Statistical Manual of Mental Disorders, 3rd ed rev. Washington, DC, American Psychiatric Association, 1987

> Contains diagnostic criteria for over 200 defined psychiatric diagnoses. Also includes information about age of onset, predisposing factors, prevalence, sex ratios and differential diagnosis for each disorder.

Berg R, Franzen M, Wedding D: Screening for Brain Impairment. New York, Springer-Verlag, 1987

> Excellent summary of neuropsychological tests that have relevance for evaluation of psychiatric patients. Gives historical information about individual tests and reviews briefer neuropsychological screening batteries.

Goodwin DW, Guze SB: Psychiatric Diagnosis. New York, Oxford University Press, 1984

> Reviews essentials of diagnosis for major psychiatric disorders and provides summary of clinical validation for each disorder, including epidemiology, natural history, and family studies.

van Riezan H, Segal M: Comparative Evaluation of Rating Scales for Clinical Psychopharmacology. Amsterdam, Elsevier, 1988

> Extensive review of psychiatric rating scales used for research and clinical purposes. Includes information on how to obtain scales and copyright considerations.

MacKinnon RA, Yudofsky SC (eds): The Psychiatric Evaluation in Clinical Practice. Philadelphia, JB Lippincott, 1986

> This book provides an authoritative and well-written discussion of the psychiatric interview and history from a psychodynamic perspective. It also provides excellent discussions of the mental status examination and other aspects of the neuropsychiatric evaluation.

Kaufman D: Clinical Neurology for Psychiatrists. New York, Grune & Stratton, 1987

> For students interested in details of the neurological exam as applied to psychiatric patients, this is a practical and lucid guide.

Principles of Behavioral Neurology by Marsel Mesulam (ed). Philadelphia, FA Davis, 1985

> This is a splendid presentation of the basic science and clinical application of behavioral neurology with a strong emphasis on neuropsychiatric assessment.

REFERENCES

American Psychiatric Association: Diagnostic and Statistical Manual of Mental Disorders, 3rd ed rev. Washington, DC, American Psychiatric Association, 1987

Bates B, Hoekelman RA: Interviewing and the health history. In Bates B (ed): A Guide to Physical Examination. Philadelphia, JB Lippincott, 1983

Berg R, Franzen M, Wedding D: Screening for Brain Impairment. New York, Springer-Verlag, 1987

Chandler JD, Gerndt JE: The role of medical evaluation in psychiatric inpatients. Psychosomatics 29:410–416, 1988

Colligan RC, Osborne D, Swenson WM, Offord KP: The MMPI: A Contemporary Normative Study. New York, Praeger, 1983

Elstein AS, Shulman LS, Sprafka SA: Medical Problem Solving: An Analysis of Clinical Reasoning. Cambridge, MA, Harvard University Press, 1978

Feighner JP, Robins E, Guze SB, et al: Diagnostic criteria for use in psychiatric research. Arch Gen Psychiatry 26:57–63, 1972

Fink PJ: Response to the presidential address: Is "biopsychosocial" the psychiatric shibboleth? Arch Gen Psychiatry 145:1061–1067, 1988

Hall RCW, Gardiner ER, Stickney SK, et al: Physical illness manifesting as psychiatric disease: II. Analysis of a state hospital inpatient population. Arch Gen Psychiatry 35:989–995, 1980

Hampton JR, Harrison MJG, Mitchell JRA, et al: Relative contributions of history-taking, physical examination, and laboratory investigation to diagnosis and management of medical outpatients. Br Med J 2:486–489, 1975

Hoffman RS: Diagnostic errors in the evaluation of behavioral disorders. JAMA 248:964–967, 1982

Koranyi EK: Somatic illness in psychiatric patients. Psychosomatics 21:887–891, 1980

Krummel S, Kathol RG: What you should know about physical evaluations in psychiatric patients: Results of a survey. Gen Hosp Psychiatry 9:275–279, 1987

LaBruzza AL: Physical illness presenting as psychiatric disorder: Guidelines for differential diagnosis. J Operational Psychiatry 12:24–31, 1981

Osborne D: The MMPI in medical practice. Psychiatr Ann 15(9):534–541, 1985.

Regier DA, Goldberg ID, Taube CA: The de facto U.S. mental health system. Arch Gen Psychiatry 35:685–693, 1978

Reich J: Personality disorders in primary care. In: Yates WR (ed): Primary Care Clinics—Psychiatry Issue Volume 14, Philadelphia, WB Saunders, 1987

Robins E, Guze SB: Establishment of diagnostic validity in psychiatric illness: Its application to schizophrenia. Am J Psychiatr 126:983–987, 1970

Rosenhan DL: On being sane in insane places. Science 179:250–258, 1979

Spitzer RL, Endicott J, Robins E: Research diagnostic criteria. Rationale and reliability. Arch Gen Psychiatry 35:773–782, 1978

Taylor MA, Sierles FS, Abrams R: The neuropsychiatric evaluation. In Hales RE, Yudofsky SC: Textbook of Neuropsychiatry. Washington, DC, American Psychiatric Press, Inc, 1987

van Riezen H, Segal M: Comparative Evaluation of Rating Scales for Clinical Psychopharmacology. Amsterdam, Elsevier, 1988

*Appendix to Chapter One**

DSM-III-R CLASSIFICATION: AXES I AND II CATEGORIES AND CODES

All official DSM-III-R codes are included in ICD-9-CM. Codes followed by a * are used for more than one DSM-III-R diagnosis or subtype in order to maintain compatibility with ICD-9-CM.

Numbers in parentheses are page numbers.

A long dash following a diagnostic term indicates the need for a fifth digit subtype or other qualifying term.

The term *specify* following the name of some diagnostic categories indicates qualifying terms that clinicians may wish to add in parentheses after the name of the disorder.

NOS = Not Otherwise Specified

The current severity of a disorder may be specified after the diagnosis as:

mild ——— currently
moderate ———— meets
severe ——— diagnostic
criteria

in partial remission
   (or residual state)
in complete remission

DISORDERS USUALLY FIRST EVIDENT IN INFANCY, CHILDHOOD, OR ADOLESCENCE

DEVELOPMENTAL DISORDERS
Note: These are coded on Axis II.

Mental Retardation (28)
317.00   Mild mental retardation
318.00   Moderate mental retardation
318.10   Severe mental retardation
318.20   Profound mental retardation
319.00   Unspecified mental retardation

Pervasive Developmental Disorders (33)
299.00   Autistic disorder (38)
            Specify if childhood onset
299.80   Pervasive developmental disorder NOS

Specific Developmental Disorders (39)
            Academic skills disorders
315.10   Developmental arithmetic disorder (41)
315.80   Developmental expressive writing disorder (42)
315.00   Developmental reading disorder (43)

*(Reprinted with permission from American Psychiatric Association: Diagnostic and Statistical Manual of Mental Disorders, Third Edition, Revised. Washington DC, American Psychiatric Association 1987.)

Language and speech disorders

315.39 Developmental articulation disorder (44)

315.31* Developmental expressive language disorder (45)

315.31* Developmental receptive language disorder (47)

Motor skills disorder

315.40 Developmental coordination disorder (48)

315.90* Specific developmental disorder NOS

Other Developmental Disorders (49)

315.90* Developmental disorder NOS

Disruptive Behavior Disorders (49)

314.01 Attention-deficit hyperactivity disorder (50)

Conduct disorder, (53)

312.20   group type

312.00   solitary aggressive type

312.90   undifferentiated type

313.81 Oppositional defiant disorder (56)

Anxiety Disorders of Childhood or Adolescence (58)

309.21 Separation anxiety disorder (58)

313.21 Avoidant disorder of childhood or adolescence (61)

313.00 Overanxious disorder (63)

Eating Disorders (65)

307.10 Anorexia nervosa (65)

307.51 Bulimia nervosa (67)

307.52 Pica (69)

307.53 Rumination disorder of infancy (70)

307.50 Eating disorder NOS

Gender Identity Disorders (71)

302.60 Gender identity disorder of childhood (71)

302.50 Transsexualism (74)
   Specify sexual history: asexual, homosexual, heterosexual, unspecified

302.85* Gender identity disorder of adolescence of adulthood, nontranssexual type (76)
   Specify sexual history: asexual, homosexual, heterosexual, unspecified

302.85* Gender identity disorder NOS

Tic Disorders (78)

307.23 Tourette's disorder (79)

307.22 Chronic motor or vocal tic disorder (81)

307.21 Transient tic disorder (81)
   Specify: single episode or recurrent

307.20 Tic disorder NOS

Elimination Disorders (82)

307.70 Functional encopresis (82)
   Specify: primary or secondary type

307.60 Functional enuresis (84)
   Specify: primary or secondary type
   Specify: nocturnal only, diurnal only, nocturnal and diurnal

Speech Disorders Not Elsewhere Classified (85)

307.00* Cluttering (85)

307.00* Stuttering (86)

Other Disorders of Infancy, Childhood, or Adolescence (88)

313.23 Elective mutism (88)

313.82 Identity disorder (89)

313.89 Reactive attachment disorder of infancy or early childhood (91)

307.30 Stereotypy/habit disorder (93)

314.00 Undifferentiated attention-deficit disorder (95)

ORGANIC MENTAL DISORDERS (97)

Dementias Arising in the Senium and Presenium (119)

Primary degenerative dementia of the Alzheimer type, senile onset, (119)

290.30 with delirium

290.20 with delusions

290.21 with depression

290.00* uncomplicated

(Note: code 331.00 Alzheimer's disease on Axis III)

Code in fifth digit:
1 = with delirium, 2 = with delusions, 3 = with depression, 0* = uncomplicated

290.1x Primary degenerative dementia of the Alzheimer type, presenile onset,

——————————— (119)

(Note: code 331.00 Alzheimer's disease on Axis III)

290.4x Multi-infarct dementia,

——————————— (121)

290.00* Senile dementia NOS
Specify etiology on Axis III if known

290.10* Presenile dementia NOS
Specify etiology on Axis III if known (e.g., Pick's disease, Jakob-Creutzfeldt disease)

Psychoactive Substance-Induced Organic Mental Disorders (123)

Alcohol

303.00 intoxication (127)

291.40 idiosyncratic intoxication (128)

291.80 Uncomplicated alcohol withdrawal (129)

291.00 withdrawal delirium (131)

291.30 hallucinosis (131)

291.10 amnestic disorder (133)

291.20 Dementia associated with alcoholism (133)

Amphetamine or similarly acting sympathomimetic

305.70* intoxication (134)

292.00* withdrawal (136)

292.81* delirium (136)

292.11* delusional disorder (137)

Caffeine

305.90* intoxication (138)

Cannabis

305.20* intoxication (139)

292.11* delusional disorder (140)

Cocaine

305.60* intoxication (141)

292.00* withdrawal (142)

292.81* delirium (143)

292.11* delusional disorder (143)

Hallucinogen

305.30* hallucinosis (144)

292.11* delusional disorder (146)

292.84* mood disorder (146)

292.89* Posthallucinogen perception disorder (147)

Inhalant

305.90* intoxication (148)

Nicotine

292.00* withdrawal (150)

Opioid
305.50*	intoxication (151)
292.00*	withdrawal (152)

Phencyclidine (PCP) or
similarly acting
arylcyclohexylamine
305.90*	intoxication (154)
292.81*	delirium (155)
292.11*	delusional disorder (156)
292.84*	mood disorder (156)
292.90*	organic mental disorder NOS

Sedative, hypnotic, or
anxiolytic
305.40*	intoxication (158)
292.00*	Uncomplicated sedative, hypnotic, or anxiolytic withdrawal (159)
292.00*	withdrawal delirium (160)
292.83*	amnestic disorder (161)

Other or unspecified
psychoactive substance
(162)
305.90*	intoxication
292.00*	withdrawal
292.81*	delirium
292.82*	dementia
292.83*	amnestic disorder
292.11*	delusional disorder
292.12	hallucinosis
292.84*	mood disorder
292.89*	anxiety disorder
292.89*	personality disorder
292.90*	organic mental disorder NOS

**Organic Mental Disorders
associated with Axis III physical
disorders or conditions, or whose
etiology is unknown** (162)
293.00	Delirium (100)
294.10	Dementia (103)
294.00	Amnestic disorder (108)
293.81	Organic delusional disorder (109)

293.82	Organic hallucinosis (110)
293.83	Organic mood disorder (111) *Specify:* manic, depressed, mixed
294.80*	Organic anxiety disorder (113)
310.10	Organic personality disorder (114) *Specify* if explosive type
294.80*	Organic mental disorder NOS

**PSYCHOACTIVE SUBSTANCE
USE DISORDERS** (165)

Alcohol (173)
303.90	dependence
305.00	abuse

Amphetamine or similarly
acting sympathomimetic
(175)
304.40	dependence
305.70*	abuse

Cannabis (176)
304.30	dependence
305.20*	abuse

Cocaine (177)
304.20	dependence
305.60*	abuse

Hallucinogen (179)
304.50*	dependence
305.30*	abuse

Inhalant (180)
304.60	dependence
305.90*	abuse

Nicotine (181)
305.10	dependence

Opioid (182)
304.00	dependence
305.50*	abuse

Phencyclidine (PCP) or
similarly acting
arylcyclohexylamine (183)

304.50*	dependence
305.90*	abuse

Sedative, hypnotic, or
anxiolytic (184)

304.10	dependence
305.40*	abuse
304.90*	Polysubstance dependence (185)
304.90*	Psychoactive substance dependence NOS
305.90*	Psychoactive substance abuse NOS

SCHIZOPHRENIA (187)

Code in fifth digit; 1 = subchronic, 2 = chronic, 3 = subchronic with acute exacerbation, 4 = chronic with acute exacerbation, 5 = in remission, 0 = unspecified.

	Schizophrenia,
295.2x	catatonic, _____
295.1x	disorganized, _____
295.3x	paranoid, _____
	Specify if stable type
295.9x	undifferentiated, _____
295.6x	residual, _____
	Specify if late onset

DELUSIONAL (PARANOID) DISORDER (199)

297.10	Delusional (Paranoid) disorder
	Specify type: erotomanic
	grandiose
	jealous
	persecutory
	somatic
	unspecified

PSYCHOTIC DISORDERS NOT ELSEWHERE CLASSIFIED (205)

298.80	Brief reactive psychosis (205)
295.40	Schizophreniform disorder (207)

Specify: without good prognostic features or with good prognostic features

295.70	Schizoaffective disorder (208)
	Specify: bipolar type or depressive type
297.30	Induced psychotic disorder (210)
298.90	Psychotic disorder NOS (Atypical psychosis) (211)

MOOD DISORDERS (213)

Code current state of Major Depression and Bipolar Disorder in fifth digit:

1 = mild
2 = moderate
3 = severe, without psychotic features
4 = with psychotic features (*specify* mood-congruent or mood-incongruent)
5 = in partial remission
6 = in full remission
0 = unspecified

For major depressive episodes, *specify* if chronic and *specify* if melancholic type.

For Bipolar Disorder, Bipolar Disorder NOS, Recurrent Major Depression, and Depressive Disorder NOS, *specify* if seasonal pattern.

Bipolar Disorders

	Bipolar disorder, (225)
296.6x	mixed, _____
296.4x	manic, _____
296.5x	depressed, _____
301.13	Cyclothymia (226)
296.70	Bipolar disorder NOS

Depressive Disorders

	Major Depression, (228)
296.2x	single episode, _____

296.3x   recurrent, _____
300.40   Dysthymia (or Depressive
          neurosis) (230)
              Specify: primary or
              secondary type
              Specify: early or late
              onset
311.00   Depressive disorder NOS

ANXIETY DISORDERS (or Anxiety and Phobic Neuroses) (235)

              Panic disorder (235)
300.21   with agoraphobia
                  Specify current severity
                  of agoraphobic avoidance
                  Specify current severity
                  of panic attacks
300.01   without agoraphobia
                  Specify current severity
                  of panic attacks
300.22   Agoraphobia without
          history of panic disorder
          (240)
              Specify with or without
              limited symptom attacks
300.23   Social phobia (241)
              Specify if generalized
              type
300.29   Simple phobia (243)
300.30   Obsessive compulsive
          disorder (or Obsessive
          compulsive neurosis) (245)
309.89   Post-traumatic stress
          disorder (247)
              Specify if delayed onset
300.02   Generalized anxiety
          disorder (251)
300.00   Anxiety disorder NOS

SOMATOFORM DISORDERS (255)

300.70*   Body dysmorphic disorder
          (255)
300.11   Conversion disorder (or
          Hysterical neurosis,
          conversion type) (257)

              Specify: single episode
              or recurrent
300.70*   Hypochondriasis (or
          Hypochondriacal neurosis)
          (259)
300.81   Somatization disorder (261)
307.80   Somatoform pain disorder
          (264)
300.70*   Undifferentiated somato-
          form disorder (266)
300.70*   Somatoform disorder NOS
          (267)

DISSOCIATIVE DISORDERS (or Hysterical Neuroses, Dissociative Type) (269)

300.14   Multiple personality
          disorder (269)
300.13   Psychogenic fugue (272)
300.12   Psychogenic amnesia (273)
300.60   Depersonalization disorder
          (or Depersonalization
          neurosis) (275)
300.15   Dissociative disorder NOS

SEXUAL DISORDERS (279)

Paraphilias (279)
302.40   Exhibitionism (282)
302.81   Fetishism (282)
302.89   Frotteurism (283)
302.20   Pedophilia (284)
              Specify: same sex,
              opposite sex, same and
              opposite sex
              Specify if limited to
              incest
              Specify: exclusive type
              or nonexclusive type
302.83   Sexual masochism (286)
302.84   Sexual sadism (287)
302.30   Transvestic fetishism (288)
302.82   Voyeurism (289)
302.90*   Paraphilia NOS (290)

Sexual Dysfunctions (290)
Specify: psychogenic only, or
psychogenic and biogenic (Note: If

biogenic only, code on Axis III)
Specify: lifelong or acquired
Specify: generalized or situational

	Sexual desire disorders (293)
302.71	Hypoactive sexual desire disorder
302.79	Sexual aversion disorder
	Sexual arousal disorders (294)
302.72*	Female sexual arousal disorder
302.72*	Male erectile disorder
	Orgasm disorders (294)
302.73	Inhibited female orgasm
302.74	Inhibited male orgasm
302.75	Premature ejaculation
	Sexual pain disorders (295)
302.76	Dyspareunia
306.51	Vaginismus
302.70	Sexual dysfunction NOS

Other Sexual Disorders

302.90*	Sexual disorder NOS

SLEEP DISORDERS (297)
Dyssomnias (298)

	Insomnia disorder
307.42*	related to another mental disorder (nonorganic) (300)
780.50*	related to known organic factor (300)
307.42*	Primary insomnia (301)
	Hypersomnia disorder
307.44	related to another mental disorder (nonorganic) (303)
780.50*	related to a known organic factor (303)
780.54	Primary hypersomnia (305)
307.45	Sleep-wake schedule disorder (305)
	Specify: advanced or delayed phase type,

	disorganized type, frequently changing type
	Other dyssomnias
307.40*	Dyssomnia NOS

Parasomnias (308)

307.47	Dream anxiety disorder (Nightmare disorder) (308)
307.46*	Sleep terror disorder (310)
307.46*	Sleepwalking disorder (311)
307.40*	Parasomnia NOS (313)

FACTITIOUS DISORDERS (315)

	Factitious disorder
301.51	with physical symptoms (316)
300.16	with psychological symptoms (318)
300.19	Factitious disorder NOS (320)

IMPULSE CONTROL DISORDERS NOT ELSEWHERE CLASSIFIED (321)

312.34	Intermittent explosive disorder (321)
312.32	Kleptomania (322)
312.31	Pathological gambling (324)
312.33	Pyromania (325)
312.39*	Trichotillomania (326)
312.39*	Impulse control disorder NOS (328)

ADJUSTMENT DISORDER (329)

	Adjustment disorder
309.24	with anxious mood
309.00	with depressed mood
309.30	with disturbance of conduct
309.40	with mixed disturbance of emotions and conduct
309.28	with mixed emotional features
309.82	with physical complaints
309.83	with withdrawal

309.23   with work (or academic)
            inhibition
309.90   Adjustment disorder NOS

PSYCHOLOGICAL FACTORS AFFECTING PHYSICAL CONDITION (333)

316.00   Psychological factors
            affecting physical condition
            Specify physical
            condition on Axis III

PERSONALITY DISORDERS (335)
Note: These are coded on Axis II.
Cluster A
301.00   Paranoid (337)
301.20   Schizoid (339)
301.22   Schizotypal (340)
Cluster B
301.70   Antisocial (342)
301.83   Borderline (346)
301.50   Histrionic (348)
301.81   Narcissistic (349)

Cluster C
301.82   Avoidant (351)
301.60   Dependent (353)
301.40   Obsessive compulsive (354)
301.84   Passive aggressive (356)
301.90   Personality disorder NOS

V CODES FOR CONDITIONS NOT ATTRIBUTABLE TO A MENTAL DISORDER THAT ARE A FOCUS OF ATTENTION OR TREATMENT (359)

V62.30   Academic problem
V71.01   Adult antisocial behavior

V40.00   Borderline intellectual
            functioning (Note: This
            is coded on Axis II.)

V71.02   Childhood or adolescent
            antisocial behavior
V65.20   Malingering
V61.10   Marital problem
V15.81   Noncompliance with
            medical treatment
V62.20   Occupational problem
V61.20   Parent-child problem
V62.81   Other interpersonal
            problem
V61.80   Other specified family
            circumstances
V62.89   Phase of life problem or
            other life circumstance
            problem
V62.82   Uncomplicated
            bereavement

ADDITIONAL CODES (363)

300.90   Unspecified mental
            disorder (nonpsychotic)
V71.09*   No diagnosis or condition
            on Axis I
799.90*   Diagnosis or condition
            deferred on Axis I

V71.09*   No diagnosis or
            condition on Axis II
799.90*   Diagnosis or condition
            deferred on Axis II

MULTIAXIAL SYSTEM

Axis I   Clinical Syndromes
            V Codes

Axis II   Developmental Disorders
            Personality Disorders

Axis III   Physical Disorders and
            Conditions

Axis IV	Severity of Psychosocial Stressors	Axis V	Global Assessment of Functioning

Axis IV
Severity of Psychosocial Stressors Scale: Adults

Code	Term	Examples of stressors	
		Acute events	**Enduring circumstances**
1	**None**	No acute events that may be relevant to the disorder	No enduring circumstances that may be relevant to the disorder
2	**Mild**	Broke up with boyfriend or girlfriend; started or graduated from school; child left home	Family arguments; job dissatisfaction; residence in high-crime neighborhood
3	**Moderate**	Marriage; marital separation; loss of job; retirement; miscarriage	Marital discord; serious financial problems; trouble with boss; being a single parent
4	**Severe**	Divorce; birth of first child	Unemployment; poverty
5	**Extreme**	Death of spouse; serious physical illness diagnosed; victim of rape	Serious chronic illness in self or child; ongoing physical or sexual abuse
6	**Catastrophic**	Death of child; suicide of spouse; devastating natural disaster	Captivity as hostage; concentration camp experience
0	**Inadequate information, or no change in condition**		

Severity of Psychosocial Stressors Scale: Children and Adolescents

Code	Term	Examples of stressors	
		Acute events	**Enduring circumstances**
1	**None**	No acute events that may be relevant to the disorder	No enduring circumstances that may be relevant to the disorder
2	**Mild**	Broke up with boyfriend or girlfriend; change of school	Overcrowded living quarters; family arguments

Code	Term	Examples of stressors	
		Acute events	**Enduring circumstances**
3	**Moderate**	Expelled from school; birth of sibling	Chronic disabling illness in parent; chronic parental discord
4	**Severe**	Divorce of parents; un-wanted pregnancy; arrest	Harsh or rejecting parents; chronic life-threatening ill-ness in parent; multiple foster home placements
5	**Extreme**	Sexual or physical abuse; death of a parent	Recurrent sexual or physi-cal abuse
6	**Cata-strophic**	Death of both parents	Chronic life-threatening illness
0	**Inadequate information, or no change in condition**		

Axis V
Global Assessment of Functioning Scale (GAF Scale)

Consider psychological, social, and occupational functioning on a hypothetical contin-uum of mental health-illness. Do not include impairment in functioning due to physical (or environmental) limitations.

Note: Use intermediate codes when appropriate, e.g., 45, 68, 72.

Code

90
|
81
Absent or minimal symptoms (e.g., mild anxiety before an exam), **good functioning in all areas, interested and involved in a wide range of activities, socially effective, generally satisfied with life, no more than everyday problems or concerns** (e.g., an occasional argument with family members).

80
|
71
If symptoms are present, they are transient and expectable reac-tions to psychosocial stressors (e.g., difficulty concentrating after family argument); **no more than slight impairment in social, occupational, or school functioning** (e.g., temporarily falling behind in school work).

70
|
61
Some mild symptoms (e.g., depressed mood and mild insomnia) **OR some difficulty in social, occupational, or school functioning** (e.g., occa-sional truancy, or theft within the household), **but generally functioning pretty well, has some meaningful interpersonal relationships.**

60
|
51
Moderate symptoms (e.g., flat affect and circumstantial speech, occasional panic attacks) **OR moderate difficulty in social, occupational, or school functioning** (e.g., few friends, conflicts with co-workers).

50
|
41
Serious symptoms (e.g., suicidal ideation, severe obsessional rituals, fre-quent shoplifting) **OR any serious impairment in social, occupational, or school functioning** (e.g., no friends, unable to keep a job).

Code

40

31
Some impairment in reality testing or communication (e.g., speech is at times illogical, obscure, or irrelevant) **OR major impairment in several areas, such as work or school, family relations, judgment, thinking, or mood** (e.g., depressed man avoids friends, neglects family, and is unable to work; child frequently beats up younger children, is defiant at home, and is failing at school).

30

21
Behavior is considerably influenced by delusions or hallucinations OR serious impairment in communication or judgment (e.g., sometimes incoherent, acts grossly inappropriately, suicidal preoccupation) **OR inability to function in almost all areas** (e.g., stays in bed all day; no job, home, or friends).

20

11
Some danger of hurting self or others (e.g., suicide attempts without clear expectation of death, frequently violent, manic excitement) **OR occasionally fails to maintain minimal personal hygiene** (e.g., smears feces) **OR gross impairment in communication** (e.g., largely incoherent or mute).

10

1
Persistent danger of severely hurting self or others (e.g., recurrent violence) **OR persistent inability to maintain minimal personal hygiene OR serious suicidal act with clear expectation of death.**

2

Biopsychosocial Assessment and Case Formulation

Alan Stoudemire

The preceding chapter focused on the basics of the psychiatric history, mental status examination, physical and laboratory assessment, and DSM-III-R as a descriptive psychiatric classification system. Based on the information gathered in this type of initial assessment, a preliminary diagnosis and treatment plan can then be made. In some patients, a more in-depth psychological evaluation, however, may then be required. Examples of patients in whom a more in-depth psychosocial or psychodynamic assessment is called for include the following:

1. Patients who appear to have complex or problematic family, marital, or interpersonal problems.
2. Patients who appear to have *repetitive* patterns of conflicts or difficulties in their interpersonal relationships.
3. Individuals who appear to have psychiatric disorders and symptoms that are apparently precipitated or exacerbated by social, occupational, family, or interpersonal factors.
4. Patients who have unexplained somatic symptoms that cannot be explained on the basis of physical or laboratory findings.
5. Children and adolescents with psychiatric symptoms.

By emphasizing the importance of psychosocial assessment, one should not necessarily assume that such factors are the direct *cause* of the patient's psychiatric disorder—this may or may not be the case. The relative contribution of psychosocial factors in precipitating the onset or exacerbation of psychiatric disorders and symptoms varies depending on the disorder being evaluated. Moreover, the relative contribution of psychosocial and psychodynamic factors to the cause of many psychiatric disorders remains highly controversial in the psychiatric literature. To take the position that psychosocial factors are important in the assessment of a patient who has a psychiatric disorder such as schizophrenia, however, is not the same as saying that schizophrenia is *caused by* psychosocial factors, because this disorder is now considered to derive primarily from predisposing genetic and biochemical factors. Nevertheless, few psychiatrists would argue against the position that psychosocial and environmental factors may be involved in relapses of schizophrenia or that schizophrenia has profound effects on the patient's social and interpersonal functioning. Likewise, vulnerability to panic disorder and the major mood disorders appears to be determined predominantly by biological factors, yet certain patients may have their symptoms precipitated or exacerbated under certain types of emotionally stressful conditions. *Hence, even though certain disorders may have a primarily genetic and biological basis in respect to their underlying pathophysiology, onset or relapse of the disorder may be affected by social or environmental factors in the biologically predisposed individual.* Even in physical disorders, acute and chronic illness always poses a form of stress for the individual that may potentially affect every aspect of their family, social, and occupational life. For example, cancer and chronic renal disease may have devastating effects on the patient's emotional and social functioning (Green, 1990). Psychological reactions to physical illness are further discussed in Chapters 10 and 19.

GOALS OF PSYCHOSOCIAL ASSESSMENT

The primary goals of a comprehensive psychosocial evaluation are to: (1) assess if psychological or social factors are important in contributing to the patient's vulnerability to psychiatric illness, (2) assess if psychosocial factors are significant in causing relapse or exacerbation of symptoms, and (3) identify areas in the psychological or social realm where treatment efforts might be focused. In addition, such an assessment also will identify areas in the patient's support system that may be a resource. In patients who suffer primarily from repetitive problems in their interpersonal relationships or who have dysfunction within the family system, the psychosocial assessment may be the only means of fully understanding their condition and planning an effective course of treatment.

PSYCHODYNAMIC ASSESSMENT

A *psychodynamic* assessment is a more specialized form of psychological evaluation that is usually performed by a psychiatrist who endorses and is trained in this method of evaluation. A psychodynamic assessment may be needed as part of the psychosocial assessment in some situations and involves examining the key developmental life experiences that may have affected the patient's personality formation, the nature of the patient's past and current family relationships, and the patient's psychological strengths and vulnerabilities. A psychodynamic assessment also evaluates current interpersonal stresses that may be affecting the patient and therefore overlaps with the general psychosocial evaluation. Individuals and important environmental and family events that have influenced the patient in either a positive or negative manner are identified, and the effect they currently have or have had on the patient is evaluated. Psychodynamic assessment is often critical not only in developing a comprehensive understanding of the patient's personality and current difficulties but also in determining whether or not psychotherapy is required, and, if so, what type of psychotherapy would be most appropriate.

Psychodynamic assessment is a form of evaluation somewhat more specialized than a general psychosocial assessment and is largely based on a psychoanalytic frame of reference. Psychodynamic assessment imparts major significance to developmental influences on the patient within the family system and potential unconscious factors that may be affecting the patient's behavior, motivations, and interpersonal relationships. Psychodynamic assessment thus focuses on the influence of early relationships on the patient's personality formation and the effects that these early relationships have on behavior.

Some psychoanalytic and psychodynamic theorists attempted to explain all psychiatric illness—including major disorders such as schizophrenia, major depression, and anxiety disorders—in its most doctrinal form as deriving from intrapsychic and unconscious mental processes. Personality disorders and other disturbances in behavior also were explained predominantly on a psychological basis as deriving from abnormal or otherwise conflicted childhood developmental experiences and dysfunction within the family system.

Recent advances in biological psychiatry and psychopharmacology in some instances have almost completely usurped primarily psychoanalytic and psychodynamic viewpoints with respect to *etiological* explanations for the major mental disorders. In addition, psychoanalytically oriented therapies based on these types of purist etiological explanations have been under serious criticism. Although considerable polarization and strain exist within the field of psychiatry regarding the relative contribution of psychodynamic factors to the cause of the major psychiatric disorders, there has been a recent trend to attempt to integrate biological and psychological viewpoints regarding the etiology and treatment of psychiatric illness (Cooper, 1985; Kandel, 1979, 1983; Reiser, 1984; van der Kolk, 1990). In addition, it is recognized that the relative contribution of psychological and biological factors varies with the psychiatric disorder being studied and that even within a given disorder (such as major depression) considerable heterogeneity exists among patients who carry the same primary diagnosis.

Further discussion of this area is beyond the scope of this text, and the position taken here will be that, given our limited knowledge of the precise cause of most psychiatric disorders, a balanced approach should be taken in patient evaluation so as to always consider the possible contributions of biological, psychological, and sociological factors relevant to the patient's condition. In some situations, an in-depth psychodynamic assessment may be important; in others it may contribute nothing to an explanation of the etiology of the patient's condition and may offer little to the treatment planning process. In almost all cases, however, some form of psychosocial assessment should be part of the patient's evaluation.

THE PRIMARY PHYSICIAN'S ROLE IN PSYCHOSOCIAL ASSESSMENT

It should be emphasized that a complete psychosocial and psychodynamic assessment may be a complex and time-consuming process. In many cases, performing such an evaluation will exceed the skills and time of even the most psychologically minded physician. In such situations it may be necessary to refer the patient to a psychiatrist for a more in-depth assessment. Nevertheless, it is still the responsibility of the primary physician to gather certain basic information to assess and identify patients who may need referral.

The responsibility of the primary physician to elicit basic psychosocial data in this situation has analogies in general medical practice. For example, a general internist will assess the signs and symptoms of a patient with chest pain and, after this initial assessment, might then refer the patient to a cardiologist for possible cardiac catheterization and definitive cardiologic diagnosis and treatment. The internist would hardly consider initiating such a referral without gathering the basic medical history and performing a physical examination. Similarly, gathering basic psychological or psychosocial information about the patient will assure that patients in need of more specialized evaluation will be identified appropriately.

PSYCHOSOCIAL ASSESSMENT: BASIC APPROACHES

When the psychosocial assessment is conducted, there are several fundamental questions that should be posed to the patient, and if adequate time is allowed for exploration of the patient's responses, an excellent initial data base can be assimilated by the primary physician regarding the patient's general developmental history and current psychosocial status.

For example, the physician may ask questions directed toward determining the key events and important people in the patient's childhood, adolescence, and adulthood that appear to have had or continue to have an effect on the patient. Were there past traumas, losses, or problems within the family system, or difficulties in other childhood and adult relationships that had a major impact on the patient? Are there conflicted or unresolved relationships with family, friends, or significant other individuals that are a source of distress for the patient? Have there been particularly difficult times in the patient's life? What have been the patient's sources of happiness and satisfaction, or unhappiness and frustration? Answers to open-ended questions of this sort will usually yield information that will form the rubric of a preliminary psychosocial and psychodynamic understanding of the patient. Patients who are guarded or who deny the significance or importance of psychological matters will require more extended psychiatric evaluations.

PSYCHOSOCIAL STRESSES AND SOMATIC SYMPTOMS

Many patients under psychosocial stress in the general medical setting will present to their primary care physicians with somatic symptoms (insomnia, headaches, gastrointestinal distress). Somatic symptoms are also extremely common and may develop as a response to even minor stresses (e.g., tension headaches). Patients will also seek help in the medical sector for somatic symptoms that are part of a major depressive disorder long before the symptoms are recognized or considered as part of a primary psychiatric syndrome.

It should not, however, be assumed that all physical symptoms with a negative medical work-up are "psychosomatic" or "stress related" in nature. Two caveats should always be kept in mind: first, symptoms of medical illness and stress/psychiatrically related symptoms may coexist and be enmeshed; hence, even if stress-related symptoms are identified as such, this does not rule out the possibility of concurrent medical illness. Second, stress and the presence of a concurrent psychiatric illness (such as depression) may greatly magnify the symptoms of clearly documented underlying physical illnesses. (See also Chapters 6, 8, and 19.)

BIOPSYCHOSOCIAL ASSESSMENT

The DSM-III-R system discussed in Chapter 1 (see Chapter 1 Appendix) is used primarily for purposes of description and classification and is based on data that can be documented objectively. Integrating the descriptive approach of DSM-III-R with a psychosocial and psychodynamic understanding of the patient, however, at times can be useful in determining what types of psychiatric treatment would be most helpful for the patient, especially in determining the need for psychotherapy.

As mentioned in Chapter 1, the biopsychosocial model uses a systems approach in attempting to integrate biological, psychological, and social aspects of the patient's condition (Alexander, 1950; Bertalanffy, 1968; Cohen-Cole, 1990; Engel, 1977; Fink, 1988; Meyer, 1957; Reiser, 1988). This approach inherently validates the potential importance of biogenetic, psychological, social, and environmental factors in the diagnosis and treatment of the patient.

The basic clinical principles of the type of biopsychosocially oriented case assessment of patients in medical *or* psychiatric settings presented in this text would take the following into consideration:

1. Genetic and biological factors are deemed to be of major potential importance in certain psychiatric disorders (such as schizophrenia and mood disorders) and also may play a part in determining the patient's resilience or vulnerability to stress.
2. Certain problematic developmental experiences and conflicted relationships within the family and social system may confer vulnerabilities to certain types of psychiatric illness; alternatively, positive developmental experiences and relationships and good social support may provide a buffering effect.
3. Current life stresses may precipitate the onset of certain psychiatric disorders and symptoms or contribute to relapses of preexisting conditions.

This chapter focuses on the practical clinical applications of these principles, and space does not permit a critical review of the scientific evidence to support the biopsychosocial model. Students are referred to selected articles in the annotated bibliography and reference list and the introductory text on human behavior that precedes this volume for substantiative information (Aneshensel, Stone, 1982; Bifulco, Brown, Harris, 1987; Birley, Brown, 1970; Bolton, Oatley, 1987; Breier, Kelsoe,

Kirwin, et al., 1988; Bryer, Nelson, Miller, et al., 1987; Cadoret, O'Gorman, Troughton, et al., 1985; Cobb, 1976; Doane, West, Goldstein, et al., 1981; Greenblatt, Becerra, Serafetinides, 1982; Harris, Brown, Bifulco, 1986, 1987; Kendler, 1988; Leavy, 1983; Lindberg, Distad, 1985; MacMillan, Gold, Crow, et al., 1986; Miklowitz, Goldstein, Neuchterlein, et al., 1987; Miklowitz, Goldstein, Neuchterlein, et al, 1988; Miller, Ingham, Davidson, 1976; Parry, Shapiro, 1986; Penkower, Bromet, Dew, 1988; Roy, 1980; Rutter, 1985; Schwartz, Myers, 1977a & b; Tennant, 1983, 1988; Tennant, Bebbington, Hurry, 1982; Tennant, Hurry, Bebbington, 1982a & b; Tennant, Smith, Bebbington, et al., 1981; Uhlenhuth, Paykel, 1973; van der Kolk, 1986, 1990; Vaughn, Snyder, Jones, et al., 1984; Warr, Jackson, 1985; Weissman, Gammon, John, et al., 1987).

CLINICAL APPLICATIONS

Diagnosis and treatment using the biopsychosocial model are multimodal and are directed toward stabilizing each sphere of the patient's life that appears to be under stress—biological, psychological, and/or social. To reiterate, in this conceptual framework it is essential to (1) accurately assess the pertinent biological and physical factors associated with the patient's condition, (2) evaluate the effects of past and present environmental, social, and family stressors, and (3) appraise the psychological significance of the illness for the patient (e.g., how the patient experiences the illness in light of his significant current and past life experiences).

The following prototypical case describes how the biopsychosocial model, the DSM-III-R descriptive approach, and a psychosocial/psychodynamic formulation can be integrated into patient evaluation and comprehensive treatment planning.

CASE STUDY: MR. A

Mr. A, a 50-year-old married attorney, presented to his internist 4 weeks after successful coronary artery bypass surgery. He appeared to have deteriorated after his successful surgery, was chronically fatigued, had severe insomnia, had lost his appetite, and had lost interest in doing almost everything, including returning to work. Because of his inability to return to work, he was sinking into financial debt, and his position in his law firm was in jeopardy. Although he had little interest in sex, he did attempt intercourse with his wife several times but was impotent.

The internist performed a complete medical evaluation and checked his laboratory profile. He was slightly hypokalemic because of the use of a thiazide diuretic. He was also taking the beta-adrenergic blocking agent propranolol for hypertension. Other than being overweight and continuing to smoke two packs of cigarettes a day, his examination was unremarkable, including a screening thyroid profile.

The internist assessed that the patient was primarily depressed, so he tapered and discontinued his propranolol (the physician knew the drug has been associated with inducing depression). He "reassured" the patient and prescribed a low dose of a cyclic antidepressant and some ben-

zodiazepine sleeping medication and scheduled a follow-up appointment for 4 weeks.

Despite these measures, the patient continued to deteriorate. He began to have crying spells, guilty ruminations, and suicidal thoughts. He took his antidepressant inconsistently. He returned to the internist after a week at his wife's insistence. The internist felt a psychiatric consultation was then necessary.

The psychiatrist evaluated the patient and, because the patient had recently had an extensive physical and laboratory evaluation, he decided to begin treatment with a cyclic antidepressant with incremental increases, giving no more than a week's supply at a time because of the possibility of a suicidal overdose. Because the patient's wife could stay with him during the day and the patient denied any suicidal plans, the decision was made to treat him initially as an outpatient with twice-weekly visits.

Before deciding on this treatment plan, however, the psychiatrist first performed a full psychiatric history and mental status examination. The patient was found to be cognitively intact, and his symptoms were all consistent with the diagnosis of major depression. The patient's personality assessment revealed marked obsessive–compulsive traits in that he was a "workaholic," a perfectionist, driven to achieve, and rarely ever "relaxed." He was generally rigid and strict with his children and emotionally aloof. Although he loved and was devoted to his family, he had severe difficulty in directly expressing any affection or personal feelings toward them or other people. Although things had gone well for him professionally, he believed he was never totally happy and had a tendency to be chronically mildly depressed, dysphoric, and dissatisfied with himself and life in general. He never believed he had "done enough" professionally and always thought he had to prove himself to others, and he had doubts about his basic self-worth. He had marked difficulties in expressing not only affectionate feelings but anger as well. When angry, he would generally "bottle it up," become preoccupied with the person or situation he was angry with, and "stew" for days.

Exploration of his developmental history revealed that his mother was generally available to him, but she had periods of apparent depressive episodes that were disabling, and she would emotionally withdraw from the family. She had never sought or received professional treatment for these apparent depressive episodes. His father was emotionally remote, cold, critical, and "pushed him" to do well in school. Because of the pressure and criticism from his father (and the fact that he felt he had to "earn" his father's love and approval), he gradually became more distant from him, silently resenting him, and sometimes "wished he were dead."

His father died suddenly of a myocardial infarction at age 49 when the patient was 15. The patient described his father's death as traumatic, not only because of the loss of his father but because he felt as if the anger and hostility he felt toward his father "had something to do with his death." Although he realized that this was not rationally possible, he nevertheless felt guilty about having been angry at his father and felt that he had to make it up to him "in some way." In addition, he felt that when his father died he had forever lost the chance to be close to him.

The patient ultimately went on to finish high school and college and decided to become an attorney, similar to his father. The patient always had a fear of dying at an early age—of a heart attack, similar to his father—but nevertheless smoked, was overweight, and did not exercise.

Based on the patient's chronic history of depression, the psychiatrist believed that, in addition to his antidepressant treatment, the patient could benefit from psychotherapy. The psychiatrist, who had a psychodynamic orientation, initially formulated the patient's case as follows: Part of the patient's problems with depression and low self-esteem were associated with problematic relationships with his parents. His mother's periodic depressions would, at times, make her unavailable to him when the patient needed support as a child, and he often interpreted her lack of interest and responsiveness as a sign of rejection. Moreover, his father was hypercritical and demanding, leaving the patient with feelings of worthlessness and guilt when he did not perfectly please his father, and he was frustrated by his inability to be close to him. In addition to this frustration, he was also resentful and angry and hated his father at times, although he also loved him and craved his attention and approval. When his father died, the patient was stricken with not only a sense of loss but also remorse and guilt. His guilt centered around his hostility toward his father in that he may have unconsciously related his father's death to his hostile feelings and blamed himself for it.

Because both parents often were unavailable to him emotionally and communication of feelings in the family was poor, he felt trapped with his loneliness and did not know to whom or how he could express his inner feelings. Because of his guilt and pattern of having to "achieve" and produce to maintain his self-esteem, he gradually became more engrossed in school and work. His compulsive work habits also served to help him avoid his inner feelings of mild depression and contributed to his compulsive personality traits. The patient nevertheless channeled his compulsive style and need for achievement into his work and did well academically and professionally. His marriage was generally stable, although his wife felt that he was always emotionally remote from her, neglected the family for his work, and could not express his feelings. He tended to be distant, hypercritical, and demanding of his own children, repeating the pattern of his own father. He had drifted further and further from both his wife and children.

The psychiatrist believed that the patient's own heart attack could have reactivated the memories and feelings associated with the grief surrounding his father's death. The patient may have identified with the father, and his own heart attack fulfilled his life-long fear that he too *would die at an early age. The psychiatrist also believed that the patient was at high risk genetically for depression because of his mother's probable history of depression and the patient's use of the beta-adrenergic blocking agent propranolol. Both of these factors may have contributed to his biological vulnerability to depression, as may have the acute stress of his coronary artery bypass surgery.*

In the course of the patient's subsequent psychotherapy, the memories and feelings related to his childhood experiences were explored. The patient gained a new understanding of the impact that his father's death had on him and came to fully realize that his angry feelings toward his father were largely justified and had nothing to do with his father's death; thus, his sense of guilt, which had been largely unconscious, was relieved. He began to realize more fully how he was still trying to "earn" approval by way of work and achievement, a central conflict related to his need to be close to his father and earn his love.

Concurrent with his psychotherapy and antidepressant medication, the patient was referred to a cardiac rehabilitation program, where he was placed on a diet, exercise regimen, and a smoking cessation program. Brief office counseling with the patient's wife reassured them both about the safety of gradually resuming normal sexual activity.

The patient complied with this multimodal approach and responded well to his antidepressant, psychotherapy, and cardiac rehabilitation program and returned to work. Formal psychotherapy was terminated after 6 months, although he continued on his antidepressant for 1 year, after which it was gradually tapered and discontinued. The patient did well subsequently.

DIAGNOSIS AND BIOPSYCHOSOCIAL ASSESSMENT

In the DSM-III-R schemata, the patient would have initially been diagnosed as follows:

Axis I: 296.23. Major depression, single episode, severe, without psychotic features
300.40. Dysthymia, primary type, early onset (provisional diagnosis)
305.10. Nicotine dependence

Axis II: Obsessive–compulsive personality traits (premorbid)

Axis III: Coronary artery disease, status postcoronary artery bypass surgery. Status posthypokalemia, essential hypertension, overweight

Axis IV: Psychosocial stressors: coronary artery bypass surgery (acute event). Severity: moderate (acute event)

Axis V: Global Assessment of Functioning (GAF): current, 45; highest GAF past year, 75

The biopsychosocial assessment applied to this case provided a structured and systematic way of understanding the patient's condition by attributing significance to each sphere of his life—psychological, biological, and social—as well as understanding key developmental influences that affected the patient's personality development and vulnerability to depression (Fig. 2-1). In this manner, the treatment interventions that were devised (medical/biological, psychotherapeutic, and rehabilitative/social) addressed *each aspect* of the patient's life and sources of stress. Hence, the descriptive approach of DSM-III-R, which is based clearly on the biopsychosocial model with its multiaxial system, combined with a basic psychodynamic assessment that attempts to analyze the meaning of an illness for patients from the standpoint of both past and current life experiences, provides a comprehensive method to formulate an integrated plan of treatment. Table 2-1 summarizes a structured treatment approach to psychiatric assessment and treatment planning based on this approach.

Although the relative *weight* attached to biological, psychological, and social aspects of each individual patient varies, it is essential that each area at least be considered to be potentially important. This philosophy and approach to patient care is the essential theme that runs throughout the course of this text.

In the remaining chapters of this text, students will become familiar with major psychopathological syndromes in clinical psychiatry and the management of behavioral and psychiatric disorders that are encountered in medical, surgical, and pediatric settings. As the student studies these conditions and encounters them in his or her

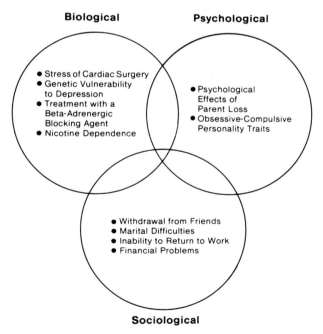

Figure 2–1. *The interaction of biologic, psychologic, and sociologic factors in the case of Mr. A.*

future medical practice, it is hoped that they will take an integrated approach to patient assessment and treatment based on the biopsychosocial model presented in these introductory chapters.

Table 2–1 **Outline of Psychiatric Assessment and Treatment Planning**

Psychiatric history
Mental status examination
Medical evaluation
Differential diagnosis: psychiatric and medical
DSM-III-R diagnoses (definitive or provisional)
   Psychiatric disorders (Axis I)
   Personality diagnosis (Axis II)
   Medical diagnoses (Axis III)
   Identification of major psychosocial stressors (Axis IV)
   Assessment of psychosocial functioning (Axis V)
Psychosocial assessment and case formulation
Treatment plan
   Psychological—need for and choice of psychotherapy; inpatient or outpatient treatment

   Biological—need for further medical/neurological evaluation or treatment; psychopharmacological treatment; rehabilitation programs

   Social—need for intervention in environmental conditions and social conditions; referral to support agencies, occupational counseling, financial or legal assistance

---

CLINICAL PEARLS

The following ten questions, which should be modified by the interviewer to be asked in an open-ended manner, will facilitate uncovering the source of psychosocial stress connected with the onset or relapse of psychiatric symptoms, assuming the patient is open and cooperative with the interviewer.

- Has there been any recent serious illness or death in your family?
- Have you been having any problems with money or with your job? Are you seriously in debt?
- Have you had any serious problems with your children, your marriage, or other close relationships?
- Have you had any recent illness or surgery, and are you on any medications?
- Have you ever thought you might have a problem with drinking too much alcohol or taking drugs?
- Have you been under any stress or pressure recently that has been difficult for you to manage?

Regarding the patient's past history, the following questions will help identify any significant psychodynamic problems or major stresses in the patient's developmental years. These are "lead" questions that will identify any major developmental traumas, but the development history should not be limited solely to these four questions.

- Tell me about growing up with your family and your relationship with your parents. Did you have any special problems with your parents or within your family when you

(continued)

CLINICAL PEARLS (continued)

were growing up? Was there frequent fighting between your parents when you were a child or teenager?

- Did either one of your parents have a problem with alcohol or drugs?
- Did your parents divorce or separate when you were a child, or did one of your parents die when you were young?
- Were you ever physically or sexually abused when you were a child or teenager?

ANNOTATED BIBLIOGRAPHY

MacKinnon RA, Michels R: The Psychiatric Interview in Clinical Practice. Philadelphia, WB Saunders, 1971

Written from a classically psychoanalytic perspective, the text is now slightly dated and doctrinal but presents the traditional psychodynamically oriented approach to patient interviewing for medical students.

Nemiah JC: Foundations of Clinical Psychopathology. New York, Oxford University Press, 1961

This is an intriguing and beautifully written text that remains a classic as an introduction to psychodynamic theory.

Balint M: The Doctor, His Patient and the Illness. New York, International University Press, 1957

Balint was a psychoanalyst who worked extensively with primary care doctors in evaluating and treating the common psychiatric conditions of general medical patients. This text remains a classic for exploring and understanding the psychological aspects of medical practice.

For students interested in excellent comprehensive resources on psychiatric interviewing, the following book is recommended:

Shea SC: Psychiatric Interviewing. The Art of Understanding. Philadelphia, WB Saunders, 1988

REFERENCES

Alexander F: Psychosomatic medicine. Its principles and applications. New York, Norton, 1950

Aneshensel CS, Stone JD: Stress and depression: A test of the buffering model of social support. Arch Gen Psychiatry 39:1392–1396, 1982

Bertalanffy L von: General system theory: A critical review. In Buckley W (ed): Modern Systems Research for the Behavioral Scientist, pp 11–30. Chicago, Aldine, 1968

Bifulco AT, Brown GW, Harris TO: Childhood loss of parent, lack of adequate parental care and adult depression: A replication. J Affective Discord 12:115–128, 1987

Birley JLT, Brown GW: Crises and life changes preceding the onset or relapse of acute schizophrenia: Clinical aspects. Br J Psychiatry 116:327–333, 1970

Bolton W, Oatley K: A longitudinal study of social support and depression in unemployed men. Psychol Med 17:453–460, 1987

Breier A, Kelsoe JR, Kirwin PD, et al: Early parental loss and development of adult psychopathology. Arch Gen Psychiatry 45:987–993, 1988

Bryer JB, Nelson BA, Miller JB, et al: Childhood sexual and physical abuse as factors in adult psychiatric illness. Am J Psychiatry 144:1426–1430, 1987

Cadoret RJ, O'Gorman TW, Troughton E, et al: Alcoholism and antisocial personality: Interrelationships, genetic and environmental factors. Arch Gen Psychiatry 42:161–167, 1985

Cobb S: Social support as a moderator of life stress. Psychosom Med 38:300–314, 1976

Cohen-Cole SA: The biopsychosocial model. In Stoudemire A (ed): Human Behavior: An Introduction for Medical Students. Philadelphia, JB Lippincott, 1990

Cooper AM: Will neurobiology influence psychoanalysis? Am J Psychiatry 142:1395–1402, 1985

Doane JA, West KL, Goldstein MJ, et al: Parental communication deviance and affective style: Predictors of subsequent schizophrenia spectrum disorders in vulnerable adolescents. Arch Gen Psychiatry 38:679–685, 1981

Engel GL: The need for a new medical model: A challenge for biomedicine. Science 196:129–136, 1977

Fink PJ: Response to the presidential address: Is "Biopsychosocial" the psychiatric shibboleth? Am J Psychiatry 145:1061–1067, 1988

Green SA: Supportive psychological care of the medically ill. In Stoudemire A (ed): Human Behavior: An Introduction for Medical Students. Philadelphia, JB Lippincott, 1990

Greenblatt M, Becerra R, Serafetinides EA: Social networks and mental health: An overview. Am J Psychiatry 8:977–984, 1982

Harris T, Brown GW, Bifulco A: Loss of parent in childhood and adult psychiatric disorder: The role of lack of adequate parental care. Psychol Med 16:641–659, 1986

Harris T, Brown GW, Bifulco A: Loss of parent in childhood and adult psychiatric disorder: The role of social class position and premarital pregnancy. Psychol Med 17:163–183, 1987

Kandel ER: Psychotherapy and the single synapse. The impact of psychiatric thought on neurobiologic research. N Engl J Med 301:1028–1037, 1979

Kandel ER: From metapsychology to molecular biology: Explorations into the nature of anxiety. Am J Psychiatry 140:1277–1293, 1983

Kendler KS: Indirect vertical cultural transmission: A model for nongenetic parental influences on the liability to psychiatric illness. Am J Psychiatry 145:657–665, 1988

Leavy RL: Social support and psychological disorder: A review. Community Psychology 11:3–21, 1983

Lindberg F, Distad L: Post-traumatic stress disorders in women who experienced childhood incest. Child Abuse Negl 9:329–334, 1985

MacMillan JF, Gold A, Crow TJ, et al: The Northwick Park study of first episodes of schizophrenia: IV. Expressed emotion and relapse. Br J Psychiatry 148:133–143, 1986

Meyer A: Psychobiology, A Science of Man. Springfield, IL, Charles C Thomas, 1957

Miklowitz DJ, Goldstein MJ, Neuchterlein KH, et al: The family and the course of recent-onset mania. In Hahlweg K, Goldstein MJ (eds): Understanding Major Mental Disorder: The Contribution of Family Interaction Research, pp 195–211. New York, Family Process Press, 1987

Miklowitz DJ, Goldstein MJ, Neuchterlein KH, et al: Family factors and the course of bipolar affective disorder. Arch Gen Psychiatry 45:225–231, 1988

Miller PM, Ingham JG, Davidson S: Life events, symptoms and social support. J Psychosom Res 20:515–522, 1976

Parry G, Shapiro DA: Social support and life events in working class women. Arch Gen Psychiatry 43:315–323, 1986

Penkower L, Bromet EJ, Dew MA: Husbands' layoff and wives' mental health. Arch Gen Psychiatry 45:994–1000, 1988

Reiser MF: Mind, Brain, Body. New York, Basic Books, 1984

Reiser MF: Are psychiatric educators "losing the mind"? Am J Psychiatry 145:148–153, 1988

Roy A: Parental loss in childhood and onset of manic-depressive illness. Br J Psychiatry 136:86–88, 1980

Rutter M: Psychopathology and development: Links between childhood and adult life. In Rutter M, Hersov L (eds): Child and Adolescent Psychiatry. London, Blackwell Scientific Publications, 1985

Schwartz CC, Myers JK: Life events and schizophrenia. I: Comparison of schizophrenics with a community sample. Arch Gen Psychiatry 34:1238–1241, 1977a

Schwartz CC, Myers JK: Life events and schizophrenia. II: Impact of life events on symptom configuration. Arch Gen Psychiatry 34:1242–1245, 1977b

Tennant C: Life events and psychological morbidity: The evidence from prospective studies. Psychol Med 13:483–486, 1983

Tennant C: Parental loss in childhood: Its effect in adult life. Arch Gen Psychiatry 45:1045–1050, 1988

Tennant C, Bebbington P, Hurry J: Social experiences in childhood and adult psychiatric morbidity: A multiple regression analysis. Psychol Med 12:321–327, 1982

Tennant C, Hurry J, Bebbington P: The relation of childhood separation experiences to adult depressive and anxiety states. Br J Psychiatry 141:475–482, 1982a

Tennant C, Hurry J, Bebbington P: The relationship of different types of childhood separation experiences to adult psychiatric disorders. Br J Psychiatry 141:475–482, 1982b

Tennant C, Smith A, Bebbington P, et al: Parental loss in childhood: Relationship to adult psychiatric impairment and contact with psychiatric services. Arch Gen Psychiatry 38:309–314, 1981

Uhlenhuth EG, Paykel ES: Symptom intensity and life events. Arch Gen Psychiatry 28:473–477, 1973

van der Kolk B: The psychological consequences of overwhelming life experiences. In van der Kolk B (ed): Psychological Trauma. Washington, DC, American Psychiatric Press, 1986

van der Kolk B: Behavioral and psychobiological effects of developmental trauma. In Stoudemire A (ed): Human Behavior: An Introduction for Medical Students. Philadelphia, JB Lippincott, 1990

Vaughn CE, Snyder KS, Jones S, et al: Family factors in schizophrenic relapse: Replication in California of British research on expressed emotion. Arch Gen Psychiatry 41:1169–1177, 1984

Warr P, Jackson P: Factors influencing the psychological impact of prolonged unemployment and of re-employment. Psychol Med 15:795–807, 1985

Weissman MM, Gammon GD, John K, et al: Children of depressed parents: Increased psychopathology and early onset of major depression. Arch Gen Psychiatry 44:847–853, 1987

3

Organic Mental Disorders

Alan Stoudemire

This chapter will discuss diagnosis and treatment of the psychiatric conditions known as organic mental disorders and syndromes in DSM-III-R, focusing on the dementias and delirium. The term "organic" is an anachronism, because it is now recognized that *all* of the *major* psychiatric disorders involve some degree of neurophysiological dysfunction and that all behavior has a neurochemical basis. Although the nomenclature is in need of revision in this regard, this chapter will nevertheless employ the terminology of DSM-III-R in the discussion of this major group of disorders, which are among the most common psychiatric disorders encountered by general medical and surgical physicians.

DSM-III-R defines the "essential features" of an *organic mental disorder* as a "psychological or behavioral abnormality associated with transient or permanent dysfunction of the brain" (DSM-III-R, 1987). If the cause of the brain dysfunction is "generally or specifically" known or can be identified (e.g., Alzheimer's disease, multiinfarct dementia, organic mental disorders caused by alcohol or substance abuse), the term "disorder" is used; if a cause or etiology is not known or cannot be specified, then the general condition is referred to as an organic brain "*syndrome.*" Before proceeding in this area, a few generic terms will be defined to guide this discussion.

1. Organic mental disorders/syndromes. As defined above, this is a broad, general category of psychiatric conditions characterized by psychological and behavioral abnormalities associated with transient or permanent dysfunction of the brain (see Chapter 1 Appendix; this table is verbatim from DSM-III-R, pp 3–12).
2. Delirium. This is an organic mental disorder, usually acute and fluctuating, characterized by an altered state of awareness and mental consciousness. Deliria may be accompanied by hallucinations, misperceptions of sensory stimuli (illusions), emotional lability, alterations in the sleep–wake cycle, psychomotor slowing, or hyperactivity. Cognitive defects in attention, concentration, think-

The editor gratefully acknowledges the help of Drs. Marshall Folstein and Paul McHugh, who supplied substantial textual material for this chapter.

ing, and goal-directed behavior and memory are almost always present. The onset is often abrupt but may be insidious in nature. The cause is usually traced to an external toxic agent, medication side effect, metabolic abnormalities, acute central nervous system (CNS) abnormality, or medication/drug withdrawal. If the cause of the delirium can be identified and corrected, the condition usually remits (Table 3-1).

3. Dementia. Dementia is an organic mental disorder, usually chronic, that denotes patients with impairments in short- and long-term memory, abstract thinking, logical judgment, personality changes, orientation, interpersonal relationships, and higher cortical functions, such as language and calculations (Table 3-2). The onset is usually insidious and slowly progressive. Unlike in delirium, the patient's *level of awareness and alertness is usually intact* in the early stages of the illness and becomes impaired usually only in the *latter stages* of the illness; the retention and stability of *alertness* is the primary distinguishing feature between *dementia* and *delirium.* Examples of dementia include Alzheimer's disease, (primary degenerative dementia in DSM-III-R), multi-infarct dementia, dementia of Parkinson's disease, and normal pressure hydrocephalus.

4. Organic anxiety disorder, organic mood disorder, organic delusional disorder, organic hallucinosis, organic personality syndrome. These organic mental disorder diagnoses are made when evidence of brain dysfunction affecting behavior exists but a *primary* dementia or delirium has been ruled out; the symptoms should occur in the presence of a clear mental status. These conditions involve abnormalities in *mood, anxiety, or personality* or the presence of *delusions* and *hallucinations* that can usually be attributed directly to some specific cause or agent. *As noted above, these diag-*

Table 3–1 **Major Signs and Symptoms of a Delirium**

Altered state of alertness, awareness, and consciousness (hyperalert or obtunded; patient's level of consciousness may vary from time to time; lucid intervals may occur)
Fluctuating course—as above
Onset may be dramatic but may be subtle and evolve over days or weeks
Disorientation and confusion
Decreased attention, concentration, and memory
Psychotic symptoms—paranoia, hallucinations (often visual), delusions
Behavioral disinhibition, emotional lability, irritability
Psychomotor retardation or agitation—may vary in a 24-hour period
Fragmented sleep/wake cycle; increased agitation at night
Usually reversible with correction of underlying etiology
Apraxia, dysgraphia, dysnomia and tremors, abnormal reflexes (myoclonus or asterixis)

Table 3-2 **DSM-III-R Diagnostic Criteria for Dementia**

A. Demonstrable evidence of impairment in short- and long-term memory. Impairment in short-term memory (inability to learn new information) may be indicated by inability to remember three objects after five minutes. Long-term memory impairment (inability to remember information that was known in the past) may be indicated by inability to remember past personal information (e.g., what happened yesterday, birthplace, occupation) or facts of common knowledge (e.g., past Presidents, well-known dates).

B. At least one of the following:
   (1) impairment in abstract thinking, as inidicated by inability to find similarities and differences between related words, difficulty in defining words and concepts, and other similar tasks
   (2) impaired judgment, as indicated by inability to make reasonable plans to deal with interpersonal, family, and job-related problems and issues
   (3) other disturbances of higher cortical function, such as aphasia (disorder of language), apraxia (inability to carry out motor activities despite intact comprehension and motor function), agnosia (failure to recognize or identify objects despite intact sensory function), and "constructional difficulty" (e.g., inability to copy three-dimensional figures, assemble blocks, or arrange sticks in specific designs)
   (4) personality change, i.e., alteration or accentuation of premorbid traits

C. The disturbance in A and B significantly interferes with work or usual social activities or relationships with others.

D. Not occurring exclusively during the course of Delirium.

E. Either (1) or (2):
   (1) there is evidence from the history, physical examination, or laboratory tests of a specific organic factor (or factors) judged to be etiologically related to the disturbance
   (2) in the absence of such evidence, an etiologic organic factor can be presumed if the disturbance cannot be accounted for by any nonorganic mental disorder, e.g., Major Depression accounting for cognitive impairment

Criteria for severity of Dementia:

Mild: Although work or social activities are significantly impaired, the capacity for independent living remains, with adequate personal hygiene and relatively intact judgment.

Moderate: Independent living is hazardous, and some degree of supervision is necessary.

Severe: Activities of daily living are so impaired that continual supervision is required, e.g., unable to maintain minimal personal hygiene; largely incoherent or mute.

(Used with permission from DSM-III-R)

---

noses are not made if the patient primarily meets diagnostic criteria for delirium or a dementia. For example, a patient with a clear mental status who becomes depressed because of *hypothyroidism* or as a result of an antihypertensive medication such as alpha-methyldopa would be considered to have an organic mood disorder; a patient severely anxious from use of theophylline would have an organic anxiety disorder; a patient who becomes emotionally labile and disinhibited as a result of temporal lobe complex partial seizures would have an organic personality disorder; and a patient hallucinating after withdrawal from alcohol who is relatively alert and cognitively intact would have organic hallucinosis. A complete review of these organic mental syndromes is beyond the scope of this text, but the most common causes of organic mood, delusional, and personality disorders are summarized in Tables 3-3 through 3-6. Readers are referred to selected references for details (Stoudemire, 1987).

5. Organic mental disorders associated with psychoactive substances. This general category of organic mental disorders is used to designate behavioral abnormalities caused by direct effects of psychoactive agents on the brain. DSM-III-R addresses 11 major classes of drugs in the area: alcohol, amphetamines and similar sympathomimetics, caffeine, cannabis, opioids, hallucinogens, inhalants, nicotine, phencyclidine and similarly acting arylcyclohexylamines, sedative-hypnotics, and anxiolytics. Table 3-7 from DSM-III-R (p 124, 1985) summarizes the signs and symptoms associated with these substances, and they are discussed further in Chapters 9 and 18.

6. Amnestic disorder. This is an organic mental disorder characterized by a relatively focal disorder of short-term memory where other cognitive functions are intact. The most common cause is alcohol. The most common neuroanatomic abnormality that has been described with the amnestic syndrome is bilateral sclerosis of the mamillary bodies probably due to hemorrhage. Degenerative changes also have been described in the dorsal medial nucleus of

Table 3–3 **Major Reported Causes of Organic Mood Syndromes (Depressed)**

Medications

Antihypertensives (reserpine, methyldopa, propranolol)
Barbiturates
Corticosteroids
Guanethidine
Indomethacin
Levodopa
Psychostimulants (amphetamine and cocaine in the postwithdrawal phase)

Medical illnesses

Carcinoid syndrome
Carcinomas (pancreatic)
Cerebrovascular disease (stroke)
Collagen-vascular disease (systemic lupus erythematosus)
Endocrinopathies (Cushing's syndrome, Addison's disease, hypoglycemia, hyper- and hypocalcemia, hyper- and hypothyroidism)
Lymphomas
Parkinson's disease
Pernicious anemia (B_{12} deficiency)
Viral illnesses (hepatitis, mononucleosis, influenza)

(Adapted from Stoudemire A: Selected organic mental disorders. In Hales RE, Yudofsky SC (eds): Textbook of Neuropsychiatry. Washington, DC, American Psychiatric Press, 1987)

Table 3-4 **Major Reported Causes of Organic Mood Syndrome (Manic)**

Medications

Antidepressants
Corticosteroids/ACTH
Decongestants (containing phenylephrine)
Levodopa
Monoamine oxidase inhibitors
Sympathomimetics/bronchodilators (containing theophylline and/or ephedrine/isophedrine)

Metabolic abnormalities

Hyperthyroidism

Seizure/neurologic disorders

Multiple sclerosis
Right hemispheric damage
Temporal lobe seizures

Neoplasms

(Adapted from Stoudemire A: Selected organic mental disorders. In Hales RE, Yudofsky SC (eds): Textbook of Neuropsychiatry. Washington, DC, American Psychiatric Press, 1987)

Table 3-5 **Major Reported Causes of Organic Delusional Syndrome (Partial Listing)**

CNS disorders

Cerebrovascular disease
Idiopathic basal ganglia calcification
Multiple sclerosis
Neoplasms
Parkinson's disease
Spinocerebellar degeneration
Temporal lobe epilepsy

Connective tissue disease

Systemic lupus erythematosus
Temporal arteritis

Deficiency states

B_{12}
Folate
Niacin

Drug/medications

Antidepressants
Antihypertensives
Antimalarials, anticonvulsants
Antiparkinsonian agents
Antituberculosis agents
Hallucinogens

Endocrinopathies

Adrenal insufficiency
Cushing's disease
Hyperthyroidism
Hypothyroidism
Hypo- and hypercalcemia
Panhypopituitarism

Miscellaneous

Amphetamines
Bromide
Corticosteroids
Heavy metal toxicity
Huntington's chorea
Pentazocine
Porphyria

(Adapted from Stoudemire A: Selected organic mental disorders. In Hales RE, Yudofsky SC (eds): Textbook of Neuropsychiatry. Washington, DC, American Psychiatric Press, 1987)

Table 3–6 **Major Reported Causes of
Organic Personality Disorder**

Adrenocortical disease
Head trauma
Heavy metal poisoning
Hypothyroidism
Multiple sclerosis
Neoplasms
Systemic lupus erythematosus
Temporal lobe seizure disorders
Vascular disease

the thalamus, which serves as a relay point between memory centers and the frontal cortex.

7. Transient global amnesia. Transient global amnesia (TGA) usually occurs in middle-aged or elderly individuals and is characterized by the sudden loss of memory of recent events and the inability to recall new information, often with secondary confusion. The level of consciousness usually is normal, and personal identity remains intact. Patients are aware of their deficits and may ask questions about their circumstances. Such episodes may last from minutes to hours, attacks usually are episodic. The "spells" often remit within 24 hours. Most experts consider the episodes to be caused by transient vascular insufficiency of the mesial temporal lobe, but other disorders such as tumors, benzodiazepine overdose, cardiac arrhythmias, cerebral embolism, migraine, polycythemia vera, and mitral valvular disease have been reported to cause TGA. Most patients with TGA also have associated risk factors for cerebrovascular stroke.

Arriving at the diagnosis of an organic mental disorder requires a carefully structured cognitive and behavioral assessment of the patient.

CLINICAL EXAMINATION OF THE PATIENT WITH COGNITIVE DYSFUNCTION: USE OF THE MINI–MENTAL STATE EXAMINATION

Perhaps the most serious clinical error made in medicine is underdiagnosis of organic mental disorders in medical and surgical settings. It is common for physicians to label a patient's abnormal behavior caused by an organic disorder erroneously as "functional" (that is, due to a "psychiatric" or emotional problem). Although the reasons for underdiagnosis or misdiagnosis of organic mental disorders are not entirely clear, they probably result from a lack of rigor and structure in performing a mental status examination, if one is performed at all. Because of this

Table 3–7 **DSM-III-R Organic Mental Syndromes Associated with Psychoactive Substances**

	INTOXICATION	WITH-DRAWAL	DELIRIUM	WITH-DRAWAL DELIRIUM	DELU-SIONAL DISORDER	MOOD DISORDER	OTHER SYNDROMES
Alcohol	X	X		X			1
Amphetamine and related substances	X	X	X		X		
Caffeine	X						
Cannabis	X				X		
Cocaine	X	X	X		X		
Hallucinogen	X (hallucinosis)				X	X	2
Inhalant	X						
Nicotine		X					
Opioid	X	X					
Phencyclidine (PCP) and related substances	X		X		X	X	3
Sedative, hypnotic, or anxiolytic	X	X		X			4

[1] Alcohol Idiosyncratic Intoxication, Alcohol Hallucinosis, Alcohol Amnestic Disorder, Dementia Associated with Alcoholism.
[2] Posthallucinogen Perception Disorder
[3] Phencyclidine (PCP) or Similarly Acting Arylcyclohexylamine Organic Mental Disorder NOS.
[4] Sedative, Hypnotic or Anxiolytic Amnestic Disorder.
(Used with permission from DSM-III-R p 124)

pervasive problem in clinical medicine, a significant portion of this chapter is devoted to presenting in some detail a structured cognitive mental status examination using the Mini–Mental State Exam (MMSE) (Folstein, Folstein, McHugh, 1975). The MMSE is a practical and efficient instrument for assessing, documenting, and tracking a patient's cognitive functioning over time. This cognitive screening instrument has been extensively validated in both clinical and research settings. Its brevity, accuracy, and efficiency make it immensely practical for routine clinical use (see appendix at end of chapter).

There are, however, several disadvantages to this approach. Symptoms such as delusions and hallucinations, which could not be quantitated as easily, are not included. A total score does not specifically characterize the patient's cognitive capacity in terms such as amnesia, aphasia, or apraxia. Hence, the MMSE is *not* to be considered a comprehensive behavioral or cognitive mental status examination but a reliable means of screening and monitoring gross changes in cognitive functioning.

Mini–Mental State Examination (MMSE)

The set of items called the Mini–Mental State Examination (MMSE) briefly surveys important cognitive functions, including language function, that are omitted from most other brief screening tests (Chapter 3 appendix). It is useful in screening patients and also is useful in teaching aspects of the cognitive examination that can be embellished by the examiner asking for such things as the interpretation of proverbs, a listing of the presidents in reverse order, or a drawing of a cube or a clock. It also can be amplified by the addition of more formal neuropsychological testing, including symbol digit and trails test, to delineate in more detail preserved and impaired functions.

The MMSE begins with a set of questions about orientation in time and place. The patient is asked, "Where are you?" and the patient is expected to be able to tell us the place they are in space and time, specific to the day of the week and the month of the year. Thus, orientation to time and place can be graded, and a patient is *more or less* oriented rather than *absolutely* disoriented or oriented. Patients can acquire 10 points out of 30 on the examination for giving a complete answer to the questions concerning *orientation*. Orientation is the first and easiest capacity to assess because it is so frequently disturbed among patients. Although disorientation can be as subtle as a mild sense of bewilderment over the date, it can be so severe that patients may not know whether they are indoors or outdoors or standing or lying in the hospital or at home.

Because one cause of disorientation might be the inability of patients to learn from an assessment of their surroundings, the disorientation could be the outcome of a memory disorder. The next set of probes tests the ability of the patient to learn and remember.

Questions in this segment of the exam begin with the test of the patient's capacity to register and repeat three simple words that are presented orally. The patient is asked to repeat three words given approximately 1 second apart, such as pony, quarter, and orange, and is given one point for each of the three correctly repeated. This task is also an assessment of the patient's capacity to hear, attend, and repeat words, as well as the capacity to remember three objects mentioned in a very short period of time. To determine their capacity to recall for a longer period of time, the patient is asked to recall the three objects a short while later, after which he or she performs another task that is presented to prevent constant rehearsal of the three objects.

During this interval, another capacity is tested; the patient is asked to attend to a task and carry it through to completion. The best tasks testing attention and concentration are those that demand a continuing focus on and performance of a serial problem. Thus, a subtraction of 7 from 100 for five consecutive subtractions requires patients to be able to attend and at the same time perform an arithmetic function without losing track of the task that they are performing. Another similar, but less difficult, task is the spelling of the word "world" backward. This task is offered to patients only when they refuse to perform the serial 7s, because the serial 7s task is more difficult.

After the assessment of attention and calculation by the serial 7s task, it is determined whether patients can recall three words presented to them previously in the registration task; thus, they are able to tap a longer-term aspect of memory.

This completes the *first section* of the MMSE. Many aspects of the tests of orientation, registration, attention and calculation, and recall depend to some extent on the patient's capacity to comprehend and use language. The second part of the examination is designed explicitly to test the patient's language capacity. It is then determined whether the patient can name a visually presented object; repeat the phrase "No ifs, ands, or buts"; follow a three-stage verbal command—"Take this piece of paper in your right hand, fold it in half, and put it on the floor"; read a simple sentence—"Close your eyes"; write a sentence spontaneously; and copy a design. This aspect of the MMSE can be supplemented with evaluation by the physician of the patient's speech—whether it is fluent, dysarthric, or of normal rate, rhythm, and prosody. Thus, one then makes make a judgment as to whether the patient speaks clearly with normal intonation or whether the speech is monotonic or slurred. In addition, it is noted whether the patient uses appropriate vocabulary or whether mistakes are made in the meaning of particular words, such as when new words are constructed or old words are pronounced incorrectly. It is also noted whether patients use appropriate syntax with complex or simple sentences in their response to questions, and finally whether the patient in the course of the examination addresses the examiner in the expected fashion, with appropriate eye contact and demeanor. In this way, in addition to being able to score the patient's performance on a series of simple tasks, it is possible to appraise the patient's phonology, semantics, syntax, and pragmatics of language function. These last aspects are not scored but should be entered as commentary on the patient's performance on the examination. The language section of the MMSE can be affected by disease processes of several types, including focal brain diseases of the left hemisphere, such as those produced by a stroke, as well as by diffuse brain disease, such as that produced by Alzheimer's disease.

Consciousness

The examination is concluded by an assessment of the patient's level of consciousness, which is rated on an analog scale from comatose to fully alert. This rating can be performed reliably and is a measure of the patient's alertness, responsiveness, and accessibility to the examiner (Anthony, LeResche, Von Korff, et al., 1985). Although this aspect of the examination is not taken into the total score, it serves to distinguish those patients who are cognitively impaired in a clear state of consciousness, as in dementia, from those who are cognitively impaired with an altered state of alertness and consciousness, as in delirium.

In a medical setting, the usual procedure is to try to determine whether the impairments as assessed by the MMSE in fact cluster into groups of symptoms, such as the syndromes of dementia and delirium. After that assessment, one then attempts to determine whether an *identifiable* pathological process is present, such as a stroke, Alzheimer's disease, or drug intoxication. In a final step of the overall evaluation, it is determined whether a recognizable risk factor or causal agent is present, such as hypertension or a genetic abnormality. Thus, one reasons from symptoms and signs to syndromes to pathology to etiology.

The Syndromes

Syndromes of cognitive impairment can be divided into two main groups, the *developmental syndromes* and the *deteriorations.* The *developmental* syndromes include those aspects of *mental retardation, developmental dyslexia, and attention deficit disorders,* which are apparently present from *birth or early childhood.* These syndromes are contrasted with the *deteriorations* of cognition, which represent a decline from a previous level of functioning. Examples of deteriorations of cognition include dementia, delirium, aphasic syndromes, and amnestic syndromes. For the purpose of this chapter, we will consider only the deteriorations that are called dementia and delirium.

Dementia

Dementia is a deterioration of multiple cognitive impairments occurring in clear consciousness and alertness and may have multiple causes (Tables 3-2 and 3-8). Dementia should be distinguished from cognitive impairments that are not deteriorating in nature and from more focal deteriorations of the brain, which may affect single functions, such as language.

The determination of brain deterioration requires confirming evidence other than what is observed directly or elicited from the patient (e.g., family members or employers who can give examples of functions that the patient could once perform but in which there has been a change). Useful functions that can be evaluated and that may indicate cognitive decline include the ability to manage finances and a checkbook, the capacity to travel without becoming lost, the ability to use the telephone and take messages, and the ability to recall the place of objects, such as the patient's wallet, keys, and eyeglasses. Observations such as these from the patient's family are correlated with impairments in orientation, recall, attention, and sometimes language function, which can be documented with the MMSE. When a decline has been reported and found to be accompanied by multiple cognitive impairments on formal examination, the syndrome of dementia can be diagnosed if the patient is otherwise generally alert.

The syndrome of dementia can occur *suddenly,* as seen after stroke, or can

Table 3–8 **Causes of Dementia (Partial Listing)**

Alcohol-related dementia
Alzheimer's disease
Amyotrophic lateral sclerosis
Bromide poisoning
Chronic granulomatous meningitis (tuberculous, fungal)
Folic acid deficiency
Head trauma
Human immunodeficiency virus (HIV)
Huntington's chorea
Hypothyroidism
Multi-infarct dementia
Multiple sclerosis
Neoplasms
Normal-pressure hydrocephalus
Parkinson-dementia complex
Parkinson's disease
Postanoxic states
Progressive supranuclear palsy
Tertiary neurosyphilis
Transmissible virus dementia (Jakob-Creutzfeldt disease)
Vitamin B_{12} deficiency

occur *insidiously and progress gradually*, as seen in association with Alzheimer's disease. The syndrome is often mostly reversible, such as when it occurs because of hypothyroidism, although the patient may be left with permanent impairments. Most dementia is irreversible, such as that associated with Alzheimer's disease. From an epidemiological point of view, most cases of dementia seen in the community are insidious, gradually progress, and are, at the present time, not reversible (Folstein, Anthony, Parhad, et al., 1985). These facts clearly are subject to revision, however, when adequate treatments are discovered.

Some authorities have found it useful to divide dementia into two types, the *cortical* type and the *subcortical* type. This distinction is based on the clinical impression or "gestalt" of the presentation of patients. For example, dementias of the *cortical* type, as in Alzheimer's disease, tend to be characterized by a profound memory deficit and often a semantic aphasia, but the patient is fluent, moderately attentive, normally responsive to questions, and normally active in his environment at home or in the office (Brandt, Folstein, Folstein, 1987).

In contrast, patients with the *subcortical* dementing illness, such as Huntington's disease and occult hydrocephalus, are alert but slowly responsive and inactive and usually are not fluent in their language. They are often dysarthric and have difficulty with forming complex sentences. These patients have little difficulty with semantic processing, however, and usually comprehend language fully, even when severely affected. They may have relatively mild disorders of memory or have marked attentional problems and show difficulty with "executive" functions, such as changing from one cognitive "set" to another, as demonstrated by the Wisconsin Card Sorting Task or the Trailmaking Test (Brandt, Butters, 1986). In addition to their cognitive features, patients with subcortical dementia frequently suffer from motor disorders, such as involuntary movements, as seen in Parkinson's disease and Huntington's disease. They often are found to have a depressive syndrome in addition to their cognitive syndrome. Thus, the patient with subcortical syndrome is slow in response, behaviorally inactive, and has a cognitive disorder associated with disorders of movement and mood. The distinction between cortical and noncortical dementias is not universally accepted by clinicians, and a significant amount of overlap exists between symptoms in the two categories.

Noncognitive Symptoms Accompanying Dementia

Disorders of mood, perception, belief, and behavior are often associated with dementia. Disorders of mood of several types are seen. A sustained depressive syndrome occurs in 30–60% of patients with subcortical dementia and 10–20% of cortical dementia patients (Rovner, Kafonek, Filipp, et al., 1986). Hence, dementia and depressive states can coexist, and the mood disorder component of the patient's condition can be responsive to antidepressants or electroconvulsive therapy.

Pathological laughter or crying occurs when the dementia syndrome is caused by bilateral corticobulbar lesions, such as in multiple strokes and multiple sclerosis. The disruption in mood may be transient, lasting seconds or minutes, and is often prompted by a meaningful psychological stimulus, such as a conversation, music, or a sentimental memory. The laughter or crying observed is often abnormal because it is expressed against the will of the patient, who does not always actually feel sad or happy and in fact is often embarrassed by it.

Irritability and explosiveness is another type of emotional disorder seen with dementia, especially with the dementia of Huntington's disease. Excessive emotional outbursts that occur after task failure have been called "catastrophic reactions" and may occur in the dementia of Alzheimer's disease. Precipitational catastrophic reactions can be modulated by educating family members so as to avoid confrontations of memory deficits.

Delusions and hallucinations occur about 10–20% of the time at some phase of the dementia process. Paranoid delusions may arise out of the cognitive impairment, as when misplaced objects are reported by the patient to be stolen; hence, the patient makes "sense" out of the fact that an object is gone by arriving at what he or she believes must be a logical explanation. It's not "there" because someone stole it.

Hallucinations of all types occur, but visual hallucinations tend to be the most common. In Parkinson's disease or diencephalic vascular disease, peduncular hallucinosis is seen. In this condition, pleasant or relatively benign simple visions, such as falling handkerchiefs, usually occur. Lilliputian hallucinations of small people often dressed in colorful costumes also occur. In addition to these primary hallucinatory experiences, patients with dementia also experience a variety of misinterpretations of environmental stimuli (illusions). Patients with agnosia often misinterpret their environment and become fearful or aggressive (Cummings, Miller, Hill, et al., 1987). A wide variety of abnormal behaviors is encountered, including suicide, aggression, agitation, emotional lability, wandering, and insomnia.

The relationship of dementia to other psychiatric disorders, such as depressive disorders, schizophrenia, and hysterical disorders, requires some clarification. Cognitive dysfunction also may occur in severe depression to the extent that it can even "mimic" dementia in some respects. When cognitive dysfunction occurs in depression or in another psychiatric disorder, it may be referred to as the "dementia syndrome of depression" or "dementia of schizophrenia" (Folstein, McHugh, 1978). Perhaps more accurately, one may refer to it as "depression with cognitive dysfunction." Clinically, cognitive dysfunction due to depression *rarely*, if ever, resembles the global progressive deficits seen in dementia unless the patient already has a preexisting dementia on which the depressive disorder becomes superimposed. Primary dementia and depression may be superimposed on each other, although depression is frequently overlooked, dismissed, or otherwise not aggressively treated in patients with dementia (Stoudemire, Hill, Kaplan, et al., 1988).

Entities Causing Dementia

Among the 6% of elderly individuals in the general population who are suffering from a dementia syndrome of some sort, approximately one third to one half are suffering from Alzheimer's disease, and approximately one fifth to one third are suffering from dementia related to stroke, with the remaining 20–30% suffering from other causes, including head trauma, alcoholism, Parkinson's disease, and miscellaneous causes (Table 3-8).

In the general community, dementia related to *reversible* disorders is extremely low; the majority is due to stroke (multi-infarct dementia) and Alzheimer's disease. In hospital settings, however, individuals with dementia syndromes are often suffering from reversible cognitive dysfunction which require treatment (Rocca, Amaducci, Schoenberg, 1986). It is also extremely common for delirium to occur concurrently with dementia in the hospitalized elderly because of unstable metabolic problems and medications (see following section on delirium).

The full evaluation of dementia (which consists of history, physical examination, laboratory tests for drug levels and toxins, electrolytes, liver function tests, calcium, phosphorus, thyroid, Venereal Disease Research Laboratory (VDRL) test, serum B_{12} level, sedimentation rate, chest x-ray, EKG, CT scan, and EEG) is usually unrevealing of reversible causes of cognitive dysfunction, although about 5–15% of patients may have a reversible or partially reversible condition affecting their cognitive dysfunction (Table 3-9).

Cortical Dementia

The leading example of a cortical dementia syndrome is Alzheimer's disease ("Primary degenerative dementia of the Alzheimer's type" in DSM-III-R) (Alzheimer, 1907). The current estimates of the prevalence of Alzheimer's disease in the community vary from 2 to 10% of the population over age 65 and from 15 to 20% of the population over age 85 (Rocca, Amaducci, Schoenberg, 1986). Patients with Alz-

Table 3–9 **Comprehensive Work-up of Dementia and Delirium**

Physical exam, including thorough neurologic exam
Vital signs
Mental status examination
Mini–Mental State Exam (MMSE)
Review of medications and drug levels
Blood and urine screens for alcohol, drugs, and heavy metals*
Physiologic work-up
    Serum electrolytes/glucose/Ca^{++}, Mg$^+$
    Liver, renal function tests
    SMA-12 or equivalent serum chemistry profile
    Urinalysis
    Complete blood cell count with differential cell type count
    Thyroid function tests (including TSH level)
    RPR (serum screen)
    FTA-ABS (if CNS disease suspected)
    Serum B$_{12}$
    Folate levels
    Urine corticosteroids*
    Erythrocyte sedimentation rate (Westergren)
    Antinuclear antibody* (ANA), C$_3$C$_4$, Anti-DS DNA*
    Arterial blood gases*
    HIV screen*†
    Urine porphobilinogens*
Chest x-ray
Electrocardiogram
Neurologic work-up
    CT or MRI scan of head*‡
    SPECT**
    Lumbar puncture*
    EEG*
Neuropsychological testing§

*If indicated by history and physical examination
†Requires special consent and counseling
‡See Table 3-10 for relative discriminating power
**May detect cerebral blood flow perfusion deficits
§May be useful in differentiating dementia from other neuropsychiatric syndromes if this cannot be done clinically
Adapted with permission from Stoudemire A, Thompson TL: Recognizing and treating dementia. Geriatrics 36:112–120, 1981)

heimer's disease constitute more than half of all patients in nursing homes. These patients in the community or in nursing homes seldom have access to adequate psychiatric care and thus present a major public health problem in terms of the prevention of complications that result from the secondary symptoms of the disease.

Alzheimer's disease (AD) is a clinical pathological entity characterized by a dementia syndrome consisting of prominent memory deficits that usually begin with short-term memory and then progress to more pervasive memory deficits and global deficits such as aphasia, apraxia, and agnosia. Alzheimer's disease has an insidious onset and a gradual progression to death on average 7 years after onset, although great variability exists in the course of the illness (Katzman, 1986). The MMSE score in AD is approximately 14 (out of 30) after 4 years of illness.

On postmortem examination, the brain is found to be small and atrophic with a remarkable accumulation of neurofibrillary tangles and neuritic plaques with amyloid core and a deposition of amyloid in blood vessels in most cases. The composition of the neuritic tangle is under active investigation. However, there is some evidence that it consists of an amyloid fibril decorated with a variety of proteins, including ubiquitin and tau. The neuritic plaque consists of a beta pleated sheet of amyloid probably derived from a transmembrane protein. Embedded in the amyloid mass are bits of neurons derived primarily from *cholinergic* and *adrenergic* systems.

Two systems of neurons appear to be primarily involved in Alzheimer's disease. One of them is the cholinergic system originating in the basal forebrain, the so-called *nucleus basalis of Meynert.* Reductions in brain acetylcholine and its rate-limiting enzyme choline acetyltransferase *are* the most consistent neurotransmitter abnormalities observed in the brains of AD patients. The other neurotransmitter system also consistently observed to be abnormal is the *adrenergic* system originating in the *locus ceruleus* (Rosser, Iverson, 1986). There is some evidence that these two systems are affected independently in the disease, because some patients can be found with more or less adrenergic involvement. Involvement of the adrenergic system may be at least partially related to the high degree of disruptions in mood and anxiety regulation seen in AD.

GENETICS OF ALZHEIMER'S DISEASE

The cause of the neuronal death and subsequent deposition of neurofibrillary plaques and tangles is currently unknown. However, some cases have been found to be linked to a restriction fragment length polymorphism (RFLP) marker on chromosome 21, and others have been found to be associated with trisomy 21. Furthermore, the gene for the regulation of the protein that is precipitated in amyloid is also found on chromosome 21. In addition, Down's syndrome appears more likely to occur in families with AD than in families without histories of AD (Heston, Mastri, Anderson, et al., 1981). DNA markers on chromosome 21 have been linked to the genetic defect causing familial AD in three of four large pedigrees (St George-Hyslop, Tanzi, Polinsky, et al., 1987). The gene that encodes amyloid, which is a major component in neuritic plaques, is located nearby on chromosome 21. Recent studies, however, have not supported the hypothesis that the genetic defect in AD involves duplication of the amyloid gene (Small, Greenberg, 1988).

Other theories of causation of AD include the excess deposition of aluminum in the brain and the possibility of a slow viral infection. A review of current theories of Alzheimer's disease is beyond the scope of this discussion, but students are referred to excellent reviews; however, they should be cautioned that research is moving so rapidly in this area that "dated" information may be only a few months old (Davies, 1988)!

For many years, Alzheimer's disease was thought to be a disorder with an early age of onset (before age 65) that was distinct from so-called "senile dementia," which occurred much later and was common in the elderly. Because the neuropathology and the clinical presentation of Alzheimer's disease, or "presenile dementia" and "senile dementia," are the same, the early-onset and later-onset types are considered to be the same entity. In recent years, however, evidence is emerging that the disorder might very well be heterogeneous, with one form having an early age of onset that is associated with more severe neuropathological changes, more rapid progression, dermatoglyphic changes similar to those found in Down's syndrome, platelet membrane abnormalities (such as increased platelet membrane fluidity), and linkage to chromosome 21. In contrast, the late-onset form has not, as yet, been found to be linked to chromosome 21 and appears to involve the locus ceruleus less often.

In some families there clearly appears to be a genetic component in the development of Alzheimer's disease. Several investigators have attempted to estimate the morbid risk among first-degree relatives of patients with Alzheimer's disease using the life-table method, which estimates the age-specific cumulative incidence of a disease in a manner that adjusts for the fact that individuals die of other causes before the disease's onset (Breitner, Folstein, 1984; Mohs, Breitner, Silverman, et al., 1987; Zubenko, Huff, Beyer, et al., 1988). Using this technique, the morbid risk among first-degree relatives of patients has been estimated to be as high as 50% by age 90 (Mohs, Breitner, Silverman, et al., 1987). These calculations have been used to suggest that there is a dominant mode of inheritance for the Alzheimer's disease gene, although it appears that the genetic predisposition to the illness shows variable penetrance.

During the next several years, the genetic basis of Alzheimer's disease may be defined, along with the factors that may influence its expression. Alzheimer's is probably not a single disease entity but rather a heterogeneous disorder with varying degrees of behavioral, neurochemical, and neuropathological differences (Small, Greenberg, 1988). A search for biological markers for Alzheimer's disease is being vigorously pursued, including ultrastructural studies of the paired helical filaments of neurofibrillary tangles and use of the monoclonal antibody Alz-50 to detect A-68 proteins in the cerebrospinal fluid (CSF) of AD patients (Alzheimer, 1987; Small, Greenberg, 1988).

BRAIN IMAGING AND ALZHEIMER'S DISEASE

Abnormalities have also been noted on computed tomography (CT), magnetic resonance imaging (MRI), single photon emission computed tomography (SPECT), and positron emission tomography (PET) scanning, but none are sensitively diagnostic as yet (Riege, Metter, 1988). Cerebral atrophic and ventricular enlargement changes have been observed on CT/MRI scanning, but these changes also can be seen in elderly patients without Alzheimer's disease; alternatively, many patients *with* Alzheimer's disease will have normal CT/MRI scans. The primary use of CT/MRI scanning is to *exclude* any potentially treatable causes of cognitive dysfunction, such as a brain tumor or chronic subdural hematoma.

The most consistent observations made to date with PET scanning have been decreases in the regional cerebral metabolic rate of glucose using the marker F-18-

fluro-2-deoxyglucose (FDG). These findings also appear to correlate with decreased cerebral blood flow, as measured by SPECT techniques. The deficits that have been observed are predominantly in the temporoparietal area but are also in frontal regions. Decreased glucose use observed by PET scanning, however, is not always uniform or symmetric in the hemispheres. In addition, there is a significant amount of interpatient variability (Riege, Metter, 1988).

PICK'S DISEASE AND JAKOB-CREUTZFELDT DISEASE

Two other disorders that are differentiated from Alzheimer's disease and are primarily cortical in their expression are *Pick's disease* and *Jakob-Creutzfeldt disease*. Pick's disease can occur in patients in their 60s and 70s and presents with an insidious and progressive change in behavior and cognition. Usually the patients show marked unpredictable and unexplainable behavioral abnormalities in association with relatively mild cognitive problems early in the illness. Although the patient subsequently develops a clear dementia syndrome, the disease is characterized by a lobar or focal atrophy that often affects the *frontal and temporal lobes* and is clearly detectable with CT or MRI scans.

Jakob-Creutzfeldt disease is a subacute dementia syndrome that affects the same age group as Alzheimer's and Pick's disease and presents with a cortical syndrome that is both insidious and progressive, usually over a period of weeks to months rather than months to years. The patient becomes moderately to severely demented 6 months to a year after the initial symptom. Patients have a typical cortical dementia syndrome with amnesia, aphasia, apraxia, and agnosia, but in addition often have tremor, ataxia of gait, and a *typical burst pattern on the EEG*. It is the rapid course of the illness that suggests the diagnosis. This condition is associated with a spongiform degeneration of the brain that is transmissible to animals and has been found to be caused by a slow virus of the scrapie type. The disease is remarkable in that it has a long latent period between exposure to the virus and subsequent expression of its effects. Although it is caused by an infectious agent, the typical inflammatory changes in the brain, which are usually associated with infection, are absent. This has led to the speculation that perhaps other psychiatric disorders, including Alzheimer's disease and even schizophrenia, could be caused by a similar virus. However, there has been no evidence of transmissibility in any of the other disorders, with the exception of the so-called Gerstmann's syndrome.

Pick's disease and Jakob-Creutzfeldt disease are rare disorders. There are other cerebral degenerations, even more rare, that are occasionally seen presenting as a dementia syndrome. These include Kufs' disease or a late-onset form of Tay-Sachs disorder, cortical striatal degenerations, and a variety of dementia syndromes associated with atypical neuropathological findings, and occasionally a case of dementia syndrome of the cortical type with an apparently normal brain. Although all of these disorders are extremely rare, they are exceptions that might reveal important mechanisms of the disease.

Subcortical Dementia

The subcortical dementias are distinguished from the cortical dementias by symptoms and pathology. An important clinical distinction is that patients with disease entities causing a subcortical dementia often have a gait disorder in the presence of a moderate dementia, whereas with Alzheimer's disease and other cortical dementia, a gait disorder occurs only late in the illness.

The discussion of subcortical disorders will begin with multi-infarct dementia. Although this is clearly a disorder that could have either cortical or subcortical signs depending on the location of the lesions, small lacunar infarctions associated with hypertension are most often found in the basal ganglia and in the subcortical white matter.

Multi-infarct dementia is a term used for a dementia syndrome associated with prominent infarctions of the brain, which can be due to a variety of causes, but is usually associated with either hypertension or atrial fibrillation with multiple cerebral emboli. The clinical diagnosis is based on the sudden and episodic appearance of worsening of the patient's mental state, usually associated with asymmetrical motor signs and CT or MRI signs of cerebral infarction. The natural history of the disease is not well described. Claims have been made that its course may be altered by vigorous treatment of hypertension (Hachinski, Lassen, Marshall, 1974).

Occult hydrocephalus or "normal pressure" hydrocephalus is a more typical subcortical disorder characterized by a triad of *dementia, ataxia,* and *urinary incontinence* and associated with a large dilatation of the cerebral ventricles with relatively mild cerebral atrophy. The disorder is caused by the defective drainage of cerebral spinal fluid, which is usually due to a blockage of reabsorption sites secondary to head trauma, previous hemorrhage, or infection. Some of these cases have been reported to respond to surgical drainage of cerebral spinal fluid; thus, diagnosis is important (McHugh, 1964).

Huntington's disease is characterized by hereditary chorea beginning in the 30s and 40s and associated with a prominent subcortical dementia syndrome. The caudate nucleus and eventually other striatal centers atrophy. Cortical atrophy is sometimes seen. The cause of the disease is an abnormal gene on the long arm of chromosome 4 whose product is unknown. However, a marked loss of n-methyl-d-aspartate receptors in the striatum is noted. The abnormality in this receptor could lead to excessive cellular excitation by incoming glutaminergic fibers and then to cell death through calcium influx, kinase activation, and eventually free radical oxygen accumulation (Folstein, Leigh, Parhad, et al., 1986).

Another subcortical dementia disorder is *Parkinson's disease,* which is characterized by the triad of akinesia, rigidity, and tremor, associated with degeneration of the dopamine-containing neurons of the substantia nigra. In recent years, Parkinson's disease has been divided into two types—that associated with the neuritic plaques and tangles of Alzheimer's disease, and that with a pure nigral degeneration. At this point, the clinical distinction between these types is uncertain.

Parkinson's disease is associated with a clear dementia syndrome. A high proportion of patients with Parkinson's disease also develop depressive disorders, and treatment of the parkinsonian patient often includes L-dopa and an antidepressant or electroconvulsive therapy, which is effective in the motoric, cognitive, and mood features of the disorder. Delusions and hallucinations are also commonly seen in Parkinson's disease and may at times be caused by L-dopa itself.

HIV (AIDS)–RELATED DEMENTIA

AIDS-related organic mental disorders. The organic mental disorders associated with AIDS are not addressed in this chapter and are dealt with in depth by Moran in Chapter 20. One should note, however, that AIDS involvement in the central nervous system has been well documented to occur as a *primary symptom of the illness with clinical signs and symptoms that may appear well before any systemic signs of immunosuppression.* In the later, more advanced stages of AIDS, behavioral observations of both delirium and dementia may be seen as a direct result of HIV infection or secondary fungal, parasitic, or viral disease (Grant, Atkinson, Hesselink, et al., 1987; Ostrow, Grant, Atkinson, 1988).

OTHER TYPES OF DEMENTIA

Multiple Sclerosis

Multiple sclerosis (MS) is characterized by multifocal lesions in the white matter of the central nervous system. Neuropsychiatric symptoms in patients with multiple sclerosis are, therefore, relatively common, particularly as the disease progresses. Because of the shifting and transient nature of both the neurological and neuropsychiatric symptoms associated with multiple sclerosis, many of these patients may be diagnosed as "hysterical" or as having conversion disorders early in the course of their illness. In the advanced stages of this illness, global dysfunction may occur in cognitive and behavioral functioning and a dementia syndrome. In addition, depression is relatively common in MS. Organic mood disorders such as depression and mania may be caused by treatment with exogenous steroids and adrenocorticotropic hormone (ACTH) treatment.

Amyotrophic Lateral Sclerosis

Amyotrophic lateral sclerosis (ALS), or Lou Gehrig's disease, is a progressive asymmetrical muscular degenerative disorder that progresses over a period of years. Although ALS is typically thought of as primarily associated with striated muscles (with the exception of the cardiac and ocular striated muscles), this disorder also may be associated with symptoms of dementia, although the pathophysiology is not understood. Lesions of the corticospinal tracks above the medulla may cause pseudobulbar palsy with loss of emotional control and spastic dysarthria and dysphagia.

Vitamin B_{12} Deficiency

Failure of the gastric mucosa to secrete intrinsic factor results in abnormal absorption of vitamin B_{12} from the ileum. B_{12} deficiency can result in peripheral neuropathy and a variety of neuropsychiatric disturbances. The megaloblastic anemia (pernicious anemia) is the most obvious hematologic manifestation of the illness. Nevertheless, *neurological changes, including CNS degeneration, may appear before megaloblastic changes.* Behavioral changes associated with vitamin B_{12} deficiency include depression, emotional lability, irritability, and the spectrum of signs and symptoms associated with dementia. Recent research has shown that typical screening tests for vitamin B_{12} serum levels may not be sufficient and that some patients will have essentially normal screening serum B_{12} levels but abnormal total serum homocysteine and methylmalonic acid (Lindenbaum, Healton, Savage, et al., 1988). Research in this area is preliminary, but clinicians should keep an index of suspicion for this disorder even when there is no megaloblastic anemia or the serum B_{12} level is normal.

Hypothyroidism (Myxedema)

Hypothyroidism may cause a form of dementia in addition to a classic organic depressive disorder. The onset may be insidious and be overlooked for months or years. The psychiatric picture is usually characterized by lethargy, mental sluggishness, and slowing of cognition. These symptoms occur in concert with the typical physical signs of the illness, which include dry skin, decreased ear canal cerumen, nonpitting edema over the face and limbs, hair loss, menstrual changes, and a "froglike" voice due to laryngeal edema. A variety of metabolic findings may be seen, including hyponatremia and hypokalemia. With progression of disease there is increased cognitive dysfunction. Gross psychosis (myxedema madness) in addition to the cognitive and depressive features may be seen. In screening patients for possible hypothyroidism, it is essential to obtain a serum thyroid-stimulating hormone level (TSH) to detect subclinical levels of the illness.

Wilson's Disease

A degenerative form of dementia is caused by Wilson's disease, which is an inherited defect in copper metabolism that affects the putamen of the lenticular nucleus and the liver (hepatolenticular degeneration). Neuropsychiatric symptoms often precede overt manifestations of the dementia syndrome. This is a disorder that usually presents in the second decade of life and is associated with cirrhosis, golden brown pigmentation on the posterior corneal surface (Kayser-Fleischer rings), tremor, and rigidity. The diagnosis can be made by presence of decreased serum ceruloplasmin in association with aminoaciduria.

DIAGNOSTIC EVALUATION OF DEMENTIA

The screening diagnostic evaluation for dementia is relatively straightforward and parallels the evaluation for a delirium, although usually without the same dramatic urgency that accompanies a patient with delirium. The basic diagnostic work-up is listed in Table 3-9, but a few special points might be considered:

1. If AIDS-related dementia is suspected, special consent and counseling will be required for HIV antibody testing.

2. As noted above, recent research has indicated that the serum B_{12} level may not be sufficient for the diagnosis by B_{12} deficiency, and serum levels of methylmalonic acid and whole blood homocysteine may be required (Lindenbaum, Healton, Savage, et al., 1988).

3. The serum VDRL may be negative in older patients with tertiary syphilis, and a serum FTA is usually recommended for a definitive answer. If the serum FTA is positive, the same test should be performed on the CSF to assess for tertiary CNS syphilis.

4. CT and MRI scanning have differential powers in assessing for dementia and other CNS lesions. While Table 3-10 (AMA Council Report, 1988) offers an excellent guide to their relative sensitivities, consultation with a neuroradiologist may be a cost-saving measure that will save both money and patient duress (the isolation involved in MRI scanning may be stressful for older patients with cognitive impairment) (see also Chapter 1).

5. The EEG is not sensitive for detecting dementia (high rate of false-negatives); however, it is quite sensitive for detecting delirium.

Table 3–10 **CT Versus MRI as a Neurodiagnostic Probe**

DISEASE	MRI	CT	METRIZAMIDE-ENHANCED CT
Cerebrovascular disease			
TIA-RIND	+ +	±	—
Emboli	+ + +	+	—
Ischemic infarction	+ + + +	+ + +	—
Vasculitis	+ + +	±	—
Intracerebral hemorrhage	+ + +	+ + + +	—
Trauma			
Craniocerebral	+ +	+ + +	—
Spinal	+ + +!	+ + +	+ + +
Tumors			
Glioma			
Low-grade (1–2)			
Supratentorial	+ + +	+ +	—
Infratentorial	+ + + +	+ +	—
High-grade (3–4)			
Supretentorial	+ + + +	+ + + +	—
Infratentorial	+ + + +	+ +	—
Metastases			
Supretentorial	+ + +	+ +	—
Infratentorial	+ + +	+	—
Meningioma			
Supratentorial	+ +	+ + + +	—
Infratentorial	+ +	+ +	—
Pituitary	+ +	+ + + +	—
Sinuses and orbits	+ + + +	+ + +	—
Demyelinating disease	+ + + +	+ +	—

(continued)

Table 3–10 *(continued)*

DISEASE	MRI	CT	METRIZAMIDE-ENHANCED CT
Dementia			
SAE	+ + + +	+ +	—
Alzheimer's, Huntington's, and PSP	±	±	—
NPH	+	+	+ + +
Cervicomedullary junction and cervical spinal cord			
Syrinx (and congenital anomalies)	+ + + +	+	+ +
Tumors (intra-axial)			
Brain stem	+ + + +	+	+ +
Cerebellopontine angle	+ + +	+ +	+ + +
Cervical spine	+ + + +	±	+ +
Tumors (extra-axial)			
Brain stem	+ + + +	+	+ +
Cervical spine	+ + + +	±	+ + +
Cervical disk disease	+ + +	+ + +	+ + + +
Lumbar disk disease	+ + +	+ + +	+ + + +
Regional cerebral blood flow	***	+ + +#	—

±, of questionable value;
+, of some value, but other technologies are definitely superior;
+ +, of moderate value at present and frequently competitive with other technologies, but should not be considered as the initial diagnostic approach;
+ + +, of definite value;
+ + + +, of definite value and the preferred initial approach;
***, research phase—of great potential importance for the future as a first-line diagnostic tool;
MRI, magnetic resonance imaging;
CT, computed tomography;
TIA-RIND, transient ischemic attacks and reversible ischemic neurological deficits;
SAE, subcortical arteriosclerotic encephalopathy;
PSP, progressive supranuclear palsy;
NPH, normal-pressure hydrocephalus;
!, roentgenographic CT is superior in visualizing bone abnormalities, while MRI may be superior in demonstrating blood and spinal cord injury;
#, roentgenographic CT combined with inhalation of stable xenon or intravenous administration of contrast medium.
(Used with permission from American Medical Association Council on Scientific Affairs, Report of the panel on Magnetic Resonance Imaging: Magnetic resonance imaging of the central nervous system. JAMA 259:1211–1222, 1988)

PHYSICIAN'S ROLE IN THE MANAGEMENT OF DEMENTIA

Beyond the diagnostic evaluation, the role of the general medical physician in the care of dementia patients is as follows:

1. Provide long-term supportive medical care for the patient
2. Provide emotional support for the patient and family as a triage point for medical and community resources
3. Provide assistance with management of disruptive behavior

In respect to the latter items, major behavioral difficulties often arise in patients with dementia, particularly dementia of the Alzheimer's type. The most problematic are agitation, insomnia, emotional lability, personality changes, and psychotic symptoms—most commonly paranoia. There are, however, a surprisingly small number of systematic studies of the psychopharmacologic treatment of the behavioral disorders of dementia. Low doses of neuroleptic agents, such as haloperidol or loxapine, will help control agitation, emotional lability, and paranoia, but often symptoms are only suppressed rather than eliminated. Disturbed sleep is an extremely common component of dementia and is probably the problematic symptom that most exhausts caregivers. Again, low-dose neuroleptic agents near bedtime may help, but other sedative-hypnotics such as chloral hydrate may be needed. Low doses of shorter acting benzodiazepines, such as temazepam, which has a short half-life (13–16 hours) and whose metabolism is not affected by aging, can help on an "as needed" basis. More recently, some clinicians have reported the efficacy of trazodone (100–300 mg), a sedating antidepressant also effective for nocturnal agitation.

If possible, psychotropic drugs should be used on an "as needed" basis, rather than given automatically for long periods of time, until the necessity of their ongoing use becomes absolutely necessary. Caution should be used, especially with the high-potency neuroleptic agents (e.g., haloperidol), because elderly patients may be quite prone to extrapyramidal reactions (see Chapter 17). Psychotropic agents are often used excessively and inappropriately in nursing home patients because they are frequently used as "chemical restraints" by overextended staffs (Beers, Avorn, Soumerai, 1988). Physicians should carefully reassess the need for psychotropic agents in this population on a regular basis.

Perhaps one of the most valuable things a physician can do for a patient's family is to refer them to a community social worker or other geriatric specialist who has an interest in geriatrics to assist in resource planning. In addition, a referral to a support organization, such as the Alzheimer's Association, will assist the family in receiving help through support groups and education as to the patient's care and management. Referral to an attorney for legal planning, in addition to getting a durable power of attorney for the family to be made when the diagnosis becomes evident, will save the family enormous amounts of time, trouble, and money (Overman, Stoudemire, 1988).

Finally, physicians should be careful to follow the patient periodically for concurrent medical problems and to continue as a source of support and information for the family. Many families often feel abandoned by their physicians if no regular plans for follow-up appointments are made. Dementia is a *chronic* illness with a duration of years, during which the family will often be under enormous emotional stress. The primary physician's role in the ongoing support of the patient and family is crucial.

DELIRIUM

As noted in the introductory comments, delirium (previously known as acute organic brain syndrome) is characterized by an alteration in the level of consciousness that often fluctuates. Patients may have either a clouding or fogging of consciousness, or they may be hyperalert and agitated at times, such as in alcohol withdrawal delirium. Multiple signs and symptoms may accompany delirium and include gross psychotic symptoms such as paranoia, delusions, and hallucinations (tactile, auditory, visual, olfactory). Patients also may exhibit evidence of thought disorganization and incoherent language that may resemble a schizophrenic psychosis.

The sleep–wake cycle may be grossly disrupted, with agitation often exacerbated during the evening hours (the same observation may be seen in relatively stable dementias)—the "sundowning" syndrome. Cognitive signs usually receive the most attention, but they may be subtle and undetected in patients who are "quietly delirious" and are not exhibiting any overt behavioral disturbances or who are overmedicated with sedatives and tranquilizers. Cognitive dysfunction may be exhibited in defects in memory, attention, concentration, and orientation. Behaviorally, the patients may be agitated, combative, and hostile. Many times the uncooperative, irritable, and aggressive nature of the delirious patient—combined with his paranoia—is assumed to be a "functional psychosis," and the underlying organic component driving the patient's abnormal behavior overlooked.

As noted earlier, the primary feature of a delirium is a diminution in the level of consciousness that fluctuates in a sine wave fashion over time. Consistent with this sine wave pattern, patients may actually experience *periods of relative lucidity.* As noted above, "clouding" of consciousness and decreased alertness are the most common symptoms, but some patients can also show hyperalert activity. Sleep is usually fragmented and poor, with the patients being anxious, irritable, and restless. Disturbances in psychomotor functioning vary from hyperactivity to lethargy, stupor, obtundation, and catatonia. Neurological signs and symptoms may be seen, such as tremor, asterixis (particularly in deliria caused by metabolic and hepatic encephalopathies), or drug intoxications or withdrawal.

Deliria by definition are usually "acute" in onset, but some, particularly those due to subtle or insidious metabolic deficits, may develop and persist over days, weeks, or months with mild forms of fluctuating cognitive dysfunction. Most cases of delirium should improve or resolve within a week to 10 days if sufficient attention is given to correcting and stabilizing the underlying condition causing cerebral dysfunction.

Delirium is an extremely common disorder within the general hospital population—particularly the elderly. One study found that as many as 35% of patients over 65 years of age will have signs and symptoms of delirium on admission, or they will develop it sometime during the course of their hospitalization (Hodkinson, 1973). Other surveys have shown prevalence rates of delirium for the hospitalized elderly to range from 16 to 25% in general medical wards (Bergmann, Eastham, 1974; Seymour, Henschke, Cape, et al., 1980) and from 10% to 15% in surgical wards (Millar, 1981). In addition, the presence of delirium is often a grave prognostic sign for survival. One study reported that one third of over 4000 patients admitted with a primary diagnosis of delirium died within a month (Bedford, 1959). Other studies have found general mortality associated with delirium and its affiliated causes to be 25% (Hodkinson, 1973; Simon, Cahan, 1963).

Diagnosis

The diagnosis of delirium is made by a combination of clinical observations and formal changes in the patient's mental status. Of paramount importance is checking on the observations of the nursing staff either verbally or by reviewing the chart. This is especially helpful in assessing for fluctuations in the patient's mental status over a 24-hour period. Documenting the patient's baseline mental status before the hospitalization or onset of the cognitive dysfunction from information provided by the family is essential. The family will also be helpful in documenting the use of drugs or alcohol.

Factors Associated with Delirium and High-Risk Groups

Lipowski (1983) has documented the most common physical illnesses associated with delirium (in the elderly), and these include congestive heart failure, pneumonia, urinary tract infections, cancer, uremia, malnutrition, hypokalemia, dehydration, hyponatremia, and cerebrovascular accidents (Flint, Richards, 1956; Hodkinson, 1973; Kay, Roth, 1955; Roth, 1955; Seymour, Henschke, Cape, et al., 1980; Simon, Cahan, 1963). Systemic illnesses that result in brain dysfunction are more common causes of delirium than are primary CNS disorders. Intoxication with medical drugs and psychotropic agents is probably the most common cause of delirium in the elderly patient, particularly iatrogenic drugs that have sedative and anticholinergic side effects (Lipowski, 1983).

Alcoholics, particularly those with a history of recent heavy drinking where there is a possibility of a withdrawal syndrome, should be watched very closely. A history of other drugs that involve significant potential for withdrawal, such as barbiturates, sedative-hypnotics, and benzodiazepines, should also be monitored carefully and treated with the appropriate detoxification regimen (see Chapters 9 and 18).

Patients with a history of trauma, especially head trauma, are at extremely high risk medically for complications. Patients with sensory impairment (blindness, deafness, history of cataract surgery, or those facing extensive bandaging or casting) are prone to become delirious because of sensory deprivation and may need special care to promote orientation to the environment. Patients with preexisting cognitive dysfunction, mental retardation, or dementia have less of an ability to organize to the strangeness of the hospital and also are prone to delirium.

The differentiation between dementia and delirium is important, and Table 3-11 lists key differentiating factors (Lipowski, 1987). It is essential to note, however, that dementia and delirium may coexist and be superimposed on one another.

Etiology

Delirium can derive from failure or dysfunction in any organ system (pulmonary, cardiac, hepatic, renal, endocrine, gastrointestinal) because of either direct or secondary metabolic abnormalities of the central nervous system (electrolyte imbalances, hypoglycemia, adrenal insufficiency, hyperosmolarity or hypoosmolarity, uremia, hypoxemia, hypercarbia, hypercalcemia or hypocalcemia, or severe hypertension). Decreases in cardiac output from congestive heart failure can lead to decreased perfusion of the CNS and confusion. Peripheral as well as central nervous infections can cause fever and sepsis, leading to altered mental status. Infiltration of the meninges from certain forms of leukemia can also cause delirium.

Direct insults to the CNS from bacterial meningitis, viral encephalitis, cere-

Table 3–11 **Differential Diagnosis of Delirium and Dementia**

FEATURE	DELIRIUM	DEMENTIA
Onset	Acute, often at night	Insidious
Course	Fluctuating, with lucid intervals, during day; worse at night	Stable over course of day
Duration	Hours to weeks	Months or years
Awareness	Reduced	Clear
Alertness	Abnormally low or high	Usually normal
Attention	Lacks direction and selectivity, distractibility, fluctuates over course of day	Relatively unaffected
Orientation	Usually impaired for time, tendency to mistake unfamiliar for familiar place and persons	Often impaired
Memory	Immediate and recent impaired	Recent and remote impaired
Thinking	Disorganized	Impoverished
Perception	Illusions and hallucinations usually visual and common	Often absent
Speech	Incoherent, hesitant, slow or rapid	Difficulty in finding words
Sleep–wake cycle	Always disrupted	Fragmented sleep
Physical illness or drug toxicity	Either or both present	Often absent, especially in Alzheimer's disease

(Used with permission from Lipowski ZJ: Delirium (acute confusional states). JAMA 258:1789–1792, 1987)

brovascular hemorrhage, subdural hematoma, strokes, and vasculitis from connective tissue diseases, such as systemic lupus erythematosus, may cause delirium with or without psychotic symptoms. Gliomas and meningiomas may cause delirium or resemble dementia, and their onset may be insidious if the tumor is growing slowly and may not be associated with focal neurological findings in their early stages.

Patients who suffer from intermittent delirium (often with psychotic features) in addition to having a history of chronic abdominal pain and a peripheral neuropathy should be suspected of having acute intermittent porphyria. The family history, if it can be reconstructed, is usually positive. Although the diagnosis is confirmed by special urine tests (porphobilinogen levels), the diagnosis has occasionally been made by exposing the patient's urine to sunlight, in which it turns beet red.

Medication side effects, particularly in the elderly and even in "therapeutic" doses, may cause delirium, especially when there are coexisting medical problems that may alter the pharmacokinetics of the drug. Common offenders include narcotic analgesics, barbiturates, benzodiazepines, and other sedative-hypnotics. Antidepressant drugs, particularly cyclic antidepressants with strong anticholinergic and sedating side effects, such as amitriptyline, are notorious for causing delirium in the elderly (anticholinergic delirium).

A variety of nonpsychiatric medications cause symptoms of delirium. These include antihistamines (some of which also have relatively potent anticholinergic effects), atropine-like drugs, cimetidine, ranitidine, phenytoin, phenobarbital, digitalis (even at "therapeutic levels"), procainamide, lidocaine, L-dopa, and antihypertensive agents if they are sedating (such as clonidine). Steroids, particularly when administered rapidly in high doses, can cause a delirium usually known as "steroid psychosis." Table 3-12 presents a partial listing of drugs reported to potentially cause delirium.

INTENSIVE CARE UNIT SYNDROMES

Special note should be made of the so-called "intensive care unit syndrome," "intensive care unit psychosis," and "postcardiotomy syndrome." Although the abnormalities that have been described in intensive care unit patients often have been called "postoperative psychosis," the majority of these patients suffer from what is best characterized as a delirium with psychotic components. Delirious states in the ICU are usually multifactorially determined and may arise from the inherent stresses of the ICU itself, particularly its sleep-depriving effects (Houpt, Stoudemire, 1984). The environmental stresses of the ICU may include being placed in a strange, technologically oriented environment; incapacitation; noisy monitors; restriction in movement by intravenous lines and catheters; and the lack of privacy. Most patients in the intensive care unit are gravely ill and compromised medically and receive multiple medications. In addition, sleep deprivation and loss of the normal diurnal light–dark rhythm in units without windows may be biologically disrupting.

Delirium after cardiothoracic surgery also has been described and has been termed "postcardiotomy delirium." This condition classically occurs 3 or 4 days after surgery. The patient may be lucid but then suffers from progressive deterioration, confusion, and other features of delirium, such as psychosis. Factors that may contribute to the development of postcardiotomy delirium include increasing age, total time spent on cardiopulmonary bypass, intraoperative hypotension, severity of illness, sleep deprivation, and sensory monotony. Postcardiotomy delirium may be related to decreased postoperative cardiac index, leading to a greater likelihood of impaired cerebral perfusion and oxygenation (Heller, Kornfeld, Frank, et al., 1979).

Diagnosis

The cardinal rule in evaluating patients with delirium is to detect and correct the underlying disorder contributing to the patient's cerebral dysfunction. Appropriate treatment must be anteceded by an extensive and thorough search for the cause of the patient's cognitive dysfunction. Although the differential diagnosis of potential causes of delirium is extensive, the actual diagnostic work-up is straightforward.

First, a review of all factors leading up to the patient's hospitalization is essential. If the patient is postsurgical, a review of the operative record also is important. In terms of premorbid factors, the presence of alcoholism, medication use, or coexisting dementia is also important. Because medications are almost always high on the list in the hospitalized elderly, the cumulative dose of medications received over the past week should be checked in the patient's chart, along with serum levels for drugs when possible (anticonvulsants, digoxin, theophylline, and so forth). Any psychotropics that the patient has been taking should be scrutinized, particularly the relationship between the onset of cognitive dysfunction and any new drugs or changes in doses. Anticholinergic agents are particularly worrisome in the elderly.

Table 3–12 **Drugs Causing Delirium (Partial Listing)**

Antibiotics

Acyclovir (antiviral)
Amphotericin B (antifungal)
Cephalexin
Chloroquine (antimalarial)

Anticholinergic

Antihistamines
  Chlorpheniramine
  Diphenhydramine
Anticholinergics
  Benztropine
  Biperiden
Antispasmodics
Atropine/homatropine
Belladonna alkaloids
Phenothiazines (especially thioridazine)
Promethazine
Scopolamine
Tricyclic antidepressants
  (especially amitriptyline)
Trihexyphenidyl

Anticonvulsants

Phenobarbital
Phenytoin
Sodium valproate

Antiinflammatory

Adrenocorticotropic hormone
Corticosteroids
Ibuprofen
Indomethacin
Naproxen
Phenylbutazone

Antineoplastic

5-fluorouracil

Antiparkinson

Amantadine
Carbidopa
Levodopa

Antituberculous

Isoniazid
Rifampicin

Analgesics

Opiates
Salicylates
Synthetic narcotics

Cardiac

Beta-blockers
  Propranolol
Clonidine
Digitalis
Disopyramide
Lidocaine
Mexiletine
Methyldopa
Quinidine
Procainamide

Drug withdrawal

Alcohol
Barbiturates
Benzodiazepines

Sedative-Hypnotics

Barbiturates
Benzodiazepines
Glutethimide

Sympathomimetics

Amphetamines
Phenylephrine
Phenylpropanolamine

Miscellaneous

Aminophylline
Bromides
Chlorpropamide
Cimetidine
Disulfiram
Lithium
Metrizamide
Metronidazole
Ranitidine
Podphylline by absorption
Propylthiouracil
Quinacrine
Theophylline
Timolol ophthalmic

Over-the-Counter (most have anticholinergic effects)

Compoz
Sleep-Eze
Sominex

(Adapted and used with permission from Wise MG: Delirium. In Hales RE, Yudofsky SC (eds): Textbook of Neuropsychiatry. Washington, DC, American Psychiatric Press, 1987)

Once the patient has been examined medically and neurologically, the history has been reviewed, and the events leading up to the hospitalization or surgery have been documented, the patient should undergo an evaluation of vital signs. The assessment is based on an organ system–by–organ system search, looking for evidence of metabolic dysfunction, such as cardiovascular (arterial blood gasses, chest x-ray), pulmonary, renal (electrolyte imbalances, uremia), endocrine (thyroid panel, hypoglycemia, calcium), liver (hepatic encephalopathy), and gastrointestinal (impaction, obstruction, ileus, hemorrhage, volvulus) disease. A search for infection (sepsis, occult abscess, meningitis, urinary tract infection, pneumonia) is crucial. *The fundamental clinical principle remains that of detecting and correcting to whatever extent possible the underlying abnormality causing the patient's altered mental status.*

Special note should be made regarding the use of the EEG in the evaluation of delirium. Although the EEG may be normal in dementia, it is almost always abnormal in delirium, making it a very sensitive test in this clinical situation. The EEG abnormalities, however, are not always characterized by slowing, and the patterns can be low amplitude–fast activity, as may be found in alcohol withdrawal and sedative-hypnotic withdrawal. EEG abnormalities, which almost always accompany delirium, may persist after the clinical manifestations of the brain syndrome remit.

Treatment

The treatment of patients with delirium primarily involves treating the underlying cause of the cerebral dysfunction as noted above. Until that can be identified and corrected, however, some environmental and psychopharmacologic strategies can facilitate keeping the patient safe and stabilizing his or her behavior. Environmental strategies include having a window from which the patient can observe normal light–dark cycles to help correct his diurnal rhythm (windows should be secured to prevent jumping, or sitters should be provided). A familiar family member or 24-hour sitters should be allowed at the bedside if at all possible to facilitate orientation. Large calendars on which days can be marked off, clocks, familiar photographs, and having a radio or television playing during waking hours can also help the patient stay connected to the outside world and provide sensory stimulation. Providing night-lights and other types of additional sensory input for heavily bandaged or casted patients can be helpful. Elderly patients with cataracts are at risk for delirium, leading to the practice of performing such procedures "one eye at a time" to prevent "black patch delirium." Patients on ventilators or who are unable to speak because of tube placement or mechanical problems should nevertheless be communicated with by handwriting, hand signals, or lap-computer keyboards.

Pharmacologic Strategies

The psychopharmacologic management of agitated and psychotic behavior will be described in other sections of this text, particularly Chapters 17 and 18. In general, however, the "higher potency" antipsychotic agents such as haloperidol are the drugs of choice in this setting because they have minimal effects on blood pressure. These drugs tend to be slightly less sedating and also have very few anticholinergic side effects. "Lower potency" antipsychotic agents such as chlorpromazine and thioridazine tend to cause hypotension.

The prototypical drug used for stabilization of delirium is haloperidol, which can be given in tablet or liquid form orally or through the intramuscular and intravenous routes (see Chapter 18). A typical starting dose of haloperidol would be 2 mg p.o. or i.m. q.1h. or until the patient is sedated. Some clinicians advocate the use of parenteral benzodiazepines such as lorazepam for this purpose as well. For example, lorazepam may be used by giving the patient 1–2 mg orally, sublingually, or intramuscularly every hour until the patient is calm and slightly drowsy. Lorazepam, however, can cause anterograde amnesia when given in this manner, and benzodiazepines may exacerbate disinhibited behavior.

If a patient is suffering from a severe anticholinergic delirium, physostigmine salicylate 1–2 mg can be given slowly intravenously or intramuscularly and repeated after 15 minutes. Contraindications to using this potent cholinergic agonist include a history of heart disease, asthma, diabetes, peptic ulcer disease, or the possibility of bladder or bowel obstruction (Lipowski, 1987).

After the patient is stabilized, haloperidol may then be given in supplemental doses every 3 to 4 hours as needed. The need for continuous medication should then be reevaluated every 24 hours and the doses decreased and discontinued as rapidly as possible commensurate with stabilization of the patient medically and the patient's overall mental status. In most instances, resolution of the delirium should be accompanied by discontinuation of the antipsychotic agent as soon as possible.

Patients also should be carefully monitored for the presence of extrapyramidal side effects, neuroleptic-induced catatonia, and neuroleptic-induced malignant syndrome. Diagnosis and management of these particular side effects of the neuroleptics are discussed in Chapters 17 and 18.

CLINICAL PEARLS

- Several of the most frequently underdiagnosed disorders in medicine are delirium and early dementia.
- The most common causes of delirium in hospitalized patients are medication side effects.
- Delirious patients are not always either obtunded or agitated; some may by hyperaroused and excitable or quietly delirious.
- The EEG is very sensitive for delirium but relatively nonsensitive in dementia.
- A mild dementia may be one of the earliest signs of HIV infection occurring before signs of systemic immunosuppression.
- Intravenous haloperidol may be given for rapid control of severely agitated delirious patients, but the necessity of its use should be carefully documented.
- Neurological signs and symptoms of B_{12} deficiency have been reported before hematologic changes and in the presence of a normal serum B_{12} level.
- Depression and dementia may coexist, and the mood disturbance may exacerbate the cognitive and psychosocial dysfunction of the demented patient. Major depression rarely mimics the pervasive and progressive picture of dementia unless the patient already has some degree of underlying dementing illness.
- SPECT scanning may reveal vascular disease and other cerebrovascular blood flow abnormalities not revealed by CT or MRI scanning.

ANNOTATED BIBLIOGRAPHY

Hales RD, Yudofsky S (eds): Textbook of Neuropsychiatry. Washington, DC, American Psychiatric Press, 1987

> This is an eminently readable textbook that provides practical reviews of the major disorders in clinical neuropsychiatry.

Lishman WA: Organic Psychiatry, 2nd ed. Oxford, Blackwell Scientific Publications, 1987

> This is a classic textbook that reviews in detail neuropsychiatric disorders.

Davies P: Neurochemical studies: An update on Alzheimer's disease. J Clin Psychiatry 49:23–28, 1988

> A superb review of the state of the art in Alzheimer's disease research as of early 1988 by one of the premier researchers in the area.

Lipowski ZJ: Delirium (acute confusional states). JAMA 258:1789–1792, 1987

> An excellent and practical review of the clinical assessment of delirium.

Perry SW, Markowitz J: Organic mental disorders. In Talbott J, Hales RE, Yudofsky S (eds): Textbook of Psychiatry. Washington, DC, American Psychiatric Press, 1988

> This chapter provides a concise and detailed overview of the organic mental disorders.

REFERENCES

Alzheimer A: About a peculiar disease of the cerebral cortex. Jarvik L, Greenson H (trans): Alzheimer Disease and Associated Disorders 1:7–8, 1987

Alzheimer A: Uber eine eigenartige Erkrankung der Hirnrinde. Allg Z Psychiatric Psychisch-Gerichtlich Med 64:146–148, 1907

American Medical Association Council on Scientific Affairs, Report of the Panel on Magnetic Resonance Imaging: Magnetic resonance imaging of the central nervous system. JAMA 259:1211–1222, 1988

American Psychiatric Association: Diagnostic and Statistical Manual of Mental Disorders, 3rd ed, rev. Washington, DC, American Psychiatric Association, 1987

Anthony JC, LeResche LA, Von Korff MR, et al: Screening for delirium on a general medical ward: The tachistoscope and a global accessibility rating. Gen Hosp Psychiatry 7:36–42, 1985

Bedford PD: General medical aspects of confusional states in elderly people. Br Med J 2:185–188, 1959

Beers M, Avorn J, Soumerai SB, et al: Psychoactive medication use in intermediate-care facility residents. JAMA 260:3016–3020, 1988

Bergmann K, Eastham EJ: Psychogeriatric ascertainment and assessment for treatment in an acute medical ward setting. Age Ageing 3:174–188, 1974

Brandt J, Butters N: The neuropsychology of Huntington's disease. Trends Neurosci 93:118–120, 1986

Brandt J, Folstein S, Folstein M: Differential cognitive impairment in Alzheimer's disease and Huntington's disease. Ann Neurol 9:21, 1987

Breitner JCS, Folstein MF: Familial Alzheimer's dementia: A prevalent disorder with specific clinical features. Psychol Med 14:63–80, 1984

Cummings JL, Miller B, Hill MA, et al: Neuropsychiatric aspects of multiinfarct dementia & dementia of the Alzheimer type. Arch Neurol 44:389–393, 1987

Davies P: Neurochemical studies: An update on Alzheimer's disease. J Clin Psychiatry 49:23–28, 1988

Engel GL, Romano J: Delirium, a syndrome of cerebral insufficiency. J Chronic Dis 9:260, 1959

Flint FJ, Richards SM: Organic basis of confusional states in the elderly. Br Med J 2:1537–1539, 1956

Folstein MF, Anthony JC, Parhad I, et al: The meaning of cognitive impairment in the elderly. J Am Geriatr Soc 33:228–235, 1985

Folstein MF, Folstein SE, McHugh PR: Mini-Mental State. A practical method for grading the cognitive state of patients for the clinician. J Psychiatr Res 12:189–198 1975

Folstein S, Leigh RJ, Parhad I, et al: Diagnosis of Huntington's disease. Neurology 36:1279–1283, 1986

Folstein MF, McHugh PR: Dementia syndrome of depression. In Katzman R, Terry RD, Bick KL (eds): Alzheimer's Disease: Senile Dementia and Related Disorders, Vol 7, pp 87–96. New York, Raven Press, 1978

Grant I, Atkinson JH, Hesselink JR, et al: Evidence for early central nervous system involvement in the acquired immunodeficiency syndrome (AIDS) and other human immunodeficiency virus (HIV) infections. Ann Intern Med 107:828–836, 1987

Hachinski VC, Lassen NA, Marshall J: Multi-infarct dementia: A cause of mental deterioration in the elderly. Lancet 2:207–210, 1974

Heller SS, Kornfeld DS, Frank KA, et al: Postcardiotomy delirium and cardiac output. Am J Psychiatry 136:337–339, 1979

Heston LL, Mastri AR, Anderson E, et al: Dementia of the Alzheimer type: Clinical genetics, natural history, and associated conditions. Arch Gen Psychiatry 38:1085–1090, 1981

Hodkinson HM: Mental impairment in the elderly. J R Coll Physicians Lond 7:305–317, 1973

Houpt JL, Stoudemire A: Diagnosis and treatment of delirium. In Kortz WJ, Lamb PD (eds): Surgical Intensive Care, pp 283–292. Chicago, Year Book Medical Publishers, 1984

Katzman R: Alzheimer's disease. Trends Neurosci 9:522–525, 1986

Kay DWK, Roth M: Physical accompaniments of mental disorder in old age. Lancet 2:740–745, 1955

Lindenbaum J, Healton EB, Savage DG, et al: Neuropsychiatric disorders caused by cobalamin deficiency in the absence of anemia or macrocytosis. N Engl J Med 318:1720–1728, 1988

Lipowski ZJ: Transient cognitive disorders (delirium, acute confusional states) in the elderly. Am J Psychiatry 140:1426–1436, 1983

Lipowski ZJ: Delirium (acute confusional states). JAMA 258:1789–1792, 1987

McHugh PR: Occult hydrocephalus. Q J Med 33:297–308, 1964

Millar HR: Psychiatric morbidity in elderly surgical patients. Br J Psychiatry 138:17–20, 1981

Mohs RC, Breitner JCS, Silverman JM, et al: Alzheimer's disease: Morbid risk among first-degree relatives approximates 50% by 90 years of age. Arch Gen Psychiatry 44:405–408, 1987

Ostrow D, Grant I, Atkinson H: Assessment and management of the AIDS patient with neuropsychiatric disturbances. J Clin Psychiatry 49:14–22, 1988

Overman W, Stoudemire A: Guidelines for legal and financial counseling of Alzheimer's disease patients and their families. Am J Psychiatry 145:1495–1500, 1988

Riege WH, Metter EJ: Cognitive and brain imaging measures of Alzheimer's disease. Neurobiol Aging 9:69–86, 1988

Rocca WA, Amaducci LA, Schoenberg BS: Epidemiology of clinically diagnosed AD. Ann Neurol 19:415–424, 1986

Rosser M, Iverson LL: Non-cholinergic neurotransmitter abnormalities in Alzheimer's disease. Br Med Bull 42:70–74, 1986

Roth M: The natural history of medical disorder in old age. J Ment Sci 101:281–301, 1955

Rovner BW, Kafonek S, Filipp L, et al: The prevalence of mental illness in a community nursing home. Am J Psychiatry 143:1446–1449, 1986

Seymour DG, Henschke PJ, Cape RDT, et al: Acute confusional states and dementia in the elderly: The role of dehydration/volume depletion, physical illness and age. Age Ageing 9:137–146, 1980

Simon A, Cahan RB: The acute brain syndrome in geriatric patients. Psychiatr Res Rep 16:8–21, 1963

Small GW, Greenberg DA: Biologic markers, genetics, and Alzheimer's disease. Arch Gen Psychiatry 45:945–947, 1988

St George-Hyslop PH, Tanzi RE, Polinsky RJ, et al: The genetic defect causing familial Alzheimer's disease maps on chromosome 21. Science 235:885–890, 1987

Stoudemire A: Selected organic mental disorders. In Hales R, Yudofsky S: Textbook of Neuropsychiatry. Washington, DC, American Psychiatric Press, 1987

Stoudemire A, Hill C, Kaplan W, et al: Clinical issues in the assessment of dementia and depression in the elderly. Psychiatr Med 6:40–52, 1988

Stoudemire A, Thompson TL: Recognizing and treating dementia. Geriatrics 36:112–120, 1981

Zubenko GS, Huff FJ, Beyer J, et al: Familial risk of dementia associated with a biologic subtype of Alzheimer's disease. Arch Gen Psychiatry 45:889–893, 1988

Appendix to Chapter 3: Mini-Mental State Examination and Instructions

Patient _____

Examiner _____

Date _____

MINI-MENTAL STATE EXAMINATION

Maximum Score	Score	
		ORIENTATION
5	( )	What is the (year) (season) (date) (day) (month)?
5	( )	Where are we: (state) (county) (town) (hospital) (floor)
		REGISTRATION
3	( )	Name 3 objects: 1 second to say each. Then ask the patient all 3 after you have said them. Give 1 point for each correct answer. Then repeat them until he learns all 3. Count trials and record.
		Trials _____
		ATTENTION AND CALCULATION
5	( )	Serial 7's. 1 point for each correct. Stop after 5 answers. Alternatively spell "world" backwards.
		RECALL
3	( )	Ask for the 3 objects repeated above. Give 1 point for each correct.
		LANGUAGE
9	( )	Name a pencil, and watch (2 points)
		Repeat the following "No ifs, ands or buts." (1 point)

Follow a 3-stage command:
  "Take a paper in your right hand, fold it in half, and put it on the floor" (3 points)
Read and obey the following:
  Close your eyes (1 point)
  Write a sentence (1 point)
  Copy design (1 point)

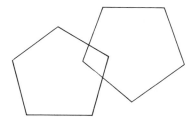

TOTAL SCORE

Perfect score = 30
Any score below 25 indicates the presence of significant cognitive dysfunction.

ASSESS level of consciousness along a continuum:

  Alert   Drowsy   Stupor   Coma

INSTRUCTIONS FOR ADMINISTRATION OF MINI-MENTAL STATE EXAMINATION

ORIENTATION

(1) Ask for the date. Then ask specifically for parts omitted, e.g., "Can you also tell me what season it is?" One point for each correct.

(2) Ask in turn "Can you tell me the name of this hospital?" (town, county, etc.). One point for each correct.

REGISTRATION

Ask the patient if you may test his memory. Then say the names of 3 unrelated objects, clearly and slowly, about one second for each. After you have said all 3, ask him to repeat them. This first repetition determines his score (0–3) but keep saying them until he can repeat all 3, up to 6 trials. If he does not eventually learn all 3, recall cannot be meaningfully tested.

ATTENTION AND CALCULATION

Ask the patient to begin with 100 and count backwards by 7. Stop after 5 subtractions (93, 86, 79, 72, 65). Score the total number of correct answers.

If the patient cannot or will not perform this task, ask him to spell the word "world" backwards. The score is the number of letters in correct order. E.g., dlrow = 5, dlorw = 3.

RECALL

Ask the patient if he can recall the 3 words you previously asked him to remember. Score 0–3.

LANGUAGE

Naming: Show the patient a wrist watch and ask him what it is. Repeat for pencil. Score 0–2.

Repetition: Ask the patient to repeat the sentence after you. Allow only one trial. Score 0 or 1.

3-Stage command: Give the patient a piece of plain blank paper and repeat the command. Score 1 point for each part correctly executed.

Reading: On a blank piece of paper print the sentence "Close your eyes", in letters large enough for the patient to see clearly. Ask him to read it and do what it says. Score 1 point only if he actually closes his eyes.

Writing: Give the patient a blank piece of paper and ask him to write a sentence for you. Do not dictate a sentence, it is to be written spontaneously. It must contain a subject and verb and be sensible. Correct grammar and punctuation are not necessary.

Copying: On a clean piece of paper, draw intersecting pentagons, each side about 1' in., and ask him to copy it exactly as is. All 10 angles must be present and 2 must intersect to score 1 point. Tremor and rotation are ignored.

Estimate the patient's level of sensorium along a continuum, from alert on the left to coma on the right.

Used with permission from Folstein MF, Folstein SE, McHugh PR: Mini-Mental State: A practical method for grading the cognitive state of patients for the clinician. J Psychiat Res 12:189–198, 1975

4

Schizophrenia and Other Psychotic Disorders

Philip T. Ninan and Rosalind Mance*

Traditionally, psychoses have been divided into "organic" (caused by organic mental disorders) and "functional." This differentiation is an oversimplification, because even "functional" psychotic disorders have, at a minimum, an underlying biochemical substrate in the brain. Nevertheless, this chapter will retain this distinction, at least for the time being, and will deal with specific "functional" psychotic disorders—schizophrenia, schizophreniform disorder, brief reactive psychosis, schizoaffective disorder, and delusional paranoidal disorder. Mood disorders with psychotic features will be dealt with in Chapter 6.

"Psychosis" is a generic descriptive term applied to behavior marked by a break from reality. This often presents as disorganization of mental processes, emotional aberrations, difficulty in interpersonal relationships, and a decrease in functional capacity. Mundane daily responsibilities can become burdensome or impossible to manage. Schizophrenia is the prototypical functional psychotic disorder and hence will be the primary focus of this chapter.

It should be emphasized before proceeding any further that psychotic symptoms may occur in multiple medical, neurological, and substance abuse disorders, and a vigorous search should be made for an organic cause of the patient's symptoms before a functional diagnosis is made (Table 4-1). In addition, psychotic symptoms may occur in a *variety* of psychiatric disorders and are *not* specific for schizophrenia (Table 4-2). For example, psychotic symptoms may be seen in mood disorders (psychotic depression and mania), in personality disorders (often during brief psychotic breaks), and in "encapsulated" form as part of a delusional (paranoid) disorder. Psychotic symptoms found in psychotic depression and mania are discussed in the appropriate chapters found elsewhere in this text. The differential diagnosis for psychosis in dementia, delirium, and other organic mental disorders may be found in Chapters 3, 18, and 19.

* Part of this chapter is adapted from Ninan PT: Schizophrenia and its pharmacological management. In Bellack AS (ed): A Clinical Guide for the Treatment of Schizophrenia, Plenum Press, New York, 1989

Table 4-1 **Brief Differential Diagnosis of Psychosis**

Organic mental disorders*

Dementia
Delirium (includes side effects of medications)
Substance-induced (e.g., amphetamine, phencyclidine, and so forth)
Organic delusional disorders
Other organic brain syndromes

Mood disorders

Bipolar disorder (mania)
Major depression with psychotic features

Psychotic disorders

Brief reactive psychosis
Schizophreniform disorder
Schizophrenia
Schizoaffective disorder
Delusional disorder

Personality disorders**

Schizotypal
Schizoid
Paranoid
Borderline

Mental retardation

Autistic disorder

*See Chapter 3
**Usually a brief reactive psychosis. See Chapter 5

Table 4-2 **DSM-III-R Psychotic Disorders**

Schizophrenia

Catatonic
Disorganized
Paranoid
Undifferentiated
Residual

Delusional paranoid disorder

Erotomanic
Jealous
Persecutory
Somatic

Brief reactive psychosis

Schizophreniform disorder

Schizoaffective disorder

Induced psychotic disorder

Psychotic disorder (atypical) not otherwise specified

SCHIZOPHRENIA

Schizophrenia is an illness that is present in all cultures. Writings indicating the presence of schizophrenia go back to the 12th century B.C. In more modern times, epidemiological studies suggest that there is a 1–2% chance that an individual will develop an episode of schizophrenia during his or her lifetime (Robins, Helzer, Weissman, et al., 1984). The cost to society is huge—over 100,000 psychiatric beds are occupied by patients suffering from schizophrenia in the U.S., and their treatment costs are estimated at $7 billion annually. What cannot be quantified is the emotional cost to the patient and loved ones.

Phenomenology and Diagnosis

Schizophrenia is a brain disorder that is characterized by abnormalities in thinking, emotions, and behavior. Because we have no laboratory test yet that can confirm the diagnosis of schizophrenia, we are dependent on a descriptive or phenomenological definition of the disorder. Unfortunately, there is no symptom that is pathognomonic of the illness or a symptom that is present in every patient with the illness. Thus, no one symptom is necessary or sufficient for the diagnosis. The criterion for diagnosis is a particular constellation of symptoms rather than a single symptom.

Such a diagnostic system defines not a homogenous group of patients with a single etiology, pathophysiology, treatment response, and outcome but a *heterogenous* group of disorders. This heterogeneity of schizophrenia has been a significant hurdle to the advancement of our understanding of schizophrenia, because failure to confirm a hypothesis in schizophrenia could be caused by the fact that findings relevant to one subgroup of schizophrenic patients are obscured by the heterogeneity of the population studied.

As our knowledge has advanced, various attempts have been made to describe the constellation of symptoms that would best make the diagnosis of schizophrenia. Different diagnostic criteria can either define the illness broadly, which results in a large number of patients meeting the criteria for the illness, or provide a narrow definition of the illness, which would result in just a small (presumably core) group of patients being diagnosed. If the illness lies along a spectrum of severity, then casting a wide net would include those patients with milder, nonpsychotic versions of the illness (schizophrenia spectrum disorders) but would also risk some nonschizophrenics being given the label (i.e., a false-positive diagnosis).

The most reliably recognized symptoms of the illness are its more dramatic ones, such as hallucinations, delusions, and bizarre behavior. These are called "positive" symptoms because they are symptoms that are added to the premorbid state. However, there is a long tradition in not considering these the central elements of schizophrenia. "Negative" symptoms, such as emotional blunting and avolition, which are symptoms marked by the absence of functions, are less dramatic in presentation. Some have postulated the negative symptoms to be the core elements of schizophrenia, but negative symptoms are agreed on less reliably. Thus, an illness defined purely by its more dramatic presentations could correctly label a group of patients as schizophrenic, but it also could potentially exclude a number of patients who suffer from the core expressions that result from the pathophysiology of the illness, but without its more dramatic manifestations.

Historical Development

Emil Kraepelin (1907) coined the term "dementia praecox," which he differentiated from manic-depressive (bipolar) illness. Dementia praecox, or the precocious development of intellectual impairment, was based on acute symptomatology marked by hallucinations, delusions, withdrawal, loss of interest, and poor attention associated with a dissociation of thought content and affect. Kraepelin believed that the illness usually began early in life and tended to result in an end state of dementia. The cause was postulated to be a disease process that affected cortical neurons. Inherent in Kraepelin's definition of dementia praecox was a cross-sectional description of psychotic symptoms that included both positive and negative symptoms, an early onset, and a deteriorating course.

Eugen Bleuler (1911) coined the term "schizophrenia" and described it as a group of illnesses. He shifted the focus from the course of illness to a purely cross-sectional approach in making the diagnosis of schizophrenia. He thus described schizophrenia as being marked by problems with association, affect, autistic thinking, and psychotic ambivalence (the four A's) and called these the fundamental symptoms of the illness. He did not include a deteriorating course as inherent in the illness. Bleuler believed that the delusions and hallucinations often associated with schizophrenia were really secondary and derived from the fundamental symptoms. Bleuler also postulated a basic organic cerebral or metabolic defect as the cause of schizophrenia. He believed that the illness of schizophrenia could present itself with the fundamental symptoms without the secondary manifestations of delusions and hallucinations and called it "simple schizophrenia." Bleuler also thought that the basic defect causing schizophrenia also could exist without expressing itself in either the fundamental symptoms or the secondary manifestations and called this "latent schizophrenia."

The inherent problem with the approach taken by Bleuler in diagnosing schizophrenia was the lack of a well-defined threshold of how prominent a symptom (e.g., autistic thinking) had to be before the diagnosis of schizophrenia could be made. Thus, nonpsychotic individuals with personality aberrations (for example, the current concept of schizotypal personality disorder) were diagnosed as having schizophrenia. The concepts of latent and simple schizophrenia blurred the distinction between patients who had schizophrenia and those who had nonpsychotic pathology.

Subsequent authors tried various methods to address the basic conflict of diagnosing an illness that required both cross-sectional symptomatology and longitudinal course of illness in its diagnostic criteria. Thus, Langfeldt (1956) developed the term *schizophreniform* to define a group of patients who had psychotic symptoms but did not have a deteriorating course. Kurt Schneider (1959) defined the list of symptoms that he thought were pathognomonic of schizophrenia. However, these have been shown subsequently to be present in functional psychotic illnesses other than schizophrenia so that the diagnostic value of these symptoms was diluted.

Current Nomenclature

The DSM-III-R has a relatively stringent approach to the diagnosis of schizophrenia that requires specific psychotic symptoms to be present for at least a week (Table 4-3). To prevent many false-positive diagnoses, the course of illness also is included in the diagnostic requirements. Thus, a deteriorating course is part of the diagnostic criteria. This combination of a cross-sectional and longitudinal approach

Table 4-3 **DSM-III-R Criteria for Schizophrenia**

A. Presence of characteristic psychotic symptoms in the active phase: either (1), (2), or (3) for at least one week (unless the symptoms are successfully treated):
  (1) two of the following:
    (a) delusions
    (b) prominent hallucinations (throughout the day for several days or several times a week for several weeks, each hallucinatory experience not being limited to a few brief moments)
    (c) incoherence or marked loosening of associations
    (d) catatonic behavior
    (e) flat or grossly inappropriate affect
  (2) bizarre delusions (i.e., involving a phenomenon that the person's culture would regard as totally implausible, e.g., thought broadcasting, being controlled by a dead person)
  (3) prominent hallucinations [as defined in (1)(b) above] of a voice with content having no apparent relation to depression or elation, or a voice keeping up a running commentary on the person's behavior or thoughts, or two or more voices conversing with each other
B. During the course of the disturbance, functioning in such areas as work, social relations, and self-care is markedly below the highest level achieved before onset of the disturbance (or, when the onset is in childhood or adolescence, failure to achieve expected level of social development).
C. Schizoaffective Disorder and Mood Disorder with Psychotic Features have been ruled out, i.e., if a Major Depressive or Manic Syndrome has ever been present during an active phase of the disturbance, the total duration of all episodes of a mood syndrome has been brief relative to the total duration of the active and residual phases of the disturbance.
D. Continuous signs of the disturbance for at least six months. The six-month period must include an active phase (of at least one week, or less if symptoms have been successfully treated) during which there were psychotic symptoms characteristic of Schizophrenia (symptoms in A), with or without a prodromal or residual phase, as defined below.
  Prodromal phase: A clear deterioration in functioning before the active phase of the disturbance that is not due to a disturbance in mood or to a Psychoactive Substance Use Disorder and that involves at least two of the symptoms listed below.
  Residual phase: Following the active phase of the disturbance, persistence of at least two of the symptoms noted below, these not being due to a disturbance in mood or to a Psychoactive Substance Use Disorder.
Prodromal or Residual Symptoms:
  (1) marked social isolation or withdrawal
  (2) marked impairment in role functioning as wage-earner, student, or homemaker
  (3) markedly peculiar behavior (e.g., collecting garbage, talking to self in public, hoarding food)
  (4) marked impairment in personal hygiene and grooming
  (5) blunted or inappropriate affect

(continued)

Table 4-3 **(continued)**

  (6) digressive, vague, overelaborate, or circumstantial speech, or poverty of speech, or poverty of content of speech
  (7) odd beliefs or magical thinking, influencing behavior and inconsistent with cultural norms, e.g., superstitiousness, belief in clairvoyance, telepathy, "sixth sense," "others can feel my feelings," overvalued ideas, ideas of reference
  (8) unusual perceptual experiences, e.g., recurrent illusions, sensing the presence of a force or person not actually present
  (9) marked lack of initiative, interests, or energy

  Examples: Six months of prodromal symptoms with one week of symptoms from A; no prodromal symptoms with six months of symptoms from A; no prodromal symptoms with one week of symptoms from A and six months of residual symptoms.

E. It cannot be established that an organic factor initiated and maintained the disturbance.

F. If there is a history of Autistic Disorder, the additional diagnosis of Schizophrenia is made only if prominent delusions or hallucinations are also present.

Classification of course

The course of the disturbance is coded in the fifth digit:

1—Subchronic. The time from the beginning of the disturbance, when the person first began to show signs of the disturbance (including prodromal, active, and residual phases) more or less continuously, is less than two years, but at least six months.

2—Chronic. Same as above, but more than two years.

3—Subchronic with Acute Exacerbation. Reemergence of prominent psychotic symptoms in a person with a subchronic course who has been in the residual phase of the disturbance.

4—Chronic with Acute Exacerbation. Reemergence of prominent psychotic symptoms in a person with a chronic course who has been in the residual phase of the disturbance.

5—In Remission. When a person with a history of Schizophrenia is free of all signs of the disturbance (whether or not on medication), "in Remission" should be coded. Differentiating Schizophrenia in Remission from No Mental Disorder requires consideration of overall level of functioning, length of time since the last episode of disturbance, total duration of the disturbance, and whether prophylactic treatment is being given.

0—Unspecified.

(Used with permission from DSM-III-R, 1987)

provides for improved reliability in the diagnosis. Patients who might have an illness that is related to schizophrenia in some ways but is atypical in others are given other diagnostic labels. For example, patients who have the symptoms of schizophrenia but recover without residual symptoms within a 6-month period of time are classified as having *schizophreniform disorder.* Patients with schizophreniform disorder also may be subclassified into those with or without good prognostic features. Good prognostic features include an acute onset, confusion, good premorbid functioning, and absence of flat affect. In patients who meet the criteria for schizophreniform disorder but have not recovered yet, the diagnosis is provisional.

If there is an affective (mood) disorder (either major depression or mania) present concurrently with schizophrenia, and the affective syndrome is present for a significant period of time relative to the schizophrenic symptoms, then the patient is given a diagnosis of either schizoaffective disorder or affective disorder with psychotic features. If the psychotic symptoms are present for 2 weeks in the absence of affective symptoms, then the patient is labeled *schizoaffective disorder.* If the psychotic symptoms are present only during an episode of affective illness, then the patient is not considered schizophrenic but has an *affective (mood) disorder (e.g., major depression) with psychotic features.* If the affective features are relatively brief and therefore do not meet the criteria for a major depressive or manic episode, then the affective features are considered to be subclinical, and the patient is diagnosed as having schizophrenia.

Schizophrenia has been subclassified into *catatonic* (dominated by motoric abnormalities such as rigidity and posturing), *disorganized* (marked by flat affect, incoherence, loose associations, and disorganized behavior), *paranoid* (paranoid symptoms in the absence of catatonic and disorganized features), and *undifferentiated* types. The prodromal phase of the illness refers to the period of time when the patient's functioning changes before the onset of frank psychotic symptoms. Because the prediction of the development of a schizophrenic break is so poor, the prodromal phase is most safely labeled in retrospect. Residual symptoms exist when the frank psychotic features, such as prominent delusions, hallucinations, incoherence, and bizarre behavior, are controlled but other symptoms (e.g., negative symptoms) remain.

The course of the illness is classified into *subchronic* (symptoms lasting up to 2 years) or *chronic* (more than 2 years), both of which can have an acute exacerbation associated with them. When the patient is free of the symptoms of the illness, then the diagnosis is changed to schizophrenia in remission.

DELUSIONAL DISORDER AND BRIEF REACTIVE PSYCHOSIS

Delusional disorder is a condition in which the patient has a nonbizarre delusion lasting for at least 1 month in the absence of prominent hallucinations or bizarre behavior. The delusion is usually confined to a single area or person (i.e., it is encapsulated). Other gross psychotic symptoms evident in schizophrenia are absent in delusional disorder. Patients with delusional disorder are subclassified into erotomania, grandiose, jealous, persecutory, and somatic types based on their symptomatic presentation.

Brief reactive psychosis is characterized by a relatively sudden onset of psychosis in the face of significantly stressful events. The patient should recover and return to premorbid levels of functioning within a period of a month to receive this diagnosis.

DIFFERENTIAL DIAGNOSIS

The functional psychotic disorders described above should be differentiated from organic mental disorders with psychotic symptoms. This can be done by gathering historical information that would provide clues as to the presence of organic factors in the illness. Principal among these would be a history of alcohol or substance abuse, especially of the stimulant (e.g., amphetamine) type. Amphetamine-induced psychosis is clinically indistinguishable in presentation from paranoid schizophrenia. A sudden, unexplained development of a psychotic illness in an otherwise well functioning individual without a family history of a psychiatric illness is a justifiable reason for exploring possible organicity. A complete physical examination, with particular emphasis on the neurological examination, also should be completed. In the mental status examination, clouding of consciousness or fluctuating levels of consciousness, memory difficulties, disorientation, and confusion should raise the possibility of an organic process underlying the psychotic presentation (see Chapter 3).

The diagnostic criteria for schizophrenia include the requirement that an organic factor cannot be established as the cause of schizophrenia. This implies that all psychotic states resembling schizophrenic psychosis have a medical, neurologic, or toxic cause ruled out before a "functional" diagnosis is made.

CASE STUDY

Clinical Case Vignette of Schizophrenia

Jim was 20 years old when his family and friends started to see a change in his behavior. During the previous months he had begun to withdraw from those around him, preferring to spend more and more time by himself. He lost interest in his scholastic work and his extracurricular activities. He seemed less interested in his personal appearance. He developed a sudden interest in philosophy and spent hours reading philosophical texts.

He had difficulty sleeping for a few nights, and his mother discovered him mumbling to himself. She noticed that he would talk to himself and pause as though he was listening, and then start talking again. When questioned about this, he would stop, turn, and walk away. He began getting suspicious, telling his mother that his friends had turned against him and were plotting to kill him. He subsequently began to read special meanings into the every day events in his life. Thus, a blue car parked on the road meant that somebody was trying to contact him.

When taken for an evaluation, he told the psychiatrist that a voice was suggesting to him that he jump in front of traffic. He was hospitalized. After a 2-day observation period and a full medical and neurological work-up, he was started on a neuroleptic agent. Within a couple of days his sleep pattern seemed to improve considerably, and he became more interested in his hygiene. Within a week he was able to follow the routine on the ward and take part in the structured activities. He seemed much less focused on the internal concerns that had preoccupied him before admission and was able to talk about current affairs without interjecting his pathological symptoms into the conversation. Although he did not think there was anything seriously wrong with him, he was willing to take medications and was discharged to outpatient treatment.

Within a few months of his hospitalization he was doing relatively well, and he attempted to return to college. He became more paranoid, however, and refused to take his medication. Over a period of a week he became more symptomatic and developed gross psychotic symptoms, resulting in a repeat hospitalization.

The next 5 years were marked by periodic hospitalizations, lasting a few weeks at a time, and outpatient treatment, which included medications and individual and family sessions. The family sessions were aimed at educating the family about the illness and helping them accept Jim's limitations. Interpersonal problems in the family were dealt with by improving communication skills. Stress management and problem-solving skills were also addressed.

Jim finally began to accept the fact that he had an illness and that he needed long-term treatment. He attended day treatment for a while and then was able to use vocational rehabilitation to begin to look for a job within his limitations. He moved out of his parents' home into a semi-structured group home. He was compliant with his medication and was able to tell his therapist when he felt an impending relapse.

Symptoms of Schizophrenia

Psychotic symptoms are marked by abnormalities in the form of thought (called formal thought disorder), content of thought, perceptual disturbances, and alterations in emotions and behavior (Andreasen, 1987).

Formal thought disorder is an abnormality in the form of thought. It is differentiated from lack of speech, which is called poverty of speech. The extreme form of poverty of speech can present itself as muteness.

Derailment or *loose associations* is a condition in which the sequential connection between ideas is difficult or impossible to follow because the patient wanders to relatively or totally unrelated subjects. This can be present in a single sentence or in a series of sentences.

Tangentiality is the tendency to wander to points that are distantly connected, but be unable to return spontaneously to the original point. Returning to the original line of thought through a circuitous route is called *circumstantiality.*

Incoherence is a condition in which even sentences are impossible to follow. It is different from derailment and loose associations, in which the connections between clauses or sentences are problematic. Lack of understanding because of incomprehensible verbalization of speech is excluded from this description.

Delusions are the result of an abnormality in the content of thought. They are false beliefs that are often fixed and cannot be explained based on the cultural background of the individual. If the intensity of the delusions is minor, patients may have some insight into their nonsensical nature and therefore may doubt them. Beliefs that can be possibly explained within the realms of reality (e.g., the patient has paranoid delusions that someone is trying to kill him) are differentiated from bizarre delusions that can have no basis in reality (e.g., the television is controlling the patient's behavior against his will). A systematized delusion (compared with an encapsulated one) is one that is complex with elaborate connections and multiple implications.

The concept of *mood congruence and incongruence* essentially assesses whether the delusions are within the context of and consistent with the overall affective state of the patient. Thus, delusions of grandeur are often associated with manic states, and nihilistic delusions can be seen in major depression with psychotic features. Mood-incongruent delusions are more likely to be associated with schizophrenic states.

The intensity of a delusion is based on how firmly the belief is held, lack of insight, whether the delusion preoccupies the individual to the exclusion of other concerns, and whether the individual bases his actions on the delusion. The different types of delusions are as follows:

Paranoid delusions are convincing feelings that one is being persecuted, in the absence of such a reality. Psychotic paranoid patients may believe that they are being followed, their personal belongings are being tampered with, their telephone is tapped, and they are being harassed. The persecution can come from individuals or organizations (such as the FBI or CIA). The delusion can be a simple isolated one or an intricate one that pervades all aspects of the individual's life such that all experiences are explained by the delusion.

Ideas and delusions of reference occur when the patient believes that some event, often of no consequence, is related to them specifically (i.e., a baby in a stroller signifies that the patient should cross the street). Often the delusions can have a paranoid flavor, whereby someone talking in the distance is misinterpreted as talking about and having designs on the patient; or a statement made on the radio or television has special reference to the patient. The questioning of these beliefs by the patient would make them ideas of reference, while their acceptance as reality would make them delusions.

Delusion of being controlled is the belief that one's actions are under the control of someone or some external force with malicious intent. The patient feels powerless in the face of such a force and will often relinquish responsibility for their actions or thoughts. The voluntary release of control over one's beliefs and actions, which is seen in cult situations, is not delusional because control is real and given voluntarily.

Thought broadcasting is the delusion that one's thoughts are broadcast so that they can be heard even in the absence of vocalizations. Some patients might feel that their thoughts are heard audibly by themselves, or that their mind can be read by someone, even in the absence of verbalization.

Thought insertion and withdrawal are delusions that the patient's mind is having alien thoughts inserted or thoughts withdrawn outside of their control.

Delusions of *jealousy* are ones in which the individual believes that a loved one is being unfaithful, in the absence of such a reality. The love might be real or imagined (where the recipient of the love does not know that he or she is the object of such admiration by the patient).

Delusions of *guilt* are ones in which patients feel that, by acts of omission or commission, they are guilty of some deed for which they blame themselves excessively. Often the delusion is based on an insignificant detail in the patient's past that he or she is unable to forget. At times the patient will confess to being the cause of major catastrophes and will focus attention on confessing a deed that is obviously not of their doing. Delusions of guilt are often in the context of overzealous religious beliefs.

Grandiose delusions are delusions in which the patient believes they have special powers that are beyond those of the normal individual. The patient may think that he or she is someone special, such as Jesus or the President, or believe that they have a special mission or significance to society and the world (e.g., developing a theory that would finally explain all of nature). A paranoid flavor is at times associated with grandiose delusions. Grandiose delusions are often associated with manic states and frequently are accompanied by excess irritability. Because paranoid delusions can be present in mania, they provide little help in differentiating schizophrenia from manic psychosis.

Religious delusions also are a frequent phenomenon and include exaggerations of conventional religious beliefs. The beliefs have to be taken within a sociocultural context before they are labeled as delusional. These can be seen in schizophrenic and affective psychosis.

Somatic delusions are false beliefs related to the body. These frequently take the form that the body or a part of it is rotting or does not exist. Similar delusions may occur in major depression with psychotic features.

Hallucinations are the experiencing of stimuli in any of the senses in the absence of external stimulation. Based on the particular sense involved, the hallucination is called auditory, visual, tactile, olfactory, or gustatory. In functional psychotic conditions, auditory hallucinations are frequent, visual hallucinations are uncommon, and hallucinations in the other senses are rare. The presence of visual hallucinations should raise the possibility of organic mental disorders, whereas the presence of olfactory hallucinations should raise the likelihood of seizure disorders, especially of the complex partial variety.

Auditory hallucinations are the most frequently reported hallucination in schizophrenic patients. These include one or more voices talking to or about the patient. Infrequently calling the patient by name is not by itself evidence that the patient is schizophrenic, but continuous hallucinations lasting all day or on and off for a couple of weeks are indicative of a schizophrenic psychosis. Typically, the patient experiences them as unpleasant, although he or she can get used to them and miss them in their absence. The voices can keep a running commentary of the patient's actions as they happen or can predict actions. The auditory hallucinations can be heard either inside the patient's head or coming from outside. At times, patients responding to treatment will report the progression of voices from outside to inside the head, to audible thoughts that may initially be alien but may later be their own before they go away. Auditory hallucinations of a self-critical or damning nature also may appear in major depression with psychotic features.

Visual hallucinations that occur with the use of hallucinogenic drugs or transiently just as the patient is about to fall asleep (hypnagogic) or wake up (hypnopompic) should not be considered schizophrenic in nature.

Bizarre behaviors include socially inappropriate behaviors such as dressing totally out of context (e.g., wearing a heavy woolen coat in the middle of summer) or disinhibition of behavior that would not be socially accepted, such as masturbating in public. The sociocultural contexts of the behavior should be taken into consideration before they are labeled as bizarre. Stereotyped behaviors are repetitive part actions, often symbolic, that have some contextual meaning to the patient.

Catatonic behavior is the presence of a marked reduction of psychomotor activity. This may present as rigidity, causing passive resistance to movement, or waxy flexibility, in which the patient maintains postures induced by the examiner. Lesser forms of catatonic behavior include mutism and negativism (passive resistance to any attempt to move).

Psychotic depression also may present with catatonic states, and catatonia is more frequently associated with affective states than schizophrenia. Catatonia also may be caused by a variety of medical and neurological disorders or may be a side effect of neuroleptic treatment.

Affect is the outward expression of emotion and is observed in facial features that routinely accompany the experience of emotions during communication. In schizophrenic patients there is a paucity of emotional expression or affect, and terms such as emotional blunting or flat affect are used to describe this situation. A dissociation between affect and behavior or cognition is described as incongruent affect.

Positive–Negative Symptoms Dichotomy

The symptoms of schizophrenia can be labeled positive or negative. Positive symptoms are symptoms that are added on to the premorbid state and include symptoms such as delusions, hallucinations, and bizarre behaviors. Negative symptoms are symptoms marked by the absence of functioning that were or should have been present in the premorbid state. Andreasen (1982) has defined the negative symptoms as affective flattening, alogia, avolition, anhedonia, and attentional impairment. There is some difficulty in differentiating negative symptoms from the "defect state" (which is the end state of chronic schizophrenia), depression, and pharmacologically induced side effects such as bradykinesia.

On the basis of the positive–negative symptom dichotomy, Crow (1985) postulated a two-syndrome concept of schizophrenia in which Type 1 schizophrenia was marked by a predominance of positive symptoms, reversible outcome, good response to neuroleptic medications, and lack of intellectual impairment, and Type II schizophrenia was characterized by negative symptoms, possible irreversible outcome, poor responsiveness to neuroleptics, and intellectual impairment.

Although such a division is potentially useful, it is difficult to divide patients into such syndromes because the vast majority of them seem to have a clinically mixed picture symptomatically and be partially responsive to treatment. However, a theory that attempts to explain the clinical manifestations of the illness, its cognitive aspects, morphological abnormalities, and response to treatment is a significant advance because it allows the proposal of testable hypotheses.

Factors in the Expression of Schizophrenia

Environmental Factors

Historical overview. At the turn of the century, emphasis by late contemporary European researchers in schizophrenia such as Kraepelin focused on the phenomenology and definition of psychotic disorders. Adolf Meyer (1866–1950) introduced the first empirical approach to investigating the role of environmental factors in the development of psychiatric disorders. Meyer advocated the use of a life chart to map life events, the relationship of which to the development of psychotic behavior and symptomatology could then be examined.

The subsequent development of psychoanalytic theory led to interest in the childhood experiences that might be responsible for the development of schizophrenia. The focus was on the child's interpersonal experience within the family, which might lead to faulty ego development and intrapsychic conflict, which in turn put the child at risk for psychotic regression in adult life. The role of the mother was the first to be cited in the search for a cause. Freida Fromm-Reichmann coined the term *schizophrenogenic mother* to describe the emotionally withholding, domineering, and rejecting attitudes she believed to be present in an excessive number of mothers whose children developed schizophrenia. This, she theorized, led to the child growing up feeling in conflict to, distrustful of, and angry toward others, which later is expressed as a psychotic illness. Other theorists noted evidence of overprotection or rejection in the mothers of schizophrenic individuals.

In the 1950s, interest shifted toward patterns of family or parental interaction that could be responsible for schizophrenia developing in a child. Three major groups of theorists emerged with different hypotheses. Bateson, Jackson, Haley, et al. (1956) described the concept of the *double bind* type of communication, which, they argued, could cause schizophrenia in a child who was repeatedly exposed to it. In a double bind message, meaning is conveyed by communication on different levels or in different modes—for example, literal or metaphorical meaning, verbal expression, and body language. Conflicting messages may thus be given simultaneously, and Bateson suggested that this type of communication could lead to deficits in interpreting meaning, which progress to a disorder of cognition and metacommunication that is seen in schizophrenia.

Theodore Lidz (1958) looked more specifically at two types of dysfunctional parental interaction that, he hypothesized, interfere with personality maturation in the offspring and lead to the development of schizophrenia. In the *schismatic* marriage, parental conflict and lack of trust and communication are seen, whereas in *skewed* marriages, the serious psychopathology of one parent is supported by the masochistic and submissive attitude of the other.

Lyman Wynne and Margaret Singer (1963) at the National Institute of Mental Health (NIMH) developed the concept of *communication deviance.* They argued that parents of schizophrenics show idiosyncratic, disconnected, and confused patterns of speech analogous to the thought disorder seen in schizophrenic patients.

In spite of significant methodologic problems associated with these studies, these theorists postulated that serious disturbances are found in a majority of families with a schizophrenic offspring. Later studies have revealed that these original studies, on which these psychological theories were based, had difficulties in methodology and interpretation and did not confirm their findings. Dysfunction in families in which a member had already developed schizophrenia may be due to the effects of living with a disturbed person. Retrospective reports of early life experience are unreliable, especially in someone who has become ill; the reported abnormal interaction patterns also are found in families of alcoholic and affectively disordered patients, making the findings nonspecific.

The etiological significance of communication deviance is continuing to be explored. It could be a subclinical manifestation of schizophrenia present in family members, a reflection of the social isolation resulting from the stigma of mental illness, or an environmental inducer of schizophrenia (a vulnerability or a causative factor) (Doane, West, Goldstein, et al., 1981). Recent controlled studies using a prospective follow-up design should shed additional light on these complex issues. For example, preliminary data suggest that disturbed adolescents in families showing communication deviance are more likely to develop one of the schizophrenia spectrum disorders later.

The possibility remains that types of psychological stresses at critical developmental stages could lead to an increased likelihood of a vulnerable individual developing schizophrenia.

Expressed Emotion

Once established, schizophrenia and the major psychoses have considerable variability in their course and outcome. Only part of this variance is related to response to medication. Thus, environmental influences on the course of illness have become a fertile area of investigation.

The course of the illness may be measured by the frequency and severity of relapse and the level of functioning between acute episodes. Follow-up studies of schizophrenic patients returning home have identified certain styles of communication in families that are positively correlated with earlier relapse (Leff, Vaughn, 1981). The critical factors as measured during a standardized family interview are criticism, hostility, and overinvolvement, known as "expressed emotion" (EE). Based on specific criteria, when families were divided into high and low EE there were large differences in relapse rates. These relapse rates were not correlated with severity of illness in the patient. Similar findings were made for families of depressed patients. In high EE families, fewer hours of face-to-face contact between patients and adult relatives significantly reduced the relapse rate in the schizophrenic but not the depressed group of patients. Use of prophylactic medications reduced the relapse rate in schizophrenics returning to high EE homes.

Life Events

Stressful life events seem to relate to the onset of relapse in major psychotic illnesses. Stressors can be divided into those that are acute and independent of the person's behavior and influence (such as an acute illness or death of a relative) and those that are chronic (such as poverty or difficulties at work or in the family environment), which also may be dependent on illness factors in the patient. In the 3 weeks before a psychotic relapse (in both schizophrenia and depression), it has been shown that there is a high frequency of independent social stressors (Brown, Birley, 1968). Moreover, the use of prophylactic medication in schizophrenics seems to protect against relapse under circumstances of acute stress, unless this is superimposed on a situation of chronic life stress.

When discussing the role of stress in the precipitation or maintenance of psychotic symptoms, one must also take into account each individual's variable response to that stress, his or her resources for dealing with it, and the degree to which he or she had control over its occurrence (Dohrenwend, Dohrenwend, 1978).

Social Class

The role of chronic life stress may be relevant to the finding that schizophrenia clusters in the lower socioeconomic classes (especially in urban environments), something that is not found in other psychotic conditions such as bipolar disorder. A second factor contributing to this clustering is the phenomenon of social drift. The higher representation of schizophrenia in lower socioeconomic classes has been shown to relate in part to the downward mobility experienced by schizophrenic individuals secondary to their disability. Studies of the occupations of both biological and adopted fathers of schizophrenics show that patients frequently fail to reach the occupational level of their parents, thus confirming that social drift occurs.

Social Network

The interaction between the effects of the environment on schizophrenia and the effects of schizophrenia on social experience is illustrated again in studies of social network. Social network refers to the circle of family members, friends, and associates with whom support and social activity is shared. Schizophrenics tend to have networks that are smaller, more family oriented, and less intimate than those of controls. This tendency becomes more prominent after repeated hospitalizations, and in many cases family members will eventually disengage and be replaced by more formal professional contacts, such as mental health staff. This finding can be explained by the difficulties schizophrenic patients have in initiating and sustaining social relationships. Because an individual's social network serves as a major buffer against the stresses of life, the patient's shrinking social network also tends to influence the progression of the illness.

Genetic Factors

There is considerable evidence that schizophrenia is an illness that runs in some families, although the majority of patients evaluated do not have a first-degree relative (i.e., sibling, parent, or child, each of whom probably shares half of the patient's genes) with schizophrenia. The morbid risk of a schizophrenic patient's relative developing schizophrenia is between 3.7 and 8.9%, based on different studies. What exactly is transmitted is not clear. Twin studies report that monozygotic twins are more likely to be concordant for schizophrenia than dizygotic twins. However, the concordance for monozygotic twins is not absolute, suggesting that the illness is transmitted only in a subset of the twins or that environmental influences can have either a triggering or protective influence in individuals. Twinning might cause vulnerability to the development of a number of conditions, including schizophrenia.

Various studies have shown that the likelihood of monozygotic twins being concordant for schizophrenia is over four times greater than that for dizygotic twins. It is important to note that approximately 50% of monozygotic twin pairs are discordant for schizophrenia, suggesting that what is transmitted is not the illness per se but the vulnerability for the development of it. Adoption studies of offspring of schizophrenic patients show that they have a greater likelihood of developing schizophrenia than do the adopted offspring of healthy individuals. The estimated heritability of a diathesis for schizophrenia based on such studies is between 60 and 70%.

Advances in molecular biology allow chromosomal analysis in which a search for linkage with known genetic markers can be done in families in which schizophrenia is prevalent. A recent report strongly suggests that, at least in a large extended family, the gene that transmits schizophrenia sits in close proximity to a known DNA marker on the fifth chromosome. Other families with an aggregation of schizophrenia clearly do not have this genetic abnormality, however, providing confirmation of the heterogeneity of schizophrenia. Such studies have tremendous potential in dividing schizophrenic patients into relevant subgroups.

Schizophrenic mothers are more likely to have pregnancy problems and perinatal problems with their children; thus, patients might have not only the genetic diathesis but also environmental insults both intrauterine and perinatally. Furthermore, children of schizophrenic mothers are more likely to have disruptive early life experiences that make developmental aberrations, including psychological ones, more likely.

There is a complex interaction between the genetic influences and environmental variables leading to the phenotypic expression of schizophrenia. These variables are interactive, not just additive. This complex interaction of nature and nurture affects not only the development of schizophrenia but also its course. In different individuals, differing genetic and environmental factors may thus play lesser or greater roles in cause and pathogenesis, thus contributing, particularly in schizophrenia, to the heterogeneity of the disorder. The most widely accepted view of the pathogenesis of schizophrenia is the stress diathesis model, in which constitutional factors determined by heredity (the diathesis) interact with environmental influences (stress) that precipitate overt expression of the clinical symptoms.

Anatomical Factors

Neuropathological studies of postmortem schizophrenic brains have attempted to find lesions that would explain the symptoms of schizophrenia. Initially, the search for the pathological lesion in schizophrenia focused on the frontal and temporal lobes. More recently, the area of interest has shifted to the limbic and diencephalic areas, although consistent results have not been reported. The pathological findings include nonspecific gliosis and cellular loss and disordered orientation of the pyramidal cells in the hippocampus. However, there is still no evidence that seems to clearly indicate a specific site for a pathological lesion in all schizophrenic patients.

Although a resurgence of interest exists in postmortem neuropathological studies of schizophrenic brains, there are a number of potential pitfalls in this methodology. These include the difficulty in dissociating the etiological factors from effects that might be the result of long-term chronic illness and effects of treatment. Other difficulties include changing ideas about diagnosis, the question of appropriate controls, the cause of death, delays in obtaining and fixing the brain after death, and so forth.

Neurochemistry also has been used in postmortem studies to unravel the mysteries of schizophrenia. A number of studies have documented increases in the number of type 2 dopamine (D2) receptors in areas such as the basal ganglia and nucleus accumbens, although such an increase could be the result of neuroleptic treatment (an issue yet to be resolved).

Imaging techniques, as they have become available, have been used to better understand the morphology and pathophysiology of schizophrenia. Computed tomography (CT) allows a noninvasive technique to be used to obtain x-rays of the brain in transverse slices. Numerous studies have documented enlargement of the lateral ventricles, increased width of the third ventricle, and sulcal enlargement suggestive of cortical atrophy. These findings are not consistently correlated among themselves and are possibly independent of each other or reflections of nonspecific insults to the brain.

Lateral ventricular enlargement is reported in schizophrenic patients in the vast majority of controlled studies (Fig. 4-1). Enlargement of the lateral ventricles is not

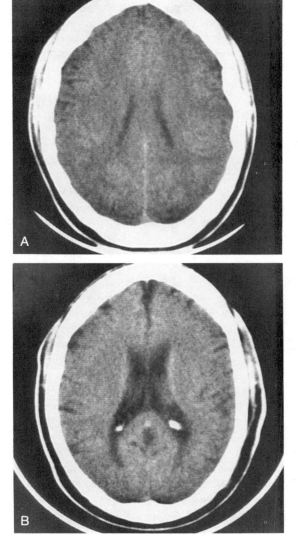

Figure 4–1. *(A) CT scan of patient with schizophrenia with normal lateral ventricles. (B) CT scan of patient with schizophrenia taken at level of bodies of lateral ventricles with enlarged lateral ventricles.*

necessarily sufficient to be read as clinically abnormal in the majority of schizophrenic patients. However, planimetric and other measurements clearly show that statistically significant enlargement of the lateral ventricle exists in the majority of schizophrenic patients. Not all schizophrenic patients have enlarged lateral ventricles, so that enlargement of the lateral ventricles is neither sufficient nor necessary for the diagnosis of schizophrenia. Lateral ventricular enlargement is not specific to schizophrenia—it is found in a number of neurological conditions and also in non-schizophrenic psychiatric conditions such as bipolar disorder.

In monozygotic twins discordant for schizophrenia, the lateral ventricles of the schizophrenic twin are enlarged compared with those of the healthy twin.

The lateral ventricular enlargement is seen very early in the onset of the illness, suggesting that it precedes the psychosis. Preliminary data suggest that the finding is not progressive. Lateral ventricular enlargement has been correlated with cognitive disturbances, negative symptoms, poor premorbid psychosocial functioning, poor response to treatment, and poor outcome.

The third ventricle is situated close to anatomical areas of particular interest in schizophrenia. It has been measured in a number of studies, and the majority report its enlargement. Sulcal enlargement also has been reported in a significant number of schizophrenic patients, suggesting diffuse cortical atrophy.

Magnetic resonance imaging (MRI) techniques provide significant advantages over CT scan studies, including better resolution; lack of exposure to radiation; the capacity to have transverse, sagittal, and coronal cuts; and the capacity to do three-dimensional reconstruction of the brain. Preliminary MRI studies appear to confirm the CT findings of enlarged lateral ventricles (Fig. 4-2). Other abnormalities noted appear to be inconsistent or nonspecific at this point.

Morphological studies can provide only a limited understanding of an illness that has some functional basis to it. Hence, static measures of structure are one step removed from physiological processes that need to be studied.

Physiological Factors

Physiological studies connect mental function to underlying physiological processes that are measurable and thus provide insights into normal and pathological psychic functioning. Physiological studies of cerebral blood flow in schizophrenia have been done with two-dimensional (xenon 133 inhalation) and three-dimensional (positron emission tomography [PET] and single photon emission computed tomography [SPECT]) techniques. Xenon is an inert gas that does not affect physiological or biochemical processes. Thus, measurement of radioactivity using gamma detectors, after inhalation of radiolabeled xenon, is a measure of regional blood flow in the brain. As neuronal activity is directly correlated with blood flow, regional cerebral blood flow is a measure of local neuronal activity.

There does not seem to be a difference in the total cerebral blood flow between schizophrenic patients and normal controls. Attempts to study differences in the resting state have resulted in inconsistent results. A number of studies have suggested a "hypofrontal pattern" to the regional distribution of cerebral blood flow with a relative decrease of blood flow to the frontal lobes.

Under activation paradigms, the functional responsivity of the various cerebral areas can be assessed. The most elegant series of studies using this methodology have

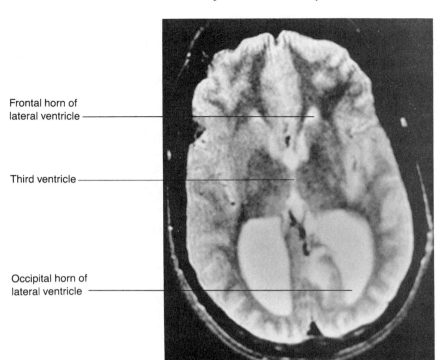

Frontal horn of
lateral ventricle

Third ventricle

Occipital horn of
lateral ventricle

Figure 4–2. *Axial MRI scan (T_2-weighted image) of a patient with schizophrenia showing enlarged lateral ventricles.*

involved the use of a cognitive task (the Wisconsin Card Sort [WCS]) that activates the dorsolateral prefrontal cortex (DLPFC) in comparison with the use of a nonspecific mental task. Schizophrenic patients failed to activate the DLPFC, and the lack of activation was directly correlated with the number of errors made on the WCS (Fig. 4-3). The interpretation of this series of studies is that schizophrenic patients have a specific abnormality in activating the prefrontal cortex—a part of the brain that is physiologically important in planning, altering strategies in problem solving, and coping with change.

Physiological studies with xenon have the advantage of repetition in individuals because of the limited radioactivity involved, but they give us only information about surface activity. To get an idea about deeper parts of the brain, we turn to techniques such as PET studies. PET allows three-dimensional quantification of physiological activity in the brain—either of blood flow or of receptor activity. Relative hypofrontality has been reported in schizophrenic patients in a number of PET studies. Using a ligand for the dopamine type 2 (D2) receptor, preliminary studies suggest a functional increase in dopamine receptor activity in the caudate nucleus of schizophrenics, including patients who have never been exposed to neuroleptic medications (suggesting that the alterations in the D2 receptors were not necessarily an effect of treatment with neuroleptics). Aside from the fact that an adequate replication of this study is still

rCBF % CHANGE ACTIVATION (WCS/NUM) MED FREE

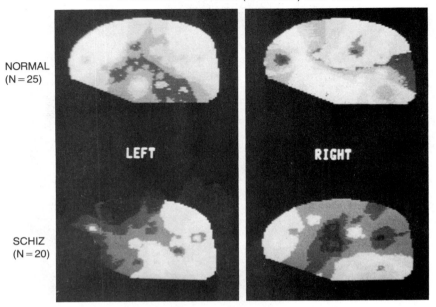

Figure 4–3. *Regional cerebral blood flow using xenon inhalation. Shows lack of activation of prefrontal cortex with Wisconsin Card Sort test compared with nonspecific number matching task in schizophrenic patients compared with controls. (Reprinted with permission from Weinberger et al)*

awaited, there are still a number of methodological issues that need to be ironed out before one accepts these findings.

Biochemical Factors

The search for a biochemical understanding of schizophrenia has been plagued by numerous discoveries that have failed to be replicated. The dopamine system has been a primary focus as a mediator of pathology that could explain the illness of schizophrenia. There is mostly indirect evidence to support a causal role of dopamine in schizophrenia. Thus, all medications that are specifically antipsychotic have the common capacity to block D2 (non–adenylate cyclase) dopamine receptors. Furthermore, indirect dopamine agonists have the capacity to induce a condition that is clinically indistinguishable from schizophrenia (as in amphetamine psychosis) or exacerbate a psychotic condition, although neither of these effects is consistent in all patients.

Thus, the suggestion that there is overactivity of the dopamine system—because of either increased firing of dopamine cells, greater release of dopamine, or alterations in the density or sensitivity of the D2 dopamine receptor—is an enticing model for explaining the biochemical underpinnings of schizophrenia.

The dopamine hypothesis has provided a conceptual framework for exploring the etiology of schizophrenia. The affinity that various neuroleptic agents had for the

D2 receptor correlated highly with the average therapeutic dose used for the control of psychotic symptoms. Such data strongly suggest that the neuroleptic action at the D2 receptor is pharmacologically relevant for the clinical benefits.

A number of dopamine systems exist in the mammalian brain. The ones of particular relevance to schizophrenia include the mesolimbic and mesocortical systems, which are thought to be integrally related to schizophrenia, and the nigrostriatal and tuberoinfundibular, which are thought to be related more to the side effects of neuroleptics.

Crow's typology of schizophrenia suggests two different pathological processes in the development of schizophrenia. The first involves the negative symptoms of schizophrenia, which could be reflections of pathological processes in the prefrontal cortex. Damage to the prefrontal cortex results in an amotivated withdrawn state with lack of initiative, thought, and emotion (Fuster, 1980). The positive symptoms, such as hallucinations and delusions, seem to be the result of pathology in the limbic system (Schmajuk, 1987).

Because both the limbic and prefrontal cortex have dopamine projections from the midbrain, it is interesting to look at these systems and their relation to pathology in schizophrenia. There are some differences between the mesocortical and mesolimbic dopamine pathways. The mesocortical dopamine pathway, like the tuberoinfundibular one, does not seem to have autoreceptors on the cell bodies and nerve terminals (Bannon, Roth, 1983). It is believed that as a result of this lack of autoreceptors, the mesocortical dopamine neurons have a higher rate of physiological activity, are less responsive to dopamine agonists and antagonists, and do not develop tolerance to chronic neuroleptic treatment. Thus, it is possible that neuroleptics are used at therapeutic doses have their predominant effect on the nigrostriatal and the mesolimbic dopamine systems, which result in control of the positive psychotic symptoms and the development of extrapyramidal side effects. At higher doses, neuroleptics may also have an effect on the mesocortical system whereby they can exacerbate negative symptoms.

Lesion studies of the mesocortical dopamine system (Pycock, Kerwin, Carter, et al., 1980) in rats result in disinhibition of the mesolimbic dopamine system with the resulting functional overactivity and up-regulation of the dopamine receptors. Such a finding is congruent with postmortem studies of schizophrenic brains (Weinberger, Kleinman, 1986). These data can suggest a model for explaining the symptomatology in schizophrenia whereby underactivity of the mesocortical dopamine system results in an overactivity of the mesolimbic system, which results in the positive symptoms of schizophrenia.

Weinberger (1987) has suggested that insult to the prefrontal cortex early in life would be silent through prepubertal development. However, when the prefrontal cortical functions come on-line with normal brain development associated with sexual maturity and the attainment of early adulthood, such a "lesion" could express itself (possibly triggered by stress) in the form of a psychotic episode. The pathophysiology of this abnormality would be in the form of decreased inhibition of subcortical dopamine systems, which are expressed as psychotic symptoms. Such a model would potentially explain the age of onset of schizophrenia.

Acute treatment with neuroleptic agents results in an increase in the firing rate

Table 4–4 Side–Effect Profiles and Dose Equivalents of Commonly Used Neuroleptics

DRUG	EQUIVALENT DOSE (MG)	DOSAGE FORMS	SEDATIVE	SIDE EFFECTS		
				Extra-pyramidal	Hypoten-sive	ANTI-CHOLINERGIC
Phenothiazines						
Chlorpromazine	100	t,i,c,s,r	+++	++	IM +++ oral ++	+++
Thioridazine	95	t,c,s	+++	+	++	++++
Mesoridazine	50	t,i,c	+++	+	++	+++
Fluphenazine	2	t,i,d,s,c	+	+++	+	+
Perphenazine	10	t,i,c	++	+++	+	++
Trifluoperazine	5	t,i,c	+	+++	+	+
Butyrophenones						
Haloperidol	2	t,i,c,d	+	+++	+	+
Thioxanthenes						
Thiothixene	5	t,i,c	+to++	++	++	+
Dihydroindolone						
Molindone	10	t,c	++	+	0	+
Dibenzoxazepine						
Loxapine	15	t,i,c	+	++	+	++
Diphenylbutylpiperidine						
Pimozide*	2	t	+	+	+	+
Clozapine†	50	t	+++	+	++	++++

0 = none, + = slight, + + = moderate, + + + = marked, + + + + = pronounced
t = tablet or capsule, c = concentrate, i = injectable, s = suspension, r = rectal suppository, d = depot injection
*Pimozide may have a greater propensity for prolonging the QT interval than other neuroleptics
†Clozapine may become commercially available in the United States in 1990.
Information in table extracted in part from:
Mason A & Granacher RP (1980). *Clinical handbook of antipsychotic drug therapy.* New York: Brunner/Mazel, pp. 19–108.
and
Baldessarini RJ (1978). Chemotherapy. In Nicholi AM (Ed.): *The Harvard Guide to Modern Psychiatry.* Cambridge: Harvard University Press, p. 390.
(Used with permission from Stoudemire A, Fogel BS: Psychopharmacology in the medically ill. In Stoudemire A, Fogel BS (eds): Principles of Medical Psychiatry, p 89. Orlando, Grune & Stratton, 1987)

of the dopamine cells and an increasing turnover of dopamine at the synaptic sites. However, chronic treatment results in a decrease in the firing rate related to depolarization block of the dopamine cells and the down-regulation of the receptor sensitivity. This is reflected in the reduction of both plasma and cerebrospinal fluid (CSF) homovanillic acid (HVA), a metabolite of dopamine. This reduction in HVA is temporally associated with clinical improvement.

Thus, a number of different lines of information from the clinical, anatomical, physiological, biochemical, and pharmacological areas are coming together to aid in understanding the complex enigma of schizophrenia.

Other Biological Findings in Schizophrenia

Numerous attempts have been made to find biological markers for schizophrenia. Abnormalities in eye tracking have been reported in about 65% of schizophrenic patients and in a lesser number of other psychiatrically ill patients. At this point it seems to be a trait marker, only partially affected by the psychotic state and unrelated to the medication status of the patient. Interestingly, some healthy family members of schizophrenic patients also have this abnormality, suggesting that it could be an abnormality that is genetically transmitted closely with schizophrenia or a vulnerability for the development of schizophrenia.

Treatment of Schizophrenia

Pharmacological Management

The pharmacology of neuroleptic (antipsychotic) medications is covered in Chapter 17. This section will focus on clinical issues in the use of neuroleptics in the treatment of schizophrenia.

Neuroleptic agents are significantly more powerful in controlling the symptoms of psychosis than are antianxiety, antidepressant, and antimanic agents, none of which is any better than placebo. There are two indications for neuroleptic agents in the treatment of schizophrenia. The first is to control the active symptoms of the illness, and the second is to provide a prophylactic effect in preventing relapse. The first is aimed at controlling the acute episode, whereas the second is aimed at maintenance management. In a significant number of patients, however, the control of symptoms is only partial, and therefore the palliative and prophylactic indications for the neuroleptics are often combined.

The neuroleptic agents in general use today are all equally effective in the treatment of psychosis (Table 4-4). Thus, in choosing a particular neuroleptic for the treatment of a patient, therapeutic effectiveness is not a factor that guides the physician in the choice of a particular neuroleptic. Even neuroleptics that have a greater sedating effect (e.g., chlorpromazine, thioridazine) seem to improve psychomotor retardation associated with psychosis, whereas less sedating neuroleptic agents (e.g., haloperidol) have a calming effect in agitated patients.

Side effects can be used when choosing which neuroleptic should be used in a particular individual. Major side effects include anticholinergic ones, postural hypertension, and extrapyramidal ones (acute dystonic reactions, pseudoparkinsonism, akathisia, and tardive dyskinesia). Less common, but with considerable morbidity and mortality, is neuroleptic malignant syndrome.

For the acute episode of schizophrenia, doses in the range of 400–600 mg of chlorpromazine or its equivalent are necessary for successful treatment (Kane 1987). Megadoses of neuroleptics (over 2000 mg of chlorpromazine or its equivalent) do not seem to result in any greater or faster improvement of schizophrenia. Combining benzodiazepines with neuroleptic agents in the early part of the treatment of an acute schizophrenic episode can be an appropriate strategy to induce sedation and control agitated behavior while using lower doses of neuroleptic agents. Use of benzodiazepines for such an indication should not be for more than a few days at a time because of the potential development of dependence.

The maintenance strategy is to find the lowest useful dose of neuroleptic that will continue to provide protection against psychotic relapse while not interfering with the psychosocial functioning of the individual and reducing the risk for tardive dyskinesia. If high doses of neuroleptics are required for control of an acute episode of schizophrenia, one should consider a slow and gradual reduction in dose once the patient has stabilized and is relatively free of stressful situations. A generic suggestion would be to reduce the dosage of chlorpromazine or its equivalent at the rate of 100 mg per month. Such a decrease in dosage should be coupled with education of the patient and significant others and attempts to monitor the development of early warning signs indicative of impending relapse. An unstable environment around the patient and emotional hostility and intrusiveness (high EE) that the patient might have to endure from close relationships are much more likely to be associated with a psychotic relapse. Hence, patients with these situations should have their medications reduced in a more conservative manner.

Neuroleptic Side Effects

Neuroleptics have numerous side effects; this chapter will focus exclusively on the extrapyramidal side effects. These are important because they have a tremendous impact on the patient's compliance with neuroleptic medications.

The extrapyramidal systems are involved in the nonconscious control of all voluntary musculature. Neuroleptics have complex effects on the extrapyramidal systems that are exacerbated by anxiety, disappear during sleep, and can be consciously controlled for a limited time with effort. Extrapyramidal side effects can be classified into those which happen early or late in treatment.

Among the early extrapyramidal side effects are acute dystonic reactions. These are involuntary spasms of voluntary muscle groups that are often painful and frightening to patients. Frequently they involve the orofacial and head and neck areas, although any part of the body may be involved. Young men on high-potency neuroleptics (e.g., haloperidol) are at the greatest risk for the development of acute dystonic reactions. Low-potency neuroleptics, especially ones that have significant anticholinergic effects (e.g., thioridazine), have less likelihood of inducing acute dystonic reactions. Acute dystonic reactions tend to happen relatively early in treatment, and there is some tolerance that develops to them. The presumed mechanism of action is an imbalance induced by neuroleptic agents blocking dopamine receptors that are in balance with the cholinergic system. The use of neuroleptics with anticholinergic agents or dopamine agonists results in reestablishment of this dopamine–cholinergic balance and the control of the acute dystonic reaction. Considering the impact of such reactions on compliance of the patient, it is worthwhile to consider using antiparkinsonian agents in a prophylactic manner in patients who are started on neuroleptics, especially the high-potency ones such as haloperidol.

Parkinsonian side effects also associated with the use of neuroleptics include tremor, rigidity, and bradykinesia. These symptoms are indistinguishable from the symptoms of Parkinson's disease, which is caused by degeneration of the dopamine cells in the substantia nigra. Neuroleptic-induced parkinsonian side effects are responsive to anticholinergic and dopamine agonist agents.

Bradykinesia is a state associated with diminished spontaneous motor movements associated with a reduction in spontaneous speech, general apathy, and difficulty initiating activities. Bradykinesia can be difficult to differentiate from depression and negative symptoms. Because anticholinergic agents are effective in treating bradykinesia, such symptoms should be aggressively treated with these agents.

Akathisia is a subjective sense of motor restlessness and is often mistaken for agitation. It is not as responsive as other extrapyramidal side effects to anticholinergic agents. Some patients with akathisia respond to the use of beta-blockers such as propranolol. The most effective treatment for akathisia is a reduction in neuroleptic dose.

Tardive dyskinesia (TD) is a late complication of neuroleptic treatment and has been described as "a syndrome consisting of abnormal stereotyped involuntary movements usually of choreoathetoid type principally affecting the mouth, face, limbs and trunk, which occurs relatively late in the course of drug treatment and the etiology of which the drug treatment is a necessary factor" (Jeste, 1982). There is roughly a 3% annual risk for the development of TD, which is cumulative annually. Only about one third of patients treated with neuroleptics seem to be at risk for the development of TD. If detected early, and the neuroleptic is discontinued, the TD is most often reversible. Continued treatment with neuroleptics results in potential worsening of the symptoms of TD and makes them more likely to be irreversible. Risk factors for the development of TD include total lifetime exposure to the dose of neuroleptic medications, older age, female sex, a history of extrapyramidal side effects, and mood disorders.

The presumed pathogenesis of TD is the development of supersensitive dopamine receptors in response to chronic blockade by neuroleptics. However, such supersensitivity probably develops in all patients treated chronically with neuroleptics, but only some go on to develop TD. Hence, supersensitive dopamine receptors might be necessary but not sufficient for the development of TD. Currently, there is no clinically successful strategy for the treatment of TD. Thus, the best approach for avoiding the risk of TD is the use of neuroleptics at the lowest possible dose necessary, regular evaluation for development of the symptoms of TD, and periodic voluntary informed consent for the continued use of neuroleptics.

Psychosocial Treatment

Psychosocial treatment of the major psychoses must be part of an integrated plan involving the use of a range of therapies appropriate to the phase of illness and the individual characteristics of each patient. Underlying goals are the treatment of symptoms, reduction of stress, mobilization of social supports, assistance with deficits in daily living skills caused by the illness, and gradual rehabilitation to the most autonomous level of functioning possible for the individual patient. Psychosocial treatment modalities include the use of hospitalization, partial hospitalization or day treatment programs, crisis intervention, individual therapy, and family treatment including psychoeducational approaches, social skills and behavioral training, and case management.

Individuals with all major psychotic disorders are likely to need long-term, often lifetime treatment. A consistent relationship with a primary clinician is of key importance, because he or she will provide support and guidance through different phases of the illness and will coordinate the different treatment modalities that may be needed. Careful attention to maintaining continuity of care between hospital and outpatient clinic, day treatment, vocational rehabilitation, and family treatment programs is of particular importance for patients whose illness may make it difficult for them to make transitions and new relationships or to negotiate complex institutional barriers. Integration of medication and psychosocial programs is essential. Psychosocial treatments are used to target problems not responsive to medications, such as negative symptoms and social and occupational deficits, and to support medication strategies that will be most therapeutic and produce the least possible side effects. Studies indicate that the combination of medication and psychosocial programs is significantly more effective than either used alone (Falloon, Lieberman, 1983).

Acute phase. In the acute phase of a psychotic illness, hospitalization is often necessary to contain disruptive and dangerous behavior and remove the individual from everyday stresses and responsibilities. Patients should always be medically reevaluated for the presence of medical, neurological, or substance disorders that may be etiologically related to the psychotic break or may have precipitated a relapse.

The push toward deinstitutionalization and community care (founded on the advent of neuroleptics), concern over the iatrogenic effects of long-term institutionalization, and the shifting of public money from state hospitals to community mental health centers has dramatically reduced the length of stay for most psychotic patients. Studies show short-term hospitalization to be at least as effective as longer stays. Interest in partial hospitalization, in which the patient lives at home but attends a structured daily program, has grown. Several studies show that this is feasible and works as well as inpatient treatment for patients who do not present a risk of violence or suicide (Weiss, Dubin, 1982).

The goals of psychosocial intervention in the acute phase of a psychotic experience are to reduce stimulation and provide a safe and structured environment where clear communication, little demand for performance, and firm limit-setting by tolerant and supportive staff can complement the use of medication in achieving a rapid resolution of symptomatic behavior. Immediate contact with the family is important in developing an alliance, providing crisis intervention to resolve stress that may have caused or been caused by the patient's relapse, and planning for future treatment. Connecting the patient with appropriate aftercare treatment is an essential part of the treatment of the acute phase of illness. This requires careful attention because in many public care systems inpatient and outpatient staff are segregated into different institutions and agencies, under different funding and administration, resulting in a high failure rate in keeping first outpatient appointments.

Follow-up treatment. After an acute psychotic episode, little should be expected of the patient for several months. The principal goals of treatment at this stage are to prevent relapse while adjusting medication to a maintenance level and to help the patient reintegrate into the community. The home environment is now often the major treatment milieu, and it is important for the clinician to attend to the major impact that an acute psychotic episode has on the family system. Emotional turmoil, disruption of family routine and coping strategies, stigma, and restriction of social network are all dimensions that need to be addressed while the family is taught to provide the most therapeutic milieu. Attempts to change specific aspects of family interaction that correlate with higher relapse rates, such as high EE or communication deviance, may be warranted. Family treatment programs involving crisis intervention, education about the illness, stress reduction, and communication skills training have been shown to reduce the risk of relapse in the first year after hospitalization. Day hospital programs can play a useful role in assisting the patient's gradual readjustment to community living and also have been shown to reduce the risk of relapse. They may be particularly helpful for many chronic patients who have little family support and return to boarding homes, halfway houses, or cooperative living arrangements, which provide little in the way of treatment. Psychosocial programs that are too demanding or stimulating are not appropriate for this phase of treatment. Major role therapy (MRT), an intensive problem-solving approach used with schizophrenic outpatients, has been shown to improve social functioning after 18 months of treatment, but if it is offered without the use of prophylactic medication, it is associated with a lower level of adjustment, indicating that too much pressure can be detrimental to patients in the recovery process.

Individual psychotherapy alone has not been shown to improve the outcome for schizophrenic patients over the use of medication alone. This does not preclude its use for a few high-functioning schizophrenic patients. For many patients recovering from an acute psychotic episode, help with living accommodations, food, clothing, income, child care, and medical care is needed immediately. Case management is the term used to describe the social work function of helping the patient access the services that will meet these needs. This model of care is now part of many aftercare systems for psychotic patients. Case management functions may be provided by the primary clinician or may be allocated to separate case managers who work with a specific target population.

For the many patients who do not return to a premorbid level of adjustment following reentry into the community, other types of psychosocial intervention may be indicated. Social skills training programs using behavioral techniques focus on teaching patients verbal and nonverbal behaviors necessary for independent living and everyday social interaction. Assessment of strengths and weaknesses is followed by instruction, modeling, rehearsal (often in role play), and positive reinforcement of behavior that is correctly carried out. This approach has been shown to be helpful for chronic patients left with marked negative symptoms.

Group psychotherapy is useful in developing social skills as well as in encouraging supportive interpersonal relationships, reality testing, giving and receiving advice with practical problems of living, and exploring fears and feelings in a safe environment. With patients who have been psychotic, the group should have a structured, task-oriented focus rather than an exploratory focus. Many mental health centers use a biweekly or monthly medication group to provide an opportunity for patient evaluation, education, and socialization as well as an extension of each patient's social network.

Patients who recover sufficiently from the acute psychotic episode may need assistance in returning to work. Vocational rehabilitation programs such as workshops, job training programs, and transitional employment are offered by state and private agencies, which usually provide a structured and sheltered work environment in which patients may rehearse general job-related skills (such as being on time, completing tasks, and responding to supervision) as well as acquire new skills in preparation for a specific job. Little research has been done to measure the effectiveness of such programs, but they nevertheless address an area of recovery that is sorely in need of help, considering that less than 30% of schizophrenic patients return to work postdischarge.

CONCLUSION

Schizophrenia is an illness that is heterogenous in its cause, pathophysiology, response to treatment, and long-term outcome. Thus, generalizations about the illness and predictability in treatment response and outcome are important factors to consider, but their predictive capacity is small.

CLINICAL PEARLS

- Psychotic symptoms are nonspecific and occur in a variety of medical, psychiatric, neurological, and substance abuse disorders.
- Always rule out an organic mental disorder first before assuming that any patient with psychotic symptoms has a "functional" psychiatric disorder.
- First-onset psychosis after age 45 generally indicates an organic mental disorder or a psychotic depression; the onset of schizophrenia after age 45 is relatively rare.
- It is now believed that schizophrenia is primarily a neurological disorder with a strong genetic component; it is possible, however, that certain types of environmental or developmental stresses in individuals who are genetically vulnerable may contribute to the onset of the illness.
- It has been well demonstrated that the most effective treatment for schizophrenia involves a combination of neuroleptic medication and psychosocial treatment modalities.
- After years of research, abnormalities in the dopaminergic system of the brain remain the most consistent theory for the biological basis of schizophrenia.
- In treating schizophrenia, neuroleptics should be used at the lowest possible dose, and the patient should be monitored closely for tardive dyskinesia. Informed consent regarding tardive dyskinesia should be given at least every 6 months.

ANNOTATED BIBLIOGRAPHY

Andreasen NC: The diagnosis of schizophrenia. Schizophr Bull 13:9–22, 1987

> An overview of the development of the criteria for diagnosing schizophrenia. Assesses both the strengths and limitations of nomenclature in psychiatry.

Arieti S: The Interpretation of Schizophrenia, 2nd ed. New York, Basic Books, 1974

> For students interested in an eloquent, psychoanalytically oriented view of the inner world of the schizophrenic, this text is a classic. Its fundamental flaw is that it considers psychological factors as being primary in the etiology of the illness, but it nevertheless enables one to understand the evolution of schizophrenia from the internal world of the patient.

Kendler KS: The genetics of schizophrenia: A current perspective. In Meltzer HY (ed): Psychopharmacology: The Third Generation of Progress, pp 705–713. New York, Raven Press, 1987

> A brilliant review of a confusing area. Frames the right questions and reviews the literature to delineate the answers that are known, and discusses the areas in which knowledge is lacking.

Kane JM: Treatment of schizophrenia. Schizophr Bull 13:133–156, 1987

> A detailed overview of the state-of-the-art knowledge on pharmacological treatment of schizophrenia. Includes strategies on how to address patients who are nonresponders.

Weinberger DR: Implications of normal brain development for the pathogens of schizophrenia. Arch Gen Psychiatry 44:660–669, 1987

> An interesting hypothesis that potentially explains the disparate aspects of schizophrenia, including its symptomatology, age of onset, biochemistry, and pharmacological response. The hypothesis connects morphological abnormality, brain development, and pathogenesis of schizophrenia.

REFERENCES

American Psychiatric Association: Diagnostic and Statistical Manual of Mental Disorders, 3rd ed, rev. Washington, DC, American Psychiatric Association, 1987

Anderson CM: Family intervention with severely disturbed patients. Arch Gen Psychiatry 34:697–702, 1977

Andreasen NC: Negative symptoms in schizophrenia: Definition and reliability. Arch Gen Psychiatry 39:784–788, 1982

Andreason NC: Comprehensive Assessment of Symptoms and History. Department of Psychiatry, University of Iowa College of Medicine, 1987

Baldessarini RJ, Cohen BM, Teicher MM: Significance of neuroleptic dose and plasma level in the pharmacological treatment of psychosis. Arch Gen Psychiatry 45:79–91, 1988

Bannon MJ, Roth RH: Pharmacology of mesocortical dopamine neurons. Pharmacol Rev 35:53–68, 1983

Bateson G, Jackson DD, Haley J et al: Toward a theory of schizophrenia. Behav Sci 1:251–264, 1956

Bleuler E: Dementia Praecox or the Group of Schizophrenias. Zinkin J (trans): New York, Int University Press, 1960 (German ed, 1911)

Brown GW, Birley JLT: Crises and life changes and the onset of schizophrenia. J Health Soc Behav 9:203–214, 1968

Crow TJ: The two-syndrome concept: Origins and current status. Schizophr Bull 11:471–485, 1985

Doane J, West KL, Goldstein MJ et al: Parental communication deviance and affective style. Arch Gen Psychiatry 38:679–685, 1981

Dohrenwend BS, Dohrenwend BP: Some issues in research on stressful life events. J Nerv Ment Dis 166:7–15, 1978

Falloon IRH, Lieberman RP: Interactions between drug and psychosocial therapy in schizophrenia. Schizophr Bull 9:543–544, 1983

Fromm-Reichmann F: Notes on the development of treatment of schizophrenics by psychoanalytic psychotherapy. Psychiatry 11:263–273, 1948

Fuster J: The Prefrontal Cortex. New York, Raven Press, 1980

Garmezy N, Neuchterlein K: Invulnerable children: Fact and fiction of competence and disadvantage. Presented at the annual meeting of the American Orthopsychiatric Association, Detroit, Michigan, 1972

Gibbons R, Lewine R, Davis J et al: An empirical test of a Kraepelinian vs a Bleulerian view of negative symptoms. Schizophr Bull 11:390–396, 1985

Gottesman II, Shields J: Schizophrenia: The Epigenetic Puzzle. New York, Cambridge University Press, 1982

Herz M: Prodromal symptoms and prevention of relapse in schizophrenia. J Clin Psychiatry 46:22–25, 1985

Hogarty GE, Anderson CM, Reiss DJ et al: Family psychoeducation, social skills training and maintenance chemotherapy in the aftercare treatment of schizophrenia. Arch Gen Psychiatry 43 (7):633–642, 1986

Hollingshead AB, Redlich FC: Social Class and Mental Illness: A Community Study. New York, John Wiley & Sons, 1958

Holzman PS: Eye movement dysfunction and psychosis. Int Rev Neurobiol 27:179–205, 1985

Jeste DV, Wyatt RJ: Understanding and Treating Tardive Dyskinesia, p 84. New York, Guilford Press, 1982

Kraepelin E: Textbook of Psychiatry (abstr). Diefendorf AR (trans): London, Macmillan, 1907

Langfeldt G: The prognosis in schizophrenia. Acta Psychiatr Neurol Scand 110:7–66, 1956

Leff JP: Schizophrenia and sensitivity to the family environment. Schizophr Bull 2:566–574, 1976

Leff J, Vaughn C: The role of maintenance therapy and relatives' expressed emotion in relapse of schizophrenia: A two-year follow up. Br J Psychiatry 139:102–104, 1981

Lidz T: Schizophrenia and the family. Psychiatry 21:21–27, 1958

Maser JD, Keith SJ: CT scans and schizophrenia—Report on a workshop. Schizophr Bull 9:265–283, 1983

Meyer A: The dynamic interpretation of dementia praecox. Am J Psychol 21:385–403, 1910

Pycock CJ, Kerwin RW, Carter CJ: Effect of lesion of cortical dopamine terminals on subcortical dopamine receptors in rats. Nature 286:74–76, 1980

Robins LN, Helzer JE, Weissman MM et al: Lifetime prevalence of specific psychiatric disorders in three sites. Arch Gen Psychiatry 41:949–958, 1984

Schmajuk NA: Animal models for schizophrenia. The hippocampally lesioned animal. Schizophr Bull 13(2):317–327, 1987

Schneider K: Clinical Psychopathology. Hamilton MW (trans): New York, Grune & Stratton, 1959

Tienari P, Sorri A, Lahti I et al: The Finnish adoptive family study of schizophrenia. Yale J Biol Med 58:227–237, 1985

Vaughn CE, Leff JP: The influence of family and social factors on the course of psychiatric illness. Br J Psychiatry 129:125–137, 1976

Weinberger DR: Implication of normal brain development for the pathogens of schizophrenia. Arch Gen Psychiatry 44:660–669, 1987

Weinberger DR, Berman KF, Zec RF: Physiological dysfunction of the dorsolateral prefrontal cortex in schizophrenia. Arch Gen Psychiatry 43:114–124, 1986

Weinberger DR, Kleinman JE: Observations on the brain in schizophrenia. In Hales RE, Frances JA: Psychiatry Update, American Psychiatric Association Annual Review, Vol 5, pp 42–67. Washington, DC, American Psychiatric Press, 1986

Weiss KJ, Dubin WR: Partial hospitalization: State of the art. Hosp Community Psychiatry 33:923–928, 1982

Wong DF, Wagner HN, Tune LE et al: Positron emission tomography reveals elevated D2 dopamine receptors in drug-naive schizophrenics. Science 234:1558–1563, 1986

Wynne L, Singer M: Thought disorder and family relations of schizophrenia. I: Research strategies. Arch Gen Psychiatry 9:191–198, 1963

This work was supported in part by U.S. Public Health Service (NIMH) grants MH 40597 and MH 42298.

5

Personality Disorders

Deborah B. Marin, Allen J. Frances, and Thomas Widiger

For centuries, ever since Hippocrates suggested a neuroendocrine model of behavior in which the relative balance of four bodily humors (blood, black bile, yellow bile, and phlegm) caused the different personality types (Allport, 1937), physicians have sought to understand how and why people's personalities differ. Behavioral regressions often accompany physical illness, and one of the features that separates a great doctor from a technician is the ability to understand how a patient's personality interacts with the stress of illness (see Chapter 1). The physician who can accurately assess patients' personality traits and manage their idiosyncrasies in the context of illness will improve his or her relationship with patients, enhance compliance, and reduce patients' stress (Kahana, Bibring, 1964). Open and comfortable two-way communication coupled with an understanding on the part of the physician of the patient's personality, sensitivities, vulnerabilities, mechanisms of defense, and ways of coping with stress will help the patient recognize that he or she is being understood.

Essential to achieving these goals is an understanding that different personality styles often entail different, yet predictable, ways of coping with illness that require specific responses from the physician. For example, as will be seen, compulsive patients who have a need to be "in control" can best be managed by being encouraged to become actively involved in treatment decisions. In contrast, the dependent person who desperately needs to be cared for and reassured will be most appropriately served by the doctor's being more directive of the decision making (Kahana, Bibring, 1964).

Physicians of all specialties can learn the techniques of personality assessment and supportive treatment to obtain optimal doctor–patient relationships. It is also a wise physician who acknowledges his or her *own* personality patterns and responses and the responses that different types of patients are likely to elicit from them. Problematic personality traits are ubiquitous in medically ill patients, and personality disorders occur in 5 to 10% of the general population and in up to 60% of inpatient psychiatry samples (Merikangas, Weissman, 1986; Docherty, Fiester, Shea, 1986). Thus, assessing and managing personality disorders is a common part of both general medical and psychiatric practice.

DEFINITION: PERSONALITY TRAITS vs. PERSONALITY DISORDERS

The fact that everyone has a personality is what makes people more or less predictable in their behaviors and reactions. *An individual's personality style is exemplified by typical behavior patterns and characteristic responses to life events and stresses.* The term *personality trait* describes such typical patterns and responses. In distinction to a "trait," a personality *disorder* occurs when an individual's traits are *inflexible* and *maladaptive,* resulting in significant impairments in social, interpersonal, and occupational functioning. Personality *disorders* are chronic behavior disturbances with an early and insidious onset that crystallize by late adolescence or early adulthood. To varying degrees, personality disorders influence all facets of personality, including cognition, affect, behavior, and interpersonal style (Widiger, Frances, 1988).

CLASSIFICATION

The *Diagnostic and Statistical Manual of Mental Disorders-III-Revised* (DSM-III-R) (American Psychiatric Association, 1987) provides the current system for classification of personality disorders. The provision of a separate axis in the DSM-III-R system (Axis II) for personality pathologies draws attention to the importance of these pathologies and emphasizes their coexistence with, and contribution to, other psychiatric disorders (Frances, Widiger, 1986; Siever, Klar, 1986). Axis I conditions include all the mental disorders that are not personality disorders. Depression, schizophrenia, and dementia are examples of such conditions. In addition, it acknowledges the coexistence of personality disorders with Axis I conditions.

The DSM-III-R personality disorders are grouped into three major clusters (Table 5-1): Cluster I includes the odd or eccentric (schizotypal, schizoid, and paranoid); Cluster II includes the dramatic, emotional, or erratic (histrionic, narcissistic, antisocial, and borderline); and Cluster III represents the anxious or fearful (avoidant, dependent, obsessive-compulsive, and passive-aggressive).

DSM-III-R also includes the sadistic and self-defeating personality disorders in an appendix, pending further research to support their inclusion in the future editions of the manual. The allowance for multiple diagnoses in the personality disorder section in DSM-III-R is very useful, because over 50% of patients with Axis II pathology

Table 5–1 **The Three Clusters of Personality Disorders**

CLUSTER I (ODD)	CLUSTER II (DRAMATIC)	CLUSTER III (ANXIOUS)
Schizotypal	Histrionic	Avoidant
Schizoid	Narcissistic	Dependent
Paranoid	Antisocial	Obsessive-compulsive
	Borderline	Passive-aggressive

meet criteria for two categories (Pfohl, 1986). Because all axes must be included in a patient's diagnoses, it is important to list every trait observed in all the Axis II categories. If a patient's symptoms are not severe enough to warrant a formal diagnosis, the presence of more subtle, subthreshold personality characteristics may be noted in Axis II using the term *traits* rather than *disorder.*

DIAGNOSIS

Several factors make the diagnosis of personality disorder difficult and should be considered carefully during the clinical assessment of the patient. *Personality characteristics reflect an enduring disposition to react in a particular way.* In contrast, *state* conditions reflect a person's condition at a *given point* in time. As an example, a widowed woman may seem dependent or compulsive because she is depressed. Distinguishing *trait* from *state* is particularly pertinent when making Axis I and II diagnoses (Frances, Widiger, 1986). It is crucial to try to ascertain whether or not a patient's behavior represents a change from his or her baseline or an enduring personality style.

When determining if a behavior is maladaptive enough to be consistent with a personality disorder, attention must also be turned to the *situation* in which the behavior occurs (Frances, Widiger, 1986). *The physician must not erroneously assign behaviors to personality traits and overlook the contribution of situational factors.* The young man questioning authority in military boot camp should not necessarily be diagnosed as having a passive-aggressive personality unless he behaves similarly in other circumstances.

Traits also must be distinguished from roles (Frances, Widiger, 1986). An observed behavior may be a response to the demands of a social role rather than a personality style. When a pathological behavior is evident only in response to a specific stressor or expected role, an adjustment disorder should be diagnosed (Frances, Widiger, 1986). In contrast, an individual with a personality disorder exhibits a maladaptive behavior that is consistent over time in many situations (Millon, 1981).

The traits that constitute the personality disorders frequently occur in diminished number or intensity in the normal population (Frances, Widiger, 1986). The personality disorders differ quantitatively, not qualitatively, from normality. Attention also must be paid to the culture in which certain behaviors occur. It is expectable that cultural norms in different countries and societies will differ significantly. Furthermore, perceptions of the threshold dividing normality from pathology may vary among those performing the evaluation. Determining this boundary is difficult and requires clinical judgment and experience (Frances, Widiger, 1986).

METHOD OF ASSESSMENT

The most frequently used methods to assess personality disorders are the clinical interview, self-report inventories, and semistructured interviews. The three major self-report inventories for assessment of personality disorders are the Minnesota Multiphasic Personality Inventory, the Millon Clinical Multiaxial Inventory, and the Personality Diagnostic Questionnaire (Widiger, Frances, 1987). The advantages of self-report instruments include ease of administration and scoring as well as documentation of symptoms without the input of a clinician's possible preconceptions and expectations (Widiger, Frances, in press). Yet, interviewing informants may indeed yield a more accurate assessment of the person's personality (Tyrer, Strauss, Cicchetti, 1983).

Semistructured interviews have facilitated much research in, and understanding of, personality disorders. Examples of such interviews, which include the Structured Interview for the Diagnosis of Personality Disorders, the Personality Disorder Examination, the Structured Clinical Interview for DSM-III-R (SCID), the Personality Interview Question, and the Diagnostic Interview for Borderlines, are reviewed by Widiger and Frances (1987). These instruments have proved that good interrater reliability can be obtained for the diagnoses of personality disorders if a set of comprehensive and specific questions is provided (Widiger, Frances, in press).

EPIDEMIOLOGY

When evaluating the prevalence of personality disorders, one must consider the population being sampled. The different rates reported below result from the differing instruments used on varied populations. *Most studies assessing the epidemiology of personality disorders have been done in psychiatric inpatients who have concurrent Axis I conditions.* In part, this is because treatment settings are more likely to facilitate comprehensive interviews and to ensure the presence of the experienced raters necessary for a valid assessment of personality traits (Merikangas & Weissman, 1986). Because instruments for establishing criteria for personality disorders in the community are lacking, there are few studies that examine the rates of personality disorders in the general population. To date, there exists no systematic study using DSM-III-R criteria to assess all personality disorders in the general population. Because most test instruments to assess personality disorders are standardized on psychiatric patients, their generalizability to epidemiologic studies in other populations is not clear.

Among patients admitted to psychiatric hospitals for depression, 23 to 67% have a concurrent personality disorder (Merikangas & Weissman, 1986). Psychiatric outpatients with mood disorders have rates of personality disorder ranging from 12 to 100% (Merikangas & Weissman, 1986). In the medical setting, a 10% rate of personality disorders has been reported in patients at risk for HIV infection (Jacobsberg, unpublished data). In random community samples, the overall rates of personality disorder appear to range from 5 to 10% (Merikangas & Weissman, 1986). Studies of the prevalence of paranoid, schizoid, and schizotypal traits show ranges of 0.03 to 28.4 per 100 people (Merikangas & Weissman, 1986). These figures reflect people who may only have *traits* of these disorders without meeting full threshold criteria for the disorders.

Personality disorders appear to be distributed equally between the sexes and to be more common in the lower socioeconomic classes. The prevalence of histrionic and borderline personality disorders ranges from 0.2 to 2.2 per 100 people. Antisocial personality disorder is the only Axis II diagnosis that has been studied in many epidemiologic studies. Antisocial traits have prevalence ranging from 0.2 to 9.4 per 100 people. Antisocial personality disorder has been shown to be more common in young men in lower socioeconomic classes, mobile populations, and in prisons (Merikangas and Weissman, 1986). There are no epidemiologic studies examining narcissistic personality disorder.

There are no studies using DSM-III-R criteria for avoidant, dependent, compulsive, and passive-aggressive personality disorders in community samples. The prevalence of avoidant traits ranges from 7 to 41 per 100. The prevalence of dependent traits ranges from 2.5 to 27.2 per 100. Compulsive personality disorders have been shown to have a prevalence of 0.04 per 100 and passive-aggressive personality changes have rates from 0.9 to 2.5 per 100 (Merikangas and Weissman, 1986). This group of diagnoses is more common in women and in lower social classes (Merikangas & Weissman, 1986).

ETIOLOGY

Personality development depends on the interaction of several variables, including the person's constitution, innate temperament, developmental experiences within the family, quality of family relationships, available role models, and opportunities for acquisition of coping skills (Rutter, 1985). Earlier writings favored *either* environment *or* biology as causative factors. In contrast, more recent literature views personality as resulting from a complex interaction of constitutional *and* developmental influences.

Very young infants already differ from one another in several variables, including biologic functioning, autonomic reactivity, sensory alertness to stimuli, adaptability to change, characteristic moods, distractibility, and persistence. These innate endowments constitute each child's *temperament,* which interacts with the environment and caregivers in ways that accentuate and modify behavior (Millon, 1981).

Twin and adoption studies are the most useful research designs for investigating the effects of environment and heredity. Such studies have examined personality traits that may be associated with schizophrenia in a family member. Schizotypal and paranoid personality disorders have been shown to have a familial and genetic association with schizophrenia (Siever, Klar, 1986). There is evidence suggesting that borderline personality disorder also runs in families (Pfohl, 1986).

The rate of Axis I and Axis II disorders in families of patients with personality disorders is coming under increasing investigation. There are data supporting an association between borderline personality disorder and mood disorder, alcoholism, and substance abuse in relatives (Pfohl, 1986). A familial transmission of obsessive-compulsive personality has also been supported (Pfohl, 1986).

According to psychoanalytic theory, the infant is born with instinctual drives that are primarily aggressive and sexual in nature. Personality development, as understood by this theory, is a process in which the child learns to control his or her instinctual impulses in order to adapt and adjust to the family environment. Organization and stabilization of this effort for adaptation result in normal behavioral tendencies. During development, if a child's needs are too intense to be satisfied adequately or if expected needs are not satisfied because of lack of response from the environment, the resulting experience may serve as a trauma that may not be completely overcome. Resultant "fixations," which represent unfulfillment of those needs, can occur during any of the major phases of development (Kahana, Bibring, 1964). Disturbances at particular critical development phases will result in certain characteristic personality formations.

It is not possible within the confines of this text to discuss psychoanalytic and other theories of the development of personality disorders in depth, although it should be reiterated that authorities consider personality to be strongly influenced by early developmental influences, the nature and quality of relationships with the parents and siblings, and the psychological adaptations that the individual makes to both positive and negative aspects of the family experience. It is also assumed that although basic personality traits crystallize by late adolescence, experiences and significant relationships with other people later in life may modify the personality. Readers are referred to comprehensive textbooks of psychiatry and selected references for a more in-depth discussion of theories of personality development in general and for discussions of the pathogenesis of specific types of personality disorders (Meissner, 1985).

Supporting the role of biogenetic factors is evidence that patients with personality disorders differ from normal and psychiatric controls in a number of biologic parameters. Schizotypal patients have been shown to have abnormalities in platelet monoamine oxidase activity, plasma amine oxidase, and smooth pursuit eye movements (Pfohl, 1986). An inverse correlation has been found between serotonin levels in the cerebrospinal fluid and aggression and suicide attempts in borderline patients (Brown, Ebert, Goyer, et al., 1982). There exists evidence both for and against the finding that patients with borderline personality disorder have high rates of serum cortisol (a proposed biological marker of mood disturbance) in response to overnight dexamethasone suppression tests (Pfohl, 1986). EEG abnormalities—in particular, slow wave activity—have been demonstrated in both antisocial and borderline personality disorders (Pfohl, 1986). Although most of these studies are being used for research purposes at present, similar biologic tests may aid in personality evaluation in the future and lend credibility to the influence of biologic substrates on personality characteristics.

TREATMENTS

Among the treatment modalities for personality disorders are psychodynamic insight-oriented, supportive, interpersonal, behavioral, cognitive, and pharmacologic therapies. Unlike the other psychotherapies, *psychodynamic psychotherapy* specifically focuses on the personality structure and the major developmental experiences in childhood that have affected the individual. The other techniques are oriented more toward target symptoms but may have a beneficial impact on personality functioning.

The precise form that psychodynamic therapy takes may vary from time-limited therapy for several months to psychoanalysis for several years (Widiger, Frances, in press). Fundamental alteration of personality style is frequently an unrealistic goal.

Therefore, this form of therapy usually strives to improve interpersonal functioning by decreasing the *inflexible* nature of the maladaptive traits and increasing the individual's awareness of his or her behaviors. *The appropriateness of psychodynamic psychotherapy depends in part on the patient's psychological-mindedness and capability and motivation for insight and character change.* Patients with schizotypal, schizoid, paranoid, and antisocial traits are less likely to benefit from such a treatment than are patients with dependent, compulsive, avoidant, histrionic, passive-aggressive, and masochistic personality disorders (Frances, Widiger, 1986).

In contrast, *supportive* psychotherapy attempts to aid patients without challenging their basic defenses or attempting to change their fundamental character structure (Widiger, Frances, in press). Supportive treatment can help the patient through periods of medical, interpersonal, occupational, or other stresses by minimizing regression and maximizing compliance. For instance, these goals may be met by admiring and being empathic with the narcissistic patient, providing detailed information to the obsessive-compulsive patient, or maintaining an appropriate and nonintrusive distance from the schizoid patient. Although psychoanalytic therapy is used for narcissistic patients, a supportive and empathic approach may aid the patient in overcoming current narcissistic injuries (Widiger, Frances, in press). The borderline patient who has difficulty tolerating insight-oriented therapy may also benefit from this approach.

Interpersonally oriented psychotherapies are particularly suitable treatments because personality disorders often represent maladaptive interpersonal styles (Frances, Widiger, 1986). This technique can be practiced in *group, family, marital,* and *system-strategic* therapy. This therapy relies on the fact that personality styles frequently elicit complementary responses in others, including the therapist (Widiger, Frances, in press). In this treatment approach, the therapist assumes an interpersonal style that encourages more adaptive and flexible functioning in the patient in order to halt the usual pattern of mutually debilitating relations.

Behavioral therapy can be used to reduce target symptoms in appropriate patients. Behavioral techniques involving assertiveness training and graded exposures for social anxiety may be useful for dependent and avoidant patients, respectively (Liebowitz, Stone, Turkat, 1986). The schizoid patient may benefit from shaping his or her social behavior. Behavior therapy for patients with antisocial personality disorder may be useful in structured settings, but the behavioral changes observed in these patients may not be sustained (Widiger, Frances, in press).

Cognitive therapy focuses on central, irrational assumptions underlying patients' beliefs and behaviors. Because personality disorders involve debilitating cognitive styles, such a therapeutic approach may be particularly appropriate in patients with these disorders (Millon, 1981). For example, the masochistic-depressive prone individual may respond to a cognitive treatment similar to that used in treating depression. The borderline patient may benefit from addressing the exaggerated attitudes in order to develop more realistic perceptions of others. Cognitive techniques that focus on assumptions of threat and inadequacy may also be beneficial for the avoidant and dependent patient. The obsessive-compulsive patient may benefit by addressing his or her irrationally rigid, severe beliefs and moral standards (Widiger, Frances, in press).

Pharmacotherapy may be useful when it focuses on such features as mood dysregulation in borderline personality disorder, perceptual disturbances in schizotypal personality disorder, or anxiety in avoidant personality disorder. Low-dose neuroleptics have been found useful for anxiety and cognitive disturbances in schizotypal and borderline personality disorders (Liebowitz, Stone, Turkat, 1986). Antidepressant regimens, including the monoamine oxidase inhibitors, may be useful for mood disorders frequently seen in patients with other Axis II disorders.

There is growing literature on the treatment of personality disorders (Siever, Klar, 1986). This increased attention to Axis II conditions is appropriate, since most patients do have some maladaptive traits that will influence the course and treatment of Axis I syndromes. A treatment chosen for Axis I conditions that considers the patient's personality traits will optimize treatment course and response (Widiger, Frances, in press).

The Relationship Between Axis I and Axis II Diagnoses

The development of the multiaxial system in DSM-III reflected the recognition that personality disorders often coexist with, and impact on, the treatment of the acute psychiatric syndromes (Axis I). A patient's personality traits affect not only the doctor–patient relationship but also compliance and outcome. Axis II psychopathology has been shown to influence predisposition, presentation, course, and treatment response of Axis I conditions (Docherty, Fiester, Shea, 1986). The exact nature of the relationship between personality disorders and the major syndromes can be conceptualized in different ways. Certain personality traits may (1) predispose toward, (2) modify, (3) represent a complication of, (4) represent an attenuated form of, or (5) coexist independently with specific Axis I disorders (Docherty, Fiester, Shea, 1986). Below is a review of how specific personality disorders have been shown to be associated with Axis I conditions.

Mood Disorders

Many investigations of the incidence of personality disorders in patients with mood disorders have focused on borderline patients (see below). Up to 61% of patients with mood disorders have been shown to have borderline pathology Docherty, Fiester, Shea, 1986). Histrionic, dependent, and avoidant personality disorders also occur frequently in depressed patients (Pfohl, 1986). The presence of character pathology in depressives has been associated with a different clinical presentation than that seen in patients with major depression only. Specifically, the presence of borderline character disorder has been associated with increased anxiety, anger, substance abuse, and attempts at suicide (Docherty, Fiester, Shea, 1986). The presence of personality pathology in general has been correlated with earlier onset and poorer treatment outcome of depression (Docherty, Fiester, Shea, 1986).

By definition, patients with personality disorders are impaired in their ability to adjust to stress. Their inflexible behavioral patterns may, indeed, provoke problematic situations. Consequently, a person with character pathology will be more likely to develop depressive, anxiety, psychotic, and other Axis I disorders. Major depression, bipolar disorder, dysthymic disorder, and cyclothymic disorder have been shown to occur in 14 to 87% of borderline patients (Docherty, Fiester, Shea, 1986). These rates are substantially higher than would be expected for the general population. Antisocial, schizotypal, compulsive, passive-aggressive, histrionic, narcissistic, self-defeating, and dependent patients not uncommonly have mood disturbances as well (Docherty, Fiester, Shea, 1986).

Schizophrenia

Because of the chronic course of schizophrenia, in which personality alterations frequently occur during and after acute psychotic decompensation, it is often difficult to determine premorbid personality traits. McGlashan noted that the most frequently diagnosed personality disorder in schizophrenics is schizotypal, followed by borderline personality disorder (McGlashan, 1983). Schizotypal and borderline patients were reported to have a 55% and 16% to 24% chance, respectively, of developing schizophrenia (McGlashan, 1983). Other studies have noted much lower rates of overlap between schizophrenia and borderline personality disorder (Docherty, Fiester, & Shae, 1986).

Other Axis I Disorders

Both borderline and antisocial patients have been noted to have an increased incidence of alcoholism (Docherty, Fiester, Shea, 1986). In the borderline patient, substance abuse may reflect an attempt to alleviate affective instability. For the antisocial patient, alcoholism may either result from or initiate an antisocial lifestyle. Social hypersensitivity and perception of threat predispose schizotypal and paranoid patients to develop anxiety disorders.

THE DISORDERS

Included in each of the descriptions of the disorders presented below is an overview of psychiatric treatment, probable presentation in the medical setting, therapeutic strategies for the nonpsychiatric physician, and indications for psychiatric consultation. When evaluating a patient's psychopathology, attention should first be paid to the differential diagnosis of Axis I disorders. *This permits the clinician to determine whether or not a patient's symptoms represent an acute change or a long-lasting pattern.* When a chronic Axis I condition exists, such as dysthymia or an anxiety disorder, Axis II diagnoses can still coexist. Conversely, the presence of an Axis II disorder makes it more likely that an Axis I disorder also will exist.

Schizotypal Personality Disorder

Schizotypal personality disorder encompasses a combination of odd or peculiar behavior, speech, thought, and perception. Patients with such disorders are usually withdrawn and display idiosyncratic and odd speech patterns, eccentric beliefs, paranoid tendencies, perceptual illusion, unusual appearance, inappropriate affect, and social anxiety. When stressed, such a patient may lapse into brief breaks with reality. *Unlike the patient who has the fully developed syndrome of schizophrenia, frank hallucinations, or delusions, the schizotypal patient experiences subtle distortions of the environment.*

When seen in a psychiatric setting, a supportive, structured, and firm approach will help combat the schizotypal patient's misperceptions and fragile grasp of reality (Widiger, Frances, in press). A supportive therapeutic approach would serve to encourage the patient to become involved in activities that are not socially frightening. Social skills training may diminish eccentric behavior and odd appearance, and help the patient to feel more at ease in social settings.

Low-dose neuroleptics may alleviate the social anxiety and cognitive symptoms of schizotypal patients (Liebowitz, Stone, Turkat, 1986). Medical illness may accentuate underlying misperceptions of physical symptoms and possible treatments. As an example, an intravenous line may be viewed by the patient as a device containing something harmful; similar reactions may occur to other medication or to the physician. Basic trust in others is usually a major problem for these individuals—as it is for schizoid, paranoid, and borderline patients.

A physician who can detect these features, understand their significance for the patient's interpersonal relationships and perception of reality, be supportive, reality test, and respect the patient's need for privacy will ease the patient's hospital course substantially. The staff may be repelled by the patient's "strangeness" and underestimate the degree of attachment such a patient may have for them. It is important to educate the staff that this patient's peculiar behaviors are not meant to be provocative. Psychiatric consultation may be necessary for management of anxiety and cognitive disturbances.

Schizoid Personality Disorder

A central characteristic of schizoid personality disorder is the inability to form relationships or to respond to others in a meaningful manner, leading to social isolation. Indifference to others and lack of response to praise, criticism, or any feelings experienced by others is typical. Yet, beneath the surface of this indifference often exists a loneliness and a desire for close relationships. Such a patient frequently experiences little pleasure or pain and has an affect that is constricted and apathetic. Unlike a schizotypal patient, this patient does not experience cognitive distortions.

Group therapy with similar individuals may demonstrate to the patient that others are also introverted and socially awkward. Behavior therapy that helps the patient with social integration may also be of value (Liebowitz, Stone, Turkat, 1986). Because such patients dislike new contacts and intrusion into their privacy, medical illness and hospitalization are particularly troubling and anxiety-provoking. A typical response to disease would therefore be further withdrawal. A physician's goal for management should consist of accepting the patient's desire for privacy while still demonstrating interest and concern. Such a therapeutic approach will help engender a perception of the doctor as being both protective and benign.

Paranoid Personality Disorder

Paranoid personality disorder is exemplified by suspiciousness, mistrust, rigidity, and hypervigilance but not grossly psychotic or delusional beliefs. Such a patient is preoccupied with perceived exploitation and infidelity by others. Paranoid beliefs may result in hostility, irritability, anxiety, and an undercurrent of anger. The paranoid patient may be hard to distinguish from the schizotypal patient, since both display mistrust of others and social anxiety.

Supportive therapy may be most efficacious for such a patient. An approach that is open, honest, and nonconfrontational will be most likely to engender trust. If the therapist is perceived as a benign, objective, and friendly helper, the patient may be more inclined to entertain alternative explanations and perceptions (Liebowitz, Stone, Turkat, 1986).

Optimal management of a paranoid patient in a *medical* setting depends on the doctor's recognizing that the patient may believe his or her illness to be due to the inconsiderateness or malice of others. The patient is likely to respond to familiarity or joviality from the physician with withdrawal and suspicious misinterpretation (Nardo, 1986). This type of behavior may cause a physician to become more guarded with the patient, and such a reaction may only engender more distrust. To foster a trusting relationship with a paranoid patient, management should include clear explanations of procedures, medications, and results. The patient's suspicion and mistrust should be met with consideration, information, and impartial recommendation of procedures rather than with annoyance and exasperation.

Histrionic Personality Disorder

The patient with histrionic (formerly known as hysterical) personality disorder tends to be attention-seeking, self-dramatizing, excessively gregarious, seductive, manipulative, exhibitionistic, shallow, labile, vain, and demanding. Such a patient may, at times, be difficult to distinguish from the borderline or narcissistic patient, and some degree of overlap exists between them. Psychoanalytic psychotherapy has traditionally been the treatment for such patients. The following is a case vignette typifying a histrionic patient admitted to a general hospital.

A CASE STUDY

A 46-year-old woman was admitted for a mastectomy after a breast biopsy revealed a malignant tumor. She refused to be admitted to a four-bedded room, stating that she did not intend to share the facilities or staff with any other patients. Her flamboyant and gregarious manner initially ingratiated her to the staff. Her seductive dress and preoccupation with her appearance seemed to overshadow her concern over the implications of her upcoming surgery. After the procedure, her demands for care became so frequent as to interfere with the staff's ability to care for the other patients on the service. She required repeated reassurance and became excessively angered when the staff did not immediately fulfill her needs.

Medical illness threatens loss of attractiveness, strength, and achievement for any patient, but these are especially profound threats to histrionic patients, whose self-image, self-esteem, and self-worth usually depend on their ability to attract and hold the attention of others with their attractive appearance and entertaining behavior. Careful attention should also be paid to identifying the male histrionic patient, who will have the need to display increased masculinity as exemplified by a "macho" image and to elicit admiration (Nardo, 1986). The physician can greatly aid these patients by complimenting them in a nonpatronizing manner on their appearance and basically acknowledging their need for special attention, while not allowing himself or herself to become overwhelmed by demands. Partially fulfilling such patients' needs combined with limit setting will ease their acceptance of certain restrictions. It is important to convey to these patients that the limits being set do not reflect the doctor's impatience, but rather pressures with which the patient must comply to get the best possible treatment. This approach will offer these patients the knowledge that people are devoted to their care while recognizing the reality of limits.

Fundamental to understanding and treating the histrionic patient is an appreciation of the fact that these patients are fundamentally insecure and are extremely sensitive to rejection by others. Behavior that may be superficially interpreted as manipulative, dependent, or even seductive is usually an effort to obtain love, support, attention and reassurance, which the patient may have been deprived of in childhood. If rejection actually occurs, or if the patient perceives that his or her needs are not being fully met—which is often difficult to do—explosive, dramatic, and turbulent outbursts of emotion may follow. Awareness of the core personality dynamics in such patients will help the physician to manage their behavior and demands in an objective yet empathic manner.

Narcissistic Personality Disorder

The narcissistic patient, in the extreme form, is egocentric, grandiose, entitled, shallow, exploitative, arrogant, and preoccupied with fame, wealth, and achievement and generally lacks empathy and consideration for the feelings of others. Such a person is, nevertheless, exquisitely hypersensitive to evaluation or criticism by others. Narcissistic individuals crave admiring attention and praise from others and place excessive emphasis on displaying the accoutrements of beauty, power, fame, and wealth. They are typically exploitative of others and use their relationships to meet their own selfish needs with little consideration for the needs of the other person. Hence, they usually show a profound lack of empathy for others in their relationships. Regardless of the situation, they feel that they are "entitled" to special rights, attention, privileges, and consideration.

Medical illness is a blow to self-esteem, particularly if it separates these patients from their admirers and other sources of support. The narcissist may try to escape the possibility of illness either by ignoring the effects of the illness or by totally denying its existence. An example of such a patient would be the person with Crohn's disease who refuses to take steroids for fear of the disfigurement caused by this medication (Nardo, 1986). Such a patient will benefit most from a medical setting where he or she feels admired, accepted, and appreciated. This is obviously difficult to do.

Psychiatric treatments ranging from long-term insight-oriented to brief, more supportive therapy are useful. These patients may be difficult to treat psychiatrically because of their tendency to be competitive and to alternately devalue or idealize the therapist. Cognitive techniques and systematic desensitization may be helpful for overcoming harsh self-criticism and evaluation anxiety. Special psychoanalytic techniques using empathic rather than confrontational approaches, originally devised by Heinz Kohut, have been recommended in the treatment of these patients.

Antisocial Personality Disorder

The antisocial (alternatively known as sociopathic) patient typically lacks empathy, social responsibility, guilt, and a sense of social, moral, and interpersonal responsibility. Such a person displays a consistent pattern of behavior that disregards the conventional limitations imposed by society. A veneer of charm and a smooth and ingratiating seductiveness that is hard to resist may mask disregard for the rights and feelings of others, because these patients are interested only in meeting their own needs.

Impulsivity, as manifested by frequent physical fights and abusive behavior, combined with a lack of appropriate responses to obvious consequences of one's actions are apparent. Encounters with the law and other authorities are frequent, as is repetitive criminal behavior.

In the psychiatric setting, antisocial personality disorder is viewed as one of the most difficult personality disorders to treat. Behavior therapy within very structured environments, like prison, may be useful. These patients may benefit from a therapeutic technique that attempts to channel their sensation-seeking behavior into more constructive activities (Liebowitz, Stone, Turkat, 1986). These patients are at high risk for suicide, depression, alcoholism, and substance abuse. In the medical setting, their manipulative behavior and disregard for the staff make them particularly difficult to treat. While avoiding the temptation to be punitive, the physician should set limits and not be manipulated or deceived into prescribing excessive medications.

Borderline Personality Disorder

Borderline personality disorder encompasses a behavioral pattern of intense and chaotic relationships with fluctuating and extreme attitudes toward others. In the extreme form, these patients are affectively unstable, impulsive, engage in self-destructive behaviors, and lack a clear sense of identity. Suicide attempts may be a frequent response to rejections or disappointments in their interpersonal relationships. They often alternate between viewing themselves—and others—as "all good" (idealizing) and as "all bad" (devaluing). Their personal lives tend to be chaotic, unstable, and marked by frequent disappointments and rejections. An underlying mood of chronic anger and depression is ubiquitous. These patients are prone to alcoholism and substance abuse.

During times of crisis or rejection, or under the influence of alcohol or substance abuse, these patients may experience transient psychotic breaks lasting from hours to days. They may show poor control of emotions and impulses that may result in aggressive and destructive behavior toward themselves and others. Borderline personality disorder frequently overlaps with histrionic, schizotypal, and antisocial personality disorders.

When diagnosing a borderline patient, attention should be drawn to the possible coexistence of a mood disorder that should be treated. Various treatment modalities have been used to treat borderline patients in the psychiatric setting. Although intensive, interpretive techniques may be useful, a more supportive, cognitive, and problem-solving approach may be most appropriate (Widiger, Frances, in press). Borderline patients frequently reenact struggles from childhood, which are often of a depriving or abusive nature, in their current relationships with their physicians by displays of excessive dependency, unrealistic expectations, and anger, hostility, and suicidal depression when their emotional needs are not met.

Self-destructive behavior may be treated by behavioral techniques or medication if it is associated with disturbances of mood, impulse, or cognition. The physician must maintain an empathic attitude while setting fair and consistently enforced limits on disruptive, manipulative, or drug-seeking behaviors. Cognitive techniques may diminish the split and exaggerated attitudes by aiding the patient to develop more realistic perceptions of self and others.

Pharmacotherapy may be useful to treat particular target symptoms. Tricyclic antidepressants, lithium, and monoamine oxidase inhibitors may be valuable in the treatment of mood disturbances (Gunderson, 1986). Lithium may attenuate impulsive, self-destructive behavior as well as anger. Neuroleptics may lessen distorted cognition (Widiger, Frances, in press). The use of psychotropics in this population may be risky, however, because of these patients' tendency to impulsively attempt suicide by overdosing during crises.

Medical illness, like other stresses, may be met with reactions ranging from intense anger to overwhelming anxiety and depression. Borderline patients may be unclear as to the cause of their physical discomfort. They may blame the pain on others and may perceive painful procedures as hostile and inappropriately intrusive acts. Because of their increased anxiety and regressive behavior in stressful situations, such patients may expect unrealistic and excessive degrees of attention from the staff. If their expectations are not met immediately, these patients may become increasingly hateful and angry.

Provocative and hostile behaviors, which include the tendency to devalue or feel devalued by caregivers, should be met by a stable and calm reaction, rather than by a yielding to demands or a rejection of the patient. The physician can help by recognizing the dependency needs of these patients and by providing hope with a sense of stability. Psychiatric consultation may be useful if the patient's extreme response to illness cannot be adequately treated by the medical staff or is accompanied by psychotic symptoms and suicidal behavior. The staff should be educated to expect the patient's tendency to idealize some caregivers and devalue others. Open and continued communication among physicians and staff who are treating the patient is absolutely critical to prevent "splitting"—that is, playing one caregiver against another—which is a classic manipulative technique employed by these patients.

Dependent Personality Disorder

Dependent personality encompasses a pattern of excessive reliance on others that is reflected in the affected person's tendency to permit others to make decisions for him or her, to feel helpless when alone, to subjugate his or her needs to those of others, to tolerate mistreatment, and to be unable to function when self-assertiveness is required. It is not uncommon for such a patient to be living with a controlling, domineering, overprotective, and infantalizing person. The avoidant and dependent personality disorders share the characteristics of interpersonal insecurity, desire for relationships, and low self-esteem.

These patients may benefit from insight-oriented, cognitive, and group therapy. Assertiveness and social skills training may also be useful for both dependent and avoidant patients. When medically ill, these individuals may complain about their suffering and clearly delineate how the physician is unable to allay it. Such patients may become angry and increasingly frustrated if their treatment fails to produce expected results. The dependent patient will often want the physician to "make all the decisions." When informing the patient about procedures, therefore, the physician should be prepared to be very active in treatment planning. Diagnosis of dependent personality disorder in the medical setting is difficult because physically ill patients often display an increase in dependent traits as part of the general behavioral regression that frequently accompanies physical illness.

Avoidant Personality Disorder

The avoidant patient is inhibited, introverted, anxious, and fearful of closeness to, and rejection by, others. Additional features include low self-esteem, apprehension, social awkwardness, and a chronic fear of being embarrassed. The criteria for social withdrawal overlap with those for schizoid personality disorder. However, the schizoid patient is indifferent to others, whereas the avoidant person desires relationships yet is too shy and insecure to obtain them.

Both insight-oriented and cognitive techniques may benefit the avoidant patient. Assertiveness training and behavior therapy with exposure to the anxiety-producing stimulus may lessen fearfulness. Group therapy will aid the patient in overcoming social anxiety and in obtaining more interpersonal trust and rapport. Anxiety and depression, which may develop in avoidant patients, may be treated by anxiolytics and antidepressants, respectively, depending on their Axis I diagnosis (Liebowitz, Stone, Turkat, 1986). Medical illness may be embarrassing to the avoidant patient both because he or she has to discuss symptoms and because he or she is being forced into a new, contact-filled situation in the hospital. Although the avoidant patient will be more fearful at first, both this patient and the dependent person will soon become quite reliant upon, and desiring of, contact with the doctor. The physician will make the patient feel more at ease in the medical setting by developing an alliance in a timely manner. Such a patient may benefit from not having new and unfamiliar staff and students frequently in rounds at the bedside. Responding to the patient's anxiety with a calm and reassuring demeanor will significantly help the patient to deal with both illness and hospitalization. Physicians should nevertheless avoid taking on a patronizing or parent-like role in treating these individuals and should expect them to take responsibility for their treatment and to participate in the decision-making process.

Obsessive-Compulsive Personality

The person with obsessive-compulsive personality disorder tends to be perfectionistic, constricted, and excessively disciplined. Behavior is rigid, formal, emotionally cool, distant, intellectualizing, and detailed. These patients may be driven, aggressive, competitive, and impatient, with a chronic sense of time pressure and an inability to relax. They have an excessive tendency to be in control of themselves, others, and life situations. They are often tormented with anxiety over matters of uncertainty and ambiguity. Because of their need for perfection, they often have difficulty making decisions and are prone to procrastinate or "obsess." On the other hand, other types of obsessional patients have a hard-driving urge to do "everything now" and expect the same level of efficiency from others. An undercurrent of anger is often visible in their general demeanor, although open expression of anger—or any other emotion—is difficult for them. Superficially, these patients may appear to be drab and monotonous personalities who drone on in excruciating detail. They are usually preoccupied with, and withholding of, money. They are often "hoarders" of both money and other items.

These individuals are also likely to be overly concerned with productivity and achievement. They usually have rigid moralistic attitudes toward life—especially sex—and are prone to criticism and moralistic judgment of others because of their rigid superego. They may also be preoccupied with orderliness, neatness, and cleanliness and expect others to meet their expectations. Inflexibility, stubbornness, rigidity, and a need for control dominate their interpersonal relationships.

These patients can benefit from both insight-oriented and cognitive techniques. Following is a case vignette exemplifying such a patient.

A CASE STUDY

A 50-year-old male lawyer with no prior medical history presented to the emergency room with crushing substernal chest pain, shortness of breath, and nausea. He reluctantly cancelled a business meeting to come for an evaluation. Laboratory studies and an electrocardiogram confirmed an acute myocardial infarction. The patient adamantly refused admission, stating that his work could not go unattended. His wife described him as a perfectionist "workaholic" who worked 7 days a week without vacations. He adhered to this rigid and demanding schedule and faulted those who did not subscribe to his standards and morals. He always prided himself on how he was in control of his business and personal affairs and could not allow his health to interfere with his obligations.

When managing a compulsive patient who has a medical problem, the physician must appreciate how illness might represent a disruption in the patient's work, orderly lifestyle, obligations, and sense of control. His or her response may be to oscillate between minimizing the illness's importance and being overwhelmed with anxiety, anger, and fear of the unknown.

These patients usually will seek as much knowledge as possible about their condition so that they can plan their hospital stay and know exactly when they will be able to return to work. Unlike dependent patients, compulsive patients will not want the doctor to be the primary decision maker and will argue and bicker until they feel they are in control and can make their own decisions about their care. Physicians may approach these patients' overconcern with work by acknowledging the importance of their work but pointing out that inappropriate actions will have harmful consequences and that taking care of themselves will allow them to go on with their responsibilities—that recuperation is a form of "work" in itself. Recognition of these patients' tendencies should lead the physician to treat them by inviting their active cooperation and by providing them with enough information to facilitate a rational understanding of their disease and its treatment. The physician should deal with power struggles and stubbornness by "backing off" and putting decisions solely in the patient's hands.

Passive-Aggressive Personality Disorder

Passive-aggressive personality disorder is reflected in a pattern of passive and indirect resistance to authority, responsibility, and obligations. Associated symptoms include complaining, irritability, whining, discontent, and disillusionment. Anger is usually expressed indirectly through resistance, delays, negativism, procrastination, and undermining attempts to help them.

Because these individuals cannot express their anger or resentment directly, they display hostile or resentful feelings by postponing or cancelling appointments, procrastinating over assignments and deadlines, not returning phone calls, withholding information, pouting, not paying bills, and being chronically late. When confronted with their actions or queried about being angry or resentful, the patient will usually deny any anger initially and evade dealing with the situation directly.

Social skills training and assertiveness training may help these patients develop alternative ways to deal with frustration. Insight-oriented therapy and behavioral techniques are also useful for such patients. The passive-aggressive patient may undermine procedures and treatment plans suggested by the physician as noted above. It is important to avoid both the power struggles and the withdrawal from the patient that may arise in these circumstances. If the patient is allowed to have a say in treatment, he or she will likely become a more facilitating and active participant in the care.

CLINICAL PEARLS

- A personality disorder is a constellation of intense chronic behavioral traits that result in enduring maladaptive behaviors across many situations.
- These disorders are not uncommon and will influence how a person reacts to the

(continued)

CLINICAL PEARLS (continued)

stress of medical illness; elements of a personality disorder are almost always exacerbated by stress and may subside when the crisis is over.

- Physicians who recognize their patients' personality styles and coping mechanisms will be in a better position to understand and appropriately respond to their characteristic responses to illness.
- Axis I and Axis II conditions frequently coexist, necessitating an evaluation for mood, anxiety, psychotic, and alcohol and substance abuse disorders.
- The hallmark of a personality disorder is repetitive patterns of problematic interpersonal relationships. Persons with severe personality disorders usually tend to deny their contribution to this pattern and externalize blame for their problems.
- A classic sign of when a physician is dealing with a personality disorder is when the doctor feels angry, frustrated, defeated, manipulated, or irritated by the patient. Patients with some types of personality disorders may be flirtatious and seductive yet "turn" on the physician suddenly.
- An objective analysis of the problematic aspects of the patient's behavior can usually only be achieved when the physician "backs off," gains some distance, and reviews the situation formally or informally with a colleague or psychiatric consultant.
- Effective management of patients with personality disorder traits depends, first, on assessing the problematic aspects of the personality and of how these are affecting compliance and the doctor–patient relationship, and second, on developing a plan adapted to accommodate the patient's personality style and characteristic ways of dealing with others.
- Adjunctive psychopharmacology agents may be helpful in treating concurrent Axis I disorders, but the patient's potential to overdose should be carefully assessed.

ANNOTATED BIBLIOGRAPHY

Charney DS, Nelson, CJ, Quinlan DM: Personality traits and disorder in depression. Am J Psychiatry 138:1601–1604, 1981

   A good description of the occurrence of Axis II pathology in depression.

Epstein S, O'Brien E: The person-situational debate in historical and current perceptive. Psychol Bull 988:513–537, 1985

   Highlights issues to be considered in diagnosing a personality disorder.

Fisher FD, Leigh H: Models of the doctor–patient relationship. In Michels R, Cavenar JO, Brodie HKH et al (eds): Psychiatry. Philadelphia, JB Lippincott, 1986

   Emphasizes the physician's obligation to consider the patient's personality in assessing the optimal doctor–patient relationship.

Frances AJ: The DSM-III personality disorders section: A commentary. Am J Psychiatry 137:1050–1054, 1980

   Offers an overview of the formulation of Axis II disorders.

Fogel BS, Martin C: Personality disorders in the medical setting. In Stoudemire A, Fogel BS (eds): Principles of Medical Psychiatry. Orlando, FL, Grune & Stratton, 1987, pp. 253–270.

   Reviews in detail specific strategies for assessing and monitoring personality disorders in the medical setting.

Phohl B, Stangl D, Zimmerman M: The implication of DSM-III personality disorders for patients with major depression. J Affect Disord 7:309–319, 1984

> Emphasizes the effects of personality disorders on the outcome of depression.

Meissner WW: Theories of personality and psychopathology: Classical psychoanalysis. In Kaplan HI, Sadock BJ (eds): Comprehensive Textbook of Psychiatry, 4th ed, vol 1. Baltimore, Williams & Wilkins, 1985

> An in-depth overview of psychoanalytic perspectives on personality development and personality disorders.

Soloff PH, George A, Nathan RS, et al: Progress in pharmacotherapy of borderline disorders. Arch Gen Psychiatry 43:691–697, 1986

> A comprehensive review of treatment options for borderline patients.

Stangl P, Pfohl B, Zimmerman M, et al: A structured interview for the DSM-III personality disorders: A preliminary report. Arch Gen Psych 42:591–596, 1985

> Reviews the use of a structured instrument that is used to diagnose personality pathology.

Stoudemire A, Thompson TL: The borderline personality in the medical setting. Annals of Internal Medicine 96:76–79, 1982.

> Practical management of the borderline personality in the medical setting.

Weissman MM, Prusoff BA, Lkerman GL: Personality and the prediction of long-term outcome of depression. Am J Psychiatry 135:798–800, 1978

> Emphasizes the impact of personality pathology on outcome of depression.

Widiger TA, Hyler SE: Axis I/II interactions. In Michels R, Cavenar JO, Brodie HKH, et al (eds): Psychiatry. Philadelphia, JB Lippincott, 1986

> Reviews the implications of the comorbidity of Axis I and II pathology.

REFERENCES

Allport G: Personality: A psychological interpretation. New York, Holt & Company, 1937

American Psychiatric Association: Diagnostic and statistical manual of mental disorder, 3rd ed., revised. Washington, DC, American Psychiatric Association, 1987

Brown GL, Ebert MH, Goyer PF et al: Aggression, suicide and serotonin: Relationships to CSF amine metabolites. Am J Psychiatry 139:741–746, 1982

Docherty JP, Fiester SJ, Shea T: Syndrome diagnosis and personality disorder. In Frances AJ, Hales RE (eds): American Psychiatric Association Annual Review, vol 5. Washington, DC, American Psychiatric Press, 1986

Frances AJ, Widiger T: The classification of personality disorders: An overview of problems and solutions. In Frances AJ, Hales RE (eds): American Psychiatric Association Annual Review, vol 5. Washington, DC, American Psychiatric Press, 1986

Gunderson J: Pharmacotherapy for patients with borderline personality disorder. Arch Gen Psychiatry 43:698–700, 1986

Kahana RL, Bibring GL: Personality types in medical management. In Zinberg NE (ed): Psychiatry and Medical Practice in a General Hospital. New York, International Universities Press, 1964

Kaplan H: History of psychosomatic medicine. In Kaplan H, Sadock J (eds): Comprehensive Textbook of Psychiatry/IV. London, Williams & Wilkins, 1983

Liebowitz MR, Stone MH, Turkat ID: Treatment of personality disorders. In Frances AJ, Hale RE (eds): American Psychiatric Association Annual Review, vol 5. Washington, DC, American Psychiatric Press, 1986

Meissner WW: Theories of personality and psychopathology: Classical psychoanalysis. In Kaplan HI, Sadock BJ (eds): Comprehensive Textbook of Psychiatry, 4th ed, vol 1. Baltimore, Williams & Wilkins, 1985

Merikangas KR, Weisssman MM: Epidemiology of DSM-III Axis II Personality Disorders. In Frances AJ, Hales RE (eds): American Psychiatric Association Annual Review, vol 5, pp 258–278. Washington, DC, American Psychiatric Press, 1986

Millon T: Disorders of personality: DSM-III Axis II. New York, Wiley, 1981

McGlashan TH: The borderline syndrome: II. Is it a variant of schizophrenia or affective disorder? Arch Gen Psychiatry 40:1319–1323, 1983

Nardo JM: The personality in the medical setting: A psychodynamic understanding. In Michels R, Cavenar JO, Brodie HKH, et al (eds): Psychiatry. Philadelphia, JB Lippincott, 1986

Pfohl B: Personality disorders. In Winoker G, Clayton P (eds): The Medical Basis of Psychiatry. Philadelphia, WB Saunders, 1986

Rutter M: Resilience in the face of adversity: Protective factors and resistance to psychiatric disorder. Br J Psychiatry 147:598–611, 1985

Siever LF, Klar H: A review of DSM-III criteria for the personality disorders. In Frances AJ, Hales RE (eds): American Psychiatric Association Annual Review, vol 5. Washington, DC, American Psychiatric Press, 1986

Tyrer P, Strauss J, Cicchetti D: Temporal reliability of personality in psychiatric patients. Psychological Med 13:393–398, 1983

Widiger T, Frances A: Interviews and inventories for the measurement of personality disorders. Clin Psychol Rev 7:49–75, 1987

Widiger TA, Frances A: Personality disorders. In Talbott JA, Hales RE, Yudofsky S. (eds): Textbook of Psychiatry, (pp 621–648) Washington, DC, American Psychiatric Press, 1988

6

Mood Disorders

Emile D. Risby, S. Craig Risch, and Alan Stoudemire

The prevalence of mood disorders in the United States is conservatively estimated to be between 5 and 8% for the general population. Some studies have estimated that from 13 to 20% of the population has some depressive symptoms at any given time (Weissman, Boyd, 1984). Data from the National Institutes of Mental Health Environmental Catchment Area project reveal that the approximate 6-month prevalence for mood disorders in the general population is as follows: major depression, 2 to 3%; dysthymic disorder, 2%; adjustment disorder with depressed mood, 2 to 3%; and bipolar disorder, 0.3% (Myers et al., 1984). In some studies, the prevalence of bipolar illness in industrialized nations was found to be as high as 0.60 to 0.88% (Weissman, Myers, 1978; Helgason, 1979). In general medical settings, which select for patients with emotional distress and physical illness, prevalence rates for depression vary from 5 to 15%. Studies in both the United States and Europe suggest that at any one time, approximately 2 to 3% of the population is hospitalized or seriously impaired because of major mood disturbances (Goodwin, Jamison, 1984). Thus, collectively, mood disorders constitute a major public health problem.

"Depression" can be used to describe an array of conditions, including normal fluctuations in mood, feelings of demoralization, episodes of bereavement, and transient psychological reactions to injury or loss (Willner, 1985). In addition, the complaint of depression can be seen in almost every psychiatric disorder. Although all of the above conditions may be associated with a depressed mood, in the clinical context the term "depression" refers to more than just a depressed mood state. Clinically, depression is a *syndrome* comprising a mood disorder, psychomotor changes, and a variety of cognitive and vegetative disturbances. And while all of these symptoms may be present in the person with depression, none (not even depressed mood itself) is essential for the diagnosis!

There are many signs and symptoms of depression. The hallmarks of depression are a subjective sense of dysphoria (sadness) and an inability to derive pleasure from life (anhedonia). Depressed individuals often feel discouraged, defeated, helpless, hopeless, and unable to cope with life. Life often loses its meaning or there is a pervasive sense of boredom and emptiness. Those affected may begin to think of themselves in negative terms, feel like failures, or feel that their families would be better off without them. They may become so self-critical and feel that life is so hopeless and worthless that they contemplate suicide. Severely depressed individuals find it impossible to motivate themselves to carry out even the most common day-to-day tasks. They may develop physical symptoms, including headaches, constipation, gastrointestinal distress, fatigue, lethargy, and difficulty with concentration and memory. "Vegetative" symptoms such as insomnia or a fragmented sleep pattern, and decreased appetite with weight loss are common.

The mood disturbance opposite of depression is mania. Although a heightened

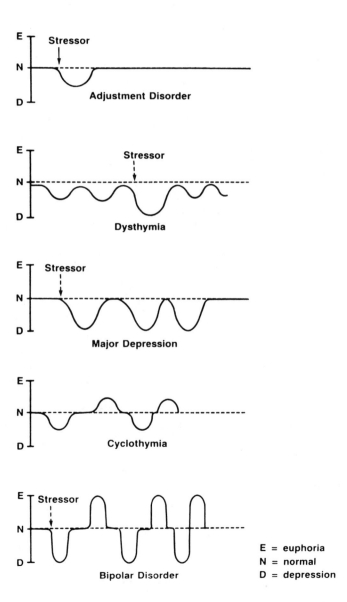

Adjustment Disorder

Dysthymia

Major Depression

Cyclothymia

Bipolar Disorder

E = euphoria
N = normal
D = depression

sense of euphoria is typical, anger and irritability may be the predominant feature in some cases. The manic patient may be hyperverbal, hyperactive, overconfident, adventuresome, and irrational.

It is only when the above signs and symptoms occur with considerable frequency and severity that a formal psychiatric diagnosis of "mood disorder" can be made. In the United States, the Diagnostic and Statistical Manual of Mental Disorders (DSM-III-R) (American Psychiatric Association, 1987) provides the most widely used system for diagnosing psychiatric illnesses. The primary mood disorders, as identified by the DSM-III-R, are adjustment disorder (with depressed mood), dysthymia, cyclothymia, major depression, bipolar disorder, organic mood disorders, and depressive disorders not otherwise specified (NOS). The type of mood disorder an individual has is determined by a number of factors, including (1) number and type of symptoms, (2) severity of symptoms, (3) duration of symptoms, (4) what happens when the patient is not depressed, and (5) the absence or presence of medical or other psychiatric illnesses. A schematic representation of some of the major mood disorders is depicted in Figure 6-1.

ADJUSTMENT DISORDER WITH DEPRESSED MOOD

In the DSM-III-R, an adjustment disorder (Table 6-1) is defined as a psychological disorder brought on by identifiable psychological stressors (such as divorce, job loss, family difficulties) that leads to maladaptive impairment in social, occupational, or interpersonal functioning. Strictly defined, the symptoms should have persisted for no longer than 6 months and have occurred within 3 months of the precipitating

◄ **Figure 6–1.** *Major mood disorders. An adjustment disorder can occur at any time and in anyone, if psychosocial stressors are severe. The affected person usually recovers, however, and regains previous levels of functioning. Dysthymia is a chronic mood disorder that has no discrete onset and is characterized by a chronically dysphoric mood. The severity of the dysphoria may fluctuate but the individual is "depressed" more times than not and has no significant periods of euphoria but may have some brief periods of euthymic mood. Major depressive episodes may develop in patients with dysthymic disorders even in the absence of any identifiable psychosocial stressors. Unipolar depressions are characterized by recurrent major depressive episodes that are separated by periods of euthymia. Early depressive episodes may be associated with psychosocial stressors, but later episodes seem to occur independent of environmental events. Note that the interval between episodes appears to get progressively shorter with time. Cyclothymia is a chronic mood disorder characterized by numerous affective episodes of insufficient severity or duration to meet the criteria for major depression or mania. Although the mood swings are diagramed as alternating with one another, there may be successive episodes of one mood state before an episode of the other occurs. There may also be periods of euthymia between these affective episodes. In bipolar disorders, major depressive and manic episodes occur in the same individual. Again, psychosocial issues may be identified early in the course of the illness but a more autonomous course soon develops. Note the tendency of the euthymic periods to shorten with time.*

Table 6–1 **Criteria for Adjustment Disorder***

1. The condition develops as a psychological reaction to identifiable stressors or events.
2. The reaction clearly reflects a change in the individual's normal personality and can be distinguished as different from the person's usual style of functioning.
3. The psychological reaction is maladaptive in that normal functioning (including social and occupational functioning) is grossly impaired or the reaction is in excess of what would normally be expected of others in similar circumstances.
4. The psychological reaction is not an exacerbation of some other mental disorder.
5. The reaction begins within 3 months of the stressor(s) but resolves within 6 months of its onset.

*May present primarily as anxiety, depression, or mixed features.
(Adapted from American Psychiatric Association: Diagnostic and Statistical Manual of Mental Disorders, Third edition, Revised. Washington, DC, American Psychiatric Association, 1987)

stressful event. Furthermore, it is assumed that the symptoms will remit when the stressors the patient is encountering are resolved (American Psychiatric Association, 1987).

There is no way to predict who will develop an adjustment disorder in the wake of adverse circumstances (e.g., physical illness, death of loved one). The severity of the adjustment disorder does not always parallel the intensity of the precipitating event. The important factor appears to be the relevance or meaning of the event (stressor) to the individual and the ability of the individual to "cope" or manage the stress. Patients with poor coping skills or inadequate social supports may be more prone to develop adjustment disorders than those with good coping skills and strong social supports.

In general, adjustment disorders with depressed mood are relatively transient and are not accompanied by the major cognitive symptoms seen in major depression (see below). For example, patients with adjustment disorders feel bad about their situation, but not necessarily about themselves. *An adjustment disorder with depressed mood is not necessarily a less serious form of depression, however, and may cause major problems in the patient's life as well as suicidal behavior.* It differs primarily from a major depressive disorder in the duration of the symptoms (less than 6 months) and the improvement in symptoms when the stressor is removed or a new level of adaptation (coping) is achieved. Note that depressed mood is only one of the nine types of maladaptive adjustment responses that may occur in response to a psychosocial stressor as defined by the DSM-III-R. Although adjustment disorders generally can be managed by the empathic primary care provider, the development of extreme withdrawal, hopelessness, or suicidal ideations, or failure to improve as circumstances improve, are clear indications for psychiatric referral. Treatment of adjustment disorders includes supportive psychotherapy, psychosocial interventions, and, occasionally, time-limited pharmacotherapy to alleviate specific target symptoms (e.g., insomnia).

DYSTHYMIA

The essential feature of dysthymia (depressive neurosis) is a *chronically depressed mood* (or possibly an irritable mood in children or adolescents), present for most of the day and occurring on more days than not, for at least 2 years (1 year for children or adolescents). Brief periods of normal mood may be present within the 2-year diagnostic period for adults but should not have lasted more than 2 months. In addition to a depressed mood, there must be some associated symptoms, such as sleep disturbance, appetite disturbance, low energy, hopelessness, and low self-esteem (American Psychiatric Association, 1987; Table 6-2). The diagnosis is not made if there is clear evidence of a major depressive episode during the 2-year period, if the disturbance is superimposed on another psychiatric disorder, or if the disturbance is judged to be induced by a concurrent medical problem or by medications. Dysthymia is classified as primary or secondary based on the presence or absence of a preexisting "non-mood" disorder, and is further divided into early or late onset based on whether the illness developed before or after age 21 (American Psychiatric Association, 1987). Dysthymia often arises in childhood or late adolescence and may become inextricably intertwined into the individual's personality, behavior and way of looking at life.

The differentiation of dysthymia from major depression can be difficult (Table 6-3). Remember that the depressed mood of dysthymia is chronic (at least 2 years) without a clear onset, is relatively persistent (patient has only brief periods of relief from depression) and is nonpsychotic in nature. The mood disturbance in patients with major depression (as will be discussed in detail later) generally has a period of

Table 6-2 **Criteria for Dysthymia**

---

1. There is a chronic, mildly depressed mood state that is generally present most of the day, on more days than not, and for a period of at least 2 years (1 year in children and adolescents).
2. There is never a 2-month period where there are no depressive symptoms.
3. The depression is associated with at least two of the following:
   I. Vegetative Symptoms
      Sleep disturbance
      Appetite disturbance
      Decreased energy or fatigue
   II. Cognitive Symptoms
      Low self-esteem
      Feeling of hopelessnes
      Poor concentration or difficulty making decisions
4. There is no unequivocal evidence of a major depressive episode during the *first 2 years* of the disturbance or of any other major mental disorder *during the course* of the illness.
5. There is no evidence of an organic etiology.

(Adapted from American Psychiatric Association: Diagnostic and Statistical Manual of Mental Disorders, Third edition, Revised. Washington, DC, American Psychiatric Association, 1987)

Table 6–3 **Comparison of Depressive Disorders**

	ADJUSTMENT DISORDER	DYSTHYMIA	MAJOR DEPRESSIVE EPISODE
Onset	Sudden	No identifiable onset (no history of sustained normal mood during adulthood)	Gradual onset (but period of normal functioning during adulthood can be identified)
Precipitating event	Always	None	Occasionally
Duration	Less than 6 months	At least 2 years	2 weeks to 2 years
Response to treatment	Good	Poor	Good

gradual onset, is episodic in nature (with periods of normal functioning between episodes) and may reach psychotic proportions. Although patients with dysthymia may be socially and occupationally impaired, patients with major depressions are often severely incapacitated by their depression. It is possible however, for patients with dysthymia to develop a major depressive episode. This combination of dysthymia and major depression is often referred to as a "double depression" (Keller, Lavori, Endicott, 1983).

Dysthymia in the psychoanalytic literature was generally looked on as a form of neurosis and/or personality disorder arising out of abnormal developmental life experiences. This type of depression was thought to stem from injuries to the individual's self-esteem that could be caused by a lack of nurturing, love, and acceptance in the home. Excessive criticism from parents could be incorporated into the child's own conscience (superego) causing the development of a personality marked by harsh self-criticism. Other developmental experiences thought to lead to dysthymia include multiple losses or separations from parents as a child, parental loss through death or divorce, neglect, sexual and/or physical abuse and alcoholism in the home. (Many of these same developmental factors have been identified in patients with major depression as well). Children of depressed parents may develop "depressive personalities" by identifying and incorporating certain aspects of their parents' feelings and attitudes into their own sense of self. Individuals with dysthymia often experience problems in their interpersonal relationships. These individuals often feel inadequate, unlovable, insecure, and lack the ability to appreciate their value to others. Some individuals may turn to alcohol or substance abuse to soothe these feelings and quell their sense of dysphoria and emptiness.

Dysthymia should not, however, be considered as just a "psychological" disorder. There are many patients with dysthymia who show vegetative and biological abnormalities that may be responsive to antidepressant medications (Akiskal, 1983). Treatment of the dysthymic patient therefore may include insight-oriented psychotherapy, cognitive therapy, behavioral therapy, and pharmacotherapy. Psychopharmacology may be particularly helpful in those patients with a family history of mood disorders and evidence of abnormal neuroendocrine functioning (see below).

MAJOR DEPRESSIONS (UNIPOLAR AND BIPOLAR DEPRESSION)

Major depression is a serious psychiatric disorder that is set apart from adjustment disorder and dysthymia by the severity of the mood and cognitive disturbances and the presence of significant somatic symptoms. The diagnostic criteria for a major depressive episode (including melancholic and psychotic subtypes) are listed in Table 6-4. The distinction of unipolar or bipolar depression is based on the presence or absence of a past history of mania or hypomania (see Bipolar Disorder below). "Depression" as defined by the DSM-III-R may represent a heterogeneous group of disorders with overlapping symptoms and etiologies (Gold, Goodwin, Chrousos, 1988). One subgroup however, the melancholic depressives, may be a more biologically homogeneous group. This group, characterized by early morning awakening, anorexia, and diurnal variation in mood, crosses the boundaries of unipolar and bipolar illnesses and accounts for 40 to 60% of all hospitalizations for depression (Klerman, 1984).

Table 6–4 **Criteria for a Major Depressive Episode**

1. There is a 2-week period of maladaptive functioning (i.e., a clear change from previous functioning) in which five of the following symptoms are present and in which one of the symptoms is either depressed mood or loss of interest or pleasure.
   a. depressed mood
   b. inability to experience pleasure or markedly diminished interest in pleasurable activities
   c. appetite disturbance (more than 5% change in body weight within 1 month)
   d. sleep disturbance
   e. psychomotor disturbance
   f. fatigue or loss of energy
   g. feelings of worthlessness or excessive or inappropriate guilt
   h. diminished ability to concentrate or indecisiveness
   i. recurrent thoughts of death of suicidal ideations
2. At no time during the disturbance have there been delusions or hallucinations for as long as 2 weeks in the absence of prominent mood symptoms. (If there have been, think schizoaffective disorder.)
3. There is no evidence of an organic etiology or other major mental disorder.

The episode is designated as mild, moderate, severe (with or without psychotic features), in remission (full or partial), chronic, melancholic, or seasonal based on the number, severity, duration, and/or pattern of the depressive episode(s).

(Adapted from American Psychiatric Association: Diagnostic and Statistical Manual of Mental Disorders, Third edition, Revised. Washington, DC, American Psychiatric Association, 1987)

Following an initial episode, severe depressions may recur at intervals through-out life. In both unipolar (depression only) and bipolar (recurrent depression and mania) patterns, the frequency of affective episodes appears to increase as a function of the number of previous episodes. Later episodes tend to be more precipitous in onset and may be more severe than earlier episodes. Corollary clinical observations indicate that psychosocial stressors are often identifiable before the first affective episodes but become increasingly less apparent as the illness progresses. Hence, as the illness evolves, its episodes appear to occur independently of life events. In general, the onset of bipolar illness occurs in the late teens or early 20s, whereas unipolar depressions tend to occur later in midlife. Untreated patients with bipolar illness can expect on the average to have more affective episodes than untreated patients with unipolar depressive illness (7 to 15 vs 3 to 5). Studies show that before drug treatments were available, untreated episodes usually last from 7 to 14 months, although 20% last 2 or more years, and the rates of suicide were between 15 and 30% (reviewed by Gold, Goodwin, Chrousos, 1988).

In general unipolar and bipolar depressed patients do not appear to differ markedly in the quality of their depression. Additionally, there is little evidence that the unipolar and bipolar depressions show a differential response to treatment. Antidepressants and electroconvulsive therapy (ECT) effectively treat both conditions. When clinical features have been controlled for, studies comparing the pro-phylactic efficacy of lithium (the treatment of choice in bipolar illness—see below) in unipolar and bipolar illness are inconsistent, with some reports showing lithium being less effective in unipolar illness and others showing it to be equally effective in both conditions (reviewed by Willner, 1985). Nonetheless, the prophylactic efficacy of lithium in both types of depression has been consistently demonstrated to be superior to placebo. Thus, the major difference in unipolar and bipolar depressives appears to be what happens to them when they are not depressed.

Psychotic Depression

Psychotic depression is considered a subtype of major depression. Psychotic depression may be characterized by paranoia, delusions, and hallucinations. Delusions may involve the idea that one has a venereal disease, that one's internal organs are rotting, that one exudes a foul odor, and the like. Certain patients with psychotic depression also may develop guilty ruminations, obsessions, or think their food is poisoned. If auditory hallucinations occur, they usually involve accusations of being bad, guilty, or evil; there may even be "command" hallucinations denoting the patients need for punishment or urging them to commit suicide. Patients may appear frantic, fearful, agitated, frightened, or withdraw into a reclusive and paranoid state.

Psychotic depressions tend to respond most predictably to ECT (as do profound melancholic depressions) although some clinicians prefer the use of cyclic anti-depressant/neuroleptic combinations. In general, response to ECT is more rapid in psychotic depression and should be considered a primary mode of treatment, espe-cially if suicidal ideation is prominent.

Theories of Depression

Most studies agree that the likelihood of entering an episode of depression is increased five- or sixfold in the 6 months following the occurrence of stressful "life events." Although reliable, the relationship between life events and depression is not particularly strong. In fact, life events appear to account for at most 10% of the variance in the incidence of depression (Lloyd, 1980).

In addition to a high level of stress or repeated stressors, a number of other factors have been identified that appear to put a person "at increased risk" for developing depression. These variables include the individual's social support system, sex, and heredity. Early parental loss also appears to be a contributing factor. There is some evidence that the absence of social supports by itself may predispose to depression (Aneshensel, Stone, 1982; Williams, Ware, Donald, 1981), and the belief that social reinforcement contributes to psychological well-being is generally well accepted. Although there does not appear to be any single personality trait that is common among all depressives, one psychological attribute that does appear to predispose to depression is introversion, a personality trait that is associated with a decrease in social contacts and support (Akiskal, Hirschfeld, Yerevanian, 1983). Women generally have higher rates of depression than men, by a factor of two to three (Boyd, Weissman, 1981; Hirschfeld, Cross, 1982). The reasons for this sex difference are not entirely clear although some investigators have suggested that social or hormonal factors may contribute to the higher incidence of depression in women. The status of childhood loss as a factor predisposing to depression has also been controversial. A review by Lloyd (1980), which considered specifically the effects of childhood bereavement, concluded that parental, particularly maternal, loss in childhood was associated with a two- to threefold increase in the likelihood of developing an adult depression. More recent research, however, has indicated that the quality of home life in which the parent loss occurred is the most critical variable in determining vulnerability to psychiatric illness in later life (Breier et al., 1988).

A separation phenomenon, consisting of protest followed by despair, is present to some extent in many species. Many investigators feel, however, that the most useful animal model of depression is that involving the separation phenomenon seen in nonhuman primates. Infant monkeys respond to maternal separation (loss of love object) by an initial stage of "protest" characterized by agitation, sleeplessness, distress calls, and screaming. After 1 or 2 days they exhibit "despair" characterized by decrease in activity, appetite, play, and social interaction and by the assumption of hunched posture and "sad" facial expression. Although the phenomenon is treatable simply by maternal reunion or by antidepressants (McKinney, Bunney, 1969; Janowsky, Risch, Neborsky, 1985), psychobiological consequences of the traumatic event may be enduring. For example, in animals with a history of separation, the drug alpha-methylparatyrosine (an inhibitor of norepinephrine and dopamine synthesis) was able to induce "depressive responses" at doses substantially lower than those needed to induce the same response in control animals (Kraemer, McKinney, 1979).

Previous exposure to stressful events has been found to sensitize neurotransmitter systems to subsequent stressors (Anisman, Zacharko, 1982). Even without prior sensitization, however, exposure to prolonged or severe stress can produce the abnormalities in hypothalamic–pituitary–adrenal axis (HPA) functioning and sleep architecture that is seen in patients with major depressions (Willner, 1985). Thus, patients whose neurologic system has already been sensitized (because of previous stress, early parental loss, or poor social support), or who have a genetic propensity to develop depression (e.g., because of low 5-HT function—see below), may be more sensitive to a multiplicity of unspecified stressors throughout life that may initiate the cascade of neurophysiological and psychological events characteristic of a major depression. Thus, depressions appear to result from the accumulation of psychological, biological, and environmental factors.

A model that attempts to account for many of the features of affective (mood) illnesses is the "kindling-sensitization" hypothesis, advanced by Post and colleagues (Post et al., 1981). In this model, repeated exposures to various stressors or losses may sensitize limbic substrates that respond to such stimuli (e.g., the induction of tearful affect). As a result, ideas and images associated with the precipitation of a depressive episode could acquire the characteristics of a conditioned stimulus capable of eliciting such an episode, even in the absence of any concrete external stress or loss. The progressive sensitization of limbic substrates may account for many features seen in affective illnesses, including the possible predisposition as a result of early stressful experiences, the gradual worsening of affective episodes over time, the progressively shorter latency between an episode's onset and its peak severity, the progressive acceleration in frequency of the cycle of mood swings in bipolar illnesses, and the gradual attainment of autonomy and spontaneity (lack of obvious stressors). The prophylactic efficacy of the limbic anticonvulsants carbamazepine and valproic acid (which inhibit certain kindled seizures) in mood disorders lends additional support for this hypothesis.

Learning Hypotheses

Cognition is defined as the process of obtaining, organizing, and utilizing intellectual knowledge. According to cognitive learning theories, depressed patients have a cognitive style that focuses on what is wrong or negative, rather than what is right or positive. Beck (1974) described a cognitive triad in depression consisting of a person's (1) negative view of self, (2) negative interpretation of experiences, and (3) negative expectation of the future. Thus, in Beck's model, people are depressed because of their negative view of themselves, the world, and the future. Depressions are viewed as a form of thought disorder, of which dysphoric mood is a secondary manifestation, in contrast to the traditional view of depression as a primary mood disorder (Willner, 1985). Depressed people tend to rate specific stressful life events as more unpleasant than do controls (Lewinsohn, Tarkington, 1979; Schless et al., 1974). Unpleasant events will precipitate a depressed mood. Depressed mood produces cognitive distortions (Willner, 1985) that increase the salience of unpleasant events, which further depresses mood. According to Beck's theory, cognitive distortions arise from early traumatic experiences (parental loss or emotional deprivation or peer group rejection), which condition the individual to think and respond to most life events in a negative way (Brown, Harris, 1978; Lloyd, 1980). Once a state of depression is established, information processing is biased in such a negative way (tendency to underestimate positives and overestimate negatives, more recall of unpleasant memories, decreased ability to experience pleasure, and increased sensitivity to adverse events) that the negative mood is reinforced and maintained.

Behaviorally, depression-prone individuals may fail to engage in actions that lead to pleasant consequences, since their behavior may be dominated by actions directed at escaping from or avoiding perceived unpleasant situations (Ferster, 1973; Lewinsohn, Weinstein, Shaw, 1969). Although there is little evidence that reduced participation in pleasant events causes depression, there is evidence that an increase in exposure to perceived unpleasant events does adversely affect mood (Willner, 1985). When depression-prone individuals do engage in behaviors that should be rewarded by others (e.g., the masochistic caregiver), they frequently view their work as "their duty" and "reject" the positive feedback. Low self-esteem may lead depressives to see themselves as unworthy of pleasure, praise, or reward. Some have proposed that the self-esteem of depressives is not low, but vulnerable in the face of stressors that others would cope with adequately.

Learned helplessness is a behavioral phenomenon consisting of passivity, withdrawal, and hypoactivity that follows exposure to uncontrollable adverse events (McKinney, Bunney, 1969). It has been demonstrated that animals who have developed learned helplessness as the result of exposure to uncontrollable shock will develop performance deficits in subsequent learning tasks. The learning deficit is accompanied by other symptoms commonly seen in depression, such as sleep and appetite disturbances. In humans, exposure to insoluble problems or to uncontrollable stress (typically loud noise) has also been found to induce performance deficits in subsequent tasks (Abramson, Garber, Seligman, 1980). Thus, depression may result from learning that one is unable to control the outcome of unexpected adverse events, which leads one to "give up" any attempt to master them. The motivational, emotional, and cognitive responses that may develop from such helplessness are consistent with what is found in many depressed individuals. It should be noted however, that adverse events as such do not engender depression unless they are perceived by the subject as being uncontrollable (Buchwald, Coyne, Cole, 1978; Seligman, 1975; Seligman, 1978).

Neurohormonal Hypotheses

The cardinal biologic manifestations of major depressive illness consist of alterations in the hypothalamic centers that govern food intake, libido, circadian rhythms, and the synthesis and release of hypothalamic hormones into the hypophyseal portal blood and the systemic circulation. Patients with melancholia typically have anorexia, decreased sexual interest, altered timing in the cycle of rest and activity (early morning awaking), diurnal variation in mood, and multiple endocrine abnormalities.

In some depressed patients (particularly those with melancholia), there is evidence that the activity of the hypothalamic—pituitary—adrenal (HPA) axis is abnormally high, resulting in elevated plasma cortisol levels (Carroll, 1977) and an inability of normal feedback mechanisms to inhibit adrenocorticotropic hormone (ACTH). The defect appears to be at or above the level of the hypothalamus, resulting in the hypersecretion of corticotropin-releasing factor (CRH) (Gold, Goodwin, Chrousos, 1988; Nemeroff et al., 1984). This hypercortisolism has been one of the most consistent findings in the biological study of depression.

The dexamethasone suppression test is used to access HPA feedback mechanisms (Arana et al., 1985). Dexamethasone is a synthetic corticosteroid that, when given orally, usually suppresses plasma ACTH and cortisol levels for at least 24 hours. The dexamethasone suppression test is normally administered by giving 1 mg dexamethasone at 2300 hours and then drawing plasma cortisol levels at 1600 and 2300 hours the next day. Depressed patients may initially show a normal suppression of blood cortisol (below 5 mg/dl) following dexamethasone, but often escape from suppression significantly earlier than normal. Therefore they may not show suppression when tested 17 to 24 hours later (Carroll, 1982). A number of studies have demonstrated that normalization of the dexamethasone suppression test may accompany or precede clinical recovery from depression (Holsboer et al., 1982; Targum, 1983). It has also been observed that a patient who appears to have recovered from depression but fails to suppress cortisol after dexamethasone administration may be at higher risk for relapse. Among depressed patients, failure of suppression on dexamethasone suppression testing appears to be more common in the melancholic subgroup (Carroll, 1982). Nonsuppression is not specific for depressive illnesses. Anorexia nervosa patients (Gerner, Gwirtsman, 1981) and dieting obese volunteers (Edelstein et al., 1983) may also fail to normally suppress cortisol. However, suppression occurs much more commonly in depressed patients than in other psychiatric patients and may be an important variable in diagnosis and treatment monitoring.

Another neuroendocrine abnormality reported in depressed patients is an abnormal thyrotropin-releasing hormone (TRH) stimulation test. TRH is a hypothalamic peptide that stimulates the release of thyroid stimulating hormone (TSH) (Jackson, 1982). Several studies have demonstrated that the TSH response (increase in basal plasma TSH concentration) to TRH is blunted in approximately 25% of major depressive patients and tends to normalize with clinical recovery (Loosen, Prange, 1982).

It should be emphasized that none of these neuroendocrine abnormalities or "biologic markers" is specific to depression nor does any of them always occur in depressed patients. For example, the results on dexamethasone suppression testing are abnormal (nonsuppression) in only about 50% of patients with major depression.

Circadian Rhythm Hypothesis

Several features of affective illness suggest abnormalities in biologic rhythms. These include the inherent cyclicity of depression, abnormalities in the sleep architecture, reported abnormalities in the "phase" of circadian rhythms, and clinical responsiveness to experimental alterations in circadian organization (Gold, Goodwin, Chrousos, 1988).

The abnormal sleep of depressed patients was one of the earliest findings in biological psychiatry. Sleep may be monitored electroencephalographically and is divided into phases of rapid eye movement (REM) and non-REM sleep (stages 1 to 4). The first REM period usually begins after a period of 70 to 100 minutes of non-REM sleep. Another three to five REM periods usually occur, mainly in the latter part of the night. REM periods generally increase in length as the night progresses (Gold, Goodwin, Chrousos, 1988; see Chapter 21).

There are a number of sleep abnormalities that distinguish endogenous ("biologic") depressives from nonendogenous (reactive, situational, or characterological) depressives and normal subjects. This is most readily apparent in such non-REM abnormalities as *prolonged sleep latency* (the period of time between going to bed and falling asleep), *shortened REM latency* (the period of time from the onset of sleep to the first REM period), *increased wakefulness, decreased arousal threshold, early morning awakening, and reduced stage 3 and 4 sleep* (Coble et al., 1976; Gillin et al., 1979).

With respect to REM sleep, in addition to a shorter REM latency (i.e., 30 to 60 minutes), depressed patients may have a redistribution of REM sleep to the first half of the night (Reynolds, Kupfer, 1987). Supersensitive cholinergic (muscarinic) receptors may be responsible for the shortened REM latency in depression (see below). In laboratory animals, REM sleep has been found to be associated with quiescence of the locus ceruleus. In general, antidepressants decrease the overall firing rate of the locus ceruleus and may restore a normal pattern of REM sleep in depression by markedly reducing the frequency and intensity of REM sleep (Hartmann, Cravens, 1973; Kupfer, Bowers, 1972). In fact, some investigators have proposed that antidepressants may exert their antidepressant effects by modifying pathologic REM sleep (Vogel et al., 1980). Like nonsuppression on the dexamethasone suppression test, abnormal REM latencies tend to normalize with clinical recovery (Kupfer et al., 1983).

Ordinarily, the cycle of sleep and waking follows the 24-hour cycle of light and darkness. When constant lighting conditions are imposed, an endogenous oscillator drives the sleep-wake cycle and other 24-hour rhythms with an intrinsic period of about 25 hours. Studies spanning several years suggest that in depression there is an advance in the timing of the circadian propensity for REM sleep (short REM latency) and of the rhythms of temperature and cortisol. Due to an advance in the timing of the initial rise in core body temperature (which is associated with arousal) the time of awakening is also advanced (early morning awakening). Drugs such as lithium and monoamine oxidase inhibitors tend to delay the phase of circadian rhythms in laboratory animals (reviewed by Gold, Goodwin, Chrousos, 1988b).

Neurotransmitter Hypotheses

Much of the biological literature on depression concerns the monoamine neurotransmitters norepinephrine (NE), dopamine (DA), and serotonin (5-hydroxytryptamine, 5-HT). Norepinephrine and dopamine are catecholamines, while serotonin is an indoleamine. Dopamine is synthesized from the amino acid tyrosine. The enzyme dopamine-beta-hydroxylase, converts dopamine to norepinephrine. The catecholamines are degraded by two enzymes, monoamine oxidase (MAO) and catechol-O-methyltransferase (COMT), which produce a variety of breakdown products. Like the catecholamines, 5-HT is also synthesized from an amino acid, tryptophan. The degradation of 5-HT is much simpler, however. One enzyme (MAO) produces its single major breakdown product, 5-hydroxyindoleacetic acid (5-HIAA). Stores of catecholamines and 5-HT are stored in synaptic vesicles and are released when a nerve impulse invades the terminal. Although MAO and COMT are both present in the region of the synapse, the major mechanism for clearing the transmitter from the synapse and aborting synaptic neurotransmission is by a process of presynaptic neuronal reuptake, rather than enzymatic degradation. Following reuptake, much of the neurotransmitter is recycled into the "functional pool" to be reused by the neuron (Willner,

1985). In addition to the catecholamines and indoleamines, other neurotransmitter systems may be important etiology of mood disorders, including acetylcholine, gammaaminobutyric acid and various neurohormones and neuropeptides.

Catecholamine Hypothesis

The first major hypothesis to address the biologic basis of major affective disorders emerged from the observation that approximately 15% of the patients who were treated for hypertension with the biogenic amine-depleting agent reserpine developed depression (Bunney, Davis, 1965; Schildkraut, 1978). Subsequently, drugs that were known to enhance monoamine functioning such as the MAO inhibitors (which interfere with the enzymatic degradation of biogenic amines); amphetamines, which promote norepinephrine release and inhibit its presynaptic reuptake; and the cyclic (bicyclic, tricyclic, tetratracyclic and heterocyclic) antidepressants (CyAD), which also block the synaptic reuptake of amines into presynaptic neurons (Hertting et al., 1961), were all found to have antidepressant properties.

These observations gave rise to the original catecholamine hypothesis of major depression, which stated that this disorder resulted from a functional deficit of norepinephrine at critical effector sites in the central nervous system (Schildkraut, 1978). Yet treatments that interfered with monoaminergic transmission or pharmacologic blockade of catecholamine synthesis do not regularly produce depression in most subjects (Willner, 1985). Another issue is the time course of antidepressant actions. Blockade of monoamine reuptake or MAO inhibition occurs within a short time after administration of the antidepressant, but the clinical effects do not usually appear until after 2 to 4 weeks. To further complicate matters, attempts to demonstrate abnormalities in norepinephrine activity by measuring plasma, urine, and cerebrospinal fluid (CSF) concentrations of norepinephrine and its major metabolite 3-methoxy-4-hydroxy-phenylglycol (MHPG) have produced conflicting data. Decreases, no change, and even increases in noradrenergic parameters have been reported in depressed subjects compared to normal controls (Davis, Bresnahan, 1987; Jimerson et al., 1983; Mass et al., 1987; Redmond et al., 1986; Roy et al., 1985). The following findings have led to a reformulation of the original catecholamine hypothesis: (1) noradrenergic measures are increased in some depressed patients; (2) chronic treatment with antidepressant medications is associated with decreases in MHPG levels in CSF and plasma; and (3) preclinical data indicate that MAO inhibitors and tricyclic antidepressants decrease the firing rate of the locus ceruleus (the major bundle of noradrenergic neurons located in the pons), thereby reducing the level of norepinephrine metabolites in the brain. The reformulated version of the catecholamine hypothesis holds that in major depression the noradrenergic system is *overactivated.* Animal models of stress-induced "depressions" support the hypothesis of an activated noradrenergic system. Thus, depression could result from "too much" norepinephrine, a state of affairs corrected by chronic antidepressant treatment (Segal et al., 1974).

Noradrenergic Receptor Functioning

In addition to changes in norepinephrine turnover, depressed patients also show some evidence of altered noradrenergic receptor function. There are two types of postsynaptic alpha adrenergic receptors, identified as *alpha-1* and *alpha-2.* Post-synaptic alpha-2 receptors have been studied using neuroendocrine research strate-gies. *In depressed patients the responsiveness of postsynaptic alpha-2 receptors appears to be reduced. Depressed patients consistently show a reduced sensi-tivity of the postsynaptic alpha-2 receptors that stimulate the secretion of growth hormone (GH).* At least five independent studies have demonstrated a blunted growth hormone response to clonidine (an alpha-2 agonist) in endogenously de-pressed patients compared with controls or patients with other psychiatric disorders (reviewed by Willner, 1985)

Two other alpha receptor–mediated stimuli to growth hormone release, de-sipramine and insulin, are also blunted in endogenously depressed patients. Taken together, these studies (growth hormone response to clonidine, desipramine, and insulin) demonstrate that in depressed patients, the responsiveness of postsynaptic alpha-receptors is reduced. There is little evidence at present however, from which to deduce the origin of this reduced postsynaptic alpha-2 receptor sensitivity (Willner, 1985). That receptor sensitivity is not static and tends to change over time in a homeostatic manner leaves open the possibility that the decreased postsynaptic alpha-2 sensitivity seen in depression is a compensatory mechanism secondary to an *increase* in presynaptic noradrenergic activity.

Some have postulated that the decreased sensitivity of postsynaptic alpha-receptors is a consequence of the changes in ACTH and cortisol secretion seen in depressed patients. Furthermore, the significance of this finding has been questioned on the grounds that chronic treatment with antidepressants does not consistently alter abnormal postsynaptic alpha-2 receptor function. If postsynaptic alpha-2 recep-tor function is important in the development of depression, one would expect anti-depressant treatments to have some "corrective" effects on this abnormality. Yet in depressed patients, the growth hormone response to clonidine was unchanged by 3 to 6 weeks of treatment with desipramine, amitriptyline, clorgyline, or electroconvulsive therapy (Willner, 1985).

By contrast, there is now considerable evidence that chronic antidepressant treatment increases the functional *efficacy* of the far more numerous postsynaptic alpha-1 receptors, even though these receptors do not appear subsensitive in un-treated depressed patients. In addition, this enhancement of postsynaptic alpha-1 receptors appears to be a general property of antidepressants. It may be that by increasing alpha-1 sensitivity, antidepressants can overcome the biologic effects of subsensitive alpha-2 receptors (Willner, 1985).

In addition to the classic postsynaptic receptors, neurons also have receptors situated presynaptically (Usdin, Bunney, 1975). These *presynaptic* receptors are sensitive to their own neurotransmitter and are therefore called *autoreceptors.* In general, autoreceptors appear to mediate inhibitory functions and to serve as negative feedback systems that act to minimize change in the activity of the cell. The presynap-tic alpha receptors have been identified as being of the alpha-2 subtype (Langer, 1980; Starke, 1981). Thus the presynaptic alpha-2 receptors situated on the cell bodies of adrenergic neurons inhibit the firing of the neuron, playing an important inhibitory role in regulating norepinephrine release.

No abnormality of presynaptic alpha-2 receptors is apparent in depressed patients. Nevertheless, a reduction in autoreceptor responsiveness has been observed following some antidepressant treatments (Svensson, Usdin, 1978; Willner, 1985). This desensitization of alpha-2 autoreceptors is not a general property of all antidepressants, however. Yet the finding of "downregulation" of autoreceptors (which will decrease inhibitory input, thereby increasing output) in conjunction with an increased responsiveness of postsynaptic alpha-1 receptors suggests that chronic antidepressant treatment may increase the overall integrated functioning of the alpha-noradrenergic system. These findings are consistent with the original hypothesis of a functional deficit in noradrenergic functioning in patients with major depression.

Beta-Adrenergic Receptors

Contrary to the predictions of the original catecholamine hypothesis of depression, but consistent with the reformulated hypothesis of increased norepinephrine activity, chronic treatment (2 to 3 weeks) with antidepressants *reduced the physiologic sensitivity* (Vetulani, Sulser, 1975) and also *reduced the number of central beta-receptors* in the brain of rodents (Banerjee et al., 1977). Thus in humans, it has been suggested that the therapeutic efficacy of antidepressants is related to or coincident with downregulation of beta-adrenergic receptor function in the CNS (Maggi et al., 1980; Sulser et al., 1978; Vetulani et al., 1976). The model used to study beta-receptor function relies on the fact that beta-receptor stimulation activates the enzyme adenylate cyclase, which leads to the production of cAMP within the cell (Greengard, 1976). Thus the cAMP response to norepinephrine serves to measure the physiologic sensitivity or responsiveness of beta-adrenergic receptors. This desensitization of beta-adrenergic receptors appears to be a property shared by virtually all antidepressants. The specific 5-HT uptake inhibitors fluoxetine and *citalopram* are the only antidepressants that have been found not to reduce the activity of the noradrenergic-stimulated cAMP generating system (Hyttel et al., 1984; Mishra et al., 1979). This decrease in functional sensitivity of beta-receptors is accompanied (in most cases) by a reduction in cortical beta-receptor binding sites as well. The decrease in beta-receptor binding reflects a decrease in the number of receptor binding sites (Bmax), with no change in receptor affinity for the ligand (Kd). This reduction of beta-receptor function appears to be a relatively specific effect of chronic antidepressant treatment that does not seem to be shared by other agents (Willner, 1985).

The effects of antidepressants on beta-receptors are firmly established, yet if these constitute the mechanism of action of antidepressants, some major paradoxes must be resolved. First of all, depression is two to three times more frequent in women than in men (Boyd, Weissman, 1981), yet beta-receptor responsiveness is lower in females than in males (Sulser, Mishra, 1982; Wagner, Davis, 1980). And although beta-receptor responsiveness is decreased by estradiol, symptoms of depression may be experienced by 50% of women taking oral contraceptives (Parry, Rush, 1979). Similarly, it has been observed that the noradrenergic-stimulated cAMP response was decreased by cortisol. Yet depressive episodes are frequently accompanied by abnormally elevated hypothalamic-pituitary-adrenal activity and there is an extremely high incidence of depression in Cushing's syndrome. Nonetheless, desensitization of beta-receptors regularly occurs with antidepressant use (Willner, 1985). There is little evidence, however, to suggest that the changes in beta-receptors represent anything more than a homeostatic mechanism that counteracts the norepinephrine-enhancing effects of antidepressants (Crews et al., 1981; Smith et al., 1981). Furthermore, the finding does not support the belief that depression is secondary to a generalized decrease in noradrenergic function.

Dopamine

As previously noted, dopamine is a precursor of norepinephrine in sympathetic nerve terminals. Histologic and pharmacologic methods for distinguishing nor-epinephrine-containing from dopamine-containing neurons leaves no doubt that the brain contains independent norepinephrine and dopamine pathways. Some depressed patients have been found to show evidence of reduced central dopamine function, as judged by the concentration of the dopamine metabolite homovanillic acid (HVA) in the cerebrospinal fluid (CSF). Measurement of HVA in the CSF is the most direct method available for studying dopamine turnover in the human brain. In studies that utilize the probenecid technique (a drug that blocks the transport of acid metabolites out of the CSF) the concentration of CSF HVA in depression has generally been shown to be decreased (reviewed by Willner, 1985). However, CSF HVA is derived primarily from the nigrostriatal dopamine system (the system that is associated with motor activity), so turnover studies may not reflect information about the functional activity of the mesolimbic or mesocortical dopamine system (the systems presumably associated with mood and cognitive functions). Reports on the effects of antidepressants on CSF HVA concentrations have been inconsistent, suggesting that chronic antidepressant treatment may have little discernible effects on dopamine metabolism and turnover (Potter, Scheinin, Golden, 1985).

The best evidence that low CNS dopamine neurotransmission may induce depression comes from studies of patients suffering from Parkinson's disease. An association between Parkinson's disease and depression is well established (Asnis, 1977; Robins, 1976). Oddly, low-dose neuroleptics have been shown to be helpful in some depressions (Robertson, Trimble, 1982) possibly by blocking dopamine auto-receptors (which are generally more sensitive to receptor blockade than postsynaptic receptors) (Usdin, Bunney, 1975). Autoreceptor blockade would activate dopamine neurons and enhance, rather than suppress, dopamine transmission. Furthermore, clear antidepressant effects, comparable to those of tricyclic antidepressants, are seen with the dopamine uptake inhibitor nomifensine (van Scheyen et al., 1977). The postsynaptic dopamine receptor agonists bromocriptine (Waehrens, Gerlach, 1981; Theohar et al, 1981) and piribedil (Post et al., 1978) have both been shown to have antidepressant effects in several studies. The observation that patients with Parkinson's disease may improve when treated with tricyclic antidepressants suggests that these antidepressants may increase central dopamine activity (Randrup et al., 1975). In fact, it has been demonstrated that tricyclic antidepressants do block synaptic dopamine reuptake (Friedman et al., 1977; Halaris et al., 1975; Hyttel, 1978). This effect is generally several orders of magnitude less potent than their effects on norepinephrine and 5-HT. It is possible, however, that changes in the concentration of dopamine in the micromolar range might be sufficient to enhance dopamine function in the brains of patients with major depression (especially if chronic low presynaptic dopamine activity has produced supersensitive postsynaptic dopamine receptors).

As reviewed by Willner (1985), the collective results from a series of independent studies failed to show any major abnormalities of dopamine receptors in depression, at least in the tuberoinfundibolar dopamine system. We have no reason to believe, however, that dopamine-mediated neuroendocrine responses bear any functional relationship to the information-processing functions of forebrain dopamine systems (e.g., the mesolimbic system). However, the lack of any consistent findings in the tuberoinfundibular system is not consistent with a picture of generalized dopamine underactivity as suggested by the dopamine metabolite (HVA) data. Nevertheless, dopamine receptor responsiveness is increased by chronic antidepressant treatments. In rodents, behaviors elicited by moderate doses of dopamine receptor agonist are enhanced, following chronic antidepressant treatments, indicating increased responsiveness of the dopaminergic system. Thus, behavioral evidence suggests that chronic antidepressant treatment causes an increase in dopamine neurotransmission. This increased postsynaptic responsiveness of the dopamine system is generally noted after most antidepressant treatments.

Indoleamine Hypothesis

There is significant evidence to implicate the indoleamines in the pathogenesis of depression as well (Lapin, Oxenkrug, 1969). Like the catecholamines, serotonin is metabolized by MAO and so 5-HT levels are elevated by MAOI's. Similarly, most antidepressants block the reuptake of both norepinephrine (NE) and 5-hydroxytryptamine (5-HT) by roughly equal amounts, though the relative potencies vary somewhat from drug to drug. The serotonin system in depression was initially thought to be functionally deficient based on the numerous studies demonstrating low levels of the serotonin metabolite 5-HIAA in the CSF of patients with major depression. Measurement of 5-HIAA in the CSF provides a reasonable estimate of brain 5-HT turnover.

Although not all patients have been found to have decreased 5-HIAA levels in their CSF, depressed patients in whom 5-HT turnover is clearly reduced are more likely to have attempted suicide than depressives with normal 5-HIAA levels (Asberg, Traskman, 1981; Banki, Arato, 1983). Yet low 5-HT turnover may not be specific for depression per se. Low CSF levels of 5-HIAA have also been noted in prison populations and in personality-disordered military personnel with a history of aggressive thinking and behavior. Thus, rather than being associated with depression specifically, it appears that low 5-HT turnover may be related to agitation and aggression, which presents clinically as sociopathic behavior or as suicide attempts (Willner, 1985).

Another finding is that low 5-HT turnover (low 5-HIAA) does not appear to be a phenomenon that accompanies an episode of depression, but rather is a state-independent marker that confers a predisposition to becoming depressed. Bipolar patients have been shown to have low CSF 5-HIAA levels while in their manic phase (Banki, 1977; Copper et al., 1972; Mendels et al., 1972). When low CSF levels of 5-HIAA are observed in depressed patients, they usually remain low during periods of remission (Goodwin, Post, Murphy, 1973; Mendels et al., 1972; van Praag, DeHaan, 1979). In addition, low CSF levels of 5-HIAA may also correlate with a family history of depression in healthy volunteers (Sedvall et al., 1980).

Both 5-HT uptake into the presynaptic neuron and the number of platelet imipramine binding sites (sites that are associated with the 5-HT uptake site) have been reported to be reduced in many depressed patients (Willner, 1985). The imipramine binding sites on blood platelets appear to be pharmacologically identical to those in the brain (Langer et al., 1980; Rehavi et al., 1980). Because reuptake of the transmitter is the primary method for replenishing the "functional pool" of neurotransmitters, a decrease in reuptake may lead to an eventual decrease in the total amount of available transmitter. Like low 5-HIAA levels, decreased platelet 5-HT uptake is a state-independent marker, since the decrease is also observed in depressed patients after recovery. Thus, the decreased 5-HT turnover (as measured by 5-HIAA concentrations) may be the result of decreased reuptake of 5-HT into the neuron where it is recycled as well as metabolized. Since MAO activity is not decreased in depressed patients, the decreased turnover of 5-HT cannot be explained by changes in 5-HT metabolism. Therefore, it may represent a reduction in the presynaptic neuronal release of 5-HT.

The evidence reviewed suggests that the activity of the CNS 5-HT system is reduced in a substantial proportion of depressed patients. The obvious interpretation is that depression is associated with a reduction in 5-HT neurotransmission—the classic "indoleamine hypothesis of depression" (Lapin, Oxenkrug, 1969). However, an alternative interpretation has been proposed in which it is suggested that as a consequence of a chronic low level of 5-HT function, depressed patients develop a compensatory "supersensitivity" of their postsynaptic 5-HT receptors, which restores transmission to normal (Aprison et al., 1982). A putative increase in 5-HT transmission secondary to stimulation of supersensitive receptors (stress has been shown to activate the serotonin system) is held to underlie depression, rather than the decrease in transmission postulated by the classic indoleamine hypothesis. Two groups have reported an increase in the number of at least one subtype of serotonin receptor, the 5-HT_2 subtype (see below), in postmortem brain samples of suicide victims (Mann et al., 1986; Owen et al., 1983). This finding has been interpreted as evidence for increased postsynaptic serotonin receptor activity, which might reflect upregulation of the postsynaptic serotonin receptor in response to diminished presynaptic activity (Mann et al., 1986).

Pharmacologic treatments that increase 5-HT function have been found to have antidepressant properties. Although drugs that reduce 5-HT transmission do not always induce depression, several investigators have reported that imipramine binding to brain or blood platelets was decreased by chronic antidepressant treatments. But why would antidepressants reduce imipramine binding or 5-HT reuptake, since these measures are already reduced in depressed subjects? There is little evidence to suggest that the functioning of the 5-HT receptors is significantly altered in depression, yet chronic antidepressant treatment has been reported to reduce maximal binding of serotonin receptors in vivo in animal studies (Wamsley et al., 1987).

There are at least two subtypes of serotonin receptors, designated as 5-HT_1 and 5-HT_2 receptors (Peroutka, Snyder, 1981). The 5-HT_1 type appears to be both pre- and postsynaptically located. The 5-HT$_2$ type appears to be only postsynaptic. On the basis of pharmacologic studies, it has been suggested that the 5-HT$_1$ and 5-HT$_2$ receptors might mediate, respectively, the inhibitory and excitatory synaptic actions of 5-HT neurons (Peroutka, Snyder, 1982). The overwhelming impression from available evidence is that antidepressant medications do not, in general, change 5-HT$_1$ receptor binding. In contrast, a large number of reports show that chronic treatments with antidepressant drugs reduce agonist binding (a measure of receptor number) to 5-HT$_2$ receptors (thus decreasing 5-HT activity postsynaptically). What makes it extremely unlikely that these changes in 5-HT$_2$ receptor binding mediate the clinical effects of antidepressants is that electroconvulsive therapy has the opposite effect. Three independent studies have reported that the number of 5-HT$_2$ receptors was increased by electroconvulsive therapy, rather than decreased (Willner, 1985).

The complexity of the serotonin system in the CNS has made it difficult to construct a simple model for the role of serotonin in mood disorders. Nonetheless, taking all the data collectively, depression does appear to be associated with a decrease in serotonin metabolism (decreased 5-HIAA) and drugs that appear to increase CNS serotonin function have antidepressant properties.

Acetylcholine Hypothesis

It has also been proposed that mood is regulated by a relative balance in activity between CNS cholinergic and catecholaminergic systems (Janowsky et al., 1972; Janowsky, Risch, 1984a). The cholinergic-adrenergic balance hypothesis suggests that depression results from a cholinergic predominance, whereas mania is secondary to an adrenergic predominance. Two major biological markers identified as being frequently abnormal in depression, decreased REM latency and increased HPA activity, might reflect cholinergic hyperactivity in depressed patients.

As already discussed, the sleep of depressed patients is classically characterized by a short REM latency. The induction of REM sleep depends on the activation of cholinergic cells in the pontine reticular formation in the brain (Jouvet, 1975; McCarley, 1982). In nondepressed volunteers, intravenous infusions of physostigmine or the muscarinic receptor agonist arecoline have been found to cause a reduction of REM latency (Gillin et al., 1978; Sitaram, Wyatt, Dawson, 1976). A number of studies have shown that physostigmine, which stimulates ACTH release via a cholinergic mechanism (Janowsky, Risch, 1984b), overrides the suppressive effects of dexamethasone on serum cortisol in nondepressed volunteers (Carroll et al., 1980; Doerr, Berger, 1983). Thus, cholinergic stimulation in normal volunteers can mimic the biological changes seen in patients with major depression.

The studies showing cholinergic induction of REM sleep and ACTH release in normal volunteers are consistent with the hypothesis that cholinergic systems are hyperactive in depression. Evidence that cholinergic receptor responsiveness is enhanced in depressed patients includes the following: (1) the ACTH responses to physostigmine may be greater in depressed patients than in controls or other groups of psychiatric patients; (2) the induction of REM sleep by arecoline is significantly faster in depressed patients than in nondepressed controls (Sitaram et al., 1980); (3) the effect of arecoline on REM latency is also evident in patients who had been previously depressed but were not at the time of testing; and (4) in nondepressed subjects with a family history of depression, there is a hypersensitivity to the arecoline effects on REM sleep (Sitaram et al., 1982). Thus, the abnormalities of REM sleep and pituitary-adrenal function in endogenous depression strongly suggest that patients with major depression, or a predisposition to become depressed, may possess a hypersensitive cholinergic system. A consequence of this would be an exaggerated response of cholinergic mechanisms when the cholinergic system is activated by stress. This is consistent with the finding that centrally active cholinergic agonists may induce depression in some individuals (Janowsky, Risch, 1984a; Risch et al., 1981).

Anticholinergics have been reported to elevate mood when used as antiparkinsonian agents (Jellinek et al., 1981; Smith, 1980) and many tricyclic antidepressants include blockade of muscarinic receptors among their other pharmacologic actions. Yet anticholinergic properties are not shared by all antidepressants. Among the tricyclic antidepressants, the correlation between anticholinergic properties and clinical potency is weak and nonsignificant. Furthermore, during antidepressant treatment, tolerance often develops to the anticholinergic effects. Thus, blockade of the proposed hyperactive cholinergic system does not in itself appear to be adequate to correct the clinical disturbance in mood (Willner, 1985). In addition, studies that have directly measured cholinergic receptors in postmortem brain samples from suicide victims have not demonstrated differences from control subjects (Stanley, Mann, 1983).

GABA Hypothesis

The inhibitory neurotransmitter gamma-aminobutyric acid (GABA) is found throughout the brain and is probably active at more synapses than any other neurotransmitter. A number of recent studies have reported data that indicate reduced GABA turnover in depression. Both CSF and plasma GABA levels tend to be low in depressed patients. The enzyme glutamic acid decarboxylase (GAD), which synthesizes GABA from glutamic acid, is released from nerve terminals along with GABA and therefore serves as another marker of GABA turnover. It has been found that depressed patients have reduced plasma GAD activity. Low GAD activity has been reported in a number of brain areas of unipolar depressed patients studied postmortem. There has been several reports documenting the antidepressant effects of some GABA agonists. Yet there is little evidence that conventional antidepressants work through GABA-ergic mechanisms or correct some GABA deficiency. Studies of GABA receptor function following electroconvulsive therapies or antidepressant drug treatments are unanimous in finding no posttreatment alterations (reviewed by Willner, 1985).

Neurotransmitter Hypothesis: Conclusion

Although the original hypotheses for the etiology of mood disorders focused on single transmitter models, subsequent neuroscientific developments have highlighted the complex interrelations among neurotransmitter systems. As already discussed, several neurotransmitter systems have been linked to depression or antidepressant action, but neither the pathophysiology of mood disorders nor the mechanism of action of antidepressants can be explained entirely by changes in any single system.

Animal studies have amply demonstrated the importance of interactions between monoamine systems, and such monoamine interactions may have considerable clinical relevance (reviewed by Hsiao et al., 1987). For example, the postsynaptic beta-adrenergic downregulation induced by chronic antidepressant treatments does not occur if serotonergic projections to the noradrenergic system are disrupted (Stockmeier et al., 1985; Janowsky et al., 1982). In addition, it has become increasingly evident that antidepressants do not confine their effects to single monoamine systems. Drugs whose "primary" pharmacologic effects are selective for one monoamine cause "secondary" changes in other monoamine systems (Bowden et al., 1985; Potter et al., 1985)

In summary, the weight of the evidence supports the position that in depression (1) the functional activity of noradrenergic systems may be reduced; (2) that low 5-HT turnover predisposes to depression; (3) that central dopamine turnover is decreased; (4) that cholinergic sensitivity is enhanced; (5) that GABA-ergic functioning may be decreased; and (6) that the balance or interactions between neurotransmitter systems appears to be important. Antidepressants seem to enhance overall adrenergic, 5-HT, and dopaminergic functioning, while having more variable effects on neurotransmitter metabolites. Antidepressants do not alter either cholinergic hypersensitivity or GABA functioning. Table 6-5 summarizes trends in the research literature.

Heritability and Depression

Genetic factors are undoubtedly important in the etiology of major mood disorders. Family studies reveal that the rate of depression is greater in the relatives of depressed patients than in controls, with the increase in relative risk ranging from two- to fivefold. The genetic evidence is much stronger for bipolar illness than for unipolar depression. First-degree relatives (parents, siblings, and offspring) of patients with bipolar illness are reported to be at least 24 times more likely to develop bipolar illness than relatives of the control subjects. The incidence of both bipolar illness and unipolar illness is much higher in the first-degree relatives of patients with bipolar illness than in the general population. First-degree relatives of patients with unipolar illness, on the other hand, have an increase only in the incidence of unipolar illness. Comparisons between the two groups reveal that bipolars are more likely to have a history of affective disorder (of either polarity) than unipolar patients (Gold, Chrousos, 1988; Willner, 1985; Pardes et al., 1989).

Unfortunately, in themselves, family studies cannot establish that an illness is hereditary since familial aggregation may also reflect a shared environment. Twin and adoption studies have attempted to address this issue. Twin studies compare the concordance rate for illness in pairs of monozygotic twins with the rate of illness in dizygotic twins and assumes that both twins are exposed to the same environment. Due to identical genes, one would expect monozygotic twins to show greater concordance for hereditary disorders than dizygotic twins. Twin studies have reported concordance rate for bipolar illness to be 79% in monozygotic twins, in contrast to 19% of dizygotic twins. Adoption studies attempt to separate the contributions of nature and nurture by studying children raised away from their biologic parents. Studies comparing the tendency of adopted children to develop the disorder of a

Table 6–5 **Receptors and Neurotransmitters in Depression**

	RECEPTOR FUNCTION		NEUROTRANSMITTER TURNOVER/METABOLISM	
	Before Treatment	After Treatment	Before Treatment	After Treatment
NA	↓ postsynaptic alpha-2	↑ alpha-1 ↓ presynaptic alpha-2 ↓ postsynaptic beta	±MHPG	↓ MHPG
DA	Normal	Functioning	↓ HVA	No change
5-HT	↓ ? presynaptic ? normal postsynaptic	↑ functioning ± 5HT-2 binding	↓ 5-HIAA	↓ 5-HIAA
GABA	Normal	No change	↓ GABA	No change
ACh	Hypersensitive	No change	—	—

? = not consistently reported in all studies or all depressed subjects

± = antidepressant medications reduce 5HT$_2$ binding, while ECT has opposite effects

NA = noradrenergic system
DA = dopaminergic system
5-HT = serotonergic system
GABA = GABAnergic system
ACh = cholinergic system

biologic parent versus the rates of biologic relatives (but not adoptive relatives) to develop the disorder of the ill adoptee lend support to the involvement of a genetic factor in the development of mood disorders. Adoption studies have shown a greater prevalence of psychiatric illness among biological relatives of patients with bipolar illness but not in adoptive relatives. Nonetheless, the most likely mode of inheritance of a mood disorder is multifactorial, that is, the expression of the illness is probably based on a combination of numerous gene effects plus an interaction between various heredity traits and environment factors (Pardes et al., 1989).

Although various phenotypic characteristics have traditionally been used to study the inheritance of specific genes in mood disorders (i.e., color blindness, glucose-6-phosphate deficiency), this method has been partly superseded by the use of molecular genetic techniques. Restriction-fragment-length polymorphisms (RFLPs), are DNA fragments that have been "digested" by specific enzymes called restriction endonucleases (Gold, Goodwin, Chrousos, 1988). In 1987, in a study of an Amish family, Egeland and colleagues reported an association between two RFLPs on the short arm of chromosome 11 and a strong predisposition to develop a major mood disorder (Egeland et al., 1987). Although this finding clearly suggests that the vulnerability to develop affective disorders is at least partially transmitted on chromosome 11, two concurrent studies failed to show a relationship between major affective disorders and the two identified RFLP's from chromosome 11 (Hodgkinson et al., 1987; Detera-Wadleigh et al., 1987). The conflicting data may simply reflect the heterogeneity of mood disorders in the general population. Nonetheless, molecular genetic strategies are expected to reveal much about the etiology and pathogenesis of mood disorders.

Diagnosis of Depressive Illnesses in the Medical Setting

As noted earlier, depressive illnesses are among the most common psychiatric problems seen in medical-surgical patients. Many factors appear to be involved in the pathogenesis of depression in medically ill patients, but common core issues include losses, helplessness, chronic disability and pain, injuries to self-esteem, and financial and marital/interpersonal strain subsequent to the illness. In some instances depressive symptoms can result from underlying physical illness or be induced by medications (see discussion of organic mood syndromes).

The issues of loss and stress (either acute or chronic) tend to be a recurrent theme in many depressed patients. The "loss" that the patient perceives may be of body parts (amputation, mastectomy), sexual functioning (spinal cord injury, radical prostatectomy), bodily functions (ostomy placement), or body image (burns). The progressive loss of autonomy, independence, and control over one's life caused by physical illness may also induce depressive reactions. Self-esteem can be damaged by loss of one's role as a productive member of the family. Individuals who feel stressed, helpless, and overwhelmed by an inability to control or predict the consequences of their situation may develop passive withdrawal, resignation, and depression. The financial stress induced by illness may also bring with it a certain degree of depression, especially if the patient begins to feel that he is now a burden to the family. The stress of illness may also bring tension to marital and family relationships. In searching for the psychological precipitants of depression, the physician must look beyond the immediate circumstances of the patient's illness to evaluate the patient's general ability to "cope," the amount of family support available, the degree of financial and occupational strain, and other conflicts, pressures, or losses with which the patient may have to struggle.

Most depressive reactions in medical-surgical patients are relatively time-limited, have identifiable causes, and resolve with stabilization of the medical condition. If major disturbances in social, occupational, interpersonal, or psychological functioning occur, a diagnosis of adjustment disorder can be made. In some instances, however, the depressive symptoms do not resolve and deteriorate into a major depressive episode.

One of the difficulties in making a diagnosis of depression in medical-surgical settings is that physical illnesses may produce symptoms that are often associated with depression (fatigue, anorexia, insomnia, etc.). In addition, the patient's "sadness" is often felt to be "normal" or "understandable," given the medical circumstances (Cohen-Cole, Stoudemire, 1987). Although a decrease in mood is expected when one has to deal with unpleasant circumstances, cognitive expressions of decreased self-esteem, worthlessness, excessive guilt, "giving up," or thoughts of death or suicide, are not normal reactions to even extreme stressors (e.g., dealing with terminal cancer). When such cognitive symptoms are present, the physician should immediately suspect the development of a depressive disorder and request psychiatric consultation. Although it is "normal" to be sad if suffering a serious medical illness, it is not "normal" to be depressed. Depression is a treatable medical/psychiatric condition.

The relation between pain, particularly chronic pain, and depression is a question that frequently arises in medical-surgical patients. High rates of pain complaints attributable to almost every organ system (e.g., headaches, abdominal pain, joint pain, back pain, and chest pain) have been observed in depressed patients. Somatic pain complaints in the absence of an obviously depressed mood have been described as "masked depressions" and the symptoms as "depressive equivalents." Thus a caveat to bear in mind in evaluating depression is that some depressions may be "masked" by the patient being unaware of, denying, or having a limited ability to verbalize feelings. Patients with certain cultural backgrounds, and often the elderly, will present with "somatizing" depressions and have a host of complaints referable to almost every organ system (dizziness, nausea, diarrhea, etc.). *Indeed, this may be the predominant way in which a majority of patients, particularly in medical settings, present with mood disturbance.* The physician should not accept denial of depression by the patient as excluding the diagnosis. Often, after medical workup has ruled out an organic basis for the patient's complaints, a therapeutic trial of an antidepressant medication may be essayed along with further probing and evaluation of the patient's psychosocial circumstances.

Chronic pain patients have a high frequency of depressive complaints (sleep disturbance, appetite changes, irritability, decreased libido, social withdrawal, and somatic preoccupation). Whether or not this symptom constellation constitutes true clinical depression remains a matter of controversy. Arguments in this area soon become circular: Chronic pain can cause significant reactive depressions, or masked depressions can present as chronic pain. At any rate, the net result is the development of a patient who exhibits chronic pain behavior (focus of life is on pain complaints and obtaining relief from pain). Invariably, however, if a mood disorder is the basis for the patient's pain complaints or if depression produces an amplification of the symptoms, antidepressant therapy will yield both improved mood and diminished pain complaints. Whether or not antidepressants work as a primary mood elevator or have a direct analgesic effect is not fully understood, since common biochemical mechanisms have been postulated for pain and depressive syndromes.

Assessment of Suicide Risk in Depressed Patients

One of the myths surrounding assessment of suicidal risk in depressed patients is that asking about suicidal ideation will bring the idea to the patient's mind or serve to "plant" the idea, increasing the chances that suicide will occur. In actuality, the opposite is true: bringing up the subject of suicide and allowing patients to ventilate their possible motives, ideas, and even plans is the best way to "diffuse" a suicidal situation. Thorough questioning regarding suicidal ideation should therefore be a part of every assessment of a depressed patient.

A number of factors may help identify patients at higher risk for suicidal intention. These include increasing age, being male, living alone, recent major loss, chronic debilitating illness (such as renal disease), and a previous history of depression and/or suicide attempts. While women tend to attempt suicide more often, men complete the act at a greater rate. Questioning the family is of prime importance, because the most lethal patient is one who has already made up his (or her) mind and is determined that no one will be allowed to intervene. Patients who suddenly begin to "get their affairs in order," make out a will, or suddenly "get better" inexplicably (because they now feel they have a way out of their intractable situation), should be evaluated carefully. In direct questioning of patients, it is important to be specific about the method. Patients who have schizophrenia, alcoholism, drug addictions, and organic brain syndromes are more likely to commit suicide because of impaired judgment and impulsivity. Obviously, depressed patients with low self-esteem, excessive guilt, and feelings of helplessness and hopelessness may be extremely suicidal. If the patient is a significant suicidal risk, he or she should receive a psychiatric consultation before being allowed to go home. The broad grounds for psychiatric "commitment" usually require that patients must have a mental illness and be immediately dangerous to themselves or others, or be so gravely incapacitated as to be unable to care for themselves. Commitment codes and procedures vary from state to state, and psychiatric consultation is advised before pursuing this avenue. Management of suicidal patients is discussed in detail in Chapter 18.

BIPOLAR DISORDER (MANIC PHASE)

The essential features of a manic episode as described by the DSM-III-R (American Psychiatric Association, 1987; Table 6-6) is a distinct period during which the predominant mood is elevated, expansive, or irritable to such a degree that it causes

Table 6–6 **Criteria for Bipolar Disorder: Manic Episode**

1. There is a distinct period of abnormally euphoric, expansive, or irritable mood, which is of sufficient severity to cause marked impairment in social or occupational functioning.
2. During the mood disturbance, at least three of the following are also present:
   a. grandiosity
   b. decreased need for sleep
   c. hyperverbal or pressured speech
   d. flight of ideas or racing thoughts
   e. distractibility
   f. increase in goal-directed activity or psychomotor agitation
   g. excessive involvement in pleasurable activities that have a high potential for painful consequences
3. At no time during the disturbance have there been delusions or hallucinations for as long as 2 weeks in the absence of prominent mood symptoms.
4. There is no evidence of an organic etiology or other major mental disorder.

Designate as mild, moderate, severe (with or without psychotic features) in remission (full or partial) based on the severity, the symptoms. If psychotic symptoms are present, designate as mood-congruent or mood-incongruent.

(Adapted from American Psychiatric Association: Diagnostic and Statistical Manual of Mental Disorders, Third edition, Revised. Washington, DC, American Psychiatric Association, 1987)

marked impairment in social or occupational functioning and necessitates hospitalization to prevent harm to self or others. In addition, the DSM-III-R lists seven other categories of symptoms: inflated self-esteem or grandiosity, decreased need for sleep, hyperverbal or pressured speech, flight of ideas or racing thoughts, distractibility, increase in goal-directed activity or psychomotor agitation, and excessive involvement in pleasurable activities which have a high potential for painful consequences.

Clinically, since unipolar depressions cannot be distinguished from bipolar depressions (depressions that cycle with hypomanic or manic episodes), it seems reasonable to assume that bipolar and unipolar depressions share some common pathophysiologic mechanisms. Data on the theories of "depression" have been presented in the previous section. However, in mania, the lack of good animal models has made preclinical investigations difficult. Yet, "drug-amine-behavioral" associations in man have shed some light on the possible pathologic mechanisms that may underlie manic episodes. The most striking pharmacologic evidence in man is the consistent finding that direct or indirect norepinephrine and dopamine agonists (those drugs that stimulate the noradrenergic and dopaminergic receptors or increase concentrations of these neurotransmitters in the brain) can precipitate mania or hypomania in patients with underlying bipolar illness. Some stimulants (amphetamines, cocaine) can induce mania-like syndromes in humans who do not appear to have an underlying vulnerability to develop a bipolar disorder. Thus, the association of mania or hypomania with hyperadrenergic and/or hyperdopaminergic states is firmly established (Potter, Rudorfer, Goodwin, 1987).

How can one illness present itself as two opposite mood states, in which the explanation for the pathophysiology of one mood state would seem to preclude the existence of the other? One possible explanation is as follows: The onset of a major depressive episode (and most bipolar illnesses begin with a depressive episode, especially in females) is associated with a "functional" deficiency in neurotransmitter transmission. The brain's compensatory response to this deficiency is to upregulate postsynaptic receptor mechanisms. In addition, due to the lack of adequate inhibitory feedback mechanisms (because neurotransmitter transmission is inadequate) presynaptic induction of neurotransmitter synthesis and release is uninhibited. The net result of these compensatory adjustments is to increase neurotransmitter transmission. Unfortunately, the regulatory mechanisms fail to adjust and soon the resultant increase in neuronal activity overstimulates the nervous system and mania develops. The manic (increased neurotransmitter activity) state, which induces postreceptor downregulation secondary to overstimulation and the depletion of presynaptic neurotransmitter stores (because of increase release), starts the cycle over again.

BIPOLAR DISORDER (DEPRESSED PHASE)

If a patient has a history of manic episodes, the patient's condition should be considered a part of a bipolar (manic-depressive) mood disorder. This differentiation may be critically important, since antidepressants, when used in depressed bipolar patients, may precipitate a manic episode or, when used on a chronic basis, may increase the cycling of the mood disorder. Hence, if the patient has a personal or family history of bipolar disorder, antidepressants (particularly tricyclic antidepressants) should be used cautiously. Lithium should be started first if cyclic antidepressants are to be used to help prevent mania. Lithium itself has significant antidepressant properties, especially in bipolar patients, and could be considered as the sole agent.

CYCLOTHYMIA

Cyclothymia can be conceptualized as a less severe form of bipolar illness. Approximately 30% of cyclothymics have a family history of bipolar illness, and the prevalence of cyclothymia in the relatives of bipolar patients is much higher than the prevalence of cyclothymia in the relatives of patients with other psychiatric disorders. The observations that about one third of patients with cyclothymic disorder subsequently develop a major mood disorder and that about half report improvement while on lithium further support the conceptualization of cyclothymia as a mild form of bipolar disorder (Kaplan, Sadock, 1988).

Cyclothymia has an insidious onset beginning in the late teens or early twenties. By definition it is a chronic mood disturbance of at least 2 years duration involving numerous hypomanic and depressive episodes that do not meet the criteria for mania or major depression, and with no periods of euthymia greater than 2 months. The mood disturbance is not severe enough to markedly impair social or occupational functioning (American Psychiatric Association, 1987).

ORGANIC MOOD DISORDERS

The essential feature of an organic mood disorder is a disturbance in mood, resembling a major mood disorder, that is due to a specific organic factor (Cohen-Cole, Harpe, 1987). Numerous medical conditions or medications may induce mood changes. The possibility of an organic mood disorder should be ruled out before attributing a patient's condition to a purely psychiatric cause. Medications that have been implicated in inducing organic mood disorders include steroids, reserpine, alpha-methyldopa, propranolol, carbonic anhydrase inhibitors, stimulants, hallucinogens; the chronic use and abuse of alcohol, sedative-hypnotics, benzodiazepines, and narcotics has also been implicated. Medical conditions that may present as mood disorders include endocrinopathies (Cushing's syndrome, Addison's disease, hypothyroidism, hypo- or hypercalcemia), malignancies (occult cancers, lymphomas, pancreatic carcinoma, gliomas), and infections (hepatitis, encephalitis, mononucleosis, HIV). A basic history and physical examination along with a medication review and appropriate laboratory screening tests will rule out the majority of organic mood disorders (Kaplan, Sadock, 1988; see also Chapter 3)

INDICATIONS FOR PSYCHOPHARMACOLOGIC TREATMENT OF DEPRESSION

The indications for antidepressant drugs are most clear for patients with symptoms of major depression (particularly the melancholic and psychotic subtypes). The presence of prominent somatic or vegetative signs and symptoms in addition to profound depression are relatively clear target symptoms that indicate an underlying biological disruption in the central nervous system's regulation of mood. Even patients who do not have prominent mood or somatic features but are plagued by severe cognitive signs of depression (low self-esteem, guilt, uncertainty, pessimism, suicidal thoughts) may respond to a trial of antidepressants. Other clinical indications that the patient's depression may be responsive to medication include a history of depression or recurrent depressions (with complete resolution of symptoms at the end of the depressive episode), previous good response to antidepressant or electrotherapy, and a family history of depression or suicide. It is important to note that even depressions that appear to have been precipitated by environmental or psychological stressors may require antidepressant medications if the symptoms are severe or do not resolve with resolution of the precipitating stressor. The primary pharmaceutical armamentarium of antidepressants includes the cyclic antidepressants, MAO inhibitors, and lithium.

The cyclic antidepressants are often the drugs of choice, followed by the MAO inhibitors if patients fail to respond. The dose range and general properties of the cyclic antidepressants may vary significantly, as shown in Table 6-7, but in general the average maintenance dose for most tricyclics in this category is about 150 mg/day. The most prominent exceptions are trazodone (300 to 600 mg/day), protriptyline (40 mg/day), and fluoxetine (20 mg/day). Fluoxetine is a straight-chain phenylpropylamine antidepressant.

In general the tricyclics should be started at low bedtime doses (25 to 50 mg) and gradually increased by 25 or 50 mg every third or fourth night over a 10- to 14-day period (with the exceptions already noted). Due to metabolic changes, elderly patients generally require lower doses than younger adults (start with 10 or 25 mg and build up dose gradually, monitoring for side effects). The half-life of most antidepressants is such that they can be administered once daily in the evening. This approach may facilitate both sleep induction and compliance. A lag time of 3 to 4 weeks may be seen before a true mood-elevating effect is seen with these drugs, and patients should be warned not to expect results overnight. Improvement in certain biological abnormalities, such as sleep disturbance, agitation, and anxiety, may be seen early in the treatment and precede the onset of true antidepressant activity. In this regard, a suicidal patient whose mood remains depressed but who is suddenly energized may become an even greater suicide risk because he or she now has the energy to attempt it. Sleep improvement is an excellent parameter to monitor as a guide for predicting treatment response and to assess if the dose of drug is sufficient.

There are no clear indications as to how long antidepressant drugs should be continued once an antidepressant effect is achieved. In general, antidepressant medications should be continued for an average of 6 to 12 months: a gradual taper can then be attempted, watching for signs of relapse. If the patient has had frequent relapses, he or she may well need to be maintained on antidepressants for longer periods of time. In conjunction with medication treatment, supportive psychotherapy or some form of counseling to deal with the conflicts, stressors, or other precipitants that may have contributed to the depression is usually important (even if the therapy is relatively brief and confined to the early stages of treatment).

Among the most bothersome side effects of many cyclic antidepressants are anticholinergic effects, such as dry mouth, blurred vision, urinary retention, constipation, palpitations, and tachycardia (American Psychiatric Association Commission on Psychiatric Therapies, 1984). Hypotensive effects are often a major concern as well, particularly in the elderly, who are most prone to develop orthostatic hypotension and are at most risk if it occurs. Orthostatic hypotension may precipitate falls and cerebrovascular or cardiac events that may preclude the attainment of therapeutic drug levels. The demethylated or secondary tricyclics are generally better tolerated and less likely to produce orthostatic changes.

Problems may also arise in patients with cardiovascular disease, particularly those with conduction delays. On the EKG, the cyclic antidepressants as a group tend to increase the P-R interval, QRS duration, and QTc time and to flatten T-waves (Stoudemire, Fogel, 1987). The drugs have a quinidine-like effect on the heart, hence their tendency to increase conduction time. If type I antiarrhythmic drugs (quinidine or procainamide) are used with a tricyclic, effects on conduction time may be additive.

Table 6-7 **Properties of Antidepressants**

DRUG	EFFECT ON SEROTONIN RE-UPTAKE	EFFECT ON NOREPINEPHRINE RE-UPTAKE	SEDATING EFFECT	ANTICHOLINERGIC EFFECT	ORTHOSTATIC EFFECT	DOSE RANGE[d] (mg)
Amitriptyline[a]	+ + + +	+ +	+ + + +	+ + + +	+ + + +	75–300
Imipramine[a]	+ + + +	+ +	+ + +	+ + +	+ + + +	75–300
Nortriptyline	+ + +	+ + +	+ +	+ +	+	40–150
Protriptyline	+ + +	+ + + +	+	+ + +	+	10–60
Trazodone	+ + +	±	+ + +	±[b]	+ +	200–600
Desipramine	+ + +	+ + + +	+	+	+ +	75–300
Amoxapine[c]	+ +	+ + +	+ +	+ +	+ +	75–400
Maprotiline	+	+ +	+ +	+	+ +	150–200
Doxepin	+ + +	+ +	+ + +	+ +	+ +	75–300
Trimipramine[c]	+	+	+ +	+ +	+ +	50–300
Fluoxetine	+ + + +	–	–	–	–	20–60
Bupropion	–	–	–	±	–	150–450

Relative potencies (some ratings are approximated), based partly on affinities of these agents for brain receptors in competitive binding studies (Richelson E: Pharmacology of antidepressants in use in the United States. J Clin Psychiatr 43:4–11, 1982)

– = none; + = slight; + + = moderate; + + + = marked; + + + + = pronounced; ± = indeterminate.

a = Available in injectable form.

b = Most in vivo and clinical studies report the absence of anticholinergic effects (or no difference from placebo). There have been case reports, however, of apparent anticholinergic effects.

c = Amoxapine and trimipramine have dopamine receptor blocking activity.

d = Dose ranges are for treatment of major depression. Lower doses may be appropriate for other therapeutic uses.

(Adapted and used with permission, from Stoudemire A, Fogel BS: Psychopharmacology in the medically ill. In Stoudemire A, Fogel BS (eds): Principles of Medical Psychiatry, p 85. Orlando FL, Grune & Stratton, 1987)

Premature ventricular contractions, however, may decrease with cyclic antidepressant treatment (Glassman, Bigger, 1981; Veith et al., 1982). In patients with pre-existing conduction disturbance (e.g., bundle branch blocks, dissociative AV heart block), the psychiatrist and cardiologist should jointly establish a schedule for monitoring cardiac effects of the antidepressants (Stoudemire, Atkinson, 1988).

Other side effects of the cyclic antidepressants include blockade of the antihypertensive effects of guanethidine, methyldopa, and clonidine and potentiation of the hypotensive effects of prazosin. They may also inhibit the metabolism of anticoagulants, causing increased prothrombin times (Stoudemire, Fogel, 1987). Because of their anticholinergic effects, cyclic antidepressants may induce a narrow-angle glaucoma crisis, delay gastric emptying, and exacerbate symptoms in patients with dysphagia. Antidepressants generally lower the seizure threshold in patients with seizure disorders, but the exacerbation of seizures is usually not a problem if seizures are under good control and therapeutic levels of anticonvulsants are maintained.

Plasma drug level monitoring may be helpful in selected patients, particularly in patients unresponsive to usual therapeutic doses or in patients at high cardiovascular risk, where the lowest therapeutic blood levels should be achieved. Cigarette smoking, oral contraceptives, alcohol, and barbiturates tend to lower plasma levels of antidepressant through hepatic enzyme induction; disulfiram (Antabuse), antipsychotics, and amphetamine derivatives tend to raise levels, as does the acute administration of other medications competing for the same hepatic enzymes. In evaluating drug levels, the clinician should strive to obtain samples under uniform conditions. A standard procedure is to draw samples in the morning, approximately 12 hours after the last dose of medication (Glenn, Taska, 1984).

MAO Inhibitors, Stimulants, and Electrotherapy

Monoamine oxidase inhibitors (MAOIs) are not widely prescribed because of their potential to produce a hypertensive crisis if the patient ingests a food source high in tyramine or some other sympathomimetic. They are generally prescribed for patients who are unresponsive to cyclic antidepressants, who develop intolerable side effects with cyclic antidepressants, or who give a history of previous response to MAOIs. However, MAOIs may be the drug of choice in patients with "atypical" depression whose mood disorder is characterized by hypersomnia, increased appetite, somatic complaints, phobias, anxiety, or hysterical features (Robinson et al., 1973; Quitkin et al., 1979).

Foods rich in tyramine should be avoided during treatment with MAOIs. Examples are aged cheese, yogurt, chianti wine, foreign beer, liver, snails, pickled herring, chocolate, broad beans, soy sauce, and avocados. Patients should avoid medications containing sympathomimetic compounds, such as amphetamines, diet pills, and over-the-counter common cold preparations. MAOIs should not be used in patients on guanethedine or sympathomimetics of any kind or in combination with narcotics or alcohol. These drugs may cause orthostatic hypotension but have no significant anticholinergic side activity (Snyder, Yamamura, 1977). Patients with congestive heart failure, liver disease, or pheochromocytoma should not receive MAOIs. There are two major types of MAOIs, the hydrazine and the nonhydrazine compounds. Phenelzine (hydrazine) and tranylcypromine (nonhydrazine) are the most frequently used MAOIs. The usual dosage range is 15 to 90 mg for phenelzine and 20 to 30 mg for tranylcypromine, given in divided doses.

Stimulants such as methylphenidate occasionally have been used to treat depressed medical patients who cannot tolerate other antidepressant drugs or who refuse electroconvulsive therapy (Katon, Raskind, 1980). However these drugs may produce rebound depression, insomnia, restlessness, agitation, and even paranoid reactions. Their antidepressant action may be short-lived and they are not approved by the Food and Drug Administration for use as antidepressants. In addition, in some patients they have great abuse potential. These agents have been reported to be effective for depression in patients with AIDS (see Chapter 20).

Electroconvulsive therapy, or electrotherapy, is clearly the most effective treatment for major depressive episodes and is the treatment of choice in depressed patients who cannot tolerate the side effects of antidepressant medications or who have severe psychotic, delusional, or obsessional symptoms. Other indications for electroconvulsive therapy are severe melancholia, refractory depressions (usually defined as failure to respond to at least two different antidepressants given for 4 to 6 weeks at therapeutic plasma levels), depressions in frail elderly patients, and some cases of acute mania, catatonia (both withdrawn and excited types), schizoaffective disorders, or acute-onset schizophrenic episodes presenting with a predominance of affective or catatonic symptoms. The only contraindications to electrotherapy are the presence of CNS mass lesions, recent myocardial infarction, or a history of malignant ventricular arrhythmia.

TREATMENT OF BIPOLAR ILLNESS AND THE USE OF LITHIUM

The efficacy of lithium carbonate in the acute and chronic maintenance treatment of bipolar illness has been well documented (Glenn, Taska, 1984). Although its onset of action is somewhat slow (5 to 10 days), 60% of patients with acute mania will respond to therapeutic blood levels of this monovalent cation alone. Maintenance therapy with lithium has been shown to be the treatment of choice in preventing or attenuating recurrence of depression and mania in bipolar illness and is superior to placebo in preventing or attenuating depressive episodes in both bipolar and unipolar illness.

Lithium has no metabolites and is therefore excreted, almost entirely by the kidney, in unchanged form. Rates of renal excretion are affected by advancing age or other conditions that may impair renal blood flow. In addition, lithium excretion is influenced by sodium intake because the two cations compete with each other at the same ion transport sites in the kidney. Nephrotoxic effects of lithium has been reported and include nephrogenic diabetes insipidus, interstitial nephritis, and renal failure. The possibility that lithium can produce clinically significant renal damage is controversial. Renal failure secondary to interstitial nephritis has been reported

(Scully et al., 1981) as have tubular atrophy, interstitial fibrosis, and glomer-ulosclerosis (Hestbach et al., 1977). Yet the risk of clinically significant renal damage in patients treated with therapeutic levels of lithium appears small if it truly exists at all. (Scully et al, 1981). The effects of lithium on thyroid function include induction of thyroid goiter and clinical manifestations of hypothyroidism. Lithium-induced changes in EKG include inversion and flattening of the T-wave—this is usually considered benign and reversible. Sinus node dysfunction and SA block and the development of ventricular irritability have been occasionally described, even at therapeutic blood levels (Glenn, Taska, 1984).

Renal function, electrolytes, EKG, and thyroid function should be evaluated before lithium therapy is initiated. To begin inpatient treatment of an acute manic episode, lithium carbonate can usually be started at 300 mg tid plus 600 mg at bedtime in healthy middle-aged or younger adults. (Baldessarini, Lipinski, 1975). Lower doses will be needed in patients who are elderly, have renal insufficiency or are otherwise compromised. Since clinical response usually requires at least a week, antipsychotic or sedative medications are frequently needed during the initial treatment. The optimal serum blood level during an acute manic episode should be at the upper spectrum of the therapeutic range (between 1.0 and 1.5 mEq/L). Serum levels should be drawn in the morning before the morning lithium dose (approximately 12 hours after the last dose). Serum levels above 1.5 mEq/L often produce signs of toxicity, and levels of 5 mEq/L can be fatal. Following the acute episode, maintenance lithium levels between 0.6 and 1.2 mEq/L are usually sufficient to prevent relapses of both bipolar and recurrent unipolar depressive illnesses (Glenn, Taska, 1984).

It should be emphasized that side effects, not serum lithium concentrations, are the ultimate criterion for lithium toxicity, and these must be closely monitored. Signs and symptoms of lithium toxicity include tremor, weakness, ataxia, drowsiness, dys-arthria, blurred vision, tinnitus, nausea, vomiting, hyperactive deep tendon reflexes, nystagmus, confusion, seizures, and coma. More benign side effects are seen with therapeutic levels of lithium. Some patients develop marked polyuria and polydipsia. These side effects are generally reversible if the dose of lithium is reduced. Lithium can produce a tremor that can be partially alleviated by the addition of 15 to 60 mg propranolol—although propranolol itself may induce depression. Gastrointestinal disturbances may develop and can best be treated by dividing total dosage or with slow-release formulations, but especially by having patients take lithium on a full stomach. Cogwheel rigidity and leukocytosis may also be induced by lithium.

Lithium should be avoided during pregnancy (especially during the first trimester) because of the reported increase in cardiovascular abnormalities in the offspring of lithium-treated mothers. Lithium should be used cautiously in patients with unstable renal or cardiovascular disease or severe dehydration and in patients receiving thiazide diuretics. Although there have been some reports of neurotoxicity in patients being treated with a combination of lithium and neuroleptics (Cohen, Cohen, 1974), in general the combination of lithium and neuroleptics is well tolerated.

The use of psychopharmacological agents in the treatment of mood disorders is more fully discussed in Chapter 17. Discussions of the use of lithium in medically complicated patients may be found elsewhere (Stoudemire, Fogel, 1987).

Table 6–8 **Findings in Depression**

Neuroendocrine Findings in Depression

1. DST nonsuppression
2. TRH stimulation test-blunted
3. Advance in rhythms of temperature and cortisol
4. Blunted GH response to alpha agonists

Sleep Abnormalities in Depression

1. Prolonged sleep latency
2. Shortened REM latency
3. Decreased stage 3 and 4 sleep
4. Redistribution of REM sleep to the first half of the night
5. Increased wakefulness
6. Decreased arousal threshold
7. Early morning awakening

DST = Dexamethasone Suppression Test
TRH = Thyroid Releasing Hormone
GH = Growth Hormone

CLINICAL PEARLS

- Major depression is best understood as a psychobiological disorder characterized by a dysregulation in the neurobiological regulation of mood (Table 6-8).
- In primary medical settings, most depressed patients present with somatic complaints.
- One of the most common somatic complaints of patients with depression in medical settings is sleep disturbance—especially early morning awakening.
- Before prescribing sleeping pills for a patient, always investigate for the primary diagnosis of depression.
- The most common cause of "refractory" major depression is noncompliance or inadequate doses of antidepressant.
- With the exception of fluoxetine, protriptyline, and bupropion, all of the cyclic antidepressants can be given near bedtime, once a day.
- Psychotic depression responds best to electroconvulsive therapy, followed by a cyclic antidepressant plus a neuroleptic.
- No one cyclic antidepressant is necessarily superior to others—when choosing a cyclic antidepressant, you are primarily selecting the side effect profile that you feel the patient can best tolerate.
- At therapeutic doses, anticholinergic effects, sedation, and weight gain are the most problematic side effects of the traditional cyclic antidepressants. Fluoxetine essentially has almost none of these problems.
- If a patient does not respond to a trial of a cyclic antidepressant after 4 weeks of treatment at a therapeutic serum level, consider stopping the cyclic antidepressant and switching to a MAOI. In some patients you may want to refer for electroconvulsive therapy before a MAOI trial, especially if the patient is psychotic, has acute and unpredictable suicidal ideation, or is severely medically compromised.
- When prescribing lithium, have the patient take it on a full stomach to decrease gastric irritation.

(continued)

CLINICAL PEARLS (continued)

- Carbamazepine may be an alternative to lithium in patients who are refractory to lithium or who cannot tolerate lithium's side effects.
- Elderly patients tolerate lithium poorly; keep serum levels at the lower end of the therapeutic spectrum.
- Manic psychosis may not be distinguishable from a schizophrenic psychosis in the acute state; always consider both possibilities in evaluating a psychotic patient in addition to ruling out an organic mental disorder.
- In the patient over 40 who has developed psychotic symptoms for the first time, consider an affective or organic disorder as the primary cause; new onset of schizophrenia after the age of 40 is rare.
- Of the traditional tricyclic antidepressants, nortriptyline and desipramine as best tolerated by patients. Of the newer drugs, fluoxetine is selective for activity on the serotonin system, has a very low side effect profile, generally does not have to be titrated to doses above 40 mg and is given in the morning rather than the evening.
- Be careful not to write off patients with chronic low-grade depression (dysthymia) as suffering from a personality disorder or "neurosis"; the presence of dysthymia does not rule out the possibility of major depression but makes the patient more *vulnerable* to the development of major depression.
- All of the cyclic antidepressants with the possible exception of trazodone, fluoxetine, and bupropion, potentially have a quinidine-like effect on the heart. Patients with evidence of cardiac conduction delays or heart block need consultation with a cardiologist to advise the safest form of treatment. MAOIs have not been demonstrated to have any quinidine-like side effects.
- Trazodone may cause priapism. Obtain informed consent before using it in males. Trazodone should also be taken on a full stomach because it can cause gastric irritation.
- Maprotiline may cause seizures in doses above 200 mg/day.
- In beginning a patient on antidepressants, give no more than 1 week's supply of antidepressants at a time and follow the patient weekly until he or she has responded and is stable.

ANNOTATED BIBLIOGRAPHY

American Psychiatric Association Commission on Psychiatric Therapies: The Psychiatric Therapies, Chapter 2. Washington, DC, American Psychiatric Association, 1984

> Reviews the use of psychotropic agents in the treatment of emotional disorders.

Arieti S, Bemporad J: Severe and Mild Depression. New York, Basic Books, 1978

> Covers psychodynamic/psychoanalytic interpretation of depressive reactions and their psychotherapeutic management in great detail. Recently, however (as discussed in Chapter 16), cognitive therapies for depression have received the most attention in the psychotherapy of depression.

Gold PW, Goldwin FK, Chrousos GP: Clinical and biochemical manifestations of depression, Part I. N Engl J Med 319:348–353, 1988

Gold PW, Goldwin FK, Chrousos GP: Clinical and biochemical manifestations of depression, Part II. N Engl J Med 319:413–420, 1988

Two-part article that reviews the diagnosis, epidemiology, biological findings, and theories of major depression. Primarily focuses on norepinephrine and depression, however, and neglects serotonin theories.

Potter WZ, Rudorfer MV, Goodwin FK: Biological findings in bipolar disorders. In Hales RE, Frances A (eds): American Psychiatric Association Annual Review, vol 6. Washington, DC, American Psychiatric Press,, 1987

Reviews biological findings in mood disorders with particular emphasis on comparing bipolar with unipolar depressions.

Veith RC, Raskind MA: Neurobiology of aging: Does it predispose to depression? Neurobiol Aging 9:101–117, 1988

Reviews epidemiology, research, and recent findings in major depression and compares these findings with those of normal aging. Contains a superb review of biochemical aspects of depression.

Willner P: Depression: A Psychobiological Synthesis. New York, Wiley-Interscience, 1985

A comprehensive review of the biological and cognitive theories of depression.

REFERENCES

Abramson LY, Gerber S, Seligman MEP: Learned helplessness in humans: An attributional analysis. In Garber J, Seligman MEP (eds): Human Helplessness: Theory and Applications. New York, Academic Press, 1980

Akiskal HS: Dysthymic disorder: Psychopathology of proposed chronic depressive subtypes. Am J Psychiatr 140:11–20, 1983

Akiskal HS, Hirschfeld RMA, Yerevanian BI: The relationship of personality to affective disorders: A critical review. Arch Gen Psychiatry 40:801–810, 1983

American Psychiatric Association: Diagnostic and Statistical Manual of Mental Disorders, Third Edition, Revised. Washington, DC, American Psychiatric Association,, 1987

Aneshensel CS, Stone JD: Stress and depression: A test of the buffering model of social support. Arch Gen Psychiatr 39:1392–1396, 1982

Anisman H, Zacharko RM: Depression: The predisposing influence of stress. Behav Brain Sci 5:89–137, 1982

Aprison MH, Hintgen JN, Nagayama H: Testing a new theory of depression with an animal model: Neurochemical-behavioral evidence for postsynaptic serotonergic receptor involvement. In Langer SZ, Takahashi R, Segawa T, Briley M (eds): New Vistas in Depression, pp 171–178. New York, Pergamon, 1982

Arana GW, Baldessarini RJ, Ornsteen M: The dexamethasone suppression test for diagnosis and prognosis in psychiatry. Arch Gen Psychiatr 42:1193–1204, 1985

Asberg M, Traskman L: Studies of CSF 5-HIAA in depression and suicidal behavior. Adv Exp Med Biol 133:739–752, 1981

Asnis G: Parkinson's disease, depression and ECT: A review and case study. Am J Psychiatr 134:191–195, 1977

Baldessarini RJ, Lipinski JF: Lithium salts. Ann Intern Med 83:527–533, 1975

Banerjee SP, Kung CS, Riggi SJ, Chanda SK: Development of beta-adrenergic subsensitivity by antidepressants. Nature 268:455–456, 1977

Banki CM, Arato M: Amine metabolites and neuroendocrine responses related to depression and suicide. J Affect Disord 5:223–232, 1983

Banki CM: Correlation between cerebrospinal fluid amine metabolites and psychomotor activity in affective disorders. J Neurochem 28:255–257, 1977

Beck AT: The development of depression: A cognitive model. In Friedman RJ, Katz MM (eds): The Psychology of Depression: Contemporary Theory and Research, pp 3–20. New York, Wiley, 1974

Bowden CL, Koslow SH, Hanin I, Mass JW, Davis JM, Robins E: Effects of amitriptyline and imipramine on brain amine neurotransmitter metabolites in cerebrospinal fluid. Clin Pharmacol Ther 37:316–324, 1985

Boyd JH, Weissman M: Epidemiology of affective disorder. A reexamination and future directions. Arch Gen Psychiatr 38:1039–1046, 1981

Breier A, Kelsoe JR, Kirwin PD, Beller SA, Wolkowitz OM, Pickar D: Early parental loss and development of adult psychopathology. Arch Gen Psychiatr 45:987–993, 1988

Brown GW, Harris T: Social Origins of Depression. London, Tavistock, 1978

Buchwald AM, Coyne JG, Cole CS: A critical evaluation of the learned helplessness model of depression. J Abnorm Psychol 87:180–193, 1978

Bunney WE Jr, Davis JM: Norepinephrine and depressive reactions: A review. Arch Gen Psychiatr 13:483–494, 1965

Carroll BJ: The hypothalamus-pituitary-adrenal axis in depression. In Burrows G (ed): Handbook on Depression, pp 325–341. Amsterdam, Excerpta Medica, 1977

Carroll BJ: The dexamethasone suppression test for melancholia. Br J Psychiatr 140:292–304, 1982

Carroll BJ, Greden JF, Haskett R, Feinberg, M et al: Transmitter studies of neuroendocrine pathology in depression. Acta Psychiatr Scand 61 (suppl 280):183–199, 1980

Carroll BJ, Mendels J: Neuroendocrine regulation in affective disorders. In Sachor EJ (ed): Hormones, Behavior and Psychopathology, pp, 193–224. New York, Raven, 1976

Christensen NJ, Vestergaard P, Sorensen T, Rafaelsen DJ: Cerebrospinal fluid adrenaline and noradrenaline in depressed patients. Acta Psychiatr Scand 61:178–182, 1980

Coble P, Foster FG, Kupfer DJ: electroencephalographic sleep diagnosis of primary depression. Arch Gen Psychiatr 33:1124–1127, 1976

Cohen WJ, Cohen NH: Lithium carbonate, haloperidol, and irreversible brain damage. JAMA 230:1283–1287, 1974

Cohen-Cole S, Harpe C: Diagnostic assessment of depression in the medically ill. In Stoudemire A, Fogel BS (eds): Principles of Medical Psychiatry. Orlando, FL, Grune & Stratton, 1987

Cohen-Cole S, Stoudemire GA: Major depression and physical illness; Special considerations in diagnosis and biologic treatment. Psychiatr Clin N Am, 10:1–17, 1987

Copper A, Prange AJ, Whybrow PC, Noguere R: Abnormalities of indoleamines in affective disorders. Arch Gen Psychiatr 26:474–478, 1972

Crews FT, Paul SM, Goodwin FK: Acceleration of β-receptor desensitization in combined administration of antidepressants and phenoxybenzamine. Nature 290:787–789, 1981

Davis JM, Bresnahan DB: Psychopharmacology in clinical psychiatry. In Holes R, Franes HJ (eds): Psychiatry Update, vol 6, pp 159–187. Washington, DC, American Psychiatric Association, 1987

Depue RA Monroe SM: The unipolar-bipolar distinction in the depressive disorders: Implications for stress-onset interactions. In Dupe RA (ed): The Psychobiology of the Depressive Disorders: Implications for the Effects of Stress, pp 23–53. New York, Academic Press, 1979

Detera-Wadleigh SD, Berrettini WH, Goldin LR, Bosrman D, Anderson S, Gershon ES: Close linkage of c-Harvey-*ras*-1 and the insulin gene to affective disorder is ruled out in three North American predigrees. Nature 325:806–808, 1987

Doerr P, Berger M: Physostigmine-induced escape from dexamethasone suppression in normal adults. Biol Psychiatr 18:261–268, 1983

Edelstein CE, Roy-Byrne P, Fawzy FI, Dornfeld L: Effects of weight loss on the dexamethasone suppression test. Am J Psychiatr 140:338–341, 1983

Egeland JA, Gerhard DS, Paris DL: Bipolar affective disorders linked to DNA markers on chromosome 11. Nature 325:783–787, 1987

Everett HC: The use of beth anechol chloride with tricyclic antidepressant. Am J Psychiatr 132:1202–1204, 1975

Ferster CA: A functional analysis of depression. Am Psychol 28:857–870, 1973

Friedman E, Fung F, Gershon S: Antidepressant drugs and dopamine uptake in different brain regions. Eur J Pharmacol 42:47–51, 1977

Gerner RH, Gwirtsman HE: Abnormalities of dexamethasone suppression test and urinary MHPG in anorexia nervosa. Am J Psychiatr 138:650–653, 1981

Gillin JC, Duncan W, Pettigrew KD, Erakel BL, Snyder F: Successful separation of depressed, normal, and insomniac subjects by EEG sleep data. Arch Gen Psychiatr 36:85–90, 1979

Gillin JC, Sitaima N, Mendelson WB, Wyatt RJ: Physostigmine alters onset but not duration of REM sleep in man. Psychopharmacology 58:111–114, 1978

Gjerris A, Rafaelsen OJ, Christensen, NJ: CSF adrenaline-low in "somatizing depression." Acta Psychiatr Scand 75:516–520, 1987

Glassman AH, Bigger JT: Cardiovascular effects of therapeutic doses of tricyclic antidepressants: A review. Arch Gen Psychiatr 38:815–820, 1981

Glenn M, Taska RJ: Antidepressants and lithium. In The American Psychiatric Association Commission on Psychiatric Therapies: The Psychiatric Therapies. Washington, DC, American Psychiatric Association, 1984

Glowinski J: Some characteristics of the "functional" and "main storage" compartments in central catecholamine neurons. Brain Res 62:489–493, 1973

Gold PW, Goodwin FK, Chrousos GP: Clinical and biochemical manifestations of depression. Part I: Relation to the neurobiology of stress. N Eng J Med 319:348–535, 1988

Gold PW, Goodwin FK, Chrossos GP: Clinical and biochemical manifestations of depression. Part II: Relation to the neurobiology of stress. N Engl J Med 319:413–420, 1988

Goodwin FK, Jamison KR: The natural course of manic-depressive illness. In Post RM, Ballenger JC (eds): Neurobiology of Mood Disorders. Baltimore, Williams & Wilkins 1984

Goodwin FK, Post RM, Murphy DL: Cerebrospinal fluid amine metabolites and therapies for depression. Sci Proc Am Psychiatr Assoc 126:24–25, 1973

Greengard PA: Possible role for cyclic nucleotides and phosphorylated membrane proteins in postsynaptic actions of neurotransmitters. Nature 260:101–109, 1976

Halaris A, Beleudiuk K, Freedman DX: Antidepressant drugs affect dopamine reuptake. Biochem Pharmacol 24:1896–1898, 1975

Hartmann E, Cravens J: The effects of long term administration of psychotropic drugs on human sleep. III: The effects of emitriptyline. Psychopharmacologia (Berlin) 33:185–222, 1973

Helgason T: Epidemiological investigation concerning affective disorders. In Scho M, Stromgren M (eds): Origin, Presentation and Treatment of Affective Disorders, pp 241–257. London, Academic Press 1979

Hertting G, Axelrod J, Whitby LG: Effects of drugs on the uptake and metabolism of 3H-norepinephrine. J Pharmacol Exp Ther 134:146–153, 1961

Hestbach J, Hansen HE, Amdisen A, Olsen S: Chronic renal lesions following long-term treatment with lithium. Kidney Int 12:205–213, 1977

Hirschfeld RM, Cross CC: Epidemiology of affective disorders: Psychosocial risk factors. Arch Gen Psychiatr 39:35–47, 1982

Hodgkinson S, Sherrington R, Gurlin H, et al: Molecular evidence for heterogeneity in manic depression. Nature 325:805–806, 1987

Holsboer F, Liebl R, Hofschuster E: Repeated dexamethasone suppression test during depressive illness: Normalization of test result compared with clinical improvement. J Affect Disord 4:93–101, 1982

Hsiao JK, Agren H, Bartko JJ, Rudolfer MV, Linnoila M, Potter WZ: Monoamine neurotransmitter interactions and the prediction of antidepressant response. Arch Gen Psychiatry 44:1078–1083, 1987

Hyttel J: Inhibition of [3H] dopamine accumulation in rat striatal synaptosomes by psychotropic drugs. Biochem Pharmacol 27:1063–1068, 1978

Hyttel J, Overo KF, Arnt J: Biochemical effects and drug levels in rats after long-term treatment with the specific 5-HT-uptake inhibitor, citalopram. Psychopharmacology 83:20–27, 1984

Jackson IMD: Thyrotropin-releasing hormone, N Engl J Med 306:145–155, 1982

Janowsky DS, el-Yousef MK, Davis KM, Srkerke JH: A cholinergic-adrenergic hypothesis of mania and depression. Lancet 2:6732–6735, 1972

Janowsky A, Okado F, Manier DH, Applegate CD, Susler F: Role of serotonergic input in the regulation of the β-adrenergic receptor-coupled adenylate cyclase system. Science 218:900–901, 1982

Janowsky DS, Risch SC: Adrenergic-cholinergic balance and affective disorders: A review of clinical evidence and therapeutic implications. In Rusch AJ, Altschuler KC (eds): New Advances in the Treatment of Depression. New York, Guilford Press, 1984

Janowsky DS, Risch SC: Cholinomimetic and anticholinergic drugs used to investigate an acetylcholamine hypothesis of affective disorders and stress. Drug Dev Res 4:125–142, 1984

Janowsky DS, Risch SC, Neborsky R: Strategies for Studying Neurotransmitter Hypothesis of Affective Disorders: In Cavener JO (ed): Psychiatry Vol 3, Ch 55. Philadelphia, JB Lippincott, 1985

Jellinek T, Gardos G, Cole J: Adverse effects of antiparkinsonian drug withdrawal. Am J Psychiatr 138:1567–1571, 1981

Jimerson DC, Insel TR, Reus VI, Kopin IW: Increased plasma MHPG in dexamethasone-resistant depressed patients. Arch Gen Psychiatr 40:173–176, 1983

Jouvet M: Cholinergic mechanisms omit sleep. In Waser P (ed): Cholinergic Mechanisms. New York, Raven Press, 1975

Kaplan HI, Sadock BJ: Mood disorders. In Kaplan HI, Sadock BJ (eds): Synopsis of Psychiatry. Williams & Wilkins, Baltimore, 1988

Karasu TB (ed): American Psychiatric Association Commission on Psychiatric Therapies, p 90. Washington, DC, American Psychiatric Association, 1984

Katon W, Raskind M: Treatment of depression in the medically ill elderly with methylphenidate. Am J Psychiatr 137:963–965, 1980

Keller MD, Lavori PW, Endicott J: "Double depression": Two-year follow-up. Am J Psychiatr 140:689–694, 1983

Kelly WF, Checkley SA, Bender DA: Cushing's syndrome, tryphophan and depression. Br J Psychiatr 136:125–142, 1980

Klerman GL: History and development of modern concepts of affective illness. In Post RM, Ballenger JC (ed): Neurobiology of Mood Disorders, pp 1–19. Baltimore, Williams & Wilkins 1984

Kraemer GW, McKinney WT: Interactions of pharmacological agents which alter biogenic amine metabolism and depression. J Affect Disord 1:33–54, 1979

Kupfer DJ, Bowers MB Jr.: REM sleep and central monoamine oxidase inhibition. Psychopharmacologia (Berlin) 27:183–190, 1972

Kupfer DJ, Thase ME: The use of the sleep laboratory in the diagnosis of affective disorders. Psychiatr Clin North Am 6:3–25, 1983

Kupfer DJ, Spiker DG, Rossi A, Coble PA, Ulrich R, Shaw D: Recent diagnostic and treatment advances in REM sleep and depression. In Clayton PJ, Barrett JE (eds): Treatment of Depression: Old Controversies and New Approaches, pp 31–52. New York, Raven, 1983

Langer SZ: Presynaptic regulation of the release of catecholamines. Pharmacol Rev 32:337–362, 1980

Langer SZ, Briley MS, Raisman R, Henry JF, Morselli PL: Specific 3H-Imipramine binding in human platelets: Influence of age and sex. Naunyn Schmiedebergs Arch Pharmacol 313:189–194, 1980

Lapin IP, Oxenkrug GF: Intensification of the central serotonergic processes as a possible determinant of the thymoleptic effect. Lancet 1:132–136, 1969

Levenson JL: Neuroleptic malignant syndrome. Am J Psychiatr 142:1137–1143, 1985

Lewinsohn PM, Tarkington J: Studies on the measurement of unpleasant events and relations with depression. Appl Psychol Res 3:83–101, 1979

Lewinsohn PM, Weinstein MS, Shaw DA: Depression: A clinical research approach. In Rubin RD, Franks CM (eds): Advances in Behavior Therapy, pp 231–240. New York, Academic Press, 1968

Lloyd C: Life events and depressive disorder reviewed. I: Events as predisposing factors. Arch Gen Psychiatr 37:529–535, 1980

Lloyd C: Life events and depressive disorders reviewed. II: Events as precipitating factors. Arch Gen Psychiatr 37:541–548, 1980

Loosen PT, Prange AJ Jr: Serum thyrotropin response to thyrotropin-releasing hormone in psychiatric patients: A review. Am J Psychiatr 139:405–416, 1982

Maggi A, U'Prichard DC, Enna SJ: Differential effects of antidepressant treatment on brain monoaminergic receptors. Eur J Pharmacol 61:91–98, 1980

Mann JJ, Stanley M, McBride A, McEwen BS: Increased serotonin and beta-adrenergic receptor binding in the frontal cortices of suicide victims. Arch Gen Psychiatr 43:954–959, 1986

Mao CC, Costa E: Biochemical pharmacology of GABA transmission. In Lipton MA, DiMascio A, Killam KF (eds): Psychopharmacology: A Generation of Progress. New York, Raven Press, 1978

Mass JW, Koslow SH, David J, Katz M, et al: Catecholamine metabolism and disposition in healthy and depressed subjects. Arch Gen Psychiatr 44:337–344, 1987

McCarley RW: REM sleep and depression: Common neurobiologic mechanisms. Am J Psychiatr 139:565–575, 1982

McKinney WT, Bunney WE Jr: Animal models of depression: Review of evidence and implications for research. Arch Gen Psychiatr 21:240–248, 1969

Mendels J, Frazer A, Fitzgerald RG, Ramsey TA, Stokes KW: Biogenic amine metabolites in cerebrospinal fluid of depressed and manic patients. Science 175:1380–1382, 1972

Mishra R, Janowsky A, Sulser F: Subsensitivity of the NE receptor coupled adenylate cyclase system in rat brain: Effects of nisoxetine or fluoxetine. Eur J Pharmacol 60:379–382, 1979

Myers JK, Weisman MM, Tischler GL, et al: Six month prevalence of psychiatric disorders in three communities 1980–82. Arch Gen Psychiatr 41:959–967, 1984

Nemeroff CB, Widerlov E, Bissette G, et al: Elevated concentrations of CSF corticotropin-releasing factor–like immunoreactivity in depressed patients. Science 226:1342–1343, 1984

Owen F, Cross A, Crow TJ, et al: Brain 5-HT$_2$ receptors and suicide. Lancet 1:1256, 1983

Papahostas Y, Lee J, Johnson L, Fink M: Neuroendocrine effects of ECT. Sci Proc Soc Biol Psychiatr (Abstr 3):35, 1980

Pardes H, Kaufmann CA, Pincus HA, et al: Genetics and Psychiatry: Past discoveries, current dilemmas, and future directions. Am J Psychiatry 146:435–443, 1989

Parry BL, Rush AJ: Oral contraceptives and depressive symptomalogy: Biologic mechanisms. Compr Psychiatr 20:347–358, 1979

Peroutka SJ, Snyder SH: Two distinct serotonin receptors: Regional variations in receptor binding in mammalian brain. Brain Res 208:339–347, 1981

Peroutka SJ, Snyder SH: Recognition of multiple serotonin receptor binding sites. In Ho BT, Schoolar JC, Usdin E (eds): Serotonin in Biological Psychiatry. New York, Raven Press, 1982

Post RM, Jimerson DC, Ballenger JC, et al: Cerebrospinal fluid norepinephrine and its metabolites in manic-depressive illness. In Post RN, Ballenger JC (eds): Neurobiology of Mood Disorders pp 539–553. Baltimore, Williams & Wilkins, 1984

Post RM, Ballenger JC, Uhde TW, Putman TW Jr, Bunney WE Jr: Kindling and drug sensitization: Implications for the progressive development of psychopathology and treatment with carbamazopine. In Sadler M (ed): The Psychopharmacology of Anticonvulsants, pp 27–53. Oxford, Oxford University Press, 1981

Post RM, Gerner RH, Carman JS, et al: Effects of a dopamine against piribedil in depressed patients. Arch Gen Psychiatr 35:609–615, 1978

Potter WZ, Rudorfer MV, Goodwin FK: Biological findings in bipolar disorders. In American Psychiatric Association Annual Review, vol 6. Washington, DC, American Psychiatric Association, 1987

Potter WZ, Scheinin M, Golden RN, et al: Selective antidepressants and cerebrospinal fluid. Arch Gen Psychiatr 42:1171–1177, 1985

Quitkin F, Rifkin A, Klein DF: Monoamine oxidase inhibitors. Arch Gen Psychiatr 36:749–759, 1979

Randrup A, Munkuad J, Fog R, et al: Mania, depression and brain dopamine. In Essman WB, Valzelli L (eds): Current Developments in Psychopharmacology, vol 2. New York, Spectrum, 1975

Redmond DE, Katz MM, Mass JW, Swann A, Casper R, David JM: Cerebrospinal fluid amine metabolites. Arch Gen Psychiatr 43:939–947, 1986

Rehavi M, Paul SM, Skolnick P, Goodwin FK: Demonstration of high affinity binding sites for 3H-imipramine in human brain. Life Science 26:2273–2279, 1980

Reynolds CF III, Kupfer DJ: Sleep research in affective illness: State of the art circa 1987. Sleep 10:199–215, 1987

Risch SC, Cohen PM, Janowsky CS, Kalin NH, Insel TR, Murphy DL: Physostigmine induction of depressive symptomatology in normal volunteer subjects. J Psychiatr Res 4:89–94, 1981

Robertson MM, Trimble MR: Major tranquilizers used as antidepressants: A review. J Affect Disord 4:173–193, 1982

Robins AH: Depression in patients with parkinsonism. Br J Psychiatr 128:141–145, 1976

Robinson DS, Nies A, Ravaris CL, Lamborn RR: The monoamine oxidase inhibitor, phenelzine, in the treatment of depressive-anxiety states. Arch Gen Psychiatr 29:407–413, 1973

Roy A, Pickar D, Linnoila M, Doran AR, Ninan P, Paul SM: Cerebrospinal fluid monoamine metabolite concentrations in melancholia. Psychiatr Res 15:281–292, 1985

Schildkraut JJ: The catecholamine hypothesis of affective disorders: A review of supporting evidence. Am J Psychiatr 122:509–522, 1965

Schildkraut JJ: Norepinephrine metabolites as biochemical criteria for classifying disorders and predicting responses to treatment; Preliminary findings. Am J Psychiatr 130:695–699, 1973

Schildkraut JJ: Current status of the catecholamine hypothesis of affective disorders. In Lipton MA, DiMascio A, Killiam KF (eds): Psychopharmacology: A Generation of Progress, pp 1223–1234. New York, Raven Press, 1978

Schless AP, Schwartz L, Goetz C, Mendels J: How depressives view the significance of life events. Br J Psychiatr 125:406–410, 1974

Scully RF, Galdabini JJ, McNely BV: Case records of the Massachusetts General Hospital. N Engl J Med 304:1025–1032, 1981

Sedvall G, Fyro B, Gullberg B, Nyback H, Wiesel FA, Wode-Helgot B: Relationships in healthy volunteers between concentrations of monoamine metabolites in cerebrospinal fluid and family history of psychiatric morbidity. Br J Psychiatr 136:366–374, 1980

Seligman MEP: Helplessness: On Depression, Development and Death. San Francisco, WH Freeman, 1975

Seligman MEP: Comment and integration. J Abnorm Psychol 87:165–179, 1978

Seqal DS, Kuczenski R, Mandell AF: Theoretical implications of drug-induced adaptive regulation for a biogenic amine hypothesis of affective disorder. Biol Psychiatry 9:147–159, 1974

Sharman DF: The catabolism of catecholamines. Br Med Bull 29:110–115, 1973

Sitaram N, Nurnberger JI, Gershon ES, Gillin JC: Faster cholinergic REM induction in euthymic patients with primary affective illness. Science 208:200–202, 1980

Sitaram N, Nurnberger JI, Gershon ES, Gillin JC: Cholinergic regulation of mood and REM sleep: Potential model and marker of vulnerability to affective disorder. Am J Psychiatr 139:571–576, 1982

Sitaram N, Wyatt RJ, Dawson S, Gillin JC: REM sleep induction by physostigmine infusion during sleep. Science 191:1281–1283, 1976

Smith JA: Abuse of antiparkinsonian drugs: A review of the literature. J Clin Psychiatry 41:351–354, 1980

Smith SB, Garcia-Sevilla JA, Hollingsworth PJ: Adrenoceptors in rat brain are decreased after long-term tricyclic antidepressant drug treatment. Brain Res 210:413–418, 1981

Snyder SH, Yamamura HI: Antidepressants and the muscarinic acetylcholine receptor. Arch Gen Psychiatr 34:235–239, 1977

Stanley M, Mann JJ: Serotonin-2 binding sites are increased in the frontal cortex of suicide victims. Lancet 1:214–216, 1983

Starke K: Presynaptic receptors. Annu Rev Pharmacol Toxicol 21:7–30, 1981

Stockmeier CA, Martino AM, Kellar KM: A strong influence of serotonin axons on β-adrenergic receptors in rat brain. Science 230:323–325, 1985

Stoudemire A: Depression. In Lubin MF, Walker HK, Smith RB (eds): Medical Management of the Surgical Patient, pp 438–444. Boston, Butterworths, 1988

Stoudemire A, Atkinson P: Use of cyclic antidepressants in patients with cardiac conduction disturbances. General Hospital Psychiatry 10:389–397, 1988

Stoudemire A, Fogel BS: Psychopharmacology in the medically ill. In Stoudemire A, Fogel BS (eds): Principles of Medical Psychiatry, pp 79–112. Orlando, FL, Grune & Stratton, 1987

Sulser F, Vetulani J, Mobley PL: Mode of action of antidepressant drugs. Biochem Pharmacol 27:257–261, 1978

Sulser F, Mishra R: Regulation of central noradrenergic receptor function and its relevance to the therapy of depression. In Langer SZ, Takahashi R, Segawa T, Briley M (eds): New Vistas in Depression. New York, Pergamon, 1982

Svensson TH, Usdin T: Feedback inhibition of brain noradrenaline neurons by tricyclic antidepressants: Alpha-receptor medication. Science 202:1089–1091, 1978

Targum SD: Application of serial neuroendocrine challenge studies in the management of depressive disorders. Biol Psychiatr 18:3–19, 1983

Theohar C, Fischer-Cornelsson K, Akesson HO, et al: Bromocriptine as anti-depressant: Double-blind comparative study with imipramine in psychogenic and endogenous depression. Curr Ther Res 30:830–842, 1981

Torgum SD: Application of serial neuroendocrine challenge studies in the management of depressive disorders. Biol Psychiatr 18:3–19, 1983

Usdin E, Bunney WE: Pre- and Postsynaptic Receptors. New York, Marcel Dekker, 1975

Van Praag HM, DeHaan S: Central serotonin metabolism and frequency of depression. Psychiatr Res 1:219–224, 1979

Van Scheyen JD, Van Praag HM, Korf J: Controlled study comparing nomifensine and chlomipramine in unipolar depression, using the probenecid technique. Br J Clin Pharmacol 4:1795–1845, 1977

Veith RC, Raskind MA: The neurobiology of aging: Does it predispose to depression? Neurobiol Aging 9(1):101–107, 1988

Veith RC, Raskind MA, Caldwell JH: Cardiovascular effects of tricyclic antidepressants in depressed patients with chronic heart disease. New Engl J Med 306:954–959, 1982

Vetulani J, Stawarz RJ, Dingell JV, Sulser F: A possible common mechanism of action of antidepressant treatments: Reduction in the sensitivity of the noradrenergic cyclic AMP generating system in the rat limbic forebrain. Naunyn Schmiedebergs Arch Pharmacol 293:109–114, 1976

Vetulani J, Sulser F: Action of various antidepressant treatments reduces reactivity of noradrenergic cyclic AMP generating system in limbic forebrain. Nature 257:495–496, 1975

Vogel GW, Vogel F, McAbee RS, Thrumand AJ: Improvement of depression by REM sleep deprivation. Arch Gen Psychiatr 37:247–253, 1980

Waehrens J, Gerlach J: Bromocriptine and imipramine in endogenous depression: A double-blind controlled trial in outpatients. J Affect Disord 3:193–202, 1981

Wagner HR, Davis JN: Decreased beta-adrenergic responses in the female brain are eliminated by ovariectomy: Correlation of [3H]-dihydroalprenolol binding and catecholamine stimulated cyclic AMP levels. Brain Res 201:235–239, 1980

Wamsley JK, Byerley WF, McCabe RT, McConnell EJ, Davison TM, Grosser BI: Receptor alterations associated with serotonergic agents: An autoradiographic analysis. J Clin Psychiatr 48:19–25, 1987

Weissman MM, Boyd JH: The epidemiology of affective disorders. In Post RM, Ballenger JC (eds): Neurobiology of Mood Disorders. Baltimore, Williams & Wilkins, 1984

Weissman MM, Myers JK: Rates and risks of depressive symptoms in a United States urban community. Acta Psychiatr Scand 57:219–231, 1978

Weissman MS, Paykel ES: The depressed woman: A study of social relationships. University of Chicago Press. Chicago, 1974.

Williams AW, Ware JE, Donald CA: A model of mental health, life events, and social supports applicable to general populations. J Health Soc Behav 22:324–336, 1981

Willner P: Depression: A Psychobiological Synthesis. New York, Wiley-Interscience, 1985

7

Anxiety Disorders

Linda M. Nagy, John H. Krystal, and Dennis S. Charney

The anxiety disorders discussed in this chapter are those included in the Diagnostic and Statistical Manual of Mental Disorders, Third Edition—Revised (DSM-III-R): Panic disorder and agoraphobia, social phobia, simple phobia, obsessive-compulsive disorder, post traumatic stress disorder, and generalized anxiety disorder (American Psychiatric Association, 1987). For each disorder, epidemiologic data, a basic description of the syndrome, similarity to and differences from other psychiatric or nonpsychiatric medical disorders, current models and theories of etiology, and treatment approaches are reviewed. An attempt is made to indicate whether information is well-documented or tentative, to guide students in forming a knowledge base to supplement as further research developments become available. It is crucial that physicians be able to recognize anxiety disorders and be aware of their appropriate treatments. These conditions are among the most common in the general population, lead to high utilization of health care services, and, when untreated, produce significant distress and disability.

ADJUSTMENT DISORDERS OF ANXIOUS MOOD

The general category of *adjustment disorder* has been mentioned in Chapter 6 in reference to depressive reactions. In the context of anxiety, an adjustment disorder with anxious mood would be defined as a *maladaptive* reaction to an identifiable environmental or psychosocial stress, accompanied predominantly by symptoms of anxiety, that interferes with the patient's functioning. Although the degree of anxiety-related stress can be disabling, the anxiety is expected to remit after the stress remits or an adaptation is made. (A similar category, "Adjustment Disorder with Physical Complaints," exists to describe patients with stress-related—albeit relatively transient—somatic symptoms.) Patients can also be designated as having "mixed emotional features" if symptoms of anxiety and depression appear enmeshed.

These types of stress-related reactions often bring patients to physicians' offices with a variety of physiological symptoms of their anxiety. Short-term use of low-dose benzodiazepines may be of benefit as long as the patient is helped to identify the stress that may have caused the symptoms and means of managing it more effectively are discussed. If the stress appears to be chronic or unmanageable by the patient, the patient may require further evaluation and possibly some form of psychotherapy. Referral for a psychiatric evaluation should be made before the long-term use of benzodiazepines becomes the only alternative for managing chronic anxiety.

PANIC DISORDER AND AGORAPHOBIA

Panic disorder is characterized by recurrent discrete attacks of anxiety accompanied by several somatic symptoms, such as palpitations, paresthesias, hyperventilation, diaphoresis, chest pain, dizziness, trembling, and dyspnea. Usually the condition is accompanied by agoraphobia, which consists of excessive fear (and often avoidance) of situations, such as driving, crowded places, stores, or being alone, in which escape or obtaining help would be difficult. Current DSM-III-R classifications include "Panic Disorder with or without Agoraphobia" and "Agoraphobia without History of Panic Disorder." In the previous classification system, agoraphobia was designated as the primary condition. Historically, other terms for what is likely the same condition have included anxiety neurosis, neurasthenia, neurocirculatory asthenia, effort syndrome, soldier's heart, irritable heart, and DaCosta's syndrome.

Epidemiology

The Epidemiologic Catchment Area Study (ECA) reports prevalence estimates based on DSM-III diagnoses, which were separated into agoraphobia (analogous to DSM-III-R diagnoses of "Agoraphobia without History of Panic Attacks" and "'Panic Disorder with Agoraphobia") and panic disorder (analogous to DSM-III-R diagnosis of "Panic Disorder without Agoraphobia"). Lifetime prevalence rates at the three sites varied between 7.8 and 23.3% for all phobias (including social and simple) and between 1.4 and 1.5% for panic disorder. Six-month prevalence rates were 2.7 to 5.8% for agoraphobia and 0.6 to 1.0% for panic disorder. The lifetime rate for females was 2.4 to 4.3 times greater than that for males for agoraphobia and 1.3 to 3.5 times greater for panic disorder; however, 6-month prevalence rates for panic disorder were either similar between sexes or increased in males (Robins et al., 1984; Myers et al., 1984). It is generally felt that there may be underreporting of these disorders by men either due to reluctance to admit to having these symptoms or through disguise by alcoholism. Alternatively, there may be a true higher rates in females because of hormonal, social, or other gender differences.

Age of onset is typically in the late teens to early thirties and is unusual after the age of 40 years. *The majority (78%) of patients describe the initial attack as spontaneous* (occurring without an environmental trigger). In the remainder the first attack is precipitated by confrontation with a phobic stimulus or use of a psychoactive drug. Onset of the disorder often follows within 6 months of a major stressful life event, such as marital separation, occupational change, or pregnancy (Breier et al., 1986).

These disorders appear to be less prevalent in the elderly. Both 6-month and lifetime rates are lower in the over-65 age group, suggesting possible underreporting, decreased survival of those with the disorder, or a cohort effect, such that the frequency of the disorder is increased in the middle age groups. Rates are generally similar for blacks and whites. Rates of agoraphobia in college graduates are about half those of noncollege graduates. Rates are higher for separated and divorced persons than married individuals. It is not yet established whether these differences reflect predisposing factors, noncausal associations, or consequences of the disorder. Panic disorder is also increased among family members of those with the disorder (see Etiology, below). A history of childhood separation anxiety disorder is reported by 20 to 50% of patients. Preliminary findings of high rates of behavioral inhibition in the offspring of patients with panic disorder are consistent with the hypothesis that the disorder may have developmental antecedents.

Description and Differential Diagnosis

Panic disorder usually begins with a spontaneous panic attack that leads the individual to seek medical treatment, often presenting to an emergency room believing that he or she is having a heart attack, stroke, losing his or her mind, or experiencing some other serious medical event (Table 7-1). Some time may pass before subsequent attacks, or the patient may continue to get frequent attacks. Patients may feel constantly fearful and anxious after the first attack, wondering what is wrong and fearing it will happen again. Some patients experience nocturnal attacks that awaken them from sleep. Usually patients gradually become fearful of situations (1) that they associate with the attacks; (2) in which they would be unable to flee if the attack occurred; (3) in which help would not be readily available; or (4) in which they would be embarrassed if others should notice they are experiencing an attack (although attacks are not usually evident to others). Typical agoraphobic situations are listed in Table 7-2. Less frequently, a history of phobia may precede the first panic attack. Before patients are educated about the symptoms of the disorder they believe they are suffering from a serious medical condition. They are often embarrassed about their symptoms and will try to hide them from others, often making excuses not to attend functions or enter phobic situations.

The differential diagnosis of panic disorder and agoraphobia includes organic anxiety disorder (usually due to endocrine disturbance, such as hyperthyroidism; withdrawal from CNS depressants such as alcohol or benzodiazepines; or intoxication by stimulants such as caffeine, cocaine, or amphetamine), other phobic conditions, generalized anxiety disorder, and psychosis. Medical illness that may produce symptoms similar to panic attacks must be excluded. Endocrine disturbances, such as pheochromocytoma, thyroid disorder, or hypoglycemia, may produce similar symptoms and can be excluded with appropriate clinical history and laboratory evaluations. When gastrointestinal symptoms of attacks are prominent one may need to exclude the diagnosis of colitis. Symptoms of tachycardia, palpitations, chest pain or pressure, and dyspnea may be confused with cardiac or respiratory conditions. Lightheadedness, faintness, dizziness, derealization, shaking, numbness, and tingling may suggest a neurologic condition. The association between mitral valve prolapse and panic disorder is controversial. The presence of mitral valve prolapse in panic disorder

Table 7-1 **DSM-III-R Criteria for Panic Disorder**

A. At some time during the disturbance, one or more panic attacks (discrete periods of intense fear or discomfort) have occurred that were (1) unexpected, i.e., did not occur immediately before or on exposure to a situation that almost always caused anxiety, and (2) not triggered by situations in which the person was the focus of others' attention.

B. Either four attacks, as defined in criterion A, have occurred within a 4-week period, or one or more attacks have been followed by a period of at least a month of persistent fear of having another attack.

C. At least four of the following symptoms developed during at least one of the attacks:
   1. Shortness of breath (dyspnea) or smothering sensations
   2. Dizziness, unsteady feelings, or faintness
   3. Palpitations or accelerated heart rate (tachycardia)
   4. Trembling or shaking
   5. Sweating
   6. Choking
   7. Nausea or abdominal distress
   8. Depersonalization or derealization
   9. Numbness or tingling sensations (paresthesias)
   10. Flushes (hot flashes) or chills
   11. Chest pain or discomfort
   12. Fear of dying
   13. Fear of going crazy or of doing something uncontrolled
   Note: Attacks involving four or more symptoms are panic attacks; attacks involving fewer than four symptoms are limited symptom attacks.

D. During at least some of the attacks, at least four of the C symptoms developed suddenly and increased in intensity within 10 minutes of the beginning of the first C symptom noticed in the attack.

E. It cannot be established that an organic factor initiated and maintained the disturbance: e.g., amphetamine or caffeine intoxication, hyperthyroidism.

Note: Mitral valve prolapse may be an associated condition, but does not preclude a diagnosis of panic disorder.

(Used with permission. American Psychiatric Association, 1987)

---

patients does not appear to alter treatment response or course, so the diagnosis of panic disorder should be made independently of mitral valve prolapse.

Panic disorder differs from generalized anxiety disorder in having recurrent discrete, intense episodes of panic symptoms, although in both disorders anticipatory anxiety and generalized feelings of anxiety may be present. Although some of the same situations may be feared, agoraphobia differs from social and simple phobias in that the fear is related to feeling trapped or being unable to escape and in that the fears often become generalized. Agoraphobics may additionally have a history of other phobias.

Panic disorder is frequently associated with major depression, other anxiety disorders, and alcohol and substance abuse. In clinical samples as many as two thirds of panic patients report experiencing a major depressive episode at some time in their lives. Similarly, studies of patients seeking treatment for major depression report high rates of panic in these patients and their relatives. Once symptoms begin, patients often describe becoming demoralized as a result of fear related to the symptoms and imagined causes, and resulting from impairment when their activities are restricted by their agoraphobia. Unlike depressed patients, panic disorder patients usually lack

Table 7-2 **DSM-III-R Criteria for Agoraphobia**

Agoraphobia is fear of being in places or situations from which escape might be difficult (or embarrassing) or in which help might not be available in the event of a panic attack. (Include cases in which persistent avoidance behavior originated during an active phase of panic disorder, even if the person does not attribute the avoidance behavior to fear of having a panic attack.) In agoraphobia without history of panic disorder, the fear is of suddenly developing a symptom that could be incapacitating or extremely embarrassing. Example include: dizziness or falling, depersonalization or derealization, loss of bladder or bowel control, vomiting, or cardiac distress. As a result of this fear, the person either restricts travel or needs a companion when away from home, or else endures agoraphobic situations despite intense anxiety.

Common Agoraphobic Situations

TRAVEL:
Airplane (Note: fear is of being trapped, not that plane will crash.)
Car
Bus
Subway
Trains
DRIVING:
Alone
Highways
Bridges
Tunnels
Heavy traffic
Inner lane of highway
PROXIMITY TO SAFETY:
May have a "safe perimeter" (a specific distance from home; in severe form can become
    housebound)
Far from medical help
Being home alone
PUBLIC PLACES:
Stores
Malls
Restaurants
Theaters
Church
Temple
Crowds
OTHER:
Sitting in a meeting
Waiting in line
Sitting far from exit (prefer last row, aisle seat) in theater/auditorium/classroom
These situations are feared because the patient feels that he or she will not be able to leave
    quickly in the event of a panic attack or will not be able to get help quickly, or feels that having
    an attack in the situation would be embarrassing or the situation will cause them to have an
    attack.

(Used with permission. American Psychiatric Association, 1987)

vegetative symptoms and have a normal desire to engage in activities but avoid them because of their phobias.

The disorder may cause personality changes. Patients' premorbid personalities may be highly independent, outgoing, and active, but while symptoms are active they can become very dependent, passive, overly agreeable, with an extreme need to please others, and may resist making appointments or social engagements.

Attempts to self-medicate the intolerable anxiety may increase the risk of alcoholism and substance abuse. Patients may require a drink before entering phobic situations. Approximately 20% of patients report a history of alcohol abuse, but the onset of alcoholism precedes the first attack in almost all patients (Breier et al., 1986). Alcoholism may also alter the course of the disorder. Preliminary data suggest panic disorder precipitated by cocaine use may be less likely to respond well to the usual pharmacologic treatments and may have less association with a family history of panic disorder.

Etiologic/Pathophysiologic Theories

Familial/Genetic Theories

Genetic epidemiologic studies have consistently demonstrated increased rates of panic disorder among first- and second-degree relatives of panic disorder probands. This observation could result from genetic, nongenetic biological, and/or cultural factors shared by family members. The reported recurrence risk of illness in first-degree relatives of panic disorder probands is 15 to 18% by patient report vs. 0 to 5% in controls, and is 20 to 50% by direct interview of proband relatives vs. 2 to 8% in controls (Crowe, 1985). Segregation analysis indicates the pattern of familial transmission is consistent with single-locus autosomal dominant transmission with incomplete penetrance, although a multifactorial mode of inheritance (additive effects of more than one gene) or genetic heterogeneity (different gene defects producing similar clinical syndromes) have not been excluded as possibilities (Pauls et al., 1980). Comparison of concordance rates in monozygotic vs. dizygotic twins is used to differentiate between genetic and environmental factors in families, since monozygotic twins share 100% of their genetic material and dizygotic twins on average share half (therefore, in an autosomal-dominant illness with complete penetrance, expected concordance rates would be 100% in monozygotic and 50% in dizygotic twins). Torgersen (1983) found concordance for anxiety disorder with panic attacks in 4 of 13 monozygotic and 0 of 16 dizygotic twin pairs. Other preliminary reports suggest identical HLA genotypes in sibling pairs concordant for panic disorder and possible genetic linkage to chromosome 16q22, although the significance level required to establish linkage was not reached (Crowe et al., 1987).

Other Biologic Theories

Investigation of biologic systems in panic disorder include examination of adrenergic, benzodiazepine, serotonergic, and opiate neurotransmitter systems, anxiogenic response to caffeine, lactate, and CO_2, models of locus ceruleus involvement, and brain imaging studies. Yohimbine, an alpha-2 adrenergic antagonist, produces greater increases in anxiety (resembling panic attacks), blood pressure, and plasma levels of the norepinephrine metabolite MHPG in panic disorder patients than in healthy subjects. Conversely, clonidine, an alpha-2 adrenergic *agonist*, which decreases noradrenergic function, produces greater decreases in blood pressure and plasma MHPG and similar increases in drowsiness and growth hormone levels in patients as compared with controls. This responsiveness appears to be specific to panic disorder patients; it is not observed in generalized anxiety disorder, obsessive-compulsive disorder, major depression, or schizophrenia. Conflicting results have been reported for isoproterenol, a beta-adrenergic agonist: in one study isoproterenol induced panic attacks, but in another study the reduced responsiveness observed in panic disorder implied a hyposensitivity to beta-adrenergic stimulation.

The benzodiazepine inverse agonist FG-7142 precipitated severe anxiety states comparable to panic attacks in healthy individuals; this is consistent with animal studies in which beta carboline produces an acute fear state. The benzodiazepine antagonist RO 15-1788 precipitated a modest level of anxiety and panic attacks in some panic disorder patients.

Preclinical studies have suggested possible serotonergic involvement in anxiety and in the mechanisms of action of medications used to treat anxiety. However, the prolactin response to the serotonin precursor tryptophan is not altered in panic disorder. The serotonin agonist m-chlorophenylpiperazine (MCPP) may elicit greater anxiety responses in panic disorder patients, but the response is not as pronounced or consistent as that observed with yohimbine or lactate.

Interactions between opiate and adrenergic systems were studied using yohimbine and naloxone, an opiate antagonist. The combination produced a synergistic effect of increasing anxiety symptoms and plasma cortisol. This is postulated to occur through opiate-noradrenergic interactions in the locus ceruleus, amygdala, cerebral cortex, or hypothalamus. Cohen's observation in 1950 that patients with neurocirculatory asthenia developed higher blood lactate levels during exercise than controls prompted Pitts and McClure to administer sodium lactate infusions to patients with panic disorder. Although provocation of panic attacks with sodium lactate is the best-replicated of the provocation procedures in panic, the mechanism by which lactate causes panic attacks is not established. Effects on noradrenergic activity, calcium, and regulation of intracellular pH and ion channels have been explored. Panic patients also demonstrate an increased anxiogenic response to breathing a mixture of air and CO_2 compared with controls. Effective antianxiety medications appear to block lactate, yohimbine, or CO_2-induced attacks.

Caffeine produces significantly greater anxiety symptoms in panic disorder patients than in controls. Therefore, patients are usually advised to eliminate caffeine from their diet. The most likely mechanism of caffeine's anxiogenic effect is antagonism of central adenosine receptors, which have neuromodulatory effects on acetylcholine, norepinephrine, and firing rates of locus ceruleus and other neurons. In animal studies of the locus ceruleus, the major norepinephrine-containing nucleus in the brain, stimulation produces a marked fear and anxiety response and ablation diminishes fear response to threatening stimuli. Additionally, many drugs which increase locus ceruleus firing in animals are anxiogenic in humans, whereas several drugs that decrease locus ceruleus discharge are anxiolytic in humans (Gorman, Liebowitz, 1986).

Preliminary results of brain-imaging studies using positron emission tomography preinfusion in patients experiencing lactate-induced attacks indicate cerebral blood flow asymmetry in the parahippocampal gyrus and temporal pole. Brain electrical mapping and magnetic resonance imaging similarly suggest temporal lobe abnormalities in panic disorder. Unlike major depression, panic disorder patients fail to show nonsuppression of cortisol following dexamethasone and worsen rather than improve with sleep deprivation (reviewed in Roy-Byrne, Cowley, 1988).

Behavioral Theories

Behavioral theories (learning theory) have mainly been applied to the development of agoraphobia. This involves contiguity learning, the paired association of events that have occurred together (e.g., a panic attack and driving over a bridge), together with instrumental learning or operant conditioning, the modification of behavior to avoid future negative events and invite future positive events (e.g., by avoiding bridges, avoid the discomfort of an attack). Stimulus generalization may occur or subsequent attacks may occur in different situations and become associated with those situations (Millon, 1986). Panic disorder has also been viewed as a phobia in which the feared stimuli are internal rather than external. Patients associate somatic sensations with immediate threat and respond with anxiety and fear. After the first panic attack, subsequent attacks begin with unexpected peripheral somatic sensations to which the patient responds with anxiety, resulting in additional somatic symptoms and a spiralling increase in anxiety and symptoms. This theory has lead to the application of relaxation, cognitive, and exposure techniques to the treatment of the attacks themselves (Rapee, Barlow, 1988).

Psychoanalytic Theories

Psychoanalytic theory stems from Freud's hypothesis that panic attacks result from incomplete repression of unacceptable impulses. Later he revised this theory to conceptualize anxiety as a signal to the ego that it is in a dangerous situation. The patient then develops neurotic symptoms to reduce the signal anxiety and avoid danger. In any case, unconscious psychological conflict is believed to be the root cause. Freud also felt agoraphobia was due to the recollection of an anxiety attack along with fear of a future attack occurring in a situation in which the patient believed he or she could not escape it. He observed constitutional variability in individuals' capacities to experience anxiety and predicted that the mechanisms of biological predispositions would be better elucidated with advancing knowledge of brain neurochemistry.

Treatment

Pharmacologic Treatment

Monoamine oxidase inhibitors (MAOIs) are probably the most effective medications for anxiety patients but are not necessarily the drugs of choice, because they necessitate a low-tyramine diet to minimize the risk of hypertensive crisis. Anxiety patients are especially fearful and need extra coaxing to take this medication. Dosing is similar to that for treatment of depression, except one may wish to begin with smaller doses. Imipramine is the best studied, but most tricyclic antidepressants probably have similar efficacy. Because of the sizable proportion of patients who exhibit sensitivity, with an activation syndrome of jitteriness, stimulant-like sensation, and insomnia, one may need to start at 10 mg/day and work up slowly. Some patients habituate to the activation syndrome but symptoms may reemerge with each dose increment. Activation syndrome may be more common with desipramine, presumably because of its greater effect on norepinephrine. In some patients these drugs have an antipanic effect at much lower doses than is required for antidepressant treatment; others will require doses similar to those needed for depression. Onset of therapeutic (antipanic) effect of MAOIs and tricyclic antidepressants is delayed until after 2 to 4 weeks once the therapeutic dose is reached, as in depression. More patience, reassurance, and encouragement is needed when these medications are used in panic disorder. Trazodone appears not to be effective in panic disorder. Preliminary reports suggest fluvoxamine may be effective, but it is not commercially available in the United States.

Alprazolam is the best studied of the benzodiazepines in panic disorder. It is very effective in reducing or blocking panic attacks. Other benzodiazepines, including lorazepam, clonazepam, and diazepam, may also be effective. Onset of therapeutic effects is fairly rapid. Some respond to low doses (i.e., 0.25 mg t.i.d. of alprazolam or equivalent) but 3.0 mg/day in divided doses is common, with some patients requiring gradual increases to 6 to 10 mg/day. Alprazolam is usually a second-line treatment for panic because of concerns about difficulty with discontinuation. Possibly because of its short half-life, patients may experience increased symptoms during taper or new withdrawal symptoms may emerge. As with tricyclic antidepressants, some patients will require chronic treatment. Benzodiazepines should be avoided in patients with alcohol or substance abuse problems. Some clinicians feel that longer-acting benzodiazepines such as clonazepam have advantages over the shorter-acting drugs such as alprazolam and lorazepam.

Despite its usefulness in treating generalized anxiety disorder, the non-benzodiazepine anxiolytic buspirone is probably ineffective in treating panic. Beta-blockers may block symptoms of palpitations or tremor but generally are not as effective against panic attacks as tricyclic antidepressants, MAOIs, or benzodiazepines. Occasionally a combination of a tricyclic antidepressant and benzodiazepine is required. If both medications are initiated together, there is some possibility that the benzodiazepine blocks the therapeutic effect of the tricyclic antidepressant, based on reemergence of symptoms on attempts to withdraw the benzodiazepine. An alternative explanation is that benzodiazepine discontinuation itself induces symptoms of panic. The combination of pharmacologic treatment with behavioral or supportive psychotherapy is very important, especially when phobias are present.

The question of how long pharmacologic treatment should be continued after symptom control has been achieved is not well studied. As already mentioned, panic attacks may increase during discontinuation of alprazolam but will often subside once the patient is medication-free. Relapse appears to be common when effective pharmacologic therapy is discontinued (including therapy with tricyclic antidepressants and MAOIs) and may be precipitated during periods of high stress. One long-term follow-up study of panic disorder patients treated with alprazolam and behavioral therapy indicated that 30% of patients were able to discontinue medication and most others substantially decreased the dosage of medication 2 to 4 years after initial treatment. Tolerance to antipanic effects of alprazolam were uncommon. The general recommendation is to continue medications for 6 months following treatment response and then attempt to taper slowly over a period of months (Krystal et al., 1988). Table 7-3 summarizes pharmacologic approaches for panic disorder/agoraphobia.

Table 7-3 **Pharmacotherapy for Anxiety Disorders**

	ALPRAZOLAM*/BENZODIAZEPINES	BUSPIRONE	IMIPRAMINE/TCA	PHENELZINE/MAOI	FLUOXETINE
Main indications†	PD, GAD, SP(?)	GAD	PD, PTSD, GAD(?), OCD(?)	PD, PTSD, SP, OCD(?)	OCD, PD(?)
Starting dose	0.25–0.5 mg TID	5 mg TID	10 mg qhs	15 mg q AM	20 mg/day‡
Initial side effects	Sedation, ataxia, memory impairment	Dizziness, nausea, diarrhea, headache, nervousness	Sedation, orthostatic hypotension, dry mouth, anxiety	Orthostatic hypotension, stimulant, tyramine reaction	Gastrointestinal, anorexia, insomnia, anxiety, drowsiness
Onset of effect	Immediate	2–4 wk delay	2–4 wk delay	2–4 wk delay	3–6 wk delay (OCD)
Common maintenance dose	.25–1.0 mg TID	5–15 mg TID	25–200 mg qhs (or divided dose)	15–30 mg TID	20–60 mg/d
Long-term side effects	Physical dependence	None known at this time	Weight gain	Tyramine reaction	Unknown
Rate of taper	0.25 mg/wk	5 mg TID/wk	50 mg/1–2 wk	15–45 mg/wk	10–20 mg/wk
Symptoms of abrupt discontinuation	Increased sensitivity to sound/light/touch, autonomic arousal, confusion, seizures	None known at this time	Flulike symptoms, anxiety, nightmares	Hypertension, anxiety, nightmares, autonomic arousal, psychosis	None known at this time

* Benzodiazepine dose equivalents: 1 mg alprazolam = 0.5 mg triazolam = 0.5 mg clonazepam = 2 mg lorazepam = 10 mg diazepam. Alprazolam is used as the prototypical benzodiazepine, but these other drugs listed are effective; longer-acting benzodiazepines may have advantages. Alprazolam and other high-potency short-acting benzodiazepines may be associated with severe withdrawal syndromes.
† PD = panic disorder; SP = social phobia; OCD = obsessive compulsive disorder; GAD = generalized anxiety disorder; PTSD = post traumatic stress disorder
(Adapted from Krystal JH, Charney DS: Advances in anxiety therapy. Internal Medicine for the Specialist 9:93–111, 1988)
‡ Fluoxetine is currently available only in a 20 mg dose form; lower starting doses may be needed in PD and other patients which require special compounding efforts to reduce the dose form to 10 mg/day.

Behavioral Treatment

Prolonged exposure in vivo (see Behavioral Therapies) appears to be the most effective behavioral treatment for agoraphobia. The usual procedure is to develop a hierarchical list of phobias, gradually enter the least phobic situations repeatedly, then work up the hierarchy to more strongly feared situations. Prolonged (2 hours), in vivo, and frequent (daily) exposure sessions are superior to brief (0.5 hours), imaginal, and spaced (weekly) exposure sessions. Good results can be achieved in groups, individually, or as a self-help or spouse-assisted program. Group therapy may have the additional advantages of being cost-effective, providing the patient with coping models, and leading to fewer dropouts. It is not essential to evoke anxiety during exposure. Follow-up studies report enduring effects several years after treatment.

Cognitive therapy appears to reduce irrational beliefs but by itself may not reduce anxiety or avoidance. The focus is to identify distorted patterns of thinking, interrupt the thought with self-instruction to stop, and substitute either distraction or positive thoughts. There is some evidence favoring the combination of relaxation training and biofeedback with cognitive therapy in the treatment of panic attacks. Similarly, assertiveness training specifically increases assertiveness. Often patients suffering from this disorder have become dependent on others to accompany them into phobic situations or for other support. They may fear abandonment and rejection and question their ability to survive or function independently. As an adaptation they become passively over-agreeable and have an excessive need to please. This makes them delightful to have as friends or acquaintances but has the negative effect of inhibiting their ability to express their own needs or to say no, and can create additional suppressed anger (usually self-directed) and anxiety. As patients overcome their symptoms and gain mastery of phobias, they can begin to address their passivity and learn to tactfully express their own needs and desires while acknowledging needs of others. Aggressive individuals may be taught to recognize their aggressive behavior and substitute assertiveness.

Psychoeducation plays a very important role in the management of these patients. Knowing their diagnosis is enormously reassuring to many patients, who tend to believe they have a rare, perhaps life-threatening condition that doctors have failed to recognize. It is important to emphasize that although they feel they will die, faint, lose control, or go crazy during attacks, this will not happen. They also should understand current theories of etiology and that, with treatment, the prognosis for a significant reduction in symptoms and improvement in functioning is very good. Also, *group treatment* is helpful for patients to recognize that others suffer from the same syndrome. These groups can provide very beneficial understanding, support, and encouragement from peers. Many communities have self-help groups for panic/agoraphobic patients.

Combinations of behavior therapies or medication together with behavior therapy are commonly employed. It is important to emphasize alternative treatments to patients expecting to receive only one form of treatment, such as individuals who are "phobic" of medications or patients expecting complete relief from a "magic pill." The possibility of noncompliance with treatment recommendations should be considered in treatment failure.

Psychodynamically oriented psychotherapy may be an important adjunctive treatment for individuals with significant interpersonal difficulties, but has no proven specific effect in alleviating panic attacks or agoraphobia.

Role of the Nonpsychiatric Physician In Patient Management

Nonpsychiatric physicians play a crucial role in the initial evaluation and recognition of panic disorder, since patients will most frequently present with symptoms of panic attacks in medical settings. Following a negative work-up for medical pathology, it is insufficient to attribute the patient's symptoms to "anxiety" or "stress." As stated above, it is very important that patients receive the appropriate diagnosis and treatment.

In ongoing pharmacologic treatment (especially with benzodiazepines), it is important to differentiate the patient's desire to alleviate symptoms with effective medication from the drug-seeking behavior of substance abusers. Once symptoms are relieved, panic patients usually do not request dose increases. On the contrary, they typically fear "addiction" and have the long-term goal of dose reduction or being medication-free. However, due to the chronic nature of the disorder, and because medications provide treatment without necessarily a cure, prolonged pharmacologic treatment or repeated courses of treatment may be necessary.

Indications for Psychiatric Consultation and Referral

In cases that are not straightforward, psychiatric evaluation can aid in establishing the diagnosis, comprehensively assessing co-morbid disorders, and selecting appropriate treatments. When a patient's response to initial treatment is inadequate, psychiatrists experienced in treatment of panic and agoraphobia may facilitate a treatment response with dosage adjustment, management of side effects, addressing resistance to treatment recommendations, and ensuring the adequacy of nonpharmacologic treatments.

CLINICAL PEARLS

- Suspect panic attacks in patients without physical pathology who present with somatic symptoms suggestive of cardiac, endocrine, and neurologic disorders.
- It may be very important in successful long-term management that a patient overcome the fear of having another panic attack.
- When using tricyclic antidepressants be sure to warn patients about a possible initial "activation syndrome" and use small doses if necessary to begin treatment.
- Benzodiazepines may be required in higher dosages and for longer periods than indicated for other disorders; tricyclics and MAOIs should be considered first lines of treatment.
- Be alert for coexisting anxiety disorders, major depression, alcoholism, and substance abuse, and address them as indicated.

SOCIAL PHOBIA

Social phobia is commonly experienced by healthy individuals, especially in initial public speaking experiences. For some people, this fear becomes persistent and overwhelming, limiting their social or occupational functioning because of intense anxiety and, often, avoidance. Social phobia is probably the least studied of the anxiety disorders; much of our current understanding is based on imprecise classifications or related phenomena and so must be considered preliminary.

Epidemiology

Preliminary estimates of 6-month prevalence rates of social phobia ascertained by screening questionnaire in the ECA study are 1.2 to 2.2% (0.9 to 1.7% in men, 1.5 to 2.6% in women). The distribution is fairly even across the age span although rates may be lower in the over-65 age group. Onset is usually between 15 and 20 years of age, and the course tends to be chronic and unremitting. Complications include interference with work or school, social isolation, and abuse of alcohol or drugs. In inpatient alcoholism treatment programs, 20 to 25% report social phobia beginning before the onset of alcoholism or persisting after 1 year of abstinence. Significant depressive symptoms may also occur in social phobia; in one study one third of social phobia patients reported a history of major depression.

Description and Differential Diagnosis

Social phobia is characterized by a persistent and exaggerated fear of humiliation or embarrassment in social situations, leading to high levels of distress and possibly avoidance of those situations (see DSM-III-R criteria; Table 7-4) Patients may become fearful that their anxiety will be evident to others, which may intensify their symptoms or even produce a situational panic attack. The fear may be of speaking in public, meeting people, eating or writing in public, and relates to fear of appearing nervous or foolish, making mistakes, being criticized, or being laughed at. Often physical symptoms of anxiety such as blushing, trembling, sweating, and tachycardia are triggered when the patient feels under evaluation or scrutiny.

Two case vignettes of social phobia follow:

CASE 1:

A 29-year-old single businessman stated that at age 12 his voice "cracked" during an audition and people laughed at him. A few years later he became very anxious when he had to speak in class. He gradually became very anxious or avoided any situation in which he might be called upon or observed, even to answer a roll call. His avoidance of professional meetings was interfering with his work.

CASE 2:

A 33-year-old single female chemist described how, during the rehearsal dinner for her best friend's wedding, she became very anxious and

Table 7-4 **DSM-III-R Criteria for Social Phobia**

A. A persistent fear of one or more situations (the social phobic situations) in which the person is exposed to possible scrutiny by others and fears that he or she may do something or act in a way that will be humiliating or embarrassing. Examples include being unable to continue talking while speaking in public, choking on food when eating in front of others, being unable to urinate in a public lavatory, hand-trembling when writing in the presence of others, and saying foolish things or not being able to answer questions in social situations.

B. If an Axis III or another Axis I disorder is present, the fear in A is unrelated to it: e.g., the fear is not of having a panic attack (Panic Disorder), stuttering, trembling (Parkinson's Disease), or of exhibiting abnormal eating behavior (Anorexia Nervosa or Bulimia Nervosa).

C. During some phase of the disturbance, exposure to the specific phobic stimulus (or stimuli) almost invariably provokes an immediate anxiety response.

D. The phobic situation(s) is avoided, or is endured with intense anxiety.

E. The avoidant behavior interferes with occupational functioning or with usual social activities or relationships with others, or there is marked distress about having the fear.

F. The person recognizes that his or her fear is excessive or unreasonable.

G. If the person is under 18, the disturbance does not meet the criteria for Avoidant Disorder of Childhood or Adolescence.

Specify generalized type if the phobic situation includes most social situations, and also consider the additional diagnosis of Avoidant Personality Disorder.

(Used with permission. American Psychiatric Association, 1987)

---

broke into a cold sweat. She began anticipating that she would perspire excessively when encountering people, which then would occur. She began avoiding any organized social event and was frustrated about this limitation on her life.

Probably the most difficult diagnostic distinctions are between social phobia and normal performance anxiety, or social phobia and panic disorder. Normal fear of public speaking usually diminishes as the individual is speaking or with additional experience, whereas in social phobia the anxiety may worsen or fail to attenuate with rehearsal. Social phobics may experience situational panic attacks resulting from anticipation or exposure to the feared social situation. Some panic disorder/agoraphobia patients avoid social situations due to fear of embarrassment if a panic attack should occur, but usually their initial panic attack is spontaneous (occurs in a situation they previously did not fear), and the subsequent development of phobias is generalized beyond social situations. Sometimes social phobia and panic disorder coexist. The diagnostic distinction between these disorders still requires validation. However, differences in response to lactate challenge and treatment may support this separation. Social phobia can be differentiated from simple phobias in that the latter do not involve social situations involving scrutiny, humiliation, or embarrassment. In major depression, social avoidance may develop from apathy rather than fear and resolves with remission of the episode. In schizoid personality disorder, social isolation is due to lack of interest rather than fear. In avoidant personality disorder, the avoidance is of personal relationships; however, if the patient develops a marked anxiety about and avoidance of most social situations, the additional diagnosis of social phobia should be given.

Etiology

Familial/Genetic Theories

Animal studies demonstrate heritability of various fear, anxiety, and exploratory, escape, or avoidant behaviors, often mediated by combinations of genes. These are reviewed by Marks (1986) and may be relevant to social phobia and other anxiety disorders. Human studies of general population samples have suggested some genetic heritability for traits such as fear of strangers, shyness, social introversion, and fear of social criticism. Torgersen found greater monozygotic than dizygotic twin concordance for social phobic features such as discomfort when eating with strangers, or when being watched eating, writing, working, or trembling. There are very few family data reported about social phobia. The strong heritability of blood-injury phobia has led to the hypothesis that blushing, for example, may be an autonomic response under genetic influence that is tied to social cues and might lead to social phobia.

Other Biologic Theories

Symptoms reported by social phobia patients in phobic situations suggest heightened autonomic arousal. When placed in a phobic situation, social phobics experience significant increases in heart rate that are highly correlated with self-perceived physiologic arousal, in contrast to claustrophobics, who experience less heart rate increase and negative correlations between perceived and actual physiologic arousal. Stressful public speaking results in two- to threefold increases in plasma epinephrine levels in normal individuals. It is not known whether social phobia patients have greater or more sustained epinephrine increases or are more sensitive. Epinephrine infusions do not appear to cause social anxiety in social phobia patients. Social phobia patients may lack normal habituation to anxiety in social situations, but this has not been studied systematically. The response of social phobia patients to lactate challenge appears to be more similar to normal controls than to panic patients.

Behavioral Theories

It is suggested social phobia may result from a lack of social skills (skills-deficit model), faulty evaluation of one's performance in social situations (cognitive inhibition model), hypersensitivity to criticism or rejection, or early traumatic social or performance experiences (conditioned-anxiety model). These models have led to application of various behavioral techniques to treatment of social phobia (see below).

Psychoanalytic Theories

Psychoanalytic theories do not differentiate between phobias, and so would explain social phobias in a manner similar to agoraphobia (above). A number of traits have been observed in social phobia, such as rigid concepts of appropriate social behavior, an unrealistic tendency to experience others as critical or disapproving, increased awareness and fear of scrutiny by others, exaggerated awareness and tendency to overreact to minimal somatic symptoms, but the relevance of these traits to social phobia and whether they cause or result from the disorder have not been studied. As adults, social phobia patients retrospectively rate their parents as less caring, more rejecting, and overprotective as compared with healthy adults' perceptions of their parents; however, the accuracy of retrospective reporting and the specificity of this finding in social phobia are not established.

Treatment

Pharmacologic Treatment

Most pharmacologic studies have been performed on mixed phobic groups or have examined social anxiety in nonpatient (subclinical analogue) populations. There are no MAOI trials in which social phobia is examined independently from agoraphobia. However, phenelzine (a MAOI) was found to be superior to placebo in four studies that included social phobia patients; one study reports significant reduction of social phobia scale ratings in all phobics treated with phenelzine. Phenelzine was found superior to the tricyclic antidepressants imipramine and amitriptyline in reducing interpersonal sensitivity in depressed outpatients. One trial of beta-blockers in social phobia failed to show superiority of propranolol over placebo. However, this trial suffers from several methodologic limitations. Several studies of performance anxiety in nonclinical populations support the use of beta-blockers to reduce subjective anxiety, physical symptoms, and observed anxiety during performance. In most trials, single doses of propranolol 40 mg, oxyprenolol 40 mg, alprenolol 50 to 100 mg, or pindolol 5 mg were administered prior to the performance situation; one study used a maintenance dose of oxprenolol 40 mg b.i.d. (reviewed in Liebowitz et al., 1985).

Tricyclic antidepressants have not received much study in social phobia. A few studies report efficacy of clomipramine in mixed phobic samples. As already noted, comparison trials of MAOIs and tricyclic antidepressants in depressed outpatients suggest MAOIs may be more effective in reducing social anxiety.

Benzodiazepines have not been systematically studied in social phobia. However, uncontrolled reports suggest possible efficacy for benzodiazepines alone or with beta-blockers.

Behavioral Treatment

Although systematic desensitization in imagination was found to be effective in analogue (nonclinical) samples, most studies find limited benefits in social phobia patients. Social-skill training was found to be superior to systematic desensitization in some studies. Cognitive restructuring has been studied as an adjunct to social-skill training, without evidence of added benefit. However, a study comparing exposure in vivo with two forms of cognitive therapy demonstrated significant decrease in anxiety in social phobics with all three treatments; only the cognitive treatments led to improvement of irrational beliefs. Therefore, social-skill training, cognitive therapy, and exposure in vivo each have some demonstrated efficacy in treating social phobia, but whether any behavioral therapy or combination is preferable and whether individual patient characteristics dictate a certain treatment is not established (Emmelkamp, 1986). The comparative efficacy of behavioral and pharmacologic treatments or their combination has not been studied.

Psychodynamic Treatments

Psychodynamic treatments or other psychotherapies may be useful in social phobia but systematic studies have not been conducted.

Patient Management and Indications for Psychiatric Consultation and Referral

Consultation with a psychiatrist may help in establishing the diagnosis, especially when features of other psychiatric disorders may be present. After identification of the disorder, a trial of beta-blockers or an MAOI before entering phobic situations may be considered. Behavioral treatments may be used alone, but are probably enhanced when used concurrently with medication.

CLINICAL PEARLS

- Social phobia is differentiated from normal social or performance anxiety by the degree of distress resulting from the fear or by the presence of social or occupational impairment. Anxiety often increases rather than attenuates in the phobic situation.
- As currently defined, social phobia patients have never experienced a spontaneous panic attack; if situational panic attacks occur they are confined to the social phobic situations.
- Systematic pharmacologic treatment studies in social phobia are lacking, but preliminary evidence supports trials of beta-blockers or MAOIs; initial reports suggest benzodiazepines may have some benefit alone or added to beta-blockers.
- Social skill training, cognitive therapy, and exposure in vivo may be effective behavioral therapies; it is not yet known whether individual patient characteristics indicate the need for a specific type of treatment, so choice of treatment is largely determined by availability or trial and error.

SIMPLE PHOBIA

Simple phobia shares many of the basic features of the other phobias, but the fear is limited to a specific object or situation, such as dogs or heights, so the extent of interference in a patient's life tends to be mild.

Epidemiology

Six-month prevalence rates of simple phobia reported in the ECA study are between 4.5 and 11.8%; rates are higher for females than for males. The onset of animal phobia is usually in childhood. Blood-injury phobia usually begins in adolescence or early adulthood and may be associated with vasovagal fainting on exposure to the phobic stimulus. Age of onset may be more variable for other simple phobias. Many childhood-onset phobias may remit spontaneously. Impairment depends on the extent to which the phobic object or situation is routinely encountered in the individual's life. Simple phobias may coexist with social phobia and panic disorder, but are believed to be unrelated.

Description and Differential Diagnosis

Simple phobia is usually a circumscribed fear of a specific object or situation (Tables 7-5, 7-6) As with the other phobias, the fear is excessive and unrealistic, exposure to the phobic stimulus produces an anxiety response, expectation of exposure may produce anticipatory anxiety, and the object or situation is either avoided or endured with considerable discomfort. However, unlike social phobia, the fear does not involve scrutiny or embarrassment and, unlike agoraphobia, the fear is not of being trapped or of having a panic attack. The nature of the fear is specific to the phobia, such as a fear of falling or loss of visual support in height phobia, or fear of crashing in a flying phobia. Isolated fears are common in the general population; a diagnosis of simple phobia is reserved for situations in which the phobia results in marked distress or some degree of impairment in activities or relationships.

Etiology

Of all the forms of anxiety disorder, blood-injury phobia has the strongest family history; 68% of probands have relatives with blood phobia. Concordance rates are higher in monozygotic than dizygotic twins. When blood-injury phobics are exposed to their phobic stimuli they exhibit a biphasic cardiovascular response with initial tachycardia followed by extreme bradycardia, which can produce syncope. It is presumed that this autonomic response is genetically determined and present at an early age (Marks, 1988).

In behavior theory, the classic case study of "Little Albert" illustrates how

Table 7–5 **DSM-III-R Criteria for Simple Phobia**

A. A persistent fear of a circumscribed stimulus (object or situation) other than fear of having a panic attack (as in Panic Disorder) or of humiliation or embarrassment in certain social situations (as in Social Phobia).
   Note: Do not include fears that are part of Panic Disorder with Agoraphobia or of Agoraphobia without History of Panic Disorder.
B. During some phase of the disturbance, exposure to the specific phobic stimulus (or stimuli) almost invariably provokes an immediate anxiety response.
C. The object or situation is avoided or endured with intense anxiety.
D. The fear or the avoidant behavior significantly interferes with the person's normal routine or with usual social activities or relationships with others, or there is marked distress about having the fear.
E. The person recognizes that his or her fear is excessive or unreasonable.
F. The phobic stimulus is unrelated to the content of the obsessions of Obsessive-Compulsive Disorder or the trauma of Post-traumatic Stress Disorder.

(Used with permission. American Psychiatric Association, 1987)

Table 7–6 **Common Simple Phobias**

Animals (dogs, snakes, mice)
Insects, spiders
Blood/injury
Claustrophobia (enclosed spaces)
Acrophobia (heights)
Air travel
Water
Thunderstorms

operant learning may produce simple phobia. A 2-year-old boy experienced a loud noise while playing with a white rat and became fearful of rats and objects resembling rats. In this example, the loud noise is the unconditioned stimulus, the fear reaction to the noise is the unconditioned response. The white rat, the conditioned stimulus, is paired with the loud noise and elicits a similar fear response, the conditioned response.

Freud's psychoanalytic theory of phobias is portrayed in the classic analytic study of "Little Hans," a 5-year-old boy who developed a fear of horses. Freud hypothesized that the phobia was a symptom of unresolved unconscious Oedipal conflict in which the boy had sexual longings for his mother but felt guilt and feared retribution from his father in the form of castration. The libidinal impulse was repressed into the unconscious and the threat of danger displaced onto the horse, an avoidable object. However, the love for and desire to marry one's opposite-sexed parent is also believed to be a normal developmental stage and it is not explained why this should result in phobic symptoms in some individuals and not others.

Treatment

The standard treatment for simple phobias is exposure to achieve habituation to or extinction of the fear response. The types of phobias in which efficacy is documented include height, darkness, animals, blood-injury, and claustrophobia. Cognitive therapy has been attempted but does not appear to add any benefit. There is some evidence supporting the use of applied relaxation techniques in patients with strong physiological reactions. When exposure to the phobic stimulus is infrequent, predictable, and difficult to practice repeatedly, such as in flying phobia, benzodiazepines on a "prn" basis may be considered. Self-medication with ethanol is probably common.

OBSESSIVE-COMPULSIVE DISORDER

Obsessions are recurrent, distressing thoughts, ideas, or impulses experienced as unwanted and senseless but irresistible. Compulsions are repetitive, purposeful, intentional behaviors, usually performed in response to an obsession, which are recognized as unrealistic or unreasonable, but again irresistible. What was considered a rare disorder with poor response to treatment has recently received more attention. Advances in treatment and exploration of the underlying etiology and pathophysiology have increased the importance of recognizing obsessive-compulsive disorder. Public awareness and decreased stigma have been fostered by the media (television talk shows, radio and newspaper features), and advocacy for obsessive-compulsive disorder sufferers is accomplished through organizations such as the OCD Foundation and the National Alliance for the Mentally Ill.

Epidemiology

Obsessive-compulsive disorder was previously thought to be a rare disorder affecting only 0.05% of the population. However, with increased awareness and detection, recent estimates of population rates have been higher. The ECA Study found lifetime population prevalence rates of 2 to 3% and 6-month prevalence rates of 1.3 to 2.0% (Robins et al., 1984; Myers et al., 1984). The diagnosis of obsessive-compulsive disorder is often very difficult to make; the accuracy of ECA diagnosis is being studied. The risk in females may be increased as much as twofold over males, but some samples have reported higher rates in males. Rates of obsessive-compulsive traits and disorder are increased in family members of patients (see Etiology, below). Age of onset is usually in adolescence or early adulthood (70% between 10 to 23 years old). Several years may pass between onset and when a patient first seeks treatment. Obsessive traits are commonly present before onset of the disorder. Most patients are unable to identify an environmental trigger as a precipitant to onset of the disorder, but once the disorder is established, many individuals experience an increase in symptoms with stressful life events. In probands with Gilles de la Tourette's Syndrome (with or without OCD), rates of both disorders are increased in biologic relatives, suggesting that in these families, OCD and Tourette's may be alternative phenotypic expressions of the same underlying genetic defect (a highly penetrent, sex-influenced, autosomal dominant trait).

The majority of obsessive-compulsive disorder patients report depressive symptoms after experiencing impairment from obsessive-compulsive disorder symptoms (Rasmussen, Tsuang, 1986). Obsessive-compulsive disorder can also coexist with panic disorder in up to 15 to 20% of patients (Breier et al., 1986). Separation anxiety disorder in childhood is also occasionally reported by obsessive-compulsive disorder patients.

Description and Differential Diagnosis

Obsessive-compulsive disorder is defined as the presence of obsessions or compulsions that produce discomfort or impairment (Table 7-7). Obsessions are thoughts, impulses, or images that are recurrent, persistent, intrusive, and recognized as senseless (at least initially). Compulsions are behaviors (rituals) that are repetitive, purposeful, and intentional; are a response to an obsession; are performed in a stereotyped fashion or according to certain rules to prevent discomfort or a dreaded event ; and are initially recognized as excessive or unreasonable. Obsessions and compulsions are not in themselves pleasurable, and patients usually attempt to ignore, suppress, or neutralize obsessions. In clinical samples both obsessions and compulsions are almost always present and multiple obsessions and/or compulsions are common.

Table 7–7 **DSM-III-R Criteria for Obsessive-Compulsive Disorder**

A. Either obsessions or compulsions:
   Obsessions (1), (2), (3), and (4):
   1. Recurrent and persistent ideas, thoughts, impulses, or images that are experienced, at least initially, as intrusive and senseless: e.g., a parent's having repeated impulses to kill a loved child, a religious person's having recurrent blasphemous thoughts
   2. The person attempts to ignore or suppress such thoughts or impulses or to neutralize them with some other thought or action
   3. The person recognizes that the obsessions are the product of his or her own mind, not imposed from without (as in thought insertion)
   4. If another Axis I disorder is present, the content of the obsession is unrelated to it: e.g., the ideas, thoughts, impulses, or images are not about food in the presence of an Eating Disorder, about drugs in the presence of a Psychoactive Substance Use Disorder, or guilty thoughts in the presence of a Major Depression.
   Compulsions (1), (2), and (3):
   1. Repetitive, purposeful, and intentional behaviors that are performed in response to an obsession, or according to certain rules or in a stereotyped fashion
   2. The behavior is designed to neutralize or to prevent discomfort or some dreaded event or situation; however, either the activity is not connected in a realistic way with what it is designed to neutralize or prevent, or it is clearly excessive
   3. The person recognizes that his or her behavior is excessive or unreasonable (this may not be true for young children; it may no longer be true for people whose obsessions have evolved into overvalued ideas)
B. The obsessions or compulsions cause marked distress, are time-consuming (take more than an hour a day), or significantly interfere with the person's normal routine, occupational functioning, or usual social activities or relationships with others.

(Used with permission. American Psychiatric Association, 1987)

Patients are often reluctant to spontaneously divulge their symptoms, so these must be inquired about directly. Reasons for the patient's difficulty in discussing symptoms include embarrassment over content which is perceived as socially unacceptable, recognition of the strangeness of the thoughts and behaviors and fear of being viewed as "crazy," and content that is disturbing to the patient. In addition, longstanding symptoms may be incorporated into the patient's lifestyle and no longer be recognized as abnormal.

Obsessive thoughts may take the form of images of a child being killed, counting rituals, or mental list-making that can occupy hours or entire days, or repeated thoughts of having sex with a dead person, which the patient finds disgusting and distressing yet is unable to dismiss. Compulsive cleaners may spend hours meticulously dusting, vacuuming, and so on. Compulsive hoarders are unable to discard useless objects, resulting in a home cluttered with mail, bags of used containers, dustballs, and so on. Some patients need to repeat tasks over and over to "get it right" or repeatedly rearrange objects so that they assume an exact pattern. Fear of contamination can result in avoidance of any contact with dirt or of any object that could possibly have come in contact with the feared contaminant or was sold in the same store as the contaminant. While driving, the thought that they hit someone may come to mind, followed by the need to repeatedly return to a location to check, despite the virtual certainty that no accident occurred. One individual feared losing his daughter and repeatedly checked billboards and envelopes for her presence, knowing that this was absurd yet being unable to pass a billboard or discard an envelope without repeated checking. Common obsessions and compulsions are lised in Table 7-8.

Symptoms may result in lateness due to time spent repeating rituals or in chapped and thickened skin from repeated washing. In one extreme case, a woman had a compulsion to lie down in the street in a north-south, then an east-west direction. She was unable to get up in time to avoid oncoming traffic and lost both legs.

The disorder may cause isolation and dependence on others: patients may make demands on family and treaters to decontaminate objects, check for them, and so on. Suicide risk must be considered since death may be perceived as the only escape from chronic symptoms.

In clinical samples, symptoms are present continuously from the time of onset until the patient seeks treatment. Occasionally, there is a chronic deterioration in which the obsessions and compulsions become more pronounced and more difficult to resist; they may consume all of the individual's time so that he or she is unable to function outside of performing rituals. An episodic course of illness is uncommon (2%) in clinical samples but may be more frequent in individuals who do not seek treatment (or go undiagnosed).

The differential diagnosis of obsessive-compulsive disorder may include schizophrenia, major depression, phobias, Gilles de la Tourette's syndrome, amphetamine intoxication, obsessive-compulsive personality, and normal thoughts and behavior. In obsessive-compulsive disorder, behavior can be bizarre and can have an impact on social and occupational functioning similar to schizophrenia. However, the behaviors are limited to the execution of compulsive rituals. When reality testing is lost, the loss is limited to convictions regarding obsessive ideas and does not extend to other areas of thinking. Occasionally, the depressive ruminations seen in major depressive episodes may be mistaken for obsessions, but the brooding has a clear depressive or guilty quality and clears with recovery from the episode. Avoidance of contaminant or other objects and situations may resemble the avoidance seen in phobic disorders, but the fear is not of being trapped as in agoraphobia, or social embarrassment as in social phobia, but is directly related to the obsessional thought. The repetitive, irresistible movement or utterances of Tourette's syndrome may be difficult to differentiate from obsessive-compulsive disorder, and the disorders may coexist. The repetitive, stereotyped behavior seen in amphetamine (or cocaine) intoxication usually is mechanical, without the intellectual quality and intention of obsessive-compulsive disorder.

Table 7–8 **Common Obsessions and Compulsions**

Obsessions	Compulsions
Contamination/illness	Checking
Violent images	Cleaning/washing
Fear of harming others/self	Counting
Perverse/forbidden sexual thoughts, images, or impulses	Hoarding/collecting
Symmetry/exactness	Ordering/arranging
Somatic	Repeating
Religious	

Obsessive-compulsive personality (see personality disorders), although similar in name, consists of ego-syntonic attitudes and behaviors that are not resisted or experienced as intrusive. Other repetitive behaviors, such as gambling, addiction, sexual behavior, and eating, are to some degree inherently pleasurable, resisted only due to deleterious consequences, and lack the senseless, unrealistic nature of obsessive-compulsive disorder symptoms. Normal checking or meticulousness is not intrusive, senseless, distressing, difficult to resist, or time-consuming to the extent of interference with usual activities.

Etiology and Pathophysiology

Familial and Genetic Theories

Possible familial and genetic contributions to obsessive-compulsive disorder have been studied in two ways: by examining the percentage of disorder in first-degree relatives of obsessive-compulsive disorder probands and by comparing concordance rates of illness in monozygotic vs. dizygotic twins. Reports of the prevalence rates of obsessive-compulsive disorder in first-degree relatives of obsessive-compulsive disorder probands range from 0 to 37%; of obsessive-compulsive personality, from 3 to 33%; of affective disorder, from 3 to 11%; and of any psychiatric disorder, from 9 to 73% (for review see Marks, 1986; Insel, 1985). Although these rates of obsessive-compulsive illness in family members of obsessive-compulsive disorder probands are clearly elevated, interpretation of these findings would be strengthened by comparison to rates of obsessive-compulsive disorder in relatives of nonobsessive-compulsive disorder probands using the same methodology, since estimates of population prevalence vary widely. Concordance rates summarized across three twin studies are 75% for monozygotic and 32% for dizygotic twin pairs. Only the two studies reporting obsessional features in co-twins of obsessive-compulsive disorder probands showed any concordance. The hypothesis that milder obsessional tendencies may be inherited is supported by the high proportion of the variance (45%) for obsessive traits and symptoms that is heriditary in normal twin pairs, as measured by the Leyton Obsessional Inventory.

Psychoanalytic Theories

Psychoanalytic theories of obsessive-compulsive disorder attribute symptoms to a disturbance in the anal-sadistic phase of development. A conflict (such as the oedipal-genital impulse) may lead to regression to use of earlier defenses, including isolation, undoing, displacement, and reaction formation, resulting in ambivalence and magical thinking.

Cognitive Theories

Obsessive-compulsive disorder patients appear to have a defect in their cognitive information-processing mechanism, with frequent mismatch between beliefs and sensory data (e.g., a patient may continue rinsing his hands because he feels the soap is not washed off or restack dishes because they do not appear to be straight).

Behavioral Theories

Psychiatrists working from a behavioral perspective have suggested a two-stage classical instrumental conditioning model of obsessive-compulsive disorder. Obsessions are thought to result from pairing mental stimuli with anxiety-provoking thoughts. Compulsions are neutral behaviors that have been associated with anxiety reduction and thereby reinforced. Avoidance of anxiogenic stimuli may also be reinforced, as in phobic disorders.

Neurobiological Theories

The predominant neurobiological hypothesis of the etiology of obsessive-compulsive disorder involves dysfunction of brain serotonin neuronal systems. These systems have been the subject of much investigation in obsessive-compulsive disorder since the potent serotonin (5-HT) reuptake blocker clomipramine was found to have therapeutic efficacy. Clomipramine was found to have greater efficacy than other antidepressants having less serotonergic selectivity or potency, and its efficacy correlated with levels of the serotonergically selective compound clomipramine rather than with desmethylclomipramine, the noradrenergically active metabolite. In one study, higher baseline CSF 5-HIAA (5-hydroxyindoleacetic acid, a serotinin metabolite) and platelet 5-HT concentrations and greater drug-induced decreases of these measures correlated with treatment response. Other treatments with serotonergic effects (L-tryptophan, lithium augmentation of tricyclic antidepressants, fluoxetine and fluvoxamine) have also been used to decrease obsessive-compulsive symptoms. Serotonin function in obsessive-compulsive disorder has been evaluated by examining differences between baseline levels and levels after stimulation with serotonin agonists. Whole-blood 5-HT levels were decreased in obsessive-compulsive disorder patients in one study. Platelet ^{3}H-imipramine binding (a possible measure of 5-HT uptake) has been reported as normal or decreased in obsessive-compulsive disorder patients relative to normal controls. CSF 5-HIAA levels have been reported as normal or increased. Brain regulation of serotonin in obsessive-compulsive disorder has been assessed using m-chlorophenylpiperazine (MCPP), a 5-HT agonist. The prolactin response to MCPP was blunted in female obsessive-compulsive disorder patients, but response to the 5-HT precursor, tryptophan, was normal. Two studies found increases in obsessive-compulsive disorder symptoms following administration of oral MCPP, but one study found no behavioral change with intravenous MCPP. The role of serotonin function in habituation has been explored in animal studies. Experimentally induced lesions of 5-HT systems in rats exacerbated amphetamine-induced preservative behavior, which may be analogous to compulsions.

Neurobiologic systems believed to be involved in other anxiety disorders have been examined in obsessive-compulsive disorder. Yohimbine, an alpha-2 antagonist, produced no consistent change in MHPG, cortisol, or behavior. Caffeine and lactate did not produce anxiogenic responses such as those in panic disorder. It has been suggested that the opiate system may mediate "drive reduction reward," and, it has been further hypothesized that a deficit in an opiate-mediated capacity to register reward may be manifested as a cognitive deficit in reaching certainty in obsessive-compulsion patients with ruminative doubt and compulsive checking behavior. To test this hypothesis, an opiate antagonist was administered and found to exacerbate obsessions in one study but produced no consistent behavioral change in another.

Possible involvement of dopamine and serotonin systems is implied by PET-scan findings of increased metabolic activity in the heads of the caudate nuclei and orbital gyri. It has been hypothesized that in obsessive-compulsive disorder functional activity in the cortex and orbital gyrus have increased beyond the caudate's ability to maintain integrative function. After successful treatment, the increase in caudate activity relative to the structures with which it interacts may represent a reestablishment of the caudate nucleus' integrative capacity (Baxter et al., 1987). Further questions of dopaminergic involvement are raised by the observation of obsessions and compulsions in postencephalitic parkinsonism. The role of dopamine dysfunction in the pathogenesis of obsessive-compulsive disorder deserves further study.

Treatment

Psychodynamic Treatment

If psychotherapy is undertaken, caution may be advisable as a searching, interpretive, in-depth approach may exacerbate introspective obsessional thinking. There are individual anecdotal reports of successful analytic treatment (Shear, Frosch, 1986).

Behavioral Treatment

A variety of behavioral techniques have been applied to obsessive-compulsive disorder and are often beneficial; however, absence of compulsions, severe symptoms, significant depression, and poor motivation limit use of behavior therapy to a subset of obsessive-compulsive disorder patients. The specific elements responsible for treatment efficacy that have been identified are prolonged exposure to ritual-eliciting stimuli together with prevention of the compulsive response. Flooding is less well tolerated and no more effective than gradual exposure. Therapist modeling and self-instructional training do not seem to enhance treatment. Home-based treatment administered by the patient, alone or with the assistance of a partner, may improve maintenance of therapeutic gains. Prolonged rather than short exposure sessions and attention-focusing instead of distraction improve outcome. Behavior therapy may be enhanced by pharmacologic treatment and assertiveness training. Obsessions appear less responsive to behavioral treatment, but prolonged exposure to obsessive material in imagination may have some benefit.

Most improvement occurs in the first month of treatment but improvement may continue with additional treatment up to 6 months. Treatment gains have been maintained at 2- to 6-year follow-up. Earlier age of onset is associated with better long-term outcome; higher initial anxiety and depression are associated with poorer short-term but similar long-term outcome (for review see Emmelkamp, 1986).

Pharmacologic Treatment

Clomipramine (CMI) was the first medication discovered to have an effect on obsessive-compulsive disorder symptoms and is the best studied. At this time it is not available for general use in the United States but is used in several research centers. It is believed that clomipramine's serotonergic effects are responsible for somewhat specific treatment for obsessive-compulsive disorder symptoms, since it has greater efficacy than antidepressants with less potent serotonergic activity. In double-blind studies CMI was superior to amitriptyline, nortriptiline, desipramine, or the MAO inhibitor corgyline. Imipramine, with intermediate inhibition of serotonin uptake, was found equivalent to CMI in two studies but ineffective in a third study.

Other serotonergically selective antidepressants also reduce obsessive-compulsive disorder symptoms. These include zimelidine, a selective serotonin reuptake inhibitor that is no longer available because of serious adverse side effects; fluvoxamine, a unicyclic selective and potent serotonin reuptake inhibitor which is still an investigational drug in the United States; and fluoxetine, a related drug, which is available.

Pharmacologic treatment response in obsessive-compulsive disorder differs from major depression in having later onset of therapeutic effect (3 to 4 weeks), more gradual improvement, and significant reduction of symptoms and disability usually without complete remission. Return of symptoms is common when effective medication is decreased or discontinued. Higher doses of tricyclic medications than typically used to treat depression may be required. MAO inhibitors may be especially helpful in obsessive-compulsive disorder patients with a history of panic attacks.

Tryptophan (temporarily withdrawn from the market because of suspected problems with eosinophilia) may reduce symptoms alone or in combination with CMI or other antidepressant drugs. However, with MAO inhibitors, tryptophan should be used cautiously, if at all, because of the risk of hypertensive and other toxic reactions. Lithium augmentation of antidepressant treatment for refractory depression has been used as a result of evidence that lithium increases presynaptic serotonin release onto postsynaptic serotonin receptors that were sensitized by prior treatment with antidepressant medications. Reports indicate lithium added to CMI, trazodone, or fluvoxamine and probably fluoxetine may further reduce obsessions and compulsions.

Benzodiazepines may reduce anxiety associated with obsessive-compulsive symptoms but do not appear to alleviate the central symptoms of the disorder. Buspirone, despite efficacy in generalized anxiety and partial serotonin agonist properties, fails to decrease obsessive-compulsive disorder symptoms.

Current evidence does not support the use of neuroleptics alone in obsessive-compulsive disorder. Preliminary reports suggest that addition of a neuroleptic (e.g., pimozide) to an antidepressant drug may have benefit when schizotypal features, delusions, or Tourette's syndrome are present. In general, electroconvulsive therapy (ECT) is not effective in obsessive-compulsive disorder but symptom response is reported in individual cases. Psychosurgery consisting of stereotactic cingulotomy has been attempted in severe, refractory cases, sometimes with good response.

Role of the Nonpsychiatric Physician in Patient Management

Initial treatment of obsessive-compulsive disorder is usually best accomplished by psychiatrists who have familiarity and experience in treating this disorder. Supportive or behavioral psychotherapies are usually necessary in addition to pharmacotherapy. Once satisfactory treatment has been initiated, ongoing pharmacologic treatment can at times be managed by a nonpsychiatric physician.

Indications for Psychiatric Consultation and Referral

Consultation with a psychiatrist can assist in establishing the diagnosis of obsessive-compulsive disorder and forming an appropriate treatment plan. In individuals with severe persistent symptoms who are unable to tolerate the distress resulting from their illness, or when concurrent depression is present, assessment of suicide potential and indications for hospitalization may require evaluation by a psychiatrist. Any patient requesting psychosurgery should have careful psychiatric evaluation to determine if less-invasive treatment options have been exhausted. Obsessive-compulsive disorder patients may also benefit from involvement in support groups; the Obsessive-Compulsive Disorder Foundation (P.O. Box 9573, New Haven, CT, 06535) is a useful resource formed by obsessive-compulsive disorder sufferers in 1987.

CLINICAL PEARLS

- Recognition of obsessive-compulsive disorder can be difficult; if the specific obsessions or compulsions the patient experiences are not directly inquired about, the diagnosis can be missed. Therefore, when you suspect obsessive-compulsive disorder, question the individual about each of the common obsessions or compulsions.
- The course of the illness is usually chronic and exacerbated by stressful life events, and treatment response is often gradual and incomplete.
- Current evidence points to involvement of brain serotonin systems in the etiology and/or pathogenesis of the disorder.
- Currently available pharmacologic treatments include imipramine, fluoxetine, tryptophan, and tryptophan or lithium added to an antidepressant medication. Clomipramine and fluvoxamine are effective investigational drugs; clomipramine will soon be generally available. Treatment usually includes behavioral and/or supportive psychotherapy.
- Depression, panic attacks, schizotypal features, delusions and Tourette's syndrome may coexist with obsessive-compulsive disorder symptoms.

POSTTRAUMATIC STRESS DISORDER

Posttraumatic stress disorder (PTSD) can be a brief reaction that follows soon after a traumatic experience or a chronic condition producing severe debilitation. Unlike the routine stresses experienced in life, this disorder results from an extreme, overwhelming, or catastrophic experience. The syndrome consists of intrusive memories, flashbacks, nightmares, avoidance of reminders of the event, numbing of affect, and hyperarousal (Table 7-9).

Epidemiology

Posttraumatic stress disorder was not recognized as an independent diagnosis until the publication of DSM-III in 1980, although descriptions of the syndrome date at

Table 7-9 **DSM-III-R Criteria for Post-traumatic Stress Disorder**

A. The person has experienced an event that is outside the range of usual human experience and that would be markedly distressing to almost anyone: e.g., serious threat to one's life or physical integrity; serious threat or harm to one's children, spouse, or other close relatives and friends; sudden destruction of one's home or community; or seeing another person who has recently been, or is being, seriously injured or killed as the result of an accident or physical violence.

B. The traumatic event is persistently reexperienced in at least one of the following ways:
  1. Recurrent and intrusive distressing recollections of the event (in young children, repetitive play in which themes or aspects of the trauma are expressed)
  2. Recurrent distressing dreams of the event
  3. Sudden acting or feeling as if the traumatic event were recurring (includes a sense of reliving the experience, illusions, hallucinations, and dissociative [flashback] episodes, even those that occur upon awakening or when intoxicated)
  4. Intense psychological distress at exposure to events that symbolize or resemble an aspect of the traumatic event, including anniversaries of the trauma

C. Persistent avoidance of stimuli associated with the trauma or numbing of general responsiveness (not present before the trauma), as indicated by at least three of the following:
  1. Efforts to avoid thoughts or feelings associated with the trauma
  2. Efforts to avoid activities or situations that arouse recollections of the trauma
  3. Inability to recall an important aspect of the trauma (psychogenic amnesia)
  4. Markedly diminished interest in significant activities (in young children, loss of recently acquired development skills such as toilet training or language skills)
  5. Feeling of detachment or estrangement from others
  6. Restricted range of affect: e.g., unable to have loving feelings
  7. Sense of a foreshortened future: e.g., does not expect to have a career, marriage, or children, or a long life

D. Persistent symptoms of increased arousal (not present before the trauma), as indicated by at least two of the following:
  1. Difficulty falling or staying asleep
  2. Irritability or outbursts of anger
  3. Difficulty concentrating
  4. Hypervigilance
  5. Exaggerated startle response
  6. Physiologic reactivity upon exposure to events that symbolize or resemble an aspect of the traumatic event (e.g., a woman who was raped in an elevator breaks out in a sweat when entering any elevator)

E. Duration of the disturbance (symptoms in *B, C,* and *D*) of at least 1 month.

Specify delayed onset if the onset of symptoms was at least 6 months after the trauma.

(Used with permission. American Psychiatric Association, 1987)

least to the Crimean and American Civil Wars. Development of the disorder by definition requires exposure to a traumatic event outside the range of usual experiences that would universally be experienced as markedly distressing. It is not known what proportion of the population has experienced such events or what proportion of those who have experienced traumatic events develop posttraumatic stress disorder. The Research Triangle Institute estimates that posttraumatic stress disorder developed in 15% of Vietnam theater veterans. Some maintain that a sufficiently severe stressor will produce symptoms in all persons exposed. Studies of Vietnam veterans suggest that exposure to atrocities, death of friends, isolation from peers during combat, and exposure to dead or dying soldiers increases the risk of developing the disorder. Other proposed vulnerability factors include severity of the stressor, genetic predisposition, psychologic/cognitive immaturity, lack of social support, prior trauma, and preexisting personality problems (Van der Kolk, 1987). A latent period of months or years may intervene between the trauma and the onset of symptoms.

The disorder may occur in childhood. Comorbidity with substance abuse, depression, and anxiety disorders may occur; these disorders may also be increased in first-degree relatives of posttraumatic stress disorder probands. Individuals with posttraumatic stress disorder may be at increased risk for impulsive behavior or suicide.

Description and Differential Diagnosis

The mental status examination should probably routinely include questions about exposure to trauma or abuse. Examples of traumatic events include war, assault, and natural or man-made disasters—events usually experienced with intense fear, terror, and helplessness. The symptoms are clustered into three categories: reexperiencing the trauma, psychic numbing or avoidance of stimuli associated with the trauma, and increased arousal. Reexperiencing phenomena include intrusive memories, flashbacks, and nightmares. Intrusive memories are spontaneous, unwanted, distressing recollections of the traumatic event. Flashbacks are dissociative states in which components of the event are relived, and the person feels and behaves as though experiencing the event at that moment. These flashbacks can last from a few seconds to as long as days. Avoidance may include thoughts, feelings, situations, or activities that are reminders of the trauma. Numbing may occur through amnesia, emotional detachment, restricted affect, or loss of interest in activities. Increased arousal may include insomnia, irritability, hypervigilance, increased startle response, or physiological symptoms triggered by exposure to reminders of the trauma.

In adjustment disorder the stressor is usually less severe, and the characteristic symptoms of posttraumatic stress disorder, such as reexperiencing and avoiding, are not present. Avoidance of trauma-associated stimuli may resemble a phobia; however, in posttraumatic stress disorder the avoidance is limited to reminders of the trauma. The physiological response to events symbolizing the trauma may resemble panic attacks but in pure posttraumatic stress disorder no spontaneous attacks occur, nor do attacks occur apart from the circumscribed trauma-stimulus. Many of the symptoms of posttraumatic stress disorder resemble those of major depression. If a full depressive syndrome also exists both diagnoses should be made; the same is true of coexisting anxiety disorders. The amnesia and impaired concentration may resemble an organic mental disorder; if the trauma involved physical injury, organic brain impairment should be considered. Reexperiencing phenomena, such as flashbacks, may appear to be psychotic.

Etiology

Posttraumatic stress disorder is unique among psychiatric disorders in that a specific causative event can be identified for the psychological, behavioral, and physiologic symptoms that comprise this syndrome. Early psychodynamic theories focused on the function of traumatic experiences in reactivating latent conflicts originating in infancy. Children's poorly developed cognitive defenses may leave them more vulnerable to psychic trauma, whereas adults may vary in the degree to which the full traumatic response is expressed. The traumatic elements believed to be required to produce the syndrome involve an extreme stress that produces high levels of arousal in a situation of helplessness. The acute reaction may involve near-cessation of affective, cognitive, and physiologic functioning, similar to that observed in catatonia, but in adults a modification or incomplete expression of this response is usually observed.

An animal model used to understand a variety of anxiety and depressive symptoms is maternal deprivation. When maternal deprivation occurs during a critical developmental phase, rhesus monkeys exhibit a protest-despair-detachment process, disturbed social behavior, and excessive arousal and fear in response to novel environmental stimuli. In addition, abnormal catecholamine and hypothalamic-pituitary-adrenal axis function are observed. The behavioral abnormalities respond to social and antidepressant treatments. Learned helplessness has been used as an animal model of depression but may actually be more analogous to posttraumatic stress disorder. In this model, effects of exposure to inescapable aversive events include deficits in learning to escape novel adverse situations, decreased motivation for learning new contingencies, chronic subjective distress, increased tumor genesis, and immunosuppression.

Psychobiologic Theories

Psychobiologic theories suggest that catecholamine depletion may be related to the "negative symptoms" of decreased motivation, poor occupational functioning, and global constriction. The hyperactivity symptoms of startle response, explosive outbursts, nightmares, and intrusive recollections may be mediated by chronic noradrenergic hypersensitivity which follows catecholamine depletion. It is possible that the downregulation of postsynaptic norepinephrine sensitivity that accompanies prolonged use of antidepressant medications also decreases the hyperactivity symptoms of posttraumatic stress disorder. In animals, prolonged stress produces changes in opiate receptors resembling those induced by opiate dependence, and cessation of the stress or opiate antagonists will produce withdrawal symptoms. The interactions between brain opiate and noradrenergic systems lead to a hypothesis of central noradrenergic hyperactivity associated with a relative decrease in opiate receptor binding in the pathophysiology of posttraumatic stress disorder.

Clinical studies with posttraumatic stress disorder patients demonstrate noradrenergic dysfunction consisting of increased 24-hour urinary norepinephrine/cortisol ratio, downregulation of platelet alpha-2 adrenergic receptors, and downregulation of lymphocyte beta-adrenergic receptors. Lactate provocation elicits flashbacks in posttraumatic stress disorder patients who also have panic attacks. Exaggerated anxiety response and autonomic hyperactivity are triggered by reminders of the trauma, especially if imaginal flooding is used.

Behavioral Models

Behavioral models of a two-stage learning theory (classical conditioning followed by stimulus generalization or higher-order conditioning) may also apply to aspects of posttraumatic stress disorder. The conditioned stimulus—the cues associated with a traumatic experience—acquires the ability to trigger the conditioned response—the inborn, involuntary reaction to environmental threat. For example, helicopter sounds may provoke the physiologic and mental experience of being in combat. This hyperarousal response may become generalized to relatively minor stimuli.

Treatment

As with other anxiety disorders, treatment for posttraumatic stress disorder often is best accomplished with a combination of pharmacologic and nonpharmacologic therapies. It has been proposed that pharmacologic treatment may be required to control the physiological symptoms so that the patient will be able to tolerate working through highly emotional material in psychotherapy. Historically, agents such as sodium amytal were used to facilitate abreaction, or release of repressed or forgotten emotion or memories. This has also been reported to occur during phenelzine treatment. A number of case reports and an open trial of successful treatment of posttraumatic stress disorder with antidepressants led to a double-blind, placebo-controlled trial of phenelzine and imipramine (Frank et al., 1988). Both agents significantly reduced intrusion symptoms (nightmares, flashbacks, intrusive recollections) but did not affect avoidance items (emotional numbing, distance from loved ones, active suppression of traumatic memories); there was some suggestion of greater efficacy for phenelzine. Usual dose ranges were 60 to 75 mg/day for phenelzine and 200 to 300 mg/day for imipramine. Open trials and case reports suggest efficacy for a variety of other medications. Clonidine 0.2 to 0.4 mg/day and propranolol 120 to 180 mg/day relieve startle, explosiveness, nightmares, and intrusive reexperiencing in some patients. Lithium decreased autonomic arousal, reexperiencing of symptoms, and ethanol use in 64% of patients; carbamazepine appeared to have similar effects.

Benzodiazepines may reduce anxiety, sleep disturbance, and nightmares but are not the optimal medication for posttraumatic stress disorder because of the high percentage of patients predisposed to abuse of ethanol and other drugs. When poor impulse control or psychotic features are prominent, neuroleptics may be considered, but due to the risk of tardive dyskinesia, their use should be limited to specific indications and the lowest dose and shortest duration necessary.

Often individual psychotherapy employing a combination of psychodynamic and cognitive techniques is useful in reviewing the events of the trauma, elucidating their meaning for the patient, and integrating the traumatic memories, affects, and physiological responses with current experiences. The process of forming a therapeutic alliance is complicated by the distrust resulting from the trauma, and sometimes from earlier life experiences. The process of therapy requires a balance between encouraging the patient to recount painful memories in detail and allowing the patient to "distance" from the material when it becomes overwhelming. Group therapy can provide a peer group in which to share common experiences and may facilitate a patient's reintegration into society.

GENERALIZED ANXIETY DISORDER

Generalized anxiety disorder (GAD) is characterized by chronic anxiety, apprehension, and somatic symptoms of anxiety such as muscle tension, trembling, autonomic hyperactivity, and hypervigilance. The anxiety is "free-floating" and unrelated to panic attacks, phobic stimuli, or obsessions. The validity of generalized anxiety disorder as a diagnosis distinct from other anxiety disorders or depression, or whether generalized anxiety disorder is a homogeneous category, is still unclear. This disorder was previously generally referred to as "anxiety neurosis."

Epidemiology

An epidemiologic study in New Haven, Connecticut, estimated a 2.5% one-month prevalence rate for generalized anxiety disorder using research diagnostic criteria. Of the patients with generalized anxiety disorder, 80% had at least one other anxiety disorder in their lifetime, and 7% had major depression. In this study generalized anxiety disorder was slightly more common in young to middle-aged females, nonwhites, those not currently married, and those of lower socioeconomic status. Rates for generalized anxiety disorder were not reported in the ECA study. Age at onset is variable, but is usually in the 20s to the 30s. Generalized anxiety disorder may begin as childhood overanxious disorder. In clinical samples the prevalence in males and females appears to be equal and the course tends to be chronic (Merikangas, Weissman, 1986).

Description and Differential Diagnosis

Generalized anxiety disorder is characterized by chronic excessive anxiety about life circumstances accompanied by symptoms of motor tension, autonomic hyperactivity, vigilance, and scanning (see DSM-III-R criteria; Table 7-10). The individual often "awakens with" apprehension and unrealistic concern about future misfortune. One patient described experiencing the anxiety of a final exam with every task he was assigned at work. The current diagnostic criteria require 6-month duration of symptoms to differentiate the disorder from more transient forms of anxiety, such as adjustment disorder with anxious mood. Generalized anxiety disorder has been a residual diagnosis covering a heterogeneous group of anxiety conditions that did not fit other diagnoses. Recently an attempt has been made to refine the definition of this syndrome and evaluate if and how it is distinct from other diagnoses. Generalized persistent anxiety may develop between attacks in panic disorder. Generalized anxiety disorder symptoms are often present in episodes of depression. In patients with somatization disorder, the focus of worries is about health concerns and physical

Table 7-10 **DSM-III-R Criteria for Generalized Anxiety Disorder**

A. Unrealistic or excessive anxiety and worry (apprehensive expectation) about two or more life circumstances: e.g., worry about possible misfortune to one's child (who is in no danger) or worry about finances (for no good reason), for a period of 6 months or longer, during which the person has been bothered more days than not by these concerns. In children and adolescents, this may take the form of anxiety and worry about academic, athletic, and social performance.

B. If another Axis I disorder is present, the focus of the anxiety and worry in *A* is unrelated to it: e.g., the anxiety or worry is not about having a panic attack in the presence of panic disorder; being embarrassed in public in the presence of social phobia; being contaminated in the presence of obsessive-compulsive disorder; or gaining weight in the presence of anorexia nervosa.

C. The disturbance does not occur only during the course of a mood disorder or a psychotic disorder.

D. At least 6 of the following 18 symptoms are often present when anxious (do not include symptoms present only during panic attacks):

Motor tension:
1. trembling, twitching, or feeling shaky
2. muscle tension, aches, or soreness
3. restlessness
4. easy fatigability

Autonomic hyperactivity:
5. shortness of breath or smothering sensations
6. palpitations or accelerated heart rate (tachycardia)
7. sweating, or cold clammy hands
8. dry mouth
9. dizziness or lightheadedness
10. nausea, diarrhea, or other abdominal distress
11. flushes (hot flashes) or chills
12. frequent urination
13. trouble swallowing or "lump in throat"

Vigilance and scanning:
14. feeling keyed up or on edge
15. exaggerated startle response
16. difficulty concentrating or "mind going blank" because of anxiety
17. trouble falling or staying asleep
18. irritability

E. It cannot be established that an organic factor initiated and maintained the disturbance: e.g., hyperthyroidism, caffeine intoxication.

---

symptoms, rather than apprehensive worry about life circumstances. As with panic disorder, medical conditions that may produce anxiety symptoms, such as hyperthyroidism or caffeinism, must be excluded.

Etiology

Torgersen's twin study found no evidence for genetic transmission of generalized anxiety disorder. Diagnostic heterogeneity of generalized anxiety disorder is suggested by the high frequency of nonanxiety psychiatric disorders in co-twins. However, a family study of generalized anxiety disorder probands reports an increased rate of generalized anxiety disorder but not other anxiety disorders in first-degree relatives, suggesting some degree of familial transmission and separation of generalized anxiety disorder from panic disorder and agoraphobia (Noyes et al., 1987).

Psychodynamic theories are based on "neuroses," which do not directly correspond to current diagnostic classification. As stated above, unconscious conflict is felt to be the underlying cause of anxiety, which as a symptom is a "signal" to the ego of the danger of expressing unacceptable impulses.

Behavioral theories consider anxiety, like panic disorder, a conditioned response to a stimulus that the individual has come to associate with danger. However, in generalized anxiety disorder it is difficult to identify specific anxiogenic stimuli. There is some suggestion that the onset of generalized anxiety disorder may be related to the cumulative effects of several stressful life events.

Biological theories relating to generalized anxiety disorder stem from preclinical animal models, basic and clinical pharmacologic studies, and pharmacologic properties of effective anxiolytic treatments in humans. Since generalized anxiety disorder is a heterogeneous disorder, it is likely that dysfunction of many brain neurochemical systems can account for the observed symptoms. There is preclinical and clinical evidence suggesting that neuronal systems involving noradrenergic, serotonergic, dopaminergic, corticotropin releasing factor, and endogenous benzodiazepine ligands may be involved. There is particular interest in the endogenous benzodiazepine system because of the marked efficacy of benzodiazepine drugs in this disorder. Recently an endogenous anxiogenic substance with strong affinity for benzodiazepine receptors in animal and human brain (DBI—diazepam binding inhibitor) has been identified (Ferrero et al., 1986). Acute anxiety and genetically determined anxiety appear to be associated with changes in benzodiazepine receptor density. Beta-carbolines, which are benzodiazepine inverse agonists, produce an acute anxiety state in animals and humans. Studies of benzodiazepine function in generalized anxiety disorder patients are needed. The efficacy in generalized anxiety disorder of buspirone, a 5-HT_{1A} agonist that reduces serotonin function, has led to interest in the role of serotonergic systems. Studies of serotonergic function using tryptophan and MCPP are being conducted. Recent data suggest that noradrenergic function in generalized anxiety disorder patients may be normal.

Treatment

Psychotherapy may be indicated for cases of generalized anxiety disorder to which the clinician feels unresolved unconscious conflict causes or perpetuates a patient's chronic anxiety (see Psychoanalytic/Psychodynamic Therapy).

Preliminary studies of behavioral treatment of generalized anxiety disorder suggest positive results with live presentation of progressive muscle relaxation to community volunteers and anxiety management (application of relaxation in response to physiologic cues of tension) in anxious outpatients. Biofeedback does not appear to have a specific value. Cognitive therapy combined with systematic desensitization in imagination or relaxation improves generalized anxiety disorder symptoms, but cognitive therapy alone is not effective. A treatment combination of biofeedback, relaxation, and cognitive therapy resulted in improvement in subjective and physiologic measures of anxiety, but it is not known which element(s) of treatment are necessary.

The most commonly used pharmacologic agents for generalized anxiety disorder are benzodiazepines such as diazepam, alprazolam, lorazepam, and clonazepam (Table 7-11). Advantages include rapid onset of efficacy and long-term safety. Disadvantages include memory impairment, sedation, dependence (particularly with alprazolam), and abuse potential. Antidepressant medications were believed to be ineffective in treating generalized anxiety disorder, but recent studies suggest imipramine may be of some benefit. Buspirone, a nonbenzodiazepine anxiolytic, may become the treatment of choice for generalized anxiety disorder. The mechanism of action is not established, but pharmacologic activity includes decrease in serotonin and increase in dopamine and norepinephrine cell firing. In contrast to benzodiazepines, therapeutic effects are delayed from 1 to 4 weeks. Side effects are usually mild and transient but may include dizziness, nausea, diarrhea, headache, or nervousness. Buspirone does not produce drowsiness or impair driving skill, and thus far appears to lack abuse potential or withdrawal symptoms with abrupt discontinuation (Sussman, 1987). The drug is not sedating. Other serotonergic agents and mixed agonist-antagonist benzodiazepines are being studied.

As with the other anxiety disorders, optimal treatment may involve a combination of psychotherapy, behavioral therapy, and/or pharmacotherapy. Comparative trials are needed to establish the relative efficacies of these treatment modalities or their combination.

Table 7–11 **Commonly Used Benzodiazepines**

TYPE	PRIMARY ROUTE OF BIOTRANSFORMATION	ELIMINATION HALF-LIFE (HOURS)
Diazepam (Valium)	oxidation	36–200
Flurazepam (Dalmane)	oxidation	50–120
Halazepam (Praxipam)	oxidation	36–200
Chlordiazepoxide (Librium)	oxidation	30–90
Alprazolam (Xanax)	oxidation	12–15
Triazolam (Halcion)	oxidation	3–5
Clorazepate (Tranxene)	oxidation	36–200
Prazepam (Centrax, Vestran)	oxidation	36–200
Midazolam (Versed)*	oxidation	2–4
Lorazepam (Ativan)	conjugation	10–20
Temazepam (Restoril)	conjugation	8–12
Oxazepam (Serax)	conjugation	8–12
Clonazepam (Klonopin)	oxidation	18–50

* IM or IV route only
(Reprinted with permission from Stoudemire A, Fogel BS: Psychopharmacology in the medically ill. In Stoudemire A, Fogel BS (eds): Principles of Medical Psychiatry, p 104. Orlando, FL, Grune & Stratton, 1987)

Role of the Nonpsychiatric Physician in Patient Management and Indications for Psychiatric Consultation and Referral

The initial step in evaluating an anxious patient is to exclude medical conditions that produce anxiety syndromes. If another anxiety disorder (such as panic attacks or phobias) or another Axis I disorder (such as major depression or psychosis) is present, more specific treatments are usually indicated for these disorders. When generalized anxiety disorder is the sole diagnosis or a residual condition, the treatments outlined above may be implemented. Psychiatric consultation can assist in excluding other diagnoses and choosing the optimal treatment.

CLINICAL PEARLS

- Exclude medical conditions that mimic anxiety.
- Exclude other psychiatric disorders and other anxiety disorders.
- Inquire about use of ethanol or other substances, *especially* caffeine. If a history of substance abuse exists, avoid use of benzodiazepines.
- Consider buspirone, antidepressant medications, or benzodiazepines (at lowest effective dose and shortest duration necessary).
- Consider psychotherapy or behavioral therapy, alone or with medication.

ANNOTATED BIBLIOGRAPHY

Emmelkamp PMG: Behavior therapy with adults. In Garfield SL, Bergin AE (eds): Handbook of Psychotherapy and Behavior Change, 3rd ed. New York, John Wiley & Sons, 1986.

> Provides a critical review of behavioral and cognitive treatment studies in each of the anxiety disorders with the exception of post traumatic stress disorder. Information is well documented and conclusions clearly stated.

Goodwin DW, Guze SB (eds): Psychiatric Diagnosis, 3rd ed. New York, Oxford University Press, 1984.

> Chapters on anxiety neurosis, obsessive-compulsive disorder, and phobic disorders provide good descriptions of clinical phenomenology.

Krystal JH, Goodwin WK, Woods SW, Charney DS: Anxiety Disorders. In Lazare A (ed): Outpatient Psychiatry, Diagnosis, and Treatment, 2nd ed, pp 416–454. Baltimore, Williams & Wilkins, 1989.

> A comprehensive overview of anxiety disorders containing both practical and theoretical information. Integration of the various etiologic constructs is emphasized in understanding the development of these disorders.

Liebowitz MR, Gorman JM, Fyer AS, Klein DF: Social phobia: Review of a neglected anxiety disorder. Arch Gen Psychiatr 42:729–736, 1985.

> A very helpful summary of social phobia discussing diagnostic validity, epidemiology, pathophysiology, and etiology, and summarizing methods and findings of treatment studies of social phobia and performance anxiety.

Marks IM: Genetics of fear and anxiety disorders. Br J Psychiatr 149:406–418, 1986.

> Reviews animal and human genetic studies of fear and anxiety and summarizes family and twin studies of panic disorder, phobic disorders and obsessive-compulsive disorder.

Rapoport JL: The neurobiology of obsessive-compulsive disorder. JAMA 260:2888–2890, 1988

> A succinct yet excellent overview of biological aspects of obsessive-compulsive disorder and its psychopharmacologic treatment.

Roy-Byrne PP, Cowley DS: Panic disorder: Biological aspects. Psychiatr Ann 18:457–463, 1988

> A concise, comprehensive, and clearly written review of biological studies in panic disorder.

Nemiah JC: Foundations of Psychopathology. New York, Oxford University Press, 1961

> Chapters 7, 8, and 9 discuss anxiety as a symptom and anxiety syndromes from a psychoanalytic perspective.

Jenike MA, Baer L, Minichiello WE, (eds): Obsessive Compulsive Disorders: Theory and Management. Littleton, MA, PSG Publishing Company, 1986

> Good text for clinical description and management of obsessive-compulsive disorder.

Van der Kolk BA: The drug treatment of post-traumatic stress disorder. J Affect Disord 13:203–213, 1987

> A good summary of the clinical syndrome, etiologic models, and psychopharmacologic treatment of posttraumatic stress disorder.

REFERENCES

American Psychiatric Association: Diagnostic and Statistical Manual of Mental Disorders, Third Edition, Washington DC, American Psychiatric Association, 1980

American Psychiatric Association: Diagnostic and Statistical Manual of Mental Disorders, Third Edition, Revised. Washington, DC, American Psychiatric Association, 1987

Baxter LR, Phelps ME, Mazziotta JC, et al: Local glucose metabolic rates in obsessive—compulsive disorder. Arch Gen Psychiatr 44:211–218, 1987

Breier A, Charney DS, Heninger GR: Agoraphobia with panic attacks: Development, diagnostic stability, and course of illness. Arch Gen Psychiatr 43:1029–1036, 1986

Britton KT: The neurobiology of anxiety. In Cavenar JO (ed): Psychiatry, vol 3. Philadelphia, JB Lippincott, 1986

Crowe RR: The genetics of panic disorder and agoraphobia. Psychiatric Developments 2:171–186, 1985

Crowe RR, Noyes R, Wilson AF, et al: A linkage study of panic disorder. Arch Gen Psychiatr 44:933–937, 1987

Emmelkamp PMG: Behavior therapy with adults. In Garfield SL, Bergin AE (eds): Handbook of Psychotherapy and Behavior Change, 3rd ed. New York, John Wiley & Sons, 1986

Ferrero P, Costa E, Conti-Tronconti B, Guidotti A: A diazepam binding inhibitor (DBI)–like neuropeptide is detected in human brain. Brain Res 399:136–142, 1986

Frank JB, Kosten TR, Giller EJ, et al: A randomized clinical trial of phenelzine and imipramine for post-traumatic stress disorder. Am J Psychiatr 145:1289–1291, 1988

Fyer AJ, Klein DF: Agoraphobia, social phobia, and simple phobia. In Cavenar JO (ed): Psychiatry, vol 1. Philadelphia, JB Lippincott, 1986

Gorman JM, Liebowitz MR: Panic and anxiety disorders. In Cavenar JO (ed): Psychiatry, vol 1. Philadelphia, JB Lippincott, 1986

Insel TR: Obsessive-compulsive disorder. Psychiatr Clin North Am 8:105–117, 1985

Krystal JH, Charney DS: Advances in anxiety therapy. Internal Medicine for the Specialist 9:93–111, 1988

Krystal JH, Goodman WK, Woods SW, et al: Anxiety disorders. In Lazare A (ed): Outpatient Psychiatry, Diagnosis and Treatment, 2nd ed. Baltimore, Williams & Wilkins, 1989

Liebowitz MR, Gorman JM, Fyer AJ, Klein DF: Social phobia: Review of a neglected anxiety disorder. Arch Gen Psychiatr 42:729–736, 1985

Marks IM: Genetics of fear and anxiety disorders. Br J Psychiatry 149:406–418, 1986

Marks I: Blood-injury phobia: A review. Am J Psychiatr 145:1207–1213, 1988

Merikangas KM, Weissman MM: Epidemiology of anxiety disorders in adulthood. In Cavenar JO (ed): Psychiatry, vol 3. Philadelphia, JB Lippincott, 1986

Millon T: Social learning models. In Cavenar JO (ed): Psychiatry, vol 1. Philadelphia, JB Lippincott, 1986

Myers JK, Weissman MM, Tischler GL, et al: Six-month prevalence of psychiatric disorders in three communities: 1980 to 1982. Arch Gen Psychiatr 41:959–967, 1984

Noyes R, Clarkson C, Crowe RR, et al: A family study of generalized anxiety disorder. Am J Psychiatr 144:1019–1024, 1987

Pauls DL, Bucher KD, Crowe RR, et al: A genetic study of panic disorder pedigrees. Am J Hum Genet 32:639–644, 1980

Rapee RM, Barlow DH: Panic disorder: cognitive-behavioral treatment. Psychiatr Ann 18:473–477, 1988

Rasmussen SA, Tsuang MT: Clinical characteristics and family history in DSM-III obsessive-compulsive disorder. Am J Psychiatr 143:317–322, 1986

Robins LN, Helzer JE, Weissman MM, et al: Lifetime prevalence of specific psychiatric disorders in three sites. Arch Gen Psychiatr 41:949–958, 1984

Roy-Bryne PP, Cowley DS: Panic disorder: Biological aspects. Psychiatr Ann 18:457–463, 1988

Shear KM, Frosch WA: Obsessive-compulsive disorder. In Cavenar JO (ed): Psychiatry, vol 1. Philadelphia, JB Lippincott, 1986

Sussman N: Treatment of anxiety with buspirone. Psychiatr Ann 17:114–120, 1987

Torgersen S: Genetic factors in anxiety disorders. Arch Gen Psychiatr 40:1085–1089, 1983

Van der Kolk BA (ed): Psychological Trauma. Washington DC, American Psychiatric Press, 1987

8

Somatoform Disorders, Factitious Disorders, and Malingering

David G. Folks, Charles V. Ford, and Carl A. Houck

Somatoform disorders, factitious disorders, and malingering represent various degrees of illness behavior characterized by the process of somatization. These distinct diagnostic categories are often conceptualized as a continuum of abnormal illness behavior, with particular attention being given to the question of whether symptoms are consciously or unconsciously produced and to whether conscious or unconscious motivations account for the production of symptoms. This chapter will cover many of the current concepts of the epidemiology, diagnosis, etiology, and clinical management of each diagnostic group. The management of chronic pain is not thoroughly covered in this chapter, which rather addresses those aspects more relevant to somatization; the reader is referred to Chapter 22 for more extensive coverage of pain management.

THE PROCESS OF SOMATIZATION

Somatization is a process by which an individual consciously or unconsciously uses the body or bodily symptoms for psychological purposes or personal gain. The observed prevalence of abnormal illness behavior characterized by somatization varies according to the clinical setting and the medical specialty, with reported figures ranging between 5 and 40% of patient visits (Ford, 1983). Somatization is thought to be more prevalent among clinical populations presenting to general practice, primary care, or internal medicine clinicians. Somatizing disorders undoubtedly result in increased use of both inpatient and outpatient medical services and significantly affect the cost of medical care. Conservative estimates indicate that at least 10% of all medical services are provided for patients who have no evidence of organic disease; these figures do not include services provided for patients with identified psychiatric syndromes (Smith et al., 1986).

Somatization is facilitated in cultures that accept physical disease as an excuse for disability but reject psychological symptoms as acceptable for entry into the "sick role." Similarly, governmental agencies, insurance companies, and other third-party payers may allow financial restitution for medical expenses, or approve disability payments for physical disease, but deny benefits for disturbances that are psychiatric. Thus, many somatizing individuals receive secondary gain for illness behavior. Ford (1986) has elucidated other specific motivations for somatization as follows: (1) the manipulation of interpersonal relationships; (2) the privileges of the sick role, including sanctioned dependency; (3) financial gain; (4) communication or ideas or feelings that are somehow blocked from verbal expression; and (5) the influence of intrapsychic defense mechanisms.

Perhaps the major conscious or unconscious motivation for somatization is the achievement of the sick role. The sick role, first examined by Parsons (1951), enables release from the normal and usual obligations of society while absolving the affected person from blame for the condition. When considering etiologic factors relevant to the process of somatization, one must also appreciate the distinction between the concepts of illness and disease (Eisenberg, 1977). *Disease* is defined as objectively measurable anatomic deformations and pathophysiologic states presumably caused by such varied factors as degenerative processes, trauma, toxins, and infectious agents. *Illness* refers to those experiences associated with disease that ultimately impact on an individual's state of being and social functioning. Therefore, illness takes into account the personal nature of suffering, alienation from one's usual gratifying activities, and a decreased capacity to participate in society, all of which significantly affect life quality itself.

Irrespective of the underlying motivation(s), all of the possible explanations for somatization encourage a thorough diagnostic investigation and therapeutic approach that focuses on the psychosocial history while formulating the extent of the patient's disease, the magnitude of the illness, and the degree to which the patient is suffering and unable to engage in his or her usual activities. Also worthy of consideration is the appropriateness of an individual's illness behavior in the context of existing disease, and the extent to which a patient's symptoms could serve to resolve life problems or represent psychological conflicts. In this regard, Brodsky (1984) has identified family factors that predispose to somatization as follows: (1) growing up in a family of somatizers; (2) being raised by parents who were demanding and unrewarding when the child was well, but caring and loving when the child was ill; (3) experiencing an environment in which one or both parents suffered illness; (4) living in an environment in which other coping mechanisms for dealing with a psychosocial crisis are unavailable; (5) developing a repertoire of reactions used to withdraw from usual life activities or to engage or punish others; and (6) consciously feigning illness to obtain something or to avoid punishment, responsibility, or required duties. *One must also consider the possibility that somatization is primarily or secondarily associated with an underlying psychiatric syndrome, a coexisting personality disorder, or a psychosocial stressor that has diagnostic significance with respect to the interpersonal or intrapsychic features of the case.*

Psychiatric referral is infrequent with somatization, probably because cases are not recognized as such or these patients lack the psychological capacity and motiva-

Table 8-1 **Somatization: Principles of Clinical Management**

1. The presentation is considered in the context of psychosocial factors, both current and past.
2. The diagnostic procedures and therapeutic interventions are based on objective findings.
3. A therapeutic alliance is fostered and maintained involving the primary care and/or psychiatric physician.
4. The social support system and relevant life quality domains* are carefully reviewed during each patient contact.
5. A regular appointment schedule is maintained for outpatients, irrespective of clinical course.
6. The patient dialogue and examination and the assessment of new symptoms or signs are engaged judiciously, and usually primarily address somatic rather than psychologic concerns.
7. The need for psychiatric referral is recognized early, especially for cases involving chronic symptoms, severe psychosocial consequences, or morbid types of illness behavior.
8. Any associated, coexisting, or underlying psychiatric disturbance is assiduously evaluated and steadfastly treated.
9. The significance of personality features, addictive potential, and self-destructive risk is determined and addressed.
10. The patient's case is redefined in such a way that management rather than cure is the goal of treatment.

* Quality of life is an elusive concept but includes the psychosocial domains of occupation; leisure; family, marital, and health; sexual and psychological functioning.

---

tion to cooperate with a psychiatric consultant. Fortunately several recommendations have evolved regarding the general therapeutic approach in the management of somatization, enabling primary care physicians and psychiatric consultants to collaborate more effectively. When the therapeutic principles outlined in Table 8-1 are employed, decreased morbidity, medical use, and cost can be expected.

SOMATOFORM DISORDERS

Somatoform disorders were included as a new category in the third edition of the American Psychiatric Association's Diagnostic and Statistical Manual (DSM-III) and have been expanded in the revised third edition (DSM-III-R; American Psychiatric Association, 1987). Somatoform disorders are characterized by physical complaints lacking known organic basis or demonstrable physical findings in the presence of psychological factors judged to be etiologic or important in the initiation, exacerbation, or maintenance of the disturbance. A comparison of the individual subtypes of somatoform disorder is presented in Table 8-2. These clinical features are fundamentally important and serve to facilitate the discussion that follows.

Somatization Disorder

Formerly "hysteria" or Briquet's syndrome, somatization disorder represents a polysymptomatic disorder beginning in early life, affecting mostly women, and characterized by recurrent, multiple somatic complaints reflected in a diffusely positive review of systems. Cases date back more than 3000 years, with the first systematic

Table 8-2 **Somatoform, Factitious or Malingering: A Comparison of Clinical Features**

DIAGNOSTIC SUBTYPE	CLINICAL PRESENTATION	DEMOGRAPHIC/ EPIDEMIOLOGIC FEATURES	DIAGNOSTIC FEATURES	MANAGEMENT STRATEGY	PROGNOSTIC OUTLOOK	ASSOCIATED DISTURBANCES	PRIMARY DIFFERENTIAL PRESENTATION	PSYCHOLOGIC PROCESSES CONTRIBUTING TO SYMPTOMS	MOTIVATION FOR SYMPTOM PRODUCTION
Somatoform Disorders									
Somatization disorder	Polysymptomatic Recurrent/chronic "Sickly" by history	Younger age Female predominance 20 to 1 Familial pattern 5–10% incidence in primary care populations	ROS profusely positive Multiple clinical contacts Polysurgical	• Therapeutic alliance • Regular appointments • Crisis intervention	Poor to fair	Histrionic personality Sociopathy Substance/alcohol use Many life problems Conversion	Physical disease Depression	Unconscious Cultural/developmental	Unconscious psychologic factors
Conversion disorder	Monosymptomatic Mostly acute Simulates disease	Highly prevalent Female predominance younger age Rural/lower social class Less educated/psychologically unsophisticated	Simulation incompatible with known physiologic mechanisms or anatomy	• Suggestion and persuasion • Multiple techniques	Excellent except chronic conversion	Drug/alcohol dependence Sociopathy Somatization disorder Histrionic personality	Depression Schizophrenia Neurologic disease	Unconscious Psychologic stress or conflict may be present	Unconscious psychologic factors
Somatoform pain	Pain syndrome simulated	Female predominance 2 to 1 Older: 4th or 5th decade Familial pattern Up to 40% of pain populations	Simulation or intensity incompatible with known physiologic mechanisms or anatomy	• Therapeutic alliance • Redefine goals of treatment • Antidepressant medications	Guarded, variable	Depression Substance/alcohol use Dependent/histrionic personality	Depression Psychophysiologic Physical disease Malingering/disability syndrome	Unconscious Acute stressor/developmental Physical trauma may predispose	Unconscious psychologic factors
Hypochondriasis	Disease concern or preoccupation	Previous physical disease Middle or older age Male/female ratio equal	Disease conviction amplifies symptoms Obsessional	• Document symptoms • Psychosocial review • Psychotherapeutic	Fair to good Waxes and wanes	Obsessional "neurosis" Depression-anxiety	Depression Physical disease Personality disorder Delusional disorder	Unconscious Stress—bereavement Developmental factors	Unconscious psychologic factors
Body dysmorphic disorder	Subjective feelings of ugliness or concern with body defect	Adolescence or young adult ? Female predominance Largely unknown	Pervasive bodily concerns	• Therapeutic alliance • Stress management • Psychotherapies • Antidepressant medications	Unknown	Anorexia nervosa Psychosocial distress Avoidant/compulsive personality disorder	Delusional psychosis Depression Somatization disorder	Unconscious Self-esteem factors	Unconscious psychologic factors

Factitious Disorders

	Definition	Characteristics	Clinical features	Management	Prognosis	Associated	Differential diagnosis	Etiology	Motivation
Factitious with physical symptoms	Feigned or simulated physical symptoms or signs or disease	Female, younger, socially conforming; Employed in medical field; Social supports often available	Feigned illness; No external goal of simulation is obvious; Organ mode of presentation varies but is physical	• Confront as appropriate • Redefine illness as psychiatric • Psychiatric referral	Fair to good except Munchausen's subtype	Depression; Borderline or other personality disorder	Malingering; Conversion disorder; Hypochondriasis; Depression; Schizophrenia	Unconscious; Developmental/family factors; Masochism, dependency, and mastery are utilized	Conscious effort to assume patient status
Factitious with psychological symptoms	Multiple hospitalizations	Female, younger, socially conforming; Employed in medical field; Social supports often available	Feigned illness; No external goal of simulation is obvious; Mode of presentation varies but is psychiatric	• Confront as appropriate • Redefine illness as psychiatric • Psychiatric referral	Fair to good except Munchausen's subtype	Schizophrenia; Borderline or other personality disorder	Malingering; Conversion disorder; Hypochondriasis; Depression; Schizophrenia	Unconscious; Developmental/family factors; Masochism, dependency, and mastery are utilized	Conscious effort to assume patient status
Munchausen's syndrome	Multiple hospitalizations	Male, younger, socially nonconforming; Social supports often unavailable	Feigned illness; Pathologic liar; Geographic wandering; Antisocial features; Frequently leaves against medical advice	• Recognize • Confront • Avoid invasive or iatrogenic procedures or treatments • Social work referral	Poor	Antisocial, histrionic, or borderline personality	Malingering; Conversion disorder; Hypochondriasis; Depression; Schizophrenia	Unconscious; Developmental/family factors; Masochism, dependency, and mastery are utilized	Conscious effort to assume patient status

Malingering

	Definition	Characteristics	Clinical features	Management	Prognosis	Associated	Differential diagnosis	Etiology	Motivation
Malingering	Feigned or simulated with physical or psychological symptoms	? Male predominance; Psychosocial stress or failure present	Feigned illness; External incentives for disease present	• Confront • Consider psychiatric or psychosocial problems	N/A	Antisocial personality; Substance abuse/dependence	Factitious disorder; Personality disorder; Ganser syndrome; Munchausen syndrome; Major psychosis; Disability syndrome	Conscious but may display other psychopathology	Conscious response to external incentives

evaluation being reported by Briquet, for whom the condition was originally named (Guze, 1975). Certain diagnostic aspects of the syndrome have been refined, resulting in the more reliable diagnostic criteria ultimately included in DSM-III-R.

Epidemiology

Estimates from the Epidemiologic Catchment Area (ECA) study show an estimated lifetime prevalence of approximately 0.4% for somatization disorder (Swartz et al., 1986). Although accurate point prevalence figures are not readily available, 1 to 2% prevalence is suggested for women with a female-to-male predominance of approximately 20 to 1. Somatization disorder is more commonly observed in lower socioeconomic groups. Between 5 and 10% of a primary care ambulatory population will meet DSM-III-R diagnostic criteria, suggesting that somatization is the fourth most common diagnostic group seen in an ambulatory medical setting. A relationship between somatization disorder and polysurgery is also well documented. A familial pattern is observed affecting 10 to 20% of female first-degree biologic relatives of females with somatization disorder; male relatives of females with this disorder show an increased risk of antisocial personality disorder and/or substance use disorder (Bohman et al., 1984). Adoption studies have indicated that both genetic and environmental factors contribute to the risk for the disorder. Several investigators have reported the tendency for somatization disorder to be associated with sociopathy, alcoholism, and drug addiction. Although no specific data exist to establish the economic impact of somatization, the prevalence and tendency to use surgery and advanced technology in diagnosis or treatment undoubtedly represents a significant cost.

Diagnosis and Differential Diagnosis

The most important diagnostic feature of somatization disorder is recurrent, multiple somatic complaints of several years duration for which medical attention has been sought. The DSM-III-R diagnostic criteria are depicted in Table 8-3. The diagnosis using these criteria has been shown to possess criterion stability, with a high degree of reliability and validity. Liskow observed that the disorder is quite heterogeneous and that other psychiatric illness is likely to coexist (Liskow et al., 1986). Histrionic and antisocial personality disorder are the most frequently associated personality disorders and may appear in conjunction with anxiety or depressed mood,

Table 8-3 **Diagnostic Criteria for Somatization Disorder**

A. A history of many physical complaints or a belief that one is sickly, beginning before age 30 and persisting for several years.

B. At least 13 symptoms from the list below. To count a symptom as significant, the following criteria must be met:

  (1) no organic pathology or pathophysiologic mechanism (e.g., a physical disorder or the effects of injury, medication, drugs, or alcohol) to account for the symptom or, when there is related organic pathology, the complaint or resulting social or occupational impairment is grossly in excess of what would be expected from the physical findings

(continued)

Table 8–3 **(continued)**

(2) has not occurred only during a panic attack
(3) has caused the person to take medicine (other than over-the-counter pain medication), see a doctor, or alter life-style

Symptom list:

Gastrointestinal symptoms:
(1) **vomiting (other than during pregnancy)**
(2) abdominal pain (other than when menstruating)
(3) nausea (other than motion sickness)
(4) bloating (gassy)
(5) diarrhea
(6) intolerance of (gets sick from) several different foods
Pain symptoms:
(7) **pain in extremities**
(8) back pain
(9) joint pain
(10) pain during urination
(11) other pain (excluding headaches)
Cardiopulmonary symptoms:
(12) **shortness of breath when not exerting oneself**
(13) palpitations
(14) chest pain
(15) dizziness
Conversion of pseudoneurologic symptoms:
(16) **amnesia**
(17) **difficulty swallowing**
(18) loss of voice
(19) deafness
(20) double vision
(21) blurred vision
(22) blindness
(23) fainting or loss of consciousness
(24) seizure or convulsion
(25) trouble walking
(26) paralysis or muscle weakness
(27) urinary retention or difficulty urinating
Sexual symptoms for the major part of the person's life after opportunities for sexual activity:
(28) **burning sensation in sexual organs or rectum (other than during intercourse)**
(29) sexual indifference
(30) pain during intercourse
(31) impotence
Female reproductive symptoms judged by the person to occur more frequently or severely than in most women:
(32) **painful menstruation**
(33) irregular menstrual periods
(34) excessive menstrual bleeding
(35) vomiting throughout pregnancy

Note: The seven items in boldface may be used to screen for the disorder. The presence of two or more of these items suggests a high likelihood of the disorder.

(Reprinted with permission from American Psychiatric Association: Diagnostic and Statistical Manual of Mental Disorders, Third Edition, Revised. Washington, DC, American Psychiatric Association, 1987)

as well as substance abuse. Conversion symptoms may also be a prominent clinical feature with somatization disorder. Antisocial behavior and occupational, interpersonal, or marital difficulties are also frequently observed.

The differential diagnosis includes schizophrenia, panic disorder, conversion disorder, factitious disorder, and psychological factors affecting physical illness (psychophysiologic disorders), in addition to physical diseases or organic disorders that present with confusing, vague somatic symptoms. Patients with somatization disorder may present in the context of acute illness, psychophysiologic symptoms or other chronic medical conditions. Thus, a mix of primarily psychogenic and organic symptoms is the rule rather than the exception, making these cases extraordinarily challenging diagnostically.

Etiology and Pathogenesis

The etiologic foundations of somatization disorder are not readily discernible, although familial incidences and association with antisocial and histrionic personality disorder, as well as substance and alcohol use disorders, suggest a biologic predisposition. Undoubtedly, a learning model or behavioral theory is equally applicable, because, as already mentioned, the general use of somatizing behavior in the family of origin or culture may predispose to the syndrome (Brodsky, 1984). Furthermore, the disorder begins early in life and serves as a prototype for the ideas discussed regarding the cultural, developmental and behavioral aspects of somatization and illness behavior. Thus, somatization disorder develops in the context of a lifelong pattern in which somatic symptoms are readily utilized to communicate distress and to cope with ongoing psychosocial stressors and interpersonal problems.

Clinical Management

The first step in the management of somatization disorder is simply to recognize the syndrome and initiate a therapeutic strategy in keeping with the principles outlined in Table 8-1. These patients see themselves as functionally disabled and readily use medical services despite the fact that no objective measures support that they are physically sick. The following case is illustrative:

A CASE STUDY

A 40-year-old woman presented to the emergency room with a complaint of chest pain. A preliminary evaluation revealed no obvious cause, but because she reported numerous symptoms in her systems review, she was admitted for a more complete evaluation. Her diagnostic work-up ultimately included cardiac catheterization, which yielded totally normal results. The medical student involved in her case learned that her twin children who had "always helped" her in illness, had recently left to attend college. Furthermore, a review of her complaints in view of the negative findings seemed to indicate that the patient was "psychosomatic." At this point a psychiatric consultant was asked to see the patient and obtained a thorough psychosocial history revealing that the patient had been sickly since about age 15, with numerous chronic symptoms arising in different organ systems: nausea, bloating, back

pain, dysuria, pain in her knees, palpitations, dizziness, dyspnea, dou-
ble vision, gait unsteadiness, weakness of her arms, trouble swallowing,
dyspareunia, and dysmenorrhea were all related at various times
throughout the interview. She dramatically related that she was "tired of
suffering" and was "frustrated" with her doctors, who had been unable
to diagnose her case or satisfactorily explain the disabling symptoms.
The psychiatrist, who recognized her problem as somatization disorder,
suggested psychotherapy as a means to help her cope with the rather ob-
vious family stresses that had precipitated her pain, but she declined,
saying that she preferred to see "a real doctor who can understand me
better."

Smith and Quill (Smith et al, 1986; Quill, 1985) suggest the following principles in the clinical approach to somatization disorder: (1) a therapeutic alliance with an empathic physician is established to minimize doctor shopping, multiple medication regimens, and the potential for substance dependence or unnecessary diagnostic procedures; (2) the symptoms are viewed as an emotional communication and some attempt is made to understand their psychological significance; (3) patients are seen at regular intervals so that they will not require new symptoms to see a physician; (4) the use of psychotropic agents, analgesics, and other such medications is minimized or avoided; and (5) psychiatric consultation is recommended for those cases that are severe or in which psychiatric complications or disturbances arise. As represented in the case above, many patients are highly resistant to psychiatric referral, thus the recommendations for treatment must first consider the general principles outlined in Table 8-1. A cure is seldom achieved, but recurrent debilitating symptoms can be relinquished and perhaps exchanged for controlled dependence on a clinic or physician. Again, the psychiatric consultant's role usually involves crisis intervention or attention to associated disturbances, with the key therapeutic interventions resulting from a developing therapeutic relationship with the primary clinician.

Conversion Disorder

Conversion symptoms have been described since antiquity and represent a type of somatoform disorder in which there is a loss or alteration in physical functioning suggesting a physical disorder but which cannot be explained on the basis of known physiologic mechanisms (Table 8-4). Conversion disorder is usually seen in ambulatory settings or emergency departments, and frequently runs a rather short-lived course, responding to nearly any therapeutic modality that offers a suggestion of cure.

Epidemiology

Conversion symptoms are exceedingly common in medical practice; estimates of 20 to 25% prevalence are given for patients admitted to a general medical setting (Ford, 1983). General hospital patients have consistently shown conversion symptoms in between 5 and 14% of all psychiatric consultations (Folks et al., 1984). Conversion symptoms are also ubiquitous among randomly selected psychiatric clinic patients, and particularly prevalent among patients with drug addiction, sociopathy, alcoholism, and somatization disorder or "hysteria." The disorder more typically occurs in women. In men the disorder tends to be associated with a history of industrial accidents or, more typically, military duty. Conversion disorder reportedly encompasses ages ranging from early childhood into the ninth decade. The disorder appears more frequently in lower socioeconomic groups, and in rural or less psychologically sophisticated populations. The more primitive and grossly nonphysiologic conversion symptoms are observed in patients of rural background; by contrast, conversion symptoms observed in better-educated populations will more closely simulate known disease.

Diagnosis and Differential Diagnosis

Diagnostic descriptions and terminology relating to conversion phenomena have changed markedly over the last 30 years. The current diagnostic criteria as listed in DSM-III-R are depicted in Table 8-4. The diagnosis is unique, implying that specific psychodynamic mechanisms account for the disturbance. In contrast with somatization disorder, which is chronic and polysymptomatic, involving many organ systems, conversion disorder is generally sporadic and monosymptomatic with a symbolic relationship between the underlying psychological conflict and the disturbance in physical functioning. *A number of traditional clinical features previously associated with conversion—for example, secondary gain, histrionic personality, and la belle indifference—appear to have no diagnostic significance; these are regarded as "soft signs," supportive of the diagnosis and having no firm diagnostic validity.* The diagnosis of conversion must ultimately rest upon positive clinical findings clearly indicating that the symptom does not derive from organic disease, such as demonstration of normal motor function in patients with "paralysis." Common examples of conversion symptoms include paralysis, abnormal movements, aphonia, blindness, deafness, or pseudoseizures, the last of which is illustrated by a case vignette:

A CASE STUDY

A 42-year-old woman was admitted to the neurology service for evaluation of seizures beginning 1 month earlier. The seizures consisted of

Table 8–4 **Diagnostic Criteria for Conversion Disorder**

A. A loss of, or alteration in, physical functioning suggesting a physical disorder.
B. Psychological factors are judged to be etiologically related to the symptom because of a temporal relationship between a psychosocial stressor that is apparently related to a psychological conflict or need and initiation or exacerbation of the symptom.
C. The person is not conscious of intentionally producing the symptom.
D. The symptom is not a culturally sanctioned response pattern and cannot, after appropriate investigation, be explained by a known physical disorder.
E. The symptom is not limited to pain or to a disturbance in sexual functioning.

Specify whether single episode or recurrent.

abrupt onset of tonic-clonic movements, lasting about 10 minutes, resolving equally abruptly, with no postictal confusion or diminished consciousness. An intensive neurological evaluation revealed no abnormal physical findings: neurological exam, routine physical exam, routine laboratory exam, head CT scan, magnetic resonance imaging of the brain, lumbar puncture, and routine electroencephalogram were all normal. The patient's brain electrophysiologic activity was then monitored continuously and showed no abnormal EEG patterns despite the occurrence of several "seizure" episodes. A psychiatric consultant was called who learned that the seizure activity—now thought to represent a conversion disorder—began within a week of learning that her husband had been unfaithful. An amobarbital interview revealed that the patient had been considering a divorce although such an alternative was unacceptable to her or her family of origin's value system.

As suggested by the case, conversion symptoms will usually conform to the *patient's* concept of disease rather than to typical pathophysiologic mechanisms or anatomical patterns. When the symptom occurs in isolation, it is appropriate to assign a diagnosis of conversion disorder; however, conversion symptoms may also occur as a part of other major syndromes, such as somatization disorder, schizophrenia, depression, organic brain syndromes, or even medical or neurological disease. The most common personality disorder purported to be associated with conversion disorder is histrionic (hysterical) personality, but data in this regard are inconsistent. Evidence of current or prior neurologic disorder is also frequently identified, and a number of neurologic cases have appeared in the literature that were initially misdiagnosed as conversion disorder (Merskey, Buhrich, 1975).

Etiology and Pathogenesis

Clinical descriptions of conversion phenomena date back to at least 1900 BC, at which time the Egyptian papyri attributed symptoms to "wandering of the uterus." Conversion symptoms result from stressful environmental events acting on the *affective* part of the brain in predisposed individuals. Some patients' symptoms conform to Freud's concept of "conversion" in reference to the concept that conversion results from the substitution of a somatic symptom for a repressed idea or psychological conflict. Conversion may also be a means to express forbidden feelings or ideas, as a kind of communication via pantomime or mimicry when direct verbal communication is blocked, or may simply serve as an acceptable means of enacting the sick role, or as an acute entry into illness behavior. The individual with conversion avoids certain responsibilities or noxious situations, and is frequently able to control or manipulate the behavior of others. Classical conditioning paradigms have provided other possible explanations for conversion phenomena. Learned symptoms of illness are then later used as a means of coping with particularly stressful situations. More recent theories have proposed social, communication, and sophisticated neurophysiologic mechanisms whose discussion is beyond the scope of this chapter (Folks et al, 1984).

Clinical Management

A wide variety of treatment techniques have been successfully used for conversion disorder. Brief psychotherapy focusing on stress and coping, and suggestive therapy—sometimes using hypnosis or amobarbital interviews that focus on symptom removal—are commonly employed with amazing efficacy. A short hospital admission also may be helpful, particularly when symptoms are disabling or alarming. Hospitalization may serve to remove the patient from the stressful situation, demonstrate to the family that the matter is important, or facilitate resolution of the psychological trauma. Many patients experience spontaneous remission of symptoms or demonstrate marked or complete recovery after a brief therapeutic intervention. In fact, prompt recovery is the rule, and few patients will need long-term management. For example, a case seen in our facility involved a healthy 29-year-old farmer who experienced acute blindness when confronted with a mortgage foreclosure notice and was ultimately "cured" with saline drops. The psychiatric consultant merely told the patient that the "special" eye drops had "cured several others in a matter of days."

Unfortunately, chronic conversion disorder carries a poorer prognosis and is notoriously difficult to treat, resembling somatization disorder and somatoform pain disorder. Behavior modification can be used in the approach to recalcitrant conversion symptoms maintained by secondary gain. The therapeutic principles outlined in Table 8-1 are particularly relevant to these chronic cases, and psychiatric consultants are often required.

Somatoform Pain Disorder

Estimates by the National Institute of Neurological Communication Disorders and Stroke suggest that as many as 75 million Americans are afflicted with chronic pain, at a cost of some 40 billion dollars per annum (Bonica, 1976). Multidisciplinary pain clinics have developed in which patients can be effectively evaluated and treated by consultants from a variety of disciplines—anesthesia, neurology, neurosurgery, orthopedics, psychiatry, psychology, and social work. Various diagnostic categories of psychological pain are encountered, including psychogenic or idiopathic (somatoform) pain, muscle tension syndromes, masked depression, and varying degrees of disability syndromes or malingering. This chapter is confined to the diagnosis and clinical management of certain aspects of somatoform pain. Therapeutic strategies for other pain syndromes are suggested in Chapter 22.

Epidemiology

No substantial information exists on the prevalence of somatoform pain disorder, although it is expected that in a significant proportion of pain patients—perhaps as many as 40%—the pain is psychogenic in origin (Stoudemire, Sandhu, 1987). The disorder may occur at any age but more frequently presents in the fourth or fifth decade, usually appearing acutely with an increase in severity over time. The disorder is diagnosed in women twice as frequently as in men. Evidence exists to suggest a familial pattern, with first-degree biologic relatives being at higher risk for developing the disorder. A known familial pattern that includes a history of depression or alcohol dependence occurs at a greater frequency than might be expected within the general population.

Diagnosis and Differential Diagnosis

The prominent diagnostic feature of somatoform pain disorder is preoccupation with pain in the absence of physical findings that might account for the pain or its intensity. As with conversion symptoms, the pain is manifested inconsistently with respect to anatomical distribution or, if it mimics a known disease entity, such as angina or sciatica, the pain cannot be adequately explained on the basis of any existing organic pathology. The DSM-III-R diagnostic criteria for somatoform pain are presented in Table 8-5. As suggested by these diagnostic criteria, pathophysiologic mechanisms should not account for the pain, and, as with conversion, the etiologic impact of any psychological factors must be appreciated, whether they (1) are clearly identified in precipitating the pain, (2) simply permit the individual to avoid some unacceptable or noxious activity, or (3) result in significant psychosocial support that might not otherwise be forthcoming. The following case presented with all three psychological factors:

A CASE STUDY

A 29-year-old radiologist complained to his family physician of constant abdominal pain so severe that he had used up all of his sick leave and was now strongly having to consider quitting his prestigious new position. An admission to the hospital led to a comprehensive but fruitless evaluation of the pain, culminating in an unremarkable exploratory laparotomy. On learning that the surgery was unrevealing, the patient appeared surprised, frustrated, and distraught, proclaiming that he was "afraid" that he would be unable to return to work with his boss, his father, the division chief.

The differential diagnosis of somatoform pain disorder must take into consideration other psychiatric syndromes, such as somatization disorder, depressive disorder, or schizophrenia, in which complaints of pain are common. Of course, a significant minority of these patients are ultimately found to be malingering (as is discussed below), and the symptoms are manifested for the sole purpose of obtaining an obviously explainable or recognizable goal, or in an attempt to secure narcotic analgesics or other addictive substances. Another important differential diagnosis is psychophysiologic disorders, such as muscle contraction headache, muscular spasm

Table 8–5 **Diagnostic Criteria for Somatoform Pain Disorder**

A. Preoccupation with pain for at least 6 months.
B. Either (1) or (2):
  (1) appropriate evaluation uncovers no organic pathology or pathophysiologic mechanism (e.g., a physical disorder or the effects of injury) to account for the pain
  (2) when there is related organic pathology, the complaint of pain or resulting social or occupational impairment is grossly in excess of what would be expected from the physical findings

back pain, proctalgia fugax affecting the musculature of the anus, or other syndromes that may involve a clear pathophysiologic mechanism that reasonably accounts for the pain syndrome.

Major depression or depressive symptoms are often present as an underlying or coexisting disorder. The changes in mood and in personality that accompany chronic pain are also frequently seen in depression (Reuler et al., 1980). Indeed, all pain patients seem to report symptoms or changes in their physiologic response, with the emergence of vegetative symptoms similar or identical to those that accompany depression. The observed personality disorders that most frequently accompany somatoform pain disorder are histrionic and dependent personality conditions (Reich et al., 1983). For a discussion of more specific pain syndromes, the reader is referred to Ford (1983), where the clinical features of psychogenic aspects of pelvic pain, phantom pain, low back pain, and atypical facial pain are discussed.

Etiology and Pathogenesis

Somatoform pain disorder is best conceptualized on the basis of psychosocial features identified on history; evidence of past somatization, the presence of a symptom model, prominent guilt, and a history of physical or psychogenic abuse by either a parent or a spouse are thought to carry some diagnostic validity. However, these "soft" findings together with negative physical or laboratory or radiographic findings do not necessarily imply that the pain symptoms are attributable to psychosocial forces. Moreover, as with all forms of somatization, a complete separation of etiology into organic or psychogenic may be difficult and in some ways unnecessary.

Full appreciation of the etiologic factors involved in any form of psychogenic pain is complicated, since the clinician must account for the economy of secondary gain or reinforcement, understand abnormal illness behavior, and evaluate the role of unconscious motivations and primary gain. Those individuals receiving compensation are prone to confound their management; compensation neurosis or disability syndromes (not covered in this chapter) are perhaps the best studied etiologic and consequential factors resulting in patients with pain syndromes.

Pain is a subjective experience and simply cannot be measured; patients consciously or unconsciously perceive or describe their symptoms in such a way as to be compatible with previous illnesses or their conception of what other persons might have experienced. The marked variation in perception of pain is likely due to the neuroanatomic nature of the brain in numerous associated pathways linking sensory cerebral cortex and the limbic system. Generally, etiologic theories are not mutually exclusive and may be deemed congruous, representing our current understanding of neuroanatomic and physiologic mechanisms, psychodynamics, and learning theories about pain. An eloquent illustration from learning theory uses transactional analysis concepts in which pain is thought to be used for interpersonal manipulation and control (Sternbach, 1974).

Psychological tests, most popularly the Minnesota Multiphasic Personality Inventory (MMPI), are used routinely in pain clinics to identify psychological factors. An elevation of scores on the three scales labeled hypochondriasis (Hs), depression (D), and hysteria (Hy), referred to as the conversion V, purportedly provides evidence that the patients are "neurotic," representing themselves as physically ill and obtaining appreciable secondary gain from their symptoms. These psychological tests should not be carried out or interpreted in a vacuum, and are unlikely to be useful diagnostically without other means of supporting data. In short, correlations do *not* distinguish organic from nonorganic patients for whom "conversion" or psychogenic forces are assumed to account for the pain.

Clinical Management

A multiplicity of treatments for somatoform (psychogenic) pain have been suggested in the literature (Stoudemire, Sandhu, 1987; Reich et al., 1983). Generally, a systems approach and a variety of therapeutic techniques are necessary. The therapeutic strategy is to initially minimize the doctor-shopping and other interpersonal "games" while establishing a strong therapeutic alliance assuring the patient that complete relief is unlikely. The therapeutic principles outlined in Table 8-1 are effective. A major task is to convince patients that they must work to modify their therapeutic expectations and attempt to manage or live with their pain. A therapeutic contract can usually be initiated and the clinician quickly discerns whether the patient is really motivated to get "better." Because stress and psychological problems are always a component of pain cases, the psychiatric consultant is an invaluable participant in the psychological treatment and should be involved early. Moreover, the possible role of psychosocial or psychological factors and the impact of stress are better considered during the initial evaluation process. Specifically, many experienced clinicians recommend involving the psychiatric consultant at the outset of the diagnostic evaluation to minimize any feelings of rejection or abandonment that may otherwise emerge when psychiatric consultation is deemed necessary.

A number of nonpharmacologic treatments are useful in pain patients; transcutaneous nerve stimulation, nerve blocks, biofeedback, and other forms of behavioral or psychotherapy. Irrespective of the selected intervention, attention must be given to the patient's psychosocial, marital, and family situation, and to the meaning and significance of the pain itself. Regarding pharmacologic modalities, narcotics or other addicting substances are rarely indicated, but the psychotropics may serve as adjuvants. The cyclic antidepressants, particularly those that act preferentially via serotonin systems, often afford pain relief at a dosage below that generally believed to be effective for depression (i.e., 50 to 100 mg daily of imipramine or 50 to 75 mg doxepin or their equivalents). MAO inhibitors have also been suggested as reasonable when combined with some of the aforementioned nonpharmacologic therapies.

Hypochondriasis

Many inconsistencies and contradictions are found in the literature on hypochondriasis, probably because of the lack of systematic research. Perhaps this is why hypochondriasis has remained in a gap between psychiatry and medicine.

Epidemiology

The actual prevalence of hypochondriasis as a disorder distinct from other somatoform disorders is unknown, with estimates varying with culture and diagnostic criteria. Only a few twin studies have been reported, and inadequate evidence exists for conclusions about the importance of genetic factors. Developmental or other predisposing factors include parental attitudes toward disease, previous physical disease, lower social class, and culturally acquired attitudes relevant to the epidemiology and etiology of the disorder. Hypochondriasis typically begins in middle or older age and is equally common in men and women—features that serve to distinguish it from somatization and conversion disorder.

Diagnosis

Pilowsky (1970) defines hypochondriasis as "a concern with health or disease in one's self which is present for the major part of the time." The preoccupation must be unjustified by the amount of organic pathology and must not respond more than temporarily to clear reassurance given after a thorough examination. The core features of hypochondriasis appear to consist of a complex of attitudes: disease fear, disease conviction, and bodily preoccupation associated with multiple somatic complaints. These features are reflected by the DSM-III-R criteria shown in Table 8-6. On presentation, the medical history is often related in great detail in the context of doctor-shopping, deteriorating doctor–patient relationships, and associated feelings of frustration and anger. Anxiety, depressed mood, and obsessive personality features are frequently encountered. The clinical course is chronic with waxing and waning of symptoms. Complications may arise secondary to numerous exposures to medical care and the dangers of repeated diagnostic procedures. The possible evolution of this pattern is illustrated by the following case:

A CASE STUDY

A 35-year-old accountant presented to a gastroenterologist with a request to be "checked for colon cancer." The patient stated that, in contrast to his usual pattern of daily bowel movements, he had been constipated for the past 3 weeks. He also stated that 6 months previously, he had been constipated and an evaluation had revealed nothing wrong. However, a family history of colon cancer and fears relating to his dietary habits were elaborated. The current episode was not associated with rectal bleeding, abdominal pain, or other symptoms. Subsequently, a thorough

---

Table 8–6 **Diagnostic Criteria for Hypochondriasis**

A. Preoccupation with the fear of having, or the belief that one has, a serious disease, based on the person's interpretation of physical signs or sensations as evidence of physical illness.

B. Appropriate physical evaluation does not support the diagnosis of any physical disorder that can account for the physical signs or sensations or the person's unwarranted interpretation of them, *and* the symptoms in A are not just symptoms of panic attacks.

C. The fear of having, or belief that one has, a disease persists despite medical reassurance.

D. Duration of the disturbance is at least 6 months.

E. The belief in A is not of delusional intensity, as in delusional disorder, somatic type (i.e., the person can acknowledge the possibility that his or her fear of having, or belief that he or she has, a serious disease is unfounded).

(Reprinted with permission from American Psychiatric Association: Diagnostic and Statistical Manual of Mental Disorders, Third Edition, Revised. Washington, DC, American Psychiatric Association, 1987)

outpatient evaluation, including digital rectal exam, flexible sigmoidoscopy, and barium enema revealed no significant abnormalities. While exploring psychological possibilities, a personal history revealed some occupational distress related to his not yet becoming a full partner in the accounting firm, which in the same breath was compared to the rather glowing career observed in his brother, recently promoted to vice-president at the local bank. The patient seemed quite irritated by the questions pertaining to his personal life and emotional wellbeing. Reluctantly he stated that he would "just have to accept the fact that everything's okay" but proceeded to question the doctor's credentials and the diagnostic validity of the completed procedures. Within 2 weeks, a letter from a gastroenterology colleague across town requested the patient's records, implying that the same complaints had been offered with a request for a "more thorough evaluation."

The most important step in the differential diagnosis of hypochondriasis is the exclusion of physical disease; a number of organic diagnoses can be difficult to identify in their early course, including myasthenia gravis, multiple sclerosis, slowly deteriorating degenerative diseases of the neurologic system, endocrinopathies, or systemic diseases such as systemic lupus erythematosus or occult neoplastic disorders. However, the diagnosis should not be one of exclusion; a positive diagnosis can be made by careful history in the absence of objective physical findings and on recognition that an emotional component contributes to the symptoms.

Among psychiatric diagnoses, the most important differential diagnosis is major depression; the entity of masked depression or "secondary hypochondriasis" is repeatedly cited in the literature (Pilowsky, 1970). One must also carefully consider the existence of other somatoform disorders, factitious disorders, or malingering, and of psychotic disorders for cases manifesting hypochondriacal delusions. Investigators have consistently reported syndromes of hypochondriasis that qualify as a delusional state.

Patients with hypochondriasis seem to perceive their bodily functions more acutely than others. Barsky's suggested term "amplifying somatic style" emphasizes that these individuals selectively perceive bodily functions and attribute their symptoms to physical disease (Barsky, 1979): *why* patients develop this type of behavior is unknown. Worry about disease and absorption in their health can be a powerful motive for attending selectively to a bodily sensation. Anxiety escalates and further serves as a motive for selective perception. Depression or dysphoria exists since the patient suffers and feels helpless or hopeless as the illness evolves. Anger may also arise as a result of unmitigated distress, conflicting diagnoses, ineffective treatments, and experiences of encountering impatient, rejecting, or hostile physicians. These emotions are compounded by doctor-shopping, medication problems, conflicting opinions from physicians, and iatrogenic phenomena, as well as the specific personality features in any individual case (Kellner, 1987). Furthermore, many hypochondriacs are alexithymic—that is, have no words for emotion and constriction of affect, little concern about psychological issues, a mechanical, repetitive way of thinking, and a general inability to describe their inner feelings (Lesser et al., 1979).

Clinical Management

The most crucial management technique in caring for the hypochondriacal patient is the inclusion of a legible psychosocial history in a prominent place in the patient's record (Brown, Vaillant, 1981). The general therapeutic principles described in Table 8-1 are applicable to the vast majority of cases. Moreover, the effective strategy for the treating physician is to appreciate the obsessional features with respect to bodily complaints and to intellectually understand the fascinating displacement of psychodynamics involved in the symptom formation while appreciating the psychosocial history.

Generally, effective treatment takes place in the context of collaboration by a consulting psychiatrist and the primary physician, who continues to offer regular appointments to the patient. The possibility of concurrent organic disease or intercurrent illness exist—indeed, these will eventually occur as life progresses. Adequate physical examination on a regular and reasonable basis is helpful, and the judicious and coordinated use of other nonpsychiatric consultants is also appropriate in order to evaluate new or justifiable physical complaints. Hypochondriacal patients are best managed in a primary care or medical setting, but psychiatric consultation should be considered when the patient requests adjunctive psychiatric treatment—usually for anxiety, depression, or psychosocial distress—or when the primary physician becomes concerned about suicide or overt symptoms of depression or is unable to manage his or her own emotional response to the hypochondriacal patient. Surprisingly, the prognosis for hypochondriasis is good in a substantial portion of patients.

Body Dysmorphic Disorder

Body dysmorphic disorder, or dysmorphophobia, has been included as a separate disorder in the revised version of the DSM-III. This syndrome had been regarded as a hypochondriacal subtype or unspecified somatoform syndrome in past literature.

Epidemiology

Because the vast majority of references involve case reports, descriptive accounts of body dysmorphic disorder offer little substantial information regarding epidemiologic or etiologic factors. Onset typically occurs in adolescence, but the initial presentation can be as late as the third decade. The condition can persist for years and significantly affect social or occupational functioning. Polysurgery or unnecessary surgical procedures complicate the cases, but currently no information is available on the predisposing factors, sex ratio, or familial pattern.

Diagnosis and Differential Diagnosis

The fundamental diagnostic feature is primarily a pervasive subjective feeling of ugliness or physical defect; the patient genuinely feels that changes are readily apparent to others (Thomas, 1984). The DSM-III-R criteria for body dysmorphic disorder are outlined in Table 8-7. Commonly, the symptoms of body dysmorphic disorder involve facial flaws such as wrinkles, spots on the skin, excessive facial hair, shape of the nose, mouth, jaw, or eyebrows and swelling of the face; rarely, they may include complaints involving the feet, hands, breast, back, or some other body part. A

Table 8–7 **Diagnostic Criteria for Body Dysmorphic Disorder**

A. Preoccupation with some imagined defect in appearance in a normal-appearing person. If a slight physical anomaly is present, the person's concern is grossly excessive.
B. The belief in the defect is not of delusional intensity, as in delusional disorder, somatic type (i.e., the person can acknowledge the possibility that he or she may be exaggerating the extent of the defect or that there may be no defect at all).
C. Occurrence not exclusively during the course of anorexia nervosa or transsexualism.

(Reprinted with permission from American Psychiatric Association: Diagnostic and Statistical Manual of Mental Disorders, Third Edition, Revised. Washington, DC, American Psychiatric Association, 1987)

slight physical defect may actually be present, but the concern expressed is grossly in excess of what might be considered appropriate. This disorder is also characterized by much distress but is not to be confused with those transient feelings commonly experienced by adolescents. A case illustration can better distinguish the pathologic state:

A CASE STUDY

A 19-year-old college student approached her campus physician with a request for him to "remove some of the bone" from her nose. She described the end of her nose as "too large," and believed that she could not attract a date because her nose was "repugnant." She conceded that perhaps her nose was really not too excessively large, but continued to worry about its impact on her social life and presented again and again wanting it "fixed." She was reluctantly referred to a plastic surgeon, who concurred that indeed no appreciable defect existed and that a surgical procedure was not justifiable. However, the surgeon was familiar with such presentations and suggested that a psychiatric colleague could "help her cope with her distress." The patient, who was somewhat compulsive, felt obliged to accept psychiatric referral. She was evaluated and ultimately became involved in group psychotherapy, which was therapeutic in helping her correct her distorted self-perceptions.

The differential diagnoses entertained with hypochondriasis are equally applicable to body dysmorphic disorder. However, the differential diagnosis must also consider anxiety syndromes, particularly phobias; personality disorders, especially avoidant and compulsive types; major depression; delusional disorder, somatic subtype; and the other somatizing disorders. Body dysmorphic disorder may also accompany anorexia nervosa and transsexualism, in which the patient displays unfounded beliefs about body weight and/or gender-related physical characteristics.

Etiology and Pathogenesis

Individuals with body dysmorphic disorder who indeed appear normal develop a low sense of aesthetic perception, whereas those who are somewhat abnormal regard their appearance in the context of a high sense of aesthetic perception. Avoidance of social or occupational situations due to anxiety or apprehension about the defect is the rule. Thus, a "neurotic" syndrome is operating with secondary features of anxiety and depression. Some authors have regarded this syndrome as rather ominous, a prodrome of schizophrenia. Furthermore, the belief in the physical defect of appearance can sometimes be delusional in its intensity. In some cases, it is unclear whether two different disorders can be clearly distinguished on the basis of whether the belief is quasidelusional or a clear delusion. Symptoms bordering on psychosis are presumed to develop more often in individuals with schizoid, narcissistic, or obsessional personality traits, but must also be distinguished from the features of personality disorder per se.

Clinical Management

Persons with body dysmorphic disorder frequently visit primary care physicians, dermatologists, or plastic surgeons repeatedly in an effort to correct the defect; depressive and obsessive personality traits and psychosocial distress frequently coexist with the disorder and require treatment. Psychiatric consultation may be useful in identifying and treating depression, anxiety, and other disturbances that require pharmacologic or psychotherapeutic intervention. Brotman and Jenike (1984) have suggested that patients with persistent anxiety or depressive symptoms be started on a trial of antidepressant therapy, either a cyclic antidepressant with serotonin-active properties or an MAO inhibitor. The antipsychotic drug pimozide has also produced startling and sustained improvement, particularly in patients whose neurotic preoccupation has become quasidelusional. However, no other antipsychotic or other pharmacologic agents have proven as effective in the treatment of this disorder. As illustrated in the above case, psychiatric intervention with individual or group therapy may be useful, again focusing on psychosocial functions and body image complaints while supporting the patient's efforts to understand their "use" of the defect to cope and receive secondary gain. Family conferences or therapy are also required in cases where the individual is not yet emancipated from the family of origin, particularly if an eating disorder, personality disorder, or other coexisting disturbance is identified.

Undifferentiated Somatization Disorder (Somatoform Disorders Not Otherwise Specified)

The revised version of DSM-III lists an undifferentiated somatoform disorder category for clinical presentations that do not meet the full symptom picture of somatization disorder or one of the other somatizing syndromes. The diagnostic criteria for this disorder are illustrated in Table 8-8. This newly added diagnosis was recently assigned in the following case:

A CASE STUDY

A 68-year-old woman presented to her family physician for an evaluation of dysuria and fatigue. She had experienced the symptoms for many years. Complete evaluation produced no evidence of a physical disease to account for her symptoms. Further questioning revealed no

Table 8–8 **Diagnostic Criteria for Undifferentiated Somatoform Disorder**

A. One or more physical complaints: e.g., fatigue, loss of appetite, gastrointestinal or urinary complaints.

B. Either (1) or (2):
   (1) appropriate evaluation uncovers no organic pathology or pathophysiologic mechanism (e.g., a physical disorder or the effects of injury, medication, drugs, or alcohol) to account for the physical complaints
   (2) when there is related organic pathology, the physical complaint or resulting social or occupational impairment is grossly in excess of what would be expected from the physical findings

C. Duration of the disturbance is at least 6 months.

D. Occurrence not exclusively during the course of another somatoform disorder, a sexual dysfunction, a mood disorder, an anxiety disorder, a sleep disorder, or a psychotic disorder.

(Reprinted with permission from American Psychiatric Association: Diagnostic and Statistical Manual of Mental Disorders, Third Edition, Revised. Washington, DC, American Psychiatric Association, 1987)

---

other physical symptoms and she did not display a depressive or associated psychiatric disorder. A consulting psychiatrist subsequently learned that the patient lost her parents, both at 65 years of age, due to cancer—leukemia in her father and renal cell carcinoma in her mother.

As illustrated, these disorders involve a single, circumscribed symptom that is not explainable on the basis of demonstrable organic findings or known pathophysiologic mechanisms. In keeping with somatoform disorders, the presentation is apparently linked with psychological factors. The circumscribed symptoms are of 6 months duration or longer and, of course, not a part of another type of somatoform disorder, sexual dysfunction disorder, mood disorder, anxiety disorder, sleep disorder, or one of the other major psychotic syndromes important in differential diagnosis. A diagnosis of somatoform disorder that cannot be otherwise specified is assigned for somatoform symptoms that are of less than 6 months duration, hypochondriacal in nature, nonpsychotic, or presenting with nonstress-related physical complaints.

FACTITIOUS DISORDER

Most clinicians will at some point in their career encounter a case of factitious disorder. These somatizing states are essentially characterized by the voluntary production of signs, symptoms, or disease for no apparent goal other than to achieve the role of being a patient. By contrast, the somatoform disorders are collectively viewed as having symptoms that are manifested unconsciously. Münchausen's syndrome, the most extreme type of factitious disorder, is characterized by a triad of features involving simulation of disease, pathological lying, and wandering. These cases frequently involve men of lower socioeconomic class who have had a lifelong pattern of social maladjustment. Several other clinical features of the Münchausen type are depicted in Table 8-9. However, most authorities concur that the vast majority

Table 8-9 **Münchausen's Syndrome: Diagnostic Features***

Essential Features

Pathologic lying (Pseudologia fantastica)
Peregrination (traveling or wandering)
Recurrent, feigned, or simulated illness

Supporting Features†

Borderline and/or antisocial personality traits
Deprived in childhood
Equanimity for diagnostic procedures
Equanimity for treatments or operations
Evidence of self-induced physical signs
Knowledge of or experience in a medical field
Most likely to be male
Multiple hospitalizations
Multiple scars (usually abdominal)
Police record
Unusual or dramatic presentation

*Patients will meet DSM-III-R criteria for a chronic factitious disorder or an atypical factitious disorder.
†May also support the diagnosis of other factitious disorders.
(Reprinted with permission from Folks DG, Freeman AM: Münchausen's syndrome and other factitious illness. Psychiatr Clin North Am 8:263–278, 1985)

of factitious disorders involve socially conforming young women of a higher socio-economic class who are intelligent, educated, and frequently employed in a medically related field. Thus, one will rarely encounter the socially nonconforming "wanderers" who satisfy the Münchausen's syndrome criteria listed in Table 8-9.

Epidemiology

The available literature provides only a few indications of the incidence of factitious illness. These disorders appear to be far more common than was once generally believed, perhaps because of the progress in medical technology and the popular medical journalism that is readily available to the lay public. The paucity of systematic studies and disproportionate number of case reports on the Münchausen syndrome have resulted in contradictory data on the age and sex ratio. Patient age averages approximately 30 years and ranges from adolescence to old age. The available epidemiographic data on factitious disorders are inadequate, but again strongly suggest a preponderance of young adults, the majority of whom are female and likely to be employed in the health professions.

Differential Diagnosis

Factitious illness is not real, genuine, or natural. Thus, physical or psychological symptoms are under voluntary control and are simulated to deceive the physician, although the manifestation of symptoms possesses a rather compulsive quality. The characteristic presenting modes and organ system subtypes of factitious disorder are listed in Table 8-10. Factitious disorder with physical symptoms is the most commonly diagnosed DSM-III-R subtype (Table 8-11). A dramatic presentation with a history of

Table 8–10 **Commonly Presenting Features of Chronic Factitious Illnesses**

Organ System Subtypes	Demeanor or Behavior
Abdominal*	Bizarre
Cardiac	Demanding
Dermatologic†	Dramatic
Genitourinary	Evasive
Hematologic*†	Medically sophisticated
Infectious	Self-mutilating
Neurologic*	Unruly
Psychatric	
Self-medication*‡	

*Original subtypes identified
†Recently reported to be more common
‡Especially insulin, thyroid, vitamins, diuretics, and laxatives
(Reprinted with permission from Folks DG, Freeman AM: Münchausen's syndrome and other factitious illness. Psychiatr Clin North Am 8:263–278, 1985)

multiple hospitalizations and, of course, the primary goal of assuming the patient role are the pertinent diagnostic features. Eisendrath (1984) suggests that factitious presentation may be manifested at one of three levels of enactment: (1) a fictitious history, (2) a simulated disease, or (3) the presence of verifiable pathophysiology. The last is illustrated by the following case vignette:

A CASE STUDY

A 32-year-old psychiatric nurse was hospitalized for uncontrolled diabetes mellitus. During her hospitalization, her serum glucose levels fluctuated markedly despite diligent efforts to regulate her insulin dosage requirements. On the fourth hospital day, the patient suggested that perhaps she needed further diagnostic testing to determine whether any other unrecognized problems might be present. Her physician discouraged further testing. The next morning the ward nurse found the patient

Table 8–11 **Diagnostic Criteria for Factitious Disorder with Physical Symptoms**

A. Intentional production or feigning of physical (but not psychological) symptoms.
B. A psychological need to assume the sick role, as evidenced by the absence of external incentives for the behavior, such as economic gain, better care, or physical well-being.
C. Occurrence not exclusively during the course of another Axis I disorder, such as schizophrenia.

(Reprinted with permission from American Psychiatric Association: Diagnostic and Statistical Manual of Mental Disorders, Third edition, Revised. Washington, DC, American Psychiatric Association, 1987)

lying comatose in her bed. A stat blood sugar showed severe hypo-glycemia. During the emergency evaluation, a medical student found a used syringe and a bottle of regular insulin lying behind the patient's nightstand. When the patient recovered and was confronted with the discovery of the covert insulin, she became highly indignant and left the hospital against medical advice.

A diagnosis of inclusion, not exclusion, factitious disorder with physical symptoms may require a high index of suspicion and clinical perseverance once the diagnosis is established. In addition to the possibility that a true disease exists and accounts for the presentation, malingering, pseudomalingering, conversion disorder, and hypochondriasis are the leading differential diagnoses.

Psychiatric or psychological symptoms may replace physical ones and dominate the clinical presentation of factitious disorder. The DSM-III-R criteria for factitious disorder with psychological symptoms is depicted in Table 8-12. Many cases involving psychological presentations of factitious illness have been reported. Factitious mourning or grief and feigned psychosis are commonly encountered. Posttraumatic stress disorder has also emerged as a newer presentation, with several reports of simulated cases appearing in the literature.

Poorly defined distinctions between factitious disorder, somatization disorder, and malingering have likely contributed to the diversity of diagnoses included in the differential diagnosis of factitious disorder. Atypical factitious illness not otherwise specified is also an appropriate DSM-III-R diagnosis for patients who do not seek hospital admission and for other atypical cases involving simulated illness, such as dermatitis artifacta. In pediatric settings Münchausen by proxy may also be encountered; in these cases a parent or caregiver presents a child with a factitial illness (Folks, Freeman, 1985). Factitial cases seen in psychiatric consultation may have already been misdiagnosed as a range of psychiatric disorders, including conversion disorder, somatization disorder, malingering, schizophrenia, or other major psychoses. Histrionic, schizotypal, borderline, antisocial, and masochistic personality disorders

Table 8-12 **Diagnostic Criteria for Factitious Disorder with Psychological Symptoms**

A. Intentional production or feigning of psychological (but not physical) symptoms.
B. A psychological need to assume the sick role, as evidenced by the absence of external incentives for the behavior, such as economic gain, better care, or physical well-being.
C. Occurrence not exclusively during the course of another Axis I disorder, such as schizophrenia.

(Reprinted with permission from American Psychiatric Association: Diagnostic and Statistical Manual of Mental Disorders, Third edition, Revised. Washington, DC, American Psychiatric Association, 1987)

often, if not always, are concurrently diagnosed on Axis II; borderline personality disorder is the most common type of personality disorder observed. (Folks, Freeman, 1985).

Etiology and Pathogenesis

Any attempt to understand the etiology of factitious disorder requires careful consideration of any developmental disturbance, personal history, and current life stressors and an appreciation of primary psychodynamic mechanisms—masochism, dependency, and mastery. The desire to be the center of interest and attention; a grudge against physicians and hospitals that is somehow satisfied by frustrating and deceiving the staff; a desire for drugs; a desire to escape the police; and a desire to obtain free room and board while tolerating the consequences of various therapeutic investigations and treatment are some of the more frequently listed reasons that might possibly motivate the self-destructive behaviors of patients with a factitious disorder.

Although patients often possess borderline personality traits, one can often obtain a history of childhood emotional insecurity; excluding or rejecting parents; and broken homes leading to foster home placement or adoption, and subsequent delinquency, antisocial behavior, or failure in psychosexual development. The possible enactment of past or present developmental disturbances within the medical setting should also be considered. In essence it seems that these patients, through their illness, also may primarily seek to compensate for developmental traumas and secondarily escape from and make up for stressful life situations. Psychodynamic explanations suggest that the factitiously disordered patient experiences satisfaction from manipulating as many aspects of his own medical and surgical care as possible (mastery), receives strong sexual gratification from diagnostic and therapeutic procedures (masochism), and enjoys the warm and personal but ambivalent care inherent in the doctor–patient relationship (dependency), culminating in the excitement of the hospital experience.

Clinical Management

The general therapeutic approach outlined in Table 8-1 is applicable to cases of factitious disorder, and a comparison with the somatoform disorders is presented in Table 8-2. The initial clinical approach also requires a clear recognition of the syndrome or a high index of suspicion that a factitious disorder is indeed present. Psychiatric consultation should be requested for all cases, and if confrontation is advisable, the primary physician (as opposed to the consultant) should confront the patient in a nonpunitive manner (Hollender, Hersh, 1970). Patients are usually less difficult to confront than might be expected, and do not show the intense anger, impulsivity, or instability of interpersonal relationships that is commonly reported with the more extreme cases representing Münchausen's syndrome (Reich, Gottfried, 1983). If confronted with the factitious nature of the illness, the patient may deny it, refuse psychiatric intervention, and resume the same behavior; may admit that the factitious illness is present but refuse psychiatric intervention; or may acknowledge the factitial nature of the illness and cooperate with psychiatric intervention (Ford,

1983; Hollender, Hersh, 1970). Confrontation is not necessarily appropriate for all cases; the psychiatrist may simply attempt to build rapport with the patient while the primary physician continues any necessary noninvasive medical treatment. Confrontation is more often favored in the hospitalized patient who has the intelligence, psychosocial supports, and personal attributes necessary for a more mature adaptation. The psychiatric consultant also serves to assist the medical staff with its negative reactions to the factitiously disordered patient. In turn, the medical staff team can protect the patient from himself or herself by avoiding potentially dangerous diagnostic or operative procedures. Family members can be especially therapeutic in providing pertinent history or assisting the medical staff in maintaining acceptable limits on the illness behavior. Treatable psychopathology such as anxiety disorders, depressive syndromes, conversion symptoms, and major psychoses should be assiduously evaluated and steadfastly treated whenever possible (Folks, Freeman, 1985).

The prognosis for factitious illness has generally been considered poor. However, careful exclusion of malingerers, severe borderline personalities, wandering patients with Münchausen's syndrome, the chronic medically ill, and the more evasive can result in a subgroup of potentially treatable patients (Folks, Freeman, 1985; Table 8-13). The prognosis is better for patients with an underlying depression than for those merely possessing a personality disorder. Reich and associates observed that once the diagnosis was established, even some of the more severe and chronic cases responded quite well to a combined medical and psychiatric approach (Reich, Gottfried, 1983). Finally, as noted with other forms of somatization, the possibility of coexisting physical disease or intercurrent illness should be appreciated in all diagnostic and therapeutic endeavors.

Table 8–13 **Aspects of Factitious Illness Potentially Amenable to Treatment**

1. Presence of treatable psychiatric syndromes, including:
   Mood disorders
   Anxiety disorders
   Psychotic disorders
   Conversion disorders
   Substance abuse disorders
   Organic mental disorders
2. Personality organization closer to compulsive, depressive, or histrionic rather than borderline, narcissistic, or antisocial.
3. Stability in psychosocial support system as manifested by marriage, stable occupation, and family ties, as opposed to the single, unemployed wanderer.
4. Ability to cope with confrontation or some redefinition of the illness behavior.
5. Capability of establishing and maintaining rapport with the treating clinicians.

(Reprinted with permission from Folks DG, Freeman AM: Münchausen's syndrome and other factitious illness. Psychiatr Clin North Am 8:263–278, 1985)

MALINGERING

The essential clinical feature of malingering is the intentional production of illness or grossly exaggerated physical or psychological symptoms that is motivated by external incentives such as avoiding military duty, obtaining financial compensation through litigation or disability, evading criminal prosecution, obtaining drugs, or simply securing better living conditions (Gorman, 1982). DSM-III-R suggests that malingering should be strongly suspected in the following circumstances: (1) a medical/legal context overshadows the presentation, (2) a marked discrepancy exists between the clinical presentation and the objective findings, (3) a lack of cooperation is experienced with diagnostic efforts or in compliance with medical regimen, and/or (4) the psychosocial history suggests the presence of an antisocial personality disorder. Thus, malingering can be fundamentally viewed as a feigning of illness: the fraudulent simulation or exaggeration of physical or mental disease or defect consciously produced to achieve a specific goal. The reasons for the illness behavior in the individual circumstances can be readily understood by an objective observer. Unlike the patient with factitious disorder, who merely wishes to assume the patient role, a malingering individual has a more clearly external motivation, and the illness behavior is intentional and consciously produced to achieve a consciously desired goal. This distinction is represented in Table 8-2 and illustrated by the following case:

A CASE STUDY

A 57-year-old man appearing thin and disheveled presented to the emergency room one cold wintry night at 2:00 a.m. complaining of chest pain. He stated that he had a history of angina; he stated that only intravenous morphine could alleviate his pain. The emergency physician, in obtaining a history of the pain, noted that it did not seem to fit the pattern of any of the common causes of chest pain; routine physical exam, laboratory screen, arterial blood gases, and electrocardiogram were surprisingly normal. However, as a precaution, the patient was admitted for further observation and evaluation. The next day, the chest pain persisted and the patient still requested narcotics. A medical student ascertained that no relatives were available, and that the patient had no reasonable plan for how he might manage following hospital discharge. On afternoon rounds, the patient, after being informed that he would be given no narcotics, reported that his pain had disappeared, and despite the physician's willingness to search further for the cause, he insisted on leaving the hospital.

Malingering may be sometimes adaptive (arguable in the case just presented) and is, to a lesser degree, observed in apparently normal children, students, test subjects, and employees; thus malingering behavior does not always represent a maladaptive or malignant form. A few clinicians have promulgated the theory that pure malingering is a mental disease worthy of a therapeutic response. Malingering has also been conceptualized as occurring on a continuum with conversion disorder (Ford, 1986). Briefly, the conscious effort to falsify symptoms may in some cases include rather complex motivations, originating in part from the unconscious. Malingering is also likely to arise in individuals with antisocial personality disorder or other various forms of feigned illness, such as Ganser syndrome, or as a component of organic mental disorder or a neurotic state. These coexisting psychiatric disturbances should be the focus of evaluation and treatment for these "mentally ill" malingerers.

Irrespective of one's views on malingering, some basic legal principles should be considered in examining for the presence or absence of malingering. In particular, before reporting malingering one should steadfastly follow the basic rules of confidentiality and privilege. Another important aspect of malingering concerns the way in which physicians perceive such behavior and their moral judgment of it. As a case in point, situations certainly exist in which this extreme form of somatization is regarded as acceptable, constructive, or even praiseworthy, as in the case of the prisoner of war who malingers to protect his country's interests. Therefore, a professional and therapeutic posture in approaching the malingering patient must initially include an examination of one's own feelings of anger, disgust, or humiliation, recognizing that the malingering behavior often threatens the very foundations of the doctor–patient relationship. Frank, nonjudgmental communication between the physician and the malingerer, and awareness that the behavior may be an ongoing reaction to stress or due to a psychiatric disorder may lead to an open discussion of the patient's needs— which may, in turn, provide a basis for an adequate therapeutic alliance or a solution to the problem (Mark et al., 1987).

Finally, a number of authors have described simulation among persons seeking compensation for work-related injuries or disease (Weighill, 1983). However, the psychological difficulties in these cases vary greatly, and the physician must be able to appreciate and assess a number of background factors, such as severity of injury, preexisting personality traits, developmental characteristics, social class, attitudinal response, and the pertinent family, social, and employment factors, as well as the actual progress of the physical condition or legal process of settlement. Unfortunately, these disability syndromes are beyond the scope of this chapter.

As a final note, a number of clinical pearls and suggested readings will serve to expand upon the material presented in this chapter. A thorough review of Tables 8-1 and 8-2 in conjunction with the Clinical Pearls section will aid in the diagnostic and therapeutic approach to each diagnostic type.

CLINICAL PEARLS

General Points for Somatoform Disorders

Somatoform disorders, factitious disorders, and malingering represent illness behavior; whether symptoms are consciously or unconsciously produced and whether the motivations for the production of symptoms are conscious or unconscious will determine what particular DSM diagnostic category is assigned.

(continued)

CLINICAL PEARLS *(continued)*

General Points for Somatoform Disorders

- Somatization is a process by which an individual consciously or unconsciously uses the body or bodily symptoms for psychological purposes or personal gain.
- Somatizing individuals are primarily motivated and secondarily receive gain for illness behavior, including the privileges of the sick role and sanctioned dependency.
- The presence of somatization encourages a thorough diagnostic investigation and therapeutic approach that focuses on psychosocial history and illness behavior in the context of existing disease, life problems, and psychological conflicts.
- Somatization may be primarily or secondarily associated with an underlying psychiatric syndrome, coexisting personality disorder, or psychosocial stressor of diagnostic significance.

Somatization Disorder

Somatization disorder is a polysymptomatic disorder that begins in early life, affects mostly women, and is characterized by recurrent multiple somatic complaints and a profusely positive review of systems.

- The disorder is commonly associated with sociopathy, alcoholism, and drug addiction.
- The disorder is heterogeneous and likely to coexist with a psychiatric disturbance or personality disorder, especially histrionic or antisocial disorder.
- Management includes a therapeutic alliance with an empathic primary care physician, regularly scheduled patient visits, appreciation of the psychological significance of symptoms, use of diagnostic or therapeutic procedures or medications based on objective findings, and use of psychiatric consultation for complications, coexisting disturbances, or crisis intervention.

Conversion Disorder

Conversion symptoms are ubiquitous among psychiatric patients with schizophrenia, somatization disorder, alcoholism, sociopathy, and drug addiction.

- Conversion disorder typically occurs in women who are of lower socioeconomic class, psychologically unsophisticated, or of rural background.
- The diagnosis of conversion disorder must ultimately rest on positive clinical findings clearly indicating that the symptom does not derive from organic disease or as a part of another psychiatric disorder.
- Conversion symptoms often accompany degenerative neurological syndromes such as multiple sclerosis, amyotrophic lateral sclerosis, and so on.
- Acute conversion disorder can usually be etiologically related to psychological conflict and allows an individual to avoid certain responsibilities or noxious situations and secondarily enables control or manipulation of the behavior of others (i.e., secondary gain).
- Treatment usually includes supportive and suppressive approaches that include some element of suggestion or persuasion using the therapeutic principles outlined in Table 8-1; a multitude of treatments have proved successful.

Somatoform Pain Disorder

In as many as 40% of patients presenting with pain, the pain will be assigned as psychogenic or idiopathic.

- The prominent diagnostic feature of somatoform pain disorder is the preoccupation with pain in the absence of physical findings that account for the pain or its intensity.
- Psychological factors must be appreciated and may include any of the following:
  - identified precipitants by history,
  - avoidance of an activity or responsibility that is unacceptable or noxious
  - acquisition of significant psychosocial support that would not otherwise be forthcoming.

(continued)

CLINICAL PEARLS *(continued)*

Somatoform Pain Disorders

- Major depression or depressive symptoms are often present and may be a component of the pain syndrome or represent a coexisting disorder.
- The best therapeutic strategy is to limit doctor-shopping and modify the patient's therapeutic expectations from "cure" to "management" of the pain, while attempting to appreciate the role of psychosocial or psychological factors and the impact of stress on the case, using psychiatric consultation as appropriate.

Hypochondriasis

Hypochondriasis is characterized by a concern or preoccupation with health or disease in oneself that is present most of the time and is not justified by the organic pathology.

- The core features include disease fear, disease conviction, and bodily preoccupation associated with multiple amplified somatic complaints.
- As with pain, the possibility of an underlying or secondary depression should be strongly considered, and physical disease should be excluded.
- Treatment is most effective when there is collaboration between a primary physician who continues regular appointments and a consulting psychiatrist who focuses on coping with the pain syndrome and treats symptoms of anxiety, depression, or psychosocial distress.

Body Dysmorphic Disorder

Body dysmorphic disorder typically occurs in adolescence or young adulthood, persists for years, and significantly affects social and occupational functioning.

- The fundamental diagnostic feature is a pervasive feeling of ugliness or physical defect that the patient feels is readily apparent to others.
- Patients frequently consult primary care physicians, dermatologists, and plastic surgeons in an effort to correct the defect.
- Depressive and anxious symptoms, obsessive personality traits and psychosocial distress frequently coexist with the disorder and provide a basis and rationale for psychiatric consultation.
- Individual therapy that focuses on psychosocial distress and group or family therapy as appropriate are the primary interventions, in keeping with the principles outlined in Table 8-1.

Factitious Disorders

Factitious disorders usually involve socially conforming young women of a higher socioeconomic class who are intelligent, educated, and frequently employed in a medically related field.

- A distinction can be drawn between "wanderers," who frequently satisfy the Münchausen's syndrome criteria, and "nonwanderers," who do not. The latter (the majority) are amenable to treatment.
- As opposed to somatoform disorders, factitious disorders are characterized by psychological or physical symptoms that are *consciously* produced with the goal of assuming the patient role; thus a patient may be confronted about the illness behavior. However, unconscious motivations are responsible for the clinical presentation and must be addressed as such (see below).
- The primary therapeutic approach involves an attempt to understand the etiology, including consideration of developmental disturbances, personal history, and current life stressors; appreciation of primary psychodynamic mechanisms (masochism, dependency, and mastery); and an appreciation of any personality disorders that might complicate treatment planning. Usually a borderline personality disorder is involved.
- Clinical management includes confrontation by the primary physician and/or referral to

(continued)

CLINICAL PEARLS (continued)

Factitious Disorders

a psychiatric consultant who redefines the illness as primarily psychiatric and offers a psychotherapeutic approach to those patients who do not represent the Münchausen's syndrome.

- The possibility of intercurrent illness or coexisting physical disease should be appreciated in all diagnostic and therapeutic endeavors. Careful follow-up by the primary physician is essential.

Malingering

The essential feature of malingering is the intentional production of illness consciously motivated by external incentives such as avoiding military duty, obtaining financial compensation through litigation or disability, evading criminal prosecution, obtaining drugs, or securing better living conditions.

- Malingering should be suspected in cases where a medical/legal context overshadows the presentation, a marked discrepancy exists between clinical presentation and objective findings, and a lack of cooperation is experienced with diagnostic efforts or in compliance with medical regimen, and possibly when the psychosocial history suggests the presence of an antisocial personality disorder.
- The malingering should be confronted in a confidential and empathic but firm manner that leaves an opportunity for constructive dialogue and appreciation of any psychological or psychosocial problems.

ANNOTATED BIBLIOGRAPHY

Ford CV: The somatizing disorders. Psychosomatics 27:327–337, 1986

> Includes an excellent overview of the process of somatization illustrating somatizing behaviors, sociocultural and interactional influences on somatization, and the specific diagnostic categories relevant to the process of somatization.

Quill TE: Somatization disorder: One of medicine's blind spots. JAMA 254:3075, 1985

> An overview of somatization disorder and management strategy in terms of the specific problems encountered in the doctor–patient relationship and in developing a therapeutic alliance.

Ford CV, Folks DG: Conversion disorders: An overview. Psychosomatics 26:371–383, 1985

> An excellent overview of conversion disorder that includes a detailed discussion of its etiology and pathogenesis as well as a review of the diagnostic and treatment approaches.

Kellner R: Hypochondriasis and somatization. JAMA 258:2718–2722, 1987

> A superb discussion of hypochondriasis and of how those affected use somatization in their clinical presentation. An excellent review follows outlining caveats in the management of hypochondriasis.

Stoudemire A, Sandhu J: Psychogenic/idiopathic pain syndromes. Gen Hosp Psychiatr 9:79–86, 1987

> A comprehensive article that reviews the various pain syndromes encountered in clinical practice with special attention to psychogenic or somatoform pain and its evaluation and treatment.

Folks DG, Freeman AM: Münchausen syndrome and other factitious illness. Psychiatr Clin North Am 8:263–278, 1985

> A thorough review of the factitious disorders distinguishing those that are potentially treatable from Münchausen syndrome and other more refractory factitial syndromes. Includes a section covering Münchausen by proxy encountered in practice.

Gorman WF: Defining malingering. J Forensic Sci 27:401–407, 1982

> An excellent overview that conceptualizes malingering on a continuum from normal to the abnormal to the pathologic forms. Provides the reader with a pragmatic conceptualization for approaching malingers therapeutically.

REFERENCES

American Psychiatric Association: Diagnostic and Statistical Manual of Mental Disorders, Third Edition, Revised. Washington, DC, American Psychiatric Association, 1987

Barsky AJ: Patients who amplify bodily sensations. Ann Intern Med 91:63–70, 1979

Bohman M, Cloninger R, Von Knorring A-L, et al: An adoption study of somatoform disorders: III. Cross-fostering analysis and genetic relationship to alcoholism and criminality. Arch Gen Psychiatr 41:872–878, 1984

Bonica JJ: Organization and structure of a multidisciplinary pain clinic. In Weisenberg M, Tursky B (eds): Pain: New Perspectives in Therapy and Research. New York, Plenum Press, 1976

Brodsky CM: Sociocultural and interactional influences on somatization. Psychosomatics 25:673–680, 1984

Brotman AW, Jenike MA: Monosymptomatic hypochondriasis treated with tricyclic antidepressants. Am J Psychiatr 141:1608–1609, 1984

Brown HN, Vaillant GE: Hypochondriasis. Arch Intern Med 141:723–736, 1981

Eisenberg L: Disease and illness: Distinctions between professional and popular ideas of sickness. Cult Med Psychiatr 1:9–23, 1977

Eisendrath SJ: Factitious illness: A clarification. Psychosomatics 25:110–116, 1984

Folks DG, Ford CV, Regan WM: Conversion symptoms in a general hospital. Psychosomatics 25:285–295, 1984

Folks DG, Freeman AM: Münchausen syndrome and other factitious illness. Psychiatr Clin North Am 8:263–278, 1985

Ford CV: The Somatizing Disorders: Illness as a Way of Life. New York, Elsevier, 1983

Ford CV: The somatizing disorders. Psychosomatics 27:327–337, 1986

Gorman WF: Defining malingering. J Forensic Sci 27:401–407, 1982

Guze SB: The validity and significance of the clinical diagnosis of hysteria (Briquet's syndrome). Am J Psychiatr 132:138–141, 1975

Hollender MH, Hersh SP: Impossible consultation made possible. Arch Gen Psychiatr 23:343–345, 1970

Kellner R: Hypochondriasis and somatization. JAMA 258:2718–2722, 1987

Lesser LM, Ford CV, Friedmann CTH: Alexithymia in somatizing patients. Gen Hosp Psychiatr 1:256–261, 1979

Liskow B, Othmer E, Penick EC, et al: Is Briquet's syndrome a heterogeneous disorder? Am J Psychiatr 143:626–629, 1986

Mark M, Rabinowitz S, Zimran A, et al: Malingering in the military: Understanding and treatment of the behavior. Military Med 152:260–262, 1987

Merskey H, Buhrich NA: Hysteria and organic brain disease. Br J Med Psychol 48:359–366, 1975

Parsons T: Social structure and dynamic process: The case of modern medical practice. In Parsons T: The Social System, pp 428–479. New York, Free Press, 1951

Pilowsky I: Primary and secondary hypochondriasis. Acta Psychiatr Scand 46:273–285, 1970

Quill TE: Somatization disorder: One of medicine's blind spots. JAMA 254:3075, 1985

Reich P, Gottfried LA: Factitious disorders in a training hospital. Ann Intern Med 99:240–247, 1983

Reich J, Tupin JP, Abramowitz SI: Psychiatric diagnosis of chronic pain patients. Am J Psychiatr 140:1495–1498, 1983

Reuler JB, Girard DE, Nardone DA: The chronic pain syndrome: Misconceptions and management. Ann Intern Med 93:588–596, 1980

Smith GR Jr, Monson RA, Ray DC: Psychiatric consultation in somatization disorder: A randomized controlled study. New Engl J Med 314(22):1407–1413, 1986

Sternbach RA: Varieties of pain games. Adv Neurol 4:423–430, 1974

Stoudemire A, Sandhu J: Psychogenic/idiopathic pain syndromes. Gen Hosp Psychiatr 9:79–86, 1987

Swartz M, Hughes D, George L, et al: Developing a screening index for community studies of somatization disorder. J Psychiatr Res 20:335–343, 1986

Thomas CS: Dysmorphophobia: A question of definition. Br J Psychiatr 144:513–516, 1984

Weighill VE: "Compensation neurosis:" A review of the literature. J Psychosom Res 27:97–104, 1983

9

Alcoholism and Substance Abuse

Robert M. Swift

Throughout history, humans have used psychoactive substances for medicinal, social, recreational, and religious purposes. Today, a variety of psychoactive substances continue to be widely used for similar, socially sanctioned purposes. Many people, however, use psychoactive substances to excess, in an uncontrolled fashion, in situations that are not socially approved, or in circumstances that have deleterious effects on health or behavior. Such individuals are considered to have a substance use disorder. The causes of substance use problems are complex and involve social, psychological, genetic, and pharmacologic factors.

SPECTRUM OF THE ALCOHOL-RELATED DISORDERS

An estimated 5 to 7% of Americans have alcoholism in a given year; 13% will have it sometime during their life. Simply defined, alcoholism is a "repetitive, but inconsistent and sometimes unpredictable loss of control of drinking which produces symptoms of serious dysfunction or disability" (Clark, 1981). There are marked sex differences in alcohol dependence/abuse rates: prevalence rates of alcoholism are about 5 to 6% for men, about 1 to 2% for women. The prevalence of alcoholism is highest in men ages 18 to 64 and in women ages 18 to 24, with a gradual drop afterwards (Regier, et al., 1988).

Alcoholism is believed to be involved in 20 to 50% of all hospital admissions, but is diagnosed less than 5% of the time (Lewis, Gordon 1983; Holden, 1985). Alcohol use is highly correlated with suicide, homicide, and accidents (Goodwin, 1967; Waller, 1966).

Substance use is etiologically related to other psychiatric disorders. Chronic alcohol use is associated with the cognitive and memory deficits of *alcoholic dementia* and the more restrictive memory deficits of *alcohol amnestic syndrome*. Patients with alcohol-related amnestic syndrome have the most difficulty with short-term memory (remembering recent events), but deficits may be noted in long-term memory as well. Patients may try to conceal or compensate for their memory loss by confabulation, making up answers or talking around questions that require them to use memory. This syndrome, previously known as Korsakoff's psychosis, is thought to be due to a deficiency of thiamine, which is required as a cofactor for neuronal transketolase. The memory deficits often are permanent, although about 30% of patients will show improvement with abstinence and thiamine repletion over time.

Alcohol use may also produce *alcoholic hallucinosis,* characterized by auditory and visual hallucinations in a patient with a relatively clear mental status; *alcoholic paranoia,* characterized by suspiciousness, and single or multiple delusions usually due to chronic alcoholism; and *alcohol withdrawal delirium* (see also Chapter 3).

RECOGNITION OF SUBSTANCE ABUSE

To recognize and treat alcoholism and other types of substance abuse and dependence, the physician must:

1. know the pharmacokinetics and pharmacodynamics of specific psychoactive substances;
2. be able to identify the presence of substance abuse or dependence;
3. know therapies for the acute management of intoxication and withdrawal of specific psychoactive substances;
4. know options for the long-term rehabilitation and treatment of patients; and
5. be aware of his or her own attitudes and biases towards patients with substance abuse problems.

This chapter provides basic information on the etiology and nosology of substance use disorders and on the identification and treatment of such disorders in medical and psychiatric patients. Management of specific drug intoxications and emergencies is discussed in Chapter 18.

Clinical Pharmacology of Psychoactive Substances

For a drug to have psychoactive effects, it must be present in a high enough concentration as free drug at its active site in the brain. The drug must enter the body, be transported by the bloodstream to the brain, and enter the brain tissue. Usually, only a small amount of the total administered drug is delivered to the site of action; the rest of the drug may be bound to serum or tissue proteins, metabolized or excreted, or otherwise unavailable. Because brain capillaries prevent the passage of many polar molecules into the brain (blood-brain barrier), most psychoactive substances are lipid soluble.

Figure 1 illustrates the competing pharmacokinetic processes that determine the availability of active drug. The potency, duration, and mode of administration of a drug can be predicted by understanding its pharmacokinetics. For example, the different potencies of cocaine hydrochloride and freebase cocaine can be explained

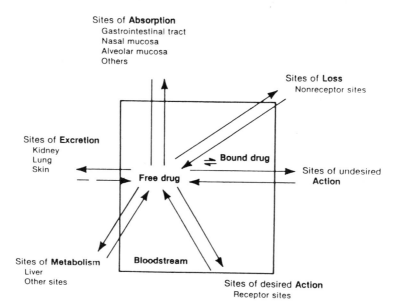

Figure 9–1. *Characteristics of drug movement across membranes. (Morgan JP. Alcohol and drug abuse curriculum for pharmacology faculty. U.S. Department HHS Publication No. (ADM) 85-1368, 1985)*

by the slower absorption of the hydrochloride from the nasal mucosa and the rapid absorption of freebase from the alveolar mucosa. The rapid absorption of alcohol from the gastric mucosa accounts for its preferred oral administration.

To have psychoactive effects, a drug also must affect some neuronal process. The way drugs act at the active site is known as *pharmacodynamics.* Many psychoactive substances, such as stimulants, sedatives, anxiolytics, and hallucinogens, bind to a specific cellular component, such as a receptor. However, other substances, such as alcohol or inhalant solvents, may nonspecifically dissolve in cell membranes and disrupt cellular functions.

Alcohol's central nervous system effects may be mediated through brain mechanisms involving the inhibitory neurotransmitter GABA. Alcohol has been shown to modify the binding of GABA to its receptors and augments the electrophysiologic and behavioral effects of GABA in animals (Hunt, 1983). Alcohol also appears to affect the binding of other sedative drugs to the inhibitory chloride channel of cell membranes, which is coupled to the GABA receptor (Seeman, 1972; Skolnick, et al, 1981). The existence of a common mechanism for the actions of alcohol and sedative-hypnotics accounts for the cross-tolerance between these substances.

Risk Factors for the Development of Substance Use Disorders

Factors determining an individual's susceptibility to a substance use disorder are not well understood. Studies of populations at risk for developing substance abuse have identified many factors that foster the development and continuance of substance use, including genetic, familial, environmental, occupational, socioeconomic, cultural, personality, life stress, psychiatric comorbidity, biologic, social learning, and behavioral conditioning. The relative contributions of these factors vary between individuals, and *no single factor appears to account entirely for the risk.*

The influence of genetic factors has been best studied for alcoholism. It is well established that alcoholism is a familial disorder: children of alcoholics, especially males, are several times more likely to become alcoholic than are children of nonalcoholics (Goodwin, 1985; Cloninger, 1987). The increased risk of alcoholism exists regardless of whether children are raised by their biologic parents or by nonalcoholic foster parents, suggesting that genetic factors are important. Children of alcoholics are also more susceptible to other types of drug dependence. A genetic predisposition for alcoholism is also supported by differences in alcoholism rates between identical and fraternal twins. The concordance for alcoholism among identical twin pairs is twice that of fraternal twin pairs (70 vs. 35%). However, environmental influences must also have effects, because 30% of male identical twins of alcoholics do not themselves become alcoholic.

Factors proposed to account for the genetic predisposition for alcoholism include genetic variations in the rate of metabolism of ethanol and acetaldehyde (Thomas et al., 1982); differences in brain electrophysiology (Porjesz and Begleiter, 1982); differential subjective sensitivity to the intoxicating effects of alcohol (Schuckit, 1985); and altered cell membrane properties.

CRITERIA FOR THE DIAGNOSIS OF SUBSTANCE USE

Describing substance use disorders is complicated by the ambiguity of the language used to describe substance use and in basic questions of whether using psychoactive substances constitutes a medical or a moral condition. In addressing these issues, organizations such as the World Health Organization (WHO) and the American Psychiatric Association (APA) consider the problem use of psychoactive substances to be a medical disorder and have formally defined criteria to determine *when* the use of psychoactive substances constitutes a formal medical disorder.

In a strict pharmacologic sense, *dependence* is often defined as a state in which a syndrome of drug-specific withdrawal signs and syndromes follows reduction or cessation of drug use (Table 9-1). *Tolerance* refers to the state in which the physiologic or behavioral effects of a constant dose of a psychoactive substance decreases over time or when a greater dose of a drug is necessary to achieve the same effect. *Withdrawal* is a physiologic state that follows cessation or reduction in the amount of drug used. In general, the behavioral effects of withdrawal are the opposite of those the drug produces (i.e., withdrawal from depressants produces psychomotor activation; withdrawal from stimulants produces psychomotor slowing).

In its Diagnostic and Statistical Manual of Mental Disorders (DSM-III-R) (APA, 1987), the APA has widened the concept of dependence to include the association of substance use with uncontrolled use or with use in spite of adverse consequences. In

Table 9–1 **Diagnosing Substance Dependence**

At least *three* of the following persisting for at least 1 month or having occurred repeatedly over a long period of time:

—Substance taken in larger amounts or over a longer time period than the person intended
—At least one unsuccessful attempt to cut down or to control substance use or a persistent desire to do so
—Considerable time spent in activities necessary to get the substance (e.g., theft), taking the substance (e.g., chain-smoking), or recovering from its effects
—Symptoms of intoxication or withdrawal occur when expected to fulfill major obligations at work, school, or home
—Important activities or obligations are given up or reduced because of substance use
—Continued substance use despite knowledge that a persistent or recurrent social, psychological, or physical problem is caused by or exacerbated by use of the substance
—Marked tolerance; need for increased amounts of the substance (at least 50 percent) in order to achieve intoxication or other desired effect; or markedly diminished effect with use of the same amount of substance
—Characteristic withdrawal symptoms (may not apply to cannabis, hallucinogens, or PCP)
—Substance use to relieve or avoid withdrawal symptoms (may not apply to cannabis, hallucinogens, or PCP)

Adapted in part from American Psychiatric Association DSM-III-R, 1987.

the DSM-III-R nomenclature, *abuse* is a residual category for patterns of drug use that do not meet the criteria for dependence. Psychoactive substance abuse is defined as a pattern of substance use of at least 1 month's duration that causes impairment in social or occupational functioning, in the presence of a psychological or physical problem, or in situations where use of the substance is physically hazardous, such as driving while intoxicated. While not specifically defined by DSM-III-R, "addiction" is often used as an equivalent for "dependence," but carries a more negative and pejorative connotation.

The acute and chronic effects of psychoactive substances are classified by DSM-III-R under two major categories:

1. *Psychoactive Substance-Induced Organic Mental Disorders*— These describe direct effects of the drug on the central nervous system, such as intoxication, withdrawal, delirium, delusions, or mood changes.
2. *Psychoactive Substance Use Disorders (Dependence and Abuse)*—These describe behavioral symptoms and maladaptive behaviors due to the acute or chronic effects of the drug.

DSM-III-R designates 11 distinct classes of psychoactive substances (Table 2): alcohol; amphetamines and similarly acting sympathomimetics; caffeine; cannabis; cocaine; hallucinogens; inhalants; opioids; nicotine; phencyclidine and similarly acting arylcyclohexylamines; sedatives, hypnotics, and anxiolytics. Each class is associated with both an organic mental disorder and a substance use disorder. Under the category "Substance Use Disorders," all the classes but nicotine are associated with

Table 9–2 **Classes of Psychoactive Substances**

Alcohol
Amphetamines or similarly acting
   sympathomimetic amines
Caffeine
Cannabis
Cocaine
Hallucinogens
Inhalants
Nicotine
Opioids
Phencyclidine and similarly acting
   arylcyclohexylamines
Sedatives, hypnotics, anxiolytics

abuse and dependence; dependence only is defined for nicotine. Patients using three categories of substances are said to have polysubstance dependence.

EVALUATING SUBSTANCE USE

The physician's primary task in evaluating a patient for substance use or dependence is to establish an effective therapeutic relationship. In the context of this relationship, the physician should take a detailed alcohol and drug history, conduct a physical and mental status examination, order and interpret necessary laboratory tests, and meet with family or significant others to obtain additional information and to facilitate their involvement in evaluation and treatment.

Assessing and treating patients who have both a psychiatric disorder and a substance use disorder (dual diagnosis) is particularly complex. The physical, psychological, and behavioral effects of psychoactive substances may be similar to symptoms of a psychiatric disorder or, alternatively, may mask the symptoms of a psychiatric disorder. The physical, psychological, and social consequences of substance use may impair treatment of other illnesses as well.

The Interview

As discussed in Chapters 1 and 2, in psychiatry the patient interview remains the single most important component of the diagnostic and assessment process. In a well-conducted interview, the physician not only may obtain information relevant to the diagnosis and etiology of a patient's substance use disorder, but also may set the tone for that patient's treatment. The physician should try to obtain a detailed substance use history and should also inquire about physical or behavioral problems suggesting substance use. Empathy and concern are necessary to instill trust. This may be difficult, as many interviewers often have negative feelings about substance users or about their prognosis. Judgmental attitudes and pejorative statements may severely limit the interviewer's ability to gather information and to initiate treatment.

In obtaining information about a patient's alcohol and drug use, the *most effective interview strategy* is to focus on whether the patient has experienced negative consequences from the use of psychoactive substances, has poor control of use, or has been criticized by others about his or her substance use. Quantity and frequency questions ("How much?" and "How often?") are not especially effective in detecting substance use. The quantity of substance consumed is not the critical factor in making a diagnosis; the effects of whatever amount is consumed are on the individual's functioning and interpersonal relationships.

Several formalized interviews are well validated in their ability to discriminate alcoholism. The CAGE questionnaire (Ewing, 1984) is a highly sensitive four-item test that uses the letters C A G E as a mnemonic. A "yes" answer to more than one question is suspicious for alcohol abuse.

Have you ever felt the need to *C*ut down on drinking?
Have you ever felt *A*nnoyed by criticisms of drinking?
Have you ever had *G*uilty feelings about drinking?
Have you ever taken a morning *E*ye opener?

Another reliable screen for heavy alcohol use is the Michigan Alcohol Screening Test (MAST). This 25-item scale identifies abnormal drinking through its social and behavioral consequences with sensitivity of 90 to 98% (Selzer, 1971). The Brief MAST, a shortened 10-item test, has been shown to have similar efficacy.

Although less documentation exists about the optimal interview to assess the drug-abusing patient, the same considerations apply: *it is more effective to ask about the behavioral consequences of drug abuse than about quantity and frequency of use.* The Drug Abuse Screening Test (DAST) developed at the Addiction Research Foundation of Toronto has been used successfully to assess drug abuse.

Even under the best interviewing circumstances, many patients who use psychoactive substances are reluctant to report the full extent of their drug and alcohol use and may deny or lie about it. Patients may deny the full extent of their substance use to themselves. In addition, the patient's family, friends, and colleagues collude in the denial of problems with substance use.

The following questions and historical data may help identify occult problem drinking and other types of surreptitious substance abuse:

1. Does the patient have a pattern of unexplained job changes?
2. Is the patient or family vague, evasive, or defensive about alcohol use?
3. Does the patient have convictions for driving under the influence or driving while impaired?
4. Are there multiple unexplained traffic accidents?
5. Does the patient have a history of impulsive behavior, fighting, or unexplained falls and scrapes?
6. Does the patient have any obvious stigmata of alcoholism (i.e., spider angiomas or a ruddy nose and face)?

7. Does the patient drink in the morning, or find he or she needs an "eye-opener"?
8. Does the patient have a history of blackouts, "lost weekends," binge drinking, "DTs," or "the shakes"?
9. Does the patient relate a history of having to drink to relax or sleep?
10. Is there a history of chronic family chaos and instability?

A "yes" answer to any of these questions may help confirm the likelihood of an alcohol- or substance-related disorder.

Obviously, patients with an altered mental status due to intoxication or withdrawal from a psychoactive substance may be incapable of providing an accurate history. In these circumstances, it is especially important to interview family members or acquaintances about the assessment. It is also helpful to examine any pill bottles or medications in the patient's possession.

The Physical Examination

The physical examination provides important information about substance use and its medical manifestations. Physical findings of interest include cutaneous abscesses and track marks of intravenous drug abuse, nasal lesions from cocaine abuse, peripheral neuropathy from alcohol use or solvent inhalation, and signs of liver disease from alcoholic or infectious hepatitis. Intravenous drug use should be suspected in any patient who is seropositive for hepatitis B or human immunodeficiency virus (HIV) or who presents with signs and symptoms of acquired immunodeficiency syndrome (AIDS). Substance use disorders should be considered in all patients who present with accidents or signs of repeated trauma, especially to the head (Skinner et al., 1984).

In addition to the physical examination, a complete mental status examination should be performed, including tests of memory, concentration, abstract reasoning, affect, mood, and form and content of thought (see Chapter One).

Laboratory Testing

Serum and urine toxicologic screens have an important role in assessing and treating patients with substance use disorders. However, it is important that such tests be properly conducted and that the results be properly interpreted. Informed consent should be obtained for all drug testing. As with all laboratory tests, both false-positive and false-negative results may be obtained; results may be affected by the methods of sample collection and the accuracy of the laboratory (Hansen et al., 1985). To minimize collection errors, all samples for toxicologic analysis should be obtained under direct observation. Both serum and urine samples should be obtained, as substances may be differentially distributed in body fluids. Positive test results should be confirmed by a second test on the same sample using a different analytic method, as closely related compounds in foods or medications may mimic illicit drugs in some drug analyses (for example, eating poppy-seed bagels has been reported to yield a positive urine test for opioids). A positive toxicologic screen may indicate past exposure to a psychoactive substance, but it may not indicate the extent of the exposure, when the exposure occurred, or whether there was behavioral impairment as a result of the exposure.

Abnormal values on diagnostic laboratory testing are widely used to diagnose substance use disorders, but they are not absolutely reliable or specific. No single laboratory test has been found to discriminate substance users from nonusers. In heavy users of alcohol, laboratory tests such as mean corpuscular volume (MCV) and liver function tests such as aspartate aminotransferase (SGOT) and gamma glutamyl transferase (GGT) may be abnormal in a high percentage of patients; however, a significant number of heavy drinkers may have normal test values. Opioid users may have abnormal liver function tests and positive serology for hepatitis B or HIV.

TREATMENT

General Considerations

To provide optimal treatment of substance use and dependence, the physician must know about therapies for the acute management of intoxicated or withdrawing patients, and about options for long-term treatment and rehabilitation. A treatment plan should be practical, economical, and based upon sound principals. The physician's initial task is to establish an effective therapeutic relationship. In the context of this relationship, the physician should engage the patient and if possible the family in short-term and long-term treatment.

There are five objectives of short-term treatment:

1. Relieving subjective symptoms of distress and discomfort due to intoxication or withdrawal,
2. Preventing and/or treating serious complications of intoxication, withdrawal, or dependence,
3. Establishing a drug- or alcohol-free state,
4. Preparing for and referral to longer-term treatment or rehabilitation, and
5. Engaging the family in the treatment process.

The objective of longer-term treatment or rehabilitation is to maintain the alcohol- or drug-free state through ongoing psychological, family, and vocational interventions. Long-term treatment should involve behavioral and psychological interventions to maintain abstinence. Changes in lifestyle, work, or friendships may be necessary to decrease the availability of drugs and to reduce the peer pressure to use drugs. Halfway houses, therapeutic communities, and other residential treatment situations may be useful. Individual and group psychotherapy can help the patient understand the role the drug plays in his or her life, can improve the patient's self-esteem, and can provide alternate methods of relieving psychosocial distress. Treatment of underlying psychiatric or medical illness may reduce the impetus for self-medication. Self-help groups such as Alcoholics Anonymous and Narcotics Anonymous provide education, emotional support, and hope to substance users and their families.

The Role of the Family in Treatment

Most patients presenting for treatment do so in the context of a family structure that is also dysfunctional. Therefore, substance dependence should be considered a chronic disorder involving the entire family. While family influences may motivate an individual to seek treatment for substance use, more often family members "enable" or facilitate the patient's substance use and may or may not be aware of their contribution. Substance use by one or more family members may maintain a pathological equilibrium in the family; eliminating the substance use may lead to interpersonal conflicts and loss of family integrity. Therefore, it is important for the physician to be aware of family dynamics and family dysfunction and to recognize the denial, defensiveness, hostility, and also the strengths that may be present in family members.

Spouses and children may experience considerable physical or emotional abuse due to the substance use within the family. The physician should try to involve family members in the patient's treatment as much as possible and should recommend psychological or substance abuse treatment for other family members when appropriate. Self-help organizations such as Al-Anon, Narc-Anon, Alateen, and groups of adult children of alcoholics (ACOA) may provide valuable emotional support and education for family members.

Alcohol Intoxication and Withdrawal:
Acute Medical Treatment

Patients presenting for alcohol treatment may show various types of impairment. Many alcoholics have profound social and financial problems that the healthcare system is ill-equipped to handle. Particularly frustrating to both physician and patient is an alcoholic with profound social needs who does not require medical treatment or who refuses medical treatment. In this case, referral to social agencies may help the patient, but in many instances no assistance can be obtained.

Acute *alcohol intoxication* results in behaviors ranging from coma to a hyperactive state with affective lability. Ingesting large amounts of alcohol may be fatal. Treatment of alcohol intoxication is essentially supportive and consists of maintaining physiologic homeostasis by supporting vital functions.

Patients presenting with *alcohol withdrawal syndrome* require evaluation of the severity of their withdrawal; they may require behavioral or pharmacologic intervention. The withdrawal syndrome is a complex physiologic process resulting from increased neuronal activity in the central and peripheral nervous systems. The consequences of this process may be minimal or may include autonomic hyperactivity, seizures, and *withdrawal delirium* (formerly known as delirium tremens or "the DTs") (Gross, Lewis, and Hastey, 1974). The severity of withdrawal depends on the amount and length of alcohol exposure, the presence of medical complications, and the patient's psychological state. In addition, chronic alcohol ingestion is associated with poor nutrition, poor hygiene, and general debilitation. Current data suggest that less than 5% of patients undergoing detoxification develop severe withdrawal delirium, with a mortality of 1 to 2%.

Physical dependence on alcohol is due to compensatory central nervous system changes that occur in response to a chronically administered depressant substance (ethanol). Historically, the signs and symptoms of the withdrawal syndrome have been reduced by administration of over 100 different pharmacologic agents, including chloral derivatives, paraldehyde, barbiturates, antihistamines, neuroleptics, anti-depressants, lithium, adrenergic blocking agents, and benzodiazepines (Sellers et al., 1980; Sullivan and Sellers, 1986; Liskow and Goodwin, 1987). Today, benzodiazepine derivatives are the treatment of choice, and their efficacy is well established by double-blind controlled studies (Sellers et al., 1983). Benzodiazepines are minimally toxic and have intrinsic anticonvulsant activity.

Thiamine should be administered to all alcohol users as soon as possible (and before the administration of glucose) to prevent the development of Wernicke's encephalopathy, which is characterized by ataxia, nystagmus, ophthalmoplegia, and mental status changes. The encephalopathic symptoms tend to improve with thia-mine repletion. Magnesium and other electrolyte levels should be obtained and deficits replaced.

Details of detoxification management are discussed in Chapter 18.

Recent studies indicate that many alcohol-dependent patients may not require drug-assisted detoxification. Social setting detoxification, a nondrug method, is used with excellent results by many alcohol-treatment facilities. This method, which in-cludes intensive peer and group support in a nonmedical environment, is effective in reducing withdrawal signs and symptoms with no increased incidence of medical complications. Questions have been raised about the possible bias in selecting health-ier patients for detoxification in these settings, but Shaw et al. (1981) have demon-strated that even within a medical setting a significant number of patients respond to supportive care and do not require pharmacologic intervention.

There is an association between alcoholism and affective illness and anxiety disorders (Von Knorring et al., 1983). Often, mood disturbances are directly related to alcohol and will resolve within 2 or 3 weeks after detoxification. Affective symptoms persisting beyond this time should be treated with antidepressants or electroconvul-sive therapy; benzodiazepines or other dependence-producing agents should not be used chronically in patients with alcoholism. In patients with severe mood symptoms or patients previously known to have mood disorders, antidepressant treatment may need to be started during detoxification.

Confronting the Patient and Family: The Initial Intervention

Effectively confronting patients with their alcohol or drug problem and then getting them into treatment requires special skills and techniques. Some authorities argue that presenting the problem to the patient and family as a *disease* is most effective. In this model, the patient is told that the use of alcohol or drugs represents a serious threat to his or her health and well-being; the evidence (historical or medical data) is pointed out in an objective and nonjudgmental manner. The physician should emphasize the effects that the alcohol or substance use has had on the patient's health, behavior, or family, and should not focus on the amount consumed. The physician should be prepared for denials, excuses, and promises to stop. Alcoholism or substance use may be explained as an addictive disease with a genetic basis; the physician can explain that the alcohol or drug has affected the brain and central nervous system to the extent that the patient can no longer control his or her intake and may have lost sight of the negative effects it is having. Blame for the disease should be placed on the alcohol or drug, not on the patient. Lecturing, cajoling, and threatening rarely work and may only heighten the patient's defensiveness, denial, and evasiveness. Most alcoholics or drug abusers have built up a pattern of denial to protect their habit, or use denial to avoid embarrassment, shame, guilt, and humiliation. Efforts by the physician to frighten patients into treatment are not usually successful in the long run.

Blaming the alcohol or drug avoids making the patient defensive, but the physician should point out that even though the disease may not be the patient's fault, now that he or she have been advised of the illness, getting effective treatment for managing the illness *is* his or her responsibility. If this type of presentation is not effective in getting the patient to agree to treatment, then consultation with a specially trained mental health alcohol/addictive disorder specialist is recommended. Even if patients tacitly agree to treatment, the physician should be careful to follow up to see if the recommendations have been followed. The physician should have handy the name and telephone number of a referral for the patient to call; a decision will have to be made as to whether the patient needs initial inpatient treatment. It is critical that the family should be involved in this process as well. Alcoholics Anonymous (AA) is a valuable resource for consultations and referral; members of AA will usually visit the prospective patient if the patient initiates the call.

Alcoholism is a family disease: families develop rigid systems of denial to cope with the drinking and maintain the family's equilibrium. The spouse often plays a *codependent* role by enabling the patient to drink, collaborating in the system of denial, and "rescuing" the patient in times of distress. Alcoholism may be the *family secret*, which the family feels would be socially humiliating and embarrassing to acknowledge. Hence, effective intervention usually means working with the entire family, not just confronting the alcoholic. This usually requires careful assessment, planning, and preparation by skilled professionals with a special interest in treating alcoholics and other patients with addictive disorders. The best strategy is to confer with a psychiatrist or other mental-health professional with a special interest in alcoholism or addiction before direct confrontation, or when an alcohol or substance abuse problem is suspected. The physician and specialist can then plan a coordinated intervention with clear plans for follow-through.

Long-Term Treatment

The goal of long-term treatment is to maintain abstinence through a comprehensive treatment program that includes psychological, family, and social interventions.

AA is an independent organization founded by a physician alcoholic in 1939. Its only goal is to help individuals maintain total abstinence from alcohol and other addictive substances, through group and individual interactions between alcoholics in various stages of recovery. While there is little objective outcome data on the efficacy of self-help groups (Emrick, 1974), they are useful for many individuals. Often, AA groups meet at hospitals, and psychiatric or medical inpatients may easily attend meetings.

Family involvement is extremely important in alcohol treatment. Alcohol use causes many family problems due to the financial and emotional stress the drinking creates. Yet alcoholic family structures often develop a pathological equilibrium that may encourage or maintain alcohol-related behaviors. Spouses and children in alcoholic families adapt to a family member's drinking with their own "wet behaviors." Educating and counseling family members about their role(s) in the patient's alcohol use and treatment is important in avoiding enabling and denial. Often, emotional distress, psychopathology, or substance use by other family members must be treated as well. Valuable emotional support and education for spouses and children may be provided by self-help organizations such as Al-Anon and Alateen.

Drugs to Reduce Alcohol Consumption/ Pharmacologic Prophylaxis

Disulfiram (Antabuse) inhibits the enzyme acetaldehyde dehydrogenase and is used as an adjunctive treatment in selected alcoholics. If alcohol is consumed in the presence of this drug, the toxic metabolite acetaldehyde accumulates, producing tachycardia, skin flushing, dyspnea, nausea, and vomiting. This unpleasant reaction provides a deterrent to the consumption of alcohol (Keventus and Major, 1979). Recently, however, several professional groups have questioned whether disulfiram's toxicity justifies its therapeutic use under any circumstances.

Patients taking disulfiram must be informed about the dangers of even small amounts of alcohol. Alcohol present in foods, shaving lotion, mouthwashes, or over-the-counter medications may produce a disulfiram reaction. The usual dose of disulfiram is 250 to 500 mg once daily. Disulfiram may interact with other medications, notably anticoagulants and phenytoin. It is contraindicated in patients with liver disease.

Antidepressants such as imipramine and amitriptyline have been reported effective in reducing alcohol consumption, via an unknown mechanism. Recent studies with serotonin reuptake blocker antidepressants such as fluoxetine and sertraline show the efficacy of these agents in reducing alcohol use in nondepressed heavy drinkers. In several studies, lithium carbonate has also been found to reduce alcohol consumption and to block the intoxicating effects of alcohol but should not be considered a sole treatment intervention.

Amphetamines and Similarly Acting Sympathomimetic Amines

The amphetamines are a group of drugs structurally related to the catecholamine neurotransmitters norepinephrine, epinephrine, and dopamine. The amphetamines release endogenous catecholamines from nerve endings and are catecholamine agonists at receptors in the peripheral autonomic and central nervous systems. Intoxication with stimulants such as amphetamines, methylphenidate, or other sympathomimetics may produce a similar clinical picture as cocaine intoxication, including sympathetic and behavioral hyperactivity. "Amphetamine psychosis" with manifestations of agitation, paranoia, delusions, and hallucinosis may follow chronic use of these drugs (Ellinwood, 1969), and paranoid states can persist even after detoxification. Antipsychotic medications such as haloperidol are useful in the treatment of stimulant psychoses; however, such patients often require psychiatric hospitalization. Severe hypertension is seen in overdose and may be treated with alpha-adrenergic blockade.

Chronic amphetamine users engage in a pattern of use similar to that of chronic cocaine users: they take escalating doses for a period of several days, then abstain from the drug. Paranoid psychosis diagnostically similar to schizophrenia may occur with chronic use and may persist for some days after cessation of stimulant use. A withdrawal syndrome with physiologic dysfunction does not follow abstinence from amphetamines; however, marked dysphoria, fatigue, and restlessness may occur. Because stimulant users may also suffer from underlying psychiatric illnesses such as affective disorders, a comprehensive psychiatric evaluation is necessary for all patients.

The use of over-the-counter sympathomimetic amines such as ephedrine and phenylpropanolamine as stimulants has increased dramatically in the past decade (Dietz, 1981). These medications are often sold as appetite suppressants, decongestants, or bronchodilators. Signs of intoxication are similar to those for amphetamines, although there tends to be less central nervous system stimulation and greater autonomic effects. Hypertensive crises have resulted from the use of these drugs.

Caffeine

Caffeine and the related methylxanthines theophylline and theobromine are ubiquitous drugs in our society. More than 80% of the population consumes these agents in coffee, tea, cola, and other carbonated drinks (Dews, 1982). Caffeine is present in chocolate and in a variety of prescription and over-the-counter medications, including stimulants (No-Doz), appetite suppressants (Dexatrim), analgesics (Anacin, APC tablets), and cold and sinus preparations (Dristan, Contac).

Methylxanthines produce physiologic effects through actions at the cellular level. They produce cardiac stimulation, diuresis, bronchodilation, and central nervous system stimulation through several mechanisms. They inhibit the enzyme cyclic AMP phosphodiesterase and increase intracellular levels of this second messenger, thereby augmenting the action of many hormones and neurotransmitters, such as norepinephrine. They also may have a direct stimulatory effect on nerve endings.

Central nervous system effects of caffeine include psychomotor stimulation, increased attention and concentration, and suppression of the need for sleep. Even at low or moderate doses, caffeine can exacerbate the symptoms of anxiety disorders and may increase requirements for neuroleptic or sedative medications (Charney, Henninger, and Jatlow, 1985). At high doses and in sensitive individuals, methylxanthines may produce tolerance and behavioral symptoms of tremor, insomnia, jitteriness, and agitation. In moderate to heavy users, a withdrawal syndrome characterized by lethargy, hypersomnia, irritability, and severe headache follows abrupt cessation of use.

Treatment of caffeine dependence consists of limiting consumption of caffeine-containing foods, medications, and beverages. In many instances, decaffeinated forms of preferred beverages such as coffee or cola may be substituted. Often, patients are unaware of the extent of their caffeine consumption and of the caffeine content of consumables. They need to be informed about the caffeine content of these substances.

Cocaine

The use of cocaine and "crack" cocaine has undergone an epidemic increase. In 1970, the Haight-Ashbury Clinic reported cocaine use in less than 1% of patients; by 1982, more than 6% were users. Based on the 1985 National Survey of Drug Abuse, 22 million Americans had tried cocaine at least once and 12 million have used it during the preceding year. Along with an increase in use, the manner of cocaine use has changed from intranasal snorting of cocaine powder to smoking or intravenous injection of the more potent form of cocaine, freebase. Freebase cocaine, known as crack, is inexpensive and widely available.

Cocaine is an alkaloid extracted from the leaves of the plant *Erythroxylon coca*, native to South America. It is a local anesthetic that blocks the initiation and propagation of nerve impulses by affecting the sodium conductance of cell membranes. It is a potent sympathomimetic agent that potentiates the actions of catecholamines in the autonomic nervous system, causing tachycardia, hypertension, and vasoconstriction. In addition, cocaine is a central nervous system stimulant, increasing arousal and producing mood elevation and psychomotor activation.

Cocaine intoxication is characterized by elation, euphoria, excitement, pressured speech, restlessness, stereotyped movements, and bruxism. Sympathetic stimulation occurs, including tachycardia, mydriasis, and sweating. Paranoia, suspiciousness, and psychosis may occur with prolonged use. Overdosage produces hyperpyrexia, hyperreflexia, seizures, coma, and respiratory arrest.

Cocaine has a rather short plasma half-life of 1 to 2 hours, which correlates with its behavioral effects (Van Dyke et al., 1978). Along with the decline in plasma levels, most users experience a period of dysphoria known as a *crash*, which often leads to additional cocaine use within a short period. The dysphoria of the crash is intensified and prolonged following repeated use.

Treatment

Optimal treatment for the chronic cocaine user has not been established. While cessation of cocaine use is not followed by a physiologic withdrawal syndrome as severe as that seen with opioids or alcohol, the dysphoria, depression, and drug craving that follow chronic cocaine use are often intense and make abstinence difficult. Psychotherapy, group therapy, and behavior modification have been found to be useful in maintaining abstinence (Rounsaville et al., 1985). Several pharmacologic agents have shown promise as adjunctive treatments. Antidepressants such as imipramine, desipramine, lithium, or trazodone reduce cocaine craving and usage (Rosecan, 1983; Tennant and Rawson, 1983; Gawin and Kleber, 1984). The dopamine agonists bromocriptine and amantadine may block cocaine craving (Dackis and Gold, 1985).

Many psychiatric and drug hospitals now offer short-term inpatient treatment of the cocaine user, providing intensive psychological treatment and drug education in a drug-free environment. For recidivists, long-term residential drug-free programs, including therapeutic communities, may be efficacious. Self-help groups such as Narcotics Anonymous may be useful both as a primary treatment modality for cocaine dependence and as an adjunct to other treatment.

Certain psychiatric disorders, such as depression and attention deficit disorder, may be common in cocaine users. Recognizing and treating these underlying disorders may be necessary to stop cocaine use. In addition, many cocaine users also use alcohol or other drugs, particularly sedatives and heroin, and may require treatment for these substances as well.

Cannabis

Cannabis sativa, also called marijuana or hemp, is a plant indigenous to India but now grown worldwide. The leaves, flowers, and seeds of the plant contain many biologically active compounds, the most important of which are the lipophilic cannabinoids, especially δ-9-tetrahydrocannabinol (THC). The biologically active substances are administered by smoking or ingesting dried plant parts (marijuana, bhang, ganja), the resin from the plant (hashish), or extracts of the resin (THC or hash oil). After inhalation or ingestion, THC rapidly enters the central nervous system. It has a biphasic elimination with a short initial half-life (1 to 2 hours), reflecting redistribution and a second half-life of days to weeks. THC is hydroxylated and excreted in bile and urine.

Although it is illegal, a high percentage of the American population has used marijuana. In 1982, 64.1% of young adults (18 to 25) had tried marijuana. Although the use may be declining, millions of individuals continue to use marihuana regularly.

Cannabis intoxication is characterized by tachycardia, muscle relaxation, euphoria, and a sense of well-being. Time sense is altered and emotional lability, particularly inappropriate laughter, may be seen. There is impaired performance on psychomotor tasks, including driving (Klonoff, 1974). Marijuana has antiemetic effects and reduces intraocular pressure; it has been used medically for these effects. Occasionally, with high doses of drug, depersonalization, paranoia, and anxiety reactions occur. Although tolerance to the effects of cannabis occurs with chronic use, cessation of use does not produce significant withdrawal phenomena. Chronic use of cannabis has been associated with an apathetic, amotivational state that improves upon discontinuation of the drug (Gersten, 1980).

Treatment

Treatment of cannabis dependence is similar to treatment of other drug dependencies. As part of the initial assessment, all patients should undergo complete psychiatric and medical examinations. Short-term goals should focus on reducing or stopping cannabis use and interventions to ensure compliance. Inpatient treatment may be necessary to achieve abstinence. Because many patients with cannabis dependence are adolescents or young adults, involving the family in assessment and treatment is important.

Long-term treatment should involve behavioral and psychological interventions to maintain abstinence. Often, a change in social situation is necessary to decrease drug availability and reduce peer pressure to use drugs. Individual and group psychotherapy may be useful for helping the patient understand the role marijuana plays in his or her life and may improve self-esteem and provide alternate methods of relieving psychosocial distress. Self-help groups such as Narcotics Anonymous can provide group and individual support.

Hallucinogens

Many drugs may be used for their hallucinogenic or psychotomimetic effects. These include psychedelics such as lysergic acid diethylamide (LSD), mescaline, psilocybin, and dimethyltryptamine (DMT); hallucinogenic amphetamines such as methylenedioxymethamphetamine (MDMA or Ecstasy) and methylenedioxyamphetamine (MDA); and anticholinergics, such as scopolamine. All can cause a state of intoxication characterized by hallucinosis, affective changes, and delusional states.

The mechanism of action of these substances is thought to involve stimulation of central nervous system dopamine or inhibition of serotonin. Recent studies indicate that administration of hallucinogenic amphetamines to animals produces persistent depletions of brain monoamines, which is consistent with a neurotoxic effect of these substances. Human neurotoxicity has not been established.

Hallucinogens are primarily used by young adults on an intermittent basis. Chronic daily use of hallucinogens is uncommon. In 1982, 21.1% of 18- to 25-year-olds reported using hallucinogens sometime during their life, although more recent statistics report a decrease in use.

The differential diagnosis of hallucinogen-induced psychosis includes schizophrenia, bipolar disorder, delusional disorder, and organic mental disorders such as encephalitis and brain tumor, and other toxic ingestions. Psychoses, including those that are drug induced, produce an analgesic state, and medical problems such as pain may be obscured.

Treatment of hallucinogen intoxication includes reducing agitation and psychosis, preventing patients from harming themselves or others, and maintaining vital functions. Agitation and psychosis usually respond to verbal reassurance and decreased sensory stimulation, but sometimes require treatment with benzodiazepines or high-potency neuroleptics. Most hallucinogen intoxications are short-lived (several hours), although prolonged drug-induced psychoses may occur, particularly in patients predisposed to psychiatric illness (Bowers and Swigar, 1983). Some patients experience brief recurrences of the psychotomimetic state (flashbacks) after a drug-free interval.

Inhalants

Inhalants are volatile organic compounds that are inhaled for their psychotropic effects. Substances in this class include organic solvents (such as gasoline, toluene, and ethyl ether), fluorocarbons, and volatile nitrates (including nitrous oxide and butyl nitrate). Inhalants are ubiquitous and readily available in most households and worksites. At low doses, inhalants produce mood changes and ataxia; at high doses, they may produce dissociative states and hallucinosis. Dangers of organic solvent use include suffocation and organ damage, especially hepatotoxicity and neurotoxicity in the central and peripheral nervous systems (Watson, 1982). Cardiac arrhythmias and sudden death may occur. Inhaled nitrates may produce hypotension and met-hemaglobinemia.

The typical inhalant user is an adolescent male. According to the National Household Survey on Drug Abuse, 9.1% of 12- to 17-year-olds and 12.8% of 18- to 25-year-olds have tried an inhalant at least once.

Optimal treatment of the inhalant user is not well established. Since most users are adolescents, treatment must involve the family. Long-term residential treatment may be helpful in the treatment of heavy users.

Nicotine

Nicotine is an alkaloid drug present in the leaves of the tobacco plant *Nicotiana tabacum*. The plant is indigenous to the New World and has been used for centuries by American Indians in ceremonies and as a medicinal herb. Since its discovery by Europeans, tobacco use has spread worldwide; today nicotine is the most prevalent psychoactive drug. More than 50 million Americans smoke cigarettes daily; another 10 million use another form of tobacco. Nicotine addiction and tobacco use are legally sanctioned forms of substance abuse. Tobacco is clearly the most lethal substance in our society, accounting for over 350,000 premature deaths per year, primarily due to cardiovascular disease and cancer. Since the publication of the Surgeon General's Report on Smoking and Health in 1964, there has fortunately been a gradual decline in the percentage of Americans who smoke. Most of this decline has occurred in men. The numbers of young women who smoke, and the use of other tobacco products such as smokeless tobacco, has increased. Tobacco companies continue their unscrupulous practice of marketing tobacco as either a chic or macho lifestyle-enhancing product; much of their advertising is directed toward young people, from whom most nicotine addicts are recruited.

To maximize the absorption of nicotine, tobacco products are usually smoked in pipes, cigars, or cigarettes or are instilled intranasally or intraorally as snuff or smokeless tobacco. Following absorption from the lungs or buccal mucosa, nicotine levels peak rapidly and then decline, with a half-life of 30 to 60 minutes.

Nicotine has several effects on the peripheral autonomic and central nervous systems. It is an agonist at "nicotinic" cholinergic receptor sites and stimulates autonomic ganglia in the parasympathetic and sympathetic nervous systems, produc-ing salivation, increased gastric motility and acid secretion, and increased cate-cholamine release. In the central nervous system, nicotine acts as a mild psychomotor stimulant, producing increased alertness, increased attention and concentration, and appetite suppression. The fact that tobacco use can prevent weight gain makes the drug attractive, particularly to young women.

Repeated use of nicotine produces tolerance and dependence. The degree of dependence is considerable: more than 70% of those who quit relapse within a year. Quitting nicotine use produces a withdrawal syndrome characterized by increased irritability, decreased attention and concentration, and an intense craving for and preoccupation with nicotine. Often, there is increased appetite and food consumption and a significant weight gain. Withdrawal symptoms may begin within several hours of cessation and typically last about a week. Craving and weight gain may persist for weeks, however.

The morbidity and mortality resulting from use of nicotine is extensive and includes an increase in cardiovascular and respiratory disease and in cancers, particularly of the lung and oropharynx. Many of the deleterious effects of tobacco are due not to nicotine but to other toxic and carcinogenic compounds present in tobacco extract or smoke.

The treatment of the nicotine-dependent patient should follow the principles of treatment common to all psychoactive substances. Short-term goals should consist of reducing and/or quitting tobacco use. Few patients can reduce tobacco use on their own, and a supportive, encouraging relationship of a physician and/or the use of a smoking cessation program is usually necessary to ensure success (Greene, Goldberg, and Ockene, 1988).

Pharmacologic therapy with nicotine gum has been shown to be safe and efficacious in the treatment of tobacco dependence. The gum is a sweet, flavored resin containing 2 mg of nicotine, which is released slowly when chewed. The patient chews the gum whenever he or she feels the need, and its use is gradually decreased over time. Proper use of the gum can reduce the craving for tobacco and can decrease the discomfort of withdrawal symptoms (Jarvik et al., 1984; Schneider et al., 1984)). Recently, the alpha$_2$-receptor agonist clonidine has also been reported as partially efficacious in reducing nicotine withdrawal symptoms (Glassman, Stetner, Walsh, et al., 1988). The most successful treatment of nicotine dependence combines pharmacologic and behavioral therapies (see also Chapter 23).

Opioids

Opioid abuse and dependence remains a significant sociologic and medical problem in the United States, with an estimated 500,000 opioid addicts. These patients are frequent users of medical and surgical services because of the multiple medical sequelae of intravenous drug use and its associated lifestyle. Intravenous opioid users now are the second largest group of persons with AIDS.

The physiologic effects of opiates are due to stimulation of receptors for endogenous hormones, enkephalins, endorphins, and dynorphins. There are at least five distinct opioid receptors, which are designated by the Greek letters mu, kappa, sigma, delta, and epsilon (Jaffe and Martin, 1985). Morphine, heroin, and methadone act primarily through mu-receptors and produce analgesia, euphoria, and respiratory depression. Drugs that appear to be mediated through the kappa-receptor include the so-called mixed agonist-antagonists, butorphanol and pentazocine, which produce analgesia, but less respiratory depression. The sigma-receptor appears similar to the receptor for the hallucinogen phencyclidine. The delta-receptor binds endogenous opioid peptides. At high doses, opioid drugs lose their receptor specificity and have agonist or antagonist properties at multiple receptor subtypes.

Treatment

Opioid overdose, a life-threatening emergency, should be suspected in any patient who presents with coma and respiratory suppression. Treatment of suspected overdose includes emergency support of respiration and cardiovascular functions. Parenteral administration of the opioid antagonist naloxone 0.4 to 0.8 mg rapidly reverses coma and respiratory suppression but does not affect depression caused by other sedatives, such as alcohol or barbiturates. Naloxone can precipitate opioid withdrawal, causing the patient whose life has just been saved to be extremely ungrateful.

The opioid withdrawal syndrome is unpleasant but not life-threatening. It is characterized by increased sympathetic nervous system activity, coupled with gastro-intestinal symptoms of nausea, vomiting, cramps, and diarrhea. Patients may also report myalgias and arthralgias. There is increased restlessness, increased anxiety, insomnia, and an intense craving for opioids. Treatment for withdrawal consists of minimizing signs and symptoms.

Opioid detoxification is performed by readministering an opioid until with-drawal symptoms cease, then gradually decreasing the dose of opioid over a period of up to 21 days, as specified by federal law (Fultz and Senay, 1975). Although any opioid could be used for detoxification, methadone is most often used due to its long half-life and once-daily oral administration. Initially, patients should be given 10 to 20 mg methadone orally every 2 to 4 hours until withdrawal symptoms are suppressed. The total initial dose is typically 20 to 40 mg for heroin addicts. This dose is then tapered over time.

The alpha$_2$-adrenergic agonist clonidine hydrochloride may also be used to suppress many of the signs and symptoms of opioid withdrawal. Clonidine acts at presynaptic noradrenergic nerve endings in the locus ceruleus of the brain and blocks the adrenergic discharge produced by opioid withdrawal (Aghajanian, 1975; Gold et al., 1979). Clonidine suppresses about 75% of opioid withdrawal signs and symptoms, especially autonomic hyperactivity, anxiety, and gastrointestinal symptoms (Gold et al., 1980; Charney et al., 1981; Watson and Resnick, 1981). Withdrawal symptoms that are not significantly ameliorated by clonidine include drug craving, insomnia, and arthralgias and myalgias. Insomnia may be treated with a short-acting hypnotic such as chloral hydrate, and pain may respond to nonnarcotic analgesics such as ibuprofen or acetaminophen. Clonidine may cause dry mouth, sedation, and orthostatic hypote-nsion. It should be used cautiously in hypotensive patients and those receiving antihypertensives, antidepressants, or antipsychotics. (See Chapter 18, Table 18-10.)

Methadone Maintenance

Since its introduction in 1965, methadone maintenance has become a major modality of long-term treatment of opioid abuse and dependence (Dole and Nyswander, 1965). Currently, about 100,000 Americans are maintained on meth-adone. The demand for treatment exceeds the availability, and many programs have long waiting lists, often up to several months. However, a physician can apply to the Drug Enforcement Administration to maintain a patient on methadone outside of an established methadone program.

In a typical methadone program, patients receive a daily dose of oral methadone, coupled with behavioral and psychological therapy. Periodic toxicologic analysis of urine is done to ensure compliance. Patients may receive methadone for various periods of time, often for years.

Methadone maintenance is clearly effective in reducing illicit drug use and criminality and in improving the social and psychological health of many heroin users. Several theories explain the efficacy of methadone maintenance, including decreasing illicit opioid use by increasing tolerance, treating an endorphin deficiency, and inducing addicts to enter a structured, rehabilitation-oriented treatment.

If hospitalized in a psychiatric or medical facility, patients on a methadone maintenance program can continue to have their daily dose of methadone in the hospital. However, it is important for the physician to keep in touch with the methadone program. If analgesia is needed, patients should receive additional opioids, such as meperidine or oxycodone. This differentiates between the use of opioids for analgesia and for maintenance and does not change the dose of methadone.

Opioid Antagonist Therapy

Detoxified opioid users may benefit from opioid antagonist therapy with naltrexone (Trexan R). Naltrexone is a long-acting orally active opioid antagonist that when taken regularly entirely blocks mu-opioid receptors, thus blocking the opioids' euphoric, analgesic, and sedative properties (Resnick et al., 1980). Naltrexone is given either in a daily dose of 50 mg or three times weekly at doses of 100 mg, 100 mg, and 150 mg. The drug appears to be most effective in motivated individuals with good social support and appears less helpful for heroin addicts. Although naltrexone may be prescribed by any physician, it is most effective as part of a comprehensive rehabilitation plan.

Drug-Free Treatment

Drug-free treatment modalities are also useful in treating the opioid abuser (Bale et al, 1984). Such programs emphasize total abstinence from opioids, alcohol, and other drugs, as well as social and psychological rehabilitation. Programs differ widely in their intensity and their theoretical orientation. Therapeutic community programs usually require a long-term treatment commitment of at least several months, during which the addict is taken out of his or her usual environment and involved in intensive psychological and behavioral individual and group therapy. Long-term residential treatment may be most useful for the chronic opioid abuser who requires a change in lifestyle.

Self-help groups such as Narcotics Anonymous (NA) may be useful either as a primary treatment modality for opioid dependence or as an adjunct to other treatment. NA, like AA, uses the 12-step philosophy and stresses total abstinence. Because NA groups often have their own orientations, patients should be encouraged to visit several groups to increase the chances that they will find a group in which they feel comfortable.

Phencyclidine and Similarly Acting Arylcyclohexylamines

Phencyclidine (PCP) and similarly acting arylcyclohexylamines, such as ketamine, are used as anesthetics in veterinary medicine and in pediatrics (ketamine). Their mechanism of action is not well understood, although recently this class of drugs has been shown to bind to the so-called sigma opioid receptor in the brain.

PCP intoxication has several definitive features. The agents produce an amnestic, euphoric, hallucinatory state, although the effects may be unpredictable and a prolonged, agitated psychosis with impulsive violence directed at self or others may occur (Petersen and Stillman, 1979; Walker et al., 1981). Vertical and horizontal nystagmus, myoclonus, ataxia, and autonomic instability are common.

As with the hallucinogens, treatment of PCP or similarly acting arylcyclohexylamine intoxication includes supportive measures to prevent patients from harming themselves or others, to maintain cardiovascular and respiratory functions, and to ameliorate psychotic symptoms. Both haloperidol and benzodiazepines have been described as useful for decreasing agitation and psychosis. Psychiatric hospitalization may be necessary in prolonged psychosis.

Sedatives, Hypnotics, Anxiolytics

Sedatives are among the most prescribed medications and are routinely used for their anxiolytic and hypnotic effects. However, they are also a major source of drug overdoses and of adverse drug reactions. Medications in this group include barbiturates such as secobarbital, butalbital, and phenobarbital; benzodiazepines such as alprazolam and diazepam; and nonbarbiturate sedative-hypnotics such as chloral derivatives, ethchlorvynol, glutethimide, meprobamate, and methaqualone. A patient who becomes dependent on sedative and anxiolytic medications often obtains them by prescription from physicians who are unaware of the patient's abuse or dependence problem.

The effects of sedative-hypnotic and anxiolytic drugs may be mediated through interactions with the GABA—chloride channel receptor complex. In the case of benzodiazepines, there is a neuronal binding site linked to the GABA receptor in both location and function. Binding of benzodiazepines to nerve cell membranes facilitates binding of GABA to its receptors and augments GABA inhibition of nerve cells (Hunt, 1983). Barbiturates, anticonvulsants, and other sedative-hypnotic drugs also have discrete binding sites closely associated with the chloride channel and affect the transport of chloride and inhibition of neurons (Seeman, 1972).

The assessment of the sedative user begins with the history, which should include drug and alcohol use, psychiatric illness, and medical history. Toxicologic screens may be useful in assessing the type of medications used.

Treatment

Treatment of the sedative abuser occurs in two stages, detoxification and long-term rehabilitation. Pharmacologic detoxification is usually necessary, as the withdrawal syndrome following cessation of drug use may be severe and may include seizures, cardiac arrhythmias, and death. The *pentobarbital challenge test* (Wesson and Smith, 1977; Wikler, 1968) is useful for predicting the need for pharmacologic-assisted detoxification to prevent severe withdrawal in heavy users. Pentobarbital 200 mg is administered orally and the patient is observed 1 hour later. The patient's condition after the test dose will range from no effect to sleep. If the patient develops drowsiness or nystagmus on a 200-mg dose, he or she is not dependent on barbiturates. If 200 mg has no effect, the dose should be repeated hourly until nystagmus or drowsiness develop. The total dose administered approximates the patient's daily sedative habit. The barbiturate dose should be tapered over 10 days, with about a 10% reduction each day.

Long-term treatment should be customized for each patient and may include residential drug-free programs and self-help groups such as AA or NA. Some patients may be found to have an underlying psychiatric disorder, such as an anxiety disorder or depression. If pharmacologic treatment is deemed necessary, antidepressants or nondependence-producing anxiolytics such as buspirone should be used.

SUMMARY

Substance use disorders are chronic disorders that involve individuals and their families. Identifying and treating such disorders requires the physician to have several skills, including:

1. Knowledge of the biological, psychological, and social substrates of substance use;
2. The ability to interview patients and their families in taking a substance use history;
3. Knowledge of acute and long-term treatment modalities for intoxication, dependence, and withdrawal; and
4. Knowledge of professionals and special programs in the community for specialized interventions and treatment.

The treatment process involves identifying the problem, making the patient and family aware of the problem, and motivating them to seek help. The process is best conducted in the context of a supportive, empathic, and ongoing physician-patient relationship.

CLINICAL PEARLS

- In diagnosing alcoholism, fully expect the patient and family to deny that a problem exists.
- Alcoholism is a family disease. Usually the entire family uses denial to cope with the alcoholic behavior and to maintain the family homeostasis. Spouses are often enablers and may deny the problem as much as the patient does. Interview and assess multiple family members in making your assessment.
- Effective intervention with alcoholic and substance-abusing patients is best carried out by specialists in intervention and treatment. Find out who is available as a resource for consultation and referral.
- In diagnosing alcoholism and substance abuse, the amount and frequency of ingestion is not the primary issue. Focus on the behavioral, medical, and social *effects* on the individual and family of whatever amount is ingested.

ANNOTATED BIBLIOGRAPHY

Gawin F, Kleber H: Pharmacologic treatments of cocaine abuse. Psychiatric Clin North America 9:573–583, 1986.

> A review of the clinical and behavioral pharmacology and medical consequences of cocaine use.

Hollister LE: Clinical pharmacology of psychotherapeutic drugs. New York: Churchill Livingstone, 1978.

> A well-written, easy-to-understand book on the actions and uses of psychoactive substances used to treat psychiatric disorders. The book also has excellent introductory chapters on basic clinical pharmacology.

Jaffe JE: Drug addiction and drug abuse. In Gilman AG, Goodman LS, Gilman A (eds): The pharmacological basis of therapeutics. 6th ed. New York, Macmillan, 1980

> An extremely comprehensive and detailed description of the clinical and behavioral pharmacology of psychoactive substances, with emphasis on chemistry and pharmacology. The bible on drugs for medical students.

Lewis DC, Williams CN (eds): Providing care for children of alcoholics: Clinical and research perspectives. Pompano Beach, FL, Heath Communications, 1986

> This short, multiauthored monograph of a conference on children of alcoholics provides an excellent review of theoretical, clinical, and policy issues related to the children and families of alcoholics.

Schultes RE, Hofmann A: The botany and chemistry of hallucinogens. 2nd ed. Springfield, IL, Charles C. Thomas, 1980

> A classic text on the chemistry and human uses of hallucinogens.

Senay E: Methadone maintenance treatment. Int J Addictions 20:803–821, 1985

> An excellent review of the principles and practice of the use of methadone to treat opioid dependence.

Stanton MD: Drugs and the family. Marriage Fam Rev 2:1–10, 1979

> A somewhat dated but useful description of the consequences of psychoactive substance use from the perspective of family functioning.

US Department of Health and Human Services: The health consequences of smoking: Nicotine addiction. A report of the Surgeon General. DHHS Publication No. CDC 88-8406, Washington DC, 1988

> The controversial Surgeon General's report on smoking has excellent sections on the clinical and behavioral pharmacology of nicotine and presents the thesis that nicotine dependence is an addiction.

West LJ: Alcoholism. Ann Int Med 100:405–416, 1984

> A good recent review of the pathogenesis and treatment of alcohol dependence.

Zinberg NE, Harding WM (eds): Control over intoxicant use: Pharmacological, psychological and social considerations. New York, Human Sciences Press, 1982

> Interesting vignettes in this well-written, somewhat controversial book describe the varieties of psychoactive substance use and the way our society deals with such use.

REFERENCES

Aghajanian GK: Tolerance of locus ceruleus neurons to morphine and inhibition of withdrawal response by clonidine. Nature 276:186–188, 1976

American Psychiatric Association: Diagnostic and statistical manual of mental disorders. 3rd ed., rev. Washington DC: American Psychiatric Association, 1987

Bale RN, Zarcone VP, Van Stone WW, et al: Three therapeutic communities: A prospective controlled study of narcotic addiction treatment process and follow-up results. Arch Gen Psychiatry 41:185–191, 1984

Bernadt MW, Taylor C, Mumford J, et al: Comparison of questionnaire and laboratory tests in the detection of excessive drinking and alcoholism. Lancet 1:325–328, 1982

Bowers MB, Swigar ME: Vulnerability to psychosis associated with hallucinogen use. Psychiatry Res 9:91–97, 1983

Charney DS, Henninger GR, Jatlow PI: Increased anxiogenic effects of caffeine in panic disorders. Arch Gen Psychiatry 42:233–243, 1985

Charney DS, Sternberg DE, Kleber HD, et al: Clinical use of clonidine in abrupt withdrawal from methadone. Arch Gen Psychiatry 38:1273–1278, 1981

Clark WD: Alcoholism: Blocks to diagnosis and treatment. Am J Med 71:275–285, 1981

Cloninger CR: Neurogenetic adaptive mechanisms in alcoholism. Science 236:410–416, 1987

Costa E, Guidotti A: Molecular mechanisms in the receptor action of benzodiazepines. Annu Rev Pharmacol Toxicol 19:231–245, 1981

Dackis CA, Gold M: Bromocriptine as treatment of cocaine abuse. Lancet 1:1151, 1985

Dews PB: Caffeine. Annu Rev Nutr 2:323–341, 1982

Dietz AJ: Amphetamine-like reactions to phenylpropanolamine. JAMA 245:601–602, 1981

Dole VP, Nyswander M: A medical treatment for diacetylmorphine (heroin) addiction: Clinical trial with methadone hydrochloride. JAMA 193:646–650, 1965

Ellinwood EH: Amphetamine psychosis: A multidimensional process. Semin Psych 1:208–226, 1969

Emrick C: A review of psychologically oriented treatment of alcoholism. Quart J Stud Alcohol 38:1004–1031, 1974

Ewing JA: Detecting alcoholism: The CAGE questionnaire. JAMA 252:1905–1907, 1984

Fultz JM Jr, Senay EC: Guidelines for the management of hospitalized narcotics addicts. Ann Intern Med 82:815–818, 1975

Gawin FH, Kleber HD: Cocaine abuse treatment: Open trial with desipramine and lithium carbonate. Arch Gen Psychiatry 41:903–909, 1984

Gay GR: Clinical management of acute and chronic cocaine poisoning. Ann Emerg Med 11:562–572, 1982

Gersten SP: Long-term adverse effects of brief marihuana usage. J Clin Psychiatry 41:60, 1980

Glassman AH, Stetner F, Walsh BT, et al: Heavy smokers, smoking cessation and clonidine: Results of a double-blind, randomized trial. JAMA 259:2863–2866, 1988

Gold MS, Redmond DE Jr, Kleber HD: Noradrenergic hyperactivity in opiate withdrawal suppressed by clonidine. Am J Psychiatry 136:100–102, 1979

Gold MS, Pottash AC, Sweeney DR, et al: Opiate withdrawal using clonidine: A safe, effective and rapid non-opiate treatment. JAMA 234:343–346, 1979

Greene HL, Goldberg R, Ockene JK: Cigarette smoking: The physician's role in cessation and maintenance. J Gen Int Med 3:75—87, 1988

Goodwin DW: Alcohol in homicide and suicide. Quart J Stud Alcohol 28:517–528, 1967

Goodwin DW: Alcoholics and genetics: The sins of the fathers. Arch Gen Psychiatry 42:171–174, 1985

Gottschalk L, McGuire F, Heiser J, et al: Drug abuse deaths in nine cities: A survey report. NIDA Research Monograph #29. Washington DC: US Gov Printing Office, 1979

Gross M, Lewis E, Hastey J: Acute alcohol withdrawal syndrome. In Kissin B, Begleiter H (eds): The biology of alcoholism, vol. 3. New York, Plenum, 1974

Hansen HJ, Caudhill SP, Boone DJ: Crisis in drug testing: Results of the CDC blind study. JAMA 253:2382–2387, 1985

Harvey SC: Hypnotics and sedatives. In Gilman AG, Goodman LS, Gilman A (eds): The pharmacological basis of therapeutics. 6th ed. New York, Macmillan, 1980

Holden C: The neglected disease in medical education. Science 229:741–742, 1985

Hunt WA: The effect of ethanol on GABAergic transmission. Neurosci Biobehav Rev 7:87–95, 1983

Jaffe JH, Martin WR: Opioid analgesics and antagonists. In Gilman AG, Goodman LS, Rall TW, et al (eds): The pharmacological basis of therapeutics. 7th ed. New York, Macmillan, 1985

Jarvik ME, Schneider NG: Degree of addiction and the effectiveness of nicotine gum therapy for smoking. Am J Psychiatry 141:790–791, 1984

Kennedy W: Chemical dependency: A treatable disease. Ohio Med 71:77–79, 1985

Keventus J, Major LF: Disulfiram in the treatment of alcoholism. J Stud Alcohol 40:428–446, 1979

Klonoff H: Marihuana and driving in real-life situations. Science 186:317–324, 1974

Lewis DC, Gomolin IH: Emergency treatment of drug and alcohol intoxication and withdrawal. Brown University Program in Alcoholism and Drug Abuse Medical Monograph II, 1982

Lewis D, Gordon A: Alcoholism and the general hospital: The Roger Williams intervention program. Bull NY Acad Med 59:181–197, 1983

Liskow BI, Goodwin DW: Pharmacological treatment of alcohol intoxication, withdrawal and dependence: A critical review. J Stud Alcohol 48:356–370, 1987

Martin WR: Naloxone. Ann Intern Med 85:765–768, 1976

McIntosh I: Alcohol-related disabilities in general hospital patients: A critical assessment of the evidence. Int J Addictions 17:609–639, 1982

National Survey on Drug Abuse. Rockville, MD, Institute of Drug Abuse, 1981

Palestine ML, Alatorre E: Control of acute alcoholic withdrawal symptoms: A comparative study of haloperidol and chlordiazepoxide. Curr Ther Res 20:289–299, 1976

Petersen RC, Stillman RC, eds: PCP (Phencyclidine) abuse: An appraisal. NIDA Research Monograph 21, DHEW. Washington DC, US Gov Printing Office, 1979

Rappolt RT, Gay GR, Inaba D: Propranolol: A specific antagonist to cocaine. Clin Toxicol 10:265–271, 1977

Regier DA, Boyd JH, Burke JD, et al: One-month prevalence of mental disorders in the United States. Arch Gen Psychiatry 45:977–986, 1988

Resnick RB, Schuyten-Resnick E, Washton AM: Assessment of narcotic antagonists in the treatment of opioid dependence. Ann Rev Pharmacol Toxicol 20:463–474, 1980

Rosecan JS: The psychopharmacologic treatment of cocaine addiction (abstract). Seventh World Congress of Psychiatry, Vienna, 1983

Rounsaville BJ, Gawin FH, Kleber HD: Interpersonal psychotherapy adapted for ambulatory cocaine users. Am J Drug Alc Abuse 11:171, 1985

Schneider NG, Jarvik ME, Forsythe AB: Nicotine vs. placebo gum in the alleviation of withdrawal during smoking cessation. Addic Behav 9:149–156, 1984

Schuckit MA: Genetics and the risk for alcoholism. JAMA 254:2614–2617, 1985

Schulz DW, Macdonald RL: Barbiturate enhancement of GABA-mediated inhibition and activation of chloride channel conductance: Correlation with anticonvulsant and anesthetic actions. Brain Res 209:177–188, 1981

Seeman P: Membrane effects of anesthetics and tranquilizers. Pharmacol Rev 24:583–655, 1972

Sellers EM, Cooper SD, Zilm DH, et al: Lithium treatment during alcoholic withdrawal. Clin Pharm Ther 20:199–206, 1976

Sellers EM, Narango CA, Harrison M, et al: Diazepam loading: Simplified treatment for alcohol withdrawal. Clin Pharm Ther 6:822, 1983

Sellers EM, Kalant H: Drug therapy: Alcohol intoxication and withdrawal. New Eng J Med 294:757–752, 1976

Selzer ML: The Michigan alcoholism screening test: The quest for a new diagnostic instrument. Am J Psychiatry 127:1653–8, 1971

Shaw JM, Kolesar GS, Sellers EM, et al: Development of optimal treatment tactics for alcohol withdrawal: Assessment and effectiveness of supportive care. J Clin Psychopharmacol 1:382–387, 1981

Skinner HA, Holt S, Schuller R, et al: Identification of alcohol abuse using laboratory tests and a history of trauma. Ann Intern Med 101:847–851, 1984

Skolnick P, Moncada V, Barker J, Paul SM: Pentobarbital: Dual action to increase brain benzodiazepine receptor affinity. Science 211:1448–1150, 1981

Tennant FS, Rawson RA: Cocaine and amphetamine dependence treated with desipramine. In Harris L (ed): Problems of drug dependence. NIDA Monograph Series 43. Rockville, MD, National Institute of Drug Abuse, 351–355, 1983

Thomas M, Halsall S, Peters TJ, et al: Role of hepatic acetaldehyde dehydrogenase in alcoholism. Lancet 2:1057, 1982

Van Dyke C, Jatlow P, Ungerer J, et al: Oral cocaine: Plasma concentration and central effects. Science 200:211–213, 1978

Von Knorring A, Cloninger CR, Bohman M, et al: An adoption study of depressive disorders and substance abuse. Arch Gen Psychiatry 20:943–950, 1983

Walker S, Yesavage JA, Tinklenberg JR: Acute phencyclidine (PCP) intoxication. Quantitative urine levels and clinical management. Am J Psychiatry, 138:674–675, 1981

Waller JA, Turkel HW: Alcoholism in traffic deaths. New Engl J Med 275:532–536, 1966

Washton AM, Resnick RB: Clonidine for opiate detoxification: Outpatient clinical trials. J Clin Psychiatry 43:39–41, 1981

Wesson DR, Smith DE: A new method for the treatment of barbiturate dependence. JAMA 231:294–295, 1975

Whitfield CL, Thompson G, Lamb A, et al: Detoxification of 1024 alcoholic patients without psychoactive drugs. JAMA 239:1409–1410, 1978

Wikler A: Diagnosis and treatment of drug dependence of the barbiturate type. Am J Psychiatr 125:758–765, 1968

Willow M, Johnston GAR: Dual action of pentobarbitone on GABA binding: role of binding site integrity. J Neurochem 37:1291–1294, 1981

Watson JM: Solvent abuse: Presentation and clinical diagnosis. Hum Toxicol 1:249–256, 1982

10

Psychological Factors Affecting Physical Conditions and Responses to Stress

Edward A. Walker and Wayne J. Katon

Although it is a difficult concept to define precisely, *stress* is a commonly experienced phenomenon. Most people have an intuitive belief that "too much of it" makes them ill, but only in the last two decades have careful methodological studies been carried out to set on firm research grounds the study of the connection between stress and medical illness. This research has elucidated several important concepts:

1. Stressful life events are correlated with increased incidence of becoming medically ill;
2. Some stressors can be perceived *positively,* others *negatively,* and this perception is mediated by cognitive "coping" mechanisms;
3. Maladaptive ways of coping with stress such as smoking and alcohol, drug, and caffeine abuse also may alter susceptibility to illness;
4. A strong social support system or network seems to buffer a patient from the effects of stress;
5. The central nervous, endocrine, and immune systems appear to have numerous previously unrecognized interconnections; and
6. An individual's response to stress may be modified by other variables such as genetic organ vulnerability (i.e., some patients develop peptic ulcers, others migraines), inherited risk of mental illness (patients with mental illness have more physical illness), and end-organ damage that results in chronic illness. This vulnerability to physical and psychological illness depends on both genetic and learned factors.

These studies have added support to the somewhat obvious idea that mind and body are inextricably intertwined and cannot be separated. Not only do stressful life events play a role in illness, but illness causes stress and affects a person's self-esteem and financial, mental, family, and vocational lives.

The Diagnostic and Statistical Manual of Mental Disorders (DSM-III-R) includes the category "Psychological Factors Affecting Physical Condition" to indicate the influence of psychological processes on the initiation or exacerbation of physical disease. It can be used to describe disorders that in the past were termed "psychosomatic" or "psychophysiologic" and may include such conditions as tension headache, diabetes, angina pectoris, obesity, gastric ulcer, rheumatoid arthritis, asthma, ulcerative colitis, and many others. In each case environmental factors must be temporally related to the onset or worsening of the symptoms or disease.

This chapter will concentrate on the role that psychological and psychosocial variables play not in causing disease but in altering individual susceptibility to disease. There is no controversy about the importance of physical factors as being etiologic in disease onset, but we will stress the notion that *the development of disease is a multifactorial process involving a complex interplay between the environment and humans as psychobiological organisms* (see Chapters 1 and 2). Finally, we will review the evidence describing the physiologic connections between mind and body: the autonomic nervous system, the neuroendocrine system, and the immune system.

A CASE STUDY

Mr. R is a 30-year-old man who presented to the family medicine clinic with a 2-month history of abdominal bloating and epigastric pain. Over the preceding 14 days, he had noticed increasing fatigue, had passed several black, tarry stools, and had been having trouble running his business as a fence builder due to lack of energy. He had a family history of peptic ulcer disease. On physical exam he was found to be quite pale and had epigastric pain to palpation and tachycardia. On lab exam he was found to have guaiac positive stool and a hematocrit of 15. The patient was admitted to the hospital and workup revealed a duodenal ulcer. The patient made a rapid recovery on cimetidine and antacids despite refusing blood transfusion due to religious beliefs (he was a Jehovah's Witness).

In reviewing the patient's life circumstances before the development of illness, many stressful life events were elicited. The patient had undergone a traumatic divorce a year and a half before admission. He and his wife had joint custody of their two children. Despite the divorce, the patient's wife handled the accounting, telephones, and business contracts for his fence-building company. A year before admission, the patient had discovered that she had embezzled $12,000, and he was already several thousand dollars in debt to the Internal Revenue Service.

The patient was raised in a family with little emotional support and a distant, critical father. He worked very hard to win his father's affection but was constantly frustrated. His style of coping with stress based on this family experience was to trust few people, to work hard, and to rely only on himself and perhaps his wife. He perceived his wife's embezzlement as a disaster financially and emotionally and felt he no longer could trust anyone. He fired his staff and worked 12 to 14 hours a day, 7 days a week, to handle the threat and anxiety of potential bankruptcy. Thus, he coped by withdrawing from people, relying even less on others (virtually no social support), working harder, and trying to deny his hurt and anger toward his wife. He began to feel progressively worn out about 6 months before admission and admitted to depressed mood, anxiety, insomnia, decreased energy, and at times feelings of hopelessness (he developed a clinical depression as his coping mechanisms were overwhelmed).

Nevertheless he continued to work hard, and about 2 months before admission began to experience abdominal pain. He admitted to distrusting doctors ("they're only out to rob you") and therefore waited until he could barely drag himself into the clinic, again using coping mechanisms of denial and minimization toward his physical condition. This was even more dramatic considering his religious beliefs prohibiting blood transfusions.

As can be seen in Figure 1, illness onset is multifactorial in origin. This is essential for the clinician to understand, because treatment can then be targeted

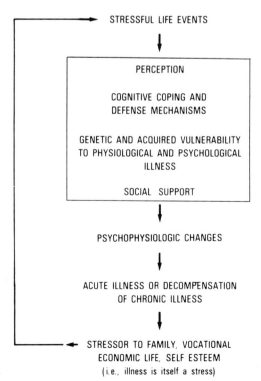

Figure 10–1. *Model of illness onset.*

specifically at both biological and psychosocial problems. For instance, the above patient's peptic ulcer was treated with cimetidine and antacids; his depression, anxiety, and rigid coping mechanisms were treated by counseling from his family physician and by training in relaxation techniques. The patient successfully used his illness experience as a chance for growth: he began to take more recreational time, hired a staff again, acquired a bank loan to stabilize his business, and became adept at relaxation techniques that decreased his anxiety. At 6-month follow-up he was asymptomatic and felt he was coping with interpersonal relationships better than before his illness.

HISTORICAL/PHILOSOPHICAL OVERVIEW

Our concepts of mind and body are the product of a long evolution that naturally followed the sociocultural, scientific, and philosophical trends of each period of history. Although the ancient Greek physicians discriminated soma (body) and psyche (mind), they frequently blurred the distinction between them. Lacking modern methods of physiological investigation, they could only speculate on the nature of this relationship, and Galen, one of the foremost physicians of his time, concluded that the brain was merely an organ required for cooling the blood.

This classical view continued as late as the 17th century, and many diseases were thought to be caused by emotions (known as "passions"). The Hippocratic legacy of physiology included combinations of four basic "humors" (yellow bile, black bile, phlegm, and blood) that corresponded with personality types such as pessimistic melancholic, irritable choleric, apathetic, phlegmatic, or optimistically sanguine. The integration of mind and body was presumed, and the intuitive appeal of this understanding must have been powerful. The physical manifestations of such mental states as fear and anger are hard to ignore, and when strong emotions precipitated symptoms such as chest pain or death it provided "evidence" for the physical potency of the passions.

A major conceptual change occurred as the new scientific method of the 17th century combined with the philosophy of René Descartes. Causality, observation, and measurement were given new emphasis as the desire increased for understanding the structure of the universe and its component parts. Against the background of this new scientific method, Descartes advanced his philosophy of separating the thinking mind (*res cogitans*) from the physical body (*res extensa*), a division that fundamentally changed the way physicians thought about the mind and body. This so-called *Cartesian dualism* persisted for centuries in a reduced, simplified, and somewhat distorted version and formed what some authorities believe to be the basis for contemporary misunderstandings about the true nature of mind and body. The legacy of this conceptual framework is seen in the thinking of many current physicians who seek to divide "organic" from "psychological" disease and who speak of "psychiatric overlays" on physical conditions, as if by removing the "overlay" the patient would return to a state of pristine organic disease. The actual contributions of Descartes' writings to dualistic notions of mind-body remain controversial.

Another landmark occurred in the late 19th century with Sigmund Freud and his contemporaries. Freud, originally a neurologist, became interested in patients with multiple somatic symptoms in whom no organic pathology could be found. These patients, known as hysterics, were problematic to his physician colleagues, who tried various remedies without relief. His followers began to postulate the existence of specific personality types and later psychodynamic conflicts and attitudes as the cause of specific physiologic conditions.

One of these theorists, Franz Alexander, formulated the *specificity theory,* the assertion that chronic suppression of emotional tension would lead to discharge in autonomic nervous system pathways, causing structural change in specific tissues and organs. The so-called "holy seven" psychosomatic illnesses (essential hypertension, bronchial asthma, neurodermatitis, ulcerative colitis, peptic ulcer, rheumatoid arthritis, and thyrotoxicosis) became the classic paradigms of this new school, with the idea that they were each caused by a specific type of psychopathology. *The experimental evidence has not supported this, and the theory is no longer widely held.* One of the only vestiges of the *specificity theory* is the possibility that the Type A personality (characterized by urgency, striving for achievement, and hostility) is a risk factor for coronary artery disease (CAD). Recent critiques of Type A personality research have found that not all the Type A personality characteristics are equally associated with this increased risk; hostility and cynicism are believed by some to be more strongly correlated with CAD (Koskenvuo et al., 1988).

The early promise of psychiatric research in providing specific connections between mind and body gradually fell into disrepute as the fragile research underpinnings by and large did not stand the test of time. (Exceptions included Pavlov's studies on conditioned reflex, Cannon's work on the "fight or flight" response, Wolff's studies of gastric acid secretion, and Selye's work on stress and cortisol.) With the tremendous technological specialty thrust of medicine, much of this psychosomatic framework fell into disregard. Medicine was taught as the study of physiologic organic illness and psychiatry as the study of psychological illness. A patient's illness was worked up biomedically, and when an organic etiology was not found, the patient could then be referred to a psychiatrist.

This dualistic view of mind and body was based on a model of the physical universe that employed the linear cause-and-effect rules of classical mechanics. During the mid-20th century, a new model of causality was developed by von Bertilanffy and Bateson, who saw the universe from a *systems perspective: systems have self-regulating properties that create a circular cause and effect.* Take, for example, a room with an unregulated heat source. Turn on the heat source, and the room will continue to grow increasingly warm, limited only by the maximum output of the heater and the insulation of the room. But connect a thermostat to the heater, and a system has been created. Now the temperature can be narrowly controlled by regulating the thermostat. All living things depend on this type of homeostatic equilibrium, nesting systems within systems to maintain life.

Noting this complexity of living things, George Engel, an internist with training in psychoanalysis, in 1977 proposed the "biopsychosocial model" as a paradigm for explaining the multiple ways in which an organism's physical health could be modified not only by physical pathogens, but also by learning, cultural norms, and mental processes. Largely derived from the psychobiological theories of Adolf Meyer, Engel popularized a model of disease not simply as a reductionistic chain of physical events, but more of a complex summation of organic, psychological, and social variables, each capable of exerting profound effects on the outcome of disease. But despite patients' instinctive grasp of these connections between mind, body, and stress, many physicians continue to maintain an archaic, dualistic philosophy that sacrifices common sense for the sake of "scientific" method.

STRESS AND DISEASE

The word "stress" has been used to refer to an aversive stimulus event, a specific physiological or psychological response, or a special type of transaction between the person and the environment (Cohen, 1981). Confusion is avoided if each of these is specified separately. Thus we will distinguish stressors (or stress events) from the psychological state of stress (feelings of threat, harm, or loss) and from stress responses (or physiologic, psychological, or social levels). Stressful life events involve change, ongoing positive or negative environmental conditions, and specific types of situations of monotony where no change has occurred when change may have been expected (i.e., there is a difference between expectation and actuality, such as not getting an anticipated promotion at work).

During the mid-19th century there was a growing awareness of the ability of stress to influence morbidity and mortality, but not until the 1950s did well-designed studies investigate this relationship. In a pioneering prospective study of pulmonary tuberculosis patients, Holmes (1961) found that those patients who got better had a number of psychosocial assets: strong family ties, steady employment, adequate income and job satisfaction, regular recreation, frequent social participation, flexibility and reliability, realistic goals, and adequate or good performance. Those patients who did not get better were lacking in these areas. He soon moved from the study of chronic illness to ask whether it was possible to make predictions about the onset of illness (i.e., why people get sick when they do).

Based on this experience, Holmes and Rahe (1967) developed the Schedule of Recent Life Events (SRE) (Table 1) to provide a unique method for a quantitative definition of life crisis. The SRE is a checklist of 43 events requiring various degrees of adaptation (losses, childbirth, catastrophe, success). Each life change is assigned a particular number of life change units (LCUs); death of a spouse, for example, is rated at 100 LCUs. Within a particular time, the individual accumulates an LCU score. Holmes and Rahe found almost linear relationships between LCU scores and the number of illnesses experienced. This effect was most marked in the 6 months after these life events. No preponderance of particular illnesses was apparent; all categories were found. Thus, the more LCUs an individual accumulated, the more likely he or she was to experience illnesses of all kinds in the following 2 years.

In retrospective studies, Holmes and Rahe found that 30 to 35% of individuals with low life change scores (in the range of 100), 50% of those in the intermediate range (200 LCU range), and 80% of those in the high range (300 LCUs) developed illness in the following 2 years. In prospective studies, a very similar picture emerged: about 80% of the high-risk group, about 50% of the medium-risk group, and about 30%

Table 10–1 **The Social Readjustment Rating Scale**

LIFE EVENT	MEAN VALUE
Death of a spouse	100
Divorce	73
Marital separation	65
Jail term	63
Death of a close family member	63
Personal injury or illness	53
Marriage	50
Fired at work	47
Marital reconciliation	45
Retirement	45
Change in health of family member	44
Pregnancy	40
Sex difficulties	39
Gain of new family member	39
Business readjustment	39
Change in financial state	38
Death of a close friend	37
Change to different line of work	36
Change in number of arguments with spouse	35
Foreclosure of mortgage or loan	30
Change in responsibilities at work	29
Son or daughter leaving home	29
Trouble with in-laws	29
Outstanding personal achievement	28
Spouse began or stopped work	26
Begin or end school	26
Change in living conditions	25
Revision of personal habits	24
Trouble with boss	23
Change in work hours or conditions	20
Change in residence	20
Change in schools	20
Change in recreation	19
Change in church activities	19
Change in social activities	18
Change in sleeping habits	16
Change in number or family get-togethers	15
Change in eating habits	15
Vacation	13
Christmas	12
Minor violations of the law	11

of the low-risk group got sick. A variety of such studies have indicated a positive relationship between life change and onset of a number of psychiatric, medical, and surgical diseases.

Across all cultures, death of a spouse is consistently rated as the most significant life change correlated with increased morbidity and mortality. Numerous studies have shown that, during the first 6 months after bereavement, there is a significant increase in death and illness of the surviving spouse, especially widowers, compared to expected rates for age (Raphael, 1987). There is emerging evidence that this involves a process of alteration of immune system function; this will be addressed later in this chapter.

Although most investigators now agree that there is a statistical correlation between life change scores and the development of illness, the correlations are low (i.e., life change units are probably only one of the variables involved). Most researchers agree that stress-induced illness is caused by chronic physiologic arousal, but evidence is mounting that the stress of adapting to new situations is buffered by the person's perception or cognitive appraisal of the events and by his or her coping or defense mechanisms, social support systems, and degree of genetic physical vulnerability.

Perception of Life Change Events

Events that are stressful for one person may not be stressful for another. Thus, if a person has adequate resources to meet a challenge or does not believe danger exists, no stress reaction may be found. Lazarus (1977) has pointed out that a stimulus can evoke a stress reaction by psychophysiological means only if it is interpreted by the individual as harmful or threatening so that coping processes are brought into play to minimize potential harm. The LCU methodology of Holmes and Rahe made no attempt to separate negative or positive life events, yet there is evidence they may have different physiological consequences. For example, although cortisol, catecholamines, and growth hormone rise after negative life events, only catecholamines show a rise after pleasant events (Rose, 1980). Further, the undesirable life events are stronger predictors of disease outcomes (Vinokur, 1975). Rahe, recognizing the impact of perception of life change, has modified the SRE so that in recent prospective studies subjects now not only list their life changes but score their own LCUs subjectively according to the degree of life adjustment needed to handle the event.

Hinkle et al. (1958) also found that episodes of illness are not randomly distributed among the population. They found in several large populations that 25% of the people experienced 50% of the episodes over a 20-year period. Individuals often experienced illnesses in clusters, and the clusters were most apt to occur when the individuals perceived they were having difficulty adapting to the environment.

Coping and Defense Mechanisms

"Coping," defined by the dictionary as struggling or contending, describes behavior that involves physical and especially emotional energy and attention to deal with some difficult circumstances. Lazarus (1977) defined two types of coping or self-regulation of a perceived stress. In one, called "direct action," the person tries to alter or master the troubled interaction with the environment (i.e., by attempting to demolish, avoid, or flee the harmful agent, or to prepare somehow to meet the danger). A student facing an important and potentially threatening examination who spends the anticipatory interval immersed in preparation is engaged in direct action forms of coping, whether these are effective or ineffective. *This sense of mastery and readiness, regardless of whether or not it is realistic, mitigates the stress reaction before the threat must be faced.*

A second coping mechanism, called "palliation," occurs when direct action is too costly to undertake, or when the person cannot successfully manage the environmental transaction. Such modes of control include ego defenses (i.e., denial, minimization), taking tranquilizers, alcohol, or sleeping pills, or engaging in techniques like muscle relaxation, jogging, or yoga. These palliative forms of coping are focused on possible ways of reducing the affective, visceral, or motor disturbances that are distressing the person, as opposed to attempts to master the environmental transaction on which the stress reaction depends. This decrease in distressing symptoms may enable the person to think more clearly and solve the problem or even confront situations he or she would normally avoid.

Numerous studies have shown that the way an individual copes may reduce physiological arousal in the face of stressful events. For example, patients with myocardial infarction who use denial and minimization as major ways of coping with their anxiety about death and disability have fewer potentially fatal arrhythmias (Freeman, 1987). It is also known that patients whose coping ability has become overwhelmed are prone to psychological decompensation and the development of mental illness such as depression, anxiety attacks, or psychosis. They subsequently have two to four times the prevalence of medical illness (Hankin, 1979). Patients who inherit or acquire (through early childhood traumatic experience) susceptibility to mental illness under stress are also more likely to develop medical illness.

Social Support

Recent research suggests that people with social support are protected in crisis from a variety of pathological states (Bebbington, 1987). It is thought that supports buffer the individual from the potentially negative effects of crisis and can facilitate coping and adaptation. There is evidence that those with social supports and assets may live longer and have a lower incidence of somatic illness and more positive mental health. Studies on marital status and health consistently reveal that married people have lower mortality rates than single, widowed, or divorced individuals (Ortmeyer, 1974). These risks are consistently higher for men than women and seem to decline with age.

Brown et al. (1978) studied the incidence of major depressive disorders in 458 women who had been exposed to stressful life events. They found that women with high degrees of stress and little support had four times the rate of depression than women with equal degrees of stress but more support. They concluded that a confiding, intimate relationship with a spouse buffered the person from high amounts of stress.

In a multivariate analysis of a 5-year prospective study of the development of new angina pectoris among 10,000 adult men, Medalie and Goldbourt (1976) found seven risk factors: anxiety, severe family problems, age, total serum cholesterol, systolic or diastolic blood pressure, certain electrocardiographic abnormalities, and diabetes mellitus. They found that the man's subjective perception of a high degree of love and support from his wife reduced the risk of angina pectoris even in the presence of high risk factors. Similarly, in a large prospective study of men who had had myocardial infarction, Ruberman et al. (1984) found that socially isolated men with high life stress had four times the risk of cardiac death compared with their non-isolated counterparts with low stress.

Dudley et al. (1977) studied 240 patients with chronic lung disease for 5 years. He found that 75% quit smoking on their own initiative, but those who could not quit had significantly less social support and less psychological stability. The patients with low psychosocial assets seemed to need cigarettes to help them cope with life.

Lack of family support also has been shown to influence the incidence of streptococcal pharyngeal infections. Meyer and Haggerty (1962) prospectively studied 76 families for a year with systematic throat cultures for hemolytic streptococci. Acute or chronic family stressors appeared to influence not only whether an individual became ill following colonization, but also the degree of postinfection antistreptolysin-O titers.

Biological Predisposition to Stress-Induced Illness

Another component in the multifactorial causation of onset of illness is the patient's health and organ susceptibility to illness. We have already alluded to biological and learned predispositions to mental illness. Many patients also have diseases such as angina pectoris, duodenal ulcers, and juvenile onset diabetes mellitus. Stress may play some role in causing especially the first two illnesses, but there is no doubt that once the disease is present these patients have an increased biological susceptibility to stress. That is, once end-organ damage has occurred, the patient is more likely to respond to stressful events with an exacerbation of chronic illness symptoms, despite a prior history of adequate coping with an identical stressor.

Thus, acute stressors appear to be greater risk factors for sudden cardiac death for individuals who already have some form of heart pathology, usually ischemic heart disease (Lown, 1980). Similarly acutely stressful life events may not necessarily predispose individuals to schizophrenia; however, they are associated with exacerbation or precipitation of an episode of the illness in some vulnerable individuals (Bebbington, 1987).

Psychophysiological Pathways

Evidence has been presented that stressful life events are important factors in the onset of illness. But what are the pathways and mechanisms that mediate the body's reaction to stress? Although much of the picture is as yet unclear, the hypothalamus appears to act as a central mediator for the coordinated regulation of the autonomic nervous, immune, and neuroendocrine systems. This phylogenetically ancient part of the brain integrates cortical (cognitive), limbic (emotional), and autonomic (visceral) inputs and controls many of the neural and endocrine systems required for both homeostasis and rapid adaptation. The affected tissues and organs complete the cycle by feeding back to the higher initiating and regulating centers. The hypothalamus appears to be the locus where psychological stress may be converted into physiological function (see Fig. 2).

The hypothalamus contains the nuclei of the autonomic nervous system, which are grouped into two divisions, the parasympathetic and sympathetic. They innervate the viscera and many hormone-secreting cells. Thus, the pancreatic insulin cells are directly contacted both by sympathetic and parasympathetic nerves, which respectively suppress and stimulate insulin secretion (Sterling, 1981).

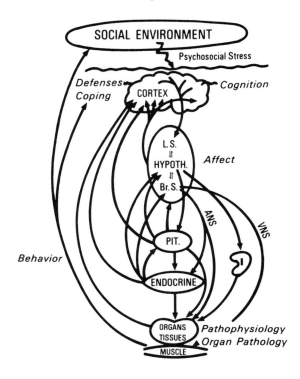

Figure 10–2. *Psychophysiologic pathways of the stress response. (Reproduced with permission from Reiser MF: The psychophysiology of stress and coping. In: Psychophysiology—Report Number 1. Philadelphia: SmithKline, 1980)*

L.S.=Limbic System
Br.S.=Brain Stem
HYPOTH.=Hypothalamus
PIT.=Pituitary
ANS=Autonomic Nervous System
VNS=Voluntary Nervous System
I=Immune System

The brain also influences the body's hormones through its own chemical messengers. Some act directly on peripheral tissues, others act on peripheral hormone-secreting cells, and still others act on the pituitary, which controls both peripheral tissues and endocrine organs. Both the cellular and humoral arms of the immune system also appear to be under the control of the brain through these hormones.

What is the reason for these central controls, since there are local self-regulating controls of physiological homeostasis (blood pressure, serum glucose level)? Neural controls permit hormonal and organ changes to occur in anticipation of changes in local feedback systems; such anticipatory changes then can reduce the size and length of metabolic fluctuations. Additionally, most processes in the body cannot be kept constant and must vary by the demands of the environment on the organism. Blood pressure must be able to vary with changes in demands (i.e., sudden fright, sexual intercourse, taking a test). If the only controls over blood pressure were local, it would be impossible to have such adaptive changes in blood pressure because every deviation from the "normal" would be automatically corrected (Sterling, 1981).

Broad Patterns of Neuroendocrine and Neuroimmune Response

Probably as a result of the experience of our primitive ancestors, we have evolved a complex but efficient energy management system that reacts flexibly to changes in our environment. Our nervous, endocrine, and immune systems have two basic states of readiness, one vegetative and reparative, the other highly responsive to impending or actual danger. The evolutionary value of both of these states is obvious in a hostile, unpredictable environment, but our primordial physiology, designed for coping with episodic, intense stress, is ill equipped to deal with the chronic, variable-level stressors of modern life.

These hormonal, autonomic, and immune system changes are under the control of subcortical centers (the hypothalamus is probably the central control) that coordinate autonomic, somatic, and psychic functions. These have been labeled ergotropic and trophotropic systems and they are reciprocally balanced (Kiely, 1974). The ergotropic system integrates functions that prepare the individual for positive action. It is characterized by alerting, arousal, excitement, increased skeletal muscle tone and sympathetic nervous system activity, and the release of catabolic hormone products. It is similar to Cannon's description of the "flight or fight" response but includes many changes in sympathetic discharge and neuroendocrine and behavioral parameters.

This ergotropic system must quickly mobilize energy to deal with the environmental demand. Complex molecules are broken down into component parts such as free fatty acids and glucose that can be rapidly converted into energy. Reproductive and reparative processes are slowed. The thymus shrinks and the levels of antibodies and white cells in the blood fall. Increased cardiac output and blood pressure speed extra blood to the tissues. Flow to the heart, muscles, and brain must be maintained or increased and flow to the gut, kidney, and skin is decreased because the blood is needed elsewhere (Sterling, 1981). Cannon in the early part of the century noted that during arousal, as in preparation for "fight or flight," there was not only an increase in blood pressure but also a change in blood flow. More blood was delivered to the heart and skeletal muscles and less to the skin, gut, and kidneys. Later, Selye showed that cortisol is also secreted during arousal and makes an important contribution to this mobilization. In recent years, with improved technology for measuring hormones in the blood, investigators have shown an increase in a whole group of hormones during arousal (see Table 2). Correspondingly, there are decreases in hormones whose functions include energy storage, growth, renewal, repair, and maintenance of surveillance against infectious agents and the body's own malignant cells.

The trophotropic system, on the other hand, reverses this process and integrates systems that promote withdrawal and conservation of energy: raising of the stimulus barrier to perceptual input, decreased skeletal muscle tone, increased parasympathetic nervous function, and the circulation of anabolic hormones. This system is turned on by relaxation or lack of perceived threat.

The anabolic hormones promote energy storage, growth, renewal, repair, and

Table 10–2 **Stress-induced Changes in Hormones**

CATABOLIC HORMONES INCREASE	ANABOLIC HORMONES DECREASE
Cortisol	Insulin
Epinephrine	Calcitonin
Glucagon	Testosterone
Growth hormone	Estrogen
Antidiuretic hormone	Prolactin
Renin	Luteinizing hormone
Angiotensin	Follicle-stimulating hormone
Aldosterone	Gonadotropin-releasing hormone
Erythropoietin	Prolactin-releasing hormone
Thyroxin	
Parathormone	
Melatonin	

(Adapted from Sterling P, Eger J: Biological basis of stress-related mortality. Soc Sci Med 15E:3–42, 1981)

maintenance of surveillance against infectious agents and the body's own malignant cells. In the anabolic state the body stores energy or glycogen, fat, and protein by polymerization of glucose, fatty acids, and amino acids. These substrates are absorbed to produce new cells to replace ones that wear out continuously. For instance, the cells lining the gut are completely renewed every 24 hours. Bone is replaced by reabsorption and redeposition of calcium salts. Wounds are healed by production of new cells and by extracellular deposition of proteins. The immune system is maintained by continuous cell and antibody production in the bone marrow, lymphoid tissue, and thymus. Blood pressure in the anabolic state is relatively low (i.e., 120/75).

These two systems have a mutually reciprocal relationship and share tonic enduring physiological activity. Mild to moderate degrees of excitation of the ergotropic system produce a corresponding degree of inhibition of the trophotropic system, and vice versa. Therefore, mild to moderate arousal turns on the sympathetic system and catabolic hormones and inhibits parasympathetic discharge as well as the release of anabolic hormones. At moderate to high degrees of excitation of the trophotropic or ergotropic activation the facilitory effects are more sharply increased and reciprocal inhibition of the opposite system is maximal. Thus, in moderate to high levels of arousal the level of ergotropic tuning is very high and trophotropic responsivity becomes nil. At this level of arousal an ergotropic response may be elicited by a stimulus that normally would produce a trophotropic response. (An example here is having a difficult day at work and coming home irritable and uptight and kicking the affectionate cat or snapping at the spouse or children.)

Finally, at maximal degrees of arousal both the ergotropic and trophotropic systems discharge simultaneously (Kiely, 1974). A clinical example is the state of anxiety in which a variety of skeletal, visceral, and psychic disturbances reflect simultaneous discharge of both systems. Flooding of the cerebral cortex by afferents from both systems may be experienced as dread; weak knees and tremulous hands represent effects of skeletal muscle tone of the mixed ergotropic and trophotropic system discharge. Simultaneous activation of sympathetic and parasympathetic divisions may be expressed as sweating, tachycardia, nausea, vomiting, and bowel and bladder hyperactivity.

In summary, accompanying the shift from relaxation to arousal there is a shift in a whole pattern of hormonal secretion, as well as a shift to sympathetic nervous system discharge. The endocrine pattern in arousal promotes the mobilization of energy at the expense of maintenance and repair processes. The catabolic processes are accompanied by auxiliary mobilization of the renovascular system for conservation of salts and water. All of these shifts are initiated by the brain via control over the autonomic and endocrine systems.

For a person to remain healthy, these periods of arousal must be balanced by periods of relaxation; otherwise, there would be no replenishing of the resources exhausted by catabolism and there would be no repair of accumulated damage or vigilance against pathogens. The hypothesis from this knowledge of psychophysiological pathways as well as from stress research is that as periods of arousal (life change units) increase there is a statistically greater chance of illness. In some patients stress may become chronic as coping mechanisms are overwhelmed and the patient develops either a psychiatric illness like depression or anxiety attacks, a physical illness, or both.

Psychoneuroimmunology

An increasing body of evidence shows that the central nervous system, the endocrine system, and the immune system may have multiple bidirectional interconnections that allow mutual modulation and feedback (Stein, 1986). Since Ader coined the term "psychoneuroimmunology" in 1964 there have been numerous studies of the relationship between the immune system and stress, psychiatric illness, and environmental factors. Although results are as yet inconclusive, strong patterns have emerged that suggest a coherent theory of CNS-immune system interaction.

One of the most impressive examples of this linkage has been the ability of the immune system to be classically conditioned (Stein, 1986). For example, by repeatedly pairing oral saccharin with cyclophosphamide (an immunosuppressant), significant immunosuppression has been demonstrated on presentation of saccharin alone. *This is important because it involves a purely behavioral stimulus that cannot engage the immune response directly through a noxious effect.*

In a double-blind study (Stein, 1986) subjects were repeatedly skin-tested with tuberculin antigen on one arm and saline on the other. After five trials the syringes were reversed, and marked diminishment or absence of reaction was noticed where the saline was expected by the subject. When the identity of the test substances was revealed, a vigorous response was obtained comparable to the antigen reaction observed previously. Whether this was due to conditioning or cognitive set, the influence of higher cortical centers in modulation of the response is likely.

Kiecolt-Glaser (Kennedy, 1988) in three separate controlled studies examined the immunologic function of 75 first-year medical students during final examinations, 38 recently separated or divorced women, and 34 relatives caring for patients with

Alzheimer's disease. She observed similar quantitative and qualitative changes in immune cells in these three groups of acutely and chronically stressed individuals, including decreases in percentages of T-helper cells, decreased numbers and function of natural killer (NK) cells, and changes in herpes virus latency. Psychological variables including loneliness, lack of attachment, and depression were related to the decrements in immunologic surveillance.

Both humoral and cell-mediated immunity seem to be modulated by stress. Stress has been reported to influence the courses of certain illnesses such as asthma, strep throat, and arthritis that involve B-cell systems, but the more robust findings involve T-cell mechanisms (Stein, 1986). The importance of T-cell regulation of the entire immunologic response has been recently underscored with the epidemic of AIDS. Studies have shown that stressors such as death of a spouse, sleep deprivation, and inability to escape from a chronic physical threat can alter T-cell regulatory patterns and response to mitogens. The protective effects of coping seem to prevent this alteration. Rats exposed to a tail shock paradigm over which they had no control showed markedly diminished T-cell mitogen response compared with a second group of rats who could control the termination of the shock. This difference existed despite the fact that the groups received an equal total amount of shock (Stein, 1986).

Current state-of-the-art research in psychoneuroimmunology shows that it is in its infancy. Many substances such as cortisol, growth hormone, substance P, endorphins, opioids, and somatostatin have been shown to be immunomodulators. Innervation of the thymus, spleen, and lymph nodes has suggested possible direct CNS effects, and the continued study of the immune cell surface has demonstrated receptors for adrenergic and cholinergic neurotransmitters (Stein, 1986). Solomon (1987) has proposed more than 30 "postulates" of immune-endocrine-CNS interaction, analogous to Koch's postulates of infectious disease. As our understanding of this complex system increases, it can only add to the continued unraveling of the mystery of stress and disease.

TREATMENT STRATEGIES

Although a thorough discussion of treatment approaches is beyond the scope of this chapter, the application of certain general principles can be useful. The overall strategy is a careful understanding of the potency of the biopsychosocial model as both a diagnostic aid and treatment guide. The biopsychosocial model is, in reality, an integrated alliance of three major heuristic models: biomedical, psychodynamic, and social-behavioral (see also Chapter 2). While the treatment plan needs to reflect the physician's understanding of the mutual interdependence of these approaches, for the sake of evaluation and planning they can be usefully separated. This involves making a biomedical diagnosis, a psychological diagnosis, and a social-behavioral diagnosis, followed by a treatment plan for each.

Let us take, for example, the case of a 29-year-old woman with chronic strep throat and a major depression. From a *biomedical* standpoint, the following observations arise:

Biomedical data:
1. Vegetative symptoms secondary to hypothalamic dysregulation
2. Decreased immunologic surveillance
3. Poor nutritional status

Biomedical diagnoses:
1. Major depression
2. Streptococcal pharyngitis
3. Impaired nutrition

Biomedical treatment:
1. Antidepressant therapy
2. Antibiotic therapy
3. Nutrition education

From a *social-behavioral* viewpoint, the following observations arise:

Social-behavioral data
1. Husband physically beats patient
2. Smoking
3. Drinks too much

Social-behavioral diagnoses:
1. Physical abuse by spouse
2. Nicotine abuse
3. Alcohol abuse
4. Maladaptive coping

Social-behavioral treatment:
1. Referral to women's shelter
2. Behavior modification plan to reduce smoking and drinking
3. Alcoholics Anonymous referral
4. Supportive counseling by physician to suggest new ways of coping

Finally the *psychological* aspect:

Psychological data:
1. Patient repeatedly chooses to return to abusive partner
2. Is an adult child of alcoholic parents

Psychological diagnoses:
1. History of childhood abuse by father
2. ACOA (adult child of alcoholic) syndrome

Psychological treatment:
1. Referral for insight-oriented psychotherapy
2. Education about ACOA syndrome
3. Referral to ACOA group

By combining the distinctive viewpoints afforded by the model, an integrated treatment plan emerges that accounts for many aspects of the patient's functioning. The prescription of an antidepressant would be ineffective in the face of continued physical assault, just as progress in insight-oriented psychotherapy would be hampered by the cognitive slowing typical of pharmacologically untreated major depression.

It would be naive to think that all aspects of this plan would be immediately implemented in the first visits. However, the longitudinal perspective of primary care allows a gradual unfolding of this strategy over time, allowing to patient to proceed at her own pace. Despite the patient's apparent complexity, this model allows thoughtful, effective treatment while building the alliance between doctor and patient.

Disease onset appears to be multifactorial. Over the past century we have learned a great deal about the biological components of susceptibility to illness, yet only in the last 20 to 30 years have we rigorously examined the psychosocial factors. The challenge to medical students now is to integrate this biopsychosocial view of patients into diagnosis and treatment in a pragmatic way. We no longer view the psychosocial problems as causes of disease but as important factors in altering susceptibility to illness. As we learn more about neuroendocrine, neuroimmune, and autonomic nervous system functions it becomes more evident how important psychosocial factors are in etiology of illness. The next step is to show the efficacy of biopsychosocial treatment as compared to unidimensional biological treatment.

As demonstrated in the case study, biological treatment of the patient's ulcer disease would include cimetidine and/or antacids. The family physician in this case also prescribed relaxation techniques to decrease patient anxiety and chronic arousal and supportive therapy to help the patient develop more adaptive coping mechanisms and to provide social support. Evidence thus far has indicated that recognizing and treating psychosocial problems in primary-care clinic patients by either short-term counseling or medication leads to decreased clinic use, decreased hospitalization, less patient-reported symptomatology, and the conservation of physician time and energy.

CLINICAL PEARLS

- In the general medical setting, patients with stress-related physical symptoms are ubiquitous. Common symptoms of stress in this setting include headaches, gastrointestinal distress, insomnia, dizziness, palpitations, chest pain, gastric distress, dysuria, urinary frequency, diarrhea, nausea, sleep disturbances, decreased appetite, fatigue, and pain complaints of almost every sort.

(continued)

CLINICAL PEARLS (continued)

- These stress-related physical symptoms may also be part of or signs of anxiety disorder or major depression, or alternately an occult medical disorder. Before attributing such symptoms to "just stress," evaluate the patient medically as the symptoms indicate and for the existence of a major psychiatric disorder.
- Ask about use of tobacco, alcohol, caffeine, and sedatives. Almost all patients will attempt some form of self-medication for anxiety before seeking medical help.
- Patients use physical symptoms as a "ticket" to get psychological help even if they may not be aware of the connection between their physical symptoms and life stresses.
- Elderly patients and patients from certain sociocultural and educational backgrounds will either deny the presence of stresses or minimize them; some patients have a limited ability to verbalize feelings and psychological stresses and express their emotional stress through somatic symptoms.
- In investigating the source of a patient's stress, it is almost always essential to speak with the spouse or other family members to identify problems that the patient may be denying or of which the patient is not consciously aware.
- Most stress involves family, employment, and money. Focus on possible problems in the patient's marriage (or other close relationships), parents, children, money, and the workplace. Focus especially on whether there have been any separations or deaths in the family.
- If psychopharmacological treatment is being considered as part of the treatment in addition to office counseling or psychotherapy, physicians should consider using low-dose, mildly sedating cyclic antidepressants for insomnia and somatic symptoms of anxiety (especially GI distress) to avoid the habituating potential of benzodiazepines. Examples would include 25 to 50 mg of doxepin or imipramine at bedtime. If major depression or panic disorder is present, then patients should be treated at higher therapeutic doses as described elsewhere in this text (Chapters 6 and 7).
- If benzodiazepines are used for stress-related anxiety, they should be used in low doses for short periods of time (usually no more than 2 to 4 weeks of continuous use at a time). These drugs in general should not be routinely refilled over the telephone. Set guidelines with the initial prescription as to how long and in what amount the drugs will be used. The same general rules apply for the use of benzodiazepine sleeping pills. Consider the use of buspirone for long term treatment of chronic anxiety.
- If somatic symptoms go unexplained for several weeks and do not remit with conservative therapy, consider a psychiatric consultation for advice on diagnosis, treatment, and long-term management.
- Always be on guard for occult or intercurrent medical illness in patients prone to "psychosomatic" symptoms: you may get burned!

ANNOTATED BIBLIOGRAPHY

Ader R, ed. Psychoneuroimmunology. New York: Academic Press, 1981.

    An excellent and comprehensive review of an emerging area in psychiatry. The field of psychoneuroimmunology is supplanting older theoretical approaches of psychosomatic illness with a solid scientific basis, and this text provides the most comprehensive treatment of the subject to date.

Engel GL: The clinical application of the biopsychosocial model. Am J Psychiatry 137:535–544, 1980

    One of the best illustrations of the biopsychosocial model, comparing the management of a myocardial infarction patient using the biomedical and biopsychosocial models.

Kahana RJ, Bibring GL: Personality types in medical management. In Zinberg N (ed): Psychiatry and medical practice in a general hospital. New York, International University Press, 1966

> A classic description of personality types found in general medical settings, and how their medical care is best managed.

Kennedy S, Kiecolt-Glaser JK, Glaser R: Immunological consequences of acute and chronic stressors: Mediating role of interpersonal relationships. Br J Med Psychology 61:77–85, 1988.

> A thorough review of social support and its modulating effect on the production of medical illness.

Lipowski ZJ: Psychosomatic medicine: Past and present. Can J Psychiatry 31:2–21, 1986

> A historical overview of the development of the concept of "psychosomatic," including a summary of current and future research trends.

Stein M, Schleifer SJ, Keller SE: Brain, behavior and immune process. In: Michels R, Cavenar JO (eds): Psychiatry. Philadelphia, JB Lippincott, 1987.

> A comprehensive summary of the latest research in psychoneuroimmunology.

Vitaliano PP, Maiuro RD, Russo J, et al: A biopsychosocial model of medical student distress. J Beh Medicine 11:311–331, 1988

> An excellent overview of the stress and coping of medical students, illuminating many of the concepts in this chapter.

Weiner H, Thalen M, Reiser MF, et al: Etiology of duodenal ulcer: 1. Relation of specific psychological characteristics to rate of gastric secretion (serum pepsinogen). Psychosom Med 19:1–10, 1957

> A classic attempt to validate Franz Alexander's specificity hypothesis. Although partially flawed, this study showed that personality characteristics could be predictive of biological performance.

REFERENCES

Bebbington PE: Psychosocial etiology of schizophrenia and affective disorders. In: Michels R, Cavenar JO (eds): Psychiatry. Philadelphia, JB Lippincott, 1987

Brown GW, Harris T: Social origins of depression. London, Tavistock, 1978

Cohen F: Stress and bodily illness. Psychiatr Clin North Am, 4:269–286, 1981

Dudley DL, Aickin M, Martin CJ: Cigarette smoking in a chest clinic population—psychophysiological variables. J Psychosomatic Res 21:367–375, 1977

Engel GL: The need for a new medical model: A challenge for biomedicine. Science 196:129–136, 1977

Freeman AM, Folks DG: Psychiatric aspects of cardiovascular disease. In: Michels R, Cavenar JO (eds): Psychiatry. Philadelphia, JB Lippincott, 1987

Hankin J, Oktary JS: Mental disorder and primary care: An analytic review of the literature. US Department of Health, Education and Welfare, Publication #(ADM) 78–661. Washington DC: US Gov Printing Off, 1979

Hinkle LE, Wolff HG: Etiologic investigations of the relationships between illness, life experiences and the social environment. Ann Intern Med 49:1373–1388, 1958

Holmes T, Joffe JR, Ketchan JW, Sheehy TF: Experimental study of prognosis. J Psychosom Res 5:235–252, 1961

Holmes TH, Rahe RH: The social readjustment rating scale. J Psychosom Res 11:213–218, 1967

Kennedy S, Kiecolt-Glaser JK, Glaser R: Immunological consequences of acute and chronic stressors: Mediating role of interpersonal relationships. Br J Med Psychology 61:77–85, 1988

Kiely WF: From the symbolic stimulus to the pathophysiological response: Neurophysiological mechanisms. Int J Psychiatr Med 5:517–529, 1974

Koskenvuo M, Kaprio J, Rose RJ, et al: Hostility as a risk factor for mortality and ischemic heart disease in men. Psychosomatic Med 50:330–334, 1988

Lazarus RS: Psychological stress and coping in adaptation and illness. In: Lipowski ZJ, Lipsitt DR, Whybrow PC (eds): Psychosomatic medicine. New York, Oxford, 1977

Lown B, Desilva RA, Reich P, et al: Psychophysiological factors in sudden cardiac death. Am J Psychiatry 137:1325–1335, 1980

Medalie JH, Goldbourt U: Angina pectoris among 10,000 men. Am J Med 60:910, 1976

Meyer RJ, Haggerty RJ: Streptococcal infections in families: Factors affecting individual susceptibility. Pediatrics 29:539–549, 1962

Ortmeyer CF: Variations in mortality, morbidity and health care by marital status. In: Erhardt CF, Berlin JE (eds): Mortality and morbidity in the United States. Cambridge, Harvard University Press, 1974

Raphael B, Middleton W: Current state of research in the field of bereavement. Isr J Psychiatry Relat Sci 24:5–32, 1987

Rose RM: Endocrine responses to stressful psychological events. Psychiat Clin N Amer 3:251–276, 1980

Ruberman W, Weinblatt E, Goldberg JD, et al: Psychosocial influences on mortality after myocardial infarction. New Engl J Med 311:552–559, 1984

Solomon GF: Psychoneuroimmunology: Interactions between central nervous system and immune system. J Neuroscience Res 18:1–9, 1987

Stein M, Schleifer SJ, Keller SE: Brain, behavior and immune process. In: Michels R, Cavenar JO (eds): Psychiatry. Philadelphia, JB Lippincott, 1987

Sterling P, Eyer J: Biological basis of stress-related mortality. Soc Sci Med 15E:3–42, 1981

Vinokur A, Selzer ML: Desirable versus undesirable life events: Their relationship to stress and mental distress. J Persp Soc Psychol 32:329–337, 1975

11

Eating Disorders

Joel Yager

Cases of women who starved themselves have been reported for hundreds of years, including cases of *anorexia mirabilis* in sainted women of the middle ages and of notorious "fasting girls" of the 16th through 19th centuries. Anorexia nervosa as we now recognize it was first described in the late 1870s, and interest in the eating disorders has grown considerably over the past two decades. The 1983 death of the popular singer Karen Carpenter from anorexia nervosa resulted in a flood of television programs and magazine articles that brought considerable attention to the eating disorders. After popular magazines featured articles revealing that several female idols, including Jane Fonda and the Olympic gymnast Cathy Rigby, had suffered from bulimia nervosa, virtually every female in the United States became aware of the existence of these disorders and their attendant dangers.

EPIDEMIOLOGY

Current studies suggest that among adolescent and young adult women in certain high school and college settings, the prevalence of clinically significant eating disorders may be as high as 1 to 5%, but their prevalence elsewhere in the population is much lower (Szmukler, 1985). Individual symptoms of eating disorders (such as body image distortion, an extreme fear of being fat that is out of line with health concerns, the desire to reduce body fat to levels below those ordinarily considered healthy, restrictive and fad dieting, amphetamine and cocaine use for anorectic effects, and purging by means of vomiting, laxative abuse, diuretic abuse, and hyper-exercise) among normal weight and even underweight individuals are relatively common. Some of these general symptoms may even be seen in the majority of certain subgroups of the female population, as in select college sororities or among female dance majors (Johnson and Connors, 1987).

Males with anorexia nervosa and bulimia form the minority of cases; 90 to 95% of cases are females. The age of onset is most typically in the teenage and early adult years, but cases with prepubertal onset and with onset in the 40s and older have been reported. Although these disorders were previously associated primarily with upper and upper-middle-class Caucasians, more recent data suggest that these disorders are now well represented among middle and lower-middle-class women, including nonwhites.

DESCRIPTION, DIAGNOSTIC CRITERIA, AND DIFFERENTIAL DIAGNOSIS

Diagnostic criteria for the eating disorders have been the subject of much discussion and recent revision. A summary of current DSM-III-R criteria is shown in Table 1. Primary symptoms for both anorexia nervosa and bulimia nervosa are a preoccupation with weight and the desire to be thinner. The two disorders are *not* mutually exclusive, and there appears to be a continuum among patients of the two symptom complexes, self-starvation and the binge-purge cycle: about 50% of patients with anorexia nervosa also have bulimia nervosa, and many patients with bulimia nervosa may have previously had at least a subclinical form of anorexia nervosa. Table 2 shows differential diagnosis of binge eating and vomiting.

Anorexia Nervosa

Although the diagnosis of anorexia nervosa requires a loss of weight to a level at least 15% below expected, many patients have lost considerably more by the time they come to medical attention. Patients engage in a variety of behaviors to lose weight. In addition to a markedly reduced caloric intake (usually 300 to 600 calories/day), strange dietary rituals include refusing to eat in front of others, avoiding entire classes of food, and using unusual spice and flavoring practices, such as putting huge quan-

---

Table 11-1 **Diagnosis of Anorexia Nervosa and Bulimia Nervosa**

Anorexia Nervosa:

The patient refuses to maintain her body weight at a minimal normal weight for age and height, leading to maintenance of body weight 15 percent below expected; or fails to gain weight as expected during growth, leading to body weight 15 percent below expected.

Even though underweight, the patient intensely fears gaining weight or becoming fat.

The patient experiences her body weight, size, or shape in a disturbed fashion (e.g., claiming to "feel fat" even when clearly underweight).

In female patients, at least three consecutive missed menstrual cycles that would otherwise be expected to occur (primary or secondary amenorrhea). (Women are considered to have amenorrhea if periods occur only following hormone administration.)

Bulimia Nervosa:

Repeated episodes of rapidly binge-eating large amounts of food in brief periods of time.

During binges, the patient feels that the eating is out of control.

The patient regularly self-induces vomiting, uses large amounts of laxatives or diuretics, fasts, diets very strictly, and/or exercises vigorously to prevent weight gain.

At least two binge-eating episodes per week for a minimum of 3 months.

Unrelenting overconcern with weight and body shape.

(Adapted from DSM III-R 1987)

Table 11–2 **Differential Diagnosis of Binge Eating and Vomiting**

Binge Eating

Bulimia nervosa
Binge eating in obesity
CNS lesions (e.g., Kleine-Levin syndrome, seizures, and rarely tumors)
Appetite increases due to metabolic conditions or drugs
Other psychiatric disorders such as schizophrenia, mania, atypical
  depression

Vomiting

CNS causes (e.g., increased intracranial pressure, tumor, seizure
  disorder)
Gastrointestinal causes (e.g., mechanical obstruction, infections, toxins,
  metabolic, allergic, "functional")
Migraine
Instrumental (goal-directed) vomiting (e.g., wrestlers before a match to
  reduce weight)
Psychogenic vomiting (other psychiatric disorders such as anxiety,
  conversion disorders)

---

tities of pepper or lemon juice on all foods. Some patients exercise compulsively for hours each day; non-eating-related compulsions such as cleaning and counting rituals are not uncommon. Although patients may initially seem cheerful and energetic, about half will develop an accompanying major depression, and all will become moody and irritable. Many complain of having no real sense of self apart from the anorexia nervosa.

Weight losses of 30 to 40% below normal are not unusual. Accompanying these losses are signs and symptoms indicative of the physical complications of starvation: depletion of fat, muscle wasting (including cardiac muscle loss in severe cases), bradycardia and other arrhythmias, constipation, abdominal pains, leukopenia, hypercortisolemia, osteoporosis, and in extreme cases the development of cachexia and lanugo (fine babylike hair over the body). Metabolic alterations that conserve energy are seen in thyroid function (low T3 syndrome) and reproductive function, with a marked drop or halt in the secretion of luteinizing hormone (LH) and follicle-stimulating hormone (FSH). All female patients stop menstruating; up to a third stop menstruating even before losing sufficient body fat to account for the onset of amenorrhea.

Anorexia nervosa appears in two general varieties, the *restrictor* and *bulimic* subtypes, although these may occasionally alternate in the same patient. The *restrictor* tends to exert maximal self-control regarding food intake and tends to be socially avoidant, withdrawn, and isolated. She tends to have an obsessional thinking style and is ritualistic in nonfood areas. In contrast, the *bulimic* subtype cannot restrain herself from frequent food binges and purges by means of vomiting. She may ingest extremely large quantities of laxatives and/or diuretics to further weight loss and is commonly depressed and self-destructive. She often displays the emotional, dramatic, and erratic personality cluster and not infrequently abuses alcohol and drugs.

Full recovery within a few years is seen in 30 to 50% of patients. Younger-onset patients and those of the restrictor subtype appear to have a better prognosis. Death from starvation, sudden cardiac arrhythmias, and suicide occurs in 5 to 10% of patients within 10 years and in almost 20% of patients within 20 years of onset (Garfinkel and Garner, 1982; Hsu 1987).

A CASE STUDY

A 24-year-old graduate student with a weight of 76 pounds and a height of 5'4" was brought in by her husband because she was fainting repeatedly and would not permit herself to eat despite his pleas and concerns for her safety. For the past 4 years her weight had never exceeded 90 pounds, and she had not had a menstrual period since age 16. She permitted herself to eat only tiny bits of white-colored food, and only from someone else's plate. She did 200 pushups and sit-ups each morning; if she lost count, she was obliged to start at the beginning. She also swam 32 laps each day. On days when she permitted herself an extra morsel and thereby considered herself "bad," she would force herself to swim an additional even number of laps in multiples of four, or she would take handfuls of laxatives to induce severe cramps and diarrhea, both as a punishment and to ensure that she lost additional weight. In spite of these limitations she was able to carry out complex and demanding intellectual assignments in her courses. Under duress, she finally agreed to gain weight, but could do so only by an extremely ritualistic diet of carefully measured amounts of cheese and ice cream.

Bulimia Nervosa

This disorder occurs predominantly in weight-preoccupied females (90 to 95%) who engage in marked eating binges and purging episodes at least twice a week for 3 consecutive months, using any or all of the purging behaviors described for the bulimic subtype of anorexia nervosa. Although most patients with bulimia nervosa appear never to have had frank anorexia nervosa, a past history of the disorder or many of its individual features is not uncommon. Patients frequently consume 2000 to 10,000 calories per binge, and binge-purge cycles may occur as frequently as several times per day. Patients always feel as if their eating is out of control and are often secretive about their problem out of shame. Up to 75% of patients have a concurrent major depression or anxiety disorder (Johnson and Connors, 1987).

Physical complications of binge-purge cycles include fluid and electrolyte abnormalities with hypochloremic hypokalemic alkalosis, esophageal and gastric irritation and bleeding, large bowel abnormalities due to laxative abuse, marked erosion of dental enamel with accompanying decay, and parotid and salivary gland hypertrophy ("squirrel face") with hyperamylasemia of about 25 to 40% above normal (Mitchell et al., 1987).

When untreated, the disorder is often chronic, lasting years to decades, but may tend toward slight spontaneous improvement in symptoms (Yager et al., 1988). Other aspects of outcome are discussed in the treatment section.

A CASE STUDY

An 18-year-old, athletically built college freshman had been bulimic since age 15, gorging an estimated 5000 to 20,000 calories of junk food each evening after her family went to bed and vomiting repeatedly when she felt painfully full. The disorder began at a time when her mother became seriously depressed about the deteriorating health of her own alcoholic mother. In addition to feeling out of control and despondent about her eating, the patient had been sexually promiscuous since age 16 and since starting college had been drinking heavily and using cocaine whenever it was available. Treatment ultimately required programs that addressed her substance abuse problems as well as the eating and mood disorders.

ETIOLOGY AND PATHOGENESIS

Theories regarding the etiology and pathogenesis of the eating disorders have implicated virtually every level of biopsychosocial organization.

Biological Theories

Several biological causes have been proposed. According to one popular theory, a hypothalamic or suprahypothalamic abnormality accounts for the profound disturbances seen in eating-disorder patients in the secretion of luteinizing hormone (LH), follicle-stimulating hormone (FSH), cortisol, and arginine-vasopressin, among other hormones and peptides, and for abnormalities in opioid and catecholamine metabolism (Garfinkel and Garner, 1982). Although this theory may prove to be at least partly valid, it is based exclusively on data from patients who are already starving or nutritionally unbalanced; no firm support for this theory is as yet available from potentially predisposed but unaffected patients such as unaffected twins or younger sisters of affected patients. Biological data from patients who have recovered and have stabilized for long enough periods of time virtually always show a return to normal values.

Another theory suggests that some eating disorders, particularly bulimic syndromes, may be variants of mood disorders. Supporting arguments include the frequent comorbidity of affective disturbances with eating disorders, an increased prevalence of mood disturbance in first-degree relatives of bulimic patients, and responses by bulimic patients to antidepressants.

Genetically transmitted vulnerability cannot be ruled out, although exactly what the vulnerability might be is obscure. Eating disorders have a familial pattern of transmission, but such patterns do not necessarily suggest genetic as opposed to environmental influences (Yager, 1982). However, the largest series of twins shows a much higher concordance for anorexia nervosa among monozygotic (about 50%) than dizygotic (about 14%) twins, suggesting that some genetic influences may be important (Crisp et al., 1985).

Still another theory suggests that the process of dieting and exercise produces an autointoxication with endogenous opioids (essentially an altered state of consciousness as a consequence of the starvation state); at a certain point, this autointoxication creates an autoaddiction to internally generated opioids. According to this theory, subsequent starvation and exercise are maintained in an effort to continue to generate enough endogenous opioids to sustain the good feelings initially produced (Marrazzi and Luby, 1986).

Aside from these speculative theories, the primary biological influences in the pathogenesis of eating-disorder symptoms are those related to starvation and malnutrition per se. Studies with starving normal volunteers have demonstrated that many of the psychopathological as well as physical signs and symptoms of eating disorders are attributable to starvation. Of course, starvation produces all the organ wasting and laboratory findings described above (Garfinkel and Garner, 1982). More interesting from the point of view of the pathogenesis of psychopathology is the observation that starved normal volunteers become depressed, irritable, and preoccupied with food. They hoard food, develop abnormal taste preferences, and binge when food is readily available. Further, in one study in which previously normal volunteers were starved over a period of several months to 25% below their usual, healthy weights, full psychological recovery did not occur until 6 months to a year after the subjects had regained all their lost weight. In other words, many of the strange and bizarre psychological symptoms, including compulsive rituals and markedly disturbed personality traits, may *result from,* rather than cause, the severe starvation. Many other psychopathological features of patients with severe anorexia nervosa, such as immature cognitive capacity as evidenced by a decrease in the ability to verbalize feelings, the complexity of cognition, and the use of fantasy, also appear related to weight loss rather than to premorbid immaturity; these symptoms improve with weight gain unrelated to psychotherapy. Of course, there do seem to be psychopathological features that antedate the severe weight loss as well.

Psychological Theories

Hypotheses regarding possible psychological factors in etiology and pathogenesis have been derived from classical, operant, cognitive, and social learning theories; psychodynamic schools, including classical psychoanalysis, ego psychology, object relations, and self psychology theories; existential psychology; and several schools of family theory (Garner and Garfinkel, 1985). Accordingly, it is thought that eating disorders may result from the following (not necessarily mutually exclusive) processes:

1. Maladaptive learned responses, based on classical or operant conditioning principles, that reduce anxiety. In the patient with anorexia nervosa these responses may take the form of food and/or weight phobias. In the patient with bulimia, inner tension states may be relieved by excessive eating. (In many families, children at a very young age learn, and may be actively taught, to use food for stress reduction.) Immediately thereafter, the anxiety generated by the shame, guilt, and loss of self control brought about by the binge is in turn relieved by purging.

2. Cognitive distortions that develop in efforts to reduce and manage anxiety in socially awkward and sensitive adolescents (as well as in others). These misguided and erroneous self-statements tend to confuse self-worth with physical appearance. The self-statements are constantly repeated as preconscious inner thoughts, cycled over and over in a ruminative fashion, and have a self-reinforcing quality so that they become overlearned shibboleths. The thinking distortions include tendencies to overgeneralize; to magnify things out of proportion (making a mountain out of a molehill); to think in "all-or-none," black-and-white terms; to take everything personally; and to think superstitiously. Examples include such self-statements as, "If I gain 1 pound, everyone will notice how fat and ugly I am;" "If I only had thinner thighs, I'd be much more popular and attractive;" "Any bite I take will immediately turn to fat;" "I am special only if I'm thin;" and "I just can't control myself. If I eat one chip I'll never be able to stop and I'll eat the whole bag."

3. Distortions of perceptions and interoceptions. Experiments with photographs, distorting mirrors, and videotape recordings generally tend to support the idea that patients with eating disorders have a greater tendency to distort and misperceive their body widths: they see themselves as much wider than they are. Although many women without eating disorders also have this tendency, the extent and degree of the distortion is much greater among women with the disorders. Patients with eating disorders also have greater difficulty than others in clearly identifying inner states such as hunger and satiety (interocepts) and in clearly identifying some of their own emotional states as well.

4. Several authorities have suggested that children who will be predisposed to eating disorders suffer developmentally from a weak sense of self and of low self-worth. As patients, they display a pervasive sense of ineffectiveness (Bruch, 1973). According to one view, these weaknesses may stem from the parents' failure to treat the child as a legitimate and authentic person in her own right. Instead, such parents are thought to take their child for granted and to value the child primarily for good behavior (so that the parents need not be bothered) and for satisfying the parents' own needs to feel valuable and to show off. The child satisfies the parents' needs by her achievements and accomplishments, which may have little intrinsic satisfaction for her; hence, a preanorexia nervosa child may be characterized as "the best little girl in the world."

The inner weakness in the sense of self may be very evident, as in the overly timid and anxious child who always clings to her mother and who has a hard time advancing and emancipating at each step of psychosocial development; this character structure may result from constitutional factors as well as from parenting style. Sometimes the weakness is well hidden, at least superficially, under a defensive personality shell that may appear strong, willful, and determined, but that lacks the adaptive flexibility of a truly strong personality structure.

5. Conflicts over adolescent development and the tasks of psychosexual maturity. Since anorexia nervosa resembles both psychological and physiological regression from the healthy adolescent state to a prepubertal one, the idea that patients may develop the disorder as a way of putting off the tasks of adolescence has had considerable appeal. In this view patients may avoid the difficult tasks of establishing a separate identity, value system, and life plan, of separating from their families, and of contending with heterosexual urges and peer pressure.

6. Family factors. A family cause for eating disorders has not been proven. A reasonable number of patients seem to come from families that are for all intents and purposes "normal," and many normal adults grow up in families that manifest the presumed pathogenetic patterns to be described. Therefore, indiscriminate "parent-bashing" (the practice of laying excessive, often undue blame on parents for their childrens' psychiatric disorders), an all-too-common practice among mental-health workers, is insupportable. Even when family problems are evident, it is far too easy to erroneously attribute the eating disorders to the family problems; even in such instances, the disorders may result from entirely different factors (Yager, 1982).

With this caveat in mind, it can be said that some families are thought to be more likely than others to produce a child with an eating disorder. Several of the hypothesized and observed parental characteristics were described earlier in this chapter. These family patterns are not idiosyncratic for eating disorders, but also are believed to produce other types of problems and possibly to exacerbate the course of illness for children with other diseases that may have "psychosomatic" components, such as asthma.

Families believed more likely to produce children with eating disorders include those in which a parent is emotionally enmeshed with a child (i.e., overinvolved to the point of being unable to distinguish the parent's needs and wishes from the child's), overt conflict between the parents or between parent and child is studiously avoided, and rules about how family members communicate with one another are so rigid that addressing the sources and even the existence of tensions in the family may not be permitted (Minuchin et al., 1978).

A family pattern characterized by "negative expressed emotion" has been empirically linked to poorer outcome for anorexia nervosa (and other psychiatric disorders such as schizophrenia and mood disorders as well). In this pattern, a family member, usually a parent, is highly emotional and unrelentingly critical of the patient, often blaming her for bringing on the disorder and for using it to harm everyone else in the family.

Social and Cultural Factors

Several factors suggest strong social and cultural influences in the appearance of eating disorders. First, *the prevalence of these disorders seems to have increased dramatically over the past several decades.* The prevalence of eating disorders parallels society's attitudes about beauty and fashion. A previous increase in eating disorders was observed in the mid-1920s, at the height of the "flapper" era, when women's fashion promoted a slim boyish look. The current increase in the prevalence of eating disorders also has been concurrent with changing cultural standards of beauty, as documented by steadily decreasing weights for height over the past two decades among fashion models, *Playboy* centerfolds, and Miss America beauty pageant winners. American first ladies have also been much slimmer since the beginning of the 1960s.

Social-feminist theorists have suggested that anorexia nervosa may signify the unconscious hunger strikes of women who have been demeaned by society. The highly skewed sex distribution, with a roughly 9:1 preponderance of women over men, has also been interpreted as due to cultural influences. Other factors may be at work, however, including the fact that psychosexual maturation occurs about 2 years earlier in women than in men, forcing them to face the associated urges and peer pressures at a younger age and perhaps rendering women more vulnerable to maturational conflicts than men. Also, men who develop anorexia nervosa may have more conflicts over sexual identity and even a higher prevalence of homosexual behavior than others. Homosexual male college students' attitudes toward their bodies and toward food fall midway between those of other male and female college students (Yager et al., 1988). Once again, such a finding may be due to cultural and/or biological influences.

Given the complexity and diversity of human nature, upbringing, and family lives, suffice it to say that although none seems to be universally true, many of the theories of etiology and pathogenesis described above find some support in clinical observations, and each has been the basis of some form of intervention.

TREATMENT

Treatment planning for eating disorders must be based on comprehensive assessment that includes attention to physical status, psychological and behavioral aspects of the eating disorders, associated psychological problems such as substance abuse and mood and personality disturbances, and the family. Each patient's problem list will be unique, and treatment components should be targeted to each specific problem (see Table 3 for medical complications of eating disorders). Treatment usually includes weight normalization and symptom reduction through cognitive and behavioral therapy programs, supportive nursing care, and dietary management and counseling; individual, group, and family psychotherapy for individual and family psychological problems; and psychopharmacological interventions for mood distur-

Table 11–3 **Medical Complications of Eating Disorders**

Related to weight loss:

Cachexia: loss of fat, muscle mass, reduced thyroid metabolism (low T3 syndrome), cold intolerance and difficulty maintaining core body temperature.

Cardiac: Loss of cardiac muscle, small heart, cardiac arrhythmias including atrial and ventricular premature contractions, prolonged His bundle transmission (prolonged Q-T interval), bradycardia, ventricular tachycardia, sudden death.

Digestive/Gastrointestinal: Delayed gastric emptying, bloating, constipation, abdominal pain.

Reproductive: Amenorrhea, low levels of luteinizing hormone (LH) and follicle-stimulating hormone (FSH).

Dermatologic: Lanugo (fine babylike hair over body), edema.

Hematologic: Leukopenia.

Neuropsychiatric: Abnormal taste sensation (?zinc deficiency), apathetic depression, mild organic mental symptoms.

Skeletal: Osteoporosis.

Related to purging (vomiting and laxative abuse):

Metabolic: Electrolyte abnormalities, particularly hypokalemic, hypochloremic alkalosis; hypomagnesemia.

Digestive/Gastrointestinal: Salivary gland and pancreatic inflammation and enlargement with increase in serum amylase, esophageal and gastric erosion, dysfunctional bowel with haustral dilatation.

Dental: erosion of dental enamel (perimyolysis), particularly of front teeth, with corresponding decay.

Neuropsychiatric: Seizures (related to large fluid shifts and electrolyte disturbances), mild neuropathies, fatigue and weakness, mild organic mental symptoms.

---

bances and some eating-disorder symptoms. As for many types of disorders, some self-help programs may be useful. At present, the best treatment approach combines elements pragmatically. The management of specific eating-disorder problems is discussed below.

Anorexia Nervosa

Low Weight

Most controlled studies have dealt with short-term weight restoration rather than with longer-term treatment, and in current practice initial attention to weight restoration is followed closely by individual and family psychotherapy (Agras, 1987; Andersen, 1985).

There is general, but not universal, agreement that weight restoration should be a central and early goal of treatment of the emaciated patient. Weight restoration per se may bring about many psychological benefits, including a reduction in obsessional thinking and mood and personality disturbance. Although some underweight patients may be successfully treated as outpatients (up to 50% in some series [Garfinkel and Garner, 1982]), such a program usually requires a highly motivated patient, a cooperative family, and good prognostic features such as younger age and a brief duration of symptoms. The large majority of severely emaciated patients (those 25 to 50% below recommended weight) require inpatient treatment in a psychiatric unit, a competently staffed general hospital unit, or a specialized eating disorders unit. The problem is how to encourage, persuade, or, in the case of the preterminal recalcitrant patient, benevolently coerce the patient into gaining weight.

Carefully designed studies have demonstrated that behavioral programs can reliably encourage weight gain (Agras, 1987). Programs that combine informational feedback regarding weight gain and caloric intake, large meals, and a behavioral program that includes both positive reinforcement (such as praise and desired visits) and negative reinforcement (such as bed rest, room and activity restrictions, and prolonged hospital stays) have the best therapeutic effects on eating and weight gain. Such programs usually require at least several weeks, and sometimes several months, in the hospital or suitable alternative such as an intensive outpatient day hospital. Compared to programs that use medications or psychotherapy as the principal forms of therapy, programs that include behavior therapy are at least more efficient, because hospital stays are generally shorter for those treated with behavior therapy. However, such programs have not proved any more effective in the long run.

Tube feeding and total parenteral nutrition programs are rarely necessary, but may sometimes be life-saving.

Psychotherapy. The role of individual and family psychotherapy in bringing about weight gain per se is difficult to evaluate. To the extent that a patient's motivation to change may be increased through such therapy, it may be valuable. Families can benefit from family therapy and counseling as soon as the problems are identified. In any event, patients often appear to make the best use of therapy, to deal with their own and their families' longstanding psychological problems, after they have regained some weight and can think more clearly.

Psychopharmacological Approaches. Many authorities avoid medications in severely malnourished patients with anorexia nervosa because such patients may be especially prone to serious side effects and because there is no evidence that medication approaches to gaining and sustaining weight have any convincing long-term advantages over nonmedication programs. In one controlled study, cyproheptadine in doses of up to 32 mg/day showed some benefit, although by no means a striking one, for lower-weight nonbulimic patients (Halmi et al., 1986). The drug's mechanism of action in this situation is uncertain, but it does seem to increase hunger; paradoxically, this makes it unacceptable to many patients. Low doses of neuroleptics or antianxiety drugs are sometimes prescribed, but existing studies do not support their general use. So far, the value of antidepressants for weight gain is unproven (Garfinkel and Garner, 1987). Medical regimens are sometimes required for patients with laxative abuse, severe constipation and other abdominal symptoms, and for associated problems.

Psychological Problems

Psychotherapeutic Approaches. For anorexia nervosa, most authorities suggest that individual psychotherapy using a highly empathic and nurturant, reality-based perspective is most useful in helping the patient examine and confront the many psychological distortions and developmental issues described above. Sessions are frequently scheduled weekly or twice weekly. The value of family therapy following hospital discharge has also been experimentally demonstrated for younger patients with anorexia nervosa (Russell et al., 1987).

Psychopharmacological Approaches. Antidepressants are often used for depression that persists following weight gain and sometimes for depression in the still-underweight patient. However, the efficacy of this approach in the underweight patient is questionable, and such patients may be more prone to cardiotoxic side effects. Low-dose neuroleptics or antianxiety drugs are sometimes used for specific target symptoms such as psychotic thinking and severe anxiety in patients with anorexia nervosa, but their use in this fashion is based solely on clinical impressions of their occasional value (Garfinkel and Garner, 1987).

Bulimia Nervosa

Binge Eating and Purging
Although with few exceptions psychotherapeutic and psychopharmacological interventions have thus far been evaluated separately from each other, in practice the various approaches are frequently combined, depending on the individual's needs.

Psychotherapeutic Approaches. Many controlled studies have shown the value of individual and group cognitive-behavioral psychotherapy. One controlled study has also shown that focal psychodynamic psychotherapy may be of value (Oesterheld et al., 1987; Wilson et al., 1986).

A *cognitive-behavioral* approach includes several stages, each consisting of several weeks or more of weekly or biweekly individual and/or group sessions. The *first* stage emphasizes the establishment of control over eating using behavioral techniques such as self-monitoring (e.g., keeping a detailed symptom-relevant diary) and response prevention (e.g., eating until satiated without being allowed to vomit), the prescription of a pattern of regular eating, and stimulus control measures (e.g., avoiding situations most likely to stimulate a binge). Patients are actively educated about weight regulation, dieting, and the adverse consequences of bulimia. The *second* stage attempts to restructure the patient's unrealistic cognitions (such as assumptions and expectations) and to instill more effective modes of problem solving. The *third* stage, which emphasizes maintaining the gains and preventing relapse, often provides 6 months to a year of weekly sessions to provide close follow-up during the time that patients are most likely to relapse (Fairburn, 1981; Wilson et al., 1986; Johnson and O'Connor, 1987). In intensive outpatient programs for bulimia, patients start their programs by attending various group programs several hours a day for several weeks.

The success rate of these methods varies considerably. For those completing the programs, about 50 to 90% experience a substantial reduction in bingeing and purging rates (the average is about 70%); about one third of patients stop these symptoms entirely. The dropout problem is considerable, however, in many groups. Available follow-up reports, generally for less than 3 years, indicate that many of the gains are maintained, although some recidivism is seen, particularly at times of severe stress.

Although long-term psychodynamic psychotherapy has often been employed in the treatment of bulimia, no controlled studies of its effectiveness in comparison to other modalities are available. Most cognitive-behavioral programs use important psychodynamically derived therapy principles, and most psychodynamically oriented therapists who treat bulimic patients often effectively use cognitive-behavioral strategies or work concurrently with other therapists who do.

Psychopharmacological Approaches. Controlled studies indicate that tricyclic antidepressants (particularly imipramine and desipramine), monoamine oxidase inhibitors (MAOIs, particularly phenelzine), trazodone, and the anticonvulsant phenytoin in their usual therapeutic dosages are useful in reducing bingeing and purging in bulimia. Common problems include medication compliance and maintaining good blood levels in the face of persistent vomiting. The tricyclics have been best studied and are used most commonly; they are effective in patients with or without concurrent major depression. With MAOIs, patients are very prone to side effects and may have difficulty following a tyramine-free diet. Results of medication treatment are similar to those with cognitive-behavioral psychotherapies, and many patients who do not respond to psychological treatment alone benefit from medication; symptoms are reduced in 70 to 90% of patients, and about one third are reported to become abstinent (Pope and Hudson, 1986; Garfinkel and Garner, 1987).

Hospitalization. Hospitalization is rarely indicated for uncomplicated bulimia nervosa. Indications include failure to respond to adequate outpatient treatment trials, worrisome medical complications not manageable in the outpatient setting, and severe mood disorder with suicidality.

ROLE OF THE NONPSYCHIATRIC PHYSICIAN IN PATIENT MANAGEMENT

The nonpsychiatric physician should play a major role in preventing, detecting, and managing patients with eating disorders. Pediatricians and family physicians should be alert to excessive concerns about dieting and appearance in preteens and their families and should teach them about healthy nutrition and the dangers of unrealistic appearance-oriented dieting and eating disorders. Because the prevalence of subclinical and full-blown forms of these disorders is so high, physicians should routinely question young female patients about what they want to weigh, their eating, dieting, and exercise practices, and their use of laxatives. Psychological problems in young women should stimulate attention to eating-disorder symptoms as well as to problems with mood, substance abuse, sexual behavior, etc. Gynecologists, internists, gastroenterologists, and dentists are also likely to encounter large numbers of eating-disorder patients in their practices.

Once an eating disorder is detected, patients merit a full physical exam, screening laboratory tests including electrolytes, complete blood count, thyroid, calcium, magnesium, and amylase studies and, for the very thin patient, an electrocardiogram or rhythm strip. The physician should consult with a registered dietitian and mental health worker knowledgeable about eating disorders to see if the problems can be ameliorated with outpatient care. With motivated patients this multidisciplinary team approach can be highly successful. The physician's role is to educate and refer and to monitor the patient's weight and laboratory tests. For the anorexic patient, monitoring should include weekly or twice-weekly office visits for stripped postvoiding weights (care should be taken that the patient has not imbibed large quantities of fluid just before being weighed) and for ongoing monitoring of any physiological abnormalities of concern.

For young adults, the physician should also be able to prescribe and monitor a course of antidepressant medication for patients with bulimia and major depression associated with an eating disorder. The extent to which the physician is willing and/or able to assume a more intense involvement with the psychological and family issues varies considerably.

INDICATIONS FOR PSYCHIATRIC CONSULTATION AND REFERRAL

Every patient with a serious eating disorder should see a psychiatrist who is knowledgeable about eating disorders for guidance to the patient, family, and referring physician about the nature, severity, and prognosis of the disorder and the available treatment options. The physician and his or her team can expect specific guidelines for psychosocial and medical management.

Specific indications for mandatory consultation include the patient's failure to respond to attempts at management in the physician's setting with deteriorating status, severe depression with suicidality, or marked family problems.

CLINICAL PEARLS

- A high index of suspicion is warranted with all female adolescents and young adults. Most want to weigh too little.
- Alerting signs include menstrual irregularities, desires to weigh 10 to 15 pounds less than reasonable for habitus, overconcern with weight or physical appearance, overuse of laxatives or diuretics, and mood disturbance.
- Signs of self-induced vomiting include puffy cheeks, scars on the knuckles, and decay of the front teeth.
- Alerting laboratory signs include mild disturbances in serum electrolytes, magnesium, and amylase.
- Patients with anorexia nervosa are often devious in providing information and in getting weighed (e.g., drinking large quantities of fluids or putting weights in their clothing). Alternative informants are always required.

ANNOTATED BIBLIOGRAPHY

Agras WS: Eating disorders: Management of obesity, bulimia and anorexia nervosa. Oxford, Pergamon, 1987
  A succinct review with special strengths in behavioral approaches to treatment.

Bruch H: Eating disorders: Obesity, anorexia nervosa and the person within. New York, Basic Books, 1973
  A seminal work by a psychoanalytically informed astute observer and experienced clinician who pioneered modern concepts.

Garfinkel PE, Garner DM: Anorexia nervosa: A multidimensional perspective. New York, Brunner/Mazel, 1982

> An excellent and comprehensive textbook covering all aspects of anorexia nervosa and bulimia.

Garner DM, Garfinkel PE (eds): Handbook of psychotherapy for anorexia nervosa and bulimia. New York, Guilford Press, 1985

> A major collection of authoritative articles describing the rationale and methods for diverse psychotherapeutic approaches including cognitive, behavioral, psychoeducational, and psychodynamic approaches to individual, group, and family therapy in the outpatient and inpatient setting.

Johnson C, Connors ME: The etiology and treatment of bulimia nervosa. New York: Basic Books, 1987

> A complete review of all aspects of bulimia nervosa.

Mitchell JE, Seim HC, Colon E, et al: Medical complications and medical management of bulimia. Ann Intern Med 107:71–77, 1987

> A thorough review of the physiological problems found in this disorder, with guidelines for the primary physician.

Pope HG Jr, Hudson JI: Antidepressant drug therapy for bulimia: current status. J Clin Psychiatry 47:339–345, 1986

> A clinically oriented review by two investigators who have published several well-conducted studies in this area.

Rock CL, Yager J: Nutrition and eating disorders: A primer for clinicians. Int J Eating Disorders 6:267–280, 1987

> A review of basic nutritional contributions to the pathogenesis of eating disorders, with corresponding nutrition-related treatment recommendations.

Russell GFM, Szmukler GI, Dare C et al: An evaluation of family therapy in anorexia nervosa and bulimia nervosa. Arch Gen Psychiatry 44: 1047–1056, 1987

> A sophisticated research study of 80 patients.

Yager J: Family issues in the pathogenesis of anorexia nervosa. Psychosom Med 44:43–60, 1982

> A review of theoretical and clinical aspects of the relationship of the appearance and course of anorexia nervosa to biological and interpersonal factors in families.

REFERENCES

Agras WS: Eating disorders: Management of obesity, bulimia and anorexia nervosa. Oxford, Pergamon, 1987

Andersen AE: Practical comprehensive treatment of anorexia nervosa and bulimia. Baltimore, Johns Hopkins, 1985

Bruch H: Eating disorders: Obesity, anorexia nervosa and the person within. New York, Basic Books, 1973

Crisp AH, Hall A, Holland AJ: Nature and nurture in anorexia nervosa: A study of 34 pairs of twins, one pair of triplets and an adoptive family. Int J Eating Disorders 4:5–29, 1985

Fairburn CG: A cognitive behavioral approach to the treatment of bulimia. Psychol Med 11:707–711, 1981

Garfinkel PE, Garner DM: Anorexia nervosa: A multidimensional perspective. New York, Brunner/Mazel, 1982

Garfinkel PE, Garner DM (eds): The role of drug treatments for eating disorders. New York, Brunner/Mazel, 1987

Halmi KA, Eckert E, LaDu TJ, et al: Anorexia nervosa: Treatment efficacy of cyproheptadine and amitriptyline. Arch Gen Psychiatry 43:177–181, 1986

Hsu LKG: Outcome and treatment effects. In Beaumont PJV, Burrows BD, Casper RC (eds): Handbook of eating disorders, part I. Amsterdam, Elsevier, 1987

Johnson C, Connors ME: The etiology and treatment of bulimia nervosa. New York, Basic, 1987

Marrazzi MA, Luby ED: An auto-addiction opioid model of chronic anorexia nervosa. Int J Eating Disorders 5:191–208, 1986

Minuchin S, Rosman BL, Baker L: Psychosomatic families: Anorexia nervosa in context. Cambridge, Harvard University Press, 1978

Mitchell JE, Seim HC, Colon E, et al: Medical complications and medical management of bulimia. Ann Int Med 107:71–77, 1987

Oesterheld JR, McKenna MS, Gould NB: Group psychotherapy of bulimia: A critical review. Int J Group Psychother 37:163–184, 1987

Pope HG Jr, Hudson JI: Antidepressant drug therapy for bulimia: current status. J Clin Psychiatry 47:339–345, 1986

Russell GFM, Szmukler GI, Dare C, et al: An evaluation of family therapy in anorexia nervosa and bulimia nervosa. Arch Gen Psychiatry 44:1047–1056, 1987

Szmukler GI: The epidemiology of anorexia nervosa and bulimia. J Psychiatric Res 19:143–153, 1985

Wilson GT, Rossiter E, Lindholm L, et al: Cognitive-behavioral treatment of bulimia nervosa: a controlled evaluation. Behav Res Therapy 24:227–288, 1986

Yager J, Kurtsman F, Landsverk J, et al: Behaviors and attitudes related to eating disorders in homosexual male college students. Am J Psychiatry 145:495–497, 1988

Yager J, Landsverk J, Edelstein CK: A 20-month followup study of 628 women with eating disorders. I. Course and severity. Am J Psychiatry 144:1172–1177, 1988

12

Dissociative Disorders

Mark E. James and Steven T. Levy

The diagnostic grouping "dissociative disorders" refers to a group of clinical conditions with the common feature of "a disturbance or alteration in the normally integrative functions of identity, memory or consciousness" (Diagnostic and Statistical Manual of Mental Disorders, 1987). The disorders in the category are listed in Table 1. These disturbances may be sudden or gradual, transient or chronic. If memory for a significant period of time is lost in the absence of an organic mental disorder, a diagnosis of *psychogenic amnesia* is made. If an individual loses memory for his or her entire previous identity and a new identity is assumed along with travel to a new location, the diagnosis is *psychogenic fugue.* If more than one distinct personality dominates consciousness at different times in any individual, a diagnosis of *multiple personality* is made. If an individual experiences him or herself as unreal, strange, or changed in some way, yet remains in contact with reality in the absence of any gross change in identity, the diagnosis is *depersonalization disorder,* as long as these symptoms are not part of any other known psychiatric disorder.

This grouping of psychiatric disorders is based both on the similarity of clinical manifestations seen in each, as well as by a presumed underlying psychological process: the phenomenon of *dissociation.* By virtue of their dramatic character, these disorders have long been of interest to psychiatrists. Explanations of dissociation play an important role in the history of modern psychiatry.

Early attempts to explore the process of dissociation did not link it exclusively with those disorders now grouped together in DSM-III-R as the dissociative disorders. Early investigators thought that a variety of other clinical entities, including hysteria, somnambulism, and other conditions, involved dissociative mechanisms.

Janet is usually given credit for first using the term "dissociation" in relation to mental disorders. By dissociation, he meant a complex of ideas that existed outside of an individual's *usual conscious* experience. Janet attributed dissociation to an inherent constitutional weakness of the patient's mind. Freud was also interested in dissociative phenomena and attributed them to psychological processes he variously termed dissociation, repression, and defense. Freud believed dissociation represented a "split" in consciousness mediated by defensive operations designed to ward off painful feelings resulting from conflict between wishful and prohibited thoughts. The idea that certain mental content can be banned from consciousness (repression) by being unacceptable to the individual became a cornerstone of dynamic psychiatry.

Table 12–1 **Dissociative Disorders**

Psychogenic Amnesia
Psychogenic Fugue
Multiple Personality Disorder
Depersonalization Disorder
Dissociative Disorder not Otherwise Specified

As a part of our modern diagnostic system, dissociative disorders are distinguished by both their clinical manifestations and a presumed common underlying psychological mechanism. This is a departure from diagnostic criteria used in other DSM-III-R syndromes, which are diagnosed only on the basis of observable signs and symptoms or known organic factors.

Since these early explorations of dissociative processes, various other explanations have been hypothesized, but none have been generally accepted. Neurologically based disturbances of cognitive integration, autohypnotic processes, and various other nondynamic factors have also been implicated. Because these disorders are rare, it has been difficult to study them in a systematic and longitudinal manner.

The capacity for gross alterations in conscious experience, such as is present in patients with dissociative disorders, represents a profound disturbance in mental life available to few individuals. When it does occur, it is usually in the face of overwhelmingly traumatic experiences or memories. Clinical manifestations vary from the mild disturbances seen in many patients with transient depersonalization experiences, to episodic and short-lived dramatic episodes of amnesia and fugue, to life-long patterns of disturbance of the greatest severity in certain patients with multiple personality disorder. The various dissociative disorders will be discussed individually in terms of description, etiology, and treatment, with common or linking trends emphasized where appropriate.

PSYCHOGENIC AMNESIA

The following often-cited case of psychogenic amnesia in colonial America was described by Benjamin Rush, "the father of American psychiatry," in his lectures (Carlson, 1981). During his preparation for an examination for the Presbyterian ministry, William Tenent developed an illness with chest pain, intermittent fever, and severe emaciation. He eventually collapsed and was believed dead. Funeral preparations were forestalled by his physician, who believed he felt a slight warmth in Tenent's body. After 3 days, the presumed corpse "opened its eyes, gave a dreadful groan, and sunk again into apparent death." This occurred again two more times, but after the last he regained consciousness.

He gradually recovered fully during the next year, but was completely amnestic for his entire life before the deathlike state. Because he also lost his ability to read or write, his brother began teaching him these skills. One day during a Latin lesson, he suddenly felt a shock in his head. He remembered reading the book before. More recollections occurred and he eventually recovered all memories of his life. He also described an experience during a 3-day coma in which he was "transported by a superior being to a place of ineffable glory." He remained healthy for the next 45 years. He became a minister, married, and had three sons.

Description

Psychogenic amnesia is defined by DSM-III-R as a "sudden inability to recall important personal information that is too extensive to be explained by ordinary forgetfulness." The amnesia must not be due to any organic causes. The most common presentation of psychogenic amnesia is a *localized* or circumscribed disturbance of recall; that is, the patient cannot recall any events that occurred during a certain time period, usually the first few hours after a severely upsetting event (Fig. 1). Less common is *selective* amnesia, in which certain but not all events within a specified time period are not remembered. On rare occasions a patient may develop *generalized* amnesia (in which the patient cannot recall any information about his or her entire preceding life) or *continuous* amnesia (in which the patient cannot remember

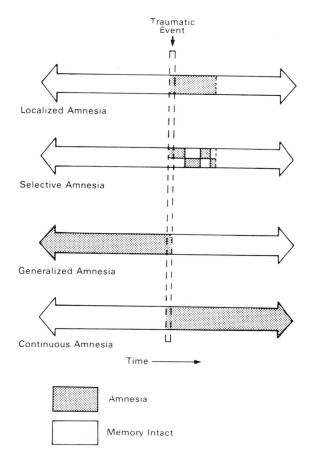

Figure 12–1. Types of psychogenic amnesia.

anything following a specific event and continuing to the immediate present). In the case above, William Tenent's amnesia was most likely the generalized type. Whether it was psychogenic or caused by his illness is open to speculation.

An episode of psychogenic amnesia is usually precipitated by a particularly intense psychological stressor, either some threat of harm or death, an intolerable, inescapable life situation, or a morally unacceptable impulse or act. In some individuals, the amnesia may be preceded by a headache or some alteration of consciousness experienced as sleepiness or dizziness. Occasionally, an amnestic patient may wander aimlessly until the police eventually bring him or her to an emergency room. Some affected individuals may be unaware of their memory disturbance until confronted by another person. Some feel distressed by the amnesia, others seem indifferent, and some may make up information to fill in what is missing.

Epidemiology

The epidemiology of psychogenic amnesia is poorly understood. It is believed to be most common in adolescent and young adult females and is most rare in the elderly. There is no information on familial transmission. During war, psychogenic amnesia may occur in as many as 5 to 8% of combat soldiers. The incidence is believed to rise during disasters.

Etiology

The precise psychological and/or neurological mechanisms of psychogenic amnesia are unknown. One hypothetical model suggests that in the face of overwhelming psychological trauma, mental mechanisms are activated in susceptible individuals that interfere with the normal retrieval of stored, anxiety-provoking information. The person can then function relatively adaptively compared to the cognitive disequilibrium that might result if the trauma continued to be experienced consciously (as occurs in patients with acute posttraumatic stress disorders). Obviously, the amnesia can itself become disabling or maladaptive.

How memories are sequestered outside of awareness is unclear. Some have suggested that a neurologically based retrieval deficit or faulty encoding and storage of information may cause psychogenic amnesia because these dysfunctions cause other types of amnesia. Because memories can often be recovered using hypnosis or sodium amobarbital interview, some capacity for storage and retrieval must remain intact on some level. The classic psychoanalytic model describes amnesia as motivated by the need to reduce anxiety or arousal, resulting in the concept of repression and other defense mechanisms. The state-dependent learning model suggests that information storage and retrieval depends on the person's state of consciousness. If memories are stored under extreme emotional turmoil, they may not be accessible in other emotional states, resulting in amnesia.

Differential Diagnosis

Any of several organic etiologies of amnesia should be ruled out by careful medical-neurological evaluation, particularly central nervous system disease, intox-

Table 12–2 **Medical and Neurological Disorders Causing Dissociative Symptoms**

Alcohol Intoxication - Blackout
Alcohol Amnestic Disorder
Postconcussion Amnesia
Complex Partial Seizures
Transient Global Amnesia
Postelectroconvulsive Therapy Amnesia
Carbon Monoxide Poisoning
Hypoglycemia
Hallucinogen Intoxication
Posthallucinogen Perception Disorder

ication, and metabolic derangement (Table 2). The classic substance-induced amnesia is the alcoholic blackout. Chronic alcohol use also may result in anterograde memory disturbances. Postconcussion amnesia may occur after head trauma. Epileptic seizures usually are accompanied by a period of amnesia. If a patient in legal trouble stands to gain by forgetting a period of time, malingering or feigned amnesia should be considered.

Diagnostic Evaluation

For all dissociative syndromes, evaluation should begin with a thorough, comprehensive history. Physical examination should include a complete neurological examination, looking especially for evidence of head injury, intoxication, or focal neurological deficits. Findings on the mental status examination that would point toward an organic cause of dissociative syndromes would include clouding of consciousness, impaired attention, disorientation, slurred speech, blunted or labile affect, disorganized flow of thought associations, difficulty with complex mental tasks, impaired cognition beyond specific memory losses, inability to learn new things, and confabulation.

Laboratory evaluation should include assessment of glucose, electrolytes, CO_2, renal and hepatic functioning, blood-alcohol level, and a urine drug screen. Finally, an electroencephalogram, computed tomography of the brain, and neuropsychological testing can be performed.

Treatment

Therapy involves two general principles: first, to remove the patient from the threatening circumstances, often by hospitalization; second, to explore his or her distress through psychotherapy. Some recommend an approach designed to retrieve the repressed memories as rapidly as possible, either through free association, hypnosis, or amobarbital interviews. Others believe this approach may be deleterious and advise instead exploring the patient's life situation and any psychological conflicts that may have resulted in the onset of amnesia under the given circumstances in a more circumspect manner.

Psychotropic medications (except for sodium amytal interviews) are rarely helpful in treating psychogenic amnesia. During therapy, the amnesia often clears rapidly, either completely or sometimes less completely.

PSYCHOGENIC FUGUE

William James described a famous case of psychogenic fugue in *Principles of Psychology* (1892):

Ansel Bourne, a 60-year-old evangelist, disappeared from Providence, Rhode Island. About 2 weeks thereafter, a man named A.J. Brown opened a small shop in Norristown, Pennsylvania. He conducted business in a quiet and orderly fashion. Six weeks later, he woke up in a frightened state. He said his name was Ansel Bourne, asked to know where he was, and said he had no knowledge of Norristown or shopkeeping. His last memory was of conducting some personal business in Providence, and he could not believe 2 months had passed. He returned home and maintained complete amnesia for the interval. James later examined Bourne under hypnosis; in this state he evoked the personality of A.J. Brown, who recounted the events in Norristown. James could never facilitate Bourne's recall of any of Brown's memories.

Description

According to DSM-III-R, this disorder involves "sudden unexpected travel away from home or customary work locale with assumption of a new identity and an inability to recall one's previous identity." During a fugue state, a person may appear perplexed or disoriented. After recovery from the fugue, there is no recall of events that took place during the episode. Patients typically present for help after the fugue, wanting to recall what happened.

Only occasionally will a fugue manifest the more dramatic and classical presentation in which a quiet, ordinary person suddenly assumes a more gregarious, uninhibited manner, travels thousands of miles, and carries on a new, complex social existence for months with a different name and a well-integrated new identity, ultimately shifting back into the former identity with no memory of the interval. More typically, the episode is less elaborate. The affected person engages in brief and apparently purposeful travel, but the new identity is less complete and socialization with others may be minimal. Most episodes last several hours to a few days.

Occurrence

As with psychogenic amnesia, the occurrence of psychogenic fugue increases during wartime or natural disasters. Many cases reported are of soldiers in combat who wandered away from duty. The age of onset is variable. Little information exists about sex ratio or familial incidence.

Etiology

The pathological cause of fugue states is unknown. The same dissociative mental mechanisms discussed under psychogenic amnesia apply to psychogenic fugue, but in fugue states a different identity is created. This phenomenon is precipitated by severe psychological stress.

Differential Diagnosis and Treatment

As mentioned, evaluation and treatment is usually sought after the fugue has resolved. As with amnesia, the differential diagnosis must include the same list of disorders. Multiple personality disorder should also be ruled out. Treatment of psychogenic fugue involves the same principles discussed under psychogenic amnesia.

MULTIPLE PERSONALITY DISORDER

Description

Multiple personality disorder is defined by DSM-III-R as "the existence within the person of two or more distinct personalities or personality states (each with its own relatively enduring pattern of perceiving, relating to, and thinking about the environment and self)." Further, "at least two of these personalities or personality states recurrently take full control of the person's behavior." The personality who presents for treatment is usually unaware of the existence of the other personalities. He or she may instead report time lapses, blackouts, or "spells," or may have been told by others about unusual episodes of behavior during which the patient referred to himself or herself by another name (the patient has amnesia for the occurrence). The patient may report hearing voices inside his or her head and may feel controlled by them. Affected individuals also often experience depression, nightmares, suicide attempts, phobias, rapid mood shifts, severe anxiety, depersonalization or derealization, and headaches (Bliss, 1984).

As diagnostic evaluation and treatment proceed, particularly if hypnosis or sodium amobarbital interview is used, the various personalities manifest themselves. Transition from one to another may also be brought about by severe life stress. The personalities are often quite different: they may appear normal or severely pathological, they may vary in age, sex, race, behavior, and habits, and they may prefer different social circles. The personalities are believed to demonstrate different psychological test profiles and different psychophysiological characteristics. Some personalities may be aware of the presence of the other personalities, while others may not.

Illustrative Case

Morton Prince described a famous patient with multiple personality, Sally Beauchamp, in *The Dissociation of a Personality* (1906). The distinctness of her three personalities was "manifested by different trains of thought, by different views, beliefs, ideals, and temperament, and by different acquisitions, tastes, habits, experiences, and memories." Her dominant, original personality was moralistic, self-righteous, and masochistic. A second personality was aggressive and ambitious. Neither one was aware of any other personalities. Her third personality, which emerged under hypnosis, was described as "an impish child" who was aware of the dominant personality. The personalities would "come and go in kaleidoscopic succession." Often her activities changed dramatically as the personality changed.

Occurrence

Although it was believed to be rare, with only about 200 reported cases in the literature, multiple personality disorder is now considered somewhat more prevalent. The exact frequency of occurrence is unknown. The disorder almost always begins in childhood, but individuals do not come to clinical attention until adulthood. It is more common in women than men and is more common in first-degree relatives of probands than in the general population.

Etiology

Almost all cases are preceded by physical, sexual, or emotional abuse or exposure to extreme, overwhelming trauma during childhood. Affected individuals seem to have an increased tendency or ability to enter dissociative states or autohypnotic states. Hypothetically, during extreme childhood abuse or trauma, this mechanism may protect the patient from being overwhelmed or incapacitated. However, if the dissociation is acquired through learning or conditioning as a coping strategy, information processed during different states of consciousness may be encoded and stored in different "circuits" inaccessible to one another, which eventually results in the development of different state-dependent personalities. Such etiologic explanations remain speculative.

Some have noted a similarity between multiple personality disorder and borderline personality disorder (see Chapter 5). Patients with either disorder often suffer from depression, anxiety, emotional instability, interpersonal turmoil, and self-destructive behavior. Both groups use "primitive" ego defense mechanisms, including splitting, denial, dissociation, and projection. Both typically have a history of abuse during childhood. Whether or not the two groups have any etiologic connection is uncertain.

Differential Diagnosis

These patients may be diagnosed as having other psychiatric disorders, particularly schizophrenia, because of the possible history of hearing voices, believing themselves to be influenced by some unknown force, expressing strange ideas, and shifting patterns of identity. As mentioned, comorbidity may include anxiety disorders, depression, and personality disorders. Psychogenic amnesia and psychogenic fugue also should be considered. As with amnesia and fugue, any medical or neurological conditions that cause alterations of consciousness, such as drug or alcohol intoxication or withdrawal, metabolic disturbances, and complex partial seizures, should be ruled out. Malingering, and factitious disorder with psychological symptoms present-ing as multiple personality disorder, should also be included in the differential diagnosis.

The diagnosis of multiple personality disorder often brings with it something verging on celebrity status to the patient among psychiatrists and other mental-health workers, who may be fascinated by the patient's symptoms. The physician must maintain a high index of suspicion for malingering or elaboration of symptoms in a patient with symptoms of multiple personality disorder who is involved in a criminal justice proceeding and may be seeking a psychiatric defense.

Treatment

Psychotropic medications are of little use in treating multiple personality. Psy-chotherapy can be used in an attempt to examine and ideally to change the use of dissociation and other pathological defense mechanisms by these patients. Some clinicians advocate using hypnosis to elicit the various personalities and eventually to reintegrate therapeutically the dissociated or split-off aspects of experience. Others believe this technique may reinforce the use of autohypnotic dissociation by patients. In therapy, the patient's past traumas and current stressors and conflicts should be explored supportively to facilitate insight and improve adaptation.

DEPERSONALIZATION DISORDER

Description

DSM-III-R defines depersonalization as "an alteration in the perception or experience of the self in which the usual sense of one's own reality is temporarily lost or changed." The experience is usually accompanied by a dreamlike state and a sense of detachment from one's mind or body. During a depersonalization episode, the person maintains intact reality testing and is generally distressed by the experience.

The symptom of depersonalization occurs in a number of disorders, including panic disorder, agoraphobia, organic anxiety disorders, hallucinogen intoxication or posthallucinogen perception disorder (e.g., LSD flashbacks), severe depression, and schizophrenia (Table 3). Patients with seizure disorders, particularly complex partial seizures (especially those of temporal lobe origin) and other brain diseases, may experience depersonalization. Finally, depersonalization can occur in normal people as a result of stress, fatigue, or sleep deprivation. When depersonalization occurs recurrently or persistently in the absence of any of the disorders listed, a diagnosis of depersonalization disorder is made.

Depersonalization may be accompanied by derealization, which involves a sense of the unreality of objects in the external world (as opposed to the alteration of perception of one's self that occurs in depersonalization). Patients with depersonaliza-tion disorder may also complain of depression, anxiety, dizziness, obsessional thoughts, somatic worries, and a fear of going insane.

This condition is usually chronic with exacerbations and remissions. Patient

Table 12–3 **Other Psychiatric Disorders Presenting with Symptoms of Dissociation**

Drug Intoxication or Withdrawal
Schizophrenia
Borderline Personality Disorder
Panic Disorder
Agoraphobia
Organic Anxiety Disorder
Depression
Malingering
Factitious Disorder with Psychological Symptoms

impairment is widely variable, and some may develop secondary alcohol or drug abuse or hypochondriasis.

Occurrence

Although single episodes of depersonalization occur in the majority of the population, the prevalence, sex ratio, and familial occurrence of depersonalization disorder are unknown.

Etiology

As with the other dissociative disorders, the etiology of depersonalization disorder is unknown. Intensely traumatic events such as military combat or physical assault may contribute to onset of the disorder. Psychoanalytic theories have viewed depersonalization as a defense against forbidden impulses, as a symptom of defective ego functioning, as a consequence of violation of one's ideals or conscience under abnormal circumstances, and as a response to interpersonal invalidation by significant others. The induction of depersonalization by hallucinogens indicates some neurologic substrate for the symptoms of this disorder.

Treatment

Psychopharmacologic interventions may be used for accompanying symptoms such as anxiety, depression, or obsessions, but the value of medication for depersonalization itself is unknown. Antipsychotics seem to make the condition worse.

The value of psychotherapy is also unknown, but a useful approach would generically include providing support, exploring ongoing stressors, examining the events and thoughts related to the onset of depersonalization experiences, and working to modify psychological defenses and intrapsychic conflicts.

DISSOCIATIVE DISORDER NOT OTHERWISE SPECIFIED

This category includes any disorders in which a dissociative symptom predominates but does not meet criteria for a particular specific dissociative disorder.

ROLE OF THE NONPSYCHIATRIC PHYSICIAN AND INDICATIONS FOR PSYCHIATRIC CONSULTATION AND REFERRAL

Most patients with dissociative disorders will present for medical evaluation or treatment with complaints of amnesia, alteration of consciousness, or deteriorating psychosocial functioning. The nonpsychiatrist should be able to recognize these disorders clinically and formulate a differential diagnosis, including both neuropsychiatric and medical diagnoses. All patients with dissociative disorders should be referred for psychiatric intervention since these conditions are complex and require specialized management. The nonpsychiatrist should not leap to the conclusion that patients with dissociative symptoms should be referred elsewhere without first conducting a thorough medical-neurological evaluation to rule out the various illnesses that cause dissociative symptoms.

The dissociative disorders are dramatic clinical entities. They stirred the interest of early psychodynamic investigators, leading to the formulation of concepts such as intrapsychic conflict, altered states of consciousness, mechanisms of defense, and unconscious mental content, which all play a role in the process described as dissociation. These dynamic mental phenomena have become part of our understanding of mental life in general and of various kinds of psychopathology. The dissociative disorders remain poorly understood manifestations of the complexity of mental life.

Patients with such disorders come to the attention of psychiatrists less often than those with more familiar clinical entities. By virtue of their dramatic presentation, such patients are often thought to be feigning their symptoms and are regularly treated with suspicion, mistrust, and even derision. Clinicians are challenged to maintain a professionally appropriate, unbiased, and technically neutral stance in attempting to understand the distress of these perplexing patients. Treatment planning must be flexible and innovative. Confronted with bizarre and somewhat theatrical behaviors, the clinician must persistently strive to be empathic, supportive, and vigorously objective. Many patients are the victims of severe past and present traumas and are reluctant to engage in any self-exploration. A negative attitude by the clinician further alienates the patient and makes a collaborative exploratory effort even less likely.

Dissociative mechanisms are particularly anxiety-provoking for physicians because, despite their bizarre appearance, they occur in patients who appear in other respects in touch with reality, and thus not radically different from those providing them with psychiatric care. Such mechanisms represent extreme instances of psychological processes that are constantly active in all individuals. Therefore, they continue to hold our scientific interest. Ideally, more systematic investigation will lead to a better understanding of them and subsequent improved responsiveness to treatment interventions.

CLINICAL PEARLS

- The dissociative disorders should be considered in the differential diagnosis of any patient presenting with alteration of consciousness, amnesia, "spells," disturbance of identity, or alteration of feelings of reality.
- A complete medical-neurological evaluation should be conducted on these patients to rule out the multiple organic causes of dissociative symptoms.
- Although the etiology of dissociative disorders is poorly understood, the best current working explanation of dissociation suggests the operation of complex psychological processes designed to interfere with information-processing and memory retrieval. These mechanisms may be motivated by a need or tendency to reduce arousal.
- Although certain medications may help reduce anxiety in these disorders, the treatment of choice continues to be psychotherapy.

ANNOTATED BIBLIOGRAPHY

Braun BG (ed): Multiple personality. Psychiat Clin North Am 7: 1984

> This issue is devoted to review articles on various topics related to multiple personality disorder.

Breuer J, Freud S: Studies on hysteria. In: The standard edition of the complete psychological Works of Sigmund Freud. Vol. 2, 1893–1895. London, Hogarth Press, 1955

> This monumental work depicts Breuer and Freud's differing conceptions of the pathogenesis of hysterical phenomena, including both conversion and dissociative mechanisms. Freud goes on to describe the psychological treatment of hysteria.

Fisher C: Amnesic states in war neuroses: The psychogenesis of fugues. Psychoanal Q 14:437–468, 1945

> This classic paper discusses the psychodynamic processes involved in dissociation, with emphasis on amnesia and fugue.

Gilmore MM, Kaufman C: Dissociative disorders. In: Michels R, Cavenar JO, Brodie HKH, et al. (eds): Psychiatry. Philadelphia, JB Lippincott, 1985

> This textbook chapter provides an excellent review of the dissociative disorders.

Kluft RP (ed): Childhood antecedents of multiple personality. Washington DC, American Psychiatric Press, 1985

> The chapters of this book describe how severe abuse during childhood can lead to the use of dissociative mechanisms and may result in the development of multiple personality.

Nemiah JC: Dissociative disorders (hysterical neurosis, dissociative type). In: Kaplan HI, Sadock BJ (eds): Comprehensive textbook of psychiatry/IV, 4th ed. Baltimore, Williams & Wilkins, 1985

> Another excellent review of dissociative disorders.

REFERENCES

Abse DW: Hysterical conversion and dissociative syndromes and the hysterical character. In: Arieti S, Brody EB (eds): American handbook of psychiatry, 2nd ed. Vol. 3. New York, Basic Books, 1974

American Psychiatric Association, Diagnostic and Statistical Manual of Mental Disorders, 3rd ed., rev. Washington, DC, 1987

Bliss EL: A symptom profile of patients with multiple personalities, including MMPI results. J Nerv Ment Dis, 172:197–201, 1984

Carlson ET: The history of multiple personality in the United States: I. The beginnings. Am J Psychiatry 138:666–668, 1981

Clary WF, Burstin KJ, Carpenter JS: Multiple personality and borderline personality disorder. Psychiat Clin North Am, 7:89–99, 1984

Gilmore MM, Kaufman C: Dissociative disorders. In: Michels R, Cavenar JO, Brodie HKH, et al. (eds): Psychiatry. Philadelphia, JB Lippincott, 1985

James W: The principles of psychology. New York, Dover, 1918

Kopelman MD: Amnesia: Organic and psychogenic. Br J Psychiatry, 150:428–442, 1987

Nemiah JC: Dissociative disorders (hysterical neurosis, dissociative type). In: Kaplan HI, Sadock BJ (eds): Comprehensive textbook of psychiatry/IV, 4th ed. Baltimore, Williams & Wilkins, 1985

Prince M: The dissociation of a personality. New York, Longman's Green, 1906

Riether AM, Stoudemire A: Psychogenic fugue states: A review. South Med J 81:568–571, 1988

13

Psychosexual Disorders

Peter J. Fagan and Chester W. Schmidt Jr.

Sexual dysfunction is a subclass of sexual disorders in which the essential feature is "inhibition in the appetitive or psychophysiologic changes that characterize the complete sexual response cycle" (DSM-III-R). Sexual dysfunction is distinguished from the other sexual disorder group, paraphilia, in which there is generally no impairment in sexual function (see Chapter 14). A third category of disorders closely related to sexuality are disorders of gender identity. Readers who wish to learn more about this diagnostic group might consult Steiner (1985) or Stoller (1985).

Sexual dysfunction is not a life-threatening condition, but the negative effects it can have on a patient's self-esteem or relationship should not be underestimated. Given the multiple biological, psychological, and social aspects of human sexual behavior, sexual dysfunctions require a careful and thorough diagnostic evaluation. Because sexuality is so central to self-esteem and ability to relate to others, a person with a sexual dysfunction deserves skillful and sensitive therapy.

EPIDEMIOLOGY

The epidemiology of psychosexual disorders can be considered from the perspectives of two groups: the general population and those with medical illnesses or postsurgical conditions. In a review of 22 sex surveys of the general population, Nathan (1986) reported the prevalence and distribution of sexual dysfunction (as defined by DSM-III) as seen in Table 1. Nathan did not report psychogenic dyspareunia and vaginismus because virtually no survey data existed about them. By a conservative estimate, these two dysfunctions occur in less than 5% of the population. No prevalence data are available for the new (DSM-III-R) diagnostic category of sexual aversion disorder.

Among those with medical illnesses or postsurgical conditions, the prevalence of sexual dysfunction due to contributing psychogenic factors has been understandably difficult to establish because of the covarying effects of the medical illness. While sample sizes of studies of specific medical conditions are generally too small for epidemiological purposes and specific psychogenic factors are usually not identified, in general sexual dysfunction is clearly highly prevalent among the medically ill

Table 13-1 **Estimated prevalence of sexual dysfunction (DSM-III) among general population (Nathan, 1986)**

SEXUAL DYSFUNCTION	MEN	WOMEN
Inhibited sexual desire	1–15%	1–35%
Inhibited sexual excitement	10–20%	indeterminate
Premature ejaculation	35%	NA
Inhibited orgasm	5%	5–30+%

(Schover and Jensen, 1988; Kolodny, Masters, and Johnson, 1979; Wise and Schmidt, 1985).

About 30% of sexually dysfunctional individuals also have an additional (Axis I) psychiatric disorder that is not a primary etiological agent in the sexual dysfunction (e.g., major depression) (Maurice and Guze, 1970; Fagan, Schmidt, Wise, et al., 1988).

DESCRIPTION

DSM-III-R suggests specifications that the clinician should make for any psychosexual dysfunction. Two of these (lifelong versus acquired and global versus situational) help clarify the phenomenology of the disorder; the third is a statement about etiology (psychogenic alone, psychogenic and biogenic, or biogenic alone).

For the present, the specification "lifelong versus acquired" states that a sexual dysfunction can either be a lifelong pattern in an individual's sexual response (or lack thereof) or a condition that has appeared at a point in life with either gradual or sudden onset. As with most developmental accomplishments, *the prognosis is better if the sexual dysfunction is a departure from a previously acquired baseline than a behavior never achieved.* Like a medical condition, the prognosis is also generally better for regaining functioning if the onset is relatively recent and acute (as opposed to chronic and insidious).

If a sexual dysfunction is global, it is assumed the psychogenic factors are located within the patient's mental and emotional life. If they are situational, one suspects that a relational problem (not excluding intrapsychic factors) is also involved. For example, if a man can function sexually in an anonymous homosexual context but cannot attain an erection with his wife, the situational aspect of the dysfunction indicates intrapsychic conflict about his bisexual behaviors as well as the quality of his relationship with his wife.

Sexual dysfunctions are best understood descriptively as deviations from the normal human sexual response cycle as described originally by Masters and Johnson (1966). This has been adapted and amplified in Figure 1 to display both the normal physiological arousal pattern (increased heart rate and blood pressure, myotonia) and the particular sexual disorders that may appear in each particular phase.

With a model of the human sexual response cycle in mind, the clinician can obtain a clear phenomenology of the specific nature of the sexual dysfunction. This can be done during an elaboration of the presenting problem by asking the patient(s)

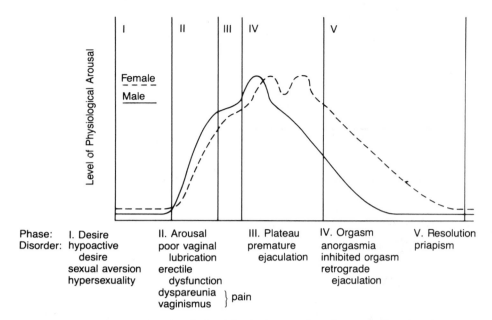

Figure 13-1. Levels of physiological arousal and sexual disorders in men and women according to phases of sexual response. (Adapted from Masters and Johnson, 1966 and Fagan and Schmidt, 1987)

to describe his or her last attempt at sexual intercourse or sexual activity. Particular attention should be paid to quantifying both time (e.g., in foreplay) and physiological response (e.g., vaginal lubrication). These data should then be compared to the human sexual response cycle described by Masters and Johnson (1966) and further elaborated in DSM-III-R. When there appears to be more than one sexual dysfunction, the clinician must determine which disorder was historically first and therefore may be etiologically connected to the secondary condition. For example, a man distressed by premature ejaculation may develop secondary erectile dysfunction.

The DSM-III-R groupings of the psychosexual dysfunctions are disorders of desire, arousal, orgasm, and pain. A fifth diagnostic category, "Sexual Dysfunction Not Otherwise Specified," provides for patients whose symptoms elude existing diagnostic taxonomy.

Disorders of Desire

DSM-III-R lists two disorders of sexual desire: "Hypoactive Sexual Desire Disorder" and "Sexual Aversion Disorder." Hypoactive sexual desire is a condition in which the patient reports usually a global lack of cognitive, emotional, and physiologic readiness to initiate or take part in sexual activity. Compared to others of the same age, sex, health status, and availability of a sexual partner, a person with hypoactive sexual desire has fewer sexual fantasies and lower orgasmic frequency (through masturbation or intercourse). If the condition is acquired, the distress shown by the patient about the low sexual desire may range from preoccupation (e.g., in the "macho" male) to indifference (e.g., in the mother of multiple preschool children). It often correlates with the distress of the partner, who in many cases initiates the consultation. In situations of longstanding hypoactive sexual desire, the condition may be quite ego-syntonic.

This disorder does not imply an inability to function sexually. Once activity is initiated, usually by the partner, the person becomes aroused and, unless there is a separate dysfunction, is orgasmic. The hallmark of this disorder is that the baseline of sexual desire (libido) remains significantly low.

Sexual aversion disorder is a new diagnostic category in DSM-III-R. Conceptualized by Helen Singer Kaplan (1987), the disorder is the aversion to and avoidance of sexual activity with a partner. Sexual desire may be normal with fantasy and masturbation frequencies appropriate for age and sex. The patient may avoid intercourse completely or may participate only infrequently out of a sense of duty to the partner. Central to the disorder is a pattern of avoidance that results in infrequent intercourse. When experienced, intercourse is merely tolerated. A sense of enjoyment, satisfaction, and collaboration ("being in control") is usually minimal or absent. Poor body image, especially regarding breasts and genitals, is common; nudity is avoided.

As a new diagnostic category, sexual aversion disorder requires further quantification of its phenomenology. Clinical researchers disagree whether this is a specific sexual disorder or whether it is a variety of avoidant behavior typical of phobia and should be included in phobic taxonomy.

Disorders of Arousal

Disorders of arousal pertain to an inability to achieve sufficient physiological or cognitive/emotional arousal during sexual activity. In women the disorder is called "Female Sexual Arousal Disorder"; in men the disorder is "Male Erectile Disorder." Insufficient physiological arousal for women consists of failure to attain or maintain adequate lubrication-swelling response of the vagina and labia for the completion of sexual activity. Intercourse may be performed, but vaginal dryness will cause pain on initial penetration or throughout coitus. In men the failure to attain or maintain erection until the completion of sexual activity is the criteria for arousal disorder. In most cases it makes intravaginal penetration and ejaculation rare. In others, ejaculation is purposefully rushed after penetration to precede penile detumescence.

In addition to the insufficient peripheral response of the genitals, a disorder of arousal exists when there is a persistent or recurrent lack of subjective sense of sexual excitement and pleasure during sexual activity. In itself, this lack of subjective arousal during sexual activity merits the diagnosis. It should be distinguished from low sexual desire, which as described previously is the baseline level of sexual drive before the initiation of sexual activity.

Orgasm Disorders

"Inhibited Female Orgasm" or "Inhibited Male Orgasm" are present when there is "a persistent or recurrent delay in, or absence of, orgasm...following a normal sexual excitement phase during sexual activity that the clinician judges to be adequate in focus, intensity and duration." DSM-III-R recognizes that some women are orgasmic during noncoital stimulation (e.g., in masturbation) but anorgasmic in coitus without manual clitoral stimulation. This latter condition is judged to be a variant of the normal female sexual response cycle. Thus, women who are anorgasmic with penile stimulation alone should not be considered to have a sexual dysfunction. The coital anorgasmia may be etiologically related to constitutional sensory thresholds rather than psychosexual conflicts (Derogatis, et al., 1986).

When evaluating a male patient with an orgasm disorder, the clinician should bear in mind the following clinical conditions. Men may ejaculate without a sense of orgasmic pleasure; this should be designated as "Sexual Dysfunction, NOS" (not otherwise specified). Others may have orgasm without the emission of ejaculate (e.g., retrograde ejaculation following surgery disrupting innervation of the bladder sphincter muscle); this is not an orgasm disorder. Finally, orgasm and ejaculation may occur without full penile tumescence. This is a disorder of arousal if maximum tumescence has been obtained after sufficient stimulation.

"Conversely Premature Ejaculation" occurs persistently with "minimal sexual stimulation or before, upon, or shortly after penetration and before the person wishes it." Premature ejaculation may occur with partial or full tumescence and is usually a condition that has been present since the male was sexually active with a partner. While no orgasmic pleasure difference is reported, a man with premature ejaculation is usually distressed that he cannot last long enough for his female partner to achieve orgasm with penile penetration. In many cases, she initiates the consultation.

Sexual Pain Disorders

There are two sexual pain disorders, "Dyspareunia" and "Vaginismus". Dyspareunia in a man or woman is "recurrent or persistent genital pain...before, during or after sexual intercourse." To assign this diagnosis in women, the dyspareunia should not be caused by a lack of lubrication ("Female Sexual Arousal Disorder") or secondary to vaginismus. In both men and women, the pain is not caused by a physical condition.

Vaginismus is "recurrent or persistent involuntary spasm of the musculature of the outer third of the vagina that interferes with coitus." Although frequently secondary to genital or sexual trauma, the disorder is not caused *exclusively* by a physical disorder. The spasms of vaginismus are reflex spasms and are not voluntary responses on the woman's part; her male partner often does not appreciate this fact and feels that his sexual advances are being willfully rejected. The condition is frequently generalized to interfere with a pelvic examination or, in rare cases, the insertion of a tampon.

ETIOLOGY

Human sexual behavior is motivated behavior in which physiological drives are expressed bodily, are experienced by a sentient person, and, if only in fantasy, are nearly always in an erotic relationship with another person (or object surrogate such as a fetish). This is what is meant when we speak of human sexual behavior as biopsychosocial. When sexual behavior fails to achieve the desired end (e.g., intercourse), then sexual dysfunction has occurred. The etiology of the dysfunction can be biogenic or psychogenic or a combination of the two. These, in fact, are the three categories of the specification that DSM-III-R suggests the clinician make when assigning a sexual dysfunction diagnosis. The social, or relational, context of the sexual behavior can be seen as an environmental support or stressor for the activity.

Biogenic Causes

Biogenic sexual dysfunction is determined by a careful review of systems as well as by physical examination (Table 2). A family history of chronic diseases should also be obtained. Symptomatology or history of endocrine, vascular, or neurologic diseases deserve special attention. Table 3 elaborates some of the more common medical and surgical causes of sexual dysfunction in men and women.

Table 13–2 **Components of physical examination of sexually dysfunctional patients**

ORGAN SYSTEM	PHYSICAL EXAMINATION
Endocrine system	hair distribution
	gynecomastia
	testes
	thyroid gland
Vascular system	peripheral pulses
Gastrointestinal	hepatomegaly, or atrophic liver with peripheral neuropathy due to alcoholism
Genitourinary system	prostate (in male)
	pelvic examination (in female)
Nervous system	
Sacral innervation	
S1-S2	mobility of small muscles of the foot
S2-S4	internal, external anal sphincter tone
	bulbocavernosus reflex (in male)
S2-S5	perianal sensation
Peripheral sensation	
Deep tendon reflexes	
Long tract signs	

Wise TN, Schmidt CW. Diagnostic approaches to sexuality in the medically ill. In RC Hall, TP Beresford, eds., Handbook of psychiatric diagnostic procedures (Vol 2). New York: Spectrum, 1985.

Table 13-3 **Organic factors which may affect sexual response in men and women**

MEN	WOMEN	BOTH
• Peyronie's disease	• Atrophic vaginitis	• Chronic systemic disease
• Urethral infections	• Infections of the vagina	• Chronic pain
• Testicular disease	• Cystitis, urethritis	• Diabetes mellitus
• Hypogonadal androgen-deficient states	• Endometriosis	• Angina pectoris
• Hydrocele	• Episiotomy scars, tears	• Hypertension
• Lumbar sympathectomy	• Uterine prolapse	• Multiple sclerosis
• Radical perineal prostatectomy	• Infections of external genitalia	• Hyperprolactinemia
		• Spinal cord lesions
		• Alcoholism
		• Substance abuse

Reprinted with permission from Schmidt. Sexual disorders. In Harvey AM, Owens A Jr, McKusick A (eds). *Principles and practice of medicine*, p 1149, 16.10-1. E. Norwalk, CT: Appleton & Lange, 1988.

Drugs are commonly a principal agent in sexual dysfunction and often contribute to the disorder in a patient whose body has already been compromised by disease. Table 4 lists many drugs reported to affect sexual response. Alcohol and drug abuse, beta-adrenergic blockers, centrally acting antihypertensives, and antiandrogens are the most commonly reported drugs implicated in sexual dysfunction (Fagan and Schmidt, 1987).

Referrals to allied medical specialties can be used to determine biogenic factors of sexual dysfunction. A urological examination for erectile dysfunction includes Doppler studies of penile blood flow and measurement of the penile-brachial index (PBI), the ratio of penile systolic pressure to brachial systolic pressure. A PBI less than 0.75 suggests possible vascular etiology for erectile dysfunction (Gerwertz and Zarins, 1985).

Endocrine studies of patients with suspected hormonal etiology should include measurement of fasting blood sugar and assays of follicle-stimulating hormone (FSH), luteinizing hormone (LH), testosterone, and prolactin as well as a general survey (e.g., SMA-18) for liver and renal disease.

Neurological assessment of the motor, sensory, and autonomic nervous system should pay special attention to the lumbosacral spinal pathways (see Table 2 and Figure 2). A cystometrogram or urinary flow studies can grossly define autonomic function in this area. The nerve-sparing technique for retropubic prostatectomy means that such patients should not be considered a priori surgically impotent (Walsh, Lepor, and Eggleston, 1983).

Nocturnal penile tumescence (NPT) studies (Karacan, 1982) monitor the duration, frequency, and amount of penile tumescence during REM sleep. NPT studies can also determine the relationship between penile blood flow and bulbocavernosus and ischiocavernosus muscle activity. In many centers there is also a rigidity challenge in which the buckling force of the erection is measured by a technician with a handheld mercury strain gauge. While NPT is the most complete evaluation of nocturnal erections, recent research (Schiavi and Schreiner-Engel, 1988; Segraves, Schoenberg,

Table 13–4 **Some drugs that may affect sexual response**

DRUG	SEXUAL DISORDER
Antihypertensives and cardiovascular	
Acetazolamide	Decreased desire
Atenolol	Inhibited excitement
Bethanidine	Inhibited excitement
Chlorthalidone	Decreased desire
Clofibrate	Decreased desire
Clonidine	Inhibited excitement
Digoxin	Decreased desire
Disopyramide	Inhibited excitement
Guanethidine	Inhibited excitement, no ejaculation
Hydralazine	Inhibited excitement
Methyldopa	Decreased desire, inhibited excitement, inability to ejaculate
Phenoxybenzamine	No ejaculation
Pentolinium	Inhibited excitement, inability to ejaculate
Prazosin	Inhibited excitement
Propranolol	Decreased desire, inhibited excitement
Reserpine	Decreased desire, inhibited excitement, decreased or no ejaculation, breast enlargement
Spironolactone	Decreased desire, inhibited excitement
Thiazide diuretics	Inhibited excitement
Timolol	Decreased desire, inhibited excitement, no ejaculation
Drugs often abused	
Alcohol	Decreased desire, inhibited excitement
Heroin	Inhibited excitement
Methadone	Decreased desire, inhibited excitement
Sedative-hypnotics	Inhibited excitement
Psychoactive drugs	
Antidepressants	
Amitriptyline	Changes in libido, inhibited excitement, inability to ejaculate
Cyclobenzaprine	Changes in libido
Doxepin	Changes in libido, inhibited excitement
Imipramine	Changes in libido, inhibited excitement, inability to ejaculate
Phenelzine	Inhibited excitement
Trazodone	Spontaneous erections or priapism in men; increased libido in women
Anxiolytic agents	
Benzodiazepines	Changes in libido
Antipsychotic agents	
Fluphenazine	Changes in libido, inhibited excitement, inability to ejaculate
Haloperidol	Changes in libido, inhibited excitement, inability to ejaculate
Lithium	Inhibited excitement
Mesoridazine	Changes in libido, inhibited excitement, inability to ejaculate
Prochlorperazine	Changes in libido, inhibited excitement, inability to ejaculate
Thioridazine	Changes in libido, inhibited excitement, inability to ejaculate, retrograde ejaculation
Trifluoperazine	Changes in libido, inhibited excitement, inability to ejaculate

(continued)

Table 13–4 **(continued)**

DRUG	SEXUAL DISORDER
Gastrointestinal drugs	
Chlordiazepoxide	Decreased desire
Cimetidine	Decreased desire, inhibited excitement
Dicyclomine hydrochloride	Inhibited excitement
Methantheline bromide	Inhibited excitement
Propantheline bromide	Inhibited excitement
Hormonal drugs	
Estrogens	Decreased desire in men
Hydroxyprogesterone caproate	Inhibited excitement
Methandrostenolone	Decreased desire
Norethandrolone	Decreased desire, inhibited excitement
Norethindrone	Decreased desire, inhibited excitement
Progesterone	Decreased desire, inhibited excitement
Others	
Aminocaproic acid	No ejaculation
Fenfluramine	Decreased desire, inhibited excitement
Homatropine methylbromide	Inhibited excitement
Metronidazole	Decreased desire
Naproxen	Inhibited excitement, no ejaculation
Phenytoin	Decreased sexual activity

Reprinted with permission from: DxRx, I, 2 (1985); Wise TN (1984, May). How drugs can help or hinder sexual function. *Drug Therapy,* pp 137–149. See also Drugs that cause sexual dysfunction (1983). *Medical Letter on Drugs and Therapeutics, 25,* 73–76, for a more complete list with references.

and Segraves, 1985) invites further exploration of the relationship between nocturnal erections and those sought or attained while awake.

If there is clear evidence that there is a biogenic cause of the sexual dysfunction and there is no indication of psychogenic factors that are, in themselves, sufficient to account for the dysfunction, the medical condition should be noted on Axis III, and an Axis I sexual dysfunction disorder should not be diagnosed. However, clinicians should be careful to avoid missing the subtle psychogenic issues that may be present, albeit somewhat overshadowed by a major illness.

Psychogenic Causes

To ascertain the psychogenic causes of sexual dysfunction, a complete psycho-social and psychosexual history should be taken. Table 5 lists the data particularly important for the sexual development and behavior of an individual. To obtain the sexual data, the clinician should establish an atmosphere of candor and relative comfort. He or she should ask every and any question that may be relevant to the diagnosis and treatment of the sexual dysfunction. If the clinician is confident that the information being obtained is important, then this attitude will be conveyed to the patient and a condition of relative comfort will exist between them.

Watching experienced clinicians taking histories of both sexes will help the

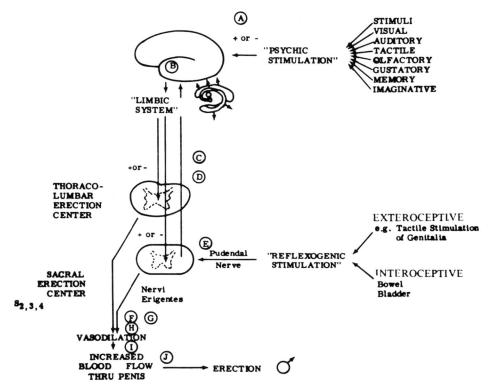

Figure 13–2. *Neurological pathways involved in human penile erection. A–J, sites where lesions could cause sexual dysfunction. (Reproduced with permission from Weiss HD: The physiology of human erection. Ann Intern Med 16:793, 1972)*

novice clinician learn the art of taking a sexual history. It is normal to be somewhat embarrassed in the initial stages of taking sexual histories, especially in patients of the opposite sex. In taking a sexual history, the clinician must be aware of and able to confront issues of sexuality in his or her own life. The discomfort or embarrassment should diminish fairly rapidly with experience. If it persists, the clinician should consult his or her clinical supervisor for assistance. Conversely, if the clinician feels absolutely no twinge of discomfort when initially taking sexual histories, he or she may lack sufficient sensitivity to the emotional issues connected with sexuality. This absence of affect should also be discussed with a supervisor.

If the sexual history follows the lifeline and developmental stages (as suggested in Table 5), the patient can have a cognitive plan of what to expect. This helps to reduce the anxiety that would be generated if the patient felt that a set of completely random questions were being asked about his or her sexual behavior in symptom checklist fashion.

To learn about the phenomenology of the sexual dysfunction, it is helpful to ask the patient to describe his or her most recent attempt at sexual experience. Questions should focus on the person's mental/emotional reactions to the sexual experience

Table 13–5 **Data Covered for Sexual History**

Childhood

First sex play with peers
Family sleeping arrangements
Sex play with siblings
Sexual abuse, incest, or molestation
Parental attitudes toward sex
Sources of sexual knowledge

Pubertal

Menarche or first ejaculation: subjective reaction
Secondary sex characteristics: subjective reaction
Body image
Masturbation fantasies and frequency
Homoerotic fantasies and behavior
Dating experiences (physical intimacies)
Intercourse
  Age at first occurrence
  Reaction to first intercourse

Young adult

Lengthy or live-in relationships
Pattern of sexual activities with others
Paraphilic behaviors
Previous marriages
  Courtship
  Parental attitudes toward spouse
  Sexual activity (dysfunction?)
  Reasons for termination of marriage
Venereal disease

Adult

Present primary sexual relationship
Development of relationship
Significant nonsexual problems (e.g., money, alcohol, in-laws)
Infertility; contraceptive practices
Children (problems?)

Sexual behaviors
Extramarital affairs
Intercourse frequency during relationship
Variety of sexual behaviors (e.g., oral-genital, masturbation)
Previous dysfunction (in either partner)
Elaboration of onset and history of present problem (without partner
  present)
Perception of partner's reaction to problem
Homosexual activity
Possible exposure to AIDS

Reprinted with permission from Fagan PJ, Schmidt CW Jr. Sexual Dysfunction in the
Medically Ill. In Stoudemire A, Fogel BS, eds. *Principles of Medical Psychiatry.* p. 312.
Orlando: Grune & Stratton, 1987.

(e.g., "Did you think about what you were doing or were you thinking about something or someone else?") as well as on the patient's physiological responses (e.g., "Were you lubricated when penetration was attempted?"). Thoughts and feelings about self and partner convey the emotional reactions. The human sexual response cycle serves as the framework for appreciating the physiological response of the patient. Even with a complete history, however, the multiple determinants of the dysfunction may not become apparent until the person or couple has been in psychotherapy for several sessions.

Psychogenic causes of sexual dysfunction are cognitions or emotions that either ignore (repress) nearly all sexual stimuli, in disorders of sexual desire, or, in the other sexual disorders, lead to a "fight-or-flight" physiological reaction in which adrenergic effects inhibit the normal human sexual response cycle. The most common example is performance anxiety, in which the man (usually) is so concerned about his sexual functioning that the anxiety itself becomes a self-fulfilling prophecy.

The etiology of these cognitions or emotions that cause sexual dysfunction can be understood from a variety of theoretical frameworks, but none totally explains the etiology of all sexual dysfunction. The major systems that have addressed sexual behavior (and by extension, sexual dysfunction) are psychoanalytic theory, behaviorism, cognitive theory, and social learning theory. What follows is a brief statement about each theory, with a clinical example of the etiology of a sexual dysfunction as explained by that theory.

A *psychoanalytic* approach to sexuality (Person, 1988) and to sexual dysfunction (Meyer, Schmidt, and Wise, 1983) most often explains the disorder as a symptom of an underlying psychological conflict. As such, the dysfunction serves as a psychosomatic symbol of an unconscious conflict and a protection (defense) against consciously experiencing the anxiety of that primary conflict (e.g., separation from a loved object). For example, most sexual dysfunction promotes sexual estrangement, in which physical intimacy is reduced. One with an arousal disorder, therefore, reduces his or her exposure to the possibility of rejection by a lover. A psychoanalytic therapist might also suspect that this fear of rejection is rooted in an infantile experience of rejection by the mother or father.

Behaviorism explains sexual behavior as it does all behavior: as a response to environmental stimuli. In classical conditioning, an object becomes paired with a stimulus so that it can provoke the same response in the organism. In operant conditioning, the organism learns to interact with the environment so that a favorable reward is obtained or a negative result avoided. Sexual pleasure is a reward; sexual pain is a negative result. If sexual intercourse has become paired with pain, including emotional pain, then any approach to it will be avoided. This is commonly seen in sexual aversion disorder. In more extreme cases, the trauma of rape or incest results in aversion disorder or vaginismus.

Social learning theory stresses the role of learning by imitating others (McConaghy, 1987). A person learns how to be sexual with others by observing how others, especially those of the same sex, act sexually. The importance of parental and familial role models in sexual development is crucial. The attitude toward sexuality, the expression of affection, and communication skills in the family of origin are precursors to later adult attitudes and the manner of expressing affection and sexuality. Conflicts about sex role (e.g., insecurity about being able to act like a "real" man or woman) or sex stereotyping can result in sexual dysfunction.

If the parents believe that sex is bad and must be controlled at all costs, then the child as an adult is likely to find it difficult to accept sexual pleasure without emotional conflict. If one "learns" early that sex can be a controlling or manipulating force over others, then sexual activity as an adult will be colored by tones of a power struggle. Sex that is used mainly as an instrument of power usually results in sexual dysfunction in one of the partners unless a primarily sadomasochistic sexual relationship has been established.

Cognitive theory stresses the importance of cognitions or beliefs that determine emotional responses and behaviors in sexual activity (Walen & Roth, 1987). In many ways it is similar to social learning theory, except that it places less stress on early childhood experiences. It is more concerned with the cognitions that are held here and now, and less with their etiology. If an individual believes, for example, that the opposite sex seeks to control, emotionally engulf, or dominate others, then those beliefs (often unrecognized) will influence the emotions the person has during sexual intimacy. Examples are a woman who is anorgasmic because she fears loss of control or a man who gets in and out of a "dangerous" situation with premature ejaculation.

Allied to cognitive etiology of sexual dysfunction are those cases in which a lack of sexual information causes dysfunction. Examples are an older man who expects to achieve an erection (as he did as a youth) without any direct penile stimulation or a menopausal woman who does not realize she may need a vaginal lubricant.

In conclusion, sexual dysfunctions that are psychogenic cannot be directly and universally related to any one specific etiologic event or psychodynamic structure. It is never a case of, "This is premature ejaculation; therefore X must have caused it." Taking a careful history, further elaborating the patient's psychological constitution in therapy, and testing etiological hypotheses in therapeutic approaches are necessary to confirm the psychogenic factors for a particular patient.

TREATMENT

General Principles

Because patients often have difficulty discussing sexual problems, their presentation of the chief complaint and the history of the present illness may be imprecise. It is therefore necessary to set aside enough time to evaluate the problem; more than one session may be necessary to complete the task. With a patient whose sexual dysfunction involves a partner or a spouse, the evaluation ideally should include the partner's view of the problem. Finally, asking patients about their notions concerning the etiology of their sexual disorder and their expectations for treatment are helpful in understanding patient biases.

The eventual development of a treatment plan depends on the specifics of each case, including several important favorable prognostic factors. Those factors include recent onset of symptoms, mild to moderate severity of dysfunction, prior history of good sexual function, identifiable situational stress factors, good mental health, absence of paraphilia, and a spouse or partner who is cooperative with the evaluation and willing to participate in treatment. Although evaluation often reveals that sexual dysfunctions may be secondary to marital or relational discord, the sexual complaint is the ticket of entry into the care system, and treatment should be provided on the basis of the presenting complaint. Once treatment has begun, relational issues may obtain priority and redirect the goals of treatment.

When patients do not require referral, the PLISSIT model developed by Annon and Robinson (1978) is very useful for evaluation and office counseling. The clinician gives permission (P) to the patient to discuss his or her sexual concerns and apprehensions by initiating discussion with appropriate solicitous questions. In response to the questions the patient may have about the sexual problem, the clinician provides limited information (LI) (i.e., enough information to enable informed decisions), without overloading the patient with accurate but excessive detail. As rapport is established between the clinician and patient, the clinician gives specific suggestions (SS) about how to maximize sexual function, taking into account the circumstances of the current relationship and other psychological stressors. Patients that do not respond are referred for intensive therapy (IT).

ORGANIC DISORDERS

Sexual disorders that are secondary to chronic illness, chronic pain, or the side effects of medications may be reversed by medical interventions. Improvement of the patient's overall physical condition and relief of pain may restore sexual function. Drug holidays, a change of medication, or discontinuance of medication may reverse dysfunctions. Dysfunction secondary to the acute side effects of substance abuse or alcoholism will often remit once the abuse is controlled. Prolactin-secreting microadenomas (which cause loss of desire and arousal disorders) may be treated by surgical resection or medically by administering bromocriptine. Inhibited desire in men and/or male arousal disorders secondary to hypogonadism are responsive to intramuscular administration of exogenous testosterone, providing there is no evidence of prostatic carcinoma.

Sexual dysfunction irreversibly impaired by trauma, disease, or the sequela of surgery is treatable by using the principles of rehabilitation medicine: quantify the loss of function, establish realistic rehabilitative goals, and develop training techniques to maximize residual functional capacities. Patients who suffer irreversible damage can be taught sexual techniques that enable them to maintain sexual relationships, a great psychological benefit to both the patient and the partner. Patients should also be referred to self-help associations (e.g., multiple sclerosis groups, ostomy and cardiac support groups), which hold group meetings and provide literature on sexual function. Dysfunctions secondary to estrogen deficiency are responsive to estrogen replacement (providing no medical contraindications exist), largely by effecting an improved sense of well-being and by increasing the ability to lubricate vaginally. Male arousal disorders can be treated surgically and/or medically.

Two types of penile prostheses are routinely implanted: silastic rods with malleable metal cores and inflatable devices. Predictors of successful adjustment to a penile prosthesis are:

1. Awareness on the patient's part of an ambivalence about the surgery;
2. A stable and mature relationship between the patient and his partner;
3. Sexual activity both before and after the onset of impotence; and
4. Good mental health (Berg, Mindus, Berg, et al., 1984).

An alternative medical treatment requires intact tissue responsive to vasodilating substances (papaverine and phentolamine), although concerns have been raised recently about tissue damage secondary to chronic injections (Turner, et al., 1988). The treatment involves injecting small amounts of the vasodilators into the corpora. Within minutes, an erection is produced that may last for 60 to 90 minutes.

PSYCHOSEXUAL DISORDERS

Desire Disorders

Loss of sexual desire is often associated with depressive disorders, which should be treated with antidepressants, psychotherapy, or both. Marital discord is a common psychogenic cause of loss of desire. Chronic discord leads to anger, and although the partners may be aware of their anger, they fail to connect their loss of sexual interest in each other with their anger towards each other. Counseling begins by reviewing current life situations to identify stressors and to highlight conflicts. Treatment focuses on resolving the situational stressors through a process of compromise, collaborative planning, and development of action plans. For example, a conflict involving in-law problems is resolved by using counseling sessions as a supportive environment in which the issue can be identified (an intrusive father-in-law). Next, action plans are developed and implemented (the couple agrees to limit the number of his visits). When counseling is successful, anger subsides and the couple returns to their baseline level of sexual function.

Physicians and patients (through self-medication) sometimes try to treat loss of sexual dysfunctions with medications such as testosterone, alcohol, antianxiety compounds, or stimulants. Unfortunately, this strategy does not work, and there is no scientific basis for using medications (except for confirmed male hypogonadal states, when testosterone is useful, and for the treatment of hyperprolactinemia with bromocriptine).

Patients suffering from sexual aversion disorders usually have experienced their dysfunction since beginning adult sexual activity. Aversion disorders exist on a spectrum: at one end is the patient who simply lacks desire to initiate sexual activity but can engage in it with reasonable gratification, and on the other end is the patient who experiences panic attacks when faced with a sexual opportunity. This reaction is clearly a more severe form of the disorder and requires aggressive treatment with chemotherapy and psychotherapy. Panic attacks are responsive to antidepressants including the tricyclics, the MAO inhibitors, and benzodiazepines. Counseling patients with the less severe form of aversion disorder is directed toward helping the unaffected partner to be more assertive in initiating sexual experiences so that the affected partner is drawn into more frequent participation in sexual relations.

Sexual Arousal Disorder

In both sexes, the inability to develop and maintain levels of sexual excitement may be the result of internal psychological events that interfere with the ability to focus on the stimuli causing sexual excitement. A common psychological distraction is preoccupation with sexual performance. This can become a powerful distraction: as concern about performance becomes more and more absorbing, the psychological activity of worrying about performance crowds out the capacity to attend to sexual stimuli, eventually resulting in the loss of arousal. Masters and Johnson named this process "spectatoring." Other common psychological interferences are worry about stressful life situations and marital discord.

Office counseling is effective for patients who present with the already described prognostic factors. The goal of counseling is to eliminate the distracting psychological event(s) so that the patient can focus on sexual stimuli. This is accomplished by first illustrating the process (i.e., spectatoring) to the patient and then teaching him or her to focus on sexual stimuli by practicing touching exercises in private. The sensate focus exercises are described by Masters and Johnson (Masters and Johnson, 1970). Prescribing small amounts of alcohol or antianxiety medications has not proven to be a successful method of chemically inducing relaxation in order to block the process of spectatoring.

INHIBITED ORGASM

Men who experience inhibited orgasm are usually found to have personality disorders and require referral for evaluation and treatment. As noted earlier, inhibited orgasm must be differentiated from retrograde ejaculation. Retrograde ejaculation has been reported as a side effect of some medications, including thioridazine (Mellaril).

Women experiencing inhibited orgasm who give evidence of the favorable prognostic factors described above, including a past history of orgasmic response, are candidates for office counseling. The current loss of orgasmic response may often be traced to recent sexual experiences during which the patient could not experience orgasm because of a psychological distraction (the process described above). Counseling is used to resolve the stress and then to shift the patient's focus of attention from her concern about orgasm to enjoyment of the total sexual experience. Again, the touching exercises (sensate focus) are prescribed to the patient and her partner. Single patients should be instructed to practice focusing on sexual stimuli during masturbation, with the expectation that a positive response (i.e., orgasmic response) will generalize to sexual experiences with a partner. As can be seen in Table I, inhibited orgasm in women is common, although few patients in the general medical setting will volunteer this complaint unless specifically asked. Many women can enjoy sex completely without achieving orgasm and derive sufficient pleasure during the plateau stage. Concern about orgasmic dysfunction varies, as does the need for specific treatment.

PREMATURE EJACULATION

Typically, the patient presents with a history of reaching orgasm as he is attempting to penetrate, just as he has penetrated, or within several thrusts after penetration. He often reports experiencing premature ejaculation since he became sexually active during late adolescence or early adulthood. Men with this dysfunction usually seek help only when their partners become exasperated with the chronic sexual frustration associated with the disorder. Single patients seek assistance when relationships fail as a result of the dysfunction.

There are two behavioral methods for treating premature ejaculation that effectively teach the patient an awareness of his progression through the sexual response cycle and help him control the timing of that progression. These goals are readily achieved when the patient has a regular sexual partner who will participate in the treatment program. Both the "squeeze" and the "stop-and-go" techniques have been used successfully. With the squeeze technique, the female partner places her thumb and first two fingers around the coronal ridge of the penis and presses firmly for 10 seconds. The pressure results in a 10 to 25 % loss of erection and a decrease in the subjective sense of arousal. The stop-and-go technique is practiced by alternately stimulating the penis and resting without touching. Either technique is introduced as an exercise following initial practice with the sensate focus exercises. Control over the pacing of the sexual experience is achieved by practicing the exercises and by using one of these techniques throughout all phases of the response cycle.

Behavioral counseling of this sort can be done in an office setting, but it requires therapist training and experience. Treatment is often complicated by the anger typically experienced and expressed by the female partner and repressed by the patient, necessitating marital therapy in addition to sexually focused treatment.

SEXUAL PAIN DISORDERS

Dyspareunia

Psychogenic dyspareunia is rare, and the diagnosis should be made only after all possible organic causes of pain have been ruled out. Patients subject to psychogenic dyspareunia are likely to have personality traits that support the disorder (e.g., the tendency to somaticize conflict). Depending on the outcome of the evaluation, the type of treatment may be individual, group, or behavioral. For some patients, it may incorporate treatment principles associated with the management of chronic pain.

Vaginismus

The diagnosis of functional vaginismus is often made when a physician attempting a pelvic examination cannot pass a finger or the smallest speculum into the vagina because of contraction of the musculature around the vaginal outlet. Successful treatment is based on behavioral methods that desensitize the patient to the experience of penetration. The couple is instructed to create a relaxing milieu by taking a bath together, followed by touching exercises (sensate focus). Next, they are asked to repeat the general touching but to include the genitals, avoiding touching that is overtly sexually stimulating. Having mastered the two sets of exercises, they are asked to repeat the bath, the general body touching, and genital touching, and then to pass a small dilator into the vagina. On subsequent days, the size of the dilators is increased until the dilator approximates the circumference of a penis. The penis is then substituted for the dilator. Patients without partners can be treated in a similar manner with the dilators self-applied. However, it is important to note that the acceptance of the dilators may not generalize to a shared sexual experience. Should this be the case, treatment should be delayed until the patient is in a relationship of sufficient commitment to permit including the partner in the treatment program.

THE ROLE OF THE NONPSYCHIATRIC PHYSICIAN IN PATIENT MANAGEMENT

Physicians in all specialities can expect to be approached by patients about sexual problems. Internists, obstetricians, gynecologists, and pediatricians are frequently questioned by patients about sexual issues. However, regardless of specialty, each physician must decide whether to evaluate the patient's complaint or make a referral. When the choice is to do an evaluation, the physician should schedule at least 30 minutes to complete an initial evaluation. Additional sessions may be necessary to complete the evaluation, to develop a diagnostic formulation, and to design a treatment strategy. Counseling methods and techniques have been described in each subsection for those physicians interested in the office management of psychosexual dysfunction. The physician should contract with the patient or the couple for a specific number of sessions (about five), for a defined amount of time per session (30 to 60 minutes), and a regular meeting date (i.e., Thursday, 2 p.m.). The scheduling details are important components of the therapeutic framework. Patients who do not respond to office counseling should be referred for further treatment.

Once the decision to refer has been made, there are several issues to consider. Should a patient be referred to a general psychiatrist or psychologist, or to someone specializing in the treatment of sexual disorders? How can a physician evaluate the credentials of therapists who state they are expert in evaluating and treating sexual disorders?

Patients with sexual complaints that are secondary to major psychiatric disorders (i.e., schizophrenia, bipolar disorder, major depression) should be referred to a general psychiatrist for the necessary psychotropic medication as well as psychotherapy. When a patient with a sexual dysfunction has a comorbid anxiety disorder or substance abuse disorder, the latter conditions should receive prompt attention from a psychiatrist or psychologist who specializes in the treatment of such disorders. In some cases, the sexual dysfunction can be treated concurrently, but generally the anxiety disorder or substance abuse must be treated first.

Individuals or couples whose major problem is their inability to relate to others (in other words, sex is just one of several issues) can be referred to a psychiatrist or psychologist, provided the patient is willing to work on general relationship issues rather than narrowly focused sexual problems. Patients whose Axis I diagnosis is a psychosexual disorder are the best candidates for sexually focused treatment. Because sexually focused treatment methods ultimately include relational issues, most therapists expert in the techniques of sexual therapy are also experienced in marital therapies and the relational issues associated with personality disorders. This combination of skills is important and useful because patients often need a course of treatment that includes several methods used in sequence.

The question of credentials may be approached in several ways. The certified generalist with the more advanced degree is likely to be better trained (for psychiatrists, board certified; for psychologists, Ph.D. and licensed). Since most states do not license or certify sexual therapists, the professional should have trained for at least a year in a sexual disorders program; the best such programs are associated with medical schools. If the referring physician has difficulty identifying a source for referral, the closest medical school is usually a safe bet for inquiring about sexual disorder programs and therapists. Several national organizations (such as the Society for Sex Therapy and Research) keep a list of qualified members, listed geographically.

Sexual dysfunctions are moderately prevalent among medical patients and, to a lesser extent, in the general population. Whether the etiology is psychogenic, biogenic, or both, the physician should take time to ascertain the nature of the disorder and the extent to which the patient is distressed. For some dysfunctions, the physician can make effective office interventions; other patients require additional evaluation and treatment. In either instance, therapeutic attention should be given to the person with sexual dysfunction.

CLINICAL PEARLS

- Neither physicians nor patients are trained to talk about sexual problems, and the terms used in most medical situations are not amenable for discussing sexual issues. It is incumbent on the physician to create an atmosphere of comfort and trust that allows the patient to explore his or her sexual difficulties. To do this, the physician must be comfortable with issues concerning human sexuality.
- When a patient is in a committed relationship, it is very helpful to have the partner's view of the problem to understand the whole story. Occasionally, a sexually functional partner will seek help to gain support for obtaining the evaluation of a dysfunctional partner; it is unusual for both partners to present with sexual dysfunctions. However, once treatment has begun, in at least 30% of the cases a sexual dysfunction will be discovered in the partner who supposedly is sexually functional.
- When evaluating or treating couples with sexual problems, extramarital relationships are sometimes uncovered. It is the responsibility of the involved partner to decide whether to reveal such a relationship. The physician should not automatically view the extramarital relationship as a threat to the primary relationship; numerous relationships have survived extramarital affairs. Until the dynamics of the relationships are well understood by the physician, it is prudent to withhold recommendations about such affairs, or to defer such decisions to a psychiatrist or psychologist.

ANNOTATED BIBLIOGRAPHY

Friedman RC: Normal sexuality and introduction to sexual disorders. In: Michels R, et al. (eds): Psychiatry. Philadelphia, JB Lippincott, 1987

> This chapter provides basic information about biopsychosocial aspects of human sexuality and contains information with which the reader of this chapter is presumed to be familiar. There is also a lengthy treatment of the history of homosexuality as a diagnostic category and of present clinical issues regarding sexual orientation.

Kaplan HS: Psychosexual dysfunctions. In: Michels R et al. (eds): Psychiatry. Philadelphia, JB Lippincott, 1987

> Dr. Kaplan provides rich clinical descriptions of sexual dysfunctions (DSM-III) and stresses an integrated treatment of them, combining behavioral, psychodynamic, and psychopharmacological modalities and interventions.

Rosen RC: Patterns of sexual response. In: Patterns of Sexual Arousal: Psychophysiological processes and clinical applications. New York: Guilford, 1988

> This chapter provides an overview of conceptualizing human sexual response; the author suggests that more attention be paid to cognitive and higher cortical stimuli. The entire book is well worth reading.

Saddock VA. Psychosexual dysfunction and treatment. In: Kaplan HI, Saddock BJ (eds): Comprehensive textbook of psychiatry/IV, vol. 1. Baltimore, Williams & Wilkins, 1985

> This chapter contains a detailed table of the physiological changes that occur during the sexual response cycle as described and documented by Masters and Johnson.

REFERENCES

Annon JS, Robinson CH: The use of vicarious learning in the treatment of sexual concerns. In: LoPiccolo J, LoPiccolo L, (eds): Handbook of sex therapy. New York, Plenum Press, 1978

Berg R, Mindus P, Berg G, et al: Penile implants in erectile impotence: Outcome and prognostic indicators. Scand J Urol Nephrol, 18:277–282, 1984

Derogatis LR, Fagan PJ, Schmidt CW, et al: Psychological subtypes of anorgasmia: a marker variable approach. J Sex Marital Ther, 12:197–210, 1986

Fagan PJ, Schmidt CW Jr: Sexual dysfunction in the medically ill. In: Stoudemire A, Fogel BS (eds): Principles of medical psychiatry. Orlando, Grune & Stratton, 1987

Fagan PJ, Schmidt CW Jr, Wise TN, et al: Sexual dysfunction and dual psychiatric diagnoses. Compr Psychiatry 29:278–284, 1988

Gerwertz BL, Zarins CK: Vasculogenic impotence. In: Segraves RT, Schoenberg HW (eds): Diagnosis and treatment of erectile disturbances. New York, Plenum Press, 1985

Kaplan HS: Sexual aversion, sexual phobias and panic disorder. New York, Brunner/Mazel, 1987

Karacan I: Nocturnal penile tumescence as a biological marker in assessing erectile dysfunction. Psychosomatics, 23:349–360, 1982

Kolodny RC, Masters WH, Johnson VE: Textbook of sexual medicine. Boston, Little, Brown, 1979

Maurice WL, Guze SB: Sexual dysfunction and associated psychiatric disorder. Compr Psychiatry 11:539—543, 1970

Masters WH, Johnson VE: Human sexual response. Boston, Little, Brown, 1966

Masters WH, Johnson VE: Human Sexual Inadequacy. Boston, Little, Brown, 1970

McConaghy N: A learning approach. In: Geer JH, O'Donohue WT (eds): Theories of human sexuality. New York, Plenum Press, 1987

Meyer JK, Schmidt CW Jr, Wise TN (eds): Clinical management of sexual disorders, 2nd ed. Washington DC, American Psychiatric Press, 1986

Nathan SG: The epidemiology of the DSM-III psychosexual dysfunctions. J Sex Marital Ther 12:267—281, 1986

Person ES: A psychoanalytical approach. In: Geer JH, O'Donohue WT (eds): Theories of human sexuality. New York, Plenum Press, 1987

Schiavi RC, Schreiner-Engel P: Healthy aging and male sexual arousal (abstract). Annual Meeting of the Society for Sex Therapy and Research, New York, March 19, 1988

Schmidt CW Jr: Sexual disorders. In: Harvey AM, Owens AH Jr, McKusick VA, et al. (eds): Principles and practice of medicine. Norwalk CT, Appleton & Lange, 1988

Schover LR, Jensen SB: Sexuality and chronic illness. New York, Guilford, 1988

Segraves RT, Schoenberg HW, Segraves KA: Evaluation of the etiology of erectile failure. In: Segraves RT, Schoenberg HW (eds): Diagnosis and treatment of erectile disturbances. New York, Plenum Press, 1985

Steiner BW (ed): Gender dysphoria: Development, research, management. New York, Plenum Press, 1985

Stoller RJ: Gender identity disorders of childhood and adults. In: Kaplan HI, Saddock BJ (eds): Comprehensive textbook of psychiatry/IV, vol. 1. Baltimore, Williams & Wilkins, 1985

Turner LA, Althof SE, Levine SB, et al: Self-injection of papaverine and phentolamine in the treatment of psychogenically impotent men. Paper delivered at the 15th annual meeting of the Society for Sex Therapy and Research, New York, March 19, 1988

Walen SR, Roth D: A cognitive approach. In: Geer JH, O'Donohue WT (eds): Theories of human sexuality. New York, Plenum Press, 1987

Walsh PC, Lepor H, Eggleston JC: Radical prostatectomy with preservation of sexual function: anatomical and pathological considerations. Prostate, 4:473–485, 1983

Weiss HD: The physiology of human erection. Ann Intern Med, 76:793–799, 1972

Wise TN, Schmidt CW Jr: Diagnostic approaches to sexuality in the medically ill. In: Hall RC, Beresford TP (eds): Handbook of diagnostic procedures, vol. 2. New York, Spectrum, 1985

Paraphilias

14

William D. Murphy and Elizabeth D. Schwarz

Paraphilias, or sexual deviations, have provoked both curiosity and abhorrence in laypersons and professionals alike. The paraphilias, as described in the DSM-III-R (APA, 1987), are a group of disorders whose essential features are recurrent, intense sexual urges and sexually arousing fantasies generally involving either nonhuman objects, suffering or humiliation of one's self or partner (not merely simulated), or children or other nonconsenting persons.

Unlike many disorders described in this text, paraphilias represent not only psychiatric or psychological problems: many are illegal and can cause significant emotional damage and sometimes physical damage to victims (Finkelhor, 1986). Therefore, in many instances the physician must be concerned not only about the presenting problem of the patient, but also about past victims and future danger. For example, in almost every state a physician must report to the local child protection agency any incident of known or suspected child sexual abuse. Many times, the clinician who elects to treat a paraphiliac patient who is involved in illegal acts assumes responsibility not only for the patient's behavior, but also for the protection of society.

Although most nonpsychiatric physicians will not provide direct psychological treatment to such patients, this chapter will serve to increase the physician's awareness of the extent of these disorders; to improve the physician's understanding of the characteristics of paraphilias, thus allowing him or her to better serve victims and family members of paraphiliacs; and to allow the physician to judge and make informed decisions about appropriate referrals. Because knowledge in this area is based largely on paraphiliacs whose behavior is illegal and causes harm to others, this chapter will focus most heavily on this particular group of patients.

EPIDEMIOLOGY

Little is known about the true prevalence of various paraphiliac disorders or other demographic factors, although there is increasing knowledge, at least in the area of victimization of children. Finkelhor et al. (1986) have extensively reviewed studies surveying college students and adults regarding their sexual contacts with adults before puberty or under the age of 18. Results vary widely: studies have found prevalence rates ranging from 6 to 62% for females and from 3 to 30% for males. For females, the average rates reported are in the 20 to 25% range, while for males they are in the 8 to 10% range. The variation in rates can be partly explained by three factors: the definition of sexual abuse used (offenses involving touching versus offenses involving hands-off experiences such as exhibitionism); the sample used; and the data collection method used (trained interviewers asking multiple questions provided higher rates than self-administered questionnaires with only one or two questions about sexual abuse). Although there is clear evidence that reporting rates of child sexual abuse have increased (Murram and Weatherford, 1988; Peters, Wyatt, and Finkelhor, 1986), an interesting finding of the Peter et al. review is that the prevalence rates of studies published in the 1940s and 1950s are quite similar to those published more recently.

Although not as extensive, survey data exist for women who have been the victims of exhibitionists. Rates range from 32% in a female college sample (Cox and McMahon, 1978) to 44% of a group of British nurses (Gittleson, Eacott, and Mehta, 1978). Moser and Levitt (1987) have reviewed similar survey studies for individuals engaging in sadomasochistic fantasies and behavior. As an example, Hunt (1974) found in a sample of 2026 respondents that 4.8% of men and 2.1% of women reported having obtained pleasure from inflicting pain; 2.5% of men and 4.6% of women reported pleasure from receiving pain. However, it is highly likely that a much smaller percentage of these individuals would meet diagnostic criteria for sexual sadism or sexual masochism.

The above data are alarming and clearly indicate the extent of the problem of child sexual abuse, but they do not give us clear evidence of the number of individuals who perpetrate such abuse and how many would actually meet the criteria for a paraphiliac diagnosis. For example, Abel et al. (1987) found that pedophiles with male targets averaged about 150 victims, while those with female targets averaged about 20 victims. Exhibitionism and voyeurism averaged 513 and 429 victims, respectively.

Little else is known about the characteristics of paraphiliacs. As the DSM-III-R indicates, the disorder is seldom diagnosed in females, except in the area of sexual masochism. Although there is evidence that a small percentage of children are sexually abused by females (Finkelhor and Russell, 1984), it seems evident that the paraphilias are primarily male disorders. There is no clear evidence to suggest that the rates of paraphilias differ between ethnic groups or between geographical areas; however, increasing evidence shows that in many paraphiliacs, the onset of the disorder is in adolescence (DSM-III-R; Knopp, 1984). The need for early intervention, before the pattern becomes fixed, is becoming increasingly recognized.

DESCRIPTION

Table 1 lists the major paraphilias included in the DSM-III-R and general diagnostic criteria. All the paraphilias require at least that the patient (1) has recurrent, intense sexual urges and sexual fantasies regarding the specific paraphilia

Table 14-1 **Major Paraphilias**

Exhibitionism: Has had over the last 6 months recurrent sexual urges and sexually arousing fantasies to expose one's genitals to strangers and has either acted on these urges or is distressed by them.

Fetishism: Has had over the last 6 months recurrent sexual urges and/or arousing fantasies that involve the use of nonliving objects as sexual stimuli (e.g., female underwear) and has either acted on these or is distressed by them. The diagnosis should not be made if the fetish objects are only female clothing used in cross-dressing or devices designed specifically for sexual arousal (e.g., vibrators).

Frotteurism: Has had over the last 6 months recurrent sexual urges that involve rubbing against or touching a nonconsenting person and has either acted on these urges or is distressed by them. The touching and rubbing itself is sexually exciting, not the aggressive nature of the act.

Pedophilia: Has had over the last 6 months recurrent sexual urges and arousing fantasies that involve sexual interactions with a prepubescent child (generally younger than 13) and has either acted on these urges or is distressed by them. In addition, the patient should be at least 16 years old and at least 5 years older than the victim.

Sexual Masochism: Has had over the last 6 months recurrent sexual urges and arousing fantasies that involve the act (not a simulation of the act) of being made to suffer, being humiliated, beaten, or bound and has either acted on these or is markedly distressed by them.

Sexual Sadism: Has had over the last 6 months recurrent sexual urges and arousing fantasies that involve acts (not simulated acts) in which suffering, either physical or psychological, that includes humiliation is found to be sexually arousing by the person and the person has either acted on these or is distressed by them.

Transvestic Fetishism: A heterosexual male who over the last 6 months has had recurrent sexual urges and arousing fantasies that involve cross-dressing, which the person has acted on or is markedly distressed by them. The individual should not meet the criteria for gender identity disorder of adolescence or adulthood nontranssexual type or transsexualism.

Voyeurism: Has had over the last 6 months recurrent sexual urges and arousing fantasies that involve observing an unsuspecting person who is either naked, disrobing, or engaged in sexual behavior, and has acted on these or is distressed by them.

Paraphilia Not Otherwise Specified: Includes paraphilias that do not fit any of the above specific categories, such as telephone scatalogia (lewdness), necrophilia (corpses), etc.

(Adapted from American Psychiatric Association, 1987)

and (2) has acted on these urges or is markedly disturbed by them. Additional criteria area listed in Table 1.

Much of our knowledge is based on subject populations who are either apprehended for a sexual crime or have sought treatment. The extent to which characteristics of this population parallel other paraphiliacs who have not been caught or who have not sought treatment is unknown. Paraphiliacs are heterogeneous; many people have multiple paraphilias, and no one characteristic will apply to all individuals. For that reason, we will not discuss in any detail personality characteristics. In the literature, paraphiliacs are many times described as shy, inhibited, nonassertive individuals who have difficulty managing anger. When these characteristics are evaluated objectively, they are found to only apply to a certain percentage of paraphiliacs; no one personality profile would characterize any one paraphilia.

Exhibitionists obtain sexual pleasure from exposing their genitals to unsuspecting strangers. However, at times an exhibitionist may also expose himself to neighbors or to children he knows. During the act, he may or may not have an erection, and may or may not masturbate. Some exhibitionists leave the exhibitionistic situation and masturbate to the fantasy of exposing themselves. The vast majority of exhibitionists expose themselves to females, although we have seen some cases of exposure to males. Targets can be adults, adolescents, or children, and generally the exhibitionist does not attempt any further contact with the victim. However, for those individuals who expose to prepubescent children, the physician should rule out that the exposure is not a prelude to more active sexual involvement with the child. In general, the exhibitionist is looking for some reaction from the victim, such as shock or surprise; some may perceive, at least in fantasy, that their victim is sexually aroused by the behavior. We have also seen some exhibitionists whose arousal is increased when the victim shows fear.

The *voyeur's* behavior involves looking at individuals either undressing, nude, or engaging in sexual activities. In voyeurism, the behavior involves people who are unaware that they are being watched; the diagnosis is not made for individuals who may watch filmed or live pornography, since in such cases the individuals are aware that they are being seen. Clinicians should also be aware a history of voyeurism is sometimes seen in rapists, and it is important to rule out that the voyeur does not have an aggressive sexual arousal pattern. At times, an individual may be arrested for voyeurism while, in actuality, he was peeping in a window with the intent of raping the victim.

The *fetishist* obtains sexual arousal from a nonliving object, commonly women's underwear, shoes, boots, or other apparel. The individual will usually masturbate while rubbing, holding, or smelling the object. The person may engage in this behavior alone or ask a partner to wear the object. At times, an individual will steal the fetish object, such as underwear, or both steal and destroy it. In such cases, it is important to consider whether there is a sadistic component to the person's arousal pattern.

If a fetish object is limited to female clothes used in cross-dressing, the appropriate diagnosis is *transvestic fetishism.* Cross-dressing in woman's clothes may be limited to single articles, such as underwear, or may involve total cross-dressing, including a wig and makeup. The transvestite may engage in this behavior alone or with a partner. Many transvestites are heterosexual, and cross-dressing is often part of sadomasochistic activity.

Frotteurs' sexual arousal arises from rubbing against or touching nonconsenting individuals. This behavior usually occurs in crowded places, such as on public transportation, and may involve such things as rubbing their genitals against the buttocks of an unsuspecting woman, grabbing the woman's breasts, or grabbing the woman's genital area. Although DSM-III-R suggests that it is the touching and not the coercive nature of the act that is sexually arousing, this is at times difficult to determine. Further research is needed to delineate more clearly the arousing stimuli to the frotteur (i.e., whether it is the actual touching or the coercion).

Pedophiles have sexual attraction to children and, along with exhibitionists, are probably the most frequent paraphilias seen by mental-health professionals. In diagnosing pedophilia, it is important to state whether the attraction is to the same sex, opposite sex, or both; whether it is limited to incest; and whether it is exclusive (only attracted to children) or nonexclusive. These factors appear to relate to the risk of recidivism since, in general, it has been found that males who molest young males have a high recidivism rate, while incest cases have the lowest recidivism rate.

Pedophiles may report sexual attraction to only one sex and to a limited age range (6 to 8 years old), although some may show attraction to all prepubescent children and either sex. Also, the age of the victim may not reflect the pedophile's true age preference, but may reflect merely the victim's availability. The behavior may be limited to fondling or may include other sexual behaviors such as oral-genital contact, digital penetration, insertion of objects in the vagina or anus, and intercourse. Pedophiles may use force, although many are quite adept at manipulating children into sexual activity. They may be very attentive to children's needs and may be involved in social activities or occupations that give them access to children. Pedophiles use numerous excuses to justify their behavior, such as it was educational for the child, the child initiated the activity, and the child got pleasure from the activity.

Sadists gain sexual pleasure from causing psychological or physical pain to their victims. In addition to pain, however, an integral part of the sadistic arousal pattern is the humiliation, degradation, and domination of the victim. The sadist may force nonconsenting victims or may engage in sadistic behavior with a consenting partner (a sexual masochist). In consenting relationships, unwritten rules usually govern how far the behavior is allowed to progress. Some sadists show progressive behavior (that is, an escalation in the degree of violence and force used). Behaviors may range from those meant to humiliate and degrade the victim (i.e., bonding, verbal abuse, locking in a cage, dressing the victim in diapers or in women's clothes, or urinating and defecating on the victim) to behaviors geared to elicit pain (spanking, pinching, burning, strangling, piercing with pins or needles, torture, mutilation, and murder).

Sexual masochism is seen as the opposite of sexual sadism, although at times sadism and masochism occur in the same individual, who may engage in both roles in sadomasochistic activity. The person may engage in the behavior alone or with a partner. Again, with a partner limits are many times agreed upon as to how far the behavior is allowed to progress. As noted by the DSM-III-R, a dangerous form of this behavior is autoerotic asphyxiation or hypoxiphilia (increasing sexual arousal by oxygen deprivation, obtained through such methods as placing a plastic bag over the head, strangling with a noose, or using chemicals such as nitrates). A number of deaths have been reported in the literature as a result of this behavior.

Differential Diagnosis

In diagnosing paraphilias, there are several factors to keep in mind. First, many paraphilias may meet the criteria for a number of the paraphiliac disorders (Abel, et al., 1983). If a patient presents complaining of one paraphilia, it is important to ask specifically about each other possible paraphilia in language understandable to the patient. Patients do not always volunteer this information spontaneously. Second, the paraphiliac fantasies, urges, and behaviors may be continuous or episodic. In some patients, the paraphiliac urges, fantasies, and behaviors may occur only during periods of stress or interpersonal conflict, while in other patients the paraphiliac fantasies or behaviors are always necessary for sexual arousal.

Differential diagnosis is less complicated by an overlap in symptomatology between disorders than by the patient's failure to provide honest details of his history. At times, paraphiliac behavior is seen in other diagnostic categories (such as schizophrenia, manic psychosis, organic mental disorders, and mental retardation), but clinical experience suggests it is unlikely that another disorder is primarily responsible for the aberrant behavior. However, in transvestism and fetishism it is important to rule out temporal lobe complex partial seizures (Blumer, 1969); numerous reports have suggested a relationship of these paraphilias to temporal lobe disorders and more recently a relationship between pedophilia and temporal lobe dysfunction has been reported (Langevin, Hucker, Wortzman, et al., in press). However, most patients with temporal lobe disorders are not paraphiliacs, and probably most paraphiliacs do not have temporal lobe disorders. It is important that these diagnoses be assessed for and appropriate treatment given if another disorder is diagnosed.

It is important to continue assessing for the presence of paraphilia, even in cases where acute psychotic episodes or other disorders have been resolved. For example, we saw one patient with clear evidence of paranoid schizophrenia. Following appropriate and reasonably successful pharmacologic treatment, this patient continued with recurrent and intense pedophiliac urges that required specific treatment in and of themselves. Similar observations have been made in patients with mental retardation and substance abuse disorders.

Because DSM-III-R criteria for paraphilia are based largely on the patient's self-report and paraphiliacs (especially those whose behavior is illegal) often provide very unreliable histories, specialists in the area have turned to other sources to assist in adequate treatment formulation and diagnosis. As part of the evaluation, extensive use is made of victims' statements, police reports, and interviews with significant others to get a clearer picture of the extent and nature of the patient's problem. Many clinical and research facilities use penile plethysmography as a means of direct assessment of sexual arousal to assist in diagnosis of sexual preference (Murphy and Barbaree, 1988).

ETIOLOGY

Data are extremely limited about the etiology of the development of paraphilias. Therefore, the information reviewed in this area should be considered speculative. Traditional theories regarding etiology follow standard psychiatric theorizing (that is, from psychoanalytic, behavioral, biological, or family systems perspectives). Some descriptive factors, however, warrant special attention.

The first is that pedophiles appear to have been victimized themselves sexually as children at a higher rate than one would expect in normals (Groth, Hobson, and Gary, 1982). Not all child molesters, however, have been sexually abused and, given the large number of males who appear to have been abused in the general population, it would appear that most young males who are sexually abused do not become sex offenders. Although being sexually abused may be a risk factor for the development of pedophilia, it would appear that there are other, unidentified factors that lead to the development of pedophilia. A number of factors could be proposed, such as whether the abuse had ever been disclosed, whether the young victim ever received treatment, adult reaction to disclosure of the abuse, and the general family stability. To date, few of these factors have been investigated, although such knowledge would allow more appropriate early interventions in individuals at risk for sexual abuse.

A second factor about paraphiliacs is that the vast majority are male. Although this might raise both biological and genetic explanations, it also brings into question the role of male enculturation in the development of paraphiliac behavior. Feminist writers (Brownmiller, 1975) and some researchers (Murphy, Coleman, and Haynes, 1986) have clearly described various aspects of male social learning that may relate to sexual aggression against adult women. Such factors include males' need for dominance, perceptions of women as objects, society's reinforcement of rape myths, and various sex role stereotypes that, at least in the past, were culturally accepted. For pedophiles, such factors might include the masculine requirement to be dominant and powerful in sexual relationships, erotic portrayal of children in advertising, male tendencies to sexualize all emotional needs, and repressive norms about sexuality (Finkelhor, 1984).

Psychoanalytic theories predominated early thinking regarding paraphilias (Karpman, 1954). Many of the early writings in this area tended to follow directly Freud's theories of infantile sexuality, in which all humans are born with primitive, reflectively unformed, instinctual sex drives. Most individuals reach adult heterosexual orientation by progressing through psychosexual levels of development, including adequate resolution of the oedipal complex. In contrast, other individuals may develop neurotic behaviors and symptoms as a result of aberrant patterns of psychosexual development. The paraphiliac, however, because of extreme castration or mutilation anxiety, expresses these infantile sexual desires directly through paraphiliac fantasies or acts. Hammer and Glueck (1957), in a study of incarcerated offenders, found that paraphiliacs feared sexual contact with adult females as a result of their failure to resolve the oedipal complex. All were found to suffer from forms of unconscious castration anxiety. The authors proposed that the various paraphilias allow the individual to resolve in unconscious ways his castration anxiety and fears of adult women. The pedophile tends to choose children, who are less threatening than mature adult women; the exhibitionist displays his genitals, therefore provoking reactions from females and proving the existence of his penis; and the transvestic fetishist may use his cross-dressing to identify with the mother figure as a defense against his castration anxiety (Blair and Lanyon, 1981; Hammer and Glueck, 1957; Wise, 1985).

Early behaviorist writers, rather than focusing on early relationship with parental figures, have instead focused on early sexual experiences and the integration of such experiences into masturbatory fantasies. The basic tenet is that paraphiliac arousal patterns are conditioned by the pairing of masturbatory fantasies with the paraphiliac stimuli (McGuire, Carlisle, and Young, 1965; Rachman, 1966; Rachman and Hodgson, 1968).

Later behavioral theorizing included other factors that at least might maintain or assist in the development of paraphiliac behavior. For example, a lack of social skills or significant heterosexual anxiety might make it difficult for the individual to develop sexual relationships with appropriate sexual partners, leaving the paraphiliac outlet as the only means of sexual gratification (Barlow and Abel, 1976; Murphy and Stalgaitis, 1987). A number of cognitive-oriented behavior therapists have focused on the role of what are called cognitive distortions (that is, the justifications paraphiliacs use to legitimize their behavior) in the maintenance of deviant sexual behavior (Conte, 1986; Murphy and Stalgaitis, 1987).

Current behavioral theorizing, then, includes several possible components to the development and maintenance of the paraphiliac pattern. These involve acquiring a paraphiliac arousal pattern by pairing the paraphiliac fantasy with masturbation, which may or may not be associated with deficits in heterosocial skills or with severe heterosocial anxiety that blocks the individual from seeking out or engaging in more corrective sexual experiences. In conjunction with the development of the deviant arousal pattern, the individual develops a cognitive system that justifies the behavior and allows the offender to overcome what internal anxiety he might feel about engaging in such behavior.

Throughout the literature on paraphilias, various case reports have associated the onset of paraphiliac behaviors with neurological or other biological abnormalities. For example, Regestein and Reich (1978) described four cases of the onset of pedophilia after illness that led to substantial cognitive impairment. Also, Berlin (1983) reports 34 cases of paraphilias (the majority pedophilic) with a variety of associated biological abnormalities, including elevated testosterone levels, schizophrenia, childhood dyslexia, Klinefelter's syndrome, and cortical atrophy. Also, as noted, temporal lobe epilepsy has been associated with fetishism and transvestite fetishism (Blumer, 1969) and more recently temporal lobe disorders have been noted among some pedophiles (Langevin, et al., 1986).

None of these studies were based on random samples of either paraphiliacs or individuals suffering from the various biological abnormalities. Therefore, it is unclear what percentage of patients with such neurological or biological findings develop paraphilias, and what percentage of paraphiliacs show such abnormalities. It cannot be assumed from studies that a biological abnormality is the factor leading to the development of paraphilia. At the clinical level, however, these case reports do suggest that the clinician needs to consider that individual paraphiliacs may have additional organic mental disorders; the clinician should try to determine whether the organic disorder has any relationship to the paraphilia. Because of the well-documented role that the temporal lobe and associated limbic structures play in regulating sexual behavior, further studies of temporal lobe disorders in paraphilias seem warranted.

Family interactions have also been implicated, at least within the subset of pedophiles involved in incest (Alexander, 1985; Larson and Maddock, 1986). Such theories have focused on factors such as the family's isolation, role confusion in the family, daughters who assume the mother's role, and a general emotional enmeshment among family members. Although it is clear to any clinician working with these families that many are quite dysfunctional, it is not clear whether this is causative or secondary to the abusive behavior (Conte, 1986).

Although a number of factors have been implicated as etiological in the paraphilias, none have produced sufficient evidence to be considered predominant. Like many psychiatric disorders, it is likely that we will find that paraphilias are multiply determined by an interaction of biological, psychological, and social/cultural variables. It is also likely that as our diagnostic abilities improve, we will be able to develop more clearly subtypes of paraphiliacs and will be better able to determine the role and importance of the various etiological factors in these subtypes.

TREATMENT

In this section, we will attempt to review the current general framework that paraphiliac treatment takes and treatment issues that are addressed in sex-offender-specific programs. In addition, recent biological approaches will be integrated into this general treatment framework, with a major focus on the antiandrogen drug Depo-Provera (medroxyprogesterone acetate, MPA), which is being used increasingly in the United States.

Treatment in general focuses heavily on the specific paraphiliac behavior or sex offense and the factors surrounding the offense, usually from a cognitive-behavioral framework. Less attention is given to early childhood experiences; therefore, psycho-dynamic or traditional psychotherapy approaches are usually not considered primary treatment modalities (Knopp, 1984). Most specialized programs use group therapy approaches with other paraphiliacs as the primary treatment modality and use male/female cotherapy teams.

In treating sex offenders, the therapist needs to be more directive and to set limits more clearly on patients' behaviors (such as having no contact with children) than in a traditional therapeutic setting. This includes having patients waive confidentiality so that treatment failure and noncompliance can be reported to appropriate agencies. Most programs work closely with the courts, parole, probation, and child protection agencies; these systems are considered active members of the treatment team rather than agencies that interfere with the therapeutic relationship. Finally, offenders are clearly told that there is no "cure" and the techniques learned in treatment should be employed on a lifelong basis.

The rest of this section will focus on specific components of treatment found in a number of treatment programs (Conte, 1985; Murphy and Stalgaitis, 1987).

Reducing Denial

Until an offender admits to the paraphiliac behavior and provides specific details of the behaviors and factors surrounding the behaviors, it is difficult for treatment to progress. Therefore, one of the initial goals of treatment is to challenge the patient's denial. Denial is sometimes total ("I didn't do it) or partial ("I didn't do everything he/she said I did"). Therapeutic approaches to reduce denial rely heavily on group confrontation, including the use of victims' statements and results of psycho-physiological assessment of sexual arousal (Abel, Cunningham-Rathner, Becker, et al., 1983).

Sexual Arousal

By definition, paraphiliacs experience fantasies of and recurrent urges to engage in paraphiliac behaviors. Therefore, most programs use some specific behavioral procedure to reduce such urges or to at least give the patient methods for controlling such urges. Although mild electrical aversive techniques were frequently used in early treatment studies (Quinsey, 1977), a number of alternative procedures have been more recently developed.

In *covert sensitization* (Cautela and Wisocki, 1971), the patient is taught to imagine a graphic picture of his paraphiliac behavior and to link it with an equally graphic description of an aversive consequence, such as going to jail or losing his family (Barlow, Leitenberg, and Agras, 1969; Brownell and Barlow, 1976; Brownell, Hayes, and Barlow, 1977). In another technique that is used either in conjunction with covert sensitization (Maletzky, 1980) or alone (Laws and Osborne, 1983), the paraphiliac stimulus or fantasy is linked with a noxious odor, such as spirits of ammonia or valeric acid. Also, many programs use some form of masturbatory satiation or verbal satiation that requires patients to verbalize their deviant fantasies for long periods of time (30 to 45 minutes) without ejaculating (Laws and Osborne, 1983; Marshall, 1979; Marshall and Lippens, 1977). This leads to a reduction in the reinforcing value of the fantasies.

A number of biologically oriented approaches have also been used to reduce sexual arousal, although these are not specific to deviant sexual arousal and are geared to reducing libido in general (Berlin, 1983; Bradford, 1985; Freund, 1980). Two antiandrogen drugs that are receiving increased attention are cyproterone acetate (CPA), which is available only in Canada and Europe, and medroxyprogesterone acetate (MPA, Depo-Provera), which has been used in the United States (Berlin, 1983; Bradford, 1985). Although CPA has been used on a larger number of sex offenders, because it is unavailable in the United States we will focus on MPA.

According to Bradford (1985), MPA reduces testosterone through a number of mechanisms, primarily by inducing A-ring reductase inhibition in the liver, therefore increasing testosterone metabolism. Berlin (1983) recommends a starting dose of 500 mg per week of the 100 mg/ml solution, with no more than 250 ml given in a single injection site. Using periodic blood levels to assess whether testosterone levels have been suppressed, the drug is then titrated so as not to cause total impotence and so the drug is not feminizing. Optimal drug levels have not yet been determined. Common side effects of MPA include weight gain, mild lethargy, cold sweats, nightmares, hot flashes, and hypertension, while elevated blood glucose, dyspnea, hypogonadism, and malignant breast tumors (in female beagle dogs) have also been reported (Berlin, 1983).

Berlin (1983) reported a series of 20 chronic paraphiliacs treated with MPA. While on the drug, only three recidivated (or only three were known to recidivate); however, nine subjects dropped out of treatment and eight of the nine recidivated while off the drug. Quinsey and Marshall (1983) criticized the use of antiandrogen drugs because of the high dropout rates, which they reported as between 30 and 100% of subjects enrolled, and because the drugs are not specific to deviant sexual arousal. Further studies are needed on the acceptability of this drug to patients and on ways to increase compliance when it is considered appropriate treatment. Given the seriousness of some of the paraphilias, it appears that antiandrogen drugs do have a role to play at least as one component of a comprehensive treatment program and do serve as a viable alternative treatment when behaviorally oriented procedures are not found effective in controlling paraphiliac fantasies.

Identifying Antecedents to Sexual Abuse and Increasing Social Competence

Paraphiliac behavior is at times influenced by certain environmental stimuli or certain emotional events (Pithers, Marques, Gibat, et al., 1983). Many paraphiliacs have trouble managing various emotional states and have difficulty with appropriate assertiveness and social skills. Therefore, programs provide a variety of structured social competency programs as part of treatment, such as stress management, anger management, interpersonal skills training, and assertiveness training.

Cognitive Distortions and Victim Empathy

Paraphiliacs whose behavior harms others tend to show limited empathy for their victims. We have hypothesized (Murphy, in press) that one reason for the lack of empathy is that patients engage in a number of distortions that they use to reduce the guilt they feel about the behavior. These include blaming the victim ("she asked for it"), denying the impact on the victim ("she/he liked it," "I didn't hurt her"), or attempting to make the behavior socially acceptable ("I was only providing sex education to the child"). Methods to challenge such belief systems involve educating the patient regarding victim impact, directly confronting the distortions, and teaching patients to identify the distortions themselves. Treatment programs commonly use books or articles written by victims or movies presented from a victim's standpoint; some programs use actual confrontations between the offender and the victim's therapist or the actual victim.

Other Treatment Issues

Several other issues need to be addressed with paraphiliac patients. For example, offenders with alcohol and drug problems or with other concurrent psychiatric problems may need treatment for those problems. Alcohol and drug issues must be addressed, and appropriate medication is warranted for patients with major affective disorders or schizophrenic disorders. Similarly, marital therapy, family therapy, or sexual dysfunction therapy may be required for paraphiliacs with partners and for incest families that plan on reuniting.

ROLE OF THE NONPSYCHIATRIC PHYSICIAN IN PATIENT MANAGEMENT AND INDICATIONS FOR PSYCHIATRIC CONSULTATION AND REFERRAL

The vast majority of patients who present to nonpsychiatric physicians, victims or perpetrators, will require referral to an appropriate mental-health professional. In almost all states, professionals are required by law to report to the proper authorities reasonable suspicion or evidence of child abuse, sexual or otherwise.

Nonpsychiatric physicians may encounter individuals who engage in paraphiliac behavior or who have paraphiliac urges that are not likely to harm others, are not likely to harm the patient or society (fetishism and transvestism, for example), and do not distress the patient. In such cases, depending on the physician's own moral beliefs and ethical standards, the physician might feel comfortable counseling the patient about the wide variety of sexual behaviors people engage in and letting the patient decide whether he needs to consult a specialist, if aspects of his own preferences are problematic for him or others. Whenever a patient's fantasies and/or behavior involve either harming others or infringing on others' rights, more specialized services are required. The physician should remember that many paraphiliacs are not forthcoming with all their fantasy material or urges. In addition, as we have noted previously, many paraphiliacs have multiple paraphilias, and even though the one being presented may not seem to be of serious harm to others, there may be other issues the patient has not addressed. Even when the paraphilia is a hands-off offense, such as exhibitionism or voyeurism, many such patients also have other paraphilias that might be more directly harmful. Also, these paraphilias in and of themselves do infringe on the privacy of others. The nonpsychiatric physician faced with such a patient should maintain a nonjudgmental stance regarding the patient and should encourage the patient to disclose further material.

In making referrals, the physician should realize that not all mental-health professionals (psychiatrists, psychologists, and social workers) have specialized training in treating paraphiliac patients; in fact, they may have very little experience with this specific diagnostic category. Many times, district attorneys, parole and probation officers, and child protection workers may have the best knowledge of individuals who specialize in the treatment of paraphiliacs in the community.

The nonpsychiatric physician can play an important role in prevention. Most primary-care physicians who provide medical care to children on a regular basis can provide their patients with information on child sexual abuse the same way they provide them with pamphlets and brochures on a variety of medical problems. Also, the nonpsychiatric physician, regardless of specialty, should continually be aware of the high frequency of sexual abuse in the population. Many patients being treated by nonpsychiatric physicians for a variety of disorders may have been sexually abused, and sometimes the physical complaints can be directly tied to the abuse. The physician should keep this in mind and should not be afraid to ask patients routinely about past or present traumatic sexual experiences as part of their diagnostic workup.

CLINICAL PEARLS

- Many paraphiliac behaviors are both a psychiatric disorder and a crime. The patient's risk to society must always be considered.
- Patients may have multiple paraphilias, and these should always be considered when evaluating the patient.
- When evaluating a paraphiliac, especially those whose behavior harms others, the clinician should never rely solely on the patient's self-report and should seek collaborative information.
- Treatment of paraphilias is specialized. Not all mental-health professionals have adequate training with this diagnostic group. Where possible, referrals should be to individuals with training in this area.
- Physicians should remember that victimization occurs frequently in our society. The nonpsychiatric physician can play a key role in identifying victims and in prevention.

ANNOTATED BIBLIOGRAPHY

Blair CD, Lanyon RI: Exhibitionism: etiology and treatment. Psychol Bull 89:439–463, 1981

A good overall review of exhibitionism both clinically and theoretically. Provides excellent description of the theoretical approach to understanding exhibitionism and common treatment techniques.

Bradford JMW: Organic treatments for the male sexual offender. Behav Sci Law 3:355–375, 1985

Reviews biological approaches to treatment of sex offenders, provides a good literature review, and discusses in some detail the pharmacology and application of antiandrogen drugs.

Finkelhor D: A sourcebook on child sexual abuse. Beverly Hills, Sage, 1986

Probably the best single source for a general presentation of the whole area of child sexual abuse with discussion of victim, offender, and prevention.

Gelder M, Gath D, Mayou R: Oxford textbook of psychiatry. Oxford, Oxford University Press, 1983

Includes a brief description of the major paraphilias, with some attention to etiology and a cursory outline of treatment.

Greer JG, Stuart IR: The sexual aggressor: Current perspectives on treatment. New York, Van Nostrand Reinhold, 1983

Fairly comprehensive review of sexual aggression against adult women. Excellent chapters on biological treatment and behavioral treatment methods.

Kaplan HI, Sadock B: Comprehensive textbook of psychiatry, 4th ed. Baltimore, Williams & Wilkins, 1985

Contains a good overview of paraphilias and their proposed etiologies including environmental, biological, and analytic formulations, highlighting clinical features and differential diagnosis, and a very brief discussion of treatment.

REFERENCES

Abel GG, Becker JV, Mittelman M, et al: Self-reported sex crimes of nonincarcerated paraphiliacs. J Interpers Viol 2:3–25, 1987

Alexander PC: A systems theory conceptualization of incest. Fam Process 24:79–88, 1985

American Psychiatric Association: Diagnostic and statistical manual of the mental disorders, 3rd ed. Washington DC, 1980

Barlow DH, Abel GG: Recent developments in assessment and treatment of sexual deviation. In: Craighead WE, Kazdin AE, Mahoney MJ (eds): Behavior modification: Principles, issues, and applications. Boston, Houghton Mifflin, 1976

Barlow DH, Leitenberg H, Agras WD: The experimental control of sexual deviation through manipulation of the noxious scene in covert sensitization. J Abnorm Psychol 74:596–601, 1969

Berlin FS: Sex offenders: A biomedical perspective and a status report on biomedical treatment. In: Greer JG, Stuart IR (eds): The sexual aggressor: Current perspectives on treatment. New York, Van Nostrand Reinhold, 1983

Blair CD, Lanyon RI: Exhibitionism: Etiology and treatment. Psychol Bull 89:439–463, 1981

Blumer D: Transsexualism, sexual dysfunction, and temporal lobe disorder. In: Green R, Money J (eds): Transsexualism and sex reassignment. Baltimore, Johns Hopkins, 1969

Bradford JMW: Organic treatment for the male sexual offender. Behav Sci Law 3:355–375, 1985

Brownell KD, Hayes SC, Barlow DH: Patterns of appropriate and deviant sexual arousal: The behavioral treatment of multiple sexual deviations. J Consul Clin Psychol 45:1144–1155, 1977

Brownell KD, Barlow DH: Measurement and treatment of two sexual deviations in one person. J Behav Ther Exp Psychiatry 7:349–354, 1976

Brownmiller S: Against our will: Men, women and rape. New York Simon & Schuster, 1975

Cautela JR, Wisocki PA: Covert sensitization for the treatment of sexual deviations. Psychologic Rec 21:37–48, 1971

Conte JR: Sexual abuse and the family: A critical analysis. In: Trepper TS, Barrett MJ (eds): Treating incest: A multimodal systems perspective. New York, Haworth, 1986

Conte JR: Clinical dimensions of adult sexual abuse of children. Behav Sci Law 3:341–354, 1985

Cox DJ, McMahon B: Incidence of male exhibitionism in the United States as reported by victimized female college students. Int J Law Psychiatry 1:453–457, 1978

Finkelhor D: A sourcebook on child sexual abuse. Beverly Hills, Sage, 1986

Finkelhor D: Child sexual abuse: New theory and research. New York, Free Press, 1984

Finkelhor D, Russell D: Women as perpetrators: Review of the evidence. In: Finkelhor D (ed): Child sexual abuse: New theory and research. New York, Free Press, 1984

Freund K: Therapeutic sex drive reduction. Acta Psychiatr Scand 62:(suppl 287) 5–38, 1980

Gittleson NL, Eacott ST, Mehta BM: Victims of indecent exposure. Br J Psychiatry 132:61–66, 1978

Groth AN, Hobson WF, Gary TS: The child molester: Clinical observations. Soc Work Hum Sexuality 1:129–144, 1982

Hammer RF, Glueck BC Jr: Psychodynamic patterns in sex offenders: A four-factor theory. Psychiatr Q 31:325–345, 1957

Hunt M: Sexual behavior in the 1970s. Chicago, Playboy Press, 1974

Karpman B: The sexual offender and his offenses: Etiology, pathology, psychodynamics and treatment. New York, Julian Press, 1954

Knopp FH: Retraining adult sex offenders: Methods and models. Syracuse NY, Safer Society Press, 1984

Langevin R, Hucker S, Wortzman G, et al: Neuropsychological impairment in pedophiles. Can J Behav Sci 18:440–448, 1986.

Larson NR, Maddock JW: Structural and functional variables in incest family systems: Implications for assessment and treatment. In: Trepper TS, Barrett MJ (eds): Treating incest: A multimodal systems perspective. New York, Haworth Press, 1986

Laws DR, Osborne CA: How to build and operate a behavioral laboratory to evaluate and treat sexual deviates. In: Greer JG, Stuart IR (eds): The sexual aggressor: Current perspectives on treatment. New York, Van Nostrand Reinhold, 1983

Maletzky BM. Assisted covert sensitization. In: Cox DJ, Daitzman RJ (eds): Exhibitionism: description, assessment and treatment. New York, Garland Press, 1980

Marshall WL: Satiation therapy: A procedure for reducing sexual arousal. J Appl Behav Anal 12:10–22, 1979

Marshall W, Lippens BA: The clinical value of boredom: A procedure for reducing inappropriate sexual interests. J Nerv Ment Dis 165:283–287, 1977

McGuire RJ, Carlisle JM, Young BG: Sexual deviations as conditioned behavior: A hypothesis. Behav Res Ther 2:185–190, 1965

Moser C, Levitt EE: An exploratory-descriptive study of a sadomasochistically oriented sample. J Sex Res 23:322–337, 1987

Murphy WD: Assessment and modifications of cognitive distortions in sex offenders. In: Marshall WL, Barbaree HE (eds): Sexual assault: Issues, theories, and treatment of the offender. New York, Plenum Press, in press

Murphy WD, Barbaree HE: Assessments of sexual offenders by measures of erectile response: Psychometric properties and decision making. Monograph Order No. 86MO506500501D. Rockville MD, National Institute of Health, 1988

Murphy WD, Coleman EM, Haynes MR: Factors related to coercive sexual behavior in a nonclinical sample of males. Violence and Victims 1:255–278, 1986

Murphy WD, Stalgaitis SJ: Assessment and treatment considerations for sexual offenders against children: Behavioral and social learning approaches. In: McNamara JR, Appel MA (eds).:. Critical issues, developments, and trends in professional psychology, vol. 3. New York, Praeger, 1987

Murram D, Weatherford T: Child sexual abuse in Shelby County, Tennessee: Two years of experience. Adolesc Pediatr Gynecol 1:114–117, 1988

Peters SD, Wyatt GE, Finkelhor D: Prevalence. In: Finkelhor D (ed): A sourcebook on child sexual abuse. Beverly Hills: Sage, 1986

Pithers WD, Marques JK, Gibat CC, et al: Relapse prevention with sexual aggressives: A self-control model of treatment and maintenance of change. In: Greer JG, Stuart IR (eds): The sexual aggressor: Current perspectives on treatment. New York: Van Nostrand Reinhold, 1983

Quinsey VL: The assessment and treatment of child molesters: A review. Can Psych Rev 18:204–220, 1977

Quinsey VL, Marshall WL: Procedures for reducing inappropriate sexual arousal: an evaluation review. In: Greer JG, Stuart IR (eds): The sexual aggressor: Current perspectives on treatment. New York, Van Nostrand Reinhold, 1983

Rachman S: Sexual fetishism: An experimental analogue. Psychol Rec 16:293–296, 1966

Rachman S, Hodgson R: Experimentally induced 'sexual fetishism': Replication and development. Psychol Rec 18:25–27, 1968

Regestein QR, Reich P: Pedophilia occurring after onset of cognitive impairment. J Nerv Ment Dis 166:794–798, 1978

Wise TN: Fetishism—etiology and treatment: A review from multiple perspectives. Compr Psychiatry 26:249–257, 1985

15

Psychiatric Disorders of Childhood and Adolescence

Mina K. Dulcan

This chapter will address the identification, evaluation, and treatment of psychiatric disorders as they occur in children and adolescents. The most detailed coverage will be given to the diagnoses that present in childhood and adolescence (see Table 15-1) and those which are most likely to be encountered in general medical, pediatric, or surgical practices.

Although phobias, obsessive–compulsive disorder, post-traumatic stress disorder, mood disorders, schizophrenia, anorexia nervosa, and bulimia nervosa occur in both children and adults, these disorders are primarily covered in the chapters on adult psychopathology. This chapter will focus primarily on the *differences* in clinical manifestations, evaluation, and treatment in adult and childhood forms of psychiatric illness.

Children and adolescents may be given any DSM-III-R diagnosis for which they meet criteria. In general, personality disorder diagnoses are not given to patients younger than 18 years old because personality development is not considered to be completed until adulthood. Space does not allow for detailed specification of DSM-III-R criteria in this chapter. They may be found in the *Diagnostic and Statistical Manual of Mental Disorders, Third Edition, Revised* (American Psychiatric Association, 1987) (see also appendix to Chapter 1).

The last section of this chapter will cover psychological aspects of medical illness in children and adolescents. This section is of particular importance to students interested in family practice, pediatrics, and surgery. Students interested in internal medicine should note that many of the emotional reactions to physical illness seen in children and their families are also seen in adults and their families (see also Chapter 19).

PSYCHIATRIC EVALUATION

When evaluating a child or adolescent, a great deal of the history is gathered from the parents or guardians. A standardized rating scale, such as the Child Behavior Checklist (Achenbach, Edelbrock, 1983) is a useful supplement (see Table 15-2).

Table 15–1 **DSM-III-R Disorders Usually First Evident
in Infancy, Childhood, or Adolescence**

Axis I	**Axis II**
Attention-deficit hyperactivity disorder	Mental retardation
Conduct disorders	Pervasive developmental disorders
Oppositional defiant disorder	Specific developmental disorders
Separation anxiety disorder	
Overanxious disorder	
Functional enuresis	
Functional encopresis	

(Used with permission. American Psychiatric Association, 1987)

When interviewing the child or adolescent, important information is gathered from direct questioning and from observations of appearance, affect, and behavior. The interview must be adapted for the age and maturity of the patient. Children and adolescents are often better reporters than their parents about feelings of anxiety and depression, or conduct problems such as stealing, truancy, or substance abuse.

A physical examination is usually indicated to search for medical causes of symptoms and to discover and treat any unrelated but coexisting medical disorders. The decision to conduct additional medical evaluations, such as a neurological exam-

Table 15–2 **Biopsychosocial History of a
Child or Adolescent**

Chief complaint

History of present illness

Development of the symptoms
Attitudes toward the symptoms
Effects on the child and family
Stressors
Prior psychiatric treatment and results
    Psychotherapy: type, frequency, duration
    Medication: exact doses, schedule, beneficial
      effects, side effects
    Environmental changes

Past history

Medical
Psychiatric

Medical review of systems

Review of psychological symptoms

Developmental history (milestones)

School history

Family history

Medical
Psychiatric
Developmental

ination and/or laboratory tests, should be made based on the findings of the medical history and physical examination. Anticipated pharmacologic treatment may require additional studies to be sure there are no contraindications to the use of medication or to establish baseline values of laboratory data.

Information from the school is always useful and is essential when there is concern about learning, behavior in school, or functioning with peers. With parental consent, the clinician may interview teachers; obtain records of testing, grades, and attendance; or have school personnel complete a standardized rating form, such as the Teacher Form of the Child Behavior Checklist (Achenbach, Edelbrock, 1986). Ideally, a visit to the school is arranged to observe the youngster in the classroom and on the playground (see Table 15-3).

Psychological testing, including an individually administered intelligence test and achievement tests, is obtained when there is any question about learning or IQ. Additional testing for specific learning disabilities is conducted as indicated by school reports and results of initial tests.

In a typical pediatric clinic, 15 to 20% of the children suffer from an emotional or behavioral problem of sufficient severity to warrant mental health care (Costello, Pantino, 1987). Parents and children, however, often do not spontaneously report their concerns about behavior, development, and/or emotional problems because they perceive physicians as "too busy," not interested, or unable to help with "nonmedical" problems (Costello, Pantino, 1987). In medical settings, parents should be asked if

Table 15-3 **Psychoeducational Test Instruments**

Estimated cognitive developmental level in very young children

Bayley Scales of Infant Development
    Age 3 months to 30 months

Intelligence

Kaufman Assessment Battery for Children (K-ABC)
    Age 2.5 to 12.5
    Less dependent on culturally based information and schooling
    Peabody Picture Vocabulary Test (PPVT-R)
    Brief test of receptive language abilities, often used as a screening test
      for IQ
Stanford–Binet
    Age 2 to adulthood
    Heavily language based
Wechsler Preschool and Primary Scale of Intelligence (WPPSI)
    Age 4–6.5
Wechsler Intelligence Scale for Children, Revised (WISC-R)
    Age 6–16
Wechsler Adult Intelligence Scale (WAIS)
    Age 16 and over

Academic Achievement

Peabody Individual Achievement Test (PIAT)
Wide Range Achievement Test (WRAT)
Woodcock Reading Mastery Tests

they have any worries about the child's intellectual, emotional, or behavioral status. Children and adolescents are asked if they have been feeling depressed or sad, or if there is anything they are worried about.

Indications for consultation with a child and adolescent psychiatrist after the initial screening assessment include:

Physical symptoms with unexplained etiology or severity
Noncompliance with medical treatment
Delays in development
Physician observation or child's or parent's report of depression, anxiety, or hyperactivity
Impaired school performance
Problems with peer or family relationships
Suspected substance abuse
Parental difficulties with child rearing

GENERAL PRINCIPLES OF TREATMENT PLANNING FOR CHILDREN AND ADOLESCENTS

The initial treatment plan is based on diagnosis, target symptoms, and strengths and weaknesses of the patient and the family. The child's environment, including school, neighborhood, and social support network, will also influence the choice of treatment strategy. Children and adolescents are usually best served by a combination of treatment modalities. Parents should be included in treatment planning by informing them of the probable course of the disorder if left untreated, as well as informing them of available treatments and the best estimate of the potential benefits and risks for their child. The child or adolescent patient is included as appropriate. With only a few exceptions, all of the treatments used for adults may be used for children and adolescents, with modifications for the patient's developmental status. In most cases, coordination of work with the parents, school, pediatrician, child welfare agency, courts, or recreation leader will be part of the treatment plan.

Virtually all parents of children and adolescents with psychiatric or learning problems need and deserve education in the nature of their child's disorder and in managing difficult behaviors. Parents spend far more time with their children than does the therapist and can powerfully assist or impede the progress of treatment. Treatment planning is an ongoing process, with reevaluations done as interventions are attempted and as additional information about the child and family comes to light.

Pharmacologic Treatment

When using psychopharmacologic agents with children and adolescents, important general principles include minimizing the use of multiple medications and *virtually never using medication as the only form of treatment.* It is important to educate the family regarding the disorder, its treatment, and the patient's different needs at each developmental stage. The physician must consider the potential meaning of using medication to the child, family, school, and the child's peer group.

In considering a specific intervention for a child or adolescent, the physician has a special responsibility to consider the "risk/benefit ratio." Both therapeutic effects and side effects must be actively evaluated, seeking information from child, parent, and other relevant adults such as teachers. There is a need to balance the potential risks of the medication with the prognosis of the untreated disorder and with what is known about the relative efficacy of medication. It is important to note that the U.S. Food and Drug Administration guidelines, as published in the *Physicians' Desk Reference* (PDR), are meant to regulate the advertising of pharmaceutical houses, not the clinical practice of physicians. This is especially relevant for the treatment of children and adolescents, because drug companies often do not go to the expense and trouble of conducting testing in children and adolescents of drugs marketed primarily for adults. This often results in overly conservative doses or lack of "approval" for certain indications. For older drugs, the PDR may recommend indications or doses that are no longer considered appropriate. The clinician should therefore rely on the scientific literature rather than the PDR.

Adjunctive Treatments

Modified school programs are indicated for those children and adolescents who cannot perform satisfactorily in regular classrooms, who need special structure or teaching techniques to reach their academic potential, or whose behavior requires a small class and special teachers.

Before being placed in a special class, youngsters must have individually administered psychological tests, including an intelligence test, achievement tests, and an evaluation for learning disabilities. Federal law 94–142 requires that all children who need them receive special services, and also that service be provided in the least restrictive environment, such as in the "mainstream" with other children and adolescents, if possible.

Learning a sport or hobby may be an especially important adjunct in the treatment of children and adolescents who lack positive relationships with peers or adults. A relationship with an adult such as a Big Brother or a YMCA counselor, or an opportunity to attend a camp, may improve peer relationships.

Placement in a foster home may be needed when parents are unwilling or unable to care for a child or adolescent. Indications are clearest in cases of physical neglect or physical or sexual abuse. Other families may be unable to provide the appropriate emotional or physical environment.

DISRUPTIVE BEHAVIOR DISORDERS
Attention-Deficit Hyperactivity Disorder (ADHD)

Children who have problems at home and school because they are fidgety, restless, overactive, inattentive, distractible, and impulsive have been described in the past as having "minimal brain damage," "minimal brain dysfunction," "hyperactivity," "hyperkinetic reaction of childhood," or "hyperkinetic syndrome of childhood." The DSM-III term was attention deficit disorder (ADD) with or without hyperactivity (APA, 1980). The more recent DSM-III-R diagnosis is attention-deficit hyperactivity disorder (ADHD).

Epidemiology

Between 14% and 20% of preschool and kindergarten boys and approximately one third as many girls have ADHD (Campbell, 1985). In elementary schools, about 3% of students have been diagnosed with ADHD by a physician. An additional 5 to 7% are rated overactive, distractible, and impulsive by parents and teachers but have not been identified or treated (Bosco, Robin, 1980; Sandoval, Lambert, Sassone, 1980). Boys outnumber girls by 4:1 to 8:1.

Description and DSM-III-R Criteria

DSM-III-R requires a pattern of behavior that appeared before the age of seven, has been present for at least 6 months, and is excessive for age and intelligence. At least eight of the following behaviors must be present often, although not necessarily all of the time or in every situation:

1. Fidgety or restless
2. Difficulty staying seated
3. Easily distracted
4. Difficulty waiting for his/her turn
5. Impulsive speech
6. Difficulty following instructions
7. Short attention span
8. Moves rapidly from one activity to another
9. Difficulty playing quietly
10. Talks excessively
11. Interrupts
12. Doesn't seem to listen
13. Loses things
14. Potentially dangerous impulsive behavior

Key features of ADHD are inattention, impulsivity, and disorganization. Excessive gross motor activity (running, jumping, climbing) in situations where it is not appropriate is frequently observed but is not required for diagnosis. Variability of symptoms from time to time and in different situations is a hallmark of ADHD. Many youngsters with ADHD can pay attention for an hour or more to a highly engaging activity of their own choosing (e.g., television, computer game).

Teachers complain that children with ADHD are frequently off task and disturb others by fidgeting, making noises, or talking. Their written work is often messy and characterized by poor handwriting and impulsive, careless errors. Virtually all youngsters with ADHD have deficits in learning, achievement, or completion of school work by the time the diagnosis is made.

Hyperactivity is no longer considered the key feature of this disorder, although the term is often used as shorthand for ADHD. Douglas (1983) views the primary deficits as:

1. Lack of investment, organization, and maintenance of attention and effort in completing tasks
2. Inability to inhibit impulsive action
3. Lack of modulation of arousal levels to meet the demands of the situation
4. Unusually strong inclination to seek immediate reinforcement

Common associated features are low self-esteem, feelings of depression and demoralization, and lack of ability to take responsibility for one's actions. In social situations, these youngsters tend to be immature, bossy, intrusive, loud, uncooperative, out of synchrony with situational expectations, and irritating to both adults and peers. As a result, they may have few friends, preferring to play with older or younger children.

Association between ADHD and neurological soft signs, minor physical anomalies, and EEG abnormalities is not clinically useful because they are not always present in ADHD and because many normal children and those with other psychiatric diagnoses have them (Rutter, 1982).

From 50% to 80% of children with ADHD continue to show symptoms of hyperactivity, impulsivity, and/or inattention in adolescence, frequently resulting in impaired academic performance, depressed mood, low self-esteem, and poor peer relationships. *In young adulthood, two thirds of grown-up hyperactive children continue to show restlessness, poor concentration, impulsivity, and/or explosiveness* (Weiss, et al. 1985).

In clinical settings, *at least two thirds* of patients with ADHD *also* have oppositional defiant disorder or conduct disorder (see below). Youngsters with coexisting attentional and conduct disorders tend to have an earlier age of onset, exhibit a greater total number of antisocial behaviors, and display more physical aggression.

Differential Diagnosis

Inexperienced or overly critical parents or teachers may confuse *normal age-appropriate overactivity* with ADHD. Onset of symptoms after age seven or a duration of less than 6 months may indicate an *adjustment disorder*, especially if there is an identifiable stressor in the child's life.

DSM-III-R includes an additional, residual category called *undifferentiated attention-deficit disorder* for children and adolescents with significant problems in attention who do not meet criteria for ADHD.

Prepubertal children with *bipolar disorder* may manifest a chronic mixed affective state marked by irritability, overactivity, and difficulty concentrating. Family history may be helpful in differentiating this from ADHD, but long-term follow-up may provide the only conclusive answer.

Children who are fidgety and preoccupied may have an *anxiety disorder* instead of, or in addition to, ADHD or undifferentiated attention-deficit disorder.

Children who are restless and inattentive only at school may have *mental retardation* or a *specific developmental disorder* rather than ADHD. ADHD can be diagnosed in addition to mental retardation if symptoms are excessive for the child's mental age. Delays in specific learning skills, such as reading, math, and language, are commonly associated with ADHD.

Symptoms resembling ADHD can be caused by *drugs* such as phenobarbital (prescribed as an anticonvulsant) or theophylline (for asthma). *Hyperthyroidism* can be differentiated from ADHD by the presence of physical signs and by laboratory measures.

Etiology

Familial factors have been strongly implicated, although teasing out genetic from environmental influences is difficult. Children with ADHD alone have an elevated rate of first-degree relatives with ADHD. Children who have both ADHD and conduct disorder tend to come from families with an increased rate of ADHD, conduct disorder, oppositional defiant disorder, and antisocial personality disorder (Biederman, et al., 1986).

Neurotransmitter abnormalities in ADHD have been suggested but have not been consistently documented. Recent studies suggest delayed or abnormal maturation of the frontal lobes of the brain.

Biological insults associated with some cases of ADHD include complications of pregnancy, maternal alcohol use or smoking, postmaturity, long labor, health problems or malnutrition in infancy, lead poisoning, phenylketonuria, and glucose-6-phosphate dehydrogenase deficiency.

Evaluation

Reports should be obtained from multiple sources, always including the teacher and preferably incorporating standardized rating scales such as the Child Behavior Checklist for parent and teacher (Achenbach, Edelbrock, 1983, 1986). The child may not demonstrate the problem behaviors in the doctor's office but may be overactive, impulsive, and distractible in the waiting room. Psychological testing should be performed to evaluate IQ and academic achievement and to search for specific developmental disorders. Patient and family should be questioned about motor or vocal tics, because patients with Tourette's disorder commonly have coexisting ADHD.

Treatment

Psychotherapy. Dynamically oriented individual therapy is not likely to be effective as a primary treatment for ADHD. These children have little insight into their behavior and its effect on others and may be genuinely unable to report their problems or to reflect on them. Supportive psychotherapy may be helpful in addressing low self-esteem and demoralization resulting from the environment's reaction to an ADHD child, or in resolving the effects of a parental divorce or other stressor. Family therapy can address problems caused by living with a difficult child or other marital or family dynamics that may interfere with consistent management. Group therapy is useful in improving social skills and peer relations.

Behavior modification. For youngsters with ADHD, behavior modification can improve both academic achievement and compliance, if they are specifically targeted. Both *noncorporal* limit setting (time out and response cost) and reward components are required. Behavioral techniques, including teaching of specific social skills, can improve peer interactions.

Behavior modification addresses symptoms that stimulants do not, but more cooperation from parents and teachers is required, and lack of generalization and maintenance is problematic. Many youngsters require programs that are intensive and prolonged (months to years). The most effective behavioral treatment programs include specific target behaviors at both home and school (see Barkley, 1981).

Classroom behavior modification techniques include specific class rules, token economies, attention to positive behavior, and response cost programs (withdrawal of reinforcers following undesirable behavior) (Pelham, Murphy, 1986). Reinforcers (e.g., praise, stars on a chart, privileges) may be dispensed by the teacher or by parents through the use of daily report cards.

Cognitive behavioral or problem-solving therapy. This form of treatment, which may be administered individually or in a group, combines behavior modification techniques, such as contingent reinforcement and modeling, with instruction in cognitive strategies, such as stepwise problem solving and self-monitoring. It was developed in an attempt to improve the generalization and durability of behavior modification techniques and directly addresses presumed deficits in control of impulsivity and problem solving (Kendall, Braswell, 1985).

Psychopharmacologic treatment. The decision to use medication is based on symptoms of inattention, impulsivity, and hyperactivity not due to another treatable cause that are persistent and of sufficient severity to cause functional impairment at school and usually also at home and with peers. Parents must be willing to monitor the medication and to attend appointments. Behavioral and school-related interventions should usually be considered first, unless severe impulsivity and noncompliance create an emergency situation.

Baseline and progress outcome measures from home and school are essential in monitoring response to treatment. Prior to starting medication, the child, family, and teacher should be educated about the use and possible positive effects and side effects of the medication. It is helpful to debunk common myths about treatment. Stimulants do *not* have a paradoxical sedative action, they do *not* lead to drug abuse, and many adolescents with ADHD continue to require and benefit from medication. The physician should work closely with parents on dose adjustments and should obtain frequent reports from teachers and annual academic testing.

It is clear that medication alone is not sufficient treatment. Every study of pharmacologic treatment of hyperactivity that has used more than one outcome measure has shown that even children who respond positively continue to show deficits in some areas.

Stimulants. Stimulants, which include methylphenidate, dextroamphetamine, and magnesium pemoline, are the drugs most used in the treatment of ADHD. They also may be effective in the treatment of undifferentiated attention-deficit disorder. Up to 20% of children who respond poorly to one stimulant medication have a positive response to another. Contrary to previous belief, normal and hyperactive children, adolescents, and adults have similar cognitive and behavioral responses to comparable doses of stimulants, except that children do not report euphoria. The most recent theory regarding their mechanism of action suggests that stimulants act by canalizing or reducing the excessive, poorly synchronized variability in the various dimensions of arousal and reactivity seen in ADHD (Evans, Gualtieri, Hicks, 1986).

Global judgments by parents, teachers, and clinicians rate 75% of hyperactive children improved on stimulants, compared with 40% on placebo. The other 25% are rated either unchanged or worse (Barkley, 1981). Stimulants reliably decrease physical activity, especially during times when children are expected to be less active (e.g., during school, but not during free play). They decrease vocalization, noise, and disruption in the classroom to the level of normal peers and improve handwriting. Stimulants consistently reduce "off-task" behavior and improve compliance to adult commands.

Stimulants produce improvement on cognitive laboratory tasks measuring sustained attention, distractibility, impulsivity, and short-term memory. Cognitive strategies the child typically uses are enhanced. Methylphenidate has been shown to increase productivity and decrease errors in tests of arithmetic, reading comprehension, sight vocabulary, and spelling, and increase percentage of assigned seat work completed (Pelham, 1983).

Methylphenidate and behavior modification at home and school have been shown to be additive in effect on motor, attention, and social measures for many ADHD children (Pelham, Murphy, 1986).

Stimulant medication should be initiated with a low dose and titrated weekly according to response and side effects within the recommended range (see Tables 15-4 and 15-5). Stimulants should be given after meals, to reduce anorexia. The need for medication after school or on weekends is individually determined.

In most cases, the presence of motor or vocal tics in the patient or family contraindicates the use of a stimulant medication. In preschool children, stimulant efficacy is more variable, and the rate of side effects is higher, especially sadness, irritability, clinginess, insomnia, and anorexia (Campbell, 1985). In children and adolescents with mental retardation, stimulants are effective in treating ADHD target symptoms, although efficacy decreases with decreasing IQ (Gadow, 1985).

Except in the most extreme circumstances, every young person on stimulants should have an annual drug-free trial, at least two weeks in the summer. Whenever possible, each youngster should have a trial off medication during the school year to assess whether it is still needed.

Tolerance has been reported occasionally, but compliance is often irregular, and noncompliance should be the first possibility considered when medication appears to lose its effect. It is not advisable for children to be responsible for their own medication. Alternatively, apparent decreased drug effect may be due to an increase in the patient's weight or to a reaction to a change at home or school.

The use of a sustained-release methylphenidate preparation has been advocated in order to avoid a midday dose at school. Unfortunately, for most ADHD children, the sustained-release preparation of Ritalin is less reliable and less effective than an equivalent dose of the standard preparation after breakfast and lunch. There is a delay in onset of action and more variability from day to day (Pelham, et al., 1987). Unpredictably high doses may result if a child chews a sustained-release tablet instead of swallowing it.

Magnesium pemoline is a longer acting, mild central nervous system stimulant structurally dissimilar to methylphenidate and dextroamphetamine. Pemoline may be able to be given once a day, although absorption and metabolism vary widely, and some children need twice-daily doses.

Table 15–4 Clinical Use of Medications to Treat ADHD in Prepubertal Children

	METHYLPHENIDATE (RITALIN)	DEXTROAMPHETAMINE (DEXEDRINE)	PEMOLINE (CYLERT)	DESIPRAMINE (NORPRAMIN)	CLONIDINE (CATAPRES)
How supplied (mg)	5, 10, 20	5, 10 (tablet) Elixir	18.75, 37.5, 75	10, 25, 50, 75, 100, 150	0.1 (scored tablet) 0.1, 0.2, 0.4 mg/day skin patch
Single dose range	0.3–0.7 mg/kg/dose	0.15–0.5 mg/kg/dose	0.5–2.5 mg/kg/dose	10–100 mg/dose	0.05–0.1 mg/dose
Daily dose range (mg/kg/day)	0.6–1.7 10–60	0.3–1.25 5–40	0.5–3.0 37.5–112.5	4–6	0.003–0.006 0.15–0.30
Usual starting dose (mg)	5 daily or b.i.d.	2.5–5 daily or b.i.d.	18.75–37.5 daily	10–25 daily (.5 mg/kg)	0.05 daily
Maintenance number of doses per day	2–4	2–4	1–2	3	3–4
Monitor	Pulse Blood pressure Growth Dysphoria Tics	Pulse Blood pressure Growth Dysphoria Tics	Pulse Blood pressure Growth Dysphoria Tics Liver functions	EKG Blood pressure	Blood pressure EKG Fasting glucose Sedation Dysphoria

ADHD, attention-deficit hyperactivity disorder

Table 15–5 **Side Effects of Stimulant Medications**

Common side effects (try dose reduction)
Anorexia
Weight loss
Irritability
Abdominal pain
Insomnia
Dysphoria and social withdrawal

Less common side effects
Rebound (try adding small afternoon or evening dose)
Impaired cognitive test performance (especially at very high doses)
Decrease in expected weight gain

Idiosyncratic side effects
Dizziness
Nausea
Nightmares
Constipation
Lethargy and fatigue
Anxiety and fearfulness
Hyperacusis
Rash or hives
Formication

Rare but potentially serious side effects (stop medication)
Tourette's disorder
Motor tics
Depression
Growth retardation (more likely with high doses)
Tachycardia
Hypertension
Psychosis with hallucinations
Compulsions or stereotyped activities

Stimulant side effects are listed in Table 15-5. Side effects seen only with pemoline include night terrors, lip licking and biting, choreiform movements, and rare hepatotoxicity manifested by elevated serum glutamic-oxaloacetic transaminase (SGOT) and serum glutamate pyruvate transaminase (SGPT), epigastric pain, or jaundice (McDaniel, 1986). There is no evidence that stimulants produce a decrease in the seizure threshold.

The combination of methylphenidate and imipramine has been associated with a syndrome of confusion, affective lability, marked aggression, and severe agitation (Grob, Coyle, 1986).

Tricyclic antidepressants. Desipramine, a drug with relatively less anticholinergic effects than other cyclic antidepressants, has been useful in the treatment of children and adolescents with ADHD, including some who are unresponsive to stimulants (Biederman, Gastfriend, Jellinek, 1986; Gastfriend, Biederman, Jellinek, 1984). Drawbacks include serious potential cardiac side effects, especially in prepubertal children, and the danger of accidental or intentional overdose. *It is used in patients who do not respond to stimulants, who develop significant depression on stimulants, or who have a history of or develop tics.* Desipramine has a longer duration of action than methylphenidate, so a dose at school is not needed and rebound is less of a problem. Prepubertal children should be given two or three divided doses to avoid excessive peaks and valleys in blood levels. The use of tricyclics in children is discussed further in the section on childhood mood disorders.

Clonidine. This alpha-adrenergic agonist, given in pill or transdermal form, is useful for a subgroup of children with ADHD, especially those with tics or a family history of Tourette's disorder (Hunt, Minderaa, Cohen, 1985). Maximum therapeutic effect may not be seen for one to two months. Vital signs, CBC, fasting glucose, and urinalysis should be obtained before starting clonidine. Some recommend an EKG. The most troublesome side effect is sedation, although it tends to decrease after several weeks. Hypotension and dizziness may occur at high doses. Dry mouth, photophobia, dysphoria, bradycardia, and abnormal glucose tolerance have been reported. The transdermal form may produce a severe skin rash. Clonidine should be tapered rather than stopped suddenly, to avoid a withdrawal syndrome consisting of increased blood pressure, pulse, and motor restlessness (Leckman, et al., 1986).

Environmental interventions. Academic deficits, learning disabilities, and/or behavior problems may necessitate tutoring, a special class for all or part of the day, or a special school. Recreational or camp programs are often useful.

Many parents ask about special diets to treat childhood behavior problems. At most, 5% of hyperactive children show minimal behavioral or cognitive improvement on the so-called Feingold or Kaiser-Permanente diet (Wender, 1986). Inducing the child to comply is extremely difficult. Controlled studies have been unable to demonstrate consistently that ingestion of sugar has any effect on the behavior or cognitive performance of normal of hyperactive children, even those identified by their parents as sugar responsive (Milich, Wolraich, Lindgren, 1986).

Conduct Disorders

The diagnosis of conduct disorder describes children and adolescents with a pattern of disruptive, willfully disobedient behavior.

Epidemiology

The prevalence of conduct disorder in children and adolescents in the United States has been estimated at 10% of males and about one-fourth as many females, although the prevalence in women is rising. The male predominance is more extreme in aggressive conduct disorders. *Conduct problems are the most common complaint in referrals to child and adolescent psychiatric clinics and hospitals.*

Description and DSM-III-R Criteria

This diagnosis requires a persistent pattern of behavior that violates the basic rights of others and age-appropriate rules of society, manifested by at least 3 of 13 specific behaviors, which include stealing, running away from home overnight at least twice (or once without returning), frequent lies (other than to avoid being abused), fire setting, repeated truancy, vandalism, cruelty to animals, and physical aggression.

DSM-III-R identifies three types of conduct disorder: group type (juvenile gang members), solitary aggressive type, and undifferentiated type (the majority). Children and adolescents who engage in a variety of significant misbehaviors have a more serious prognosis (Loeber, Schmaling, 1985).

Conduct disorder is a purely descriptive label for a heterogeneous group of children and adolescents and carries no presumption of etiology. Many patients seem to lack appropriate feelings of guilt or remorse, empathy for others, and a feeling of responsibility for their own behavior. Irritability, tantrums, cheating, low frustration tolerance, inability to delay gratification, and provocative behavior are common. Precocious and promiscuous sexual activity are often seen. Social skills are poor with both peers and adults. *This is a potentially serious disorder, because a substantial minority of patients will develop antisocial personality disorder or alcoholism in adulthood.*

Differential Diagnosis

Rule-violating behavior may be placed on a continuum. The least severe is the *normal* occasional lying and stealing seen in children less than 6 years old. A single occurrence of serious misconduct would be diagnosed *childhood or adolescent antisocial behavior* (a DSM-III-R V code). Behavior problems that are not as severe as those seen in conduct disorder and that are less persistent than those in *oppositional defiant disorder* are diagnosed *adjustment disorder with disturbance of conduct* if there is an identifiable stressor.

Etiology

A number of causal factors have been implicated, but there is no known single cause, and all factors are not present in each case. ADHD and oppositional defiant disorder may precede the development of conduct disorder. Conduct disorder symptoms may result from depression (Puig-Antich, 1982), mania, or psychosis. Mentally retarded youth may be led into antisocial acts by peers, or their lack of more adaptive coping strategies may result in aggression or stealing.

It is likely that in many cases conduct disorder results from an interaction among the following factors:

1. *Temperament* characterized by an initial resistance to child rearing, poor adaptability to change, high activity level, intense reactivity, and low threshold of responsiveness
2. *Parents who provide attention to problem behavior and ignore good behavior,* who tend toward prolonged negative interactions with the child, who do not provide adequate supervision, and whose discipline is inconsistent, ineffective, and either lax or extremely severe and even abusive (see Patterson, 1975)
3. *Parental modeling* of impulsivity and rule-breaking behavior
4. Genetic predisposition
5. Parental marital conflict
6. Placement of the child outside of the home
7. Poverty
8. Low IQ or brain damage (especially in violent delinquents)

Evaluation

Reports from both parent and child, and often community sources, are required to accurately assess the severity of the behavior. A search should be made for the common concurrent diagnoses, especially ADHD, anxiety and mood disorders, substance abuse, specific developmental disorders (especially developmental reading disorder and expressive language disorder), and mental retardation.

Because of the high frequency of brain damage in patients with violent conduct disorders, the physician should conduct a careful search for symptoms suggestive of complex partial seizures. An EEG may be useful.

Treatment

Psychotherapy. Dynamically oriented individual therapy is not usually an effective treatment for children and adolescents with conduct disorders. They are treated more effectively in family or group therapy, or a structured milieu such as a psychiatric hospital or residential treatment center.

Behavior modification. Several effective parent management training programs, based on social learning theory, exist for parents of noncompliant oppositional and aggressive children (Forehand, McMahon, 1981; Patterson, 1975). Parents are taught to use clear and consistent rules, to positively reinforce good behavior, and to use noncorporal discipline (limit setting) effectively. One frequently used negative contingency is the time out, so called because it puts the child in a quiet, boring area where there is a "time out" from positive reinforcement. Treatment is usually more effective the earlier it is begun.

Cognitive behavior modification is a technique that combines problem-solving skills training with behavior modification (Kazdin, et al., 1987). Children are taught to delay action and to consider alternative ways of resolving conflict. Functional family therapy (Alexander, Parsons, 1982) combines techniques from family systems theory and behavior modification to improve behavior by altering family communication and interaction patterns.

Psychopharmacologic treatment. *Neuroleptics* such as haloperidol and molindone may reduce aggression, hostility, negativism, and explosiveness in severely aggressive children (Campbell, Green, Deutsch, 1985; Greenhill, et al., 1985). (See section in this chapter on schizophrenia for more detail on the use of neuroleptics.)

Lithium may be considered in the treatment of severe impulsive aggression, especially when accompanied by explosive affect (Campbell, Green, Deutsch, 1985). (See section in this chapter on mood disorders for more details on lithium use.)

Carbamazepine may benefit patients with severe impulsive aggression with emotional lability and irritability who have an abnormal EEG or a strong clinical suggestion of epileptic phenomena (Evans, Clay, Gualtieri, 1987; O'Donnell, 1985). Medical and behavioral side effects of carbamazepine are similar to those seen in adults (Evans, Clay, Gualtieri, 1987; Herskowitz, 1987; Pleak, et al., 1988) (see Chapter 17).

Propranolol, a beta-adrenergic blocker, may be useful in patients with otherwise uncontrollable rage reactions and impulsive aggression, especially those with evidence of organicity (O'Donnell, 1985; Williams, et al., 1982). If the conduct disorder is secondary to a major depression, successful treatment with *antidepressants* leads to remission of the conduct symptoms (Puig-Antich, 1982). In patients with coexisting ADHD, *stimulant* treatment may decrease impulsive conduct symptoms as well as overactivity and inattention.

Environmental interventions. Community-based recreation programs or a Big Brother may be helpful. A special education placement may be needed to manage behavior, remediate learning disabilities and academic deficits, and provide vocational training. Hospitalization may be required for severe aggression. Effective residential treatment programs use close supervision and a strict token economy, combined with instruction in adaptive social and educational skills. Legal sanctions may be necessary to enforce cooperation with treatment.

The role of the non-psychiatrist physician. These children and adolescents are at high risk for injuries and accidents, resulting in frequent hospitalizations and emergency room visits. The primary care physician must be alert to possible medical complications (e.g., venereal disease, pregnancy, and sequelae of drug abuse).

Oppositional Defiant Disorder (ODD)

This is a new diagnostic category, which first appeared in DSM-III (APA, 1980). *It was intended to describe milder forms of behavior problems than those seen in conduct disorder.* Young children diagnosed as oppositional defiant disorder (ODD) may be at risk for developing a conduct disorder.

Epidemiology

Boys outnumber girls 2-3 : 1 (Anderson, Williams, McGee, Silva, 1987). This disorder is extremely common among children referred to psychiatric services.

Description and DSM-III-R Criteria

Children with ODD display a chronic pattern of stubborn, negativistic, provocative, hostile, and defiant behavior *without* serious violation of the rights of others. They are often irritable, resentful, and quick to take offense. Swearing and verbal threats are common. These children are usually most difficult to manage at home, but problems extend to school and peers. They often continue to resist even when cooperation would be in their own best interest. Specific DSM-III-R criteria include loss of temper; arguments with adults; refusal to follow commands, directions, or minor rules (noncompliance); blaming others, and vindictiveness.

Differential Diagnosis

Oppositional defiant disorder must be distinguished from milder forms of *stubbornness*. Negativity and tantrums are *normal* prior to three years of age, as are arguments with adults and resistance to rules in early adolescence. Intentional and provocative noncompliance characteristic of ODD should be differentiated from the noncompliance resulting from impulsivity and inattention in *ADHD*, although both are often present. In that case, both should be diagnosed. Oppositional behavior that is limited to school may be a result of *mental retardation* or a *specific developmental disorder*.

Etiology

Hypothesized factors include an inherited predisposition (perhaps mediated by way of difficult temperament), modeling of parental oppositional and defiant behavior, and parental inability to reward positive behavior or to set firm, fair, and consistent limits.

Evaluation

Symptoms are more prominent when the patient is with familiar people. Behavior may not seem abnormal in a diagnostic interview, especially if few demands are placed on the child. Parent and teacher reports are important. Psychological testing may be needed to discover low IQ or learning disabilities.

Treatment

Behavior modification. An operant approach, using environmental positive and negative contingencies to increase or decrease the frequency of behaviors, is the most useful. A token economy is one type of operant approach where points, stars, or tokens can be earned for desirable behaviors (and lost for problem behaviors) and exchanged for back-up reinforcers. These may be money, food, toys, television, privileges, or time with an adult in a pleasant activity. Techniques can be taught to parents (see Forehand, McMahon, 1981) and can be used by teachers in classrooms.

Psychopharmacology. In children with coexisting ADHD and ODD, stimulant medication may reduce oppositional behavior and improve compliance as well as address inattention, impulsivity, and hyperactivity.

ANXIETY DISORDERS

The prevalence of anxiety disorders in children and adolescents has been estimated to be 2 to 8%, depending on severity (Kashani, Orvaschel, 1988; Weissman, et al., 1984). There is considerable overlap among anxiety disorders and with depressive disorders (Last, Strauss, Francis, 1987). After puberty, anxiety disorders are more common in girls than in boys. There is substantial continuity in anxiety disorders, both from generation to generation and in the childhood histories of adult patients with anxiety disorders.

Etiology

Familial factors are strongly implicated, although sorting out genetic predisposition from family dynamic factors and imitation of a fearful parent is difficult. In patients with separation anxiety disorder seen in a clinical setting, 83% of the mothers had an anxiety disorder and 63% had a mood disorder (Last, Strauss, Francis, 1987).

Children identified at age 2 as extremely inhibited, quiet, and restrained in unfamiliar situations tend to remain shy and socially avoidant at age 7. They have greater sympathetic reactivity than outgoing children, as measured by heart rate acceleration and early-morning salivary cortisol levels. Two-year-olds who are uninhibited tend to remain fearless and outgoing (Kagan, Reznick, Snidman, 1988).

Traditional Freudian theory proposed that phobias result from unconscious defenses against unacceptable wishes and feelings, as described in the classic case of "Little Hans." Oedipal dynamics were thought to be prominent in childhood phobias.

According to classical conditioning theory, phobias are learned by way of the generalization of fears to other objects or situations that are similar or that are coincident in time or place. Phobias persist because avoiding the feared object reduces anxiety. This removal of an aversive stimulus strengthens the preceding behavior (the phobic avoidance).

Certain medications, such as propranolol (for headache) and haloperidol (for Tourette's disorder), may produce symptoms of separation anxiety and school refusal.

Evaluation

Techniques of assessment are similar for all of the anxiety disorders in children and adolescents. Children who are anxious about being interviewed or who are having difficulty separating from their parents may be helped by being seen together with the parent initially. A medical history and physical exam will generally rule out a medical cause for somatic complaints such as headaches, abdominal pain, nausea, or vomiting. In *separation anxiety disorder*, somatic symptoms are worst on evenings and mornings before school and are absent on weekends and holidays, except the night before school starts. Extensive medical evaluations should be avoided unless there are clear indications for them. Information should be sought regarding any possible advantage or "secondary gain" that results from the patient's symptoms. The clinical interview with the young person is especially important because parents usually underreport phobic and anxiety symptoms. A detailed history of school experiences should be taken, and a search should be made for other anxiety and mood disorders in the child and family.

Treatment

A variety of treatment techniques are applicable to all of the anxiety disorders in children and adolescents.

Psychotherapy. Individual psychotherapy may be useful, with special attention to the child's relationship to the therapist and to separations that occur in the therapy. Supportive psychotherapy may permit children to deal with their anxiety in a more adaptive way. Insight-oriented, psychodynamic individual psychotherapy, using verbal and play techniques, aims to resolve the underlying psychological conflicts and promote more functional defenses.

Cognitive therapy techniques aim to reduce anxiety and improve coping skills by using specific training to change the patient's maladaptive, self-defeating thoughts to ones that describe the child or adolescent as competent (Ollendick, Francis, 1988). Family therapy may be valuable to reduce parental modeling or subtle encouragement of fearful behavior.

Behavior modification. Behavioral techniques used to treat anxiety disorders include relaxation training, systematic desensitization, assertiveness training, shaping, and operant conditioning (Ollendick, Francis, 1988). *Behavioral treatments are generally the treatment of choice for children with one or two phobias.* Symptom substitution (i.e., the appearance of a new symptom if the phobia is removed without addressing the presumed underlying conflicts) is not a problem if attention is paid to removal of secondary gain and to ensuring that the child has the skills and the opportunities to deal with the problem situation in other ways.

Psychopharmacologic treatment. Diazepam may be used in the short-term treatment of children and adolescents with severe anticipatory anxiety. Infants and children absorb diazepam faster and metabolize it more quickly than adults (Simeon, Ferguson, 1985). The initial dose of diazepam is 1 to 2 mg, with a range of 2 to 30 mg (in adolescents) per day (McDaniel, 1986). Side effects are similar to those seen in adults (Campbell, Green, Deutsch, 1985; Simeon, Ferguson, 1985).

In patients with school phobia and separation anxiety who are resistant to psychological treatments such as family therapy, behavior therapy, and modification of the school situation, imipramine may facilitate return to school (Gittelman-Klein, Klein, 1971; Klein, Gittelman, Quitkin, Rifkin, 1980).

Separation Anxiety Disorder

Description and DSM-III-R Criteria
This disorder is characterized by excessive anxiety for the patient's age, lasting for at least 2 weeks, concerning separation from parents (or others to whom the child is attached). Specific criteria include severe and persistent worries that something terrible will happen to the child or his or her parents that will keep them apart, reluctance or refusal to go to school in order to stay home with a parent, refusal to sleep alone or away from home, avoidance of being alone, nightmares about separation, and excessive distress and/or physical symptoms in anticipation of or during separation from parents. In the past, this disorder was considered synonymous with "school phobia."

Differential Diagnosis
Normal age-appropriate separation anxiety may transiently worsen under stress, especially in children under 6 years of age. Avoidance of school may be due to separation anxiety disorder or to a number of other causes. In *truancy,* the child stays away from home, and the parents are not usually aware, unless told by the school. Some families may keep a child home from school to help with family tasks. The child may have a *realistic fear* (e.g., of a bully), a *simple phobia* of something in the school environment, or a *social phobia.* Anxiety may be related to academic performance at school. *Major depression* may lead to avoidance of school due to social withdrawal and lack of energy.

The Role of the Primary Care Physician
Mild cases of school avoidance secondary to separation anxiety disorder can be managed by the primary care physician, with encouragement to the child, family, and school. The child should be sent to school unless there are objective signs of illness, such as a fever. If the child stays home, he or she should rest in bed and not be allowed to engage in activities that are fun. If school refusal persists for more than a week,

immediate referral for psychiatric evaluation and treatment should be made, because the longer the child is out of school, the more difficult treatment becomes.

The primary physician can use a contingency management program for young children whose separation anxiety is manifested primarily by refusal to sleep in their own bed. This includes an explanation to child and parents, supporting the parents in insisting that the child stay in his or her own room, helping to devise a schedule of rewards for successful performance, and increasing motivation by the physician's own attention and praise for sleeping alone.

Overanxious Disorder

The child or adolescent with overanxious disorder suffers from and verbalizes excessive or unrealistic worry in multiple areas. Specific characteristics include worry about future events, past behavior, and the child's own competence; somatic complaints; self-consciousness; excessive need for reassurance; and marked feelings of tension. Associated features may include such habits as nail biting, thumb sucking, and hair pulling or twisting.

Phobias

Normal fears are common in children. Specific fears vary with age. For example, infants react with fear to loss of physical support, loud noises, and rapidly approaching large objects. Fear of strangers develops around 7 months. Toddlers (age 1 to 3) are frightened by loud noises, storms, certain animals, the dark, and separation from their parents. These fears continue to be prevalent among 3 to 5-year-olds, joined by fears of monsters and ghosts. All of these fears tend to decline after age 6. Common fears observed in school-age children (6 to 12 years) are those relating to bodily injury, burglars, being kidnapped, being sent to the principal, being punished, and failure. Fears of tests in school and of social embarrassment take the lead from puberty through adolescence (Ollendick, Francis, 1988). Girls generally report more fears than boys, although it is not clear whether they actually *have* more fears or are simply more willing to report them.

A *phobia* is defined as a persistent, specific fear that is out of proportion to the actual danger and that leads to impairment in social and/or academic functioning because of the need to avoid the feared object or situation.

Children and adolescents with a *social phobia* fear one or more situations in which they will be observed by others and in which their actions may lead to humiliation or embarrassment. Answering questions or speaking in front of the class are commonly feared, leading to impaired grades in school, despite adequate learning. If severe, the phobia may lead to an avoidance of school altogether, or "school phobia."

Post-traumatic Stress Disorder (PTSD)

Description and DSM-III-R Criteria

Post-traumatic stress disorder (PTSD) is characterized by the development of specific, long-lasting emotional and behavioral symptoms following a shocking, unexpected event that is outside the range of usual human experience and during which the individual feels intensely fearful and helpless (see Chapter 7). Symptoms include reexperiencing the traumatic event, avoidance of reminders of the event, and increased arousal. The precipitant may be experienced directly (e.g., rape, physical injury, kidnapping), by observation (as it occurs to another person), or vicariously (after learning about a traumatic event or a severe threat to a close friend or relative).

The clinical phenomena seen in children differ in some ways from those seen in adults (Terr, 1987). Immediate effects include fear of separation from parent(s), fear of death, and fear of further fear. Children withdraw from new experiences. Perceptual distortions occur, most commonly in time sense and in vision, but auditory, touch, and olfactory misperceptions have been described. Many details of the experience are accurately remembered, but sequencing and/or duration of events is often altered.

In children, reexperiencing the event is likely to occur in the form of nightmares, daydreams, and/or repetitive, potentially dangerous reenactment in symbolic play or in actual behavior. Despite obvious similarities between the reenactments and the original event, most children are unaware of the connection. Even children younger than age 3 demonstrate through play and/or dreams memories of traumatic events that they cannot describe verbally.

A variety of fears develop of repetition of the experience and of other situations that may involve separation or danger or remind them of the event. Children may experience somatic symptoms, such as headaches and stomachaches. Later, many traumatized children develop a sense of pessimism and hopelessness about the future. As late as 4 to 5 years after the event, children remain deeply ashamed of their helplessness in the face of danger.

Increased arousal is most often demonstrated in children by sleep disturbances, which may add to functional impairment in other areas (Pynoos, et al., 1987). Children commonly regress (i.e., show behaviors characteristic of a previous developmental stage).

Associated symptoms may include anxiety and/or depression. Impulsivity, difficulty concentrating, and decreased motivation may interfere with school performance. Guilt due to surviving if others do not and/or to perceived or actual deficiencies in attempts to save others is often experienced. The normal cognitive egocentricity and magical thinking of children may contribute to a false belief that they somehow caused the event by a thought or action.

Etiology

Children with preexisting stressors, previous loss, anxiety, or depression are at risk for more severe and prolonged symptoms, but a sufficiently severe stressor may produce the disorder in a person without any predisposition. Degree of exposure to life threat is directly related to severity of PTSD (Pynoos, et al., 1987). The changes in living circumstances caused by disasters, such as the loss of the family home, isolation from usual social supports, and even the death of parents or other family members, can exacerbate PTSD. Symptoms may be partially ameliorated by a stable, cohesive, supportive family.

Evaluation

There should be a high index of suspicion of PTSD in a child or adolescent who has had a significant change in behavior. A clinical interview technique for child and adolescent victims begins with the use of play and fantasy, using a projective drawing and story-telling task. The interviewer then structures a detailed recounting of the traumatic event, including affective responses and fantasies of revenge. The concluding stage includes a review of the child's current life concerns, a reassessment of the traumatic experience, anticipatory guidance regarding reactions that the child may experience, and efforts to support the child's self-esteem (Pynoos, Eth, 1986).

Treatment

Individual insight-oriented play and verbal psychotherapy is the modality that is most commonly used (Terr, 1987b). Time-limited focal psychotherapy may be effective in some cases (Pynoos, Eth, 1986). Group therapy, organized in schools or in the community, with victims who have been exposed to the same event may be helpful in decreasing distortions and reducing the spread of post-traumatic fears and symptoms. On the other hand, mixed groups of victims who have experienced different but similar events (e.g., rape or incest) may actually lead to contagion of fears (Terr, 1987b).

Supportive therapy for parents and siblings can provide information about the child's symptoms and their cause, as well as deal with vicarious trauma experienced by family members, and can reduce contagion.

ELIMINATION DISORDERS

One of the most common developmental problems seen by primary care physicians is the child who has not attained, or who has lost, bladder or bowel control. These disorders are called "functional" enuresis and encopresis, to differentiate from medically caused incontinence. In fact, both disorders have significant physiologic components.

Functional Enuresis

Epidemiology

Most children achieve urinary control between 18 months and 4 years of age. Daytime dryness usually precedes nighttime sphincter control. On average, boys are slower in achieving continence than girls. Family history of enuresis in a first-degree relative is positive in 75% of cases. The spontaneous remission rate is high. Among 5-year-olds, 14% of boys and girls wet at least once a month. Approximately 10% of first-graders are still nocturnally enuretic. By age 14, 1% of boys and 0.5% of girls remain enuretic (almost exclusively nocturnal).

Description and DSM-III-R Criteria

This disorder is defined as a pattern of involuntary or intentional voiding of urine into bed or clothes after the age at which continence is expected. The diagnostic criteria require a frequency of at least twice a month for children between age 5 and 6 and at least once a month for older children. *Diurnal* is used to describe wetting in the daytime, and *nocturnal* for wetting only during sleep; the latter is by far the more common form. Children with *secondary* enuresis (about 20%) have had at least 1 year of urinary continence. Children with *primary* enuresis have not had such a period.

Enuresis may result in family conflict and punitive treatment or shaming of the child, teasing by peers, restriction of social activities due to peer rejection and fear of embarrassment, and low self-esteem.

Differential Diagnosis

Transient loss of urinary control is common in young children when physically or psychologically stressed. Some children are careless in wiping or leave the toilet before urination is complete, leading to the appearance of enuresis.

Specific medical causes of urinary incontinence include:

Urethritis secondary to use of bubble bath
Urinary tract infections
Diabetes mellitus
Diabetes insipidus
Seizure disorders
Neurogenic bladder (e.g., secondary to spina bifida)
Genitourinary tract malfunction, malformation, or obstruction
Pelvic masses

Etiology

Nocturnal enuresis in younger children is largely a consequence of delayed maturation of bladder control mechanisms. General neuromaturational delay, small bladder capacity, and lack of systematic training may contribute to enuresis. Constipation has also been implicated as a causative factor (O'Regan, Yazbeck, Hamberger, Schick, 1986).

Common physiologic causes of diurnal enuresis in females are: vaginal reflux of urine, "giggle incontinence," and urgency incontinence.

Enuresis is occasionally related to other psychiatric disorders. In young children it may be a symptom of an adjustment disorder. Anxious children may experience urinary frequency, resulting in incontinence if toilet facilities are not immediately available. Children with oppositional defiant disorder may refuse to use the toilet as part of their battle for control. Many children with ADHD wait until the last minute to use the bathroom and may lose control on the way. Avoidance of dirty, dangerous, or insufficiently private toilet facilities in school may also lead to incontinence. Recent research does *not* show a relationship between enuresis and specific sleep stages for children with or without other psychiatric diagnoses.

Evaluation

The history includes details of wetting, including time of occurrence, amount, frequency, precipitants, details of toilet training, and family history of enuresis. A careful medical history, physical and neurological examination, and urinalysis are indicated in all cases. Urine cultures should be obtained in girls. Radiologic studies or instrumentation of the genitourinary tract are not indicated unless there are specific indications of abnormality on the history or physical exam.

Treatment

Environmental interventions. Nocturnal enuresis in children younger than 7 years old should be treated with patience while waiting for the child to mature. Secondary symptoms should be minimized by discouraging the parents from punishing or ridiculing the child. Children can be taught to change their own beds, in order to reduce negative reactions from parents. Measures such as restricting fluids and waking the child during the night to urinate are not notably successful. Exercises to increase bladder capacity may reduce nocturnal enuresis, and "start and stop" exercises may strengthen the bladder sphincter muscles and improve control.

Behavior modification. If treatment of uncomplicated enuresis is necessary, behavioral methods are the first choice, although parent and child motivation and participation are required. The first step is a simple monitoring and reward procedure using a chart with stars to be exchanged for rewards. For children and adolescents who do not respond to simple interventions, more elaborate programs (Azrin, Foxx, 1974), or a urine alarm or bell and pad device, may be used (Schmitt, 1982; Houts, Liebert, Padawer, 1983).

Children who are secondarily enuretic (having previously been dry) and those who have accompanying psychiatric problems are more difficult to treat. Referral to a child and adolescent psychiatrist for specialized evaluation and treatment may be necessary.

Psychotherapy. Individual or family psychotherapy may be indicated primarily to deal with secondary effects of the enuresis or coexisting psychiatric disorders that may be exacerbating the problem.

Psychopharmacologic treatment. Low doses of the tricyclic antidepressants imipramine, amitriptyline, desipramine, and nortriptyline are partially effective in the treatment of nocturnal enuresis (Campbell, Green, Deutsch, 1985). The mechanism remains unclear, but it does not seem to be altered sleep architecture, treatment of depression, or peripheral anticholinergic activity. Wetting usually returns when the drug is discontinued (Klein, Gittelman, Quitkin, Rifkin, 1980). Imipramine may be useful on a short-term basis or for special occasions (e.g., camp).

Before starting medication, baseline frequency of wet and dry nights is recorded. Daily charting is then used to monitor the child's progress. Tolerance may develop, necessitating a dose increase. In some children, tricyclics lose their effect entirely. Parents must take special precautions to avoid overdoses by the patient or siblings.

If medication is used chronically, the child or adolescent should have a drug-free trial at least every 6 months to see if medication is still required, because enuresis has a high spontaneous remission rate.

Functional Encopresis

Epidemiology

Bowel control is usually achieved between 2.5 and 4 years of age. The prevalence of encopresis is approximately 1.5% after age 5 and decreases with age. In late adolescence it is almost nonexistent in the absence of severe mental retardation, psychosis, or conduct disorder. Boys outnumber girls 4:1. Encopresis is slightly more common in lower socioeconomic classes. Encopresis is less often an isolated symptom than enuresis is. Twenty-five percent of encopretics seen in psychiatric settings are also enuretic.

Description and DSM-III-R Criteria

This disorder is characterized by repeated involuntary or, rarely, voluntary passage of feces into clothing or other places other than the toilet (e.g., the floor, closets) at least once a month for at least 6 months. Chronologic and mental age of the child must be at least 4 years. In *secondary* (or discontinuous) encopresis, the child has been without soiling for at least a year. *Primary* (or continuous) encopresis is not preceded by a period of fecal continence as long as a year. Encopresis rarely occurs during sleep. The older the child, the more resistant he or she is to treatment and the more negative the prognosis. Rejection by peers, school, and family increases with age.

Differential Diagnosis

Transient loss of continence may follow a stressor such as hospitalization or parental divorce. Organic causes of fecal incontinence include:

Metabolic—hypothyroidism, hypercalcemia
Dietary—lactase deficiency, overeating of fatty foods
Lower gastrointestinal tract
 Congenital aganglionic megacolon (Hirschsprung's disease)
 Anal fissure
 Rectal stenosis
Neurologic, e.g., myelodysplasia

Etiology

Children with functional encopresis may be divided into three groups according to etiology. The first includes children who have never been systematically toilet trained, who are retarded, or who have neuromaturational delays.

The second group is characterized by chronic severe constipation. This may be involuntary, due to dietary factors, pain on defecation caused by skin rash or an anal fissure, or lack of opportunity to use the toilet. Voluntary stool withholding may result from punitive toilet training, improper management of common toilet-related fears, or environmental interference with normal toilet habits (e.g., unsafe or dirty bathrooms, or lack of privacy). As a result of the constipation, the child develops impaired colon motility and contraction patterns, stretching and thinning of the walls of the colon (functional megacolon), and decreased sensation or perception of the urge to defecate or of the actual passage of stool. Impaction results, with leakage of loose stool around the obstruction ("overflow incontinence"). The child becomes habituated to the smell and often does not know when he/she has soiled (a fact difficult for adults to believe).

In the third group, encopresis is secondary to another psychiatric disorder (e.g., oppositional defiant disorder, attention-deficit hyperactivity disorder, conduct disorder, phobia, or adjustment disorder).

Familial factors are suggested by the 15% rate of childhood encopresis in fathers of encopretic children.

Evaluation

A complete medical history, physical examination, and routine laboratory tests are indicated. An x-ray of the abdomen or a barium enema may be required. Urinalysis will detect an associated urinary tract infection, which is common in encopretic girls. A detailed history is needed to distinguish between passage of full bowel movements (likely to be volitional), overflow of loose stool around an impaction, and staining of underwear due to careless wiping after toileting. A history of toilet training and bathroom environments is needed.

Treatment

Psychotherapy. Traditional individual psychotherapy may be used in addition to other treatments. Children with encopresis are often angry and may benefit from improving their ability to express their emotions verbally. Psychotherapy may also be useful in improving self-esteem.

Behavioral treatments are essential in most cases. Parents should be helped to avoid hostile or punitive responses to the child's incontinence and should be cautioned that relapses may occur.

The role of the primary care physician. Medical treatment is essential for children with chronic constipation and resulting functional megacolon. Children and parents are educated in the physiology and anatomy of the lower bowel. Enemas and suppositories are used to evacuate the bowel. A bowel "retraining" program follows, using orally administered mineral oil, a high-roughage diet, development of a regular toileting routine, and a mild suppository (e.g., Dulcolax) if necessary (Levine, 1982; Wright, Walker, 1978). Routine administration of enemas by parents is contraindicated, because that alone does not improve bowel function and is toxic to the parent–child relationship.

Because children with encopresis more commonly have associated psychiatric disorders than do those with enuresis, psychiatric consultation is indicated for most encopretic children older than 6 years of age and for those with secondary encopresis.

MOOD DISORDERS

Mood disorders in children and adolescents are potentially quite serious, long-lasting, and recurrent (Kovacs, et al., 1984a; Kovacs, et al., 1984b). This section will focus on age-related differences from mood disorders in adults (covered in Chapter 6).

Epidemiology

The prevalence of major depression has been estimated at 2% in prepubertal children and 4.7% in adolescents. Dysthymic disorder (without coexisting major depression) is found in 3.3% of adolescents (Kashani, et al., 1987). Mania is quite rare before puberty. In late adolescence, the incidence approaches 20% of the adult rate.

Before puberty, depression is more common in boys than girls, with a change to the adult sex ratios in adolescence.

Description and DSM-III-R Criteria

DSM-III-R criteria are essentially the same for children as for adults. The behaviors may be manifested in different ways, appropriate for developmental level. Somatic complaints or reduction in school performance and activities with friends may be key indicators of depression.

Among adolescents with major depression, subsequent bipolarity is predicted by precipitous onset of symptoms, psychomotor retardation, psychotic features, psychopharmacologically precipitated hypomania, and family history of bipolar disorder (Strober, Carlson, 1982).

Differential Diagnosis

Adolescent mania is frequently misdiagnosed as *schizophrenia* because of the psychotic manifestations and regression common to both. In a subgroup of children with *conduct disorder,* a major depression precedes the development of the conduct problems (Marriage, 1986; Puig-Antich, 1982).

Secondary mania may result from prescribed (e.g., steroids, carbamazepine, tricyclic antidepressants) or abused (e.g., cocaine, amphetamines) *drugs, metabolic abnormalities, neoplasm,* or *epilepsy.*

Children less than 4 years of age may develop a clinical picture similar to major depression when separated from their parents. Children suffering from *reactive attachment disorder* secondary to parental abuse or neglect who present with lethargy, apathy, and withdrawal may appear depressed.

Evaluation

Children can be asked direct questions related to depression, although the wording must be adjusted for their level of cognitive and emotional development. Young children have more difficulty recognizing and verbalizing their feelings and may use idiosyncratic words such as "bored" to describe dysphoria or anhedonia. "Cranky" may mean more to a child than "irritable." Although some children report their mood states more accurately than their parents can, observation of depressed affect by a trained clinician is often essential. Family history and longitudinal course are important.

It is crucial to assess the degree of suicidality. Children can be questioned regarding ideation, plans, and attempts just as adults can. This questioning will *not* increase the likelihood of self-destructive behavior. If a child or adolescent is seen following a suicide attempt, a detailed evaluation should be made of the circumstances preceding and following the attempt, history of substance abuse or impulsive behavior, wishes to die or to influence others at the time of the attempt and at the time of evaluation, whether a friend or family member has committed suicide, and coping skills and supports in the patient and family.

Treatment

Psychotherapy

Individual and family psychotherapy are cornerstones of the management of depression in childhood and adolescence. Even after successful treatment with medication, impaired interpersonal relations with peers and family members may require individual, group, or family therapy to address developmental deficits or sequelae of the depression (Puig-Antich, et al., 1985).

Cognitive therapy techniques developed for the treatment of depression in adults are being adapted for use with children and adolescents (Emery, Bedrosian, Garber, 1983).

Behavior therapy techniques such as social skills training or contingency management to reduce withdrawal may be useful adjunctive treatments.

Psychopharmacologic Treatment

The evidence for efficacy is less than that found with adults, and drugs should be used in conjunction with other treatments. For nonpsychotic depression, psychotherapy should be the first step, with medication added if there is no improvement in 4 to 6 weeks.

Tricyclic antidepressant drugs may be useful in the treatment of children and adolescents with major depression (Preskorn, et al., 1987; Puig-Antich, Ryan, Rabinovich, 1985; Ryan, Puig-Antich, 1986). Tricyclic pharmacokinetics differ before puberty. The smaller ratio of fat to muscle in children leads to a decreased volume of distribution, and they are not protected from excessive dosage by a large volume of fat in which the drug can be stored. Children have more rapid absorption and lower protein binding (Winsberg, et al., 1974) and a larger liver relative to body size, leading to faster metabolism of tricyclics than that found in adults (Sallee, et al., 1986). As a result, prepubertal children are likely to need a higher milligram per kilogram dose than adults and are prone to rapid, dramatic swings in blood levels from toxic to ineffective. Medication should be divided into three daily doses to produce more stable levels (Puig-Antich, Ryan, Rabinovich, 1985). Tricyclics may be given once daily in adolescents.

The starting dose of imipramine, amitriptyline, and desipramine is 1.5 mg/kg/day, which may be increased every 4 days by 1 mg/kg/day to a maximum dose of 5 mg/kg/day. Nortriptyline may have fewer side effects and a more precise therapeutic window of 60 to 100 ng/ml. It has a longer half-life than imipramine and can be given twice a day in children. Milligram per kilogram doses are lower than for imipramine, and variation in metabolism is greater (Geller, Cooper, Chestnut, 1986).

Parents must be reminded to supervise closely administration of medication and to keep pills in a safe place to prevent intentional overdose or accidental poisoning not only by the patient but by other family members, especially young children.

Tricyclics have a quinidinelike effect. At doses of more than 3 mg/kg/day of imipramine or desipramine, children and adolescents develop small but statistically significant EKG changes (intraventricular conduction defects) (Biederman, et al., 1985). A small group of children and adolescents may have a genetic inability to metabolize tricyclics normally, resulting in high risk for cardiotoxicity (Rancurello, 1985).

An initial EKG is essential for all patients to establish a baseline and to detect preexisting Wolff-Parkinson-White syndrome or other cardiac conduction abnormalities that could result in fatality because of interaction with the quinidinelike effect of tricyclics. In prepubertal children the EKG should be repeated at dosage increases and monitored periodically thereafter. Blood pressure and pulse should be taken initially and when the dose is increased. The dose should be decreased if any of the following limits are reached:

Pulse > 130
Systolic BP > 140 mm Hg, diastolic BP > 85 mm Hg
EKG PR interval > .22 seconds, QRS interval > 130% of baseline
   (Puig-Antich, Ryan, Rabinovich, 1985)

Plasma levels are recommended in patients who fail to respond to usual doses (possibly low levels) or those who have severe side effects at usual doses (possibly very high levels) (Puig-Antich, et al., 1987; Ryan, et al., 1986).

Anticholinergic effects and other side effects are similar to those in adults (Herskowitz, 1987). Tricyclics may cause lowering of the seizure threshold, with worsening of preexisting EEG abnormalities, and rarely a seizure. Central nervous system toxicity, which may be mistaken for a worsening of the original depression, is manifested by irritability, psychotic symptoms, agitation, anger, aggression, nightmares, forgetfulness, or confusion, especially at plasma levels of imipramine + desipramine > 450 ng/ml. (Preskorn, et al., 1988). Depressed children who are withdrawn and nonverbal may show a transient apparent worsening of sadness, crying, irritability, and aggression as their depression responds to medication.

Sudden withdrawal of moderate or higher doses results in a flulike gastrointestinal syndrome with nausea, cramps, vomiting, headaches, and muscle pains (Klein, et al., 1980). Other withdrawal manifestations may include social withdrawal, hyperactivity, depression, agitation, and insomnia (Campbell, Green, Deutsch, 1985). Tricyclics should therefore be tapered over a 1 to 2-week period rather than being abruptly discontinued. The short half-life of tricyclics in prepubertal children may produce daily withdrawal symptoms if medication is given only once a day or if a dose is missed (Puig-Antich, Ryan, Rabinovich, 1985).

Monoamine oxidase inhibitors (MAOIs) such as phenelzine and tranylcypromine may be useful in the treatment of unipolar and bipolar depressed children and adolescents who do not respond to tricyclics (Puig-Antich, Ryan, Rabinovich, 1985). Suicidal and impulsive outpatients should be excluded because of the risk of severe reactions resulting from dietary indiscretions or drug interaction (Puig-Antich, Ryan, Rabinovich, 1985; Ryan, Puig-Antich, 1986). In any case, careful dietary instruction and review are necessary.

Lithium may be considered in the treatment of children and adolescents with bipolar affective disorder, mixed or manic. Lithium should not be prescribed unless the family is willing and able to comply with regular multiple daily doses and with lithium levels. The medical work-up is the same as in adults. Growth and thyroid and kidney function should be monitored at least annually. Opinions differ on the extent of renal function studies required, but at a minimum, urinalysis and serum creatinine should be obtained every 3 to 6 months.

Therapeutic lithium blood levels are the same as for adults, 0.6 to 1.2 mEq/liter, which can usually be attained with 900 to 1200 mg/day, in divided doses, although daily doses of up to 2000 mg may be required (Campbell, Green, Deutsch, 1985). After initial calibration, saliva may be used to monitor lithium levels (Weller, et al., 1987).

Since lithium excretion occurs primarily through the kidney, and most children have more efficient renal function than adults, they may require higher doses for body weight than adults (Puig-Antich, Ryan, Rabinovich, 1985; Weller, Weller, Fristad, 1986). Lithium should be taken with food to minimize gastrointestinal distress.

Children are at risk for the same side effects as adults but may experience them at lower serum levels (Campbell, Green, Deutsch, 1985). In growing children, the consequences of hypothyroidism are potentially more severe than in adults. *Because of its teratogenic potential, lithium is contraindicated in sexually active girls* unless the patient is compliant with birth control. The calcium mobilization from bones that has been noted in adults might cause a significant problem in growing children (Herskowitz, 1987). Lithium's tendency to aggravate acne may also be of more clinical significance, especially in adolescents.

Adequate salt and fluid intake is necessary to prevent levels rising into the toxic range. The family should be instructed in the importance of preventing dehydration from heat or exercise and in the need to stop the lithium and contact the physician if the child or adolescent develops an illness with fever, vomiting, diarrhea, and/or decreased fluid intake. Erratic consumption of large amounts of salty snack foods may cause fluctuations in lithium levels (Herskowitz, 1987).

Carbamazepine may be useful in the treatment of mania that is resistant to lithium and neuroleptics or rapidly cycling. Chapters 6 and 7 discusses its use in adults.

SCHIZOPHRENIA

Schizophrenia in adults is covered in Chapter 4. The presentation of schizophrenia in adolescence is similar to that in adulthood. Features in children are rather different.

Epidemiology

Childhood schizophrenia has been estimated to be present at a rate of .5 per 1000. The prevalence increases after puberty, approaching adult levels in late adolescence.

Description and DSM-III-R Criteria

DSM-III-R criteria are the same as in adults, with the exception that failure to reach expected levels of adaptive functioning may be seen instead of regression. Schizophrenic children are characterized by markedly uneven development and insidious onset. Language and social behavior are usually delayed and are qualitatively different from those of normal children at any developmental stage. Visual hallucinations are more common in children than in adults.

Differential Diagnosis

Acute hallucinations are not uncommon in children, resulting from *acute phobic reactions, physical illness* with fever or metabolic aberration, or *medications.*

Treatment

Psychotherapy

Individual psychotherapy may be useful as part of a comprehensive treatment plan for schizophrenic children (Cantor, Kestenbaum, 1986). Family psychoeducational treatment (Anderson, Hogarty, Reiss, 1980) may prove beneficial. Token economies may be useful in shaping adaptive behavior and reducing inappropriate behaviors.

Psychopharmacologic Treatment

Clinical experience indicates that neuroleptics (also called major tranquilizers) are less likely to be effective in schizophrenic children and adolescents than in adults (Campbell, 1985; Campbell, Green, Deutsch, 1985; Realmuto, et al., 1984). Neuroleptics should be used only in conjunction with a comprehensive treatment program. Target symptoms that may respond include overactivity, aggression, agitation, stereotyped movements, delusions, and hallucinations.

The dose range for haloperidol in children is 0.5 to 16 mg/day (0.02 to 0.2 mg/kg/day) (Campbell, 1985). An initial trial of about 4 weeks is needed to assess efficacy. Laboratory studies should be monitored at regular intervals. A drug-free trial after 4 to 6 months may be useful in assessing continued need for medication.

Acute extrapyramidal side effects occur as in adults and may be treated with oral or intramuscular diphenhydramine 25 to 50 mg depending on age. Chronic extrapyramidal side effects in adolescents can be treated with diphenhydramine or the anticholinergic drug benztropine in doses of 1 to 2 mg/day, in divided doses. Adolescent boys seem to be more vulnerable to acute dystonic reactions than adult patients, so prophylactic antiparkinsonian medication may be indicated. In children, reduction of neuroleptic dose is preferable to the use of antiparkinsonian agents (Campbell, Green, Deutsch, 1985).

Tardive or withdrawal dyskinesias, some transient but others irreversible, are seen in 8 to 51% of neuroleptic-treated children and adolescents (Campbell, 1985) and are one of the major reasons why these drugs should not be used casually. Tardive dyskinesia has been documented in children and adolescents after as brief a period of treatment as 5 months (Herskowitz, 1987). A careful examination for abnormal movements, using a structured scale such as the Abnormal Involuntary Movements Scale (AIMS), should be conducted before placing the patient on a neuroleptic, and periodically thereafter. Parents and patients (as they are able) should receive regular explanations of the risk of movement disorders.

Weight gain may be problematic with the long-term use of the low-potency neuroleptics. Abnormal laboratory findings seem to be less often reported in children than in adults, but the clinician should be alert to the possibility, especially of blood dyscrasias and hepatic dysfunction. If an acute febrile illness occurs, medication should be withheld and complete blood count with differential and liver enzymes should be determined (Campbell, Green, Deutsch, 1985).

Of particular concern is behavioral toxicity, manifested as worsening of preexisting symptoms or development of new symptoms, such as hyper- or hypoactivity, irritability, apathy, withdrawal, stereotypies, tics, or hallucinations (Campbell, Green, Deutsch, 1985). The so-called low-potency antipsychotic drugs such as chlorpromazine and thioridazine can produce cognitive dulling and sedation, interfering with ability to benefit from school (Campbell, Green, Deutsch, 1985), and are probably best avoided. Children and adolescents are more sensitive to sedation than adults (Realmuto, et al., 1984).

Abdominal pain may occur, especially early in treatment. Enuresis has been reported (Realmuto, et al., 1984). Photosensitivity due to chlorpromazine may be a problem when youngsters play outside.

Environmental Interventions

The best outcome is obtained with an intensive school-based treatment program that incorporates multiple methods of intervention. Hospitalization and/or long-term residential treatment may be needed.

EATING DISORDERS

Rumination Disorder of Infancy

This potentially fatal disorder is one of the key differential diagnoses in the evaluation of children seen on pediatric services with failure to thrive (unexplained failure to gain weight).

Epidemiology

Rumination appears in infants between 3 months and 1 year of age and in persons with moderate and severe mental retardation. In both groups, males predominate 5:1 (Mayes, et al., 1988).

Description and DSM-III-R Criteria

This disorder is characterized by repeated voluntary regurgitation of food, without apparent nausea or associated gastrointestinal illness, accompanied by failure to make expected weight gain or weight loss. Rumination appears to be an enjoyable source of pleasurable stimulation or a means of tension release. When not ruminating, the child may appear apathetic and withdrawn, irritable and fussy, or may seem quite normal.

Differential Diagnosis

Other causes of vomiting include gastroesophageal reflux due to esophageal sphincter dysfunction or hiatal hernia, gastrointestinal infections, congenital malformations such as pyloric stenosis, or hyperactive gag reflex. Failure to gain weight may result from inadequate feeding, malabsorption syndromes, systemic infection, or inborn errors of metabolism.

Etiology

About one third of infants with rumination disorder have a history of obstetrical complications; one fourth have developmental delays attributed to mental retardation or pervasive developmental disorder. Abnormalities in parental caretaking have been implicated, either understimulation with neglect or excessive stimulation out of phase with the infant's needs accompanied by harsh handling. Cases with no apparent abnormalities in the infant or in the mother–child relationship may represent habit disorders that were encouraged by characteristics of the child's gastrointestinal physiology or triggered by a transient organic illness.

Evaluation

Pediatric hospitalization is usually required for evaluation, with a search for possible causes and for sequelae such as dehydration, electrolyte imbalance, and malnutrition. Calorie counts and weight should be recorded. A detailed history is taken of physical and emotional development and of feeding. Upper gastrointestinal contrast and esophageal motility studies may be indicated. The mother–child interaction is observed during times of feeding and playing. It is important not to confuse the anxiety, frustration, and disgust the child's constant vomiting and unrewarding weight gain *induce* in the mother with deficits in the mother that may have *caused* the disorder. Some infants are so irregular and unpredictable in their rhythms and labile in their responses that the best parent has a difficult time. The child should be evaluated for developmental delay, and the parents for possible primary psychiatric disorders.

Treatment

Psychotherapy. Supportive psychotherapy for the parents, with attention to any psychopathology that may have become apparent in the evaluation, is indicated. Parents and child may be seen together, to model feeding techniques and ways of interacting with the baby that will be rewarding to both.

Behavior modification. Treatment programs using social rewards such as cuddling and playing, combined with mild noncorporal punishments (brief ignoring, scolding) for rumination, may be useful.

Environmental interventions. Pediatric hospitalization may be necessary to restructure the feeding behavior of both parent and child and to reduce parental anxiety. A visiting nurse or homemaker may be arranged to support a mother who is overwhelmed. Developmentally delayed infants may benefit from an organized stimulation program.

If parents refuse to cooperate with treatment, or parenting ability is so impaired that the infant is in danger, laws in all states mandate reporting to a child protective services agency.

The role of the primary care physician. The pediatrician is the key player in cases of rumination disorder, conducting the medical evaluation and working together with social services and the child psychiatrist on psychosocial evaluation and treatment. These families require close and prolonged pediatric care to monitor progress and mobilize additional resources.

Anorexia Nervosa and Bulimia Nervosa

These disorders are covered in Chapter 11. Anorexia nervosa frequently has its onset at puberty or in early adolescence. Family treatment has a more central role in the care of adolescent patients than it does with adults (see Annotated Bibliography).

Obesity

Obesity virtually always has its onset in childhood. An estimated 10 to 20% of American children and adolescents are overweight. The majority of obese children over the age of 10 become persistently obese adults. Obesity in adults is covered in Chapter 23.

The most effective treatment programs actively involve both parents and child and include education, a balanced diet, and exercise. Contingency management programs may be useful for children, while adolescents benefit from cognitive strategies, such as those used for adults (see Annotated Bibliography).

MENTAL RETARDATION

Epidemiology

The prevalence of mental retardation in the United States has been estimated at 1 to 3%. Males predominate 1.5:1.

Description and DSM-III-R Criteria

Mental retardation (coded on DSM-III-R Axis II) is defined as significantly subaverage general intellectual functioning, as demonstrated by an IQ of 70 or below on an individually administered intelligence test, accompanied by deficits in adaptive functioning, with onset before the age of 18. The four degrees of severity are seen in Table 15-6.

Table 15–6 **Categories of Severity of Mental Retardation**

DESCRIPTION	RANGE OF IQ	PROPORTION OF RETARDED POPULATION (%)
Mild ("educable")	50–55 to 70	85
Moderate ("trainable")	35–40 to 50–55	10
Severe	20–25 to 35–40	3–4
Profound	Below 20–25	1–2

(Used with permission. American Psychiatric Association, 1987)

Differential Diagnosis

Children who have been severely *neglected* may test in the retarded range. True intellectual capacity can only be assessed after a period of remediation. Children with *specific developmental disorders* have delays in circumscribed areas with normal functioning in other areas. The DSM-III-R "V code" *borderline intellectual functioning* is used for children with IQ scores between 71 and 84. These youngsters are primarily impaired in the school setting.

Children with *autistic disorder* have uneven developmental delays and qualitative abnormalities of behavior and emotions. Many have mental retardation *in addition to* autistic disorder. Some children identified by schools as having *ADHD* are, in fact, mentally retarded. It may be difficult to determine whether children with *sensory impairments*, such as deafness or blindness, or *neurological disorders*, such as cerebral palsy, actually are mentally retarded as well or whether their disabilities interfere with testing to such an extent that their scores are falsely low.

Etiology

Mental retardation is a diverse category with a large number of etiologies. Identifiable single gene or chromosomal abnormalities and metabolic, traumatic, and toxic causes are more common in those with moderate to profound retardation. In mild retardation, etiology is more often attributed to a genetic endowment at the low end of the normal distribution or to psychosocial factors such as poverty and lack of stimulation. Many cases are idiopathic.

Evaluation

Intelligence testing is administered by a psychologist skilled in working with children in a setting that will encourage the child's cooperation. Commonly used tests of intellectual functioning are listed in Table 15-3. Adaptive functioning is evaluated by history, clinical observation, and rating scales such as the Vineland Adaptive Behavior Scales. A medical evaluation is indicated to seek causative disorders, sensory handicap, and associated physical problems such as congenital malformations, inborn errors of metabolism, or epilepsy. Genetic evaluation may be important in counseling the parents regarding the risk in future children. Psychiatric evaluation may be necessary to define associated psychiatric disorders, which are three to four times as common in the retarded as in the general population.

Treatment

Psychotherapy

Individual psychotherapy and parent counseling may be useful in dealing with developmental or situational crises or in the treatment of coexisting disorders. Parents may need assistance in dealing with their grief over having a defective child. Specific behavioral programs are useful in teaching adaptive behaviors and reducing stereotypic behaviors, aggression, and self-injury.

Environmental Interventions

Mentally retarded children and adolescents require special education programs. Moderate to profoundly retarded youth benefit from comprehensive multidisciplinary habilitation programs. Specialized infant stimulation and preschool programs can reduce intellectual and adaptive deficits. Institutionalization is now indicated only for the most severely affected, usually those with accompanying medical disorders or severe behavior problems. Adolescents and young adults benefit from vocational training programs, sheltered workshops, and group homes in the community.

The national organization, Association for Retarded Citizens, has state and local chapters that provide assistance to retarded persons and their families.

PERVASIVE DEVELOPMENTAL DISORDERS (PDD)

This category contains *autistic disorder,* formerly known as infantile autism, and a residual category called *pervasive developmental disorder not otherwise specified* (NOS) for children with similar features who do not meet full criteria for autistic disorder. These patients are characterized by an uneven pattern of development that includes both severe delays and qualitative abnormalities.

Description and DSM-III-R Criteria

Autistic disorder is characterized by severe impairment, relative to chronological and mental age, in three areas:

1. Reciprocal social interaction
2. Verbal and nonverbal communication and imaginative activity
3. Repertoire of activities and interests

The onset is in infancy or childhood. Autistic persons do not view other people as having thoughts or feelings. They do not seek out adults or peers for emotional gratification, although they may cling mechanically to their parents when frightened. They do not engage in social or imaginative play, preferring stereotyped activities with objects. There is often strong attachment to an object, such as a string or rubber band. Speech and language development are both markedly delayed and abnormal in content, form, and tone. Echolalia, incorrect use of pronouns, and idiosyncratic meanings for words are common. Even when grammatically correct speech and language develop, there is impairment in the ability to initiate or sustain conversation due to inability to make use of social cues and a lack of understanding of the other's point of view. Stereotyped body movements, such as hand flicking or head banging, are common. Changes in the environment or in routines often produce extreme distress. There is marked restriction in interests and a preoccupation with parts of objects or a narrow area of knowledge.

Development may be markedly abnormal from early infancy, with lack of eye contact and indifference or aversion to cuddling. Some children may initially appear normal, with symptoms appearing at age 2 or 3 as more complex communication and social interaction are expected.

Differential Diagnosis

Children with pure *mental retardation* have a more even pattern of delays and do not have bizarre behaviors or deficits in social relatedness. Most children with PDD *also* have mental retardation, however, usually in the moderate range. In *aphasia, developmental language disorders,* or *deafness,* the deficits in language are partially compensated for by nonverbal gestures, and social interest is normal.

History and clinical examination can distinguish PDD from *reactive attachment disorder of infancy* or severe reactions to trauma or separation from parents. *Degenerative diseases* may transiently resemble PDD.

Etiology

There is no evidence that child-rearing practices contribute to the development of this disorder. PDD is more common following a wide range of chromosomal, infectious, and traumatic insults to the central nervous system. Among the more common are maternal rubella during pregnancy and fragile X syndrome. Recent magnetic resonance imaging studies of autistic persons have shown developmental hypoplasia of two discrete areas in the cerebellum (Courchesne, et al., 1988). Pedigree studies have indicated a genetic contribution to a spectrum that includes PDD, language disorders, dyslexia, and mental retardation. In some families, an autosomal recessive inheritance appears likely.

Evaluation

Medical evaluation is needed to seek sensory deficits, possible treatable disorders, and degenerative diseases. The physician should be alert to the possibility of epilepsy, because seizures develop in 35 to 50% of patients with PDD by age 20. In evaluating family dynamics, the reciprocal effects on parents of the child's behavior must be taken into account. Baseline measurements are taken in cognitive level, social communication skills, language function, and additional psychiatric symptoms such as hyperactivity or severe anxiety.

Treatment

Psychotherapy
Group therapy, with autistic or normal peers, may significantly improve social functioning. Supportive psychotherapy may be of benefit to parents. Behavioral techniques are valuable in increasing learning and reducing maladaptive or injurious behaviors. These should be taught to parents and incorporated into the school setting.

Psychopharmacologic Treatment
No medications are known to affect the autistic disorder per se, and medication should not be used as the sole treatment.

Neuroleptics. In some hyperactive or normoactive autistic children, haloperidol (in doses of 0.5 to 3.0 mg/day) decreases behavioral target symptoms such as hyperactivity, aggressiveness, temper tantrums, withdrawal, and stereotypies, and in combination with a structured behavioral/educational program, it may enhance language acquisition. In general, hypoactive autistic children do not respond well to haloperidol (Campbell, Green, Deutsch, 1985). (See section on schizophrenia in this chapter for the use of neuroleptics in children and adolescents.)

Stimulants. Contrary to previous belief, recent reports indicate that methylphenidate in doses similar to those used to treat ADHD may reduce overactivity in autistic children and improve attention span without producing psychosis or increasing stereotyped behaviors (Birmaher, Quintana, Greenhill, 1988; Strayhorn, et al., 1988).

Early enthusiasm for the efficacy of fenfluramine in the treatment of autistic children has not been supported (Campbell, et al., 1988).

Environmental Interventions

The best outcome is obtained with a specialized therapeutic educational program, integrating social, language, and behavioral components, beginning as early as possible (age 2 to 4 years). Sufficiently intensive early treatment can avert institutionalization for all but the most handicapped. Adolescents and young adults can benefit from sheltered workshops, vocational training programs, and group homes in the community. Support and advocacy groups for parents are useful.

The role of the primary care physician. The pediatrician is usually the first to whom parents bring their concerns about a child with PDD, often in the first 18 months of life. It is essential for the physician to take these concerns seriously. If a screening examination indicates delay or deviance in development, immediate arrangements for definitive diagnosis and early intervention are indicated. Whenever possible, referral should be made to a center with experience in this rare disorder where a multidisciplinary team assessment can be conducted. The primary physician will maintain an important role in coordinating medical care for these patients, whose medical disorders may be difficult to diagnose and treat because of lack of verbal ability and cooperation.

SPECIFIC DEVELOPMENTAL DISORDERS

Description

This group of disorders is characterized by developmental delay, relative to that expected for mental age in a specific area of development, that results in functional impairment and that is not due to a diagnosable physical disorder, a visual or hearing impairment, a pervasive developmental disorder, mental retardation, or inadequate educational opportunities. It is common for a child to have more than one specific developmental disorder (Table 15-7). Common secondary symptoms include low self-esteem, demoralization, refusal to exert effort in school, and behavior problems.

Table 15–7 **Specific Developmental Disorders**

DISORDER	ESTIMATED PREVALENCE, AGE 5–12 (%)
Academic skills disorders	
Developmental arithmetic disorder	Unknown
Developmental expressive writing disorder	2–8
Developmental reading disorder (dyslexia)	2–8
Language and speech disorders	
Developmental articulation disorder	5–10
Developmental expressive language disorder	3–10
Developmental receptive language disorder	3–10
Motor skills disorder	
Developmental coordination disorder	6
Developmental disorder not otherwise specified	Unknown

(Used with permission. American Psychiatric Association, 1987)

Etiology

Genetic factors are suggested by clustering of specific developmental disorders in families. Etiology is presumed to relate to cortical delayed or abnormal maturation or damage.

Evaluation

Early diagnosis is crucial in facilitating remediation and reducing secondary emotional and behavioral symptoms. Assessment requires psychological testing (see Table 15-3) to establish IQ, followed by academic achievement tests and/or tests of specific language, speech, and motor functions. Visual and hearing impairment must be ruled out. A careful history should be taken of school attendance and performance and of the quality of teaching.

Treatment

Psychotherapy

Supportive psychotherapy may be required to deal with low self-esteem, passivity, lack of motivation, anxiety, or depression resulting from the learning difficulties. Family therapy can deal with sequelae of parental criticism and child failure. Behavioral techniques may be useful in motivating children to practice and learn skills that are difficult for them.

Environmental Interventions

Most important is specific remediation of the deficits, using teaching techniques tailored to the child's strengths and weaknesses. Special educational programs may be needed, ranging from tutoring to a resource room several periods a week, to full-time special classes. The most severe cases may require a special school or residential treatment program. Articulation or language therapy provided by a specially trained professional is indicated for language and speech disorders. Physical or occupational therapy may be needed.

MEDICAL ILLNESS IN CHILDREN AND ADOLESCENTS

Response of Child and Family to Physical Illness

Infancy

When infants less than 6 months old are hospitalized, they are usually most upset by changes in their usual routine. It is helpful to have the parents do as much of the care as possible and to arrange for consistency of nurses. For the older infant who has formed strong differential attachments, separation is traumatic, especially in the foreign hospital environment and when accompanied by physical discomfort and medical procedures. Stranger anxiety adds to the baby's distress. The infant's immature language development exacerbates the problem, because explanations are not helpful.

The constant presence of a parent is extremely important. In the absence of an attachment figure, the baby's thrashing, refusal to eat, and inability to sleep may have serious medical consequences. Fortunately, most pediatric hospital settings not only permit but encourage parents to "live in" while their young child is hospitalized.

Early Childhood

Hospitalized children aged 1 to 3 years react primarily to separation from their parents. They may react by rejecting parents when they visit, being aggressive toward the medical staff, regressing in bowel and bladder control, and refusing to eat. If parents are absent, children may develop depression, sleep disturbance, diarrhea, or vomiting. Maximizing parental presence and providing the child with familiar items from home are helpful. Toddlers also have great concern for the intactness of their bodies.

For children aged 3 to 5 years, separation from parents by hospitalization is still difficult, even for a child who is comfortably able to separate in other circumstances. Anesthesia and surgery are especially frightening because this is a time of normal fears of bodily injury. Children believe that illness and painful treatments are punishment for real or fantasied misbehavior. When possible, preparation by simple explanations and a visit to the hospital may help. Constant presence of a parent is important.

School Age

Children age 6 to 12 usually tolerate acute illness and hospitalization relatively well, especially if they are prepared, parents visit daily for substantial periods, and preceding development was normal. They may still have irrational explanations of illness (e.g., that they are being punished, or that their parents were unable to protect them). Behavioral regression or oppositional behavior often occurs.

Adolescence

Adolescents have more realistic fears regarding the outcome of illness, especially regarding changes in appearance or inability to continue favorite activities. An injury may make impossible a planned career (e.g., sports or the military). Loss of autonomy and privacy are especially painful.

Parents

At the time of diagnosis, the parents of an ill or handicapped child must go through a period of mourning. The stages are similar to those following a death: anger, denial, grief, and resignation. Medical problems in a child may be viewed by the parent (and others) as a negative reflection on the parent. Parents feel guilty, especially for genetic diseases or complications that may be attributed (rightly or wrongly) to maternal behavior. The parents' anger, resentment, guilt, and/or denial may interfere with their ability to work together with the pediatric team. Realistic additional caretaking and financial burdens may stress parents beyond their ability to cope.

Chronic Illness

Sequelae of chronic illness include interference with normal developmental tasks attained through school, peers, sports, and other activities. Autonomy and control of the child's own body are jeopardized. Children and adolescents with chronic illness, but without disability, are twice as likely as controls to have a psychiatric disorder. Those with disability as well as chronic illness are even more likely to have emotional and attention deficit disorders, social isolation, and school performance problems. The majority of chronically ill youngsters do not, however, have mental health problems or difficulties with social or school adjustment (Cadman, et al., 1987).

Compliance

Lack of compliance with medical regimens (medication, diet, exercise) is a major problem in the care of children and adolescents. Factors that contribute to noncompliance are seen in Table 15-8. Attention to and remediation of specific causes of noncompliance will improve medical management.

Specific Interventions for Medically Ill Children and Adolescents

A child and adolescent psychiatrist or pediatric psychologist can offer consultation and treatment for emotional and behavioral problems. Coexisting psychiatric disorders are treated as described above.

Psychotherapy

Supportive individual, family, and/or group psychotherapy is often valuable for both patient and parents. Instruction in social problem solving and coping skills may also be beneficial.

Table 15–8 **Causative Factors in Noncompliance**

Patient factors

Denial or lack of acceptance of the disorder
Frustration with the outcome or nature of treatment
Wish to obtain parental attention or special privileges
  by way of symptoms
Wish to regain control
Rebellion against parents
Lack of knowledge or skills
Inability to resist peer pressurre
Lack of relationship or miscommunication with healthcare team
Psychopathology
  Depression
  Suicidal intent
  Attention-deficit hyperactivity disorder
  Oppositional defiant disorder
  Anorexia nervosa or bulimia

Family factors

Unresolved guilt, denial, anger, and/or fear
Lack of knowledge and skills
Inability to encourage adolescent independence
Competition with medical personnel
Lack of support system
Other stressors on family
Family conflict acted out through the child's medical care
Rivalry between patient and healthy siblings

Treatment-related factors

Interference with usual activities
Side effects of drugs (pain, nausea, weight gain, hair loss)
Clarity of connection between noncompliance and sequela
Disinterested, inconsistent medical personnel

Behavior Modification

Techniques such as behavioral contracting with contingency management and self-monitoring with self-reinforcement are invaluable in improving medical and behavioral compliance. Children who refuse or are unable to swallow oral medication can be taught to take pills using instruction, modeling, contingent rewards, and shaping pill-swallowing using successively larger candies or placebos (Pelco, et al., 1987).

Behavioral medicine techniques have been adapted for the level of the youngster's cognitive or emotional development. Relaxation training has been used in the treatment of pediatric migraine, juvenile rheumatoid arthritis, hemophilia, asthma, and hyperventilation in patients with cystic fibrosis. Hypnosis can be used in the treatment of physical symptoms with a psychological component or to help a child manage severe pain or nausea associated with a physical disorder or its treatment.

Behavioral therapy techniques in the management of chronic pain include operant techniques, self-monitoring, and stress management planning. Emphasis is placed on fostering a sense of control and mastery and promoting normal functioning in spite of pain (Masek, Spirito, Fentress, 1984; Varni, et al., 1986).

"Stress-inoculation" uses education, modeling, systematic desensitization, hypnosis, contingency management, and training and practice in coping skills such as imagery and breathing exercises. It is useful in the prevention of stress and anxiety in children before medical and dental procedures and in chronically ill children for reduction of anxiety, pain, or other discomfort connected to repeated procedures such as spinal taps, bone marrow aspirations, and chemotherapy injections (Melamed, Klingman, Siegel, 1984; Varni, et al., 1986).

Psychopharmacologic Treatment

Tricyclic antidepressants may be used to treat depression. Situational and anticipatory anxiety related to procedures may benefit from hydroxyzine, diazepam, or alprazolam (Pfefferbaum, et al., 1987).

Environmental Interventions

Peer activities and school should be normalized as much as possible. Chronically ill children may benefit greatly from special camps and recreation programs with medical supervision. Families may require a variety of concrete assistance to provide for an ill child.

The Role of the Physician.

Members of the medical team will be more successful if they are able to deal with their own feelings of guilt, helplessness, inadequacy, and anxiety. Staff support groups may be useful. In dealing with adolescents, efforts to respect and reinforce the patient's competence and autonomy, to give information in a way that permits the adolescent to understand and to save face, and to encourage questions will be rewarded with improved compliance and psychological adjustment. Children and adolescents with potentially fatal illnesses appreciate accurate information, titrated to their ability to understand and their emotional readiness to hear.

CLINICAL PEARLS

- Emotional and behavioral reactions should be anticipated in the context of medical illness.
- Explain in advance as much as the child's age and coping style and the medical situation allow.
- Minimize separations from parents, especially for children under 8 years old.
- Try to understand the meaning of the illness to the child, and correct misconceptions.
- Understand that the child or adolescent needs to control *something* in the environment, and arrange the milieu so that this will not interfere with treatment.
- Do not blame the child or parents for or criticize regressive behavior.

BIBLIOGRAPHY

General

Adams PL, Fras I: Beginning Child Psychiatry. New York, Brunner/Mazel, 1988
> An introductory text.

Dulcan MK, Popper CW: Concise Guide to Child and Adolescent Psychiatry. Washington, DC, American Psychiatric Press, 1989
> A brief paperback handbook.

Lewis M: Clinical Aspects of Child Development, 2nd ed. Philadelphia, Lea & Febiger, 1982
> Good coverage of both normal and pathological development.

Popper CW: Disorders usually first evident in infancy, childhood or adolescence. In Talbott JA, Hales RE, Yudofsky SC (eds): The American Psychiatric Press Textbook of Psychiatry. Washington, DC, American Psychiatric Press, 1988
> A chapter in a comprehensive text.

Rutter M, Hersov L: Child and Adolescent Psychiatry: Modern Approaches. Oxford, Blackwell Scientific Publications, 1985
> A comprehensive, data-based text.

Evaluation and Treatment

Campbell M, Green WH, Deutsch, SI: Child and Adolescent Psychopharmacology. Beverly Hills, CA, Sage Publications, 1985

Cohen DJ, Schowalter JE (eds): Child Psychiatry. Volume 2 of Psychiatry (Cavenar J, ed). Philadelphia, JB Lippincott, 1985
> Chapter 20. Lewis M: General psychiatric assessment of children and adolescents
> Chapter 21. Sparrow SS, Fletcher JM, Cicchetti DV: Psychological assessment of children
> Chapter 59. Popper CW: Child and adolescent psychopharmacology
> Chapter 61. Kazdin AE: Behavior therapy
> Chapter 62. Silver M, Liebman R: Family-oriented treatment of children and adolescents
> Chapter 63. Riddle MA, Vitulano LA: Group psychotherapy for children and adolescents
> Chapter 64. Harper G, Geraty R: Hospital and residential treatment

Dulcan MK: Treatment of children and adolescents. In Talbott JA, Hales RE, Yudofsky SC (eds): The American Psychiatric Press Textbook of Psychiatry. Washington, DC, American Psychiatric Press, 1988

Simmons JE: Psychiatric Examination of Children, 4th ed. Philadelphia, Lea & Febiger, 1987

Attention-Deficit Hyperactivity Disorder

Dulcan MK: Comprehensive treatment of children and adolescents with attention deficit disorders: The state of the art. Clin Psychol Rev 6:539–570, 1986

Dulcan MK: Attention deficit disorder. In Last CG, Hersen M (eds): Handbook of Child Psychiatric Diagnosis. John Wiley & Sons, 1988

Shaywitz SE, Shaywitz BA: Attention deficit disorders. In Cohen DJ, Schowalter JE (eds): Child Psychiatry. Volume 2 of Psychiatry (Cavenar J, ed). Philadelphia, JB Lippincott, 1985

Conduct Disorders

Lewis DO: Conduct disorder. In Cohen DJ, Schowalter JE (eds): Child Psychiatry. Volume 2 of Psychiatry (Cavenar J, ed). Philadelphia, JB Lippincott, 1985

Oppositional Defiant Disorder

Forehand R, McMahon RJ: Helping the Non-Compliant Child: A Clinician's Guide to Parent Training. New York, Guilford Press, 1981

Anxiety Disorders

Eth S, Pynoos RS (eds): Post-traumatic Stress Disorder in Children. Washington, DC, American Psychiatric Press, 1985

McDermott JF, Werry JS, Petti TA, et al: Anxiety disorders. In Cohen DJ, Schowalter JE (eds): Child Psychiatry. Volume 2 of Psychiatry (Cavenar J, ed). Philadelphia, JB Lippincott, 1985

Ollendick TH, Francis G: Behavioral assessment and treatment of childhood phobias. Behav Modif 12:165–204, 1988

Rapoport JL: Annotation childhood obsessive compulsive disorder. J Child Psychol Psychiatry 27:289–295, 1986

Sheehan KH, Sheehan DV, Shaw KR: Diagnosis and treatment of anxiety disorders in children and adolescents. Psychiatr Ann 18:146–157, 1988

Enuresis

Azrin N, Foxx R: Toilet Training in Less Than a Day. New York, Simon & Schuster, 1974

Gross RT, Dornbusch SM: Enuresis. In Levine MD, Carey WB, Crocker AC, Gross RT (eds): Developmental-Behavioral Pediatrics. Philadelphia, WB Saunders, 1983

Schmitt BD: Daytime wetting (diurnal enuresis). Pediatr Clin North Am 29:9–20, 1982

Schmitt BD: Nocturnal enuresis: An update on treatment. Pediatr Clin North Am 29:21–36, 1982

Encopresis

Levine MD: Encopresis: Its potentiation, evaluation, and alleviation. Pediatr Clin North Am 29:315–330, 1982

Mood Disorders

Poznanski EO: Affective disorders. In Cohen DJ, Schowalter JE (eds): Child Psychiatry. Volume 2 of Psychiatry (Cavenar J, ed). Philadelphia, JB Lippincott, 1985

Weller EB, Weller RA (eds): Current Perspectives on Major Depressive Disorders in Children. Washington, DC, American Psychiatric Press, 1984

Schizophrenia

Cantor S: Childhood Schizophrenia. New York, Guilford Press, 1988

Tanguay PE, Asarnow R: Schizophrenia in children. In Cohen DJ, Schowalter JE (eds): Child Psychiatry. Volume 2 of Psychiatry (Cavenar J, ed). Philadelphia, JB Lippincott, 1985

Eating Disorders

Bithoney WG, Rathbun JM: Failure to thrive. In Levine MD, Carey WB, Crocker AC, Gross RT (eds): Developmental–Behavioral Pediatrics. Philadelphia, WB Saunders, 1983

Chatoor I, Kickson L, Einhorn A: Rumination: Etiology and treatment. Pediatr Ann 13:924–929, 1984

Woolston JL: Eating disorders in childhood and adolescence. In Cohen DJ, Schowalter JE (eds): Child Psychiatry. Volume 2 of Psychiatry (Cavenar J, ed). Philadelphia, JB Lippincott, 1985

Obesity

Epstein LH, Wing RR: Behavioral treatment of childhood obesity. Psychol Bull 101:331–342, 1987

Neumann CG: Obesity in childhood. In Levine MD, Carey WB, Crocker AC, Gross RT (eds): Developmental–Behavioral Pediatrics. Philadelphia, WB Saunders, 1983

Mental Retardation

Corbett JA: Mental retardation: Psychiatric aspects. In Rutter M, Hersov L (eds): Child and Adolescent Psychiatry: Modern Approaches, 2nd ed. Oxford, Blackwell Scientific Publications, 1985

Kirman BH: Mental retardation: Medical aspects. In Rutter M, Hersov L (eds): Child and Adolescent Psychiatry: Modern Approaches, 2nd ed. Oxford, Blackwell Scientific Publications, 1985

Sparrow SS, Fletcher JM, Cicchetti CV: Psychological assessment of children. In Cohen DJ, Schowalter JE (eds): Child Psychiatry. Volume 2 of Psychiatry (Cavenar J, ed). Philadelphia, JB Lippincott, 1985

Pervasive Developmental Disorders

Volkmar FR, Cohen DJ: Pervasive developmental disorders. In Cohen DJ, Schowalter JE (eds): Child Psychiatry. Volume 2 of Psychiatry (Cavenar J, ed). Philadelphia, JB Lippincott, 1985

Specific Developmental Disorders

Paul R: Specific developmental language disorders. In Cohen DJ, Schowalter JE (eds): Child Psychiatry. Volume 2 of Psychiatry (Cavenar J, ed). Philadelphia, JB Lippincott, 1985

Popper CW: Disorders usually first evident in infancy, childhood, or adolescence. In Talbott JA, Hales RE, Yudofsky SC (eds): The American Psychiatric Press Textbook of Psychiatry, pp 717–729. Washington, DC, American Psychiatric Press, 1988

Sparrow SS, Blachman BA: Developmental learning disorders. In Cohen DJ, Schowalter JE (eds): Child Psychiatry. Volume 2 of Psychiatry (Cavenar J, ed). Philadelphia, JB Lippincott, 1985

Medically Ill Children

Van Dongen-Melman JEWM, Sanders-Woudstra JAR: The chronically ill child and his family. In Cohen DJ, Schowalter JE (eds): Child Psychiatry. Volume 2 of Psychiatry (Cavenar J, ed). Philadelphia, JB Lippincott, 1985

Van Dongen-Melman JEWM, Sanders-Woudstra JAR: The fatally ill child and his family. In Cohen DJ, Schowalter JE (eds): Child Psychiatry. Volume 2 of Psychiatry (Cavenar J, ed). Philadelphia, JB Lippincott, 1985

REFERENCES

Achenbach, TM, Edelbrock, CS: Manual for the Child Behavior Checklist and Revised Child Behavior Profile. Burlington, VT, University Associates in Psychiatry, 1983

Achenbach TM, Edelbrock, CS: Manual for the Teacher's Report Form and Teacher Version of the Child Behavior Profile. Burlington, VT, University of Vermont Department of Psychiatry, 1986

Alexander JF, Parsons BV: Functional Family Therapy. Monterey, CA, Brooks/Cole, 1982

American Psychiatric Association: Diagnostic and Statistical Manual of Mental Disorders, 3rd ed. Washington, DC, American Psychiatric Press, 1980

American Psychiatric Association: Diagnostic and Statistical Manual of Mental Disorders, 3rd ed rev. Washington, DC, American Psychiatric Press, 1987

Anderson CM, Hogarty GE, Reiss DJ: Family treatment of adult schizophrenic patients: A psycho-educational approach. Schizophr Bull 6:490–505, 1980

Anderson JC, Williams S, McGee R, Silva PA: DSM-III disorders in preadolescent children: Prevalence in a large sample from the general population. Arch Gen Psychiatry 44:69–76, 1987

Azrin N, Foxx R: Toilet Training in Less Than a Day. New York, Simon & Schuster, 1974

Barkley RA: Hyperactive Children: A Handbook for Diagnosis and Treatment. New York, Guilford Press, 1981

Biederman J, Gastfriend DR, Jellinek MS: Desipramine in the treatment of children with attention deficit disorder. J Clin Psychopharmacol 6:359–363, 1986

Biederman J, Gastfriend DR, Jellinek MS, Goldblatt A: Cardiovascular effects of desipramine in children and adolescents with attention deficit disorder. J Pediatr 106:1017–1020, 1985

Biederman J, Munir K, Knee D, et al: A family study of patients with attention deficit disorder and normal controls. J Psychiatr Res 20:263–274, 1986

Birmaher B, Quintana H, Greenhill LL: Methylphenidate treatment of hyperactive autistic children. J Am Acad Child Adolesc Psychiatry 27:248–251, 1988

Bosco JJ, Robin SS: Hyperkinesis: Prevalence and treatment. In Whalen CK, Henker B (eds): Hyperactive Children: The Social Ecology of Identification and Treatment. New York, Academic Press, 1980

Cadman D, Boyle M, Szatmari P, Offord DR: Chronic illness, disability, and mental and social well-being: Findings of the Ontario Child Health Study. Pediatrics 79:805–813, 1987

Campbell M, Adams P, Small AM, et al: Efficacy and safety of fenfluramine in autistic children. J Am Acad Child Adolesc Psychiatry 27:434–439, 1988

Campbell M, Green WH, Deutsch SI: Child and Adolescent Psychopharmacology. Beverly Hills, CA, Sage Publications, 1985

Campbell SB: Hyperactivity in preschoolers: Correlates and prognostic implications. Clin Psychol Rev 5:405–428, 1985

Cantor S, Kestenbaum C: Psychotherapy with schizophrenic children. J Am Acad Child Adolesc Psychiatry 25:623–630, 1986

Costello EJ, Pantino T: The new morbidity: Who should treat it? J Dev Behav Pediatr 8:288–291, 1987

Courchesne E, Yeung-Courchesne R, Press GA, et al: Hypoplasia of cerebellar vermal lobules VI and VII in autism. N Engl J Med 318:1349–1354, 1988

Douglas VI: Attentional and cognitive problems. In Rutter M (ed): Developmental Neuropsychiatry. New York, Guilford Press, 1983

Emery G, Bedrosian R, Garber J: Cognitive therapy with depressed children and adolescents. In Cantwell DP, Carlson GA (eds): Affective Disorders in Childhood and Adolescence: An Update. New York, Spectrum Publications, 1983

Evans RW, Clay TH, Gualtieri CT: Carbamazepine in pediatric psychiatry. J Am Acad Child Adolesc Psychiatry 26:2–8, 1987

Evans RW, Gualtieri CT, Hicks RE: A neuropathic substrate for stimulant drug effects in hyperactive children. Clin Neuropharmacol 9:264–281, 1986

Forehand RL, McMahon RJ: Helping the Noncompliant Child: A Clinician's Guide to Parent Training. New York, Guilford Press, 1981

Gadow, KD: Prevalence and efficacy of stimulant drug use with mentally retarded children and youth. Psychopharmacol Bull 21:291–303, 1985

Gastfriend DR, Biederman J, Jellinek M: Desipramine in the treatment of adolescents with attention deficit disorder. Am J Psychiatry 141:906–908, 1984

Geller B, Cooper TB, Chestnut BS: Preliminary data on the relationship between nortriptyline plasma level and response in depressed children. Am J Psychiatry 143:1283–1286, 1986

Gittelman-Klein R, Klein DF: Controlled imipramine treatment of school phobia. Arch Gen Psychiatry 25:204–207, 1971

Greenhill LL, Solomon M, Pleak R, Ambrosini P: Molindone hydrochloride treatment of hospitalized children with conduct disorder. J Clin Psychiatry 46:20–25, 1985

Grob CS, Coyle JT: Suspected adverse methylphenidate–imipramine interactions in children. J Dev Behav Pediatr 7:265–267, 1986

Herskowitz J: Developmental toxicology. In Popper C (ed): Psychiatric Pharmacosciences of Children and Adolescents. Washington, DC, American Psychiatric Press, 1987

Houts AC, Liebert RM, Padawer W: A delivery system for the treatment of primary enuresis. J Abnorm Child Psychol 11:513–520, 1983

Hunt RD, Minderaa RB, Cohen DJ: Clonidine benefits children with attention deficit disorder and hyperactivity. J Am Acad Child Psychiatry 24:617–629, 1985

Kagan J, Reznick JS, Snidman N: Biological bases of childhood shyness. Science 240:167–171, 1988

Kashani JH, Carlson GA, Beck NC, et al: Depression, depressive symptoms, and depressed mood among a community sample of adolescents. Am J Psychiatry 144:931–934, 1987

Kashani JH, Orvaschel H: Anxiety disorders in mid-adolescence: A community sample. Am J Psychiatry 145:960–964, 1988

Kazdin AE, Esveldt-Dawson K, French NH, et al: Problem-solving skills training and relationship therapy in the treatment of antisocial child behavior. J Consult Clin Psychol 55:76–85, 1987

Kendall PC, Braswell L: Cognitive-Behavioral Therapy for Impulsive Children. New York, Guilford Press, 1985

Klein DF, Gittelman R, Quitkin F, Rifkin A: Diagnosis and Drug Treatment of Psychiatric Disorders in Adults and Children, 2nd ed. Baltimore, Williams & Wilkins, 1980

Kovacs M, Feinberg TL, Crouse-Novak MA, et al: Depressive disorders in childhood: I. A longitudinal prospective study of characteristics and recovery. Arch Gen Psychiatry 41:229–237, 1984a

Kovacs M, Feinberg TL, Crouse-Novak MA, et al: Depressive disorders in childhood: II. A longitudinal study of the risk for a subsequent major depression. Arch Gen Psychiatry 41:643–649, 1984b

Last CG, Strauss CC, Francis G: Comorbidity among childhood anxiety disorders. J Nerv Ment Dis 175:726–730, 1987

Leckman JF, Ort S, Caruso KA, et al: Rebound phenomena in Tourette's syndrome after abrupt withdrawal of clonidine. Arch Gen Psychiatry 43:1168–1176, 1986

Levine MD: Encopresis: Its potentiation, evaluation, and alleviation. Pediatr Clin North Am 29:315–330, 1982

Loeber R, Schmaling KB: The utility of differentiating between mixed and pure forms of antisocial child behavior. J Abnorm Child Psychol 13:315–336, 1985

Lyons JA: Posttraumatic stress disorder in children and adolescents: A review of the literature. J Dev Behav Pediatr 8:349–356, 1987

Marriage K, Fine S, Moretti M, Haley G: Relationship between depression and conduct disorder in children and adolescents. J Am Acad Child Adolesc Psychiatry 25:687–691, 1986

Masek BJ, Spirito A, Fentress DW: Behavioral treatment of symptoms of childhood illness. Clin Psychol Rev 4:561–570, 1984

Mayes SC, Humphrey FJ, Handford HA, Mitchell JF: Rumination disorder: Differential diagnosis. J Am Acad Child Adolesc Psychiatry 27:300–302, 1988

McDaniel, KD: Pharmacologic treatment of psychiatric and neurodevelopmental disorders in children and adolescents (part 1). Clin Pediatr 25:65–71, 1986

Melamed BG, Klingman A, Siegel LJ: Individualizing cognitive behavioral strategies in the reduction of medical and dental stress. In Meyers AW, Craighead WE (eds): Cognitive Behavior Therapy with Children. New York, Plenum Press, 1984

Milich R, Wolraich M, Lindgren S: Sugar and hyperactivity: A critical review of empirical findings. Clin Psychol Rev 6:493–513, 1986

O'Donnell DJ: Conduct disorders. In Wiener JM (ed): Diagnosis and Psychopharmacology of Childhood and Adolescent Disorders. New York, John Wiley & Sons, 1985

Ollendick TH, Francis G: Behavioral assessment and treatment of childhood phobias. Behav Modif 12:165–204, 1988

O'Regan S, Yazbeck S, Hamberger B, Schick E: Constipation: A commonly unrecognized cause of enuresis. Am J Dis Child 140:260–261, 1986

Patterson GR: Families: Applications of Social Learning to Family Life. Champaign, IL, Research Press, 1975

Pelco LE, Kissel RC, Parrish JM, Miltenberger RG: Behavioral management of oral medication administration difficulties among children: A review of literature with case illustrations. J Dev Behav Pediatr 8:90–96, 1987

Pelham WE, Murphy HA: Attention deficit and conduct disorders. In Hersen M (ed): Pharmacological and Behavioral Treatment: An Integrative Approach. New York, John Wiley & Sons, 1986

Pelham WE, Sturges J, Hoza J, et al: The effects of Sustained Release 20 and 10 mg Ritalin b.i.d. on cognitive and social behavior in children with attention deficit disorder. Pediatrics 80(4):491–501, 1987

Pfefferbaum B, Overall JE, Boren HA, et al: Alprazolam in the treatment of anticipatory and acute situational anxiety in children with cancer. J Am Acad Child Adolesc Psychiatry 26:532–535, 1987

Pleak RR, Birmaher B, Gavrilescu A, et al: Mania and neuropsychiatric excitation following carbamazepine. J Am Acad Child Adolesc Psychiatry 27:500–503, 1988

Preskorn SH, Weller EB, Hughes CW, et al: Depression in prepubertal children: Dexamethasone nonsuppression predicts differential response to imipramine vs. placebo. Psychopharmacol Bull 23:128–133, 1987

Preskorn SH, Weller EB, Hughes CW, Weller RA: Relationship of plasma imipramine levels to CNS toxicity in children. Am J Psychiatry 145:897, 1988

Puig-Antich J: Major depression and conduct disorder in prepuberty. J Am Acad Child Adolesc Psychiatry 21:118–128, 1982

Puig-Antich J, Lukens E, Davies M, et al: Psychosocial functioning in prepubertal major depressive disorders: II. Interpersonal relationships after sustained recovery from affective episode. Arch Gen Psychiatry 42:511–517, 1985

Puig-Antich J, Perel JM, Lupatkin W, et al: Imipramine in prepubertal major depressive disorders. Arch Gen Psychiatry 44:81–89, 1987

Puig-Antich J, Ryan ND, Rabinovich H: Affective disorders in childhood and adolescence. In Wiener JM (ed): Diagnosis and Psychopharmacology of Childhood and Adolescent Disorders. New York, John Wiley & Sons, 1985

Pynoos RS, Eth S: Witness to violence: The child interview. J Am Acad Child Adolesc Psychiatry 25:306–319, 1986

Pynoos RS, Frederick C, Nader K, et al: Life threat and posttraumatic stress in school-age children. Arch Gen Psychiatry 44:1057–1063, 1987

Rancurello MD: Clinical applications of antidepressant drugs in childhood behavioral and emotional disorders. Psychiatr Ann 15:88–100, 1985

Realmuto GM, Erickson WD, Yellin AM, et al: Clinical comparison of thiothixene and thioridazine in schizophrenic adolescents. Am J Psychiatry 141:440–442, 1984

Rutter M: Syndromes attributed to "minimal brain dysfunction" in childhood. Am J Psychiatry 139:21–33, 1982

Ryan ND, Puig-Antich J: Affective illness in adolescence. In Frances AJ, Hales RE (eds): American Psychiatric Association Annual Review, Vol 5. Washington, DC, American Psychiatric Press, 1986

Ryan ND, Puig-Antich J, Cooper T, et al: Imipramine in adolescent major depression: Plasma level and clinical response. Acta Psychiatr Scand 73:275–288, 1986

Sallee F, Stiller R, Perel J, Rancurello MD: Targeting imipramine dose in children with depression. Clin Pharmacol Ther 40:8–13, 1986

Sandoval J, Lambert NM, Sassone D: The identification and labeling of hyperactivity in children: An interactive model. In Whalen CK, Henker B (eds): Hyperactive Children: The Social Ecology of Identification and Treatment. New York, Academic Press, 1980

Schmitt BD: Nocturnal enuresis: An update on treatment. Pediatr Clin North Am 29:21–36, 1982

Schuster CR, Lewis M, Seiden LS: Fenfluramine: Neurotoxicity. Psychopharmacol Bull 22:148–151, 1986

Simeon JG, Ferguson HB: Alprazolam effects in children with anxiety disorders. Can J Psychiatry 32:570–574, 1987

Simeon JG, Ferguson HB: Recent developments in the use of antidepressant and anxiolytic medications. Psychiatr Clin North Am 8:893–907, 1985

Strayhorn JM, Rapp N, Donina W, Strain PS: Randomized trial of methylphenidate for an autistic child. J Am Acad Child Adolesc Psychiatry 27:244–247, 1988

Strober M, Carlson G: Bipolar illness in adolescents with major depression: Clinical, genetic, and psychopharmacolgic predictors in a three- to four-year prospective follow-up investigation. Arch Gen Psychiatry 39:549–555, 1982

Terr LC: Childhood psychic trauma. In Call JD, Cohen RL, Harrison SI, et al (eds): Basic Handbook of Child Psychiatry, Vol 5. New York, Basic Books, 1987a

Terr LC: Chowchilla revisited: The effects of psychic trauma four years after a school-bus kidnapping. Am J Psychiatry 140:1543–1550, 1983

Terr LC: Treatment of psychic trauma in children. In Call JD, Cohen RL, Harrison SI, et al (eds): Basic Handbook of Child Psychiatry, Vol 5. New York, Basic Books, 1987b

Varley CK: Effects of methylphenidate in adolescents with attention deficit disorder. J Am Acad Child Psychiatry 4:351–354, 1983

Varni JW, Jay SM, Masek BJ, Thompson KL: Cognitive-behavioral assessment and management of pediatric pain. In Holvman AD, Turk ED (eds): Handbook of Psychological Treatment Approaches. New York, Pergamon Press, 1986

Weiss G, Hechtman L, Milroy T, Perlman T: Psychiatric status of hyperactives as adults: A controlled prospective 15-year follow-up of 63 hyperactive children. J Am Acad Child Adolesc Psychiatry 24:211–220, 1985

Weissman MM, Leckman JF, Merikangas KR, et al: Depression and anxiety disorders in parents and children. Arch Gen Psychiatry 41:845–852, 1984

Weller EB, Weller RA, Fristad MA: Lithium dosage guide for prepubertal children: A preliminary report. J Am Acad Child Adolesc Psychiatry 25:92–95, 1986

Weller EB, Weller RA, Fristad MA, et al: Saliva lithium monitoring in prepubertal children. J Am Acad Child Adolesc Psychiatry 26:173–175, 1987

Wender EH: The food additive–free diet in the treatment of behavior disorders: A review. J Dev Behav Pediatr 7:35–42, 1986

Williams DT: Hypnosis as a psychotherapeutic adjunct. In Harrison SI (ed): Basic Handbook of Child Psychiatry, Vol 3. New York, Basic Books, 1979

Williams DT, Mehl R, Yudofsky S, et al: The effect of propranolol on uncontrolled rage outbursts in children and adolescents with organic brain dysfunction. J Am Acad Child Psychiatry 21:129–135, 1982

Winsberg BG, Perel JM, Hurwic MJ, Klutch A: Imipramine protein binding and pharmacokinetics in children. In Forrest IS, Carr CJ, Usdin E (eds): The Phenothiazines and Structurally Related Drugs. New York, Raven Press, 1974

Wright L, Walker CE: A simple behavioral treatment program for psychogenic encopresis. Behav Res Ther 16:209–212, 1978

16

The Psychotherapies: Basic Theoretical Principles, Techniques, and Indications

Robert J. Ursano, Edward K. Silberman, and Alberto Diaz, Jr.

Psychotherapy is the "talking cure." Through verbal means directed toward understanding, guidance, support, and the provision of new experiences, the psychotherapist aims to eliminate symptoms and increase the patient's productivity and enjoyment of life. One should always remember that the brain itself is the target of psychotherapy. Behavior, thoughts, and emotions all derive from brain activity and have a neuroanatomical, neurochemical, and neurophysiologic basis. The psychotherapies aim to alter brain "patterning" and functions. Psychopathology frequently limits a patient's ability to see and experience options and choices. The patients' behaviors, thoughts, and feelings are constricted by their psychiatric illness. Through the various psychotherapies, the therapist attempts to increase the patients' range of behavioral options and decrease painful constricting symptoms.

Psychotherapeutic approaches to psychopathology vary widely and reflect different conceptualizations of mental life, personality development, the evolution of abnormal behavior, and the role of environmental and biological determinants. An increasing understanding of the nature of the interaction of human beings with each other as individuals and as members of social groups has facilitated the application of some of the principles of the psychotherapy relationship as a treatment tool. Experience has taught that an integrated approach to treatment is the most successful approach. Different patients benefit from different types of psychotherapy. In addition, patients may benefit substantially from the appropriate combined use of medications and psychotherapy. Because of this, the medically trained psychiatrist can provide the most comprehensive evaluation for a psychotherapeutic treatment. The psychiatrist can use combined medication and psychotherapeutic treatments and is trained to recognize and manage the interactions of these two treatments. The psychiatrist is also alert to medical health changes that can be a cause of or a result of psychiatric illness. Patients with significant medical illness as part of their health history (e.g., migraine, ulcers, psychosomatic illnesses, and so forth) are best treated by the psychiatrist who, as a physician, is knowledgeable of these disorders and their effects on feelings, behaviors, and life adjustment and is a skilled psychotherapist.

In the following pages, the major psychotherapies are reviewed. An understanding of these techniques and the basic theoretical concepts involved in patient selection is a basic component of the treatment armamentarium in inpatient, outpatient, and consultation–liaison psychiatric practices as well as in general medical practice.

PSYCHOANALYTIC PSYCHOTHERAPIES

Psychoanalysis

Psychoanalysis was developed by Sigmund Freud beginning in the late 19th century. Freud found that patients' life difficulties were related to unrecognized (unconscious) conflicts that arise in the course of child development and continue into adult life. Such conflicts are typically between libidinal and aggressive wishes on the one hand, and fear of loss, condemnation or retaliation, the constraints of reality, or the opposition of other incompatible wishes on the other hand. "Libidinal wishes" are longings for both sexual and emotional gratification. Sexual gratification in psychoanalysis refers to the broad concept of bodily pleasure, the state of excitement and pleasure experienced in various bodily sensations beginning in infancy. Aggressive wishes may either be primary destructive impulses or arise in reaction to perceived frustration, deprivation, or attack. Such (neurotic) conflicts may give rise to a variety of manifestations in adulthood, including anxiety, depression, and somatic symptoms, as well as work, social, or sexual inhibitions and maladaptive ways of relating to other people.

The goal of psychoanalysis is to understand the nature of the patient's childhood conflicts (the "infantile neurosis") and their consequences in adult life. This is accomplished through reexperiencing these conflicts in relation to the analyst (the "transference neurosis"). This is a major undertaking that requires a reasonably high functioning individual to sustain the treatment. It requires individuals who are able to access their fantasy lives in an active and experiencing manner and are able to "leave it behind" at the end of a session. Psychoanalysis is frequently criticized for being used to treat reasonably healthy people. However, all medical treatments require certain capacities of the patient (e.g., an intact immune system for successful antibiotic therapy). As with a generally healthy person with a relatively focal, stable, yet painful and medically problematic physical disorder that impairs his or her functioning, a generally healthy person may have severe neurotic conflicts that interfere with both work and personal life and deserve treatment.

Psychoanalysis focuses on the recovery of childhood experiences as they are recreated in the relationship with the analyst (Sandler, 1973). This re-creation in the doctor–patient relationship of the conflicted relationship with a childhood figure is called the "transference neurosis" (see Table 16-1). In the therapeutic relationship with the analyst, the emotional conflicts and trauma from the past are relived. The feelings and conflicts toward major figures in the child's development, most frequently the parents, are "transferred" to the analyst. When the transference neurosis is present, the patient emotionally experiences and reacts to the analyst in a very real

Table 16–1 **Psychoanalysis**

GOAL	Resolution of symptoms and major reworking of personality structures related to childhood conflicts
SELECTION CRITERIA	No psychotic potential
	Able to use understanding
	High ego strength
	Able to experience and observe intense affect states
	Psychiatric disturbance derived from a childhood conflict
TECHNIQUE	Focus on fantasies and the transference
	Free association
	Couch
	Interpretation of defenses and transference
	Frequent meetings
	Neutrality and abstinence
DURATION	3–6 years

manner "as if" he or she was the significant figure from the past. Frequently, this experience is accompanied by other elements of the past being experienced in the patient's life. Countertransference, the analyst's transference response to the patient, is increased by life stress and unresolved conflicts in the analyst. It can appear as either an identification with or a reaction to the patient's conscious and unconscious fantasies, feelings, and behaviors. Understanding countertransference reactions can allow the analyst to recognize subtle aspects of the transference relationship and better understand the patient's experience.

Psychoanalytic treatment attempts to set up a therapeutic situation in which the patient's observing capacity can be used to analyze the transference neurosis (Stone, 1961). *Transference reactions occur throughout life in all areas and are a frequent accompaniment of the doctor–patient relationship in the medical setting.* However, psychoanalysis is unique in its efforts to establish a setting in which the transference, when it appears, can be analyzed and worked through in an intense manner to facilitate recovery from psychiatric illness.

Modern psychoanalysis requires four to five sessions per week (45 to 50 minutes per session) continued, on the average, for 3 to 6 years. This extensive amount of sessions is necessary for patients to develop sufficient trust to explore their inner life and their subjective experience. Likewise, given the number of events that occur daily in one's lifetime, the frequent meetings are necessary for the patient to be able to explore fantasies, dreams, and reactions to the analytic situation instead of focusing only on daily reality-based crises and stresses. Individuals who are in severe crisis and, therefore, are perpetually concerned with and focused on the crises in their life are generally not candidates for psychoanalysis. If major crises do occur during analysis, formal analysis may be temporarily suspended for a more supportive psychotherapeutic approach. In general, psychoanalytic patients are encouraged to use a recumbent position on the couch to further facilitate their ability to freely associate and verbalize their thoughts and feelings. In addition, the analyst usually sits out of view to assist unencumbered process of *free association.*

Free association, the reporting of all thoughts that come to mind, is a major element in psychoanalytic technique. In point of fact, free association is difficult to attain, and much of the work of psychoanalysis is based on identifying those spots at which free association breaks down (the occurrence of a defense, clinically experienced by the analyst as "resistance"). When the patient is able to achieve the highest level of free association, the neurotic conflicts have been largely removed and termination of treatment is near.

Early in treatment, the analyst establishes a *therapeutic alliance* with the patient that allows for a reality-based consideration of the demands of the treatment and for a working collaboration between analyst and analysand (patient) directed toward understanding the patient. The analyst points out the defenses the patient uses to minimize awareness of conflicts and disturbing feelings. Dreams, slips of the tongue, and symptoms provide avenues to the understanding of unconscious motivations, feelings, and ideas.

The specific treatment effects of psychoanalysis result from the progressive understanding of defensive patterns and, most important, the feelings, cognitions, and behaviors that are "transferred" to the analyst from significant individuals in the patient's past. In the context of the arousal associated with the reexperiencing of these figures from the past and the simultaneous understanding of the experience, behavioral change occurs. Interpretation is an important technical procedure in psychoanalysis. An interpretation links the patient's current experience with the analyst to an experience with a significant childhood figure during development.

The analyst operates under several rules that facilitate the analysis of the transference. These include the *rule of neutrality,* by which the analyst favors neither the patient's wishes (id) nor the condemnations of these wishes (superego), and the *rule of abstinence,* whereby the analyst does not provide emotional gratification to the patient similar to that of the wished-for childhood figure.

Medications are infrequently used in psychoanalysis, although in the present climate some analysts are attempting to integrate psychoanalytic treatment with medication, particularly for mood disorders. In general, however, the necessity for the use of medication may indicate the patient's need for greater support and structure than can be provided in the psychoanalytic treatment.

The assessment of a patient for psychoanalysis must include diagnostic considerations as well as an assessment of the patient's ability to make use of the psychoanalytic situation for behavior change. This includes the patient's psychological-mindedness, the availability of supports in his real environment to sustain the psychoanalysis (which can be felt as quite depriving), and the patient's ability to experience and simultaneously observe highly charged emotional states. Because of the frequency of the sessions and the duration of the treatment, the cost of psychoanalysis can be prohibitive. However, low-fee clinics frequently make a substantial amount of treatment available to some patients who could not otherwise afford it. Psychoanalysis has been useful in the treatment of obsessional disorders, conversion disorders, anxiety disorders, dysthymic disorders, and moderately severe personality disorders. Individuals with chaotic life settings and an inability to establish long-term, close relationships are usually not felt to be candidates for psychoanalysis. In the present cost-effective climate, psychoanalysis is more frequently recommended after a course of brief psychotherapy has proved either ineffective or insufficient. Little empirical research is available on the efficacy of psychoanalysis compared with other psychotherapies. In general, those patients who can use understanding, introspection, and self-observation to modify their behavior find the treatment beneficial and productive.

Intensive (Long-Term) Psychoanalytically Oriented Psychotherapy

Psychoanalytically oriented psychotherapy, also known as psychoanalytic psychotherapy, psychodynamic psychotherapy, and explorative psychotherapy, is a psychotherapeutic procedure that recognizes the concepts of transference and resistance in the psychotherapy setting (Bruch, 1974; Reichmann, 1950). Both long-term and brief psychodynamic psychotherapy are possible. (See following section for brief psychodynamic psychotherapy.) Psychoanalytic psychotherapy is usually more focused than is the extensive reworking of personality undertaken in psychoanalysis. In addition, psychoanalytic psychotherapy is somewhat more "here and now" oriented, with less attempt to completely reconstruct the developmental origins of conflicts.

However, the psychoanalytic techniques of interpretation and clarification are central to psychoanalytic psychotherapy. Psychoanalytic psychotherapy makes more use of supportive techniques, such as suggestion, reality testing, education, and confrontation, than does psychoanalysis. This allows for its application to a broader range of patients, including those with psychotic regressive potentials.

Patients in long-term psychoanalytic psychotherapy are usually seen two or three times per week. Patient and therapist meet in face-to-face encounters with free association encouraged. Psychoanalytic psychotherapy may extend several months to several years, at times being as long as a psychoanalysis. The length is determined by the number of focal problem areas undertaken in the treatment. Medications can be used in psychoanalytic psychotherapy and provide another means of titrating the level of regression a patient may experience.

The same patients who are treated in psychoanalysis can be treated in psychoanalytic psychotherapy (see Table 16-2). The psychosocial problems and internal conflicts of patients who cannot be treated in psychoanalysis, such as those with major depression, schizophrenia, and borderline personality disorder, can be addressed in a long-term psychoanalytic psychotherapy. In long-term psychoanalytic psychotherapy, the regressive tendencies of such patients can be titrated with greater elements of support, the use of medication as needed, and greater reality feedback through the face-to-face encounter with the therapist. Few empirical data are available on the efficacy of psychoanalytically oriented psychotherapy, although it is highly valued by many clinicians and patients.

Table 16–2 **Psychoanalytically Oriented Psychotherapy**

GOAL	Understanding conflict area, in particular, defense mechanisms used
	More "here and now" than psychoanalysis
SELECTION	Similar to psychoanalysis
	Also includes personality disorders with psychotic potential (Borderline, Narcissistic)
	Some major depressions and schizophrenia may be helped when combined with medication during periods of remission for the treatment of psychosocial features
TECHNIQUE	Face to face—sitting down
	Free association
	Interpretation and clarification
	Some supportive techniques
	Medication as adjunct
DURATION	Months to years

Brief Psychodynamic Psychotherapy

Following World War II there was a rapid growth in the demand for psychotherapy that considerably increased the pressure upon psychiatrists to develop briefer forms of psychotherapy. In addition, the community mental health movement and, more recently, the increasing cost of mental health care have stimulated efforts to find briefer forms of psychotherapy. At present, brief psychotherapy is a necessary part of the psychiatrist's armamentarium rather than the "second-best" alternative, as it was viewed in the 1950s (Ursano, Dressler, 1974).

The goals of brief psychotherapy are described by most authors as facilitation of health-seeking behaviors and the mitigation of obstacles to normal growth. From this perspective, brief psychotherapy focuses on the patient's continuous development throughout adult life in the context of conflicts relating to environment, interpersonal relationships, biological health, and developmental stages. This picture of brief psychotherapy supports modest goals and the avoidance of "perfectionism" by the therapist.

While many of the selection criteria emphasized in the literature of brief psychotherapy are common to all kinds of psychodynamic psychotherapy, certain unique selection criteria are required because of the brief duration of treatment (see Table 16-3). Patients in brief psychodynamic psychotherapy must be able to engage quickly with the therapist, terminate therapy in a short period of time. The necessity of greater independent action by the patient mandates high levels of emotional strength, motivation, and responsiveness to interpretation. The importance of the rapid establishment of the therapeutic alliance underlies a substantial number of the selection and exclusion criteria.

One set of exclusion criteria for brief psychotherapy has been devised by Malan (1975). He excludes patients who have had serious suicidal attempts, drug addiction, long-term hospitalization, more than one course of electroconvulsive therapy (ECT),

Table 16–3 **Brief Psychodynamic Psychotherapy**

GOAL	Clarify and resolve focal area of conflict which interferes with current functioning
SELECTION CRITERIA	High ego strength
	High motivation
	Can identify focal issue
	Can form strong interpersonal relationships, including with therapist, in a brief time
	Good response to trial interpretations
TECHNIQUES	Face to face
	Interpretation of defenses and transference
	Setting of time limit at start of therapy
	Focus on patient reactions to limited duration of treatment
DURATION	12–40 sessions; usually 20 sessions or less

chronic alcoholism, incapacitating severe chronic obsessional symptoms, severe chronic phobic symptoms, or gross destructive or self-destructive behavior. Patients who are unavailable for therapeutic contact or those who need prolonged work to generate motivation, penetrate rigid defenses, deal with complex or deep-seated issues, or resolve intense transference reactions are also not suited for brief psychotherapy.

The importance of focusing on a circumscribed area of current conflict in brief psychotherapy is mentioned by many authors (Davanloo, 1980; Malan, 1975; Mann, 1973; Sifneos, 1972). They also emphasize the importance of the evaluation sessions to determine the focus of treatment. The formulation of the focus to the patient may be, for example, in terms of the patient's conscious fears and pain, but it is important for the therapist to construct the psychodynamic focus at a deeper level in order to understand the work being done. Maintaining the focus is the primary task of the therapist. This enables the therapist to deal with complicated personality structures in a brief period of time. Resistance is limited through "benign neglect" of potentially troublesome but nonfocal areas of personality. The elaboration of techniques of establishing and maintaining the focus of treatment is critical to all brief individual psychodynamic psychotherapies.

Transference interpretations (that is, making comments that link the patient's reactions to the therapist to feelings for significant individuals from the patient's past) are generally accepted as important in brief psychotherapy. However, the manner and rapidity in which transference is dealt with varies considerably.

There is remarkable agreement on the duration of brief psychotherapy. Although the duration ranges from 5 to 40 sessions, authors generally favor 10 to 20 sessions. The duration of treatment is critically related to maintaining the focus within the brief psychotherapy. When treatment extends beyond 20 sessions, therapists frequently may find themselves enmeshed in a broad character analysis without a focal conflict. Change after 20 sessions may be quite slow. Clinical experience generally supports the idea that brief individual psychodynamic psychotherapy should be between 10 and 20 sessions unless the therapist is willing to proceed to long-term treatment of greater than 40 or 50 sessions.

COGNITIVE PSYCHOTHERAPY

Cognitive psychotherapy is a method of brief psychotherapy developed over the last two decades by Aaron T. Beck and his colleagues at the University of Pennsylvania primarily for the treatment of mild and moderate depressions and for patients with low self-esteem (Beck, 1976; Rush, Watkins, 1981). It is similar to behavior therapy in that it aims at direct removal of symptoms rather than the resolution of underlying conflicts, as in the psychodynamic psychotherapies. However, unlike traditional behavioral approaches, the subjective experience of the patient is a major focus of the work. Cognitive therapists view the patient's conscious thoughts as central to producing and perpetuating symptoms such as depression, anxiety, phobias, and somatization. Both the content of thoughts and thought processes are seen as disordered in people with such symptoms. Therapy is directed to identifying and altering these cognitive distortions.

The cognitive therapist sees the interpretations that depressed persons make about life as different from those of nondepressed individuals. Depressed people tend to make negative interpretations of the world, themselves, and the future (the negative cognitive triad). Depressed individuals interpret events as reflecting defeat, deprivation, or disparagement and see their lives as filled with obstacles and burdens. They view themselves as unworthy, deficient, undesirable, or worthless and see the future as bringing a continuation of the miseries of the present. These evaluations are the result of the negative biases inherent in depressive thinking and applied regardless of the objective nature of the individual's circumstances. Other psychiatric conditions have their own characteristic cognitive patterns that determine the nature of the symptoms. The "thinking" distortions in depression include arbitrary inferences about an event, selective use of details to reach a conclusion, overgeneralization, overestimating negative and underestimating positive aspects of a situation, and the tendency to label events according to one's emotional response rather than the facts.

Such cognitions (verbal thoughts) often feel involuntary and automatic. This kind of thinking is so automatic in response to many situations, and the resultant cognitions so fleeting, that people may often be virtually unaware of them. Such automatic thoughts differ from unconscious thoughts in that they can easily be made fully conscious if attention is directed to them. A large portion of the work of cognitive psychotherapy is to train patients to observe and record their automatic thoughts.

Cognitive theory postulates a chronic state of depression-proneness that may precede the actual illness and remain after the symptoms have abated. Depression-prone individuals have relatively permanent depressive cognitive structures ("cognitive schemas") that determine how new stimuli are perceived and conceptualized. Typical schemas of depression include: "I am stupid," or "I cannot exist without the love of a strong person." Unlike automatic thoughts, patients are not typically aware and cannot easily become aware of such underlying general assumptions. These must be deduced from many specific examples of distorted thinking. Schemas, such as "I am stupid," may lie dormant much of the time only to be reactivated by a specific event, such as difficulty in accomplishing a task. These enduring self-concepts and attitudes are assumed to have been learned in childhood on the basis of the child's experiences and the reactions of important family members. Once formed, such attitudes can be self-perpetuating.

Just as depressive thoughts can be triggered by events, episodes of depressive illness may, from the cognitive perspective, be triggered by sufficient stress. Such stresses may be specific to the individual and his or her particular sensitivities developed in childhood. Alternatively, sufficient degrees of nonspecific stress may precipitate depression in vulnerable individuals. Experiences of loss, a setback in a major goal, a rejection, or an insolvable dilemma are especially common precipitants of depression. The onset of medical illness, with its attendant limitations and associated meanings, is also seen as likely to trigger depression in many people.

Researchers have accumulated considerable evidence that depressed individuals do indeed manifest negative biases in their views of themselves, their experiences, and the future. In addition, they have attitudes (schemas) that distinguish them from nondepressed subjects as well as distortions in logic and information processing. It is less clear whether all depressed people show the thinking distortions that Beck has described. Much of the cognitive depression research has been criticized because the studies have been on nonpatient populations, such as student volunteers, with relatively mild degrees of depression. These individuals may be very different from actual psychiatric patients. Whether cognitive distortions are a predisposing factor to depression is also unclear. Most researchers have found that most distorted thinking disappears when depression is successfully treated, even with antidepressant medication, suggesting that these distortions are a symptom of depression rather than an enduring trait of depression-prone people. Clearly, further research is needed to test the causality of cognitive factors in depression.

Technique of Cognitive Psychotherapy

Cognitive psychotherapy is a directive, time-limited, multidimensional psychological treatment. The patient and therapist together discover the irrational beliefs and illogical thinking patterns associated with the patient's depressive affects (see Table 16-4). They then devise methods by which patients themselves can test the validity of their thinking. The therapist helps patients to become aware of their irrational beliefs and distorted thinking ("automatic thoughts") and to see for themselves whether their ideas are objectively true or logical.

Cognitive psychotherapy was developed for unipolar, nonpsychotic, depressed outpatients. The presence of bipolar illness, delusions or hallucinations, or extremely severe depression is a contraindication for cognitive psychotherapy as the sole or primary treatment modality. Other contraindications include the presence of underlying medical illness or medications that may be causing the depression, the presence of an organic mental disorder, or an ongoing problem of substance abuse. In addition, cognitive psychotherapy may not be indicated as the sole form of treatment for major or "endogenous" depression (which may be accompanied by endocrine, sleep, or other

Table 16–4　**Cognitive Psychotherapy**

GOAL	Identify and alter cognitive distortions
SELECTION	Unipolar, non-psychotic depressed outpatients
	Contraindications include delusions, hallucinations, severe depression, organic brain syndrome, ongoing substance abuse, enmeshed family system
TECHNIQUE	Behavioral assignments
	Reading material
	Taught to recognize negatively biased automatic thoughts
	Identify patients' schemas, beliefs, attitudes
DURATION	Time limited: 15–25 weeks

biological abnormalities in which antidepressant medication or ECT is needed) or for a patient enmeshed in a family system that maintains a fixed view of him as helpless and dependent. Cognitive psychotherapy may be useful in patients who refuse to take, fail to respond to, or are unable to tolerate medication, as well as those who prefer a psychological approach in the hope of greater long-term benefits.

Cognitive psychotherapy is generally conducted over a period of 15 to 25 weeks in once-weekly meetings. With more severely depressed patients, two or three meetings per week are recommended for the first several weeks. While cognitive psychotherapy was developed and is usually administered as an individual treatment, its principles have also been successfully applied to group settings.

A course of cognitive psychotherapy proceeds in a succession of regular stages. The first stage is devoted to introducing the patient to the procedures and rationale of the therapy, setting goals for the treatment, and establishing a therapeutic alliance. The therapist may assign reading material on the cognitive theory of depression. In the next stage, the therapist begins to demonstrate to the patient that cognitions and emotions are connected. Patients are taught to become more aware of their negatively biased automatic thoughts and to recognize, both during and outside of the psychotherapy hours, that negative affects are generally preceded by such thoughts. Behavioral assignments may be used.

In the next phase, which normally comprises the majority of the work, the emphasis shifts to a detailed exploration of the patient's cognitions and their role in perpetuating depressive feelings. In the final stage of psychotherapy, the patient will have had a great deal of experience in recognizing his or her habitual thought patterns, testing their validity, and modifying them when appropriate, with the result of substantial symptomatic relief. Psychotherapy then focuses on the attitudes and assumptions that underlie the patient's negatively biased thinking. For example, the patient might assume that, "If I'm nice, bad things won't happen to me." A logically equivalent assumption would then be, "If bad things happen to me, it is my fault because I am not nice." Target symptoms that might be the focus of a session include intense sadness, pervasive self-criticism, passivity and avoidance, sleep disturbance, or other affective, motivational, or cognitive manifestations of depression. The therapist repeatedly formulates the patient's beliefs and attitudes as testable hypotheses and helps the patient to devise and implement ways of verifying them. The therapist maintains an inquiring attitude toward the patient's reactions to the therapist and the therapeutic procedures. Such reactions are explored for evidence of misunderstanding and distortion, which are then dealt with in the same way as the patient's other cognitions.

A great variety of different techniques are used by cognitive therapists to break the cycle of negative evaluations and dysfunctional behaviors. Behavioral methods are often useful in the beginning of psychotherapy, particularly when the patient is severely depressed. Activity scheduling, mastery and pleasure exercises, graded task assignments, cognitive rehearsal, and role-playing may all be used.

More cognitively oriented methods are applied in the middle and late stages of psychotherapy as psychotherapy progresses. The therapist and patient explore the patient's inner life in a spirit of adventure. The patient becomes more observant of his peculiar construction of reality and usually focuses more on actual events and their meanings. The fundamental cognitive technique is teaching the patient to observe, record, and validate his cognitions.

Efficacy of Cognitive Psychotherapy

In contrast to most other psychotherapies, there is a small but growing literature on the efficacy of cognitive psychotherapy. Although the number is still relatively small, all studies examining the outcome of cognitive psychotherapy have found it to be an effective treatment at least in ambulatory outpatients with mild to moderate degrees of depression. Cognitive psychotherapy has been shown to be more effective than no psychotherapy in treating both depressed volunteers and psychiatric patients with diagnoses of depression.

It should be emphasized that the choice of treatment for a depressed patient should often involve a combination of both psychotherapy and antidepressant medication. To withhold antidepressants from a patient who has a clear biological component to his or her depression, based on their signs and symptoms and family history, because of a "bias" toward one sort of psychotherapy or another is unjustifiable on clinical grounds. Hence, integrated psychotherapeutic *and* pharmacologic treatment is often indicated and should be considered in every patient.

INTERPERSONAL PSYCHOTHERAPY

Interpersonal therapy (IPT) is a short-term psychotherapy developed by Klerman and colleagues (Klerman, et al., 1984b). IPT is generally brief (12 to 16 weeks in duration) and focuses on current interpersonal problems in outpatient nonbipolar, nonpsychotic, depressed patients. IPT has been the major psychotherapeutic modality used in combined psychotherapy and pharmacologic treatment studies. IPT has also been used in treating drug abuse; however, it did not add significantly to outcome when patients were already in a well-run treatment program that included weekly group psychotherapy. IPT derives from the interpersonal school of psychiatry that originated with Adolf Meyer and Harry Stack Sullivan. The theoretical underpinning for this form of psychotherapy is that of social supports and attachment. IPT focuses on reassurance, clarification of feeling states, improvement in interpersonal communication, testing of perception, and interpersonal skills rather than personality reconstruction.

IPT is a focused individual psychotherapy. The therapist focuses on the current social functioning (see Table 16-5). A complete inventory of current and past significant interpersonal relationships, including the family of origin, friendships, and relations in the community, is part of the evaluation phase. Patterns of authority, dominance and submission, dependency and autonomy, intimacy, affection, and activity are observed. Cognitions are generally seen as beliefs and attitudes about norms, expectations and roles, and role performance. Defense mechanisms are explored in terms of interpersonal relations. Similarly, dreams may be examined as a reflection of current interpersonal problems. The IPT therapist may explore distorted thinking by comparing what the patient says with what he does or by identifying the patient's view of an interpersonal relationship.

IPT has been used primarily in the treatment of depressed patients. In the opening phase of such a treatment, a detailed symptom history is taken, usually using a structured interview. The symptoms are reviewed with the patient, and the patient receives explicit information about the natural course of depression as a clinical condition. There is an emphasis on legitimizing the patient in the sick role. A second major task of this phase is the assessment of interpersonal problem areas. There is an attempt to identify one or more of four problem areas: grief reactions, interpersonal disputes, role transition, or interpersonal deficits. Each of these areas is felt to be related to depression. The middle phase of treatment is directed toward resolving the problem area(s). Clarifying positive and negative feeling states, identifying past models for relationships, and guiding and encouraging the patient in examining and choosing alternative courses of action constitute the basic techniques for handling each problem area. The focus is kept on current rather than past dilemmas and past interpersonal relationships. Interpersonal events rather than intrapsychic or cognitive events are the building blocks of IPT.

Much of IPT is based on psychodynamic theory. The therapist's attitude is one of exploration similar to other insight-oriented psychotherapies when applied in a medical model. Applying the dictum of working "from the surface to the depths" results in much of psychodynamic psychotherapy resembling IPT. However, Klerman and his colleagues have found it useful to highlight the differences between these approaches to standardize a psychotherapeutic technique (Klerman and Weissman,

Table 16–5 **Interpersonal Psychotherapy**

GOAL	Enhanced interpersonal/social functioning
SELECTION	Depressed outpatients
TECHNIQUES	Reassurance
	Clarification of feeling states
	Interpersonal communication
	Testing perceptions
	Interpersonal skills
DURATION	Time limited: 12–16 weeks

1984). Collaborative clinical trials have demonstrated the advantage of maintenance IPT in enhancing social functioning in recovery from depression and in reducing symptoms and improving functioning during the acute phase of a depressive episode. These effects require 6 to 8 months to become apparent. Depressed patients on combined pharmacologic treatment and IPT have the best outcomes.

SUPPORTIVE PSYCHOTHERAPY

Supportive psychotherapy aims to help patients maintain or reestablish the best level of functioning given the limitations of their illness, personality, native ability, and life circumstances (see Table 16-6). In general, this goal distinguishes supportive psychotherapy from the change-oriented psychotherapies that aim to reverse primary disease processes and symptoms or restructure personality.

The line between supportive and change-oriented psychotherapy, however, is frequently not clear. The situation is somewhat analogous to the medical treatment of viral versus bacterial infections. Treatment of the former is basically supportive in that it aims to maintain normal bodily functions (e.g., fever reduction, control of cerebral edema, dietary compensation for liver failure) in the face of infection, while in the latter, the aim is to eliminate the infection. However, in addition to the supportive aspects of treating bacterial infections, antibiotic treatment itself is supportive in the sense that it works as an adjunct to the body's natural immune system, without which it is relatively ineffective. However, there are supportive elements in all effective forms of psychotherapy, and the terms "supportive" and "change-oriented" merely describe the balance of efforts in a particular case.

Patients who are generally very healthy and well adapted but who have become impaired in response to stressful life circumstances, as well as those who have serious

Table 16–6 **Supportive Psychotherapy**

GOAL	Maintain or reestablish best level of functioning
SELECTION	Very healthy individuals exposed to stressful life circumstances (e.g., Adjustment Disorder)
	Individual with serious illness, ego deficits, e.g., Schizophrenia, Major Depression (psychotic)
	Individuals with medical illness
TECHNIQUES	Available, predictable therapist
	No/limited interpretation of transference
	Support intellectualization
	Therapist acts as a guide/mentor
	Medication frequently used
	Supportive techniques: suggestion, re-enforcement, advice, teaching, reality testing, cognitive restructuring, reassurance
	Active stance
	Discuss alternative behaviors, social/interpersonal skills
DURATION	Brief (days–weeks) to very long-term (years)

illnesses that cannot be cured, can receive supportive psychotherapy. Supportive psychotherapy may be brief or long-term. The "healthy" individual, when faced with overwhelming stress or crises (particularly in the face of traumas or disasters), may seek help and be a candidate for supportive psychotherapy. The relatively healthy candidate for supportive psychotherapy is a well-adapted individual with good social supports and interpersonal relations, flexible defenses, and good reality testing who is in acute crisis. This individual continues to show evidence of well-planned behaviors and a healthy perspective on the crisis, making use of social supports, not withdrawing, and anticipating resolution of the crisis. Although the patient is functioning below his or her usual level, this patient remains hopeful about the future and makes use of resources available for problem-solving, respite, and growth. This patient uses supportive psychotherapy to more rapidly reconstitute, to avoid errors in judgment by "talking out loud," to relieve minor symptomatology, and to grow as an individual by learning about the world.

The more typical candidate for supportive psychotherapy has significant deficits in ego functioning, including poor reality testing, impaired impulse control, and difficulties in interpersonal relations. Patients who have less ability to sublimate and are less introspective are frequently treated in supportive psychotherapy, where more directive techniques and environmental manipulation can be used.

Ego strength and the ability to form relationships may be more important than diagnosis in the selection of patients for supportive psychotherapy (Werman, 1984). The ability of the patient to relate to the therapist, a past history of reasonable personal relationships, work history and educational performance, and the use of leisure time for constructive activity and relaxation bear importantly on the treatment recommendation. Almost no information is known regarding which characteristics of the patient may predict a good result from supportive psychotherapy rather than merely a poor response to the change-oriented psychotherapies. Delineation of the minimum level of personal strengths needed to benefit from supportive individual psychotherapy is an important task for future research.

Technique of Supportive Psychotherapy

Psychoanalytic theory provides the major contributions to the theory of the supportive psychotherapy. In-depth psychological understanding of patients in supportive psychotherapy is as necessary as in the change-oriented, explorative psychotherapies (Pine, 1986; Werman, 1984). Understanding unconscious motivation, psychic conflict, the patient–therapist relationship, and the patient's use of defense mechanisms is essential to understanding the patient's strengths and vulnerabilities. This knowledge is critical to providing support as well as insight.

The therapist who is predictably available and safe (i.e., who accepts the patient and puts aside his or her own needs in the service of the treatment) assumes some of the holding functions of the "good parent." In such a therapeutic situation, the patient is able to identify with and incorporate the well-functioning aspects of the therapist, such as the capacity for self-observation and the ability to tolerate ambivalence (Pine, 1986).

The containment of affect and anxiety is also an important supportive function.

Patients in need of supportive psychotherapy typically fear the destructive power of their rage and envy. They may be helped to modulate their emotional reactions by the reliable presence of the therapist and the therapeutic relationship that remains unchanged in the face of emotional onslaughts.

The therapist fosters the supportive relationship by refraining from interpreting positive transference feelings and waiting until the intensity of feelings has abated before commenting about negative transference feelings. Interpretations of the negative transference are limited to those needed to assure that the treatment is not disrupted. While maintaining a friendly stance toward the patient, the therapist must respect the patient's need to establish a comfortable degree of distance. The therapist must not push for a more intimate or emotion-laden relationship than the patient can tolerate. The rapport with the patient, which the supportive psychotherapist tries to establish, differs from the "therapeutic alliance" of insight-oriented therapy. The doctor–patient relationship does not require the patient be able to observe and report on his or her own feelings and behavior to the same extent as in the change-oriented, explorative psychotherapies. The therapist tends to act more as a guide and a mentor.

There is virtually unanimous agreement among writers on supportive psychotherapy that fostering a good working relationship with the patient is the first priority. The therapist must be available in a way that is regular and predictable. Rather than approach the patient as a "blank screen," the therapist must actively demonstrate concern, involvement, sympathy, and a supportive attitude. The therapist acts as an "auxiliary ego" for the patient. The auxiliary ego functions of the therapist appear in the therapist's use of suggestion, reinforcement, advice, teaching, reality testing, cognitive restructuring, and reassurance. In taking such an active stance, it is especially important for the therapist to guard against grandiosity and personal biases so as not to "become an omnipotent decision maker" but rather to "act as a strong, benign individual who is reasonably available when needed." To the extent that the patient develops the capacity to observe himself, the psychotherapy may proceed beyond support and take on features of the explorative and change-oriented psychotherapies.

The defenses of denial and avoidance may be handled by encouraging the patient to discuss alternative behaviors, goals, and interpretations of events. Reassurance has a variety of forms in supportive psychotherapy, including: supporting an adaptive level of denial (such as a patient may employ in coping with a terminal illness); the patient's experience of the therapist's empathic attitude; or the therapist's reality testing of the patient's negatively biased evaluations of himself or his situation. Reassuring a patient is not easy. Reassurance requires a clear understanding of what the patient fears. Overt expressions of interest and concern may be reassuring to a patient who fears rejection but threatening to one who fears intrusion. Interpretations in supportive psychotherapy are limited to those which will decrease anxiety and strengthen (rather than loosen) defenses, particularly the defenses of intellectualization and rationalization.

The therapist's expressions of interest, advice giving, and facilitation of ventilation reinforce desired behaviors. Expressions of interest and solicitude are positively reinforcing. Advice can lead to behavioral change if it is specific and applies to frequent behaviors of the patient. Desired behaviors can be rewarded by the therapist's approval and by social reinforcement. Ventilation of emotions is useful only if the therapist can help the patient safely contain and limit them, thus extinguishing the anxiety response to emotional expression. Cognitive and behavioral psychotherapeutic interventions that strengthen the adaptive and defensive functions of the ego (e.g., realistic and logical thinking, social skills, containment of affects such as anxiety) can contribute to the supportive aspects of psychotherapy.

Efficacy of Supportive Psychotherapy

Most data on the effectiveness of supportive psychotherapy come from studies in which supportive psychotherapy has been used as a control in testing the efficacy of other treatments. In such studies, the procedures used in supportive psychotherapy tend to be poorly specified, and no attempts are made to correlate individual supportive techniques with outcome. There are no studies in which supportive psychotherapy is compared with no treatment or minimal treatment. However, despite its limitations, the research literature offers some evidence that supportive psychotherapy is an effective treatment, particularly when combined with medication. This appears to be true in the treatment of depression, anxiety disorders, and schizophrenia.

There is a larger body of research indicating that supportive psychotherapy is an effective component of the treatment of patients with a variety of medical illnesses, including those with ulcerative colitis or myocardial infarction and cancer patients undergoing radiation treatment. In general, patients in supportive psychotherapy improve emotionally and have fewer days in the hospital, fewer complications, and more rapid recovery.

The evidence to date, though preliminary, suggests that supportive psychotherapy can be effective in both psychiatric and medical illnesses and is frequently more cost-effective than more intensive psychotherapies for some disorders. More research is needed on the indications, contraindications, and techniques of supportive psychotherapy.

BEHAVIORAL THERAPY

Behavioral therapy (behavior modification) is based on the concept that all symptoms of a psychological nature are learned maladaptive patterns of behavior in response to environmental or internal stimuli. It does not concern itself with the intrapsychic conflicts that are the focus of the psychodynamically oriented psychotherapies. Rather, it uses the concepts of learning theory to eliminate the involuntary, disruptive behavior patterns that constitute the essential features of psychopathology and substitutes these with highly adaptive and situation-appropriate patterns (Lazarus, 1971). Behavioral therapy has been useful in a wide range of disorders when specific behavioral symptoms can be targeted for change and this change is central to recovery. Eating disorders, chronic pain syndromes and illness behavior, phobias, sexual dysfunction, and conduct disorders of childhood are frequently treated with behavioral therapy techniques.

Techniques of Behavioral Therapy

A variety of techniques exist that permit the modification of undesirable and unwanted behaviors when applied by therapists skilled in their use (see Table 16-7). These approaches require careful history taking and behavioral analysis in order to identify the behaviors to be targeted for extinction or modification. Often, adjunctive techniques, such as the use of hypnosis and drugs, are used to facilitate behavior modification but are not requisite for therapeutic success. Present-day behavioral therapists are usually alert to interpersonal and emotional aspects of psychiatric symptoms and the doctor–patient relationship. Psychodynamic, cognitive, and inter-personal techniques are frequently integrated into the therapy but are not seen as central to the therapeutic effect. Four of the more common behavioral techniques are as follows.

Systematic Desensitization

Systematic desensitization refers to a technique whereby individuals suffering primarily from phobic responses are gradually exposed to anxiety-provoking situations or objects in small increments. The therapist first identifies a hierarchy of behaviors directed to approaching the phobic object or situation. Relaxation techniques are used to decrease anxiety at each stage of the hierarchy. The patient moves up to the next level of intensity when the stimulus no longer provokes intense anxiety. This particularly effective technique is useful in an office setting as well, because experience has demonstrated that the patient can confront the anxiety-provoking stimulus in his imagination with very much the same effects. Again, a hierarchy of increasingly anxious imaginary scenes is constructed. The patient visualizes each scene and reexperiences the anxiety associated with it and then uses relaxation techniques to gradually become comfortable with the fantasy. The patient moves up the hierarchy of images until he or she is able to fully visualize the phobic object/situation without undue anxiety. Usually, this in vitro technique will be accompanied by in vivo practice exposures. Hypnotic procedures and the use of anxiolytic drugs are

Table 16–7 **Behavioral Therapy (Behavioral Modification)**

GOAL	Eliminate involuntary disruptive behavior patterns and substitute appropriate behaviors
SELECTION	Habit modification
	Targeted symptoms
	Phobias
	Some psychophysiologic responses: headache, migraine, hypertension, Raynaud's phenomena
	Sexual dysfunction
TECHNIQUES	Systemic desensitization
	Implosion therapy and flooding
	Aversive therapy
	Biofeedback
DURATION	Usually time limited

useful adjuncts in certain types of patients. There is some controversy regarding the mechanisms underlying the effect of systematic desensitization. Various explanations have been suggested regarding the underlying mechanisms. It is possible, for example, that the graduated exposure to the anxiety-provoking situation represents nothing more than a sequential or progressive "flooding" technique (see next section). It is also possible that by exposing the individual to only small, and therefore more tolerable, amounts of anxiety, the individual is able to develop more appropriate and successful coping mechanisms. Other authors have suggested that the key to systematic desensitization lies in the suppression of anxiety, which can be achieved by evoking a competitive physiological response such as deep muscle relaxation.

Implosion Therapy and Flooding

These two techniques vary only in the presentation of the anxiety-eliciting stimulus. Animal behaviorists discovered early on that avoidant behavior, which by its very nature can be expected to be highly resistant to extinction, could be extinguished rather rapidly by submitting the subject to a prolonged conditioned stimulus while restraining it and making the expression of the avoidant behavior impossible. In the therapeutic situation, the patient is directly exposed to the stressful stimulus until the anxiety subsides. This is in contrast to the graded exposure of systematic desensitization. In theory, each session should result in ever-decreasing intervals between exposure and cessation of anxiety. In implosion therapy the patient uses mental images as substitutes for the actual feared object or situation, whereas in the flooding approach the therapist conducts the procedure "in vivo." Results appear to indicate that both approaches are equally effective. Some have questioned the ethics of submitting patients to such painful experiences, especially when other alternatives are available. A risk associated with this technique is the danger that the patient may refuse to submit himself or herself to such an uncomfortable experience and may terminate the exposure prior to the abatement of the anxiety. This will result in a successful "escape" and will therefore reinforce the phobic response.

Aversive Therapy

This treatment modality has its roots in classical and operant conditioning. Controversial by its very nature, it has nevertheless found acceptance as a potentially useful avenue of therapy for a narrow range of disorders and unwanted habits. Perhaps the most common form of aversive therapy is the use of disulfiram (Antabuse) in alcoholics. This treatment approach is based on the fear of an extremely unpleasant, and indeed sometimes fatal, physiologic response (the unconditioned stimulus) when someone who has been taking Antabuse then imbibes alcohol (which becomes the conditioned stimulus). In theory, the alcoholic patient on Antabuse therapy will avoid alcohol to avoid the alcohol–Antabuse reaction. The use of mild aversive stimuli has also been found to be useful in smoking-cessation programs. Because of safety considerations, and to ensure continued patient participation, aversive stimuli used under these conditions are often mild and may not constitute much more than having to hold the smoke in the oral cavity for a prolonged period of time. Various aversive techniques have also been used in the treatment of sexual offenders and have included the use of such stimuli as mild electric shocks and unpleasant odors. Ethical considerations, understandable patient reluctance to participate in treatment, and pejorative associations by the general public with torture and other forms of maltreatment have resulted in rather limited applications for these techniques. In addition, its effectiveness has been more variable than that of other behavioral techniques.

Biofeedback

Biofeedback is not a type of behavioral therapy per se but rather a tool or technique that can be integrated with other operant procedures for the management of a number of psychophysiological disorders. Among some of the conditions in which there is some documented efficacy of biofeedback techniques are: hypertension, migraine headaches, tension headaches, some cardiac arrhythmias, and Raynaud's phenomenon. This approach presumes that many pathological psychophysiologic responses could be subject to modification if the individual could become aware of their existence and of positive changes incurred as a result of learned responses (Gaarder, Montgomery, 1977). For the conditioned response to be reinforced and learning to take place, the organism must be aware that a response has taken place. The biofeedback techniques consist of the use of sophisticated instrumentation to detect changes in skin temperature, muscle tension, or heart rate. Biofeedback first burst on the scene amid great publicity and exaggerated claims regarding its efficacy. This was followed by an expected period of disenchantment and skepticism. Nevertheless, for selected patients, especially those suffering from psychophysiologic disorders characterized by measurable vascular and neuromuscular changes, such as chronic tension headaches, this approach may be of some use either by itself or in conjunction with other therapies, including medication and formal psychotherapy. Biofeedback is expensive and is often administered in clinics by technicians. There is a paucity of evidence that for tension-related syndromes such as chronic headache it is any more effective than simple relaxation exercises.

Effectiveness of Behavioral Therapies

The behavioral approaches have proved to be of considerable value in the treatment of a wide spectrum of disorders, particularly phobias and muscle tension, as well as migraine headaches. They also may be considered as valuable adjunct techniques in the overall management of psychiatric and other medical conditions such as headaches and eating disorders. Often, much time and effort are devoted to discussing the relative merits of the behavioral techniques versus the psychodynamic therapies. Elements from each approach play a significant factor in the other. Even in the most dynamically oriented therapy situation, the achievement of new insights, improvements in the quality of life, and the lessening of anxiety facilitate the progress toward wellness. Similarly, there has been little research into the nature of the relationship between the patient and his or her behavioral therapist. The degree to which conflicts between the behavioral therapist and the patient may re-create past relationships and how this is handled and influences treatment progress are not well known.

GROUP THERAPIES

In its most basic form, group therapy can be described as the attainment of therapeutic goals through the skilled manipulation of group processes or mechanisms. The changes effected can be limited and situation-specific or they can be far-reaching and foster personality development and growth. Family therapy and couples therapy are specific forms of group therapy directed to the family and the couple—usually the marital couple—in special group/interpersonal settings. In contrast to the individual therapies, the group therapies have direct access to the interpersonal processes of the patient with individuals of varying age and sex. Intrapsychic, interpersonal, communication, and system theories, as well as a knowledge of family and couple development and roles, are used to elucidate various aspects of behavior and increase the patient's awareness. In addition, new behaviors can be tried in the group with the therapist present (Yalom, 1985). The different types of group therapy emphasize different theoretical perspectives and may have different group compositions (see Table 16-8). All groups provide members with support, a feeling of belonging, and a safe, secure environment where change can be effected and tried out first. The therapist uses the vast array of processes at work in a group to facilitate interaction among its members and to guide the work of the group toward the desired goal. Skill, training, and a keen understanding of group dynamics are required. Particular awareness of group fantasies (Bion, 1961), projections, scapegoating, and denial are a part of most group therapy work. Frequently, cotherapists run the group. This often increases the ability to attend to the many processes occurring in the group and aids in the avoidance of countertransference pitfalls.

Group Psychotherapy

Group psychotherapists use a variety of techniques derived from knowledge of the dynamics and behavior of social groups to foster desired change in the individual

Table 16-8 **Group Therapies**

GOAL	Alleviation of symptoms
	Change interpersonal relations
	Alter specific family/couple dynamics
SELECTION	Varies greatly based on type of group
	Homogeneous groups target specific disorders
	Adolescents and personality disorders may especially benefit
	Families and couples where the system needs change
	Contraindications: substantial suicide risk, sadomasochistic acting out in family/couple
TYPES	Directive/Supportive Group Psychotherapy
	Psychodynamic/Interpersonal Group Psychotherapy
	Psychoanalytic Group Psychotherapy
	Family Therapy
	Couples Therapy
DURATION	Weeks to years; time limited and open-ended

members. The theoretical framework supporting the various therapeutic modalities, however, varies with the goals and purposes of the group, the type of group, and the composition of the group. A review of the literature reveals widely diverging definitions and classifications. Different approaches achieve a measure of fame and popularity, such as the so-called encounter groups, then recede from the scene. In general, however, groups can be divided into three separate and distinct categories: (1) directive, (2) psychodynamic/interpersonal, and (3) analytic. This classification is based largely on the degree to which the group fosters the exploration and evocation of repressed, unconscious material. As a result, each group type will vary widely in approach, techniques, composition, conceptual model, and defined goals.

Directive/Supportive Group Psychotherapy

These groups usually have very specific, well-defined, and relatively limited goals. Good examples are the Alcoholics Anonymous (AA) and Overeaters Anonymous groups. The groups function within a very narrow set of guidelines defined by a specific philosophy, set of values, or religious orientation. In the case of AA, for example, the members help each other achieve sobriety and cope with everyday problems of living by adhering to "The Twelve Steps" and entrusting their fate to a "Higher Power." The group leader serves as a role model, stressing common-sense, reality-oriented solutions to problems while using the group to apply peer pressure, enhance self-esteem, foster a feeling of togetherness and belonging, and provide a supportive and nurturing environment. Members usually share at least one major attribute in common (for example, alcoholism), but in many other respects the group is very heterogeneous in composition. There may be a wide divergence in social background, education, personality types, and even the absence or presence of major psychiatric disorders. Behavioral techniques are often applied in similar group situations to treat individuals with phobias while using group support and encouragement to enhance efficacy.

Psychodynamic/Interpersonal Group Psychotherapy

These groups address the individual members' psychopathology, foster the development of insight, promote the development of better interpersonal and social skills, and, in general, promote improved coping skills for the here and now. Defenses are identified and challenged in an atmosphere of support and acceptance. Positive change is encouraged and reinforced. These groups may adhere to any of a wide variety of theoretical models (such as gestalt therapy, psychodrama, and so forth) or may be eclectic in their approach and incorporate aspects of these into the system to fit the needs and characteristics of the group. They tend, however, to focus on the individual's subjective experience and interpersonal behaviors.

Psychoanalytic Group Psychotherapy

This type of group essentially uses the psychoanalytic approach as applied in individual therapy. The therapist remains neutral and nondirective, thus promoting a transference neurosis that can be analyzed. Defenses are identified and resistances interpreted. The group focuses on past experiences and repressed unconscious material as the underlying factors in psychopathology. The therapist attempts to identify individual transferences of the members as well as shared group fantasies or assumptions.

In general, most patients who benefit from individual psychotherapy benefit from group psychotherapy. Empirical data are lacking except in support of various directive/supportive group psychotherapy approaches (e.g., AA, Overeaters Anonymous, type A personality). The differences and similarities in behavior change following group and individual psychotherapy are largely unknown. Although there is no hard evidence for the greater or lesser efficacy of either technique applied to appropriate patients, not all patients will do well in all groups, and some patients should not be considered for inclusion in a treatment group under any circumstances. Specifically, severely depressed and suicidal individuals should not be assigned to outpatient groups. Their emotional state will prevent them from becoming integrated into the group, and the lack of an initial strong therapeutic relationship with a specific therapist may increase the risk of suicide. Such patients should be considered for individual and other more intensely supportive modalities, and inpatient hospitalization when indicated. Manic patients tend to be disruptive to group process, and their impulsivity and lack of control prevent them from obtaining any real benefit from group work. Some types of personality disorders, such as explosive, narcissistic, borderline, and antisocial personalities, may also present insurmountable difficulties for treatment with this modality. Schizophrenics may do well in highly directive groups with emphasis on reality testing and improving interpersonal coping skills. Group therapy can be used as a useful adjunct to either individual psychotherapy or psychotropic medications. Inpatient group psychotherapy is a very common treatment modality and differs from outpatient treatment because of the high heterogeneity of the group and its frequent change in membership. Group psychotherapy may be particularly helpful with adolescents who are highly sensitive to peer group support and influence. Groups also provide a powerful arena in which individuals with personality disorders can become increasingly aware of their interpersonal problems.

Family Therapy

In family therapy, psychological symptoms are considered to be the pathological expression of disturbances in the social system of the family. For the purposes of this discussion, the latter can include any members, ranging from the basic couple to children, grandparents, distant relatives and, in some cases, even close friends of the family. The essential feature is the relationship among the various members and how their behavior can affect the group as a whole as well as the individual family members. The theoretical models may run the whole gamut of therapeutic approaches, ranging from the psychoanalytic to the behavioral (Beels, 1988).

Most family therapists agree that family groups are extremely complex and dynamic systems with a definite hierarchical structure that is a result of cultural and societal proscribed roles, repetitive behavior patterns, and ingrained ways in which the family members have interrelated. Family structure can be seen as a self-regulating system with multiple control mechanisms designed to ensure some degree of a homeostatic equilibrium. The family system seeks stability and inherently resists change. When the system is subjected to internal or external stresses, the family may respond by "designating" one of its members as the "patient," and his or her "illness" may act as a safety valve to maintain system integrity. This same resistance to change will of course oppose any therapeutic efforts and may take the form of refusal to explore family issues by the other members of the family, missed appointments, no apparent therapeutic progress, and so forth. Some change does occur in any family as the passage of time thrusts on the system irresistible forces such as maturation of children, illness, death, old age, and, of course, personal growth and maturity. The family system may thus be conceived as three-dimensional: highly structured, homeostatic, but slowly evolving and changing its character over long periods of time.

The clinical indications for family therapy are very broad. Psychopathology in any member of a family will undoubtedly influence family dynamics, and vice versa. The treatment of children and adolescents frequently requires family therapy to deal with the environment that may be causing or sustaining the symptoms. Recent research indicates the particular value of family therapy in the treatment of schizophrenic patients in reducing rehospitalization rates. Practical considerations such as geographical distance, economic situation, or refusal to participate can rule out family participation. When family members are being extremely destructive to the family unit or important familial relationships, family therapy should not be instituted or should be suspended for a brief time. The treatment of childhood disorders, eating disorders, alcoholism, and substance abuse generally requires a family therapy intervention.

Each clinician brings to the field his or her own conceptual framework, clinical experience, philosophical orientation, and training background. The orthodox psychoanalyst may conceive of family therapy as the individual treatment of the symptomatic member, while at the other end of the spectrum, the social worker specializing in this form of treatment may include any or all members of the family in the sessions and may use a highly directive approach including didactic presentations and environmental manipulation. The focus of most family therapy is on current issues (the here and now) and achievement of discrete changes toward an identifiable goal. Developmental conflicts, communication patterns, boundary management, flexibility, familial conflict resolution techniques, and roles accepted and proscribed by the system for each member are areas of therapeutic attention. Exploration of individual unconscious material is usually avoided. The use of family (or couples) therapy, when an individual psychotherapy is stalled, can help resolve environmental and family system variables that are inhibiting further individual progress. In such cases, a course of family (or couples) therapy can frequently reestablish the momentum of an individual treatment. Family therapy can be an important adjunct to inpatient treatment to facilitate discharge and psychosocial readjustment.

No single technique or procedure dominates family therapy. Therapists may see one or two members of the family or they may see the entire group. The family may be seen together by a single therapist, individually by different therapists, together by more than one therapist, or more than one family may be seen in special forms of multifamily group therapy. Similarly, the therapeutic techniques can range from inducing change by crisis to focusing on small aspects of how the family functions in order to create positive changes that the system can assimilate and incorporate over varying periods of time.

Couples Therapy

Couples therapy is the treatment of dysfunctional couples. In modern society, this includes both married and unmarried "dyads" as well as homosexual couples. It is very similar to, and, in fact, may be described as a form of, family therapy. The same theoretical concepts and treatment approaches described above apply. If the couple has an extreme sadomasochistic relationship, therapy may be blocked. During times when one partner is being overly destructive to the relationship or the other partner, the therapist may need to directly intervene. If this cannot be limited in the treatment, a brief individual therapy with each partner separately may sufficiently resolve the tension to allow the couples therapy to continue. The goal of treatment may be to resolve conflict and reconstruct the dyadic relationship or to facilitate disengagement in the least painful way possible.

SEXUAL DYSFUNCTION THERAPY

The term "sexual dysfunction therapy" encompasses the entire spectrum of accepted psychotherapies from the purely behavioral techniques to the psychodynamically oriented approaches. Treatment may be restricted to a single form of therapy or may consist of a combination of approaches. The focus, however, is the resolution of a specific sexual dysfunction, such as premature ejaculation, impotence, orgasmic dysfunction, or vaginismus (Masters, Johnson, 1970). Most sex therapists emphasize focusing on symptom relief with the use of behavior modification techniques followed by attempts at resolution of underlying conflicts (which may represent the core of the disorder) by more traditional insight-oriented dynamic methods (see Table 16-9). In general, the brief focused therapies, whether used singly or in combination with other forms, seem to have a greater success rate with specific symptom relief than do the longer term treatments.

The evaluation of sexual dysfunction should include a complete investigation of possible organic causes (see Chapter 13). A considerable number of physical illnesses,

Table 16–9 **Sexual Dysfunction Therapies**

GOAL	Resolution of specific sexual dysfunctions
SELECTION	Couples
	Sexual dysfunction: impotence, premature ejaculation, vaginismus, orgasmic dysfunction
	Rule out organic causes
TYPES	Behavior modification techniques, including systematic desensitization, homework, education
	Psychodynamic approaches
	Hypnotherapy
	Group therapy
	Couples therapy as needed to deal with the system dynamics
DURATION	Weeks to months

injuries, and congenital malformations can result in symptoms suggestive of a psycho-sexual disorder and, if not addressed, will render all other therapies useless. Intraab-dominal adhesions and masses, for example, can result in pain during intercourse. Endocrine disturbances may affect sexual drive, and spinal injuries can inhibit penile erections. Similarly, a number of medications can result in dysfunctional symptoms causing great distress to the patient. Thioridazine, a commonly used neuroleptic, is often associated with reversible retrograde ejaculation in the otherwise normal male. In this situation, simple counseling and reassurance may suffice to calm the patient. Thus, the role of careful history taking, a complete physical examination, and indi-cated laboratory testing cannot be overemphasized.

The Diagnostic and Statistical Manual of Mental Disorders (Third Edition, Revised) divides the human sexual response cycle into four distinct phases: (1) appetitive (baseline), (2) excitement, (3) orgasmic, and (4) resolution. For the purposes of our discussion, the last phase bears little relation to disturbances in sexual functioning. The psychosexual disorders may be grouped according to where the dysfunction occurs in the response cycle. Sexual desire disorders are part of the appetitive phase; sexual arousal disorders are part of the excitement phase; and orgasmic disorders are part of the orgasmic phase. Sexual pain disorders are difficult to assign but may directly or indirectly affect the cycle at any level. This classification must be borne in mind when deciding upon the most appropriate therapeutic regi-men. Disorders affecting the orgasmic phase are readily treatable by simple behavioral techniques, and the results appear to be dramatic and long lasting. Disorders affecting the appetitive phase, however, reflect deep-seated conflicts and are much more resistant to therapeutic intervention. They often require the use of insight-oriented therapies and the uncovering of repressed material in conjunction with behavioral therapy. The disturbances of the excitement phase fall somewhere between these two in terms of prognosis and choice of treatment.

Choice of Therapeutic Approach for Sexual Dysfunction

Proponents of the various therapeutic approaches can make a case for the efficacy of their methods in the treatment of these disorders. A basic understanding of the more commonly used and successful treatments is essential for appropriate treatment planning or selection of optimal referral sources.

Individual Psychodynamic Therapy

Individual brief-term psychodynamically oriented psychotherapy remains one of the more useful and effective techniques available when dealing with psychosexual disorders that have complex intrapsychic conflicts at their roots with pervasive negative influences over many other aspects of the individuals' lives. In actual prac-tice, individual psychotherapy by itself may not bring about the desired results, but its efficacy may be greatly enhanced by the application of one of the many behavioral therapies in conjunction with the more traditional approach.

Behavioral Therapy

The use of behavioral techniques such as systematic desensitization and, to a lesser degree, implosion or flooding therapy is often extremely useful in treating sexual dysfunctions—particularly those associated with disturbances of the orgasmic phase. The actual techniques differ very little from the tried and true methods used in other disorders amenable to treatment by these methods (see Chapter 13). The therapist performs a detailed behavioral analysis and develops a hierarchical list of anxiety-producing situations during the sexual act that culminate in the pathological response, be it premature ejaculation, retarded ejaculation, or inhibited orgasm. Through gradual exposure to the anxiety-provoking stimulus, the patient eventually learns to cope in a more appropriate fashion and to perform sexually in an enjoyable, rewarding fashion. As noted earlier, these techniques are particularly effective when dealing with disorders of the orgasmic phase, but their primary value when treating disturbances of the appetitive phase is as an adjunctive technique. Specific techniques of behaviorally oriented therapy for specific types of sexual dysfunction are discussed in Chapter 13.

Hypnotherapy

Hypnotic suggestion can be used effectively to convince a patient that he or she does not need to feel pain during intercourse and to relieve disabling anxiety that may impair performance or consummation and enjoyment of the sexual act.

Group Therapy

Group therapy may be of value for selected patients whose perceived inadequacies and concerns about their symptoms may make them feel "different," socially isolated, and unable to share their feelings, fears, and irrational fantasies. Support from other members of the group with whom they can relate and identify may result in decreased anxiety and improvement in symptoms and may make the patient more amenable to participation in other forms of treatment, such as behavioral therapy.

Dual Sex (Couples) Therapy

This variant of behavioral therapy was initially proposed by Masters and Johnson and in its original form approached sexual dysfunction disorders as a "dyad" issue, that is, a patient suffering from a psychosexual disorder did so in the context of his relationship with his sexual partner. The two would be treated together as members of the "dyad" unit by a team consisting of a male and a female therapist. The latter not only directed what was for all intents and purposes a behavioral treatment approach, complete with educational sessions and schedule of assignments (systematic desensitization), but also served as role models for the same-sex member of the "dyad." In recent years, adherence to the male–female team and male–female "dyad" concept has not been as strict, and the makeup of the participants has been tailored to fit individual circumstances. Nevertheless, it remains an extremely effective approach that uses education, behavioral modification, modeling, and couples therapy to effect change in sexual dysfunction.

Summary

The psychotherapies are important components of the treatment plan for nearly all psychiatric illnesses. Both short- and long-term techniques are available. Which psychotherapy for which patient with which therapist is less clear. Psychotherapy provides the patient with new problem-solving techniques. Some patients prefer one type of problem solving or can learn one type and not another.

How the outcomes from the different psychotherapies may differ and what this may mean for long-range health/relapse warrant further research. Increasingly, data indicate the effectiveness of the psychotherapies in reducing hospitalization rates and the use of other medical resources. Studies on the use of psychotherapy as an adjunct in the treatment of various physical illnesses also tend to indicate cost benefits in overall medical care dollars. The ability to use a range of psychotherapies is important in the treatment of psychiatric illness and in obtaining maximum benefit from medical case management and the therapeutic effectiveness of the doctor–patient relationship.

For the nonpsychiatrist physician, a referral for psychiatric assessment is essential when psychotherapy may be indicated. The psychiatric consultant can evaluate the interplay of biological, psychological, and social context variables that may be causing or maintaining illness in the patient. A comprehensive treatment plan and goals can then be formulated. Prior to referring a patient, the physician should educate the patient. Many patients will have the belief that psychiatric illness is fake or imaginary. They should be reassured that their distress and pain are real and that there is a wide array of possible treatments. Patients are best prepared when they can understand the role of medication in providing possible relief of symptoms and the role of the psychotherapies in learning new ways to handle the problems that may be precipitating their distress. For instance, the physician refers a patient to physical therapy to learn a new way to walk when the patient has developed a limp to compensate for chronic pain. (The limp may persist even after the pain is relieved by medication.) Similarly, the psychotherapies teach, through various means, new problem-solving techniques to relieve patterns of behaviors, feelings, and thoughts that are causing or maintaining impairment.

Finally, as noted earlier, it should be emphasized that the best form of treatment is often integrated psychotherapy and pharmacotherapy. Psychiatrists or nonpsychiatric clinicians who are polarized one way or the other may offer a narrow range of treatment and overlook a biological or psychological therapy that might potentially be dramatically effective for the patient. Hence, in making a referral for an initial evaluation, it is recommended that one consult a clinician with a balanced, integrated approach. If there are clearly no medical or organic factors involved, or if there is no indication for psychopharmacologic treatment, referral to a nonmedical therapist can be made directly. The success of a referral for psychiatric evaluation or psychotherapy is *critically* dependent on the attitude, confidence, and enthusiasm of the referring physician.

CLINICAL PEARLS

- It is important to exhibit confidence and enthusiasm when making a referral for psychiatric evaluation or psychotherapy. Patients will detect ambivalence and skepticism on the physician's part about the need for such treatment. It is usually helpful to recommend a psychiatrist or other mental health professional who is known *personally* by the physician.
- Always present the psychiatric referral as part of the patient's ongoing medical care. Some patients will view a psychiatric referral as a means to "dump" them onto another doctor or as a "rejection." Patients should be reassured that any psychiatric treatment will be in parallel with their ongoing medical care.
- Have the name and telephone number of your referral source readily available to give to the patient.
- Call the psychiatrist to personally explain the reason and need for the referral and what role you would like to continue to play in the patient's care.
- Make the appointment for the psychiatric evaluation while the patient is still in the office or clinic.
- Be sure to schedule a follow-up appointment after the date of the psychiatric evaluation to check on the patient's reaction to the referral and his response to initial treatment (Kriseman, Fiore, Stoudemire, 1990).

ANNOTATED BIBLIOGRAPHY

Balint M, Ornstein P, Balint E: Focal Psychotherapy. Philadelphia, JB Lippincott, 1972

> This book is one of the first written in the area of brief psychodynamic psychotherapy. It is a superb demonstration of a case of brief psychotherapy in an individual with moderately severe psychopathology. The case illustrates the exceptional clinical skill and technical requirements in carrying out a brief psychodynamic psychotherapy.

Bruch H: Learning Psychotherapy. Cambridge, MA, Harvard University Press, 1974

> This eloquent and well-written introduction to psychotherapy presents basic principles of psychotherapeutic relations of the management of psychotherapy that are applicable to nearly all psychotherapeutic endeavors. It is based on the author's extensive career as a psychotherapist. An excellent introduction to psychotherapy.

Coleman J: Aims and conduct of psychotherapy. Arch Gen Psychiatry 18:1–6, 1968

> This is a clearly written, classic article that articulates without jargon the basic doctor–patient relationship, goals, and orientation maintained by the psychiatrist in conducting psychotherapy.

Smith ML, Glass GV: The Benefits of Psychotherapy. Baltimore, Johns Hopkins Press, 1980

> This book is a metaanalysis of all psychotherapy studies examining the question of the efficacy of psychotherapy. Overall, this detailed and comprehensive analysis indicates that the efficacy of psychotherapy as a medical treatment is equivalent to that of other types of medical interventions.

Stone L: The Psychoanalytic Situation. New York, International University Press, 1961

> This brief book describes the structural elements of psychoanalysis—setting, organization, techniques, and contribution to the treatment. Well written.

Sullivan HS: The Psychiatric Interview. New York, WW Norton, 1954

> This excellent introduction to the psychiatric interview is written from the perspective of the interpersonal school of psychiatry. However, its basic presentation is applicable to all of the psychotherapies. It provides a basic science to the application of talk as a curative agent.

Ursano RJ, Hales RE: A review of brief individual therapies. Am J Psychiatry 143(12):1507–1517, 1986

> This article is an overview of both individual and group brief psychotherapies. It has a detailed list of references and presents the psychotherapies as medical interventions with substantive technical and selection criteria. In addition, there is a brief overview of the cost benefit issues in psychotherapy.

Ursano RJ, Silberman EK: Individual psychotherapies. In Talbott JA, Hales RE, Yudofsky SC (eds): Textbook of Psychiatry. Washington, DC, American Psychiatric Press, 1988

> This chapter reviews the individual psychotherapies and, in particular, contains an extensive review of supportive psychotherapy, perhaps the most widely used and understudied of all of the psychotherapies.

Werman DS: The Practice of Supportive Psychotherapy. New York, Brunner/Mazel, 1984

> This book is one of a very few that describe supportive psychotherapy in a technical manner. It is a substantive contribution to the literature and to the clinician's ability to learn supportive psychotherapy as a technique.

Yalom ID: The Theory and Practice of Group Psychotherapy. New York, Basic Books, 1985

> This book is the basic text of group psychotherapy. It is a comprehensive review with technical directions for the application of the technique by clinicians.

REFERENCES

Beck AT: Cognitive Theory and the Emotional Disorders. New York, International Universities Press, 1976

Beels CC: Family therapy. In Talbott JA, Hales RE, Yudofsky SC (eds): Textbook of Psychiatry. Washington, DC, American Psychiatric Press, 1988

Bion WR: Experiences in Groups. New York, Basic Books, 1961

Bruch H: Learning Psychotherapy. Cambridge, MA, Harvard University Press, 1974

Davanloo H (ed): Short-Term Dynamic Psychotherapy. New York, Jason Aronson Press, 1980

Gaarder K, Montgomery P: Clinical Biofeedback. Baltimore, Williams & Wilkins, 1977

Kaplan HS: The New Sex Therapy. New York, Brunner/Mazel, 1974

Klerman GL, Weissman MM, Rounsaville BJ, et al: Interpersonal Psychotherapy of Depression. New York, Basic Books, 1984b

Kriseman N, Stoudemire A: The family in human development and medical practice. In Stoudemire A (ed): Human Behavior: An Introduction for Medical Students. Philadelphia, JB Lippincott, 1990

Lazarus A: Behavior Therapy and Beyond. New York, McGraw-Hill, 1971

Malan DH: A Study of Brief Psychotherapy. New York, Plenum Press, 1975

Mann J: Time-Limited Psychotherapy. Cambridge, MA, Harvard University Press, 1973

Masters WH, Johnson VE: Human Sexual Inadequacy. Boston, Little, Brown & Co, 1970

Pine F: Supportive psychotherapy: A psychoanalytic perspective. Psychiatr Ann 16:524–534, 1986

Reichmann FF: Principles of Intensive Psychotherapy. Chicago, University of Chicago Press, 1950

Rush AJ, Watkins J: Group versus individual cognitive therapy: A pilot study. Cog Ther Res 5:95–104, 1981

Sandler J, Dare C, Holder A: The Patient and the Analyst. New York, International Universities Press, 1973

Sifneos PE: Short-Term Psychotherapy and Emotional Crisis. Cambridge, MA, Harvard University Press, 1972

Stone L: The Psychoanalytic Situation. New York, International Universities Press, 1961

Ursano RJ, Dressler DM: Brief versus long-term psychotherapy: A treatment decision. J Nerv Ment Dis 159:164–171, 1974

Werman DS: The practice of supportive psychotherapy. New York, Brunner/Mazel, 1984

17

Biological Therapies for Mental Disorders

Jonathan M. Silver, Robert E. Hales, and Stuart C. Yudofsky

GENERAL CONSIDERATIONS IN SELECTING A SOMATIC THERAPY

The use of a somatic treatment for a psychiatric illness is a decision that should be made only after careful consideration of many factors for that individual patient. Medication alone is never *the* treatment for a patient; rather, medications may be important components of a larger overall treatment plan. All psychiatric patients require a skilled and thorough psychiatric, neurologic, and physical evaluation. A key component of a well-considered decision to use a somatic treatment is the specification of *target symptoms*. One should list those specific symptoms which are designated for treatment and monitor response of these symptoms to treatment. However, a frequent and dangerous clinical error is the treatment of specific symptoms of a disorder with multiple drugs rather than treating, more specifically, the underlying disorder. For example, it is not uncommon for a psychiatrist to be referred a patient who is taking one type of benzodiazepine for anxiety, a different type of benzodiazepine for insomnia, an analgesic for unspecific somatic complaints, and a subtherapeutic dose of an antidepressant (e.g., 50 mg/day of imipramine) for feelings of sadness. Often, the somatic complaints, insomnia, and anxiety are components of the underlying depression, which is aggravated by the polypharmaceutical approach inherent to symptomatic treatment. In such circumstances, full explanation to the patient of the syndrome of depression, with emphasis on the necessity of adequate doses and duration of treatment with an antidepressant, should precede discontinuation of the benzodiazepine and analgesic medications and the proper administration of an antidepressant agent. After the decision has been made to initiate psychopharmacologic treatment, the clinician must select the specific drug. Usually, this choice is made on the basis of the patient's prior history of response to medication, the side effect profile of the drug chosen, and the patient's most likely response to those specific side effects.

Choice of Medication

Choice of a medication also involves an understanding of the *pharmacokinetics* of a particular drug as well as a familiarity with the relative benefits of the available routes of administration of that medication. Most antidepressant and antipsychotic drugs have sufficiently long half-lives to permit a once-a-day dosing regimen, which may increase compliance. The choice of a particular medication may depend on whether that drug is available in injection and liquid forms in addition to tablet, pill, or capsule forms.

Once a decision has been made as to the need for and the choice of a specific drug, attention must be paid to issues related to patient information about indications for and risks and benefits of the medication. A general principle is that the more the patient understands about his or her illness and the reason that medications have been chosen to treat the illness, the more compliant the patient will be. The clinician must also consider the physical, intellectual, and psychological capacities of the patient and his or her caretakers when selecting a new medication. For example, impulsive patients with a history of suicide attempts and alcohol abuse may not safely or reliably be treated with a monoamine oxidase inhibitor because of the need to follow a strict dietary regimen. In general, the more complicated the instructions, or the more medications that are prescribed, and the greater number of times per day the medication is to be taken, the more difficulty the patient will have in complying.

A major component of the treatment plan should comprise the evaluation of response and criteria for discontinuation of the medication. Far too frequently, medications are discontinued with the assumption of "failure of response to the medication" without an adequate (i.e., dose, serum level, and duration) drug trial. Different treatment approaches range from a second trial with a related class of medication to the use of complementary or different treatment modalities.

Finally, for those patients whose specific target symptoms do respond to somatic intervention, an end point for treatment must be determined. It is not uncommon that patients are continued on medications beyond the point that therapeutic benefit is derived. A common example is the use of benzodiazepines for the treatment of anxiety; patients may be maintained on this drug for years without the assessment of its therapeutic benefit by gradual discontinuation.

ANTIPSYCHOTIC DRUGS

Available antipsychotic drugs may be categorized into several classes: the phenothiazines (including their derivatives), the thioxanthenes, the butyrophenones, and the dibenzoxazepine, dibenzodiazepine, and indole derivatives. These drugs are shown in Table 17-1.

Although there are many therapeutic agents available in parenteral, oral, and depot preparations, the choice of a drug in treating psychosis is determined largely by

Table 17–1 **Selected Antipsychotic Drugs and Dosages (see also Table 4-4)**

CLASS/GENERIC NAME	TRADE NAME	DOSE EQUIVALENT (mg)	*USUAL MAINTENANCE DAILY ORAL DOSE (mg)
Phenothiazines			
Aliphatic			
Chlorpromazine hydrochloride	Thorazine	100	200–600
Triflupromazine hydrochloride	Vesprin	26–30	50–150
Piperidine			
Thioridazine hydrochloride	Mellaril	90–104	200–600
Mesoridazine besylate	Serentil	50–62	150–200
Piperacetazine	Quide	11	20–40
Piperazine			
Trifluoperazine	Stelazine	2.4–3.2	5–10
Fluphenazine hydrochloride	Prolixin Permitil	1.1–1.3	2.5–10
decanoate enanthate	Prolixin	0.61	10 mg/day oral fluphenazine = 12.5–25 mg/2 weeks fluphenazine decanoate
Perphenazine	Trilafon	8.9–9.6	16–24
Acetophenazine	Tindal	22–24	60
Thioxanthenes			
Chlorprothixene	Taractan	36–52	75–200
Thiothixene	Navane	3.4–5.4	6–30
Butyrophenones			
Haloperidol	Haldol	1.1–2.1	2–12
Haloperidol decanoate			10 mg/day oral haloperidol = 100–200 mg/4 weeks haloperidol decanoate
Dibenzoxazepine			
Loxapine	Loxitane	10	20–60
Indole derivatives			
Molindone hydrochloride	Moban Lidone	5.1–6.9	15–60
Pimozide	Orap	N/A	2–10
Dibenzodiazepine			
Clozapine	Clozaril	50	200–900

(Adapted from Silver JM, Yudofsky SC: Psychopharmacology and electroconvulsive therapy. In Talbott JA, Hales RE, Yudofsky SC (eds): The American Psychiatric Press Textbook of Psychiatry, pp 707–854. Washington, DC, American Psychiatric Press, 1988)
*Dose ranges required for patients varies. Adjustment in doses may be required depending on the patient's clinical status and responsiveness to medication.

the side effect profile of the specific drug and the ability of the individual patient to tolerate or benefit from those side effects. Clozapine has a unique pharmacologic profile when compared with currently available antipsychotic drugs. It will be discussed in a separate section in this chapter.

Mechanisms of Action

The prevailing theory regarding the mechanism of action of antipsychotic drugs is based on the observation that all of the currently available antipsychotic drugs have a similar action on the dopamine system: the blocking of the binding of dopamine to the postsynaptic dopamine receptor in the brain. The dopamine-2 (D-2) receptor, which is not linked to adenylate cyclase, is believed to be responsible for the action of this class of drugs. The theory that psychosis is a result of an excess of dopamine or the result of abnormal activity of certain dopamine receptors has been confirmed by the observation of increased dopamine concentrations and an increased number of dopamine-2 receptors in the brains of some patients with schizophrenia (see Chapter 4).

There are several dopamine pathways in the brain that are affected by the antipsychotic drugs. The nigrostriatal system is involved in motor activity. A relative deficiency of dopamine after administration of antipsychotics due to the blockage of the dopamine receptor leads to extrapyramidal disorders, such as those seen in Parkinson's disease. As a result of this, antipsychotic drugs have been termed "neuroleptics" because their actions imitate a neurologic illness. Dopamine receptors in the pituitary and hypothalamus (the tuberoinfundibular system) affect prolactin release, appetite, and temperature regulation. Since dopamine inhibits the release of prolactin, the antipsychotic drugs result in an increase in prolactin levels. Dopamine pathways also connect the limbic system, the midbrain tegmentum, septal nuclei, and mesocortical projections. These areas are believed to be involved in thought and emotion and may be responsible for the antipsychotic action of these drugs.

Indications and Efficacy

The most common use of antipsychotic drugs is in the treatment of acute psychotic exacerbations and in the maintenance of remission of these psychotic symptoms in patients with schizophrenia. Psychotic symptoms include abnormal thought content such as delusions, perceptual abnormalities such as hallucinations, and abnormal thought form such as disorganized speech.

The impressive data on the effectiveness of antipsychotic drugs as maintenance treatment for schizophrenia have been reviewed thoroughly by Davis and Andriukaitis (1986). Without continued treatment with antipsychotic medication after remission of acute psychotic symptoms, there is a relapse rate of approximately 8 to 15% per month for patients with schizophrenia (Davis, Andriukaitis, 1986). Patients maintained on drugs have a relapse rate ranging from 1.5 to 3% per month.

Antipsychotic drugs are effective in ameliorating psychotic symptoms that result from diverse etiologies such as mood (affective) disorders with psychotic features, drug toxicities such as "steroid psychoses" (delirium), and brain disorders such as Huntington's disease or post–head injury. Acute manic symptoms are effectively treated with antipsychotic drugs, with a more rapid response than with lithium. Patients with borderline and schizotypal personality disorders have been treated with antipsychotic drugs. Brief treatment with relatively low-dose antipsychotic drugs may be effective in alleviating the symptoms of somatization, anxiety, and psychotic ideation in these patients. Patients with psychotic or delusional depression may be successfully treated with a combination of antipsychotic and antidepressant drugs, but not with antipsychotic drugs alone.

The sedative side effect of antipsychotic drugs may often lead to their misuse in several clinical situations. These drugs frequently are improperly prescribed as hypnotic or anxiolytic agents. In addition, the antipsychotic drugs are administered to patients who are chronically agitated and violent. Because of the potential long-term risks of these drugs (see section on tardive dyskinesia), antipsychotics are not recommended for the treatment of anxiety or insomnia. Similarly, although these drugs are valuable for acute episodes of agitation and aggression, they should generally not be used for the treatment of chronic aggression and agitation except under special circumstances.

Clinical Use of Antipsychotic Drugs

General Principles

Drug potency refers to the milligram equivalence of drugs, not to the relative efficacy. For example, although haloperidol is more potent than chlorpromazine (2 mg haloperidol = 100 mg chlorpromazine), therapeutically equivalent doses are equally effective (12 mg haloperidol = 600 mg chlorpromazine). These doses are listed in Table 17-1. By convention, the potency of antipsychotic drugs is compared with a standard 100-mg dose of chlorpromazine. As a rule, *the high-potency antipsychotic drugs with an equivalent dose of less than 5 mg have a high degree of extrapyramidal side effects (EPS) and a low level of sedation and autonomic side effects* (e.g., haloperidol, thiothixene, fluphenazine). Low-potency antipsychotic drugs have an equivalent dose of greater than 40 mg (e.g., chlorpromazine and thioridazine). These have a high level of sedation and autonomic side effects and a low degree of EPS. Those antipsychotic drugs with intermediate potency (equivalent dose between 5 mg and 40 mg) have a side effect profile that lies between these two groups (e.g., loxapine).

Treatment with antipsychotic medication must be tailored to the individual patient. Flexible guidelines that are supported by scientific principles and research should be followed. These guidelines are outlined in Table 17-2.

Risks, Side Effects, and Their Management

Extrapyramidal Reactions

Serious side effects of antipsychotic use result from the blockade of the postsynaptic dopamine receptor. A variety of extrapyramidal symptoms may emerge, including acute dystonic reactions, parkinsonian syndrome, akathisia, akinesia, "rab-

Table 17–2 **Guidelines for Antipsychotic Drug Therapy**

1. Obtain thorough medical evaluation, including evaluation for tardive dyskinesia
2. Select drug on the basis of side effect profile, risk/benefit ratio, and history of prior use and response
3. Inform the patient and family of risk of tardive dyskinesia
4. Initiate drug therapy at low dose (chlorpromazine [CPZ] equivalent 50 mg orally three times a day)
5. Use prophylactic anticholinergic medication with high-potency antipsychotic drugs or in patients younger than 40 years old
6. Gradually increase dose (50–100 mg CPZ equivalent every other day) until improvement or usual maximum dose of 600 mg CPZ equivalent is reached
7. Maintain maximum dose for 2 to 4 weeks
8. Consider using sedative drugs or beta-blockers for agitation
9. If response is inadequate, obtain plasma level of drugs
10. If level is low, increase dose to equivalent of 1000 mg CPZ
11. Maintain dose for 2 to 4 weeks. If improvement is inadequate, gradually decrease drug and substitute with an antipsychotic from a different class
12. Monitor patient closely for therapeutic effects and side effects of treatment
13. Decrease dosage of antipsychotic medications as soon as possible after initial control of psychotic symptoms

(Adapted from Silver JM, Yudofsky SC: Psychopharmacology and electroconvulsive therapy. In Talbott JA, Hales RE, Yudofsky SC (eds): The American Psychiatric Press Textbook of Psychiatry, pp 707–854. Washington, DC, American Psychiatric Press, 1988)

bit syndrome," tardive dyskinesia, neuroleptic-induced catatonia, and the neuroleptic malignant syndrome.

Among the most disturbing and frightening adverse drug reactions that occur with the administration of antipsychotic drugs are *acute dystonic reactions.* This reaction most frequently occurs within hours or days of the initiation of antipsychotic therapy. *The most common feature of this syndrome includes uncontrollable tightening of the face and neck and spasm and distortions of the head and/or back (opisthotonus).* If the extraocular muscles are involved, an oculogyric crisis may occur, wherein the eyes are elevated and "locked" in this position. Laryngeal involvement may lead to respiratory and ventilatory difficulties.

Intravenous or intramuscular administration of anticholinergic drugs provides rapid treatment of acute dystonia. Table 17-3 lists the drugs and dosages used to treat dystonic reactions. Note that the anticholinergic drug given to reverse the dystonia will wear off after several hours. Since antipsychotic drugs may have long half-lives and duration of action, additional oral anticholinergic drugs should be prescribed for several days after the dystonic reaction has occurred.

The *parkinsonian syndrome* has many of the features of classic idiopathic Parkinson's disease: diminished range of facial expression (masked facies), cogwheel rigidity, slowed movements (bradykinesia), and "pill-rolling" tremor. The onset of this side effect is gradual and may not appear for weeks after neuroleptics have been

Table 17–3 **Drugs for Treatment of Extrapyramidal Disorders**

GENERIC NAME (TRADE NAME)	STARTING DOSE
Anticholinergic drugs	
Benzotropine (Cogentin)	P.O. 0.5 mg t.i.d.
	I.M./I.V. 1 mg
Biperiden (Akineton)	P.O. 2 mg t.i.d.
	I.M./I.V. 2 mg
Diphenhydramine (Benadryl)	P.O. 25 mg q.i.d.
	I.M./I.V. 25 mg
Ethopropazine (Parsidol)	P.O. 50 mg b.i.d.
Orphenadrine (Norflex, Disipal)	P.O. 100 mg b.i.d.
	I.V. 60 mg
Procyclidine (Kemadrin)	P.O. 2.5 mg t.i.d.
Trihexyphenidyl (Artane)	P.O. 1 mg t.i.d.
Dopamine agonists	
Amantadine (Symmetrel)	P.O. 100 mg b.i.d.
Beta-blockers	
Propranolol (Inderal)	P.O. 20 mg t.i.d.

(Adapted from Silver JM, Yudofsky SC: Psychopharmacology and electroconvulsive therapy. In Talbott JA, Hales RE, Yudofsky SC (eds): The American Psychiatric Press Textbook of Psychiatry, pp 707–854. Washington, DC, American Psychiatric Press, 1988)

administered. Drugs used in the treatment of the parkinsonian side effects of antipsychotic agents are listed in Table 17-3.

Akathisia is an extrapyramidal disorder consisting of an unpleasant feeling of restlessness and the inability to sit still. It is a common reaction and most often occurs shortly after the initiation of antipsychotic drugs. Unfortunately, *akathisia is frequently mistaken for an exacerbation of psychotic symptoms, anxiety, or depression.* The patient may pace or may become agitated or angry with the inability to control symptoms associated with akathisia. If the dose of antipsychotic medications is increased, the restlessness continues or exacerbates. Lowering the dose may improve the symptoms. In the past, anticholinergic drugs were suggested as the first line of therapy, but they often are ineffective. Benzodiazepines, such as diazepam, may be effective. The treatment of choice of akathisia is beta-adrenergic blocking drugs, particularly propranolol.

Akinesia is characterized by diminished spontaneity, few gestures, unspontaneous speech, and apathy. As with the parkinsonian syndrome, this may appear only after several weeks of therapy. This syndrome may be mistaken as depression in patients treated with antipsychotic agents. The anticholinergic drugs in the dose ranges suggested in Table 17-3 are effective in treating akinesia.

The "rabbit syndrome" consists of fine, rapid movements of the lips that mimic the chewing movements of a rabbit. This side effect occurs late in neuroleptic treatment and is treated effectively with anticholinergic drugs. It has been found to be present in approximately 4% of patients receiving neuroleptic therapy (without concomitant anticholinergics) (Yassa, Lal, 1986).

Tardive dyskinesia (TD) is a disorder characterized by involuntary movements of the face, trunk, or extremities. The syndrome is related to exposure to dopamine-receptor blocking agents, most frequently the classic antipsychotic agents (see Table 17-4). Chronically hospitalized psychiatric patients have been estimated to have a prevalence of TD of approximately 20 to 25% (Jeste, Wyatt, 1982). The most commonly hypothesized mechanism for the development of TD is that postsynaptic dopamine receptor supersensitivity develops after use of dopamine-receptor blocking drugs. Other hypotheses have also been proposed.

The most significant and consistently documented risk factor for the development of TD is increasing age of the patient. Other risk factors may include the dose of antipsychotic medication, the total time on antipsychotics, a history of drug holidays (a greater number of drug-free periods is associated with an increased risk), the time since the first exposure to antipsychotic drugs (including drug holidays), the presence of brain damage, and diagnosis (especially the presence of a mood disorder).

The issue of informed consent with respect to antipsychotic medications and the risk of TD has been extensively reviewed (Munetz, Roth 1985). It is usually difficult, if not impossible, to obtain informed consent from an acutely psychotic patient. A general guideline is to inform and educate the patient's family about the risks of TD before starting the antipsychotics and to educate the patient gradually about this disorder as soon as possible after agitation and psychosis remit. In many

Table 17-4 **Clinical Features of Tardive Dyskinesia**

The following abnormal movements may be seen in tardive dyskinesia:

Facial and oral movements

Muscles of facial expression: involuntary movement of forehead, eyebrows, periorbital area, cheeks; involuntary frowning, blinking, smiling, grimacing

Lips and perioral area: involuntary puckering, pouting, smacking

Jaw: involuntary biting, clenching, chewing, mouth opening, lateral movements

Tongue: involuntary protrusion, tremor, choreoathetoid movements (rolling, wormlike movement without displacement from the mouth)

Extremity movements

Involuntary movements of upper arms, wrists, hands, fingers: choreic movements (i.e., rapid, objectively purposeless, irregular, spontaneous), athetoid movements (i.e., slow, irregular, complex, serpentine). Tremor (i.e., repetitive, regular, rhythmic)

Involuntary movement of lower legs, knees, ankles, toes: lateral knee movement, foot tapping, foot squirming, inversion and eversion of foot

Trunk movements

Involuntary movement of neck, shoulders, hips: rocking, twisting, squirming, pelvic gyrations

(Adapted from National Institute of Mental Health: Abnormal Involuntary Movement Scale. In Guy W: ECDEU Assessment Manual. Rockville, MD, U.S. Department of Health, Education, and Welfare, 1976)

circumstances, true informed consent may be impossible to obtain from an acutely psychotic patient for several weeks. The psychiatrist also needs to be aware that some states legally mandate that informed consent be obtained from patients before the initiation of antipsychotic treatment (e.g., California and New Jersey). All such discussions with patients and their families should be documented in the patients' records. An informed consent that is exclusively in the written form has been shown to be less effective in communicating information to the patient than an oral consent obtained in conjunction with education of the patient (Munetz, Roth, 1985). The psychiatrist must designate adequate time to the provision of informed consent consistent with the confusional state and cognitive capabilities of the patient.

Prevention is the most important aspect of TD management. Periodic assessments must be made to determine the patient's requirement for continuing antipsychotic drug therapy. In addition, every 6 months a reevaluation is required to ascertain the lowest possible dose of antipsychotic drug that still proves to be effective in the treatment of psychotic symptoms.

There is no reliable treatment of TD other than discontinuing the antipsychotic medication. If discontinuation of the antipsychotic drug is possible in light of the severity of the patient's psychotic symptoms, improvement in the TD may be gradual. Worsening of the involuntary movements often initially occurs with discontinuation of neuroleptics. The new neuroleptic clozapine does not appear to cause TD, although it has the major liability of possibly causing agranulocytosis (see below).

Neuroleptic malignant syndrome. In rare instances, patients on antipsychotic medications may develop a potentially life-threatening disorder known as neuroleptic malignant syndrome (NMS). While most frequently occurring with the use of high-potency neuroleptics (haloperidol), this condition may emerge after the use of any antipsychotic agent. The patient with NMS becomes severely rigid and occasionally catatonic. There is fever, elevated white blood cell count, tachycardia, abnormal blood pressure fluctuations, tachypnea, and diaphoresis. Creatinine phosphokinase (CPK) levels are elevated due to muscle breakdown, and CPK levels are an excellent parameter to check for the presence of the disorder and response to treatment. A prodrome to neuroleptic malignant syndrome is *neuroleptic-induced catatonia*, wherein the prominent signs are extrapyramidal symptoms and a catatonic behavioral state that may be mistaken for a worsening of the psychosis. Neuroleptic-induced catatonia is best treated with amantadine 100 mg b.i.d. over several weeks.

The key treatment steps after recognition of NMS are discontinuation of all medications, thorough medical evaluation, and physical support. Several treatments have been suggested to control NMS. These include amantadine, electroconvulsive therapy, and benzodiazepines. As noted above, amantadine appears more useful in the treatment of neuroleptic-induced catatonia than do the anticholinergic drugs. Dantrolene sodium (a direct-acting muscle relaxant) and bromocriptine (a centrally active dopamine agonist) appear to be the most successful agents in the treatment of NMS, but their efficacy over supportive care has not been definitively proven. Because these two agents may treat differing symptoms of NMS and act through separate mechanisms, they also may be useful in combination. Unfortunately, no controlled clinical trials related to the somatic treatment of NMS have yet been conducted.

Anticholinergic Effects

In the treatment of a patient with antipsychotic drugs, anticholinergic side effects may be caused by either the neuroleptic or the anticholinergic drug that has been prescribed to alleviate extrapyramidal side effects. Anticholinergic effects are categorized as peripheral or central. Among the peripheral side effects, the most common are dry mouth, decreased sweating, decreased bronchial secretions, blurred vision (due to inhibition of accommodation), difficulty in urination, and constipation. Central side effects of anticholinergic drugs include impairment in concentration, attention, and memory. In cases of toxicity, anticholinergic delirium, which includes hot, dry skin, dry mucous membranes, dilated pupils, absent bowel sounds, and tachycardia, may appear.

Other Side Effects

Blockade of alpha-adrenergic receptors can result in orthostatic hypotension and dizziness. Mesoridazine, chlorpromazine, thioridazine, and clozapine are the most potent alpha-1 blockers of the antipsychotic drugs. Changes in hormonal function have been reported to occur with neuroleptic treatment. Because of the dopamine blocking effect, prolactin levels increase, which may result in gynecomastia in both men and women. Galactorrhea, although unusual, also may occur. Additional neuroendocrine side effects of neuroleptics mediated by hyperprolactinemia include amenorrhea, weight gain, breast tenderness, and decreased libido.

Sexual dysfunction also may be caused by neuroleptic therapy. In men, difficulty in achieving or maintaining an erection, decreased ability to achieve orgasm, and changes in the quality of orgasm are reported. Thioridazine may cause painful retrograde ejaculation in which semen is ejected into the bladder. Women may experience changes in the quality of orgasm and decreased ability to achieve orgasm with antipsychotic use. Menstrual irregularities also may occur.

Pigmentary changes in the skin and eyes may occur, especially with long-term treatment. Pigment deposition in the lens of the eye does not affect vision. Pigmentary retinopathy, which can lead to irreversible blindness, has been associated specifically with the use of thioridazine. Although pigmentary retinopathy has most often been reported with doses above the recommended dosage ceiling for thioridazine (i.e., 800 mg/day), cases exist where this condition has occurred at usual clinical doses. Almost all patients on neuroleptics, especially the aliphatic phenothiazines (e.g., chlorpromazine), become more sensitive to the effects of sunlight, which can lead to severe sunburn. Especially in the summer months, patients should avoid excess sun exposure and use ultraviolet blocking agents, such as sunscreens that contain para-aminobenzoic acid (PABA).

Several of the antipsychotic medications have cardiac effects that can be detected on the electrocardiogram. For example, thioridazine is associated with prolonged QT intervals, and this change is related to plasma level concentration. There have been reports of other arrhythmias and sudden death with antipsychotic agents probably due to their quinidine-like effects.

Increases in liver function enzymes have been rarely associated with antipsychotic treatment. Many cases of this reaction were linked to impurities in the original formulation of chlorpromazine, and the incidence has profoundly decreased over the years. Transient leukopenia and, in rare cases, agranulocytosis have been associated with neuroleptic treatment. These are idiosyncratic reactions that usually occur within the first 3 to 4 weeks after the initiation of treatment with an antipsychotic drug. Clozapine has a special propensity for this side effect.

The antipsychotic drugs have been shown to lower seizure threshold, a phenomenon that has been confirmed in animal models. Special precautions must be taken with the use of antipsychotic agents in those patients with a history of convulsions who are not on anticonvulsant therapy and in those patients with episodic aggression whose dyscontrol may result from "subictal seizures."

Antipsychotic drugs directly affect the hypothalamus and suppress control of temperature regulation. In combination with the alpha-adrenergic receptor and cholinergic receptor blocking effects of antipsychotics, this effect becomes particularly serious in hot, humid weather.

As a general guideline, antipsychotic drugs should be used in pregnant patients only if absolutely necessary, at the minimal dose required, and for the briefest possible time.

Unlike other antipsychotic drugs, clozapine does not elevate prolactin levels and has not been reported to induce dystonia or tardive dyskinesia. Unfortunately, clozapine has a known 2% risk of producing agranulocytosis, which is reversible if the medication is discontinued. This fact has prevented clozapine from previously being developed for use in the United States. Recent investigations have shown that clozapine has significantly superior efficacy when compared with other antipsychotic drugs in the care of "treatment-resistant" patients with schizophrenia. This drug should be available in 1990 under specific guidelines, including weekly complete blood counts as a prerequisite for obtaining weekly supplies of clozapine. Further discussion of the use of neuroleptics in schizophrenia and other conditions may be found in Chapters 4 and 18.

ANTIDEPRESSANT DRUGS

The modern era of drug treatment of depression began in the 1950s when iproniazid, a monoamine oxidase inhibitor (MAOI) used for the treatment of tuberculosis, was noted to elevate the mood of these patients. Imipramine, the first of the "tricyclic antidepressants" (TCAs), was developed as a derivative of chlorpromazine with the hope that the drug would be more effective as an antipsychotic agent. Although imipramine did not exhibit antipsychotic efficacy, it was found to be effective in the treatment of depression.

Since that time, many other antidepressant drugs have been approved for use in the United States. Among this group are other derivatives of the TCA family, drugs with related structures (e.g., tetracyclics), drugs of the MAOI family, and atypical antidepressants. For simplicity, the term "cyclic antidepressants" (CyAD) will be employed in this chapter to describe TCAs, tetracyclics, and heterocyclic antidepressants. The currently available antidepressants in the United States are listed in Tables 6-7, 17-5, and 17-6).

Table 17-5 **Selected Antidepressant Drugs and Dosages**

CLASS/GENERIC NAME	TRADE NAME	USUAL DAILY MAXIMUM ORAL DOSE (mg)
Tertiary amine tricyclics		
Imipramine	Tofranil	300
	Tofranil PM	
	SK-Pramine	
	Janimine	
Amitriptyline	Elavil	300
	Endep	
Doxepin	Adapin	300
	Sinequan	
Trimipramine	Surmontil	200
Secondary amine tricyclics		
Desipramine	Norpramin	300
	Pertofrane	
Nortriptyline	Aventyl	150
	Pamelor	
Protriptyline	Vivactil	60
Tetracyclic		
Maprotiline	Ludiomil	200
Dibenzoxazepine		
Amoxapine	Asendin	400
Triazolopyridine		
Trazodone	Desyrel	600
Bicyclic		
Fluoxetine	Prozac	60
Unicyclic		
Bupropion	Wellbutrin	450

Table 17-6 **Selected Monoamine Oxidase Inhibitors Drugs and Dosages**

CLASS/GENERIC NAME	TRADE NAME	USUAL DAILY MAXIMUM ORAL DOSE (mg)
Hydrazines		
Phenelzine	Nardil	90
Isocarboxazid	Marplan	50
Nonhydrazines		
Tranylcypromine	Parnate	60
Pargyline	Eutonyl	150

(Adapted from Silver JM, Yudofsky SC: Psychopharmacology and electroconvulsive therapy. In Talbott JA, Hales RE, Yudofsky SC (eds): The American Psychiatric Press Textbook of Psychiatry, pp 707–854. Washington, DC, American Psychiatric Press, 1988)

Mechanisms of Action

Antidepressant drugs acutely affect the serotonergic and catecholaminergic systems in the central nervous system. The CyAD block the presynaptic reuptake of serotonin (5-HT) and/or norepinephrine (NE) and thereby increase the amount of these neurotransmitters available at the synapse. The MAOIs intensify mono-aminergic transmission by blocking the catabolism of several biogenic amines, including NE, 5-HT, tyramine, phenylephrine, and dopamine (DA).

These acute effects of antidepressants on neurotransmitters were translated into the catecholamine hypothesis of depression, which postulated that depression was caused by a relative deficiency of catecholaminergic neurotransmitters that was "corrected" by antidepressant drugs (see Chapter 6). Two major subtypes of depression were hypothesized to prevail. The first was characterized by a deficiency of norepinephrine. For this type of depression, the appropriate medication would be one with primary effects on reuptake inhibition of NE. For the second subtype, depression that was characterized by a lack of serotonin, an antidepressant that blocked the reuptake of 5-HT was advocated. The relative affinities of the CyAD on the inhibition of presynaptic reuptake of 5-HT or NE are listed in Table 6-7).

Monoamine oxidase (MAO), through oxidative deamination, inactivates biogenic amines such as norepinephrine, serotonin, dopamine, and tyramine. Monoamine oxidase inhibitors block this inactivation and thereby increase the amount of these transmitters available for synaptic release. Currently available MAOIs are either hydrazine or nonhydrazine derivatives. The hydrazine derivatives, isocarboxazid and phenelzine, are related to iproniazid. The nonhydrazine derivatives include tranylcypromine and the antihypertensive drug pargyline (Table 17-6). MAO must be regenerated before the activity of the enzyme is reestablished. In practical terms, this means that the effects (including risks of drug and food interaction) of the "irreversible" MAO inhibitors will last until sufficient MAO has been regenerated. For this reason, the clinician must wait 10 to 14 days after discontinuation of these drugs before instituting other antidepressants or permitting certain drugs or foods that may interact adversely with the MAOIs.

Indications and Efficacy

Although the antidepressant drugs have many potential therapeutic uses, the primary approved indication for these drugs is the treatment of depression that corresponds to the diagnosis of major depressive disorder, with or without melancholia, in the *Diagnostic and Statistical Manual of Mental Disorders (Third Edition-Revised) (DSM-III-R)* (American Psychiatric Association, 1987). Approximately 70 to 80% of depressed patients respond to an adequate trial of an antidepressant. Among the other disorders that may respond to antidepressants are panic disorder, obsessive–compulsive disorder, peptic ulcer disease, enuresis, chronic pain, migraine headaches, bulimia, and attention-deficit disorder.

Patients with depression that is characterized by the symptoms of oversleeping, overeating, mood reactivity, and prominent anxiety ("atypical depressions") may show a preferentially positive response to MAOIs. Monoamine oxidase inhibitors have even been suggested as the treatment of choice in this group of patients.

The role of lithium in the prevention and treatment of episodes of bipolar illness is discussed in detail in a later section. For patients with recurrent unipolar depressions, maintenance CyAD with and without lithium are effective in decreasing the chance of relapse.

Panic disorder responds to drugs from both the CyAD (imipramine, desipramine) and MAOI (phenelzine, tranylcypromine) families of antidepressants. The treatment of panic disorder is discussed in detail in Chapter 7.

Clinical Use of Antidepressants

The psychiatric history, current symptoms, physical examination, and mental status of patients with depressed mood are major factors in the choice of the appropriate therapeutic modality. Diagnostic factors that may influence the choice of antidepressant drug include a history of manic or hypomanic episodes, the presence of psychosis, the prior course of episodes of depression, and the presence of "atypical" symptoms.

A history of previous episodes of mania or hypomania should alert the clinician to the possible precipitation of these episodes with antidepressants. If hypomania occurs while the patient is on antidepressant therapy, a reduction in dosage should be attempted as a first effort to control these symptoms, or lithium alone should be used. Patients with bipolar disorders may experience more frequent mood cycling when treated chronically with CyAD. Precipitation of hypomania or mania in a depressed patient treated with CyAD or MAOI usually indicates that the patient has a bipolar affective disorder. Pretreatment with lithium in usual therapeutic doses before the administration of antidepressant drugs should be considered in depressed patients who have experienced previous manic episodes.

As noted, antidepressants have been shown to decrease the interval between affective episodes and increase "cycling" in bipolar patients. For bipolar patients who develop mixed manic-depressive states or increased cycling on antidepressants, lithium or carbamazepine should be started, and the antidepressant drug should be gradually tapered. This effect should also be considered in unipolar depressed patients. Because of the demonstrated efficacy of lithium in the prevention of relapse in unipolar and bipolar patients (see section on lithium), the use of lithium should be considered in patients in whom the interval between episodes has been decreasing.

Patients with delusional (psychotic) depression respond poorly to treatment when antidepressant medications are used as the sole agent. Patients with delusional depression respond better to combined treatment of antidepressants *and* antipsychotics than to either alone but generally show the best response to electroconvulsive therapy.

Psychotherapy is vitally important in the treatment of patients with depression. Studies have demonstrated that the response to the combination of psychotherapy and medication is superior to that of either treatment as the sole modality (Conte, et al., 1986).

Treatment of depressed patients with pharmacologic agents must be guided by scientific principles that are tailored to the needs of individual patients. This requires guidelines for initiation of therapy (see Table 17-7) in addition to an overall treatment

Table 17–7 **Guidelines for Use of Cyclic Antidepressant (CyAD) Drugs***

1. Complete a thorough medical evaluation, especially with regard to cardiovascular and thyroid status.
2. Select drug on the basis of side-effect profile (stimulating effect, sedating effect, anticholinergic effect, and cardiovascular effect) and history of previous response.
3. Inform the patient and family of risks and benefits. Emphasize the expected 2–3-week "delay" in therapeutic response and anticipated side effects and their management.
4. Initiate and increase dose of CyAD slowly (e.g., for imipramine, start at 25 mg qHs and increase by 25 mg every third day). Fluoxetine is usually given in the morning at 20 mg/day and if necessary can be increased to 40–60 mg/day.
5. Increase dosage until dose equivalent of 150–200 mg imipramine is reached. Stabilize at that dose for 1 week. Trazodone and amoxapine have higher therapeutic dose ranges (200–600 mg/day). Fluoxetine (20–40 mg/day) and protriptyline (10–40 mg/day) have a lower therapeutic range.
6. If there is no significant therapeutic effect after 2 weeks, slowly increase dosage to maximum recommended dose.
7. If there is no significant improvement after 14–21 days, obtain plasma level (if appropriate) and electrocardiogram, and adjust dose as needed (e.g., increase by 50 mg per week). An electrocardiogram should be obtained before each dose increase in patients with severe heart disease. Serum levels stabilize on a given dose after 7–10 days. Therapeutic serum levels are best established for imipramine, desipramine, and nortriptyline.
8. A therapeutic trial is defined as a 6-week treatment with antidepressant, with at least three weeks with a therapeutic serum level. Then consider an MAOI after a washout period or go to ECT immediately. Reevaluate diagnosis.
9. Elderly and medically ill patients may require lower dose ranges than those noted above.
10. Most of the currently available CyAD can be given once a day at bedtime; fluoxetine and protriptyline should be given early in the day. Bupropion requires multiple daily doses.

* Note special exemptions *especially for fluoxetine.*
MAOI, Monoamine oxidase inhibitor; ECT, electroconvulsive therapy.
Adapted from Silver JM, Yudofsky SC: Psychopharmacology and electroconvulsive therapy. In Talbott JA, Hales RE, Yudofsky SC (eds): The American Psychiatric Press Textbook of Psychiatry, pp 707–854. Washington, DC, American Psychiatric Press, 1988)

---

strategy. As with the antipsychotic drugs, the choice of which CyAD to use is often dependent on the side effect profile of the drug. In general, drugs with more potent effects on inhibiting norepinephrine reuptake are more stimulating. Thus, desipramine may be poorly tolerated in agitated, depressed patients. Drugs with marked antihistaminic effects and predominantly serotonergic effects (amitriptyline, doxepin, trazodone) are sedating. This effect may be advantageous in patients with marked initial insomnia but undesirable in patients with psychomotor retardation. Fluoxetine has no anticholinergic effects and does not cause weight gain, a troublesome side effect of many other antidepressants, but can cause insomnia.

The initial therapeutic response of the depressed patient to medications may be detected as early as the first week with the patient showing improvement in sleep and energy. Mood, however, may not respond for 1 to 2 weeks after medication has been initiated. Of crucial importance is the fact that the patient may have a return of energy while still experiencing the hopelessness that characterizes the depression. Thus, the patient may be at an increased risk of suicide at this time, for he or she may regain energy requisite for the completion of a suicidal act that was not present before treatment.

A complete trial of antidepressant medication consists of treatment with therapeutic doses of a drug for a total of 6 weeks before concluding that the depression is refractory to standard pharmacotherapy. Once the patient's depressive symptoms have resolved, the dose of the antidepressant and the length of time necessary for continuance on the medication must be determined. Results from a National Institutes of Mental Health (NIMH) collaborative study indicate that antidepressant therapy should not be withdrawn before there have been 4 to 5 symptom-free months (Prien, Kupfer, 1986). After the maintenance phase of treatment, antidepressants should be gradually tapered over several months and discontinued.

For patients who have not responded to an adequate trial of one particular antidepressant, several strategies may be taken in choosing a drug for a subsequent trial. If the patient did not respond to a CyAD of the "noradrenergic" type (e.g., desipramine), one that is more serotonergic may be tried, although there is no evidence to suggest that switching from one CyAD to another has any real benefit other than adjustment in side effect profiles. In some patients who have shown an incomplete response to a single antidepressant, the addition of lithium has resulted in prompt and dramatic alleviation of the depressive symptoms. Thyroid hormone supplementation with T_3 preparations also has been reported to possibly potentiate antidepressant effects in tricyclic nonresponders.

Despite concerns over severe reactions that may occur with concomitant treatment with CyAD and MAOIs, the combination may be safely prescribed, provided specific precautions are taken, such as starting the medications together and ensuring that frequent, daily BP monitoring takes place during the "loading" phase of treatment. *Please note that it is extremely hazardous to add the CyAD to established MAOI treatment.*

Risks, Side Effects, and Their Management

The side effect profile of a specific antidepressant drug in large part determines the selection of a particular drug for an individual patient. In addition, patients have varying reactions to side effects when they occur. For example, for some patients, the almost omnipresent anticholinergic effects (i.e., dry mouth, blurred vision) of most CyAD are intolerable, while other patients note the presence of these side effects without complaint.

The antidepressant drugs vary greatly in their relative potential to produce anticholinergic side effects (see Table 6-7). Because of the anticholinergic effects, patients with prostatic hypertrophy and narrow angle glaucoma must be treated with caution. The precautions and evaluations of these complications are outlined in the section on antipsychotic drugs. Trazodone has anticholinergic effects only in higher doses, and fluoxetine is almost devoid of such effects.

Trazodone, trimipramine, amitriptyline, and doxepin are most sedating. If this property is adversely experienced by the patient, a less sedating antidepressant should be prescribed (e.g., desipramine or protriptyline). Fluoxetine has a generally activating effect and should be given in the morning.

Orthostatic hypotension is the cardiovascular side effect that most commonly results in serious morbidity, especially in the elderly and in patients with congestive heart failure. The symptoms of orthostatic hypotension usually consist of dizziness or lightheadedness when the patient changes from a lying to sitting or sitting to standing position. Although orthostatic hypotension may occur from any CyAD (especially the tertiary CyAD), nortriptyline has been found to cause less orthostatic hypotension than imipramine. Fluoxetine also probably has major advantages in this regard. The MAOIs also may cause significant hypotension.

Carefully controlled studies have demonstrated that some CyAD, with the possible exception of trazodone, are potent antiarrhythmic agents and possess quinidinelike properties. Even trazodone has been reported to cause heart block as an idiosyncratic effect in a few patients. The effects of the CyAD on the cardiac conduction system are of great clinical importance. Because prolongation of the PR and QRS intervals can occur with CyAD use, these drugs should not be used in patients with preexisting heart block, such as second-degree heart block, or markedly prolonged QRS and QT intervals. In such patients, CyAD can lead to second-degree or third-degree heart block—a life-threatening condition. Patients with relatively focal, benign, and stable right bundle and left bundle branch blocks may at times be treated with CyAD after clearance by cardiology and dosing initiated in the inpatient setting with frequent cardiac monitoring.

Sexual dysfunctions associated with CyAD antidepressants include impotence, ejaculatory dysfunction, and decreased interest and enjoyment of sexual activities for both men and women. Trazodone is the only antidepressant that has been associated with priapism, which may be irreversible and require surgical intervention. Sexual dysfunction is a common occurrence in patients treated with MAOIs and most frequently includes anorgasmia and impotence.

Patients treated with CyAD may experience an undesirable weight gain. This does not appear to relate to improvement of mood, as changes in weight and appetite are not correlated to response to treatment. Treatment of depressed patients with fluoxetine may actually be associated with weight loss.

As with most drugs, allergic and hypersensitivity reactions may occur with antidepressants but are extremely rare and may be connected to those pill forms that contain yellow dye with tartrazine. For more serious skin eruptions, the drug should be discontinued, preferably over several days to reduce the possibility of antidepressant withdrawal symptoms.

Tremor is a common side effect of antidepressants, such as imipramine and desipramine, that affect predominantly the noradrenergic system. Dose reduction or changing the type of antidepressant may ultimately be required to alleviate the tremor.

The potential of antidepressants to induce seizures is difficult to assess. Maprotiline has been associated with seizures in both therapeutic and toxic doses, especially at doses above 200 mg/day. Amoxapine and desipramine may have a higher risk of seizures after overdosage than other antidepressant drugs. Amoxapine has dopamine-blocking activity and may cause extrapyramidal symptoms and rarely even tardive dyskinesia with chronic treatment.

Because the incidence of suicide and suicide attempts is high in depressed patients, deliberate overdosage with antidepressant drugs is a common occurrence. As many as 10,000 cases of antidepressant overdoses each year are attributed to suicide attempts. It is unfortunate that a population that is at high risk for suicide is trusted with drugs that have a low LD_{50}—a relatively low ceiling for toxic doses. For patients at high suicide risk, clinicians should consider giving only a week's supply of antidepressants.

The major complications from overdose with CyAD drugs include those that arise from neuropsychiatric impairment, hypotension, cardiac arrhythmias, and seizures. Because most antidepressants have significant anticholinergic activity, anticholinergic delirium often occurs when the CyAD are taken in high doses. Other complications of anticholinergic overdose include agitation, supraventricular arrhythmias, heart block, hallucinations, severe hypertension, and seizures. These drugs also lower the seizure threshold and can result in prolonged seizures.

Because the CyAD are metabolized by the liver, drugs that induce hepatic microsomal enzymes will result in a decrease in plasma levels of the antidepressant drugs. These agents include alcohol, anticonvulsants, barbiturates, chloral hydrate, glutethimide, oral contraceptives, and cigarette smoking. Antipsychotic drugs, methylphenidate, and increasing age are associated with increased plasma levels of CyAD.

Most clinical concern regarding the use of the MAOIs stems from the reaction that occurs when ingested tyramine is not metabolized because of the MAOI inactivation of intestinal monoamine oxidase. This reaction has been called the "cheese reaction" because tyramine is present in relatively high concentrations in aged cheese. Tyramine may act as a false transmitter and displace norepinephrine from presynaptic storage granules.

Patients receiving MAOI treatment should be instructed to avoid cheeses (except cottage cheese and cream cheese), alcohol (except clear spirits and white wine), yeast extract, broad beans, smoked or pickled fish, beef or chicken liver, fermented sausage, and stewed bananas (Folks, 1983). In addition, certain general anesthetics and drugs that have sympathomimetic activity—including certain decongestant sympathomimetics such as phenylpropanolamine—should not be taken while a patient is being treated with an MAOI. Ephedrine and pseudoephedrine may be constituents of "over-the-counter" drugs. Local anesthetics that contain epinephrine must not be used. Appetite suppressants must be avoided. Synthetic and natural opioids should be used with caution. Meperidine (Demerol) must be absolutely avoided because of a potentially catastrophic lethal interaction with MAOIs.

The tyramine reaction can range from mild to severe. In the most mild form, the patient may complain of sweating, palpitations, and a mild headache. The most severe form manifests as a hypertensive crisis, with severe headache, increases in blood pressure, and possible intracerebral hemorrhage. The severity of this reaction cannot be predicted by MAOI dose, food type or amount ingested, or even prior history of a crisis. For example, a patient may ingest cheese without any reaction at one time but may have a life-threatening hypertensive crisis on a subsequent occasion when he combines the same amount of cheese with the same dose of MAOI. For this reason, patients should be carefully instructed not only about prevention but also about not gaining false confidence if dietary guidelines are broken without immediate consequences.

There is no adequate published study that establishes the optimum treatment of this reaction. Treatment strategies have relied on clinical experience and published case reports. If patients on MAOIs experience a severe or even moderately painful occipital headache, they should immediately seek medical assessment, which will include having their blood pressure monitored. If the blood pressure is severely elevated, a drug with alpha-adrenergic blocking properties, such as intravenous phentolamine (Regitine) 5 mg or intramuscular chlorpromazine 25 to 50 mg, may be administered. Because treatment with phentolamine may be associated with cardiac arrhythmias or severe hypotension, however, this should be done only in an emergency room setting by qualified medical personnel with proper monitoring equipment. It is advisable to have patients on MAOIs carry an identification card or Medic Alert bracelet as notification to emergency medical personnel that the patient is currently taking MAOIs. Patients should always carry lists of prohibited foods and medications and should be told to notify physicians that they are taking an MAOI before accepting a medication or anesthetic. A frequently encountered situation is when the patient has dental procedures performed. In this instance, local anesthetics must be used without vasoconstrictors (e.g., epinephrine). Carrying supplies of nifedipine to take in case of emergency (10 mg sublingually) has also been recommended. Practical details of treating patients with CyAD and MAOIs are also discussed in Chapter 6.

ANXIOLYTICS, SEDATIVES, AND HYPNOTICS

Anxiety disorders are the most frequently diagnosed psychiatric illnesses in the general population, with a 6-month prevalence rate approaching 16% (Reich, 1986) (see also Chapter 7). Approximately one third of the population suffers from insomnia during the course of a year, and 4% of adults use a medically prescribed drug to produce sleep (Mellinger, Balter, Uhlenhuth, 1985).

Given these figures, it is to be expected that drugs that produce sedation and reduce anxiety historically have been the most widely used drugs. The commonly used anxiolytics and hypnotics and usual dosages are shown in Table 17-8.

Mechanisms of Action

The existence of benzodiazepine receptor-binding sites has been confirmed by positron emission tomography (PET) using radiolabeled benzodiazepines. These receptors are intimately linked with the receptor for gamma-aminobutyric acid (GABA), the major inhibitory neurotransmitter in the brain. Administration of GABA results in an opening of chloride channels and a decrease in neuronal activity.

The mechanism of action of buspirone, a non-benzodiazepine anxiolytic, remains unclear. The drug has effects on many systems, especially the serotonergic and dopaminergic systems. Few of these actions are similar to those of the benzodiazepines, and cross-tolerance does not exist between buspirone and the benzodiazepines.

Table 17-8 **Selected Anxiolytic Drugs: Dosages and Half-Lives**

CLASS/GENERIC NAME	TRADE NAME	USUAL DAILY DOSE (mg)	APPROXIMATE ELIMINATION T½ INCLUDING METABOLITES
Benzodiazepine anxiolytics			
Alprazolam	Xanax	0.75–1.5, generalized anxiety disorder 2–6, panic disorder	12 hours
Chlordiazepoxide hydrochloride	Librium Libritabs	15–100	1–4 days
Clorazepate dipotassium	Tranxene	15–60	2–4 days
Clonazepam	Klonopin	1–4	1–2 days
Diazepam	Valium Valrelease	4–40 15–45	2–4 days
Halazepam	Paxipam	40–160	2–4 days
Lorazepam	Ativan	2–6	12 hours
Benzodiazepine hypnotics			
Oxazepam	Serax	30–120	12 hours
Prazepam	Centrax	20–60	2–4 days
Flurazepam hydrochloride	Dalmane	30	3 days
Temazepam	Restoril	30	12 hours
Triazolam	Halcion	0.125–0.25	4–6 hours
Barbiturates			
Phenobartibal		30–120	2–4 days
Amobarbital	Amytal	50–300	1–2 days
Secobarbital	Seconal	100–200	1–2 days
Nonbenzodiazepines/nonbarbiturates			
Hydroxyzine hydrochloride	Atarax	75–400	Less than 4 hours
hydroxyzine pamoate	Vistaril	200–400	
Diphenhydramine*	Benadryl	25–50	
Chloral hydrate		750 (sedation) 500–1000 (hypnotic)	Less than 12 hours
Azapirone			
Buspirone	Buspar	15–60	2–7 hours

*Diphenhydramine, while an antihistamine, is also a hypnotic and has strong anticholinergic properties.
(Adapted from Silver JM, Yudofsky SC: Psychopharmacology and electroconvulsive therapy. In Talbott JA, Hales RE, Yudofsky SC (eds): The American Psychiatric Press Textbook of Psychiatry, pp 707–854. Washington, DC, American Psychiatric Press, 1988)

Indications and Efficacy

Benzodiazepines

The efficacy of the benzodiazepines in the treatment of anxiety, including symptoms of worry, psychic anxiety, and somatic symptoms (gastrointestinal and cardiovascular), has been clearly and repeatedly demonstrated in many well-controlled studies.

Benzodiazepines have been shown effective in the treatment of panic attacks. These include alprazolam (Xanax), diazepam (Valium), lorazepam (Ativan), and clonazepam (Klonopin). Some clinicians have raised concerns about the development of dependency on these drugs when used in the long-term treatment of panic disorder.

Although only a few benzodiazepines have specific FDA-approved indications for the treatment of insomnia, almost all benzodiazepines may be used for this purpose. The three benzodiazepines most commonly used as hypnotics are flurazepam (Dalmane), temazepam (Restoril), and triazolam (Halcion). Each has different pharmacodynamic and pharmacokinetic profiles that importantly influence clinical application.

Buspirone

Double-blind, controlled studies have shown that buspirone is efficacious in the treatment of anxiety, and its efficacy is not statistically different from that of the benzodiazepines. It is reported that buspirone, unlike the previously available anxiolytics, is not sedating, has no dangerous interactions with alcohol, has a low dependence liability, and does not impair psychomotor performance.

Clinical Use of Anxiolytic and Sedative Drugs

Pharmacotherapy of Generalized Anxiety Disorder

The first step in the treatment of a patient with anxiety is a thorough medical, neurological, and psychiatric evaluation. Many patients with the symptoms of generalized anxiety disorder either have or have had panic disorder. The presence of panic attacks changes the focus of treatment. Medications should be considered as only one component in the treatment of anxiety. Psychotherapy is required to help the patient understand and control the circumstances that surround the anxiety. For most patients, anxiolytic medications are indicated only for relatively short-term use (i.e., 1 to 2 months), although some patients may require more prolonged treatment. The benzodiazepines generally are contraindicated in patients with sleep apnea and patients with a history of alcohol and drug abuse.

Because benzodiazepines frequently cause sedation, may impair performance on tasks that require a high degree of mental alertness, and may lead to dependence, this class of drugs should be used for as brief a period of time as possible in the lowest effective dose (see Table 17-9).

Several clinically important facets of the anxiolytic response to buspirone differentiate it from the benzodiazepines. Buspirone does not interact with other sedating drugs (including alcohol), does not seem to impair mechanical performance such as driving, and is not associated with dependence, tolerance, or withdrawal. It also does not have muscle relaxant or anticonvulsant properties, as do the benzodiazepines. Studies suggest that response to buspirone occurs in approximately 2 weeks, as compared with the more rapid onset associated with benzodiazepines.

Pharmacotherapy of Panic Disorder

Many patients who have the symptoms of generalized anxiety disorder either currently have or have had a history of panic disorder. Anxiety may develop in response to frequent spontaneous panic attacks, termed "anticipatory anxiety." Breier, Charney, and Heninger (1986) have reported that over 80% of patients with

Table 17–9 **Guidelines for Anxiolytic Treatment with Benzodiazepines**

1. Complete a thorough medical evaluation, especially with regard to thyroid status, caffeine intake, and current medications. Include a thorough evaluation of drug and alcohol history. Patients with sleep apnea should not receive benzodiazepines.
2. Evaluate patient for psychodynamic and social factors that may contribute to or precipitate anxiety.
3. Initiate benzodiazepines at a low dose (e.g., diazepam 2 mg three times a day) and increase every few days until sedation or therapeutic effect is obtained (up to 15 mg three times a day).
4. Caution patient on sedative properties, performance impairment, dependence properties, and drug and alcohol interactions.
5. Set guidelines for duration of expected treatment clearly to the patient in advance.
6. Reevaluate need for medication every month. Avoid refills by telephone.
7. Taper medication as soon as possible, by approximately 10 percent per week for patients on long-term treatment (greater than 3 months).
8. In patients with chronic anxiety or prone to anxiety and requesting or needing chronic therapy, obtain a psychiatric consultation.

(Adapted from Silver JM, Yudofsky SC: Psychopharmacology and electroconvulsive therapy. In Talbott JA, Hales RE, Yudofsky SC (eds): The American Psychiatric Press Textbook of Psychiatry, pp 707–854. Washington, DC, American Psychiatric Press, 1988)

panic disorder or agoraphobia with panic attacks have anticipatory or generalized anxiety that is responsive to treatment with benzodiazepines.

Drugs from several families of psychotropic medications may be used in the treatment of panic disorder. The benzodiazepines, specifically alprazolam and clonazepam, have been shown effective. These medications should be initiated at relatively low doses (e.g., alprazolam 0.25 mg t.i.d. or clonazepam 0.5 mg b.i.d.) and increased gradually over 1 to 2 weeks. After successful treatment of panic disorder with alprazolam, withdrawal and discontinuation of medication are difficult because of increased panic attacks and occurrence of withdrawal symptoms, including malaise, weakness, insomnia, tachycardia, lightheadedness, and dizziness. Discontinuation of these medications should be extremely slow (10% per 1 week).

Because panic disorder usually requires a prolonged period for successful treatment, benzodiazepines may be associated with an increased risk of dependence. Therefore, we recommend the use of antidepressants be considered as the initial treatment of panic disorder. For most patients, imipramine, desipramine, or nortriptyline should prove effective. A decision as to which of these drugs to choose should be based on the same factors discussed in the section on antidepressant drugs. Monoamine oxidase inhibitors are usually reserved for patients who have not responded to CyAD, although they may be used as a primary treatment. The doses, durations, and side effects of antidepressants used for the treatment of panic disorder parallel those described in the previous section for the treatment of depression.

Patients with panic disorder are exceedingly sensitive to a temporary exacerbation or worsening of symptoms in the first weeks of treatment with CyAD. Therefore, doses should be started very low and increased in lower increments. The treatment of panic and other anxiety disorders is discussed in detail in Chapter 7.

Pharmacotherapy of Insomnia

A complete medical, sleep, and psychiatric history is required before administration of drugs to produce sleep. There are multiple causes for insomnia, and the differential diagnosis of sleep disorders must be considered before the prescribing of any hypnotic. Among the common disorders associated with insomnia are depression, psychoses, anxiety, central nervous system disorders, and other medical illnesses associated with pain and discomfort. Stimulants (including caffeine) as well as alcohol may lead to insomnia.

The individual hypnotic benzodiazepines have varying pharmacodynamic and pharmacokinetic profiles that importantly influence their use in clinical practice. For example, flurazepam is rapidly absorbed and metabolized into compounds with a half-life as long as several days and may result in daytime sedation. Triazolam is a benzodiazepine hypnotic with an intermediate rate of absorption and a very short half-life (1.5 to 5 hours). The rapid elimination of this drug may lead to early-morning awakening, rebound insomnia, dissociative reactions, and anterograde amnesia. More detailed discussion of the evaluation of insomnia, including sleep hygiene assessment, is discussed in Chapter 21.

Pharmacotherapy of Obsessive–Compulsive Disorder

It appears that the usual antidepressants and anxiolytics are not generally effective in the treatment of obsessive–compulsive disorder. A new antidepressant, fluoxetine, which is a specific serotonin reuptake inhibitor, has been reported to be effective in the treatment of obsessive–compulsive disorder in higher doses (60-80 mg/day). Clomipramine has been extensively studied in the treatment of this disorder and is significantly beneficial when standard therapies have been ineffective. At the time of this writing it can be obtained only through the manufacturer (Ciba-Geigy) under a physician-sponsored investigational new drug (IND) application (see also Chapter 7).

Risks and Side Effects of Anxiolytic and Hypnotic Drugs

The production of sedation by benzodiazepines may be considered either a therapeutic action or a side effect. Hypnotics are expected and required to produce sedation to be efficacious. However, when the patient complains of sleepiness the following day, this therapeutic action becomes a side effect.

Physical dependence may occur when benzodiazepines are taken in dosages higher than usual or for prolonged periods of time. If precipitously discontinued, severe withdrawal symptoms (hyperpyrexia, seizures, psychosis, and death) may occur. Other symptoms of withdrawal may include tachycardia, increased blood pressure, muscle cramps, anxiety, insomnia, panic attacks, impairment of memory and concentration, and perceptual disturbances. These withdrawal symptoms may begin as soon as the day after discontinuing benzodiazepines and may continue for weeks to months.

As a general principle for all drugs, discontinuation should be accomplished gradually. For patients treated with benzodiazepines for longer than 2 to 3 months, we suggest that the dose be decreased by approximately 5 to 10% a week. Thus, for a patient receiving 4 mg/day of alprazolam, the dose should be tapered by 0.25 mg per week for 16 weeks. The last few dosage levels may be the most difficult to discontinue, and the patient will require increased attention and support from the physician at this time. Clonazepam may be substituted for alprazolam to assist with the discontinuation process. Since clonazepam has a prolonged half-life, tapering can be accomplished with less rebound anxiety than occurs with alprazolam withdrawal.

Buspirone, when administered to subjects who had histories of recreational sedative abuse, showed no abuse potential. Buspirone has a relatively low abuse potential.

Overdose

Benzodiazepines are remarkably safe when taken in overdose. Dangerous effects occur when the overdose includes several sedative drugs, especially alcohol. As with most medications, use of anxiolytics during pregnancy or when breastfeeding should be avoided whenever possible.

Drug Interactions

Most sedative drugs, including narcotics and alcohol, potentiate sedation from benzodiazepines. Cimetidine, oral contraceptives, acute alcohol intake, propranolol, and disulfiram inhibit the hepatic metabolism and increase the elimination half-life of benzodiazepines that are metabolized by oxidation, which include diazepam and chlordiazepoxide. However, benzodiazepines such as lorazepam, oxazepam, and temazepam are metabolized by glucuronide conjugation, and therefore their half-life is not affected by liver disease, aging, and medication, all of which affect oxidative capacities in the liver associated with the drugs just cited. Buspirone does *not* appear to interact with alcohol to increase sedation and motor impairment.

Barbiturates

The use of barbiturates for the treatment of anxiety (and insomnia) has been largely supplanted by the much safer benzodiazepines. With barbiturates, potentially fatal respiratory depression can occur at only several times the standard therapeutic dosages. Barbiturates are potent inducers of hepatic microsomal enzymes and therefore interact with many other drugs that are metabolized in the liver.

The clinical use of barbiturates is determined by their respective onsets of action and half-lives. The ultra-short barbiturates thiopental (Pentothal) and methohexital (Brevital) are used primarily as intravenous agents for the induction of general anesthesia. Amobarbital (Amytal), pentobarbital (Nembutal), and secobarbital (Seconal) have been used as sedative agents. Amobarbital is also valuable for the acute management of agitated patients when administered parenterally in doses of approximately 250 mg. Phenobarbital, a long-acting barbiturate, may be used as an anxiolytic agent, although tolerance to this effect occurs after several weeks. The principal clinical application of phenobarbital is as an anticonvulsant drug.

Alcohol Detoxification

Because of the cross-tolerance of benzodiazepines and alcohol, the benzodiazepines are used frequently for the treatment of alcohol withdrawal and detoxification. A relatively simple procedure for treating alcohol withdrawal is the benzodiazepine loading dose technique. This technique takes advantage of the long half-life of benzodiazepines such as diazepam and chlordiazepoxide. Unit doses of 20 mg diazepam (or 100 mg chlordiazepoxide) are administered hourly to patients until there are no signs or symptoms of alcohol withdrawal. Thereafter, no further doses of benzodiazepines are administered. Because of the long half-lives of benzodiazepines, the therapeutic plasma level of the benzodiazepine is maintained during the period of risk for alcohol withdrawal symptoms (see also Chapters 9 and 18).

ANTIMANIC DRUGS

Clinical investigations have conclusively demonstrated that lithium is effective in the prophylaxis of recurrent mood (affective) disorders. For the patient with acute mania, treatment with antipsychotic drugs and electroconvulsive therapy is efficacious. In fact, these treatments elicit responses more rapidly than does lithium carbonate, and they are often administered while awaiting the therapeutic response to lithium. Other classes of drugs with different chemical structures and with apparently different mechanisms of actions have been reported to be effective in the prophylaxis and treatment of mania. Among these are the anticonvulsant drugs carbamazepine (Tegretol) and valproic acid (Depakote), the calcium channel-blocking drug verapamil (Calan and Isoptin), the alpha-adrenergic agonist clonidine (Catapres), the benzodiazepine anticonvulsant clonazepam (Klonopin), and the beta-adrenergic receptor-blocking drug propranolol (Inderal). In this section we will review the clinical use of lithium and carbamazepine for which the efficacy in bipolar disorder is well established (Table 17-10). The other drugs mentioned above are not routinely used to treat bipolar illness and their efficacy is not well established.

Table 17-10 **Amtimanic Drugs**

CLASS/GENERIC NAME	TRADE NAME	USUAL DOSE RANGE (mg/day)
Lithium		
Lithium carbonate	Eskalith	600–1800
	Lithane	
	Lithonate	
	Lithotabs	
Time-release	Lilthobid	
	Eskalith CR	
Lithium citrate (syrup)	Cibalith-S	
Carbamazepine	Tegretol	800–1200

Lithium

Mechanism of Action

Despite extensive investigations, the precise mechanism of action of lithium remains unknown, but it may reduce the sensitivity of neurotransmitter receptors (including dopamine, acetylcholine, serotonin, and opiates) as well as reduce receptor density of multiple transmitter systems. The antidepressant efficacy of lithium is most likely due to its ability to enhance serotonergic activity. Antimanic effects may result from effects in super-sensitive, dopaminergic receptors or muscarinic–cholinergic enhancing action.

Indications and Efficacy

Lithium, usually administered as the carbonate salt, has been shown efficacious in the treatment of many of the mood disorders. Acute manic episodes respond to treatment with lithium within 7 to 10 days. Because manic episodes have so great a potential for psychosocial disruption, behavioral control is usually desired before lithium becomes effective. Supplemental medication (most often antipsychotic drugs), therefore, is administered on an acute basis. Lithium has been proved effective and is the drug of choice for preventing both manic and depressive episodes in patients with bipolar disorder (Consensus Development Panel, 1985). Patients with less severe bipolar illness, such as cyclothymia or bipolar II disorder (patients with episodes of major depression punctuated by periods of hypomania), may also exhibit improvement with lithium therapy.

Lithium may be effective in the prevention of future depressive episodes in those patients with recurrent unipolar depressive disorder (Consensus Development Panel, 1985) and as an adjunct to antidepressants in patients partially refractory to treatment with antidepressants alone (discussed in the section on antidepressants). Finally, lithium may be useful in the maintenance of remission of depression after electroconvulsive therapy.

Clinical Use

Before the initiation of treatment, patients should be informed of side effects that occur commonly with lithium treatment, which include nausea, diarrhea, polyuria, polydipsia, thirst, fine hand tremor, and fatigue. These may be transient or, in some patients, may persist with therapeutic lithium levels.

Because of the narrow range between the therapeutic and toxic doses of lithium, the optimum dose for an individual patient cannot be based on the dosage administered but rather should be based on the concentration of lithium in the plasma. Thus, appropriate use of lithium requires familiarity with its pharmacokinetics. Lithium is completely absorbed by the gastrointestinal tract and reaches peak plasma levels in 1 to 2 hours. The elimination half-life is approximately 24 hours. Steady-state lithium levels are obtained in approximately 5 days.

Therapeutic plasma levels for patients on lithium therapy range from 0.5 to 1.5 mEq/liter. Most healthy patients may be conservatively started on a 300 mg b.i.d. dosage of lithium, and this dose may be increased by 300 mg every 3 to 4 days. Larger "loading" doses may be used in acute manic states (e.g. 1200 mg/day in divided doses).

Elderly patients are extremely sensitive to the neurotoxic side effects of lithium and generally should be treated with doses of lithium that produce serum levels at the lower end of the therapeutic range. In the healthy patient with no renal function impairment, plasma level determinations are obtained biweekly. Since steady-state plasma levels are not obtained until the patient has been on a constant dose regimen for at least 5 days, this method may slightly underestimate the steady-state level. Lithium levels must consistently be obtained 12 hours after the last lithium dose. After therapeutic lithium levels have been established, levels should be monitored every month for the first 6 months and every 2 to 3 months thereafter.

The frequency of lithium dosing needs to be considered individually for each patient. Since lithium has a serum half-life of approximately 24 hours, the administration of lithium as a single daily dose is possible. For example, for the patient receiving a maintenance dose of lithium of 1200 mg/day, a dosing regimen of either 1200 mg once a day or 300 mg four times a day is theoretically possible. In addition, there are slow-release formulations available that maintain a higher plasma level throughout the day, while multiple doses with the usual carbonate salt will result in several peak levels throughout the day that rapidly decrease after ingestion of each dose. Both regimens are therapeutically effective and well tolerated by most patients. However, there are specific reasons for choosing differing dose regimens. The multiple-dose regimen will expose the kidney to four peak levels of intermediate concentration, while the single daily dosing regimen will expose the kidney to one higher peak dose. It has been suggested that nephrotoxicity (if indeed it occurs with lithium) is related to the duration of exposure to high lithium levels and not the absolute level of a single peak level. For this reason, single daily dosing with the usual formulation may be preferable. Gastric irritation may be associated with the duration of the peak plasma level, and lithium should always be taken on a full stomach (see Table 17-11).

Risks, Side Effects, and Their Management

Most of the effects of lithium on the kidney are reversible after discontinuation of the drug. Although permanent morphologic changes in renal structure have been reported, the exact clinical implications of these changes have yet to be established. Renal function tests are required before lithium therapy is initiated and at specified intervals throughout the course of treatment.

The most noticeable effect of lithium on renal function is the vasopressin-resistant impairment in the kidney's ability to concentrate urine. This is nephrogenic diabetes insipidus (NDI), and it may result in polyuria. A majority of patients on lithium therapy may complain of increased frequency of urination. Preventive and management strategies for NDI include decreasing the daily lithium dose and increasing liquid intake. Amiloride 5 mg b.i.d. has been suggested as a treatment for polyuria because of its effect on blunting the inhibitory effect of lithium on water transport in the renal collecting tubule (Battle, et al., 1985). This treatment was reported to be effective and did not increase lithium levels. Nevertheless, it is prudent to continue to monitor serum lithium levels when amiloride is combined with lithium.

Lithium nephropathy, characterized by tubular interstitial nephritis, has been reported as a consequence of long-term lithium therapy. Although mild decreases in the glomerular filtration rate (GFR) occur in some patients treated with lithium, there

Table 17–11 **Guidelines for Lithium Treatment**

1. Complete a thorough medical evaluation.
2. Complete appropriate medical laboratory evaluations.
3. Inform patient and family of proper use of lithium. Include common side effects, importance of monitoring lithium levels, exact procedures for accurate lithium monitoring, early signs and symptoms of toxicity, potential long-term side effects, and warnings regarding pregnancy during treatment (if patient is female).
4. Initiate therapy at 300 mg twice a day and increase by 300 mg every 3 to 4 days.
5. Obtain lithium levels (12 hours after last dose) twice a week, until lithium level is approximately 1.0 mEq/liter.
6. Treatment of acute manic symptoms may require concomitant therapy with antipsychotic medications.
7. Repeat lithium levels every month for the first 6 months, then every 2 to 3 months.

(Adapted from Silver JM, Yudofsky SC: Psychopharmacology and electroconvulsive therapy. In Talbott JA, Hales RE, Yudofsky SC (eds): The American Psychiatric Press Textbook of Psychiatry, pp 707–854. Washington, DC, American Psychiatric Press, 1988)

have been no published reports of irreversible renal failure as a result of chronic nontoxic lithium therapy.

In all patients treated with lithium, renal function tests should be monitored, but whether or not lithium has any nephrotoxic effects with long-term use is controversial. Preliminary laboratory evaluations include serum testing for blood urea nitrogen (BUN), creatinine, and electrolytes, and a urinalysis. Some conservative clinicians recommend a 24-hour collection of urine to measure the creatinine clearance. Impairment in concentrating urine may be assessed by the 12-hour fluid deprivation test, wherein the patient first refrains from drinking any fluid for 12 hours. After this time, a urine specimen is collected, and the urine osmolality is measured. A urine specific gravity of less than 1.010 may imply disordered kidney function and may indicate that further specific renal function studies are required.

Hypothyroidism may occur in as many as 20% of patients treated with lithium (Myers, et al., 1985). Many patients have an elevation of thyroid antibody titer during lithium treatment. Lithium-induced hypothyroidism may be unlikely in patients who do not have antithyroid antibodies present before treatment.

Initial laboratory tests include T3 RU (resin uptake), T4 RIA (radioimmunoassay), T4I (free thyroxine index), and thyroid-stimulating hormone (TSH). TSH is the most sensitive of these tests for detecting hypothyroidism. Because of the association between the presence of antithyroid antibodies and the subsequent development of hypothyroidism, antithyroid antibodies should also be measured before lithium treatment. Thyroid-stimulating hormone should be reassessed after every 6 months of lithium therapy. If laboratory tests indicate the development of hypothyroidism, the patient should be evaluated clinically for signs and symptoms of hypothyroidism and be referred to an endocrinologist for any further tests. In collaboration with the endocrinologist, the psychiatrist should decide on the appropriate treatment.

The effects of lithium on calcium metabolism may be related to rare reports of possible lithium-induced hyperparathyroidism. Hyperparathyroidism is associated with neuropsychiatric symptoms, which include mood changes, anxiety, psychosis, delirium, and dementia.

Lithium therapy may be associated with several types of neurologic dysfunction. Fine resting tremor is a neurologic side effect that may be detected in as many as one-half of patients in lithium treatment. Severe neurotoxic reactions occur with toxic lithium levels, and these symptoms include dysarthria, ataxia, and intention tremor, which also may occur with lithium levels in the "therapeutic range." Complaints of impairment of memory and concentration are relatively infrequent. Elderly patients are more sensitive to these reactions, and they occur at lower serum levels.

Mitchell and Mackenzie (1982) reported changes in T-wave morphology on the electrocardiogram (flattening or inversion) in 20 to 30% of patients on lithium. Before the initiation of treatment with lithium, all patients should have a complete cardiac evaluation, including history and physical examination pertinent to the cardiovascular system and an electrocardiogram in patients over 40 years old. Clinically significant cardiac side effects with lithium are extremely rare.

Weight gain is a frequent side effect of lithium treatment. Patients with polydipsia may drink fluids with a high caloric content, such as carbonated soft drinks, and thereby gain weight. Weight gain may also be a direct effect of lithium therapy. Possible mechanisms include influences on carbohydrate metabolism, changes in glucose tolerance, or changes in lipid metabolism.

The most frequent dermatologic reaction is skin rash, which is reported in up to 7% of lithium-treated patients. Hair loss and hair thinning have also been reported.

Gastrointestinal difficulties are frequent, especially nausea and diarrhea. While these symptoms may be manifestations of toxicity, they also occur at lithium levels within the therapeutic range. Gastrointestinal symptoms may improve with reducing the dose, changing to a slow-release formulation, or ingesting lithium with meals.

The most frequent hematologic abnormality detected in patients on lithium is leukocytosis (approximately 15,000 white blood cells per mm^3). This change is generally benign and may, in fact, be used to treat several conditions associated with depressed granulocytes. Lithium-induced leukocytosis is readily reversible with discontinuation of lithium therapy. Before initiation of therapy with lithium, a white blood cell count with differential should be obtained and should be repeated at yearly intervals thereafter.

Because of the narrow range between therapeutic and toxic plasma lithium levels, the psychiatrist must allow sufficient time to inform the patient and the family about the signs, symptoms, and treatment of lithium toxicity (see Table 17-12). The patient must be made aware of circumstances that may increase the chances of toxicity, such as drinking insufficient amounts of fluids, becoming overheated with increased perspiration, or ingesting too much medication. The psychiatrist must emphasize the prevention of lithium toxicity through the maintenance of adequate salt and water intake, especially during hot weather and exercise. The signs and symptoms of lithium toxicity can be divided into those which usually occur with lithium levels at 1.5–2.0 mEq/liter, 2.0–2.5 mEq/liter, and >2.5 mEq/liter; these are

Table 17–12 **Signs and Symptoms of Lithium Toxicity**

Mild to moderate intoxication (lithium level 1.5–2.0 mEq/liter)

Gastrointestinal
  Vomiting
  Abdominal pain
  Dryness of mouth
Neurological
  Ataxia
  Dizziness
  Slurred speech
  Nystagmus
  Lethargy or excitement
  Muscle weakness

Moderate to severe intoxication (lithium level 2.0–2.5 mEq/liter)

Gastrointestinal
  Anorexia
  Persistent nausea and vomiting
Neurological
  Blurred vision
  Muscle fasciculations
  Clonic limb movements
  Hyperactive deep tendon reflexes
  Choreoathetoid movements
  Convulsions
  Delirium
  Syncope
  Electroencephalographic changes
  Stupor
  Coma
  Circulatory failure (lowered blood pressure, cardiac arrhythmias, and
    conduction abnormalities)

Severe lithium intoxication (lithium level >2.5 mEq/liter)

Generalized convulsions
Oliguria and renal failure
Death

listed in Table 17-12. The drug should *not* be given to women who are pregnant or who are likely to become pregnant, due to toxic fetal effects.

Drug Interactions

Diuretics increase lithium levels and should be used with caution when treating lithium-induced diabetes insipidus. Specific nonsteroidal antiinflammatory drugs (NSAIDs) such as indomethacin also can increase the plasma lithium level. Theophylline will increase renal clearance and result in a lower lithium level.

Lithium has been reported to increase the intracellular levels of some antipsychotic drugs and may aggravate the inherent neurotoxicity of these agents as well. Thiazide diuretics raise lithium levels if used warrants close monitoring of lithium levels. Furosemide and spironolactone appear to affect lithium levels minimally.

Carbamazepine

Evidence from controlled studies indicates that carbamazepine is effective in both the acute treatment and the prophylactic treatment of mania in some patients with bipolar disorder. These findings have largely been confirmed in bipolar patients unresponsive to lithium or in bipolar patients unable to tolerate lithium-induced side effects (Post, et al., 1984). Also, patients with frequent recurrences (including rapid cycling bipolar patients) may respond more favorably to carbamazepine.

Mechanism of Action

Carbamazepine has multiple effects on the central nervous system that may have a role in the treatment of psychiatric disorders. Of particular interest is the effect of carbamazepine on "limbic kindling" and the hypothesis that this mechanism relates to the pathophysiology of affective disorders. In the process of kindling, repetitive stimuli eventually may lead to either a behavioral or convulsive response. Carbamazepine has been shown to inhibit the development of this response.

Clinical Use

Carbamazepine should be initiated at a dosage of 200 mg twice a day. Dose increments of 200 mg/day every 5 to 7 days should be made until a plasma level of 4 to 12 μg/ml is obtained. Too-rapid increases in dose may lead to dizziness, ataxia, and other adverse reactions. Although the maximum recommended dosage of carbamazepine by the manufacturer is 1200 mg/day, some investigators have administered higher dosages for the treatment of mania. Treatment principles for the use of carbamazepine are listed in Table 17-13.

Risks, Side Effects, and Their Management

The most serious toxic hematologic side effects of carbamazepine are aplastic anemia, with a prevalence rate of less than 1/50,000 (Hart, Easton, 1982), and

Table 17–13 Evaluation and Monitoring of Carbamazepine Treatment

1. Complete medical evaluation (see numbers 7 and 8).
2. Inform patient and family of potential side effects of treatment and of the importance of monitoring serum levels.
3. Initiate carbamazepine at 200 mg twice a day.
4. Increase dose by 200 mg twice a day.
5. Obtain carbamazepine levels every week until therapeutic levels are obtained (4–12 μg/ml).
6. Monitor levels every month for the first 3 months and every 3 months thereafter.
7. Hematologic monitoring: obtain complete blood count and platelet count every 2 weeks for the first 2 months of treatment and every 3 months thereafter.
8. Liver function monitoring: obtain SGOT, SGPT, LDH, and alkaline phosphatase every month for the first 2 months of treatment and every 3 months thereafter.

SGOT, serum glutamic-oxaloacetic transaminase; SGPT, serum glutamate pyruvate transaminase; LDH, lactate dehydrogenase.
(Adapted from Silver JM, Yudofsky SC: Psychopharmacology and electroconvulsive therapy. In Talbott JA, Hales RE, Yudofsky SC (eds): The American Psychiatric Press Textbook of Psychiatry, pp 707–854. Washington, DC, American Psychiatric Press, 1988)

leukopenia (total white blood cell count of less than 3,000 cells per mm^3), with a prevalence of approximately 10%. Persistent leukopenia and thrombocytopenia occur in approximately 2% of patients, and "mild anemia" occurs in fewer than 5% of patients.

Hart and Easton (1982) recommend obtaining blood and platelet counts before carbamazepine therapy and complete blood counts every 2 weeks for the first 2 months, and quarterly thereafter (see Table 17-13). Patients with abnormal results on baseline tests should be considered at high risk and require a risk–benefit assessment before treatment is initiated. During therapy, the development of leukopenia necessitates follow-up laboratory evaluations every 2 weeks. If the counts do not return to normal in 2 weeks, the drug dose should be reduced.

Carbamazepine occasionally may result in hepatic toxicity. This is usually a hypersensitivity hepatitis that appears after a latency period of several weeks and is associated with elevations in SGOT (serum glutamic-oxaloacetic transaminase), SGPT (serum glutamate pyruvate transaminase), and LDH (lactic dehydrogenase). Cholestasis is also possible, with increases in bilirubin and alkaline phosphatase.

Carbamazepine has anticholinergic activity, which may lead to blurred vision, constipation, and dry mouth. In addition, patients may also complain of dizziness, drowsiness, and ataxia. These symptoms may often occur at therapeutic plasma levels, especially in the early phases of treatment. The development of rashes is also common. Weight gain does not appear to be a side effect of carbamazepine therapy. Concurrent use of verapamil with carbamazepine can result in increases in carbamazepine leads into the toxic range. For this reason, these drugs should not be used concomitantly.

Carbamazepine is essentially a tricyclic agent and, similar to the CyAD, has quinidinelike side effects.

PSYCHOSTIMULANTS

The use of psychostimulants such as methylphenidate is primarily limited to treating attention-deficit hyperactivity disorder (ADHD) (see Chapter 15). In neurology, psychostimulants such as methylphenidate, dextroamphetamine, and pemoline are used to treat narcolepsy (see Chapter 21). Some psychiatric research has suggested that these drugs may be of benefit in depression or as an adjunct to cyclic antidepressants, or they may predict responsiveness to cyclic antidepressants. Their use for these purposes, however, is not generally accepted in psychiatric practice, and psychostimulants are primarily employed in adjunctive polypharmacy regimens in refractory depressions.

Despite the very limited use for psychostimulants in most mood disorders, several clinical situations exist in which they may be of some definite benefit. Some general hospital psychiatrists advocate their use in anergic, apathetic, and withdrawn medical patients, such as those recovered from cerebrovascular stroke or other debilitating medical illnesses. The short-term use of methylphenidate 10 to 40 mg/day or dextroamphetamine 10 to 20 mg/day has been recommended to "activate" such anergic and apathetic patients. The clinical efficacy of such strategies has mostly been reported in short-term uncontrolled studies. More recently, the use of methylpheni-date for depression associated with AIDS has also received some support (see Chapter 20).

Psychostimulants, however, may cause restlessness, anxiety, agitation, insomnia, and, primarily with amphetamines, paranoid psychotic reactions, and dependency may occur. In addition, a rebound depression is quite common after the drugs are discontinued in patients who have become dependent on them. For these reasons, the use of psychostimulants is still largely reserved for carefully selected patients.

ELECTROCONVULSIVE THERAPY

Electroconvulsive therapy (ECT) is the use of electrically induced convulsions (i.e., grand mal or motor seizures) to treat psychiatric illnesses such as depression and mania or psychiatric symptoms such as psychosis or catatonia. Although ECT was first used in the late 1930s, the treatment today remains clinically relevant because of its high degree of efficacy, safety, and utility.

Mechanisms of Action

The mechanisms of action of ECT are complex and not completely understood. Nevertheless, ECT has been found to affect many of those transmitters and receptors that have been implicated in depression and its treatment. In studies involving both humans and animals, ECT has been found to affect such brain transmitters as serotonin, gamma-aminobutyric acid (GABA), endogenous opiates and their recep-tors, and catecholamines, including dopamine, norepinephrine, epinephrine, and their receptors. It also affects a wide variety of other neurotransmitters, neuropeptides, and neuroendocrine pathways.

Indications

ECT is primarily indicated in the treatment of severe depression—particularly depression in which symptoms are intense, prolonged, and accompanied by profound alterations in the patient's level of vegetative functioning, including sleep, appetite, libido, and activity level. As has been demonstrated in previous sections of this chapter, CyAD and MAOIs are the primary somatic treatments for depression. In patients with major depression with psychotic features, severe obsessional features, or active suicidal ideation, ECT is considered by some investigators and clinicians as the first-line treatment. In general, schizophrenic patients with affective and catatonic symptoms respond the best to ECT, whereas those patients with chronic symptoms often fail to respond. There is no indication that ECT alters the fundamental psycho-pathology of schizophrenia.

Yudofsky (1981) outlined special clinical situations in which ECT may be advantageous over other treatment approaches and may be the "first line" of treat-ment. Among these situations are the following:

1. Patients whose severe mood disorders have not responded to adequate psychopharmacologic treatment.
2. Patients with delusional (psychotic) depression (see Chapter 6).
3. Patients who cannot tolerate the side effects of antidepressant or antipsychotic agents.
4. Patients whose acute symptoms are so severe that a rapid and dramatic response is required.
5. Patients with histories of depressive episodes that have responded successfully to previous electroconvulsive treatments.

Contraindications

The contraindications to ECT are relatively few. First, patients with clinically significant space occupying cerebral lesions must not receive this treatment because of the risk of brain stem herniation. Second, patients with significant cardiovascular problems that may include recent (within 6 months) myocardial infarction, severe cardiac ischemia, and uncontrolled hypertension are at higher risk for complications. Such patients may or may not be safely given ECT and must be evaluated before treatment by a cardiologist and an anesthesiologist familiar with the potential side effects of ECT. Before the use of muscle relaxants in electroconvulsive therapy technique, degenerative diseases of the spine and other bones comprised a significant risk from ECT. Today, however, adequate anesthetic techniques render ECT generally safe in patients with these disorders. Patients should generally be discontinued from their monoamine oxidase inhibitors for at least 2 weeks before the initiation of ECT to prevent dangerous increases in blood pressure during treatment.

Medical Evaluation Before Treatment

Before receiving ECT, a patient should have a complete medical and neurological examination, complete blood count, blood chemistry analysis, urinalysis, electrocardiogram, and x-ray of the lumbosacral region of the spine if orthopedic problems are suspected. A chest x-ray must be obtained because of the use of positive-pressure respiration during general anesthesia. Electroencephalogram and a computerized tomographic (CT) scan may be required for patients with suspected organic brain disease.

Because of the high degree of fear and misinformation related to ECT, we encourage that ample time be devoted to discussion of the risks, benefits, and techniques of ECT with both the patient and his or her family.

Technique

In the United States, ECT treatments are generally given on an every-other-day basis (three times a week) for 2 to 3 weeks for a total of 6-9 treatments on average. Seizure lengths of between 25 and 60 seconds per treatment are considered adequate for therapeutic purposes. Recently, it has been substantiated that placement of electrodes *unilaterally* on the nondominant hemisphere (i.e., the electrodes over the right hemisphere for a right-handed individual) results in a therapeutic seizure with markedly fewer side effects of cognition and memory. The number of treatments administered is generally determined by the patient's clinical response (i.e., when successive treatments do not elicit further beneficial effects).

Side Effects

For each treatment there is an initial confusional period that lasts for approximately 30 minutes. Memory impairment that occurs with ECT is highly variable. While certain patients report no problems with their memory, others report that their memory "is not as good as it used to be" after receiving ECT. It has been found that patients who experience retrograde amnesia (i.e., diminished ability to recall information that was recently learned before ECT was administered) following bilateral ECT seem to have recovered complete memory function by 6 months after treatment, with little evidence that new learning ability is still deficient at this time. In those patients who do have memory impairment following bilateral ECT, information acquired during the days and weeks before, during, and for several weeks following ECT may be permanently lost.

Electroconvulsive therapy remains an effective treatment for those patients with severe depressions that include those with delusional and suicidal features. ECT is only one component of a larger treatment plan that includes psychosocial interventions. Finally, it is almost always advisable to maintain patients on CyAD prophylactically after ECT is completed to hedge against relapse.

CLINICAL PEARLS

- A relatively easy way to remember the differential side effects of the antipsychotic or neuroleptic drugs is that the "low-potency" drugs such as chlorpromazine and thioridazine have relatively *high* anticholinergic and orthostatic hypotensive side effects and low extrapyramidal side effects. The "high-potency" drugs such as haloperidol, thiothixene, and fluphenazine conversely have *low anticholinergic and orthostatic hypotensive side effects* and a *high propensity for extrapyramidal side effects.* Hence, the side effects in the "high-potency" and "low-potency" drugs vary inversely in this respect.
- Monitoring serum CPK levels is an excellent way to identify the prodrome or the presence of neuroleptic malignant syndrome as well as to monitor the course of the patient's illness.
- It is imperative that patients being considered for long-term use with neuroleptic (antipsychotic) agents be given informed consent, that they be monitored frequently for extrapyramidal side effects using structured rating instruments such as the AIMS scale (Abnormal Involuntary Movements Scale), and that informed consent is updated every 6 months. Neuroleptic drugs should always be used in the lowest possible dose, and the need for continued treatment should be periodically documented.
- In respect to the antidepressant drugs, one usually chooses a drug based on its side effect profile, matching the side effects of the drug with the symptoms and physiologi-

(continued)

CLINICAL PEARLS *(continued)*

cal vulnerabilities of the patient. For example, patients with severe anxiety, agitation, and insomnia may benefit more from relatively sedating antidepressants such as imipramine. Alternatively, patients who are more apathetic and anergic may benefit from more "stimulating" drugs such as fluoxetine and desipramine.

- Most antidepressant drugs, with the exception of fluoxetine and bupropion, should be given once a day, usually 7 hours before bedtime. Fluoxetine and protriptyline, because of their stimulant properties, are usually best given in the early parts of the day.
- The most common reasons for "refractory" depression are noncompliance with medication and patients being treated with inadequate doses of antidepressants.
- Patients who have Parkinson's disease with psychotic symptoms should be considered for treatment with the new experimental antipsychotic clozapine. This drug not only has very few if any extrapyramidal side effects that could possibly worsen the Parkinson's disease, but some investigators have reported that it actually improves the symptoms of Parkinson's disease.
- The most problematic aspect of treating elderly patients with cyclic antidepressants is the development of orthostatic hypotension. Of the traditional cyclic antidepressants, nortriptyline has the fewest orthostatic side effects, and of the new antidepressants, fluoxetine appears to have the definite advantage.
- Of the traditional tricyclic antidepressants, desipramine appears to have the fewest anticholinergic side effects. Of the newer drugs, fluoxetine appears to have the advantage over both the older and newer drugs in this respect.
- The benzodiazepines can be best differentiated into two classes. Oxazepam, temazepam, and lorazepam are all primarily metabolized by conjugation, and therefore their half-lives are not affected by aging or liver disease. Practically all of the other drugs are metabolized by way of oxidative mechanisms and therefore may be affected by age, liver disease, or other medications that may affect hepatic enzymatic activity.
- Lorazepam and midazolam are the only two benzodiazepines that may be reliably absorbed by the intramuscular route and are the preferred benzodiazepines to be given intravenously.
- Lorazepam is reliably and rapidly absorbed when given sublingually.
- Shorter-acting benzodiazepines such as triazolam and lorazepam may cause anterograde amnesia.
- In respect to the cardiovascular side effects of the cyclic antidepressants, almost all of them, with the exception of trazodone, fluoxetine, and probably bupropion, have quinidinelike side effects. Carbamazepine also is a tricyclic compound with quinidinelike side effects.
- Electroconvulsive therapy is often the safest and most predictable treatment for certain patients with profound depressions and those who are elderly and medically debilitated who may not be able to tolerate the side effects of the cyclic antidepressants. The primary risk with electroconvulsive therapy is in patients who have expanding intracranial mass lesions, patients who have experienced a recent myocardial infarction, or patients with severe cardiovascular disease in which the hypertension and tachycardia associated with seizure activity may place an excessive demand on the myocardium. These latter side effects can be effectively managed through appropriate autonomic blockade with agents such as labetalol.

ANNOTATED BIBLIOGRAPHY

Dubovsky SC: Psychopharmacologic treatment in neuropsychiatry. In Hales RE, Yudofsky SC (eds): The American Psychiatric Press Textbook of Neuropsychiatry, pp 411–438. Washington, DC, American Psychiatric Press, 1987

> This is a succinct review of the use of psychopharmacologic agents in patients with neuropsychiatric disorders.

Guttmacher L: Concise Guide to Somatic Therapies. Washington, DC, American Psychiatric Press, 1988

> This is a short but succinct reference for biological therapies in psychiatry.

Hales RE: Psychopharmacologic side effects and drug interactions of importance in the critical care unit. Prob Crit Care 2:134–148, 1988

> This is a review of the benefits and risks of using psychopharmacologic drugs in the intensive care unit setting.

Schatzberg AF, Cole JO: Manual of Clinical Psychopharmacology. Washington, DC, American Psychiatric Press, 1986

> This is an excellent short guide to practical clinical psychopharmacology that is well referenced and contains excellent tables.

Silver JM, Yudofsky SC: Psychopharmacology and electroconvulsive therapy. In Talbott JA, Hales RE, Yudofsky SC (eds): The American Psychiatric Press Textbook of Psychiatry, pp 767–854. Washington, DC, American Psychiatric Press, 1988

> This is an expanded discussion of many of the basic principles discussed in this chapter.

Stoudemire A, Fogel BS: Psychopharmacology in the medically ill. In Stoudemire A, Fogel BS (eds): Principles of Medical Psychiatry. Orlando, Grune & Stratton, 1987

> This is an expanded and detailed discussion of the special modifications that must be made in the use of psychopharmacologic agents in medically ill patients. It deals on a specialty-by-specialty basis with each of the major organ systems and the possible vulnerabilities of medically ill patients to psychopharmacologic agents.

Stoudemire A, Atkinson P: Use of cyclic antidepressants in patients with cardiac conduction disturbances. Gen Hosp Psychiatry 10:389–397, 1988

> This review article discusses in depth the special considerations that must be made in choosing psychopharmacologic agents in patients with cardiac conduction disturbances.

Meltzer H (ed): Psychopharmacology: The third generation of progress. New York, Raven Press, 1987

> This is a superb and encyclopedic source on clinical psychopharmacology. It covers almost every aspect of clinical psychopharmacology from basic neuropharmacologic mechanisms to practical clinical applications. Excellent as a reference source for special study or complex clinical situations.

REFERENCES

American Psychiatric Association: Diagnostic and Statistical Manual of Mental Disorders, 3rd ed rev. Washington, DC, American Psychiatric Association, 1987

Baldessarini RJ: Chemotherapy in Psychiatry: Principles and Practice. Boston, Harvard University Press, 1985

Baldessarini RJ: Drugs and the treatment of psychiatric disorders. In Gilman AG, Goodman LS, Murel F (eds): The pharmacologic basis therapeutics, 7th ed, pp 385–445. New York, Macmillan, 1985

Battle DC, VonRiotte AB, Gaviria M, et al: Amelioration of polyuria by amiloride in patients receiving long-term lithium therapy. N Engl J Med 312:408–414, 1985

Breier A, Charney DS, Heninger GR: Agoraphobia with panic attacks: Development, diagnostic stability, and course of illness. Arch Gen Psychiatry 43:1029–1036, 1986

Consensus Development Panel: Mood disorders: Pharmacologic prevention of recurrences. Am J Psychiatry 142:469–476, 1985

Conte HR, Plutchik R, Wild KV, et al: Combined psychotherapy and pharmacotherapy for depression: A systematic analysis of the evidence. Arch Gen Psychiatry 43:471–479, 1986

Davis JM, Andriukaitis S: The natural course of schizophrenia and effective maintenance drug treatment. J Clin Psychopharmacol 6:2S–10S, 1986

Folks DG: Monoamine oxidase inhibitors: Reappraisal of dietary considerations. J Clin Psychopharmacol 3:249–252, 1983

Hart RG, Easton JD: Carbamazepine and hematological monitoring. Ann Neurol 11:309–312, 1982

Jeste DV, Wyatt RJ: Understanding and treating tardive dyskinesia. New York, Guilford Press, 1982

Mellinger GD, Balter MB, Uhlenhuth EH: Insomnia and its treatment: Prevalence and correlates. Arch Gen Psychiatry 42:225–232, 1985

Mitchell JE, Mackenzie TB: Cardiac effects of lithium therapy in man: A review. J Clin Psychiatry 43:47–51, 1982

Munetz MR, Roth LH: Informing patients about tardive dyskinesia. Arch Gen Psychiatry 42:866–871, 1985

Myers DH, Carter RA, Burns BH, et al: A prospective study of the effects of lithium on thyroid function and on the prevalence of antithyroid antibodies. Psychol Med 15:55–61, 1985

National Institute of Mental Health: Abnormal involuntary movement scale. In Guy W (ed): ECDEU assessment manual. Rockville, MD, U.S. Department of Health, Education, and Welfare, 1976

Post RM, Ballenger JC, Uhde TW, et al: Carbamazepine in manic-depressive illness: Implications for under-lying mechanism. In Post RM, Ballenger JC (eds): Neurobiology of mood disorders. Baltimore, Williams & Wilkins, 1984

Prien RF, Kupfer DJ: Continuation drug therapy for major depressive episodes: How long should it be maintained? Am J Psychiatry 143:18–23, 1986

Reich J: The epidemiology of anxiety. J Nerv Ment Dis 174:129–136, 1986

Silver JM, Yudofsky SC: Psychopharmacology and electroconvulsive therapy. In Talbott JA, Hales RE, Yudofsky SC (eds): The American psychiatric press textbook of psychiatry, pp 767–854. Washington, DC, American Psychiatric Press, 1988

Yassa R, Lal S: Prevalence of the rabbit syndrome. Am J Psychiatry 143:656–657, 1986

Yudofsky SC: ECT in general hospital psychiatry: Focus on new indications and technologies. Gen Hosp Psychiatry 3:292–296, 1981

18

Psychiatric Emergencies: Recognition and Management

William R. Dubin

Emergency management of psychiatric disorders is one of the unique areas of medicine in which physicians must have a broad knowledge of both medicine and psychiatry. The interplay between physical illness and psychological functioning is dramatic. This chapter's purpose is to provide an introduction to evaluating and intervening in psychiatric emergencies by highlighting the major syndromes most commonly seen in the emergency department (ED). Topics include the evaluation and treatment of psychosis, violence, suicide, rape, child and spouse abuse, and legal issues pertaining to emergency psychiatry.

ACUTE PSYCHOSIS: DIFFERENTIATING ORGANIC MENTAL DISEASE FROM FUNCTIONAL ILLNESS

The most important decision in evaluating a psychotic patient is to differentiate an organic mental disorder (OMD) from a functional (nonorganic) psychiatric illness. Between 3.5 and 18.4% of patients considered to be primarily psychiatric in nature have undetected medical illness (Dubin and Weiss, 1984). Clinicians often make a premature psychiatric referral in patients with OMD because of:

1. *Bias against psychiatric patients or patients with psychiatric symptoms.* Psychiatric patients often make physicians uncomfortable or anxious because of their bizarre or disruptive behavior. Physicians may not view such patients with the same urgency or seriousness as they do patients with cardiovascular disease or physical trauma. In a recent report, for example, a homeless street person with undiagnosed severe hypothyroidism was initially treated for psychiatric illness (Shader and Greenblatt, 1987). Too

often, initial decisions are based on a single piece of data, symptom, item of past history, or previous diagnosis (Leeman, 1975).

2. *Disordered perceptions.* A common misconception is that delusions, hallucinations, and disorganized thoughts are synonymous with functional psychiatric illness. On the contrary, these symptoms, like pain or headache, are ubiquitous and occur in functional *and* organic illness. Psychotic symptoms may also occur transiently in certain personality disorders during times of emotional crisis.

3. *Violence.* Because violence makes clinicians anxious, they quickly tend to refer any violent or potentially violent patient for psychiatric evaluation. However, 17% of violence that occurs in psychiatric settings results from underlying *organic* illness (Tardiff and Sweillam, 1980). Violence, like disordered perceptions, is etiologically nonspecific.

4. *Self-induced illness.* The least tolerated patients are those who are believed to create their own disease, such as alcoholics, drug abusers, or suicidal patients (Weissberg, 1979). Consequently, clinicians tend to minimize these patients' symptoms. An example is a patient who presents with a suicide attempt by overdose with antidepressants who initially is fully alert and clinically stable. In patients like this, physicians tend to trivialize the seriousness of the overdose. But in a recent study, half the patients who died from a tricyclic antidepressant overdose presented fully alert and stable, but had a catastrophic deterioration within 1 hour after admission to the ED (Callaham and Kassel, 1985).

5. *Ageism.* Clinicians often fail to take seriously or follow up the complaints and illnesses of elderly patients, attributing these complaints to old age or hypochondriasis (Goodstein, 1985). This problem may be further exacerbated in the patient with dementia. The term "dementia" is used generically to describe chronic irreversible and progressive deterioration of higher intellectual functioning. But 30 to 40% of all patients who present with symptoms of dementia have potentially treatable and sometimes completely reversible underlying causes for their altered mental status (Dubin, 1984). Premature labeling can preclude the exhaustive physical, neurological, and laboratory evaluation necessary to determine the etiology of a patient's cognitive dysfunction.

Organic Mental Disorders

Delirium is the most common manifestation of OMD encountered in the ED. Delirium specifically refers to a (usually) reversible disturbance of cerebral functioning due to a toxic, structural, neurological, or metabolic disturbance. The onset is acute, generally developing over a 6- to 96-hour period, and is characterized by impairment of alertness, thinking, memory, perception, concentration, and attention

(Lipowski, 1967). The incidence varies from 5 to 15% (Wise, 1987). The level of consciousness is altered and fluctuates in a sine-wave fashion between clouded alertness and hyperalertness and agitation.

Several common clinical features are highly suggestive of delirium: clouding of consciousness, age over 40 with no previous psychiatric history, disorientation, abnormal vital signs, visual hallucinations, and illusions (Dubin, Weiss, and Zeccardi, 1983; Hall, Popkin, and Devaul, 1978).

The differential diagnosis of delirium is so extensive that physicians may tend to avoid searching for an etiology (Wise, 1987). For example, an elderly delirious patient may have multiorgan disease (e.g., pulmonary insufficiency, cardiac failure, pre-existing brain damage) and may be taking multiple medicines (Wise, 1987). In such a patient, each problem is a potential contributor to the delirium and should be pursued and evaluated independently.

For the sake of differential diagnosis, clinicians should consider two categories of illness severity: *emergent* and *urgent.* Emergent conditions are life threatening; they require immediate attention and are of major concern to the psychiatrist (Table 1) (Anderson, 1987). Most other causes of delirium, while not life threatening, may require treatment in the ED (Table 2) (Dubin and Weiss, 1985).

Laboratory studies that will help rule out emergent illnesses include a complete blood count, glucose, serum electrolytes, blood urea nitrogen, chest radiograph, electrocardiogram, arterial blood gases, and a urinary drug screen. Patients who present with an acute behavioral change and/or clouded consciousness unexplained by this laboratory evaluation may require computerized axial tomography followed by a lumbar puncture.

At times, extreme agitation can significantly impede the evaluation. In these cases pharmacologic intervention (rapid tranquilization with antipsychotic drugs) will be helpful so that the appropriate medical-neurological examination can be completed. This procedure is discussed later under the section about violence.

In addition to medication, psychological support is important. Patients should have a staff member, if available, or a family member with them at all times during the evaluation. This can be reassuring to patients and can reduce mishaps such as pulling out intravenous lines or falling out of bed (Wise, 1987). Delirium is also discussed in Chapter 3.

Table 18–1 **Life-Threatening Causes of Delirium (Selected List)**

Meningitis and encephalitis
Hypoglycemia
Hypertensive encephalopathy
Diminished cerebral oxygenation
Anticholinergic intoxication
Intracranial hemorrhage
Wernicke's encephalopathy
Drug or alcohol withdrawal or intoxication

Table 18–2 **Selected Treatable Causes of Cognitive Dysfunction**

Cardiac	**Electrolyte Imbalance**
Arrhythmias	Hyponatremia
Congestive heart failure	Hypernatremia
Myocardial infarction	Hypercalcemia
Pulmonary	**Vitamin Deficiencies**
Chronic Obstructive Pulmonary Disease	Thiamine
Pulmonary emboli	Niacin
Hepatic	Riboflavin
Cirrhosis	Folate
Hepatitis	Ascorbic Acid
Wilson's Disease	Vitamin A
	Vitamin B_{12}
Renal	**Drug Induced**
Worsening of mild nephritis by urinary tract infection	Alcohol
	Tranquilizers
Dehydration with elevation of blood urinary nitrogen (BUN) over 50 mg/dl.	Over-the-counter preparation
	Any drug used to treat medical illness, e.g. Dilantin, aminophylline, digitalis, steroids
Vascular	**Exogenous Toxins**
Subdural hematoma	Carbon monoxide
Cerebrovascular accident	Bromide
Infection	Mercury
Endocrine Disease	Lead
Thyroid Disease	**Tumors**
Cushings Disease	**Normal Pressure Hydrocephalus**
Diabetes	**Depression**
Addison's Disease	
Hypoglycemia	

Functional Psychiatric Illness

The ED physician's task is (1) to differentiate OMD from functional psychiatric illness and to rule out any life-threatening causes of aberrant behavior, (2) to medically and/or psychiatrically stabilize the patient, and (3) to determine the most appropriate treatment setting (inpatient, outpatient, partial hospital). Ultimately, correctly diagnosing patients with functional psychiatric illness is essential because there are specific treatments for each illness (i.e., lithium for bipolar disorder, antidepressants for depression, antipsychotic medications for schizophrenia). However, for the few hours that the patient is in the ED, the treatment of aberrant behavior, agitation, excitement, and potential violence is the overriding priority. In this setting, the primary interventions include psychotherapy, pharmacotherapy, and at times physical restraints. While psychotropic medication has greatly enhanced our ability to attenuate the behavioral emergency effectively, verbal intervention remains an integral part of successful treatment.

THE EMERGENCY DEPARTMENT INTERVIEW

Treatment is inextricably interwoven with the evaluation process (Dubin and Stolberg, 1981). The initial interview not only serves to elicit important diagnostic information, but may also be therapeutic in itself. The goal of the interview is to gather information about the present illness, past psychiatric and medical history, family and occupational history, and drug and alcohol use. *The interviewer should not be distracted by the patient's bizarre behavior or verbalizations.* Such behavior often makes physicians feel uncomfortable; as a result, they are indifferent or overtly hostile. This approach may exacerbate the patient's symptoms. A controlled, patient professional composure on the physician's part is very reassuring to psychotic and organic patients, who may feel very much out of control. Even the most psychotic patient usually has enough self-awareness to form a rudimentary alliance when addressed with respect and dignity.

Emergency psychiatry work with hostile, uncooperative, or insulting patients can be especially difficult and frustrating. Hanke (1984) presents a thorough and comprehensive review of working with such difficult patients. She notes that the most common negative feelings are various forms of anger, anxiety, and despair. While clinicians may be aware of strong negative feelings, most commonly we express them in an indirect way that we may not recognize. Negative feelings may impede clinical judgment and decision making in the following ways:

1. *Arbitrary inferences,* or jumping to a conclusion based on inadequate or incorrect data ("Nothing will help this patient").
2. *All-or-nothing thinking,* or seeing situations as strictly black and white ("No one talks to me like that").
3. *Personalization,* or taking too much blame or too much credit without an objective reason ("With a little crisis intervention, I solved the patient's problem").

In general, if a clinician has an extremely negative reaction toward a patient, it suggests that the patient has struck an area of emotional vulnerability in the physician. Hanke (1984) suggests five guidelines to help manage negative responses to patients:

1. View the patient's maladaptive behavior as symptomatic of his or her condition rather than as a personal attack.
2. View negative reactions as overreactions.
3. Find a rational reaction to overreactions by identifying the type of response (i.e. arbitrary inference, all-or-nothing thinking, or personalization).
4. Generate alternate reactions. For example, instead of viewing a patient as "a manipulative sociopath," try to see him as pitiful or self-destructive, or as someone's son.
5. Maintain a larger perspective on negative reactions by attributing multiple causes to the negative reaction; for example, the negative feelings come from the patient's profanity (50%), the clinician's fa-

tigue from being on call all night (25%), and the overcrowded waiting area (25%).

While it is difficult to eliminate negative feelings completely, we should try to neutralize them to prevent distorting our clinical judgment in a way that impedes optimum care.

To begin the interview, the physician should introduce himself or herself and address the patient as "Mr. Smith" or "Ms. Jones." If the patient does not pose an imminent risk, the physician should sit. Standing over the patient may impede rapport by implying domination or intimidation. To establish a friendly atmosphere, it often helps to offer the patient food or a drink (avoid hot liquids) or to offer to call a friend.

One of the major paradoxes in emergency medicine occurs in respect to emergency psychiatry. Most emergency departments focus on rapid intervention and disposition, but in emergency psychiatric interventions *time is a major treatment variable.* The intensity of a patient's symptoms often diminishes in a structured, supportive environment with "tincture of time." Therefore, clinicians must restrain the impulse to "get right to the heart of the matter." The interview should begin with very nonspecific, less intrusive questions. After the patient begins to show some comfort with the interviewer, the physician can then start to ask about specific details. Questions should be open-ended to avoid simple "yes" or "no" answers. The physician should keep the interview format flexible, without trying to adhere to a predetermined rigid structure.

When interviewing an acutely disturbed agitated patient, the physician often must structure the interview by asking straightforward questions. If the patient begins to ramble, the interviewer should then restructure the interview to help the patient to pick up the trend of his or her thinking. The interviewer should not take a passive role but should be an active, involved participant.

With patients with hallucinations or delusions, it is important not to use simple logic in an attempt to convince them that their perceptions are wrong. This maneuver tends to make patients feel more defensive and misunderstood and may destroy any rapport that may have developed.

Except with the extremely paranoid patient, "laying on of hands" often helps establish rapport. This can be done by asking patients if the interviewer can take their pulse or blood pressure or feel their forehead. Unless there is some reason not to do it, the physician should offer to shake the patient's hand during the introduction.

An important element of the interview is helping patients identify their feelings. The patients' need to protect their integrity and self-control may initially make them reluctant to engage in the interview. If patients are resistant to the idea of talking, it is useful to elicit their feelings about the situation and to try to understand their predicament of being in the hospital and not knowing what will happen.

When a psychotic patient does not respond to questioning, the interviewer should then use whatever data is available to make contact with the patient. This may include noting the patient's words, expressions, appearance, or behavior, as well as the physician's subjective reactions and feelings that are illicited by the patient. Comments should be as specific as possible ("I don't know what Jesus says to you" or "I see you are in a bathrobe. I gather you were brought to the hospital unexpectedly.").

But despite the physician's most empathic and sensitive interventions, some patients will remain mute. Muteness is usually an angry response symbolizing an attempt to control the environment (Robbins and Stern, 1976). While medical and neurologic illnesses have been reported as etiologic for cases of mutism, it is rarely a sign of neurologic disease (Wells, 1980). When patients are mute, the first step is to indicate that appropriate responses are expected. If the patient continues to remain silent, the interviewer then should pause and observe what the silence is communicating. At no time should the clinician indicate a sense of futility by angrily and repeatedly asking questions and getting no reply. If the clinician cannot engage the patient in conversation, he or she should try to gather diagnostic information from the patient's family, friends, or spouse. If time permits, a sodium amytal interview may sometimes lead to dramatic improvement. If muteness persists, admission to a psychiatric unit for evaluation and treatment is indicated.

The most difficult patients for even experienced psychiatrists to interview are the *paranoid* patients. Perry (1976) has outlined an excellent approach to interviewing paranoid patients. If the patient is frightening, physicians should *not* ignore their own fear. Patients can quickly sense this discomfort and may become frightened themselves, leading to an escalation of symptoms. Sometimes clinicians may have to acknowledge their fears by saying to the patient, "The way you're looking makes me feel that you're on the verge of striking out. What can we do to help you feel more in control of things?" If the physician remains professionally confident and in control, patients are usually reassured. The patient's anxiety can be further ameliorated if the interview is conducted with the door open or if additional staff is present.

It is important to be tactful with paranoid patients because they are defensive, irritable, and easily humiliated. Paranoid patients who are angry often begin with a tirade of accusations about being mistreated. The clinician may have to interrupt and say to the patient, "How do you feel I might help you?" With the angry, paranoid patient, the physician should always maintain a professional demeanor by not becoming too friendly, intrusive, or controlling and by avoiding jokes or patronizing reassurance.

Occasionally, severely paranoid patients can make the interviewer feel defensive and foolish by twisting the meaning of the interviewer's words, making it impossible to sustain any direction in the interview. Under these circumstances, the interviewer should alter the course of the interview by explaining to the patient that he or she is making the interviewer uncomfortable and suggesting that they discuss reasons for doing this. If meaningful contact cannot be made, the interview should be terminated until the situation and the patient's condition permit a more productive interaction, usually after the patient has been medicated (see below).

THE VIOLENT PATIENT

The most frightening patient to interview in the ED setting is the violent or potentially assaultive patient. These patients can usually be successfully treated in the ED if the clinician approaches the patient in an objective, systematic manner and understands the dynamics of violence (Dubin, 1981). Simply stated, most patients tend to become violent when they feel helpless or passive (Lion, 1972). Successful interventions often alleviate these feelings and diminish the chances of behavioral dyscontrol.

Usually, a prodromal pattern of behavior precedes overt violence. Fortunately, sudden, unexpected physical assault is rare, and most violence is a predictable culmination of a 30- to 60-minute period of escalation. This prodrome can often be observed in the patient's posture, speech, and motor activity. Most violence is preceded by a period of increasing restlessness and pacing. Hyperactivity itself may be a sign of a psychiatric emergency that requires immediate intervention. Patients who manifest rigid postures by literally "having their back up in the air," those who clench their fists and jaws, and those whose temporal arteries are visibly pulsating are in the early stages of escalation. As part of the prodromal syndrome, patients are often verbally abusive and profane. *The clinician's response to such verbal stridency is central to the outcome of the intervention.* When verbal abuse is personalized and the clinician reacts defensively or angrily, the risk of violence is increased. *It is important to remember that verbal abuse is an attempt by the patient to assert autonomy and diminish feelings of helplessness.*

Treatment of Violence

As with psychotic patients, verbal intervention can be strikingly effective with potentially assaultive patients. Even with patients who appear to be on the verge of total loss of control, appropriate and well-timed verbal interventions can have a positive impact on behavior. Patients are terrified of losing control and welcome therapeutic efforts to restore it and prevent their acting out (Lion and Pasternak, 1973). The agitated, fearful, panicky feeling that is especially common in psychotic patients prior to their assaultiveness can be attenuated by empathic verbal interventions. Talking gives the patient an outlet for the tension that is being generated and is important for ventilating angry, hostile feelings (Lion, 1972).

During the interview, the clinician should focus on the patient's underlying feeling state or affect. Efforts to calm a patient through rationalization and intellectualization are usually not therapeutic and may only increase the patient's frustration and feelings of being misunderstood. Physicians often are reluctant to have patients express their anger, fearing that this will only escalate their loss of emotional control. On the contrary: ventilating angry feelings reduces the agitation. Often the hostile feelings frighten the patient, and by acknowledging these feelings some degree of emotional catharsis can be achieved, diminishing the need for further aggression (Lion, Levenberg, and Strange, 1972).

During the interview, the clinician should stay at least an arm's length from the patient. Never leave potentially violent patients alone, as this could be interpreted as rejection or could permit them to hurt themselves. An interviewer who feels anxious or unsure of how the patient will respond should ask the police, security personnel, or the family to remain nearby to help control the patient if necessary. There is some disagreement as to whether the patient or the interviewer should be closer to the door during the interview; a compromise would be to have both equal distance from the door.

As noted earlier, as part of verbal intervention it can be helpful to offer the patient food or a drink (again, avoiding hot liquids for obvious reasons). Offering food symbolizes friendship and caring and often helps alleviate a patient's angry affect. During the interview, it is also important to observe the patient's behavior; it may suggest that the patient is not as threatening as he or she may sound. When patients have their hands behind their backs or in their pockets or comply with all the interviewer's requests, they are less likely to become violent despite their strident speech.

The ultimate threat comes from patients with weapons. If a patient admits to having a weapon, never immediately ask for it, but explore the fear that led the patient to arm himself or herself. A weapon symbolizes a defense against feelings of helplessness and passivity. An immediate request to give up a weapon may heighten these feelings and further exacerbate the threat. During the interview, if the patient agrees to give up the weapon, the interviewer should *never* accept the weapon directly from the patient. Instead, the patient should be asked to put the weapon on the table or the floor so that the interviewer can pick it up at the end of the interview. If the patient refuses to give up the weapon, the clinician should immediately notify hospital personnel. If the patient actually threatens the interviewer with the weapon, the clinician should avoid exacerbating the patient's feelings of helplessness and shame. Nonthreatening expressions of a desire to help, coupled with an expression of fear, is the response most likely to avert physical harm ("I want to help you, but I'm too frightened to think with a gun pointed at me") (Dubin, Wilson, and Mercer, 1988).

While staff often voice concern about the threat of armed patients, consideration must also be given to weapons, especially guns, carried by police officers and security personnel. Generally, it is preferable to have them disarmed while in the ED. There are several anecdotal reports of patients who have taken guns from police officers in such situations and injured themselves and/or others. In several instances this occurred with patients who were not under the supervision of the police. Table 3 summarizes basic techniques in managing the violent patient.

Rapid Tranquilization

While verbal intervention is the mainstay of evaluation and treatment, medication is often necessary. In rapid tranquilization (RT), varying doses of antipsychotic medication are given at 30- to 60-minute intervals; ideally, patients respond significantly within 30 to 90 minutes (Dubin, Weiss, and Dorn, 1986). The target symptoms for RT include *tension, anxiety, restlessness, hyperactivity,* and *motor excitement.* Core psychotic symptoms such as hallucinations, delusions, and disorganized thought are usually not affected by RT and may require 7 to 10 days of appropriate antipsychotic drug treatment to attenuate. *The goal of RT is to calm patients so that they can cooperate in their evaluation, treatment, and disposition.* Sedation is not necessarily a desired end, since this can delay evaluation and disposition. Occasionally, there is concern that RT will obscure the patient's mental status and that antipsychotic treatment should be withheld until a diagnosis is made. This specious argument can lead to withholding an effective treatment and may prolong the risk of violence. A psychiatric diagnosis is not made on a single mental-status evaluation and, as stated earlier, definitive psychiatric treatment is not the primary task in the ED.

Table 18–3 **Dos and Don'ts of Treating Violent Patients**

DO	DON'T
Anticipate possible violence from hostile, threatening, agitated, restless, abusive patients or from those who lack control for any reason.	Don't ignore your gut feeling that a patient may be dangerous.
Heed your gut feeling. If you feel frightened or uneasy, discontinue the interview and get help.	Don't see angry, threatening, restless persons right away.
Summon as many security guards or orderlies as possible at the first sign of violence. Patients who see that you take them seriously often will not act out further. If they do, you will be prepared.	Don't compromise your ability to escape a dangerous situation. Don't sit behind a desk or between a patient and the door.
Ask if the patient is carrying a weapon. These must be surrendered to security personnel. Never see an armed patient.	Don't antagonize the patient by responding angrily or being patronizing.
Offer help, food, medication. Bolster the patient by commenting on his/her strength and self-control.	Don't touch or startle the patient or approach quickly without warning.
If restraint becomes necessary, assign one team member each to the patient's head and to each extremity. Be humane but firm, and do not bargain. Search the patient for drugs and weapons.	Don't try to restrain a patient without sufficient backup.
If the patient refuses oral medication, offer an injection after a few moments. Be prepared to administer it if the patient continues to refuse.	Don't neglect looking for organic causes of violence.
Keep a close eye on patients who are sedated and/or restrained. Restrained patients should never be left alone.	Don't bargain with a violent person about the need for restraints, medication, or psychiatric admission.
Hospitalize patients who state their intention to harm anyone, refuse to answer questions about their intent to harm, are abusing alcohol or drugs, are psychotic, have an organic brain syndrome, or refuse to cooperate with treatment.	Don't forget medicolegal concerns, such as full documentation of all interventions and the duty to warn and protect. If the patient is transferred, tell the admitting physician about any specific threats and victims.
Warn potential victims of threatened violence and notify the appropriate protection agencies.	Don't overlook family and friends as important sources of information.
Follow up on any violent person and document this in the chart.	

(Used with permission from Dwyer B, Weissberg M. Treating violent patients. Psychiatric Times p. 11, December 1988.)

At times, clinicians also withhold antipsychotic medication for fear that it will obscure or worsen underlying medical conditions; instead, they physically restrain patients while they attempt a physical evaluation and laboratory work-up. Besides the questionable accuracy of a physical examination done on a restrained, agitated patient, restraints carry significant medical risks (Gutheil, Tardiff, 1984; Johnson, Alvarez, and Freinhar, 1987). With the exception of anticholinergic delirium (which can be worsened by RT due to the anticholinergic properties of some neuroleptics), the safety of high-potency antipsychotic medication in medically ill patients has been repeatedly demonstrated (Dubin, Weiss, and Dorn, 1986).

RT is effective across all diagnostic categories regardless of the etiology of the aggression. It is effective in psychosis secondary to functional psychiatric illness such as schizophrenia or mania, as well as in organic mental syndromes such as agitation secondary to dementia, delirium, or alcohol and substance abuse or withdrawal (Dubin, Weiss, and Dorn, 1986). However, in substance and alcohol abuse patients, RT should be used for behavioral dyscontrol only. Cross-tolerant agents such as benzodiazepines for alcohol withdrawal are preferred for treatment of the withdrawal syndrome itself.

In general, the mainstay of rapid tranquilization has been high-potency antipsychotics (i.e., thiothixene, haloperidol, fluphenazine, and loxapine). The most common side effects of these high-potency neuroleptics are extrapyramidal symptoms, in contrast to the low-potency neuroleptics (e.g., chlorpromazine and thioridazine), whose primary side effects are hypotension and sedation (see Chapter 17).

While most studies used intramuscular (IM) medication as the preferred route of administration in RT, some studies suggest that oral concentrate is an effective alternative to IM medication (Dubin, Weiss, Dorn, and 1986; Dubin, et al., 1985). Oral concentrate offers the additional benefit of being less painful and intrusive. Administering IM medication may symbolize a patient's lack of choice and role as a passive, helpless recipient of treatment, whereas concentrate offers the patient a more active role in treatment.

The dosages used during RT are generally modest, and most patients respond in one to three doses given over 30 to 90 minutes (Table 4) (Dubin, Weiss, and Dorn, 1986). While some patients may require higher doses, there are currently no predictive clinical variables for this subgroup. No ceiling doses have been established, and the ultimate number of doses is an empirical decision based on an assessment of the patient's clinical status. During RT, medication is given at 30- to 60-minute intervals; most studies have found 60-minute intervals sufficient. An important caveat is to try to use the minimum dosage over the maximum amount of time clinically feasible.

While RT was conceptualized as an ED procedure, its use has expanded to the intensive care unit (ICU) setting. In the ICU, the delirious agitation and combativeness of patients frequently impedes medical treatment and sometimes can be life threatening. Several studies have clearly demonstrated the efficacy and safety of RT in

Table 18–4 **Antipsychotic Medication Dosages for Rapid Tranquilization***

DRUG	IN YOUNGER PATIENTS		IN OLDER PATIENTS	
	CONCENTRATE	IM	CONCENTRATE	IM
Thiothixene (Navane)	20 mg	10 mg	10 mg	5 mg
Trifluoperazine (Stelazine)	20 mg	10 mg	10 mg	5 mg
Haloperidol (Haldol)	10 mg	5 mg	5 mg	2.5 mg
Loxapine (Loxitane)	25 mg	10 mg	15 mg	5 mg

*While these are not the doses recommended by the Physicians' Desk Reference, these are the doses the authors have found to be the most effective.

critically ill delirious patients in the ICU (Dudley, Rowlett, and Loebel, 1979; Adams, 1984; Sos and Cassem, 1980; Tesar, Murray, and Cassem, 1985).

Intravenous (IV) administration of medication is frequently the preferred route of choice in the ICU. Patients for whom IV administration may be useful include those with lowered cardiac output who will not absorb IM medication, those incapable of taking oral medication, and those with extensive tissue damage, such as burn patients. While IV antipsychotic medication is safe and effective, the onset of action is variable. Some investigators used the IV route when a more rapid effect was desired (Clinton, et al., 1987), while others found the onset of action variable (i.e., 10 to 40 minutes) (Tesar, Murray, and Cassem, 1985); one report noted that it took up to 3 hours for some patients to become sedated (Dencker, 1976). The incidence of side effects from IV administration appears to be no greater than with other routes of administration. A recent study suggests that patients who receive IV haloperidol actually have a lower incidence of extrapyramidal symptoms compared to patients receiving oral medication (Menza, et al., 1987). Goldstein (1987), in an excellent review of RT in the ICU, provides a useful guideline for the IV use of antipsychotics (Table 5). One caution: haloperidol is not *specifically* approved for IV use, and documentation of the rationale for this maneuver should be made.

Side Effects During RT. Side effects during RT are generally few, mild, and reversible. Most studies have found that fewer than 10% of patients develop extrapyramidal symptoms (muscle rigidity, drooling, dystonias, akathisia, bradykinesia,

Table 18–5 Treatment Guidelines for the Use of Intravenous Haloperidol in the Intensive Care Setting

STARTING DOSE	
Degree of Agitation	**Dose**
Mild	0.5 to 2.0 mg
Moderate to severe	2.0 to 10 mg

TITRATION AND MAINTENANCE:

Allow 20 to 30 minutes before the next dose.

If agitation is unchanged, administer double dose every 20 to 30 minutes until patient begins to calm.

If patient is calming down, repeat the last dose at the next dosing interval.

Adjust dose and interval to patient's clinical course. Gradually increase the interval between doses until the interval is 8 hours, then begin to decrease the dose.

Once stable for 24 hours, give doses on a regular schedule and supplement with PRN doses.

Once stable for 36 to 48 hours, begin attempts to taper dose.

When agitation is very severe, very high boluses (up to 40 mg) may be required (Tesar, Murray, and Cassem, 1985).

*Haloperidol is not specifically approved by the FDA for the intravenous route; careful documentation for the necessity and rationale for its use should be made.
(Used with permission from Goldstein MG. Intensive care unit syndromes. In: Stoudemire A, Fogel BS, eds. Principles of medical psychiatry. Orlando: Grune & Stratton, 1987.)

etc.) within the first 24 hours of RT (Dubin, Weiss, Dorn, 1986). Extrapyramidal symptoms are not dose-related and can occur even after one dose. By far the most common extrapyramidal symptoms are *dystonic reactions*, which are involuntary turning or twisting movements produced by massive and sustained muscle contractions. (Mason and Granacher, 1980). They are sudden in onset and can be bizarre in presentation, which often leads to a misdiagnosis of hysterical conversion reaction. Dystonia usually involve muscles of the back, neck, and oral area. The back may be extended (opisthotonos) or the head may arch severely backward (retrocollis) or sideways (torticollis) (Hyman and Arana, 1987). The eyes may be pulled upward in a painful manner (occulogyric crisis). At times, patients may complain of thickness of the tongue or difficulty swallowing.

The most serious form of dystonia is laryngospasm. This contraction of the muscles of the larynx can compromise the airway and lead to severe respiratory distress. While it is extremely rare, clinicians should be alert for it.

A side effect that can be frequently misdiagnosed as a psychotic decompensation is *akathisia*. This Greek word literally means "inability to sit still." Patients feel uncomfortably restless, and pacing is their only relief. They will often say they feel "unable to relax," "tense," "all wound up like a spring," "irritable," or "like jumping out of my skin" or that they have "restless" legs (Van Putten and Marder, 1987). *Severe* akathisia can lead to a psychotic decompensation, and in its most severe manifestation patients have committed suicide and homicide (Van Putten and Marder, 1987). In the ED, akathisia is likely to occur under one of the following scenarios:

1. A patient is being rapidly tranquilized and after two or three doses appears to be worsening behaviorally.
2. A patient responds to RT and then several hours later becomes agitated, with the psychosis appearing to break through.
3. A patient who is known to comply with drug treatment has been taking medication and is brought to the hospital because of an apparent relapse.

The treatment for dystonia and akathisia is the same: benztropine (Cogentin) 2 mg or diphenhydramine (Benadryl) 50 mg IM or IV. These doses can be repeated at 5-minute intervals, up to three doses. Generally, relief occurs within 1 to 3 minutes after injection. While the response is dramatic in most patients, a few may not respond. In these cases, diazepam (Valium) 5 mg IV or IM or lorazepam (Ativan) 2 to 4 mg IV or IM may be helpful. In severely thought-disordered, agitated patients, it may be impossible to differentiate akathisia from psychotic excitement (Van Putten and Marder, 1987). Occasionally, treating the patient first for akathisia will resolve the diagnosis if the patient has a positive response to benztropine or diphenhydramine.

The issue of prophylactic treatment during RT is unresolved (Dubin, Weiss, and Dorn, 1986). In the first 24 hours after RT, the occurrence of extrapyramidal symptoms appears to be low, and most patients do not need antiparkinsonian agents. Yet it is clinically appropriate to use prophylactic antiparkinsonian drugs with patients who have a previous history of extrapyramidal symptoms, who are reluctant to take medication for fear of extrapyramidal symptoms, or who are paranoid and in whom extrapyramidal symptoms may lead to noncompliance. If a patient is rapidly tranquilized in the ED and then admitted to the hospital, benztropine or diphenhydramine should be ordered on a PRN ("as needed") basis since dystonia or akathisia can occur *several hours* after medication is given. If a patient is discharged from the ED, he or she should be given several 2-mg benztropine tablets, informed of the possible extrapyramidal side effects, and told when to take the benztropine.

Of major concern to many clinicians is *neuroleptic malignant syndrome* (NMS) (see also Chapter 17). This *extremely serious,* life-threatening idiosyncratic reaction to neuroleptics causes autonomic instability with hyperthermia, hypertension, and "lead-pipe" rigidity as hallmark symptoms (Mueller, 1985). It is an ill-defined sensitivity reaction that may occur in about 1% of patients on antipsychotic medication. Variables that place patients at risk for NMS are young, chronic, male patients who are dehydrated, malnourished, and placed in poorly ventilated seclusion rooms or in restraints (Mueller, 1985). To date, there have been no reports of this syndrome occurring with RT in the ED. There has been a single case report of a gynecology patient developing NMS after an injection of haloperidol 5 mg for sedation before surgery (Konikoff, et al., 1984). Another case was recently reported of a psychiatric patient who developed NMS 18 hours after receiving a total of haloperidol 45 mg over 18 hours (O'Brien, 1987). Despite these reports, concern about NMS should not deter the clinician from using an effective treatment such as RT unless the patient has a history of NMS.

Hypotension is a major concern with the use of low-potency antipsychotics such as chlorpromazine. When it occurs, treatment consists of keeping the patient supine or in the reverse Trendelenberg position, administering IV fluids for hypovolemia, and giving only noradrenergic drugs such as levarterenol or metaraminol (Bassuk, Panzarino, and Schoonover, 1984). Mixed α and β or β—adrenergic drugs such as isoproterenol and epinephrine should never be used because they could further reduce blood pressure (Bassuk, Panzarino, and Schoonover, 1984).

The risk of *tardive dyskinesia* (TD) has not been well defined in RT patients. However, since most patients who develop TD have been on antipsychotic medication for long periods of time, it does not appear that a patient is at risk from RT. *Seizures* from antipsychotic medications are rare, with only two reported seizures occurring in patients on low-potency drugs during RT (Hamid and Wertz, 1973; Man and Chen, 1973). Patients in alcohol withdrawal and drug intoxication do not appear to be at higher risk for seizures when treated for extreme agitation with antipsychotic medication (Dubin, Weiss, and Dorn, 1986). There are no reports of sudden death related to RT. The cardiovascular safety of antipsychotic medication has been demonstrated repeatedly, often in patients with severe, unstable cardiovascular illness (Dubin, Weiss, and Dorn, 1986). Other potential side effects generally develop from long-term use and are not of concern in RT.

Alternatives to Neuroleptics in RT. While studies have repeatedly demonstrated the safety and efficacy of antipsychotic medication in RT, there continues to be concern about potential untoward side effects such as NMS, TD (especially in patients with affective disorders), and extrapyramidal symptoms. As a result, many investigators have begun exploring alternatives to antipsychotics for RT.

Among the classes of drugs most often discussed are benzodiazepines; in particular, lorazepam and clonazepam have generated interest as potential non-antipsychotic drugs for RT and as an adjunct to reduce the total daily dose of antipsychotic medication (Dubin, 1988). Benzodiazepines have proven especially efficacious in patients with mania. While dosing regimens have varied, lorazepam 2 to 4 mg intramuscularly (0.05 mg/kg) at hourly intervals is the most frequent drug of choice. Most patients are well controlled on 10 mg or less per 24 hours. Side effects include ataxia, nausea and vomiting, amnesia, and confusion.

Benzodiazepines are used to control symptoms of hyperactivity, tension, anxiety, and restlessness; however, this class of drugs does not have demonstrated antipsychotic properties and will not be effective for core psychotic symptoms. To date, the literature is most convincing for using benzodiazepines for the management of acutely manic patients. Better designed, prospective studies are still necessary to determine the effectiveness of benzodiazepines for RT in patients with schizophrenia.

Physical Restraint

At times, verbal intervention and rapid tranquilization will not be sufficient, and additional personnel may be necessary. A show of force often induces compliance. Security personnel should be called in a quiet, nonthreatening manner. Patients should never be threatened with, "Either you cooperate or we are going to call security." The security force should never be presented as a challenge to a patient's masculinity or a threat to his or her passivity. When security guards are present, it is usually sufficient to have them visible, but not threatening; it is rarely necessary to have them in the interview room. The presence of security guards conveys to the patient that his or her impulses are going to be controlled and also allays the staff members' fears. When used in this manner, security guards should be unarmed, and they should should never approach patients while carrying weapons. The risk is too great that the patient may take the weapon if a physical struggle develops.

The ultimate method of behavior control is restraints, which should be used when patients may be harmful to themselves or others or when they remain agitated and noncompliant and violence seems imminent. Patients should not be threatened with restraints, but when they are inevitable maximum force should be used immediately and without belligerence (Bell and Palmer, 1981). Restraints provide a sound means for calming patients who do not respond to medication. Contrary to most clinicians' concerns, restraining a patient does not interfere with the therapeutic alliance; in the end, the patient is grateful that he was prevented from acting destructively. The procedure for using restraints is outlined in Table 6. In all restraint episodes, documentation should clearly outline the behavior requiring restraint, efforts that were made to attenuate the patient's behavior before the use of restraints, the use of all medication, continuous documentation of all efforts to remove the patient from restraints, and monitoring of the patient to prevent injury (5-minute checks of extremities to ensure adequate circulation, adequate hydration and exercise of limbs when appropriate). All clinicians should review and thoroughly understand restraint guidelines (Gutheil and Tardiff, 1984).

The final decision to be made in the ED is which setting (outpatient or inpatient) is most appropriate for continued treatment. Criteria for hospitalization are summarized in Table 7 (Dubin and Stolberg, 1981). Psychiatric consultation is almost always indicated in this situation.

Table 18–6 **Guidelines for Using Restraints**

At least four, and preferably five, persons should be used to restrain the patient. Leather restraints are the safest and surest type of restraints.

Explain to the patient why he/she is going into restraints.

A staff member should always be visible and reassuring the patient while he/she is being restrained. This helps alleviate the patient's fear of helplessness.

Patients should be restrained with legs spread-eagled and one arm restrained to one side and the other arm restrained over the patient's head.

Restraints should be placed so that intravenous fluids can be given if necessary.

Raise the patient's head slightly in order to decrease the patient's feelings of vulnerability and reduce the possibility of aspiration.

The restraints should be checked every 5 minutes for safety and comfort.

After the patient is in restraints, the clinician should begin treatment using verbal intervention or RT. Even in restraints, most patients still take antipsychotic medication in concentrated form.

After the patient is under control, one restraint at a time should be removed at 5-minute intervals until the patient has only two restraints on. Both of these remaining restraints should be removed at the same time. It is inadvisable to have only one limb in restraints.

(Adapted from Dubin WR, Weiss KJ. Psychiatric emergencies. In: Michels R, Cavenar JO, Brodie HK, et al., eds. Psychiatry, vol. 2. Philadelphia: JB Lippincott, 1985.)

THE SUICIDAL PATIENT

Suicide is one of the most dire consequences of mental illness and occurs in all diagnostic psychiatric categories. Emergency department clinicians are frequently the first to encounter patients who have either completed suicide, attempted suicide, or have suicidal ideation. Important in the evaluation and treatment of these patients is knowing the risk factors for suicide and having the skill to elicit key clinical features that differentiate the truly suicidal patient from the attention-seeker. *Never dismiss any patient as a nonrisk before a thorough evaluation is completed, even if the patient is well known to the ED staff or has a previous history of multiple nonlethal attempts.*

Table 18–7 **Criteria for Hospital Admission**

The patient shows no improvement with medication and interview.

The patient improves, but remains so psychotic that he or she cannot care for his or her daily needs (i.e., work, housing, grooming, etc).

The patient poses a physical threat to himself or herself or others.

The patient is having command hallucinations.

The physician is in doubt about the severity of the condition.

The patient is toxic from drugs and/or alcohol or prescribed medication.

The patient is psychotic and has exhausted caregivers or all sources of external support.

In assessing patients, a number of risk factors have been enumerated (Dubin and Stolberg, 1981). These factors are only guidelines that can help the physician judge the ultimate risk of suicide for each individual patient. One of the most important risk factors is the *lethality of attempt.* For example, someone whose gun misfires when he tries to shoot himself has made a much more lethal attempt than someone who swallows five aspirin. *In general, the more lethal the attempt, the greater the risk of suicide.* The concept of lethality, however, must also be based on the patient's perspective (Dubin and Weiss, 1985). For example, many patients overdose on benzodiazepines, believing they are fatal; others overdose on aspirin, thinking a household drug must be harmless. The benzodiazepine patient may be the more suicidal of the two, but the aspirin patient is more likely to die of medical complications.

Another important indicator of suicidal risk is the *imminence of rescue;* that is, the less imminent the chance of rescue, the greater the risk of suicide. Other factors that increase the risk of suicide are (Dubin and Stolberg, 1981):

Older, divorced, or widowed males
Caucasians
Unemployment
Poor physical health
Past suicide attempts
Family history of suicide, especially parent
Psychosis
Alcoholism/drug abuse
Chronic, painful disease
Sudden life changes
Patient living alone
Anniversary of significant loss

Treatment

The ED treatment of the suicidal patient is a complex problem that should generally be managed by a psychiatrist. Suicide attempts, gestures, or thoughts are always tinged with ambivalence about death, and the patient's presence in the ED may be a manifestation of part of the desire to live (Dubin and Stolberg, 1981).

It is important to instill hope in the patient. Confront the patient's sense of hopelessness by helping the patient to develop a realistic, concrete approach to his or her problems. Emphasize the patient's past successes in dealing with similar situations. Point out that the patient's negative beliefs are a result of a viewpoint that is perhaps distorted and hopeless; they are not necessarily the way things really are. Stress the patient's positive traits and accomplishments. Mobilize the patient's support system by asking family, spouse, parents, and friends to come to the ED; this will enhance the patient's sense of self-esteem and increase his or her feeling of being loved.

Approach the suicidal patient in an objective, nonjudgmental, and concerned manner. Avoid reprimanding the patient for the suicide attempt. When evaluating the suicidal patient, phrase questions concerning suicide in the general context of feelings of depression and hopelessness (i.e., How bad do you feel? What do you feel the future has in store for you? If you felt this bad before, can you describe what was happening?). Question the patient specifically about the suicide plan. *It is a myth that asking about specific suicide plans and thoughts will plant the idea of suicide.* Exploring the patient's feelings can be cathartic. Encouraging patients to discuss their feelings and fantasies often dispels the mystique of suicide, and they will begin to consider other alternatives to resolve their conflict.

The central issue in the treatment of suicidal patients is educating them about other solutions to their problems. This is done by listening to the patient and providing guidance, interpretation, and education. Involving significant others when appropriate can increase the patient's feelings of emotional support and control. Using ancillary systems such as social services, job programs, welfare assistance programs, and psychiatric outpatient and inpatient programs can further enhance support. The physician can also increase the patient's feelings of support by making such statements as, "I'm going to help you by giving you medication to relax you, by making an appointment for you, by calling your family, etc." The important phrase is "I'm going to help."

Nonverbal communication (i.e., a patient who comes to the emergency room with a bag packed and expects to be admitted) frequently gives clues to the nature of suicidal intent. Patients who recently made a will or straightened out their financial affairs may not be expecting to live too long. If the patient is in treatment, the treating psychiatrist or therapist should be notified of the suicidal gesture/attempt while the patient is in the ED. He or she often can provide information that will facilitate emergency treatment.

Disposition

Table 8 outlines the general indications for hospitalization of suicidal patients (Dubin and Stolberg, 1981; Walker, 1983). If the patient is hospitalized, he or she should be continuously observed; a staff member should accompany the patient to the bathroom. The patient should wear a gown, and ties, belts, shoelaces, or stockings should be removed.

Under no circumstances should a suicidal patient be allowed to leave the

---

Table 18–8 **Indications for Hospitalization of Suicidal Patients**

Psychosis

Intoxication with drugs or alcohol that cannot be evaluated and treated over a period of time in the emergency department.

No change in affect or symptoms despite the intervention of the physician, family, and friends.

Command hallucinations.

Low availability of outpatient resources.

Family exhaustion.

Escalating number of suicide attempts.

Uncertainty about the risk of suicide.

emergency department until an evaluation by a psychiatrist is completed. If the patient insists on leaving before such an evaluation, he or she should be detained under the appropriate legal guidelines until a reasonable assessment can be made. The patient's rights are secondary to this potentially life-threatening situation. When a patient is discharged from the ED, all efforts should be made to have friends or relatives accompany the patient home and spend the next 24 hours with him or her. *Almost without exception, a patient who presents with suicidal ideation or gestures should not be sent home alone.* The patient should be given the name and phone number of the treating ED physician and reassured that he or she can call at any time. Ideally, the patient should have an outpatient appointment the next day, if outpatient treatment is deemed safe.

ACUTE ALCOHOL AND DRUG INTOXICATION AND WITHDRAWAL

Substance abuse emergencies are a common ED problem. The treatment of substance abuse is complicated because patients often ingest multiple substances. Intoxication and withdrawal states frequently present both a medical and behavioral emergency, requiring close collaboration between the psychiatrist and other ED physicians. Since substance abuse is extensively reviewed in Chapter 9, only highlights pertaining to the ED will be addressed here.

Assessment

Many patients are brought to the ED because of acute alcohol intoxication. Treatment with such patients begins with the initial interview, which can strongly influence the course of treatment. Interviewers should be tolerant and nonthreatening and should accept the intoxicated patient just as they accept insults and rudeness as part of the illness. Food and support will often serve to calm the patient. The availability and presence of security personnel can deter the belligerent patient from violent outbursts and will help reassure the interviewer. The patient will respond in a calmer fashion if placed in a quiet room with minimal stimulation. Intoxicated patients should be prevented from harming themselves or others; physical restraints may be needed.

A physical examination is mandatory to rule out other medical conditions that may accompany alcohol intoxication, such as bleeding, cardiac arrhythmias, pneumonitis, and head injuries. Use caution with stuporous patients. Before letting them sleep it off, rule out head injury or make sure the patient did not overdose with other drugs.

Usually, the preferred disposition is to send patients home with support of family and friends and refer them to an alcohol program the next day. Part of the follow-up includes a referral to Alcoholics Anonymous. No ataxic patient should ever be discharged. Criteria for hospitalizing a patient withdrawing from alcohol are summarized in Table 9 (Greenblatt and Shader, 1977).

A frequently misdiagnosed syndrome in the ED is the Wernicke-Korsakoff

Table 18–9 **Criteria for Hospitalization of a Patient Withdrawing From Alcohol**

Alcohol withdrawal delirium (Delirium tremens)
Hallucinosis
Seizure in patient with no known seizure disorder
Presence of acute Wernicke's and/or Korsakoff's syndrome (alcohol amnestic disorder)
Fever over 101° F
Head trauma with a period of unconsciousness or altered sensorium
Clouding of sensorium
Presence of major medical illness (e.g., respiratory failure or infection, hepatic decompensation, pancreatitis, gastrointestinal bleeding, severe malnutrition)
Known history of delirium, psychosis, or seizures in previous untreated withdrawals

(Reprinted with permission from Greenblatt DJ, Snader RI. Treatment of the alcohol withdrawal syndrome. In: Snader RI, ed. A manual of psychiatric therapeutics. Boston: Little, Brown, 1977.)

syndrome, which is characterized by ophthalmoplegia, nystagmus, impaired recent memory, peripheral neuritis, and ataxia (Reuler, Girard, and Cooney, 1985). This patient requires immediate intervention, as many of the neurologic signs are reversible if treated in a timely fashion. Treatment usually begins in the ED with thiamine 100 mg intramuscularly, which should be continued throughout treatment. The patient should be hospitalized and withdrawn from alcohol and should receive vigorous vitamin therapy. (See also Chapter 9.)

Patients in delirium tremens (DTs) or alcohol withdrawal delirium are often referred to psychiatrists because of their extreme agitation and hallucinations. DTs is a serious withdrawal syndrome that occurs 3 to 4 or as late as 10 days after cessation of drinking. Mortality has been reported between 1 and 10%, with hyperthermia and peripheral vascular collapse as the usual causes of death. Symptoms of DTs are similar to those found in delirium, with waxing and waning of symptoms, visual hallucinations, disorientation, gross tremors, and elevated autonomic signs. DTs is a medical emergency requiring immediate, aggressive intervention.

In a comprehensive review of inpatient management of alcohol withdrawal and DTs, Frances and Franklin (1987) note that benzodiazepines are clearly the medication of choice because of their relatively high therapeutic safety index, the option of oral, IM, or IV administration, and their anticonvulsant properties. In contrast, barbiturates, which once were a popular treatment intervention, have fallen into relative disuse because of a high incidence of respiratory depression and a low therapeutic safety index. All benzodiazepines are equally efficacious; special circumstances may favor a particular drug (Frances and Franklin, 1987). The long half-lives of chlorodiazepoxide and diazepam (24 to 36 hours) give an advantage of a smooth induction and gradual decline in blood levels so that there are fewer symptoms on discontinuation of lower dosage. Chlorodiazepoxide gives greater sedation, while diazepam has greater anticonvulsant activity, which may make it more preferable for patients with a history of seizures. In elderly patients or those with liver diseases, lorazepam or oxazepam, which have short half lives, are preferred. Lorazepam also has the advantage of being the only benzodiazepine other than midazolam that has rapid and complete absorption following IM administration. Relative potencies are as follows: diazepam 10 mg = chlorodiazepoxide 25 mg = lorazepam 1 mg. A standard management regimen for alcohol withdrawal as suggested by Frances and Franklin (1987) is outlined in Table 10.

Table 18–10 **Treatment of Alcohol and Substance Intoxication and Withdrawal States**

Alcohol Withdrawal States
(Frances and Franklin, 1987;
Hyman and Arana, 1987)

	Chlorodiazepoxide—25–100 mg po QID on first day; 20% decrease in dose over 5 to 7 days plus 25–50 mg po QID PRN for agitation, tremors, or change in vital signs
	Thiamine 100 mg po QID
	Folic acid 1 mg po QID
	Multivitamin one per day
	Magnesium sulfate 1 mg IM q 6 hr x 2 days (if status post withdrawal seizures)
	Lorazepam 2 mg orally q 2 hr for elderly patients or patients with liver disease
*Extreme agitation	Lorazepam, 2–4 mg IM q 1 hr or rapid tranquilization (see Table 18–3)

Barbiturate Withdrawal

	Pentobarbital challenge test
	Give pentobarbital 200 mg po and observe patient for 1 hr. If:
	patient asleep —not barbiturate dependent
	no effect —repeat 200 mg hourly until nystagmus or drowsiness develops
	nystagmus and/ or drowsiness—total dosage is starting point for detoxification with 10% reduction each day, tapered over 10 days

Cocaine and Amphetamine Intoxication

Mild to moderate agitation	Diazepam, 10 mg orally q 8 hr
Severe agitation	Thiothixene, 20 mg concentrate or 10 mg IM
	Haloperidol, 10 mg concentrate or 5 mg IM

Phencyclidine (PCP) Intoxication

	Ammonium chloride, 2.75 mEq/kg/dose in 60 ml of saline given by nasogastric tube in conjunction with ascorbic acid (2 g/500 ml IV) q 6 hr until urine pH is below 5

(continued)

Table 18–10 **(continued)**

Hyperactive, mild agitation, tension, anxiety, excitement	Diazepam, 10–30 mg orally Lorazepam, 3–4 mg (0.05 mg/kg) IM may be considered as an alternative in uncooperative patients
Severe agitation and excitement with hallucinations, delusions, bizarre behavior	Haloperidol, 5–10 mg IM q 30–60 min.
Opioid Withdrawal	
	Methadone, 10–20 mg orally Clonidine, 0.1 mg BID or TID may be used as an adjunct to methadone or alone to decrease the hyperadrenergic symptoms
Anticholinergic Delirium	
	Use of phystostigmine has been questioned; should be used with the supervision of a medical consultant in doses of 1–4 mg IM or IV

*Rapid tranquilization in alcohol withdrawal states is for severe agitation and behavioral dyscontrol. The actual treatment of withdrawal is with a cross-tolerant medication.

Drug Intoxication and Withdrawal

The evaluation of patients intoxicated or withdrawing from controlled substances can pose one of the more complex problems in the ED. Frequently, patients ingest multiple medications; at other times, they may self-medicate their own withdrawal, thereby presenting a confusing picture. Often, because of the patient's agitated behavior, treatment is necessary before the results of blood screens are available. The most common problem is extreme agitation secondary to intoxication from cocaine, amphetamines, or phencyclidine. Treatment interventions are outlined in Table 10 (Dubin, Weiss, and Dorn, 1986). The signs and symptoms of intoxication and withdrawal with various drugs are discussed in Chapter 9.

VICTIMS OF VIOLENCE

Rape

Rape is an act of aggression and hostility in which victims are often brutalized; if ED diagnostic and treatment procedures are handled in an insensitive, disrespectful manner, a "second rape" may occur (Goodstein, 1984). Evaluations are often undertaken without offering an explanation to the patient or getting her consent. Multiple questions from clinical personnel, family, and legal staff are often asked in a negative tone and may involve off-color comments by the interviewer. The legal aspects of the case are often delayed and protracted, and newspapers may publish the victim's name and address (25% of the cases). Clinical follow-up for pregnancy, venereal disease, and vaginal infections may be lengthy. This entire process psychologically prolongs the rape.

In approaching the rape victim, it is important to realize that patients have several important psychological, medical, and legal needs. The phenomenon of AIDS has cast another specter over the trauma of rape.

Evaluation and Treatment

Psychological Interventions. The victim's response may vary widely from confusion, guilt, agitation, and terror to some evidence of fear and anxiety. Some patients may display complete calm and even occasionally smile, indicating they are essentially still in a state of emotional shock. Since patients may resent the offer of psychiatric help, immediate psychiatric intervention should be reserved for complicated cases or for dealing with families. However, psychological care begins the moment the patient arrives. The patient should have immediate attention and privacy and should be asked to sign consent forms for examination and future release of medical records. *Police officers should not be present during the history and physical examination, nor should family members and friends.* However, rape patients should never be left alone and a female should be with female victims.

Many patients tend to blame themselves for their handling of the rape encounter. The patient will need support and reassurance that whatever she did was appropriate, because it helped her come out of the encounter alive. At times, patients will need to repeat the story continuously. An important task is to listen and to allow the patient to share her feelings of pain, anger, and embarrassment. Patients who are unwilling to talk about the experience and their feelings even after being encouraged to do so should be respected.

Burgess and Holmstrom (1980) describe two phases of psychological reaction to a rape: disorganization and gradual reorganization. In the disorganization phase, emotions may be expressed openly (crying, shaking, and inappropriate smiling) or victims may feel numb and empty and unable to express emotion. Fear and physical symptoms are prominent. The reorganization phase usually begins 2 to 3 weeks after the rape. The victim may change the locks on her doors, move to a new residence, or change her phone number. Nightmares, phobias, and hyperactivity may occur. The victim may resort to maladaptive solutions such as drugs, alcohol, or suicidal or homicidal plans. During the reorganization phase, symptoms gradually diminish and within months to years, the victim returns to normal functioning.

Before being discharged from the ED, patients should be counseled as to the potential psychological sequelae of the rape and told where they can receive psychological help if necessary (perhaps the name of a psychiatrist and information about Women Organized Against Rape, a local counseling center, or support groups). Patients should not be sent home alone. All efforts should be made to arrange for family or friends to be with her for at least 24 hours after she is discharged to provide continued emotional support.

Medical Interventions. Hanke (1984) outlines the following steps for the treatment of the physical trauma of the rape:

1. Obtain the patient's permission to have needed physical exams done, specimens collected, photographs taken, and releases of information completed.

2. Before doing the physical exam, be sure the patient will agree to it. If the patient is reluctant to allow an exam, reassure her of the need for the exam for her physical safety and legal defense.

3. Obtain specimens from the vaginal pool for the police laboratory to test. Obtain cervical and rectal cultures for gonorrhea and obtain a serology for syphilis.

4. *Establishing that a rape occurred is a legal decision, not a medical diagnosis.* Record the history in the patient's own words, document laboratory work, and save all clothing. Defer the diagnosis of rape.

5. To prevent pregnancy, offer a 5-day course of medroxyprogesterone or diethylstilbestrol. If the patient is taking oral contraceptives or has an intrauterine device, medication is not needed.

6. To protect the patient against venereal disease, penicillin should be given. If the patient is allergic to it, use oral tetracycline or intramuscular streptomycin.

Spouse Abuse

Spouse abuse is generally wife abuse. It is rarely the presenting complaint, and many women will not volunteer information unless asked. Spouse abuse occurs in all social classes and ethnic groups, but the highest incidence is among the poor. Specific recommendations for clinical recognition of wife abuse include the following (Goodstein, 1984):

1. Consider abuse in women who present with injuries to the head, face, back, and arms. Familiar excuses for bruises and lacerations are "I walked into a door" or "I fell off a chair."

2. Suspect abuse if there are chronic injuries or a substantial delay between the time of injury and presentation for treatment.

3. Ask patients wearing sunglasses to remove them, as they may be used to hide black eyes.

4. Ask about abuse in women who come for treatment with strong themes of separation anxiety from the spouse or who have the triad of trauma, depression, and problems with children.

5. Inquire about other violence at home, especially child abuse and incest.

Emergency treatment centers around caring for any acute trauma and ensuring the immediate safety of the woman and her children. If it is not safe for them to go home, they can be referred to emergency shelters for abused women. Hospitalization is not indicated unless trauma requires it or the woman is seriously suicidal or homicidal. ED treatment is difficult because the patient will be distressed by the intensity and range of her feelings, which include loss of control, helplessness, fear, anger, shame, doubts about sanity, and ambivalence about the abuser. It is very unlikely that an abusive cycle can be broken during a single emergency visit, but the first step towards intervention in a dangerous relationship can be taken. Referral to private therapy, a mental health agency, or community service should be made from the ED. If therapy is not possible for the couple, the victim should be encouraged to seek help alone. In an excellent review of the battered-wife syndrome, Goodstein (1984) outlines in depth a variety of psychosocial interventions.

Child Abuse

There are four types of child abuse: *physical abuse, sexual abuse, neglect,* and *emotional abuse.* ED clinicians should be familiar with their state laws; most states require that reports of suspected abuse or neglect be filed immediately. Interviews with family about child abuse should be handled in a nonthreatening, supportive, empathic manner and should involve both the child and the broader family unit. Hanke (1984) suggests leading up to the question of physical abuse by obtaining more general information such as difficulties during pregnancy, labor, or delivery, feeding or sleeping problems, and presence of colic. Other initial questions include whether the child is provocative, is always getting into trouble, has temper tantrums, or gets into fights with siblings and peers. Questions about actual abuse should aim at getting a clear picture of the parent's and child's behavior before, during, and after an episode of abuse.

Parents may become angry or defensive and deny that they have harmed the child or have done anything wrong. The task is not to blame the parents or get them to admit to wrongdoing, but to make sense of the history and physical findings. The interview should focus on how the child's behavior leads the parents to overreact. The clinician should avoid trying to rescue the child from parents. The main focus of the interview is to convince the parents that physical abuse of the child is a family problem that you would like to help them with. When all data point to child abuse as the most likely diagnosis, or there is other evidence to reasonably suspect the diagnosis, it is wise to review the case with a social work consultant and to file a report as specified by state law.

Sexual abuse in children should be suspected in the following situations (Hanke, 1984):

1. Gynecologic symptoms in prepubertal children
2. Pregnancy in a girl under 12 years old
3. Abrupt changes in behavior or school performance
4. Suicidal behavior in a preadolescent girl
5. Vague somatic complaints from the child or the mother
6. Overstimulation between father and daughter (bathing together, wrestling, excessive physical contact).

Sexual abuse is a sensitive topic. The interview should be conducted in a nonjudgmental and empathic but fact-finding manner. The procedure for data collection is the same used in suspected child abuse. ED interventions are directed toward protecting the child and family from further abuse and engaging the family in treatment.

FORENSIC ISSUES:
COMPETENCY AND COMMITMENT

Commitment laws vary throughout the United States, and clinicians must be familiar with the commitment laws of their state. There are two types of commitment (Hanke, 1984). In *voluntary commitment,* a patient agrees to be admitted to a psychiatric unit for hospitalization. Generally, patients are admitted to unlocked units. Criteria for release from the unit vary from state to state; some states require the patient to request discharge in writing, after which he or she may be allowed to leave or may be detained for variable periods of time. *Involuntary commitment* is undertaken when a patient is mentally ill and refuses to be admitted voluntarily for treatment. In the broadest sense of the term, most involuntary commitments are allowed when patients either pose a danger to themselves or others or demonstrate a lack of ability to care for themselves to such an extent that without intervention they would be at medical risk for death. The evidence needed to determine or predict dangerous behavior is controversial: some state laws require evidence of an imminent act, while others require that a threatened act or steps towards commission of an act be documented. Some states actually require that suicidal or homicidal acts be committed before involuntary commitment can take place. Since most states require that psychiatric treatment occur in the least restrictive setting, involuntary commitment is viewed as a treatment of last resort when other treatments or approaches have failed.

Informed Consent

Informed consent means that before providing treatment of any sort, patients must be informed about what the treatment is, what it will do for them, and what may occur with respect to side effects or morbidity. Patients should also be told what alternative treatments are available, including possible outcomes and side effects, and what will probably happen if they refuse treatment (Sadoff, 1984). It is important that patients be competent to receive the information, to understand it, and to implement it in their thinking and consent. However, in the event of a bona fide emergency ("a valid emergency which would be recognized by any reasonable physician") such as imminent suicide or imminent violence to others, immediate intervention to protect the patient and others takes precedent.

Competency

The issue of competency is separate from that of commitment but is partially related to informed consent (Sadoff, 1984). In the ED, the question of competency most often arises when patients refuse an urgently needed medical or surgical procedure, but do not meet the criteria for involuntary commitment. Many organically impaired patients are not competent to make decisions about emergency treatment. When evaluating such patients, the physician must determine if the patient understands (Sadoff, 1984):

the nature of his or her condition
the risks and benefits of treatment
the risks and benefits of alternative treatment
the medical consequences of refusing treatment.

Failure to understand these issues constitutes incompetency. Most cities have judges or magistrates on call who will grant emergency authorization by phone to proceed with treatment if a patient meets the criteria for incompetency. However, in an emergent situation where immediate medical intervention is necessary to prevent

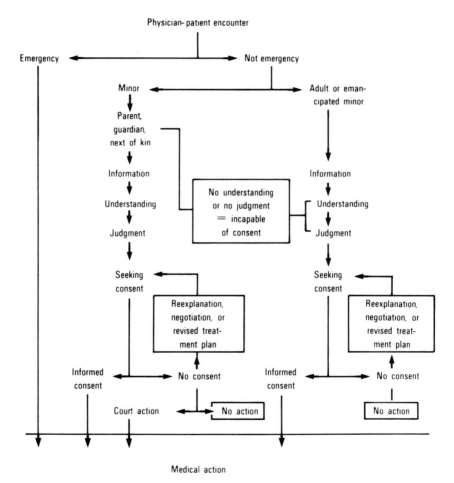

Figure 18–1. *Seeking and obtaining informed consent. (Reproduced with permission from Groves JE, Vacarino JM. Legal aspects of consultation. In: Hackett TP, Cassem NH, eds. Massachusetts General Hospital handbook of general hospital psychiatry, 2nd ed, p 601. Littleton, MA: PSG Publishing Co., 1987)*

death or prolonged morbidity, the doctrine of *implied consent* may be invoked. Specifically, this allows the treating physician to evaluate and treat the emergent condition (Mills and Daniels, 1987). In such situations, the clinician should carefully document all findings that led to his or her conclusion and decision to intervene.

The issue of competency is complex in its relationship to informed consent. In an extensive review of this issue, Groves and Vaccarino (1987) point out that patients may be competent in some situations but not in others. Incompetency may be temporary as mental states fluctuate. The guideline for informed consent from minors varies from state to state, as does the definition of an emancipated minor. A useful decision tree (Groves and Vaccarino, 1987) outlines an approach for obtaining informed consent (Fig. 1) in the ED.

ANNOTATED BIBLIOGRAPHY

Hanke N: Handbook of emergency psychiatry. Lexington, Mass., The Collamore Press, 1985

Walker JI: Psychiatric emergencies: Intervention and resolution. Philadelphia, JB Lippincott, 1983

These two handbooks on emergency psychiatry are comprehensive without overwhelming the reader with detail. They cover all aspects of emergency psychiatry and present them in a concise, clinically pertinent format. The information is clinically relevant and immediately applicable. The books are easy to read, the print is attractive, and the tables are used in a way that summarizes information in a readily retrievable format.

Dubin WR, Weiss KJ, Dorn JM: Pharmacotherapy of psychiatric emergencies. J Clin Psychopharmacol 6:210–222, 1986

This article is a comprehensive review of most of the studies in the literature that have addressed drug management of psychiatric emergencies. In addition to this comprehensive review, the authors propose basic guidelines for the drug management of psychiatric emergencies. The extensive, comprehensive bibliography is useful for those who wish to read the literature on rapid tranquilization.

Bellak L: Emergency psychotherapy and brief psychotherapy. New York, Grune & Stratton, 1965

Though this book is over 20 years old, it still remains a classic for those students interested in the application of psychodynamic principles and psychotherapy in the treatment of psychiatric emergencies and in crisis intervention. The book outlines the basic theoretical background for brief and emergency psychotherapy and offers a step-by-step approach on how to apply crisis-intervention theories in the acute psychiatric emergency. The authors describe the major clinical syndromes encountered in the psychiatric emergency service and emphasize dynamic considerations and therapeutic procedures. Very helpful illustrative case histories are given for each syndrome.

Lion JR: The evaluation and management of the violent patient. Springfield, Ill., Charles C. Thomas, 1972

This classic still remains the most definitive book on managing violent patients. The author provides rich clinical examples and a basic therapeutic approach to the management of aggressive patients. Covered are issues of diagnosis and verbal, chemical, and physical interventions. Also reviewed are staff and legal issues centering on the treatment of the violent patient.

Van Putten T, Marder SR: Behavioral toxicity of antipsychotic drugs. J Clin Psychiatry 48(9 Suppl):13–19, 1987

This article presents an excellent discussion of the antipsychotic drug side effects of akathisia and akinesia. Of importance is the excellent discussion of akathisia, which is often misdiagnosed in the treatment of psychiatric emergencies. The discussion is clinically pertinent with excellent clinical examples. The discussion on akinesia is also comprehensive in its clinical description and clinical vignettes. This is an important article for clinicians who will be using antipsychotic drugs in their daily practice.

REFERENCES

Adams F: Neuropsychiatric evaluation and treatment of delirium in the critically ill cancer patient. Cancer Bull 36:156–160, 1984

Anderson WH: The emergency room. In Hackett TP, Cassem NH (eds): Massachusetts General Hospital handbook of general hospital psychiatry, 2nd ed. Littleton, Mass., PSG Publishing Co., 1987

Bassuk EL, Panzarino PJ, Schoonover SC: General principles of pharmacologic management in the emergency setting. In Bassuk EL, Birk AW (eds): Emergency psychiatry: Concepts, methods, and practices. New York, Plenum, 1984

Bell CC, Palmer JM: Security procedures in a psychiatric emergency service. J Natl Med Assoc 73:835–842, 1981

Burgess AW, Holmstrom LL: Rape trauma syndrome. Am J Psychiatry 137:1336–1347, 1980

Callaham M, Kassel D: Epidemiology of fatal tricyclic depressant ingestion: Implications for management. Ann Emerg Med 14:1–9, 1985

Clinton JE, Sterner S, Stelmachers Z, et al: Haloperidol for sedation of disruptive emergency patients. Ann Emerg Med 16:319–322, 1987

Dencker SJ: High-dose treatment with neuroleptics in the acute phase of mental disorder. Proc R Soc Med 69:(Suppl 1) 32–4, 1976

Dubin WR: The evaluation and management of the violent patient. Ann Emerg Med 10:481–484, 1981

Dubin WR: Assessment and management of psychiatric manifestations of organic brain disease. In Dubin WR, Hanke H, Nickens HW (eds): Clinics in emergency medicine: Psychiatric emergencies. New York, Churchill Livingstone, 1984

Dubin WR: Rapid tranquilization: Antipsychotics or benzodiazepines. J Clin Psychiatry 49(Suppl):S-11, 1988

Dubin WR, Stolberg R: Emergency psychiatry for the house officer. Jamaica, N.Y., Spectrum, 1981

Dubin WR, Waxman H, Weiss K, et al: Rapid tranquilization: The efficacy of oral concentrate. J Clin Psychiatry 46:475–478, 1985

Dubin WR, Weiss KJ: Diagnosis of organic brain syndrome: An emergency department dilemma. J Emerg Med 1:393–397, 1984

Dubin WR, Weiss KJ: Psychiatric emergencies. In Michels R, Cavenar JO, Brodie HK, et al. (eds): Psychiatry, vol. 2. Philadelphia, JB Lippincott, 1985

Dubin WR, Weiss KJ, Dorn JM: Pharmacotherapy of psychiatric emergencies. J Clin Psychopharmacol 6:210–222, 1986

Dubin WR, Weiss KJ, Zeccardi J: OBS: The psychiatric imposter. JAMA 249:60–62, 1983

Dubin WR, Wilson S, Mercer C: Assaults against psychiatrists in outpatient settings. J Clin Psychiatry 49:338–345, 1988

Dudley DL, Rowlett DB, Loebel PJ: Emergency use of intravenous haloperidol. Gen Hosp Psychiatry 1:240–246, 1979

Dwyer B, Weissberg M: Treating violent patients. Psychiatric Times, p. 11, December 1988

Frances RJ, Franklin JE: Alcohol-induced organic mental disorders. In Hales RE, Yudofsky SC (eds): Texbook of neuropsychiatry. Washington DC, American Psychiatric Press, 1987

Goldstein MG: Intensive care unit syndromes. In Stoudemire A, Fogel BS (eds): Principles of medical psychiatry. Orlando, Grune & Stratton, 1987

Goodstein RK: Situational emergencies. In Dubin WR, Hanke N, Nickens HW: Clinics in emergency medicine: Psychiatric emergencies. New York, Churchill Livingston, 1984

Goodstein RK: Common clinical problems of the elderly camouflaged by ageism and atypical presentation. Psych Ann 15:299–312, 1985

Greenblatt DJ, Shader RI: Treatment of the alcohol withdrawal syndrome. In Shader RI (ed): A manual of psychiatric therapeutics. Boston, Little Brown, 1977

Groves JE, Vaccarino JM: Legal aspects of consultation. In Hackett TP, Cassem NH (eds): Massachusetts General Hospital handbook of general hospital psychiatry, 2nd ed. Littleton, MA, PSG Publishing Co., 1987

Gutheil T, Tardiff K: Indications and contraindications for seclusion and restraint. In Tardiff K (ed): The psychiatric uses of seclusion and restraints. Washington DC, American Psychiatric Press, 1984

Hall RCW, Popkin MK, DeVaul, RA, et al.: Physical illness presenting as psychiatric disease. Arch Gen Psych 35:1315–1320, 1978

Hamid TA, Wertz WJ: Mesoridazine versus chlorpromazine in acute schizophrenia: A double-blind investigation. Am J Psychiatry 130:689–692, 1973

Hanke N: Handbook of emergency psychiatry. Lexington, Mass., The Collamore Press, 1984

Hyman SE, Arana GW: Handbook of psychiatric drug therapy. Boston, Little Brown, 1987

Johnson SB, Alvarez WA, Freinhar JP: Rhabdomyolysis in retrospect: Are psychiatric patients predisposed to this little-known syndrome? Int J Psychiatry Med 17:163–171, 1987

Konikoff F, Kuritzky A, Jerushalmi Y, et al.: Neuroleptic malignant syndrome induced by a single injection of haloperidol (letter). Br Med J 289:1228–1229, 1984

Leeman CP: Diagnostic errors in emergency room medicine: physical illness in patients labeled "psychiatric" and vice versa. Int J Psychiatry Med 6:533–540, 1975

Lion JR: Evaluation and management of the violent patient. Springfield, Ill., Charles C. Thomas, 1972

Lion JR, Levenberg LB, Strange RE: Restraining the violent patient. J Psychiatric Nurs and Ment Health Serv 10:9–11, 1972

Lion JR, Pasternak SA: Countertransference reactions to violent patients. Am J Psychiatry 130:207–210, 1973

Lipowski ZJ: Delirium, clouding of consciousness and confusion. J Nerv Ment Dis 145:227–255, 1967

Man PL, Chen CH: Rapid tranquilization of acutely psychotic patients with intramuscular haloperidol and chlorpromazine. Psychosomatics 14:59–63, 1973

Mason AS, Granacher RP: Clinical handbook of antipsychotic drug therapy. New York, Brunner/Mazel, 1980

Menza MA, Murray GB, Holmes VF, et al: Decreased extrapyramidal symptoms with intravenous haloperidol. J Clin Psychiatry 48:278–280, 1987

Mills MJ, Daniels ML: Medical-legal issues. In Stoudemire A, Fogel BS (eds): Principles of medical psychiatry. Orlando, Grune & Stratton, 1987

Mueller PS: Neuroleptic malignant syndrome. Psychosomatics 26:654–661, 1985

O'Brien PJ: Prevalence of neuroleptic malignant syndrome (letter). Am J Psychiatry 144:1371, 1987

Perry S: Acute psychotic states. In Glick RT, Meyerson AT, Robbins E, et al. (eds): Psychiatric emergencies. New York, Grune & Stratton, 1976

Reuler JB, Girard DE, Cooney TG: Wernicke's encephalopathy. NEJM 16:1035–1039, 1985

Robbins E, Stern M: Assessment of psychiatric emergencies. In Glick RA, Myerson AT, Robbins E et al. (eds): Psychiatric emergencies. New York, Grune & Stratton, 1976

Sadoff RL: Legal issues in the care and treatment of psychiatric emergencies. In Dubin WR, Hanke N, Nickens HW (eds): Clinics in emergency medicine: Psychiatric emergencies. New York, Churchill Livingstone, 1984

Salamon I: Violent and agressive behavior. In Glick RA, Myerson AT, Robbins E et al. (eds): Psychiatric emergencies. New York, Grune & Stratton, 1976

Shader RI, Greenblatt DJ: Back to basics—Diagnosis before treatment: Hopelessness, hypothyroidism, aging and lithium. J Clin Psychopharmacol 7:375, 1987

Sos J, Cassem NH: Managing postoperative agitation. Drug Ther 10:103–106, 1980

Swift RM: Alcohol and drug abuse in the medical setting. In Stoudemire A, Fogel BS (eds): Principles of medical psychiatry. Orlando, Grune & Stratton, 1987

Tardiff K, Sweillam A: Assault, suicide, and mental illness. Arch Gen Psychiatry 37:164–169, 1980

Tesar GE, Murray GB, Cassem NH: Use of high-dose intravenous haloperidol in the treatment of agitated cardiac patients. J Clin Psychopharmacol 5:344–347, 1985

Van Putten T, Marder SR: Behavorial toxicity of antipsychotic drugs. J Clin Psychiatry 48(9 Suppl):13–19, 1987

Walker JI: Psychiatric emergencies: Intervention and resolution. Philadelphia, JB Lippincott, 1983

Weissberg MP: Emergency room medical clearance: An educational problem. Am J Psychiatry 136:787–790, 1979

Wells CE, Duncan GW: Neurology for psychiatrists. Philadelphia, FA Davis, 1980

Wise M: Delirium. In Hales RE, Yudofsky SC (eds): Textbook of neuropsychiatry. Washington DC, American Psychiatric Press, 1987

19

Psychiatric Aspects of Medical Practice

James L. Levenson

Psychiatric disorders are common in medical patients, although the measured frequency varies depending on the criteria used. A reasonable estimate would be that 25 to 30% of medical outpatients and 40 to 50% of general medical inpatients have diagnosable psychiatric disorders. The most common psychiatric syndromes are depression, anxiety, and substance abuse in medical outpatients (Von Korff et al., 1987; Kessler, Cleary, and Burke, 1985) and organic mental disorders, depression, and substance abuse in medical inpatients (Wallen et al., 1987; Fulop et al., 1987). Non-psychiatric physicians underdiagnose and undertreat psychiatric disorders in the medically ill (Jencks, 1985; Cavanaugh, 1983). This is unfortunate because (1) many patients with serious psychiatric illnesses depend on primary care physicians, not mental health professionals, for their mental health care (Schurman, Kramer, and Mitchell, 1985; Shapiro et al., 1984) and (2) without recognition and intervention, coincident psychopathology increases medical care utilization and costs (Hankin et al. 1982; Fulop et al., 1987; Wallen et al., 1987).

The goals of this chapter are to examine the sources and consequences of psychiatric symptoms and disorders specific to medical patients and to understand the physician's corresponding responsibilities and opportunities for treatment. Major psychiatric disorders that are often encountered in the medical setting are also discussed individually elsewhere in this book, including organic mental disorders (Chapter 3), personality disorders (Chapter 5), mood disorders (Chapter 6), somatoform disorders (Chapter 8), substance abuse (Chapter 9), and psychophysiological disorders (Chapter 10).

This chapter focuses on special aspects of psychiatry in medical practice not discussed in depth in the earlier chapters. First, *psychological and emotional reactions to physical illness* will be discussed, including the management of these reactions in the general medical setting. Second, the nature of *grief and mourning* and the *dying patient* will be considered. Third, *drugs and medical disorders that can produce psychiatric symptoms* will be reviewed. Finally, guidelines are provided for the evaluation of patients' *competency* and for *obtaining psychiatric consultation.* (See also Chapter 18 for the latter.)

COMMON PSYCHOLOGICAL REACTIONS TO MEDICAL ILLNESS AND TREATMENT

Regression and Dependency

Regression, a return to more childlike patterns of behavior and feeling, is a universal human reaction to illness. Sick patients wish to be comforted, cared for, and freed from the responsibilities of adult life. In moderation this is adaptive, as the ill must give up some control over their bodies and lives and accept some dependency on others. Regression is problematic when it becomes more extreme. It is difficult to care for a patient who has minimal pain tolerance, cannot tolerate being alone, and is infantile, overly needy, whining, and too easily upset or frustrated.

Not all patients regress in the same fashion. The varieties of regression are similar to the developmental phases of early childhood. Like young infants, some regressed patients are overdependent and seem to want "feeding" on demand, constantly pushing the nurses' call button in the hospital or, as outpatients, telephoning the physician too much. They let others make decisions, complain petulantly about their care, and avoid sharing responsibility.

Other regressed patients resemble children in the "terrible twos." They have an excessive need to control their medical care in the hospital environment and get into struggles over less critical elements of their care. They may have tantrums over getting their way and tend to be perfectionistic and intolerant of any irregularities, disarray, or tardiness.

Like many 3- to 4-year-olds, some patients who regress need to feel powerful and admired. They tend to be aggressive and narcissistic, oblivious to the needs of other patients around them. They may be sexually provocative, particularly if the illness has assaulted their sense of self-esteem and power (e.g., acute paraplegia or myocardial infarction).

These developmental descriptions of regression are illustrations that do appear as described, but also appear at milder, more easily tolerated levels. When ill, we all regress more or less along each of these lines: the need to be cared for, the need for control and order, the need for increased self-esteem. Some patients find such regression comfortable (ego-syntonic), particularly if it elicits comforting responses from those around them. Others are very uncomfortable with their regression (ego-dystonic), feeling embarrassed at the unexpected emergence of childlike feelings or actions.

Sources

As noted, moderate regression is adaptive. In the face of illness, adults hope to receive the nurturance, reassurance, and care provided by parents during childhood. Patients who regress too far often have preexisting psychopathology, particularly personality disorders. Those who use a narrow range of inflexible defenses become more helpless and regressed when serious illness overwhelms them. Patients who find regression too comfortable have usually received significant secondary gain from previous illnesses. Those who suffered serious deprivation in childhood, with emotionally or physically absent or dysfunctional parents, may experience the care of physicians and nurses as the only nurturant experiences they have ever had. As adults they unconsciously yearn to recreate this experience and so may regress excessively when ill.

Intervention

When regression is marked, physicians and nurses become impatient and angry, especially with those patients whom they feel should not act "childishly" (e.g., patients who are healthcare professionals). As with other reactions to illness, physicians should avoid scolding or shaming patients (a parallel regression in the physician). Instead, the physician can explain to the patient that feeling more dependent or needy is part of an expected reaction to illness. Patients who make repeated, unreasonable, or unrealistic demands may require limit-setting. While tolerating some necessary regression, the physician takes steps to mobilize the patient physically and emotionally to participate in treatment and rehabilitation. Psychiatric consultation should be sought if regression is too great or persists too long, creating significant interference in treatment, distress for the patient, or unnecessary invalidism.

Anxiety

Anxiety occurs with the same symptoms in the medically ill as in healthy individuals, but a correct diagnosis is more difficult with coexistence of physical disease because the signs of anxiety may be misinterpreted as those of physical disease, and vice versa. Many somatic pathophysiological events share symptoms with anxiety states, such as tachycardia, diaphoresis, tremor, shortness of breath, or abdominal or chest pain. Panic attacks present with so many prominent somatic symptoms that they are routinely misdiagnosed as a wide variety of physical illnesses. On the other hand, autonomic arousal and anxious agitation in a medically ill patient may be prematurely attributed by the physician to "reactive anxiety," when they also can be signs of a pulmonary embolus or cardiac arrhythmia.

Physicians tend to become desensitized in working with seriously ill patients and may lose sight of the spectrum of normal anxious reactions. For example, having diagnosed diabetes mellitus in an asymptomatic young adult patient, the physician may assume that a diagnosis of "just chemical diabetes" ought not to cause too much anxiety. The physician may not notice that the patient is frightened, or if the physician does notice, he or she may conclude that the patient is responding with pathological anxiety. The patient may be thinking about serious complications (amputations, blindness, and kidney failure) witnessed in relatives with the disease, leading to more anxiety than the physician expected.

Sources

There are many reasons for anxiety in the medically ill patient. Different individuals will react to the same diagnosis, prognosis, treatment, and complications with widely varying concerns. Patients may be very aware of some fears, but simultaneously affected by less conscious ones. Ideally, the physician explores this with the patient by inquiring about those aspects of the illness that are causing anxiety and by observing the patient's behavior.

Fear of death frequently occurs during the course of an illness, but not necessarily in proportion to the severity of disease. Many other factors may magnify or diminish this fear (e.g., previous losses, religious beliefs, personality, intractable pain, and previous experiences in the medical care system, including witnessing other patients' deaths). While for some patients with minor illness the fear of death can be overwhelming, for others, with major or even terminal illness, it may be less important than other fears.

Fear of abandonment ("separation anxiety") occurs in the medically ill as the fear of being alone. It may occur under the same circumstances that give rise to the fear of death, but here an individual is less concerned about the end of life and more concerned with the thought of being separated from loved ones. For some individuals who are immature, overly dependent, or overwhelmed, being hospitalized may itself precipitate acute separation anxiety. The patient must leave the security of home, family, and friends for the impersonal and anonymous institution of the modern hospital.

Closely related to separation anxiety is the *fear of strangers* ("stranger anxiety"). Visiting a physician when ill requires a patient to answer personal questions and to be physically examined by and put one's trust in (usually) previously unknown physicians and other members of the healthcare team. As patients become more acutely ill, or face a terminal illness, the fear of abandonment tends to be much greater than the fear of strangers. The sick and dying very rarely wish to be left alone. Residents and interns are often surprised at how anxious some patients become when it comes time for physicians to rotate to a new service each month, not recognizing how important they have become to their patients. What has become routine for the house staff is a repetitive source of anxiety for patients.

The morbidity and disability caused by physical disease produce a number of other fears. *The fear of loss of, or injury to, body parts or bodily functions* includes fear of amputations, blindness, and mutilating scars and is particularly highly charged when directed at the genitalia ("castration anxiety"). *The fear of pain* is universal, but the threshold varies greatly among individuals. Some patients experience intense *fear of loss of control.* Involving the outer world, this is the fear that one will no longer be able to manage a career, family, or other aspects of one's life. Directed inwardly, individuals may be frightened by loss of control over their own bodies, including fear of incontinence, metastasis, or autoimmune disease. Closely related is the *fear of dependency.* Here, it is not so much the loss of control of one's body or life that frightens the patient, but having to depend on others. For some this fear of dependency is part of a more general *fear of intimacy.* Certain individuals (particularly schizoid, avoidant, paranoid, and some obsessive-compulsive personalities) are frightened of getting too close to people in any setting. Physical illness is very threatening to them because they must allow physicians and nurses to penetrate the interpersonal barriers they have constructed.

Finally, some patients experience *guilty fears* ("superego anxiety") related to their anticipation that others will feel angry or disappointed by them. This is particularly common with illnesses attributable to patients' habits (smoking, diet, alcohol, etc.) and in situations where patients have not complied with physicians' advice. Some patients may feel their illness is a punishment from God or has some special punitive significance for past "sins."

Consequences

Some degree of anxiety is adaptive during physical illness because it alerts the individual to the presence of danger and the need for action. An appropriate and tolerable amount of anxiety aids patients in getting medical help and adhering to physicians' recommendations. The total absence of anxiety may be maladaptive, promoting a cavalier attitude of minimizing disease and the need for treatment. In most such cases, however, the absence of anxiety is only an apparent one—the patient is often extremely anxious unconsciously and is resorting to defenses like denial (see below) in order not to be overwhelmed by the illness. Too much anxiety is also maladaptive, leading to unnecessary invalidism. Becoming paralyzed with fear of disease progression or relapse, such patients give up functioning occupationally, socially, and/or sexually. In most diseases a modicum of anxiety is expectable and adaptive, but occasionally even a normal amount of anxiety can pose some risk. For example, immediately after an acute myocardial infarction, any anxiety-associated increases in heart rate and blood pressure may be considered dangerous and warrant treatment.

Intervention

First, the physician should explore the particular patient's fears. If the physician wrongly presumes to know why the patient is anxious without asking, then the patient is likely to feel misunderstood. Facile, nonspecific reassurance can undermine the physician-patient relationship, as the patient is likely to feel the physician is out of touch with and not really interested in what he or she is actually feeling.

Knowing the patient's specific fears leads the physician to appropriate therapeutic interventions. Unrealistic fears can be reduced by cognitive interventions. For example, the patient who is frightened of having intercourse after a heart attack can be reassured that it is unnecessary to give up sex. Fears of closeness can be reduced by taking extra care to respect the patient's privacy. When fears of pain, loss, or injury to body parts are not unrealistic, it is helpful for the physician to emphasize the ways in which medical care can reduce suffering and enhance functioning through rehabilitation. Physicians should tell patients about disease-specific support organizations for patients and families, which provide a continuing antidote for anxiety.

When clarifying the patient's anxieties and intervening in one of these ways is insufficient, the judicious, short-term use of benzodiazepines may be helpful (see Chapters 7 and 17). However, drug therapy for anxiety is no substitute for the reassurance and support that can be provided through the doctor-patient relationship. Antianxiety medication is best directed at new symptoms of anxiety that have been precipitated by an identifiable recent stressor (e.g., hospitalization). Drug therapy of anxiety in the medically ill should be time-limited (usually 1 to 3 weeks), because tolerance and dependence may develop with long-term use. If benzodiazepines are abruptly discontinued, significant withdrawal symptoms may occur, including rebound anxiety and insomnia, agitation, psychosis, confusion, and seizures.

While benzodiazepines are relatively safe in the medically ill, their most common side effect, sedation, may intensify confusion in delirium and dementia, suppress respiratory drive in severe pulmonary disease, and interfere with optimal participation by patients in their medical care. Sustained use of benzodiazepines or other sedatives will aggravate depression. Antianxiety medication prescribed during a medical hospitalization should not be automatically continued after discharge.

In deciding whether psychiatric consultation and intervention are required, it is important to distinguish normal, expectable anxiety from more serious "pathological" anxiety. Anxiety is usually a symptom of a psychiatric disorder when it remains unrealistic or out of proportion despite the physician's clarification and reassurance, as described above. Other signs that anxiety requires psychiatric intervention are sustained disruption of sleep or gastrointestinal functions, marked autonomic hyperarousal (tachycardia, tachypnea, sweating), and panic attacks. Psychiatric consultation should also always be requested when anxiety fails to respond to low doses of benzodiazepines, is accompanied by psychosis, or renders patients unable to participate in their medical care (including those who threaten to leave against medical advice).

Depression

In addition to clinical psychiatric depressions, depressed states in the medically ill may include grief, sadness, demoralization, fatigue, exhaustion, psychomotor slowing, and organic depression of the central nervous system. The same pitfalls of under- or overdiagnosis described for anxiety also occur with depression. The vegetative signs and symptoms of depression (e.g., anorexia, weight loss, weakness, constipation, insomnia) may be incorrectly attributed to a physical etiology and lead the physician to undertake unnecessary diagnostic evaluation. On the other hand, the physician must also guard against prematurely concluding that somatic symptoms are due to depression, as an occult medical disease (e.g., malignancy) may be missed. Desensitization to illness and suffering may make physicians unaware of, or impatient with and intolerant of, normal reactive depression. Physicians sometimes err in the other direction and regard a serious (and treatable) coexisting psychiatric depression as merely a "normal" response to physical illness.

Sources

Medically ill patients feel sad or depressed about many of the same issues discussed above under anxiety. When a feared event has not yet taken place, patients are anxious; when the loss or injury has already occurred, the patient becomes depressed. Thus, depression may arise secondary to loss of relationships, loss of body parts or functions, loss of control or independence, chronic pain, or guilt. Hospitalization results in separation of the patient from loved ones, which is a potential source for depression, especially for young children and mothers of infants. Medical illness also may reawaken dormant grief and sadness when a patient recalls the parent or sibling who died from the same disease the patient has. Patients who cannot express anger, either because they have always had difficulty doing so or because they are afraid of offending those with whom they are angry (e.g., physicians), are at higher risk for depression.

Another explanation for depression in the medically ill is *learned helplessness,* a behavioral model derived from animal experiments. When repeatedly exposed to painful or other aversive stimuli while being prevented from controlling or escaping from such stimulation, many species become passive, withdrawn, and unmotivated. In patients, the course of physical illness, particularly when there are multiple relapses, relentless progression, and/or treatment failure, may produce a very similar state of helplessness, giving up, and the perception that one has no control over one's fate. Both experimentally and clinically, learned helplessness can be reduced by increasing the subject's sense of control. Physicians may unwittingly add to some patients' helplessness by not actively eliciting patients' participation and preferences in decision-making about their health care.

Consequences

In the face of disease and disability, patients frequently feel discouraged, dejected, and helpless and need physicians who are able and willing to listen to such feelings. When feelings of sadness become too great, and demoralization or clinical depression occurs, a number of maladaptive consequences may ensue, including poor compliance, poor nutrition and hygiene, and giving up prematurely. If severe, patients may become actively or passively suicidal (e.g., a transplant patient who deliberately misses doses of maintenance immunosuppressive drugs). Recognizing these serious consequences helps the physician to distinguish pathological depression from normal depressive reactions, including grief (see below).

Intervention

As with the anxious patient, the first step for the physician is to listen and understand. Physicians can help patients by encouraging them to openly express sadness and grief related to illness and loss. Physicians should avoid premature or unrealistic reassurance or an overly cheerful attitude as this tends to alienate depressed patients, who feel that their physician is insensitive and either does not understand or does not want to hear about their sadness. Physicians *should* provide specific and realistic reassurance, emphasizing a constructive treatment plan, and mobilize the patient's support system. For patients who seem to be experiencing learned helplessness, enabling them to have a sense of more control over their illness will be helpful. Physicians can accomplish this by encouraging patients to express preferences about their health care, by giving them more control over the hospital and nursing routines, and by emphasizing active steps patients can undertake, rather than just passively accepting what is prescribed by others for them. Patients who are demoralized before beginning or at the start of major treatment (e.g., transplantation, dialysis, chemotherapy, colostomy) can benefit from speaking with successfully treated patients who have had the same disorder.

Normal depressive reactions to illness must be differentiated from pathological depression, which requires psychiatric consultation and intervention (antidepressants and psychotherapy). Patients experiencing normal degrees of depression retain their abilities to communicate, make decisions, and participate in their own care when encouraged to do so. Depression usually constitutes a psychiatric disorder when depressed mood, hopelessness, worthlessness, withdrawal, and vegetative symptoms (e.g., insomnia, anorexia, fatigue) are persistent *and* out of proportion to coexisting medical illness. Urgent psychiatric referral should always be obtained when the patient is thinking about suicide (see below) or has depression with psychotic symptoms. Psychiatric consultation should also be obtained if less serious depression fails to improve with the physician's support and reassurance and becomes prolonged, if antidepressant medication is needed, or if patients remain too depressed to participate in their own health care and rehabilitation.

Assessing Suicide Risk in Medical Patients

All physicians should be able to screen patients for suicide risk in the medical setting. Chapter 18 addresses assessment of suicide in the emergency setting. Suicide is a common preventable cause of death in the medically ill, and patients frequently drop hints to their physicians about suicidal impulses or plans. Chronic illness and chronic pain are risk factors for suicide. The physician's concern should increase when other risk factors are present. These include major mood disorder, alcoholism, schizophrenia, organic mental disorders, recent loss of a loved one, divorce, loss of a job, or family history of suicide.

Whenever patients appear depressed or despondent, physicians should explicitly ask about suicidal feelings and plans. Physicians are sometimes reluctant, fearing that they will "put ideas into the patient's head" or offend the patient. Others simply are not sure how to ask. The great majority of patients who are experiencing suicidal thoughts are relieved to discuss them with a caring physician. The physician should ask gradually and directly, with a series of questions like: "How bad have you been feeling? Have you ever felt bad enough to not go on with life? Have you ever thought of doing something about it? What did you think of doing?". Ominous signs indicative of serious suicide risk include:

1. The motive behind the suicidal wish is entirely self-directed, with no apparent intent to influence someone else
2. Detailed suicide plans are contemplated over an extended period of time
3. Lethal means have been considered by and are available to the patient
4. A suicide attempt was made in an isolated setting where the individual was unlikely to be discovered
5. The individual is putting affairs in order, i.e., making out a will, reviewing life-insurance coverage, or giving away prized possessions
6. Hints or direct statements are made about feeling suicidal. Spontaneous statements like "I'm going to kill myself" should never be dismissed as "just talk," but always carefully and thoroughly explored by the primary physician.

The presence of any suicidal ideation, with or without any attempt, is an indication for psychiatric consultation, and it is the physician's responsibility to ensure that it is obtained. Physicians must also guard against unwittingly providing the means for suicide: for significantly depressed patients, physicians should prescribe all medications in carefully monitored, small supplies (usually 1 week at a time).

Denial

Denial is a defense mechanism that reduces anxiety and conflict by blocking conscious awareness of thoughts, feelings, or facts that an individual cannot face. Denial is common in the medically ill, but varies in its timing, strength, and adaptive value. Some patients are aware of what is wrong with them but consciously suppress this knowledge by avoiding thinking about or discussing it. Others cope with the threat of being overwhelmed by their illness by unconsciously repressing it and thereby remain unaware of their illness. Physicians may sometimes misperceive as deniers patients whose lack of awareness stems from not having been sufficiently informed about and/or not understanding the nature of their disease. While denial of physical disease may accompany and be a symptom of a major psychiatric disorder (e.g., schizophrenia), outright denial also occurs in the absence of other significant psychopathology. Marked denial, in which the patient emphatically refuses to accept the existence or significance of obvious symptoms and signs of a disease, may be seen by the physician as an indication that the patient is "crazy," because the patient seems impervious to rational persuasion. In the absence of other evidence of major psychopathology (e.g., paranoid delusions), such denial is not often a sign of psychosis but rather is a defense against overwhelming fear.

Denial also occurs as a direct consequence of organic disease of the central nervous system, commonly in dementia along with other cognitive deficits and rarely as an isolated finding with parietal lobe lesions (anosognosia).

Sources

Denial is a defense mechanism used in the face of intolerable anxiety or unresolved conflict. The medically ill patient, threatened with any of the fears outlined above, may resort to denial. Individuals who deny other life stresses, such as marital or occupational problems, are particularly likely to use denial in the face of clinical illness. Denial is also common in individuals who are threatened by dependency associated with illness, for whom the sick role is inconsistent with their self-image of potency and invulnerability.

To avoid fear and conflict, the patient may deny all or only part of the disease and its consequences. Some will deny that they are ill at all; others will accept the symptoms but deny the particular diagnosis (usually displacing it to a more benign organ system, e.g., interpreting angina as indigestion), the need for treatment, or the need to alter lifestyle.

Consequences

Denial is not always a pathologic defense and may serve several adaptive purposes. When denial occurs as part of the initial shock upon learning of a serious diagnosis or complication, it allows the individual sufficient time to adjust to the bad news and avoid overwhelming, full, immediate awareness. A lesser, continuing degree of denial helps patients function without being overly preoccupied with full consciousness of the morbidity or mortality associated with their diseases.

The adaptive value of denial may vary depending on the nature or stage of illness. For example, myocardial infarction and sudden death may occur when denial prevents an individual with symptoms of coronary artery disease from acknowledging the symptoms and promptly seeking medical care. Those who delay going to the hospital after the acute onset of coronary symptoms have greater morbidity and mortality. Physicians seldom have an opportunity to affect denial at that stage of illness (that is, prior to seeking medical care), except by educating the general public. Moderate denial during hospitalization may be very adaptive, perhaps even reducing morbidity and mortality in some diseases (Levenson et al., 1989). If not excessive, such denial reduces anxiety but does not prevent the patient from accepting and cooperating with medical treatment.

Denial after hospital discharge may also be helpful or harmful. Too little denial may leave the patient flooded with fears of disability and death, resulting in unnecessary invalidism. However, excessive denial may result in the patient's rushing back to full-time work, disregarding the rehabilitation plan, ignoring modifiable risk factors, and adopting a cavalier attitude toward medication or other treatment.

Intervention

When a patient's denial does not preclude cooperation with treatment, the physician should leave it alone. The physician does have an ethical and professional obligation to ensure that the patient has been informed about his or her illness and treatment. Following that, if the patient accepts treatment but persists in what seems an irrationally optimistic outlook, the physician should respect the patient's need to use denial to cope. For some the denial is fragile, and the physician must judge whether the defense should be supported and strengthened, or whether the patient would do better by giving up the denial to discuss fears and receive reassurance from the physician. The physician should not support denial by giving the patient false information but rather by encouraging hope and optimism.

When denial is extreme, patients may refuse vital treatment or threaten to leave against medical advice. Here the physician must try to help reduce denial, but not by directly assaulting the patient's defenses. Since such desperate denial of reality usually reflects intense underlying anxiety, trying to scare the patient into cooperating will intensify denial and the impulse to flight. A better strategy for the physician is to avoid directly challenging the patient's claims while simultaneously reinforcing concern for the patient and maximizing the patient's sense of control. Involving family members should be considered, as they may be more successful in convincing the patient that accepting medical care is in his or her best interests. Psychiatric consultation is very helpful in cases of extreme or persistent maladaptive denial and should always be obtained if the denial is accompanied by symptoms of a major psychiatric disorder.

Noncompliance

Noncompliance with medical treatment is a frequent behavioral response to medical illness. It may occur in up to 90% of those receiving short-term medication regimens and probably averages about 50% in the drug treatment of patients with chronic disease (Eraker, Kirscht, and Becker, 1984). Physicians generally underestimate its occurrence, misled both by wishful thinking and by stereotypes of the noncompliant patient. Noncompliance is common in patients who poorly understand their treatment, in those who are hostile to medical care, in those with major psychiatric disorders, and in those who flatly deny their illness. However, noncompliance also occurs in "ideal" patients and is not confined to any socioeconomic or ethnic group. Physicians are also misled because patients overestimate their compliance when asked. They may be embarrassed by their failure to stick to the regimen, frightened of the consequences (including fear of angering their physician), or unconscious of the problem. The physician will be more likely to get accurate information by asking in a friendly, nonjudgmental way without any threats, accusations, or anger. The physician must avoid shaming or infantilizing the patient through scolding or patronizing.

Labeling a patient as "noncompliant" implies that the physician's recommendations are entirely correct, but sometimes our instructions are unnecessary, debatable, or even wrong. Physicians must also avoid concluding noncompliance whenever there is unexplained failure of the patient to respond to the usual treatment. This may be an appropriate time to suspect noncompliance, but the physician should not reach a conclusion without evidence.

A patient is noncompliant when the patient and physician both share the belief that treatment is warranted, but the patient fails to follow through. However, physicians must remember that patients have their own value and belief systems that guide their actions. Scientific principles and the medical literature are as not compelling for most patients as they are for physicians. Religious beliefs, cultural values, and the patient's own theories of causation and treatment, which may be culture-bound or idiosyncratic, all influence patient responses to physicians' recommendations.

Noncompliance is not a monolithic behavior. While some patients are globally noncompliant, others are only with a particular aspect of treatment. Some have difficulty keeping appointments, others with taking medication. Many have difficulty complying with recommended changes in habits or lifestyle, including patterns of work and sleep, smoking, diet, and exercise. Others may follow recommendations coming from one trusted doctor (often a primary-care physician), while ignoring the advice of unfamiliar consultants. Some individuals are only intermittently noncompliant (for example, only during periods of depression).

Sources

As suggested above, preexisting beliefs the patient has about diagnosis and treatment are a major source of deviation from the treatment plan. Many ethnic subcultures have their own traditional theories of disease and therapy that may influence how members take medications. Such patients tend to hide this from physicians who are not members of the same ethnic/cultural group, because the patients think their beliefs will not be accepted or because they are embarrassed to acknowledge "old-fashioned," "superstitious" ideas. A similar phenomenon is seen with those who believe various "counterculture" theories of disease like homeopathy or naturopathy and with followers of religions that practice faith-healing. Some patients have deep and powerful beliefs about the right and wrong way to treat their illness, based on past personal or family experience. If a severe side effect has previously occurred with dire consequences or, alternatively, the patient knows someone who did well despite refusing treatment, the physician may find the patient very reluctant to accept treatment.

Noncompliance is more likely to occur when the treatment regimen is too complex (i.e., multiple drugs on different dosage schedules), expensive, inconvenient, or long-term, or if it requires alteration of lifestyle. Misunderstanding or lack of knowledge may be the most common source of apparent noncompliance. Physicians widely overestimate patients' understanding of the reasons for treatment, the method and schedule prescribed, and the consequences of not following through. Physicians tend to assume that they are understood by patients, when they are often not. One study showed that "q6 hours" was correctly understood by only 36% of the patient sample. (Mazzullo, 1976).

The previously described emotional and defensive reactions to illness (anxiety, depression, denial, and regression) are also major causes of noncompliance. Patients may be frightened by the treatment itself, or simply avoid carrying out the treatment or habit-change because it reminds them of the feared disease. Patients who are depressed may do a poor job of following treatment recommendations because of poor concentration, low motivation, pessimism, or acting out of suicidal feelings. Individuals who need to feel strongly in control of their lives may get into struggles with physicians over compliance as a way of maintaining a sense of power over their lives and disease.

Consequences

Noncompliance results in inadequate treatment, poor follow-up, and failure to reduce risk factors, with consequent increased morbidity and mortality. Noncompliance also causes much frustration and consternation for the physician and strains the doctor-patient relationship. A vicious circle may be established in which the patient, finding that the physician becomes angry over incomplete compliance, volunteers less and less about it. The physician in turn feels increasingly upset that the patient seems to be ignoring instructions and is not being forthright.

Intervention

Trying to scare the patient into compliance is rarely successful. Patients who are noncompliant because they are already frightened will become even more anxious and harder to work with. The physician should inform patients of the consequences of not following recommendations, but preferably by emphasizing the benefits of treatment. Positive reinforcement to motivate behavior is almost always more effective than negative reinforcement or punishment, a truism well established in behavioral psychology. Scolding, shaming, or threatening seldom has a beneficial effect. It is also important to maintain a nonjudgmental, nonpunitive attitude when a patient confesses noncompliance, so that the patient will be open about deviations later in the course of treatment.

Physicians can also enhance compliance by careful attention to treatment recommendations. The regimen should be simplified by minimizing the number of drugs and the number of times per day they need to be taken. Even the most highly motivated patients will have difficulty if they must take one drug q.i.d., one t.i.d, one b.i.d., and one every other day. When a regimen remains necessarily complex, the physician should help the patient determine which aspects of treatment are most important. It is also helpful to implement the complex regimen gradually, adding one drug at a time, and to tailor dosage schedules to the patient's lifestyle. Compliance is also enhanced by incorporating the patient's preferences, which may be based on realistic factors (e.g., differing side effect profiles) or on less objective beliefs (e.g., the drug that the patient's sister did well on).

Physicians should also exercise some restraint pursuing therapeutic goals. While physicians have an ethical responsibility to maximize patients' health, therapeutic perfectionism fails to recognize that, for a particular patient, other values may counterbalance some aspects of treatment. Physicians also have an ethical responsibility to respect the individual patient's autonomous wishes and not to ignore them in the pursuit of an ideal therapeutic outcome. Compromise with the patient is not only ethically justified, but is also a practical way of enhancing compliance with the most essential aspects of treatment.

Psychiatric consultation is appropriate whenever noncompliance appears linked to a major psychiatric disorder. It may also be very helpful whenever physician and patient are at a standoff, although the physician should not expect the psychiatrist to compel the patient to become compliant. Instead, the psychiatrist helps arbitrate the dispute by eliciting the patient's values and motivation, recognizing psychological factors like anxiety or a personality disorder that may be interfering, and repairing misunderstandings in the patient's relationship with the primary physician.

Discharges Against Medical Advice

Leaving the hospital against medical advice (AMA) might be viewed as a drastic extension of noncompliance. Approximately 1% of all general hospital discharges are AMA. Patients who leave AMA have many different motives. Some are patients whose psychological reactions to illness are so intense that they try to flee (e.g., a patient phobic about undergoing general anesthesia who leaves AMA the night before surgery). Some patients are angry, feeling mistreated, misinformed, ignored, or insulted by medical or nursing staff members. Such perceptions may conform to actual experience, may be distortions arising from a patient's disordered personality, or more often may be both. Any patient who suddenly, and for no apparent reason, wishes to leave during the first few days of hospitalization may be dependent on alcohol or other substances. Agitation and irritability may reflect early withdrawal symptoms, and the patient may wish to leave the hospital to gain access to the abused substance and avoid further withdrawal. Another segment of potential AMA discharges are patients who are delirious or demented. If the physician has not recognized that the patient has an organic brain syndrome, the patient's attempt to leave the hospital may be misperceived as rationally motivated, when instead it results from the patient's confusion and misperception of reality.

The direct consequence of AMA discharges is the disruption or cessation of medical care. Such discharges are rarely if ever amicable, leaving patients, physicians, and other hospital staff resentful, hurt, and indignant. Rather than approaching the widening breach in the relationship as something to be repaired, physicians and staff may respond in a legalistic and bureaucratic manner. Patients may in turn become more upset, feeling further misunderstood and not cared for.

When a patient first expresses the intention of leaving the hospital AMA, the physician should not coerce, threaten, or try to scare the patient into remaining. The first step is to try to restore the alliance by listening to the patient's grievances, giving them legitimate consideration, and trying to work out compromises. Suspected withdrawal syndromes should be appropriately treated. If the patient still wishes to leave, the physician should calmly explain the potential consequences, emphasizing the benefits further hospitalization can offer.

If these initial steps do not lead to constructive negotiations, psychiatric consultation is indicated. The actual AMA form used by many hospitals should not be overvalued: while it serves an administrative purpose, it is unnecessary and is insufficient to protect against future lawsuits. Rather, the physician's ethical and legal obligation in such a situation is to ensure that the patient is making an informed choice. The patient's reasons for leaving and the physician's concerns that have been communicated to the patient should be documented in the patient's chart. If it appears that the patient is incapable of understanding the need for continued treatment due to mental illness or severe medical illness or both, this too should be documented, and the possibility of involuntary medical treatment should be considered.

Doctor-Shopping

Physicians commonly encounter patients who appear to be shopping around for medical care, either visiting a succession of doctors or several simultaneously for the same complaints. Some are patients with strong psychological motivations for staying in the sick role (e.g., hypochondriacs). Others may be seeking a particular diagnosis, treatment approach, or personality style in their physician and will continue searching until they find it. A few are unconsciously gratified by frustrating and defeating the efforts of physicians (e.g., factitious disorder, the so-called Munchausen's syndrome). Of course, there are also those who shop around because they have received bad medical care elsewhere and/or have an illness that has defied correct diagnosis. Certain medical and psychiatric diagnoses are notorious for eluding diagnosis, and it is not unusual for the patient to have visited many physicians before being correctly diagnosed. Panic disorder is typically misdiagnosed as various medical illnesses because of the prominent somatic symptoms; myasthenia gravis, in its early stages, is often mistaken for "stress" or depression because routine physical and laboratory examinations are normal.

On first seeing a patient who appears to have been doctor-shopping, the physician should carefully and objectively consider the chief complaint and previous evaluation and treatment. The physician should not pursue extensive diagnostic evaluation or aggressive treatment solely because of strong pressure from the patient to "do something!" There is neither an ethical nor a legal obligation to duplicate workups when they are not clinically indicated. Were the patient's evaluation and treatment elsewhere adequate? Were they optimal? What led the patient to change physicians?

Some patients are shopping around not because they want more procedures, but because they are looking for a physician who will spend adequate time listening to them.

In all cases, one should temper enthusiasm with moderation. The physician should not tell the patient that "there is nothing wrong," nor should the physician be overconfident. Do not promise that you will "certainly find out what is wrong and take care of it." This is particularly important for patients who have visited several good physicians and are still frustrated. Acknowledging the limitations of medicine is often better than promising too much. Psychiatric consultation is indicated if the physician suspects underlying primary psychopathology, such as depression or panic disorder. The physician must recognize that many doctor-shoppers may refuse psychiatric consultation, particularly those who are receiving substantial secondary gain by staying in the sick role.

NORMAL AND PATHOLOGICAL GRIEF

Normal Grief

Grief is the psychological response to loss. We are most familiar with grief following the death of a loved one, but analogous reactions follow other losses (e.g., body parts or functions, independence, affection). Grief, and the mourning process through which it is resolved, follow a typical course with recognizable manifestations (Fig. 1) (Brown and Stoudemire, 1983). Psychological symptoms of grief begin with an initial state of shock and disbelief, followed by painful dejection, despair, helplessness, protest, and anger. Social dysfunction occurs with loss of interest in life's activities, social withdrawal, apathy, and inertia. While some individuals retreat into silent sadness, others are affectively very demonstrative and cry and yell. Somatic symptoms accompanying grief include insomnia, anorexia and weight loss, tightness in the throat, chest or abdomen, and fatigue.

The initial phase of shock and numbness lasts days and is followed by a period of preoccupation with the deceased. During the day, thoughts focus on recalling the life of the deceased and on one's own relationship with the deceased. Anger, jealousy, and resentment about the lost loved one may resurface, along with guilt over unresolved conflicts and regret over missed opportunities. The living experience self-blame, wishing they had acted or felt differently in the past, ruminating over why they have been the ones to survive, and wondering if they should have done something more during the terminal illness. Sleep is delayed by these obsessive thoughts and is often interrupted by dreams about the deceased. Fleeting hallucinations may occur in which the dead seem to appear at one's bedside or in a crowd, or in which the deceased's voice calls out, usually the name of the living.

The length and intensity of the phases of shock and preoccupation are affected by the suddenness of the death. When there has been no warning, the period of shock and disbelief is prolonged and intense; when death has been long expected, much of the mourning process may occur while the loved one is still alive, leaving an anticlimactic feeling after the death. In normal grief, the intensity of symptoms gradually abates, so that by 1 month after the death, the mourner should be able to adequately

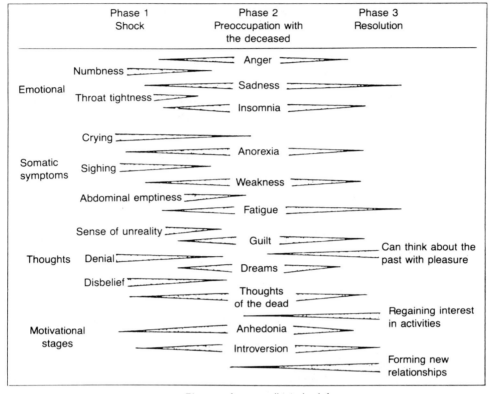

Phases of uncomplicated grief

Figure 19–1. *Phases of grief. (Reproduced with permission from Brown JT, Stoudemire A. Normal and pathological grief. JAMA 250:378, 1983)*

sleep, eat, and function at work and at home. Crying and feelings of longing and emptiness do not disappear but are less intrusive. By 6 to 12 months most normal life activities will have been resumed. For major losses, the grieving process continues throughout life, with the reappearance of the symptoms of grief on anniversaries of the death or other significant dates (family holidays, wedding anniversaries, birthdays).

Distinguishing Grief From Depression (Table 1)

Many of the psychological, social, and vegetative symptoms of depression also occur in grief. Distinguishing them is important for physicians, for the indicated interventions are quite different. As noted, in normal grief intense symptoms should abate after about a month, while in depression symptoms persist longer. While wishes to join the deceased are normal in acute grief, frank suicidal ideation (especially with a plan) is not, and suggests a major depression. Transient hallucinatory experiences occur with grief, but not the more sustained psychotic symptoms (e.g., delusions of

Table 19–1 **Distinguishing Grief from Major Depression***

	GRIEF	MAJOR DEPRESSION
Time course	Intense symptoms ≤1–2 months	Longer
Suicidal ideation	Usually not present	Often present
Psychotic symptoms	Only transient visions or voice of the deceased	May have sustained depressive delusions
Emotional symptoms	Pangs interspersed with normal feelings	Continuous pervasive depressed mood
Self-blame	Related to deceased	Focused on self
Response to support and ventilation	Improvement over time	No change or worsening

*It should be noted that depressed *symptoms* are a pervasive part of the grief response and that a clear delineation—grief *vs* depression is not always possible.

decay, nihilism, or guilt) indicative of a psychotic depression. Crying and intense feelings of sadness and loneliness occur in both grief and depression, but in grief they occur as "pangs" interspersed with periods of more normal feeling; in depression they are more continuous. Self-reproach is experienced in both, but not equivalently. In grief, self-blame is focused on the deceased, e.g., what one could have done differently. The depressed are primarily negative about themselves, feeling worthless, guilty, and helpless, not just in regard to the deceased. Finally, grief and depression respond differently to intervention. The grieving welcome emotional support from others, congregate with them, and feel better after ventilating their feelings. Those who have major depression tend to withdraw from reassurance and feel worse when encouraged to ventilate.

Pathological Grief

In some individuals, grief and mourning do not follow the normal course. Grieving may become too intense or last too long, be absent, delayed, or distorted, or result in chronic complications. Risk factors for pathological grief in the mourner include sudden or terrible deaths, an ambivalent relationship with or excessive dependency on the deceased, traumatic losses earlier in life, social isolation, and actual or imagined responsibility for "causing" the death. Grief that is too intense or prolonged exceeds the descriptions given of normal grief and can lead to an inability to function occupationally or socially for months. *Absent or delayed grief* occurs when the feelings of loss would be too overwhelming and so are repressed and denied. Such avoidance or repression of affect tends to result in the later onset of much more prolonged and distorted grief, and in a higher risk for developing a major depression, especially at later significant anniversaries. Physicians should be careful not to assume that grief is absent just because the individual is quiet and not affectively demonstrative. This may be a matter of personal or cultural style; what counts is the individual's internal experience of grief.

Distorted grief occurs when any one facet of grieving becomes disproportionate in magnitude or duration. "Survival guilt" refers to the feeling that one does not deserve to have outlived the deceased, and is especially common in those who have shared a traumatic experience with the deceased (e.g., same organ transplant program, airplane crash, or concentration camp). It is normal in moderation, but can become so pronounced that the survivors remain too guilty to ever return to full lives.

Some degree of identification with the deceased is also normal. Grief is partly resolved through intensification of traits shared with or admired in the deceased, and the treasuring of special inherited possessions. When conscious or unconscious identification is too strong, it leads to a variety of maladaptive outcomes. The living may abdicate personal life or identity to pursue the interests of the deceased. Through a process of conversion, mourners may develop symptoms identical to those of the loved one's illness. When denial of the loss is very pronounced, there may be an attempt to maintain the deceased's room and belongings entirely unchanged.

Prolonged pathological grief results in chronic complications, including major affective disorder, substance abuse, hypochondriasis, and increased morbidity and mortality from physical disease.

The Physician's Role

Physicians are in a critically important position to identify and help manage grief, especially if they have long-established relationships with patients and their families. During the acute phase of shock following a death, the physician can help the family accept the reality of the loss, and provide a calm and reassuring presence that facilitates both the release of emotion and the planning necessary by those grieving. The physician must sit down, not stand, when talking with anyone experiencing acute grief; otherwise, the physician will be perceived as too busy or uncomfortable or eager to leave. Patients frequently seek out their personal physicians when they are acutely suffering from grief, often focussing on the somatic manifestations. The physician can explain the normal symptoms and process of grief and mourning, reassuring patients that they are not "losing their minds" (a common fear, especially if vivid nightmares or fleeting hallucinatory phenomena have been experienced). Family members who wish to should be allowed (but never pressured) to see the body of the deceased in the hospital, after the physician prepares them for any distortion of appearance due to the fatal disease, accident, or treatment.

Physicians should resist the temptation to sedate the individual suffering from acute grief, since this tends to delay and prolong the mourning process. Antidepressants should not be prescribed for acute grief but rather reserved for a possible subsequent major depression. If insomnia is severe and not spontaneously improving after several days, a brief course of a benzodiazepine hypnotic may be prescribed, but extended use will be more harmful than beneficial.

THE DYING PATIENT

Helping dying patients is a major responsibility of the physician. Elizabeth Kubler-Ross drew professional attention to this long-neglected subject 20 years ago and described five sequential stages that characterize the typical response to impending death: denial, anger, bargaining, depression, and acceptance (Kubler-Ross, 1969). As we have learned more, there does not appear to be a unique or correct order. Individual patients will experience each of these reactions (and others) in varying degrees, combinations, and sequences.

Cultural and religious background profoundly influence how patients respond when they learn they are dying. Knowing this background is important for the physician, but it can also be misleading, as the prospect of death may produce abrupt changes in the patient: an agnostic may become deeply religious; a lifelong skeptic of medicine may become obsessed with medical progress; patients who have been very distant from their families may seek to reunite; and those who have been close may begin to withdraw from their relationships in anticipation of ultimate separation. Most patients take comfort through some form of sustaining hope, including hopes for miraculous cures, new medical discoveries, the resolution of personal conflicts or alienated relationships before death, or something as simple as enough improvement to briefly leave the hospital and walk in the garden.

Physicians' Reactions

Physicians' reactions are also important in the management and support of the dying patient. Many physicians, as do most people, have an aversion to death. The dying patient may make the physician feel like a failure, since treatment has been ineffective and it appears that there is nothing more to offer the patient. This is especially likely to occur with younger patients because it is harder for the physician to resort to fatalistic rationalizations (e.g., "she lived a full life" or "he died due to the inevitable progression of old age"). Even experienced physicians feel sad if the dying patient has become well-known to them. Sadness in the physician is also likely if the physician is reminded of a personal loss in his or her own life. Sadness, helplessness, and a feeling of failure in the physician may interfere with optimal care in a number of ways. The physician may avoid the patient, spending little or no time with him or her on rounds, which the physician rationalizes as not wanting to disturb the patient. Avoidance is particularly unfortunate because most patients have a fear of dying alone and because the physician is less available to provide specific comfort-care measures. The secure belief that the physician's attention will continue unceasingly until death is a benefit to patients often underestimated by physicians.

Some physicians take an overly cheerful approach, trying thereby to instill hope. When this is excessive it alienates patients, who contrast their fate with that of the seemingly happy physician, creating a gulf between them. Believing that they ought to be truthful, some physicians are overly blunt, announcing to the patient, "Nothing more can be done; we have done everything we can think of." This robs patients of hope. It is possible to be truthful without being so disheartening. Other physicians have difficulty accepting that further treatment is useless and resort to excessive heroics, needlessly prolonging death. Finally, many well-meaning physicians, sensing a patient's need to talk about dying, may prematurely refer the patient to a psychiatrist, social worker, or chaplain. At best, the patient will take this as a sign that the physician is uncomfortable discussing these issues; at worst, the patient may worry that the physician thinks there is something wrong with how the patient is reacting, or that the feelings are too unimportant for the physician's attention. Most patients prefer talking about death and dying directly with their primary physician.

Intervention

How to inform a patient of a grave diagnosis and prognosis is part of the art of medicine. The physician must gauge how much to tell and at what rate, taking into account the patient's intellectual abilities and emotional and physical state. The questions the patient asks are an indicator of whether the physician is going too fast or too slow. Important information may require repetition within the same session and over several visits. Shock induced by the initial pronouncement may interfere with the patient's registering other needed information. Physicians must balance their truth-telling obligation with some respect for different patients who want to know more or less about the details of a grave prognosis.

Another important responsibility for the physician is to discuss the patient's preferences and values regarding future treatment decisions, particularly those involving the termination of aggressive treatment. This should not be raised too quickly after the patient has been first told of a serious diagnosis, both because the patient may be too overwhelmed to participate meaningfully in such a discussion and because the patient may misinterpret the discussion as a sign that the physician is ready to give up. However, physicians tend to err in delaying such discussion until the patient's illness has progressed to the point when it can no longer be avoided. Unfortunately, by then the patient may no longer be competent to express preferences. Even if the patient is competent, the physician will feel less certain that the patient's preferences have not been unduly influenced by physical discomfort, family pressure, or financial worries. This problem is avoidable by initiating discussion before the final stages of illness.

In the face of serious illness, physicians feel better "doing something." Anticipating a patient's inevitable and impending death, physicians should focus on what can be done. Quality of life during the process of dying can be significantly improved through adequate pain control (which even now is often underprescribed), attention to bowel and bladder function, hygiene, and other comfort measures. For some patients comfort is the primary goal, while other patients may be willing to sacrifice some comfort for greater mobility and the chance to even briefly leave the hospital. Physicians should encourage patients to make wills and put their affairs in order, and help mobilize the patient's support system.

Patients with grave illnesses often have questions about what to tell their children. Most children do not develop a firm concept of the finality of death until between ages 8 and 11, but children, like adults, vary in the intellectual and emotional maturity necessary to comprehend death. Patients and families should be urged to gauge their answers by the nature of their children's questions. Questions spontaneously asked by a child of any age should be answered truthfully in language the child can understand. The adult should indicate his or her continued availability for further questions and comfort. Should children attend funerals? If the child wishes to go this should be respected and supported. If the child appears very reluctant or refuses, this too should be respected. When in doubt, it is probably helpful for the child to attend, as funerals are rituals that have evolved in our cultures to help us collectively deal with death.

As noted, psychiatric consultation should not be sought prematurely as a substitute for direct conversation between patient and physician. Psychiatric consultation is indicated for the terminally ill patient when suicidal ideation appears, for assistance with management of intractable pain, and for the emergence of major unresolved emotional conflict.

The fundamental fear of dying patients is usually not the fear of death itself, but the fear of being abandoned or deserted by others, including their physician, and dying alone. Perhaps the most reassuring comment that a physician can make to a patient with a terminal illness is, "No matter what happens or how bad things get, we're in this thing together and I'll stick by you no matter what happens. You don't have to worry about suffering alone. As long as you are ill, I'll be here to help you with whatever comes, including making sure you'll be comfortable and kept out of pain."

DRUGS THAT CAUSE PSYCHIATRIC SYMPTOMS

Drugs used to treat medical illnesses frequently cause psychiatric symptoms or side effects through a variety of mechanisms. Most drugs at toxic levels produce signs of central nervous system disturbance, including drugs that are normally benign with few side effects, such as aspirin. Certain medications frequently cause psychiatric symptoms even at therapeutic drug levels (e.g., L-dopa). This may occur via a direct effect of the drug on the central nervous system (e.g., lidocaine), a metabolic effect of the drug (e.g., hypokalemia caused by thiazide diuretics), or drug interactions. Some drugs may precipitate an underlying psychiatric disorder in vulnerable patients, such as reserpine-induced depression or sympathomimetic-induced panic attacks. Physicians must be vigilant for the possibility of psychiatric side effects induced by medications the patient may be taking without the doctor's knowledge. This is particularly true if the patient is doing this surreptitiously and is embarrassed to tell the physician (e.g., the excessive use of over-the-counter nasal decongestants or inhalers).

Table 2 shows many of the drugs that can cause psychiatric symptoms. Most of those shown can cause a wide variety of symptoms, influenced by the patient's premorbid psychopathology and personality style, metabolic status, and preexisting central nervous system pathology. When the effect on the brain is mild to moderate, most of the listed drugs can cause anxiety, depression, sleep disorders (insomnia, hypersomnia, nightmares), and sexual dysfunction. When severe, psychosis (schizophreniform, manic, or depressive), delirium, or dementia may occur, sometimes resulting in seizures and coma. (See also Chapter 3.)

MEDICAL DISORDERS THAT CAUSE PSYCHIATRIC SYMPTOMS

Many medical disorders produce psychiatric symptoms as part of their pathophysiology, sometimes as the initial presentation of the disease. This should be distinguished from the development of secondary psychiatric symptoms on a psycho-

Table 19–2 **Drugs That May Cause Psychiatric Symptoms***

Depression	**Psychosis (Hallucinations or Delusions)**
*Antihypertensives (especially reserpine, methyldopa, beta-blockers, clonidine)	*Anticholinergics
Amphotericin B	Antihistamines (cimetidine, ranitidine, diphenhydramine, etc)
*Corticosteroids	Antiarrhythmics (esp. lidocaine, tocainide, mexiletine, quinidine)
Anticonvulsants	
Sedative-hypnotics	*Dopamine agonists
Oral contraceptives	L-dopa
Antipsychotics	Bromocriptine
Metoclopramide	Amantadine
Indomethacin (and other nonsteroidal anti-inflammatory drugs)	*Corticosteroids
	Digitalis
Antineoplastic drugs	Antidepressants
Procarbazine	Opiates
Tamoxifen	Meperidine
Vinblastine	Pentazocine
Asparaginase	Antimalarials
Ethionamide	Anticonvulsants
Carbonic anhydrase inhibitors (anti-glaucoma)	Antiviral drugs
Mania	Acyclovir
	Vidarabine
*Corticosteroids	Interferon
Sympathomimetics (esp. nonprescription decongestants and bronchodilators)	Zidovudine (AZT)
	Podophyllin
Isoniazid	Antineoplastic drugs
Dopamine agonists	Asparaginase
Antidepressants	Methotrexate
Zidovudine (AZT)	Vincristine
Stimulants	Cytarabine
Anxiety	Fluorouracil
	Disulfiram
Sympathomimetics	Sympathomimetics
*Theophylline	Beta-blockers
*Caffeine	Metrizamide
*Stimulants	Methysergide
Antidepressants	Baclofen
*Sedative-hypnotics (withdrawal)	Cycloserine
	Cyclosporine

*Denotes especially "high-risk" drugs for causing symptoms in question.

logical basis, discussed earlier in this chapter. Here we focus on psychiatric symptoms that are a consequence of the disease process itself through either direct effects on the central nervous system or derangement in metabolism or homeostatic regulatory mechanisms. Some diseases cause a wide range of different neuropsychiatric symptoms in different individuals, largely determined by which areas of the brain have been affected by the disease. These disorders are listed in Table 3. Table 4 shows diseases that commonly cause specific psychiatric symptoms. While most of these also can cause a range of symptoms, they typically present with the indicated psychiatric syndromes. Symptoms and signs in other organ systems serve as clinical clues to help

Table 19–3 **Medical Disorders Causing a Wide Range of Psychiatric Symptoms**

Traumatic Brain Injury
Stroke
Systemic Lupus Erythematosus and other forms of Cerebral Vasculitis
Brain Tumor (Primary or Metastatic)
Encephalitis (Acute or Chronic)
AIDS/HIV Encephalopathy
Infectious Endocarditis

the clinician suspect a particular cause, but psychiatric symptoms may precede the onset of other clinical signs in most disorders.

When a patient presents with unexplained psychiatric symptoms, certain clues should heighten the physician's suspicions that an underlying medical disorder may be responsible. An underlying medical disorder as etiology should be considered whenever: (1) psychiatric symptoms increase and decrease in concert with prominent physical symptoms; (2) when the "vegetative symptoms" of an apparent psychiatric disorder are disproportionately greater than the psychological symptoms (e.g., a patient with a 50-lb. weight loss and only mild depressive ideation is unlikely to have major affective disorder as the explanation for the weight loss); (3) when significant cognitive abnormalities are present in the mental status examination, particularly changes in level of consciousness, attention, and memory; (4) when the age of onset or course of psychiatric illness is very atypical (e.g., new onset of "schizophrenia" in an 85-year-old patient); and (5) whenever there are objective findings of central nervous system disease (e.g., pathological reflexes, abnormal EEG or CT or MRI scan, or changes in spinal fluid). As with drug-induced psychiatric symptoms, medical illnesses may cause mild to moderate changes in affect, personality, sleep, or sexual function, which can be easily missed or misattributed. When severe, medical illnesses produce psychosis, delirium, or dementia, which are less likely to be missed but whose nature or causation may still be misinterpreted.

The physician should also keep in the mind those diseases that do not produce psychopathology per se but may be mistaken for it. Recurrent pulmonary emboli may be misdiagnosed as anxiety or panic attacks because of episodic autonomic arousal. Early myasthenia gravis is often mistaken for depression or conversion hysteria because the clinician finds a normal examination in a patient who complains of weakness and fatigue whenever he or she works too hard. Multiple sclerosis may be misdiagnosed as conversion hysteria because the pattern of the patient's symptoms seems changing and inconsistent and does not conform to simple neuroanatomical localization.

COMPETENCY

When a patient refuses diagnostic procedures or treatment, or seems unable to make medical care decisions, physicians often question whether the patient is competent. Strictly speaking, "competency" is a legal concept and is determined by the

Table 19–4 **Psychiatric Presentation of Selected Medical Disorders**

	PSYCHIATRIC PRESENTATION	CLINICAL CLUES	SCREENING DIAGNOSTIC EVALUATION
Endocrine Disorders			
Hypothyroidism	Retarded depression (+ psychosis)	Weight gain, fatigue, cold intolerance, hoarseness, bradycardia, constipation, hair loss	Free T_4, TSH
Hyperthyroidism	Anxiety, panic attacks, agitated depression (often retarded in the elderly)	Tremor, tachycardia, heat intolerance	Free T_4, T_3-RIA
Hyperadrenalism (Cushing's)	Depression or mania	Hypertension, diabetes, hirsutism, moon facies, weight gain	Dexamethasone suppression test
Hypoadrenalism (Addison's)	Depression	Postural hypotension, nausea, vomiting, skin pigmentation, weight loss	Cosyntropin stimulation test
Pheochromocytoma	Panic attacks	Labile hypertension, headache, sweating, nausea, palpitations	24-hour urinary catecholamines and metanephrines
Metabolic Disorders			
Hypoglycemia	Anxiety, panic attacks	Sweating, tachycardia, headache	Blood glucose during symptoms
Hypokalemia	Depression	Weakness, EKG changes	Serum K^+
Hyponatremia	Depression, psychosis	Weakness, nausea, vomiting, seizures	Serum Na^+
Hypercalcemia	Retarded depression	Bone disease, weakness, nausea	Serum Ca^{++}
Hypocalcemia	Anxiety	Tremor, tetany, paresthesias	Serum Ca^{++}
Hypermagnesemia	Retarded depression	Hypotension, nausea, vomiting	Serum Mg^{++}
Hypomagnesemia	Anxiety, psychosis	Tremor, tetany	Serum Mg^{++}, Ca^{++}
Hypophosphatemia	Depression	Weakness, paresthesias	Serum PO_4^-
Vitamin B_{12} deficiency	Psychosis, dementia	Megaloblastic anemia, peripheral neuropathy, myelopathy (but may occur in absence of these)	Serum B_{12}

Disorder	Psychiatric Manifestations	Clinical Features	Diagnostic Tests
Hepatic encephalopathy	Confusion, psychosis	Asterixis, jaundice	Liver function tests, serum NH_3
Uremia	Depression, dementia	Anemia, nausea, edema	BUN, creatinine
Porphyria (acute intermittent)	Psychosis	Episodic abdominal pain with nausea and vomiting, constipation, neuropathy	Blood and urine porphyrin screen
Lead poisoning	Personality change, depression	Colic, anemia, peripheral neuropathy	Serum FEP*
Neurologic Disorders			
Normal pressure hydrocephalus	Depression, dementia	Gait apraxia, urinary incontinence	CT scan
Multiple sclerosis	Depression	Multiple intermittent neurological symptoms over time	Neurological evaluation, MRI, CSF (oligoclonal bands)
Huntington's disease	Personality disorder, psychosis	Movement disorder, family history	Neurological exam
Parkinsonism	Depression, dementia	Bradykinesia, tremor, rigidity	Neurological exam
Wilson's disease	Psychosis	Movement disorder, liver disease, Kayser-Fleischer rings	Slit-lamp exam, serum ceruloplasmin
Neoplastic Disorders			
Pancreatic cancer	Depression	Weight loss, abdominal pain	Abdominal CT scan
Paraneoplastic limbic encephalitis (usually associated with small-cell carcinoma of the lung)	Psychosis, dementia	Seizures, fluctuating course	EEG, lumbar puncture
Infectious Diseases			
Infectious mononucleosis	Depression	Lymphadenopathy, hepatosplenomegaly, sore throat, malaise	CBC, Monospot
Whipple's disease	Depression, dementia	Diarrhea, weight loss, arthritis, lymphadenopathy	Malabsorption studies, small bowel biopsy

*FEP, free erythrocyte protoporphyrin

court; physicians, including psychiatrists, render opinions about competency based on their clinical assessment of the patient's mental status. What physicians must decide is whether the patient appears to have the capacity to participate in rational and reasoned decision making (President's Commission, 1982). Are limited intelligence, a psychiatric disorder, or a medical disease preventing the patient from thinking rationally about medical care? Most determinations of this kind are made by clinicians at bedside; frequency and the need for timely resolution make it impractical to seek judicial action on every case.

While psychiatric consultation is often requested to help determine if the patient is competent, primary physicians can determine this themselves in most cases. Does the physician actually suspect impaired mental capacity, or do the patient and the physician simply disagree? The test of whether a patient possesses the capacity to participate in healthcare decision making is a simple, functional one: does the patient understand the particular decision at hand? First, the physician must ensure that the patient has been fully informed. Then, the following questions should be asked, taking into account that patients will answer in their own language, not in "medically correct" terms: (1) Can the patient describe what the physician believes is wrong with the patient?; (2) Does the patient understand the diagnostic procedure or treatment proposed and the reasons for it?; (3) Does the patient understand any alternative procedures or treatments that may exist?; (4) Does the patient understand the risks and benefits of each course of action, including the consequences of refusing treatment? If the answer is "yes" to all of these questions, the patient possesses the capacity for decision making. To be viewed as competent, the patient does not necessarily have to have a good reason for disagreeing with the physician, but the patient must be able to demonstrate an understanding of the physician's advised plan.

Since this clinical competency test focuses on particular proposed treatments, it is possible that some patients may be judged able to make some but not all decisions, or that their ability varies over time. Others may be so mentally impaired that it is obvious that they entirely lack decision-making capacity.

Some patients will give answers that demonstrate their ability to understand what the physician has said, but they will persist on an irrational course based on psychotic delusional thinking. This too may be grounds for a determination of incompetence, and indicates the need for psychiatric consultation. Psychiatric consultation is also helpful if the primary physician remains unsure of the patient's level of understanding, if there is disagreement among the physicians caring for the patient, or if legal action is considered likely.

If the physician determines that the patient does not possess sufficient capacity, a surrogate decision-maker will be required. If the surrogate is a family member, as it is in most circumstances, this does not necessitate going to court. A court-appointed guardian should be sought when the family members remain intractably divided over healthcare decisions, when they appear unable to act in the best interests of the impaired patient, or when the treatment is controversial. (See also Chapter 18, Fig. 18-1.)

PSYCHIATRIC CONSULTATION

From the other parts of this chapter, it is evident that there are many reasons for a physician to seek psychiatric consultation. Unfortunately, some physicians are reluctant to do so or do not ask for psychiatric assistance very effectively. Some physicians fear that seeing a psychiatrist will upset the patient, who may feel that the physician thinks he or she is crazy. Other physicians approach patients with the belief that all organic pathology should be absolutely ruled out before considering psychological explanations for symptoms. It is certainly reasonable to avoid prematurely concluding that a patient's symptoms are psychogenic, but the relentless pursuit of an organic etiology is costly, exposes patients to unnecessary risks, reinforces a disregard for psychological factors by the patient, and neglects treatable psychiatric disorders.

Some physicians hesitate to obtain psychiatric consultation simply because they are unsure how to tell the patient. It is a mistake to ask for consultation without telling the patient, since this makes it more likely that the patient will misunderstand the physician's intentions. If not told, patients may well wonder if their physician thinks them mentally ill or may believe that their physician is frustrated and wants to transfer their care to someone else. Several studies have demonstrated that when patients are informed by physicians of the purpose of a psychiatric consultation, the great majority have little difficulty accepting it.

The physician should explain that the psychiatrist is a consultant who will advise the patient and the physician, and that the physician is still the primary doctor committed to helping the patient recover. The specific purpose for the consultation should be explained in terms the patient can understand (e.g., "Besides having heart failure, your spirits seem very low. I'd like to have our psychiatrist see if there is anything we can do to help you feel better emotionally as well as physically.").

The physician should always formulate a specific question or problem for which the consultant's help is desired (see Table 5). If the physician is unsure if psychiatric

Table 19–5 **Common Indications for Psychiatric Consultation**

Suicidal ideation or behavior.
Verbal threats or dangerous behavior.
Psychosis (hallucinations, delusions, thought disorder).
Need for psychiatric medication or change of dose.
Psychiatric disorder in need of treatment.
Psychiatric disorder complicating medical illness.
Psychiatric symptoms thought to be caused by medical illness.
Psychiatric symptoms thought to be due to medication.
Competency evaluations.
Noncompliance, AMA discharges.
Significant problems in doctor-patient relationship (or nurse-patient
  relationship).
Evaluation of organic mental disorder.

consultation would be helpful, the physician should discuss this with the consultant. Occasionally, the physician may anticipate problems in persuading the patient to see a psychiatrist. Here, too, discussion with the consultant ahead of time will be helpful. With careful explanation and a respectful approach, a skilled psychiatric consultant can persuade the great majority of patients who initially refuse consultation to agree to be interviewed.

When the patient has unexplained symptoms, physicians should avoid "either/ or" thinking (that is, considering the symptoms as either organic *or* psychogenic). Otherwise, the physician may be misled into thinking too narrowly about causation. Physicians should never diagnose by exclusion (i.e., conclude that symptoms must be psychogenic because physical and laboratory examinations have revealed only "normal" results). An organic ("occult") disease may still be present. Psychiatric diagnoses should be made on the basis of positive criteria, not solely on the absence of identifiable physical pathology. In evaluating symptoms of unclear causation, when the physician suspects the possibility of psychogenic origin, psychiatric consultation should not be delayed until the end of hospitalization. Such delays are unfortunate because they leave little time for the psychiatrist to do his or her job, they reinforce the patient's (possibly false) belief that the symptoms are organic, they promote unnecessary diagnostic testing, and they leave the patient with the implied message that the physician is at the end of his or her rope and is giving up the patient to the care of a psychiatrist.

Even when symptoms clearly appear to be due to conversion, hypochondriasis, or malingering, the physician should never tell the patient, "There's nothing wrong" or "It's all in your head." Patients experience such remarks as humiliating and insulting, and consequently the doctor-patient relationship is seriously strained. Instead, patients can be reassured that extensive diagnostic testing has not turned up any grave or malignant etiology for their illness, and that it appears they have a physical symptom exacerbated by stress for which help is available.

ANNOTATED BIBLIOGRAPHY

Drugs that cause psychiatric symptoms. The Medical Letter 28:81, 1986.

Drugs that cause sexual dysfunction. The Medical Letter 29:65, 1987.

> These two articles provide concise tabular summaries.

Hackett TP, Cassem NH (eds): Massachusetts General Hospital handbook of general hospital psychiatry, 2nd ed. Littleton, Mass., PSG Publishing Co., 1987

> This compact handbook provides a ready and portable reference for managing the most common psychiatric disorders encountered in general hospital patients.

Houpt JL, Brodie HKH (eds): Consultation-liaison psychiatry and behavioral medicine. In Michael R, Cavenar JO, Cooper AM, et al. (eds): Psychiatry, pp. 76–129. Philadelphia, JB Lippincott, 1987

> The chapters in this section of the textbook cover in great detail all areas of dealing with the psychiatric problems of medically ill patients. Sections on behavioral medicine and psychotherapy are included.

Levenson JL: Dealing with the violent patient. Postgrad Med 78:329–335, 1985

> This brief paper offers practical guidelines.

Rodin G, Voshart K: Depression in the medically ill: An overview. Am J Psychiatry 143:696–705, 1988

This is an excellent review article that discusses conceptual and practical issues in evaluating and treating depression in the medically ill.

Stoudemire A, Fogel BS (eds): Principles of medical psychiatry. Orlando, Grune & Stratton, 1987.

This is a definitive reference source for dealing with the psychiatric problems of the medically ill. Each major subspecialty is covered in terms of biological, psychological, and sociologic factors relevant to medical illness that may affect psychiatric functioning. It contains detailed discussions of diagnostic and psychopharmacologic treatment issues in treating the medically ill patient with psychiatric disturbances.

REFERENCES

Brown JT, Stoudemire GA: Normal and pathological grief. JAMA, 250:378–382, 1983

Cavanaugh SC: The prevalence of emotional and cognitive dysfunction in a general medical population: Using the MMSE, GHQ, and BDI. Gen Hosp Psychiatry 5:15–24, 1983

Eraker SA, Kirscht JP, Becker MH: Understanding and improving patient compliance. Ann Intern Med 100:258–268, 1984

Fulop G, Strain JJ, Vita J, et al.: Impact of psychiatric comorbidity on length of hospital stay for medical/surgical patients: A preliminary report. Am J Psychiatry 144:878–882, 1987

Hankin JR, Steinwachs DM, Regier DA, et al.: Use of general medical services by persons with mental disorders. Arch Gen Psychiatry 39:225–231, 1982

Jencks SF: Recognition of mental distress and diagnosis of mental disorder in primary care. JAMA 253:1903–1907, 1985

Kessler LG, Cleary PD, Burke JD: Psychiatric disorders in primary care. Arch Gen Psychiatry 42:583–587, 1985

Kubler-Ross E: On death and dying. London, Macmillan, 1969.

Mazzullo J: Methods of improving patient compliance. In Lasagna L (ed): Patient compliance. Mount Kisco, New York, Futura Publishing, 1976

President's Commission for the Study of Ethical Problems in Medicine and Biomedical and Behavioral Research: Making health care decisions: A report on the ethical and legal implications of informed consent in the patient-practitioner relationship. Washington DC, U.S. Government Printing Office, 1982

Levenson JL, Mishra A, Hamer R, Hastillo A: Denial and medical outcome in unstable angina. Psychosom Med 51:27–35, 1989

Schurman RA, Kramer PD, Mitchell JB: The hidden mental health network: Treatment of mental illness by nonpsychiatrist physicians. Arch Gen Psychiatry 42:89–94, 1985

Shapiro S, Skinner EA, Kessler LG, et al.: Utilization of health and mental health services: Three epidemiologic catchment area sites. Arch Gen Psychiatry 41:971–978, 1984

Von Korff M, Shapiro S, Burke JD, et al.: Anxiety and depression in a primary care clinic. Arch Gen Psychiatry 44:152–156, 1987

Wallen J, Pincus HA, Goldman HH, Marcus SE: Psychiatric consultations in short-term general hospitals. Arch Gen Psychiatry 44:163–168, 1987

20

Psychiatric Aspects of Acquired Immune Deficiency Syndrome

Michael G. Moran

At the turn of the century, the saying "By knowing syphilis, one knows medicine" was common in medical circles. As we approach the new century, the disease that includes more of medicine than any other, demands more of the physician than any other, and taxes our society more than any other is surely acquired immune deficiency syndrome (AIDS). By knowing AIDS, one will know much of medicine, including psychiatry. This syndrome is a psychological malignancy: the patient's defenses and coping mechanisms are attacked and eroded by repeated assaults on livelihood, relationships, sense of integrated identity, and, in the end, on sanity and the very ability to think. AIDS presents a myriad of psychiatric pictures and complications. A patient can appear angry, inhibited, depressed, manic, psychotic, or demented as a result of AIDS and its sequelae.

The broad scope of this syndrome confronts physicians with their limitations, sometimes in a brutal way. Diagnostic efforts can seem endless and futile. Avenues of treatment may appear few in number, and without substance. But there are certain principles that can help the physician conduct a thorough search for treatable causes of the psychological dilemmas and psychiatric complications of AIDS. This chapter seeks to introduce the medical student to current approaches and techniques in the psychiatric management of these patients. An outline of the most common complications of the illness and the complications of treatment is given. A section is included on how and when a psychiatric consultation may be helpful. Following the chapter is a brief list of the current review literature on the psychiatric aspects of AIDS, for students with a special interest in this area.

EPIDEMIOLOGY AND DEMOGRAPHICS OF INFECTION WITH HUMAN IMMUNODEFICIENCY VIRUS (HIV)

Human immunodeficiency virus (HIV), the causative agent of AIDS, is transmitted chiefly through the exchange of body fluids (Table 1). The most common routes of exchange are sexual intercourse, especially anal intercourse; use of contaminated needles during the intravenous administration of drugs; and administration of contaminated blood and blood products. An infected pregnant woman can also transmit the virus to her unborn fetus.

The virus is lymphotropic and neurotropic. It attacks the T4 lymphocyte and causes a time-dependent and progressive destruction of that cell. The clinical results are the development of severe, often life-threatening infections with organisms against which the T4 lymphocyte usually defends or helps defend. The clinical results of the neurotropism are seen in almost all levels of the neuraxis, but cerebral involvement is the most common.

Subacute encephalitis or subcortical dementia are the most common neuropsychiatric presentations. Heightened susceptibility to deliria from a variety of causes may then ensue. It should be noted that primary CNS infection with HIV may occur before overt systemic signs of immunosuppression appear. This is a critical factor that will be discussed in more detail later in this chapter.

Worldwide, homosexual and bisexual men account for about 65% of all AIDS cases; heterosexual intravenous drug users, about 17%; women, about 11% (worldwide). Most of the women are intravenous drug users, and the rest are prostitutes or sexual partners of men at risk. Hemophiliacs and other recipients of blood and blood products constitute less than 5% of AIDS patients (Centers for Disease Control, 1988).

Table 20–1 **High-risk and Low-risk Behavior Concerning HIV Contagion**

High-Risk Behavior

Sharing drug needles and syringes.
Anal sex, with or without a condom.
Vaginal or oral sex with someone who shoots drugs or engages in anal sex.
Sex with strangers (a pickup or a prostitute) or with individuals with a history of multiple indiscriminately chosen sexual partners.
Unprotected sex (without a condom) with an infected person.

Safe Behavior

Not having sex (abstinence).
Sex with one mutually faithful, uninfected partner.
Not shooting drugs.

(Adapted from: U.S. Department of Health and Human Services. Understanding AIDS. Public Health Service, 1988.)

PSYCHIATRIC ASPECTS OF AIDS: THE CLINICAL PICTURE

AIDS-Related Organic Mental Disorders

After infection with HIV, the clinical presentations are shaped by the target systems of the virus's attack (the immune system and the nervous system, especially the brain) and by the psychiatric reactions to the diagnosis of the illness and to its immunologic and neurologic complications. The psychiatric problems resulting primarily from immune dysfunction are chiefly deliria that stem from severe infections, their metabolic complications, and the measures used to treat them. The psychiatric problems that arise from the *neurotropism* of the virus can be seen as a species of dementia. The dementia then renders the patient more susceptible to the insults that cause the aforementioned deliria, and some of the causes of the deliria, if they are prolonged, can add to or produce a picture of dementia. Less common manifestations of neurologic complications of AIDS include a vacuolar myelopathy, similar to that of cobalamin deficiency; cranial nerve syndromes, often caused by localizations of systemic infections; and Landry-Guillain-Barré syndrome. All told, central nervous system disease occurs in *at least* 40% of AIDS patients, and is the initial symptom of the syndrome in at least 10% (see Table 20-2).

To further complicate this picture, sequelae of the immune deficiency, namely certain neoplasms, can occur in the central nervous system and cause neurologic disease; examples are Kaposi's sarcoma and lymphomas of various types. Other psychiatric symptoms are best characterized as psychological and are associated with the meanings of the events already catalogued here. These are discussed in a later section.

Delirium in AIDS

Delirium, or acute confusional state, in AIDS is caused by many potential factors; accurate diagnosis requires meticulous and careful clinical investigative work. It occurs in about one third of hospitalized patients with AIDS. Sometimes no specific etiology is found, and empiric treatment must be instituted in any case. More often, more than one candidate can be found as a cause for the delirium. Intracranial and systemic infections (often presenting as a diffuse encephalopathy), electrolyte and volume abnormalities, hypoxemia, and medication side effects are the chief offenders (Glatt, Chirgwin, and Landesman, 1988). The delirious patient may be only mildly disoriented and agitated, in which case a careful mental status exam may be the key to detecting the disorder. The spectrum of delirium can range, however, to combativeness and psychosis, with hallucinations and visual illusions. Misdiagnosis of the patient as "schizophrenic" or "manic" in this setting can result in improper treatment. Undiagnosed delirium is a cause of significant morbidity and mortality. Once delirium is suspected, a search for the infectious agent or metabolic derangement should begin. Some of the most common infectious causes of delirium are discussed below.

Pneumocystis carinii pneumonia (PCP) affects more than 80% of patients. It is the initial opportunistic infection in 60%. Progressive dyspnea with chest pain, fatigue, and fever constitute the clinical picture. Hypoxemia from the pneumonia can

Table 20-2 **Neuropsychiatric Complications of HIV Infection**

Delirium
    Infectious causes: viral (incl. HIV), mycobacterial, parasitic, bacterial
    Metabolic: volume depletion, electrolyte disturbances
    Medications: CNS depressants and anticholinergics
    Intracranial mass lesions: hematoma, neoplasm
Dementia
    Sequelae of chronic deliria; see above
    HIV infection of the brain
        Subcortical dementia is most common
        No specific treatment
        May present initially as aseptic meningitis
Vacuolar myelopathy
    Resembles cobalamin deficiency
    Mechanism is unknown
Peripheral nervous system involvement
    Local infections or neoplasms
    HIV polyneuropathy

be severe, and when cerebral functioning is already marginal because of an intra-cranial infection or dementia, delirium can result.

Systemic infections can be caused by viruses (probably including HIV), fungi, parasites, and bacteria (including *Mycobacterium* species). Sites of entry into the systemic circulation include focal infections, such as pneumonia, as well as less localized sites such as erosions of the gastrointestinal tract and skin. In such settings, delirium can accompany fever, seeding of the bloodstream with the infectious agent(s), and the metabolic and fluid derangements caused by diarrhea, nausea and vomiting, and decreased ability or desire to eat and drink. These infections are diagnosed by blood culture as well as by examination and culture of the appropriate body fluid.

Toxoplasma gondii causes a focal encephalitis characterized by a picture ranging from mild headache and fever to seizures, neurologic deficits, delirium, and coma (Glatt, Chirgwin, and Landesman, 1988). Extracerebral involvement is unusual. CT scan may show the characteristic but nonspecific constellation of multiple lesions in the cortical and subcortical regions, enhancing with contrast (Pitchenik, Fischl, and Walls, 1983).

Cryptococcal meningitis is most often unimpressive in AIDS patients in its first stages. It may resemble depression, with lethargy, fatigue, and irritability. A devastat-ing and rapidly progressive illness with meningitic signs, severe delirium, and eventual extraneural involvement is uncommon. CT scan is not helpful in making the diagnosis (Wheelan et al., 1983).

Infections with mycobacteria, especially *Mycobacterium avium-intra-cellulare*, are common in AIDS patients. *M. tuberculosis* infections are usually reactivations of earlier acquired disease and are most common in patients with a high background prevalence of the illness. Atypical presentations of *M. tuberculosis* infection are common, and bronchoscopy with biopsy of lung tissue, or biopsy of other tissue suspected of involvement, may be necessary for diagnosis. Intermediate-strength purified protein derivative (IPPD) tuberculin skin tests are too insensitive to be reliably helpful, and late in the course of the illness the patient may not be able to mount the inflammatory immune response that gives the positive reaction.

M. avium-intracellulare is an infective complex that is usually found in immunocompromised hosts. The presentation is generally that of a chronic pulmonary infection that responds poorly to antibiotics, even when in vitro sensitivity has been demonstrated. In AIDS patients, the infection can be disseminated widely, affecting the lungs, liver, bone marrow, and lymph nodes. Biopsy of these tissues yields the diagnosis, as can culture of the blood. A "wasting syndrome" is associated with *M. avium-intracellulare* infections in AIDS patients and consists of malaise, weakness, diarrhea, fatigue, weight loss, and fever (Hawkins et al., 1986). The mechanism of symptom production has not been determined. When the fever or diarrhea are severe, delirium can result, even without primary central nervous system infection. The prognosis for patients with *M. avium-intracellulare* infections is poor; there is no effective therapy at this time.

Cytomegalovirus is commonly a disseminated illness in the AIDS patient. The organism probably causes a subacute encephalopathy with associated delirium, but can also cause colitis with diarrhea, adrenalitis, and retinitis.

HIV itself produces an acute encephalopathy very similar to that supposedly seen with CMV. Altered mentation, varying alertness, apathy, depressive affect, and decreased mental and verbal acuity and spontaneity are seen. The syndrome can progress and result in paranoid ideation, impulsive behavior, and psychotic symptoms of hallucinations and illusions. Psychotic delirium can be the initial presentation of AIDS (Thomas and Szabadi, 1987). Only autopsy reveals the diagnosis with certainty. Other viruses that can cause acute meningitis and possibly encephalopathic presentations include several in the herpes group: Epstein-Barr virus, varicella zoster, and herpes simplex. The latter commonly presents as an intracerebral mass lesion in patients without AIDS; in AIDS patients, such a picture is unusual. A more diffuse encephalopathic syndrome, or widespread mucocutaneous lesions without CNS involvement, can be seen.

Fluid, electrolyte, and oxygenation abnormalities can have profoundly adverse effects on AIDS patients who are already suffering cerebral compromise. Sedating and anticholinergic medications (among others), at doses normally tolerated well by other patients, may induce confusion, disorientation, and psychotic symptoms in severely ill AIDS patients. The door towards diagnosing these problems is opened by a high index of suspicion. Careful attention to variations in mental status, laboratory values, and the list of medications the patient is taking is essential for uncovering the cause(s) of delirium.

Dementia in AIDS

Dementia can result from the chronic sequelae of most of the causes of delirium: severe electrolyte imbalance, hypoxemia, or meningitis, to name a few. However, cerebral infection with HIV probably causes a large proportion of cases of dementia seen in AIDS patients. The exact percentage of patients who become demented is hard to estimate, but studies suggest that over one third of patients with debilitating dementia had evidence of active HIV infection at autopsy. The virus has been recovered even from patients who have neurologic symptoms and signs but do not have AIDS or any evidence of immune deficiency. Detailed neuropsychological testing and MRI scanning can reveal abnormalities even before there is symptomatic evidence of CNS disease or of systemic signs of immunosuppression (Grant et al., 1987). One patient had a rapidly progressive dementing syndrome with motor deficits, hallucinations, and paranoia, but no clinical manifestations of immune compromise (Beckett, Summergrad, and Manschreck, 1987).

The neuropathologic picture is rather distinct, as is the early clinical presentation: *subcortical dementia.* Subcortical and white-matter changes dominate in these cases; gray matter is relatively spared. Macrophages, lymphocytes, and perivascular collections of multinucleated giant cells further characterize the microscopic appearance. Inclusion bodies are present in those infected with cytomegalovirus. CMV can cause dementia in AIDS patients too, but is probably less common as a true etiology for the dementia, and occurs after CNS infection with HIV.

Clinical features of subcortical dementia (of any origin) include mental slowness, apathy, impaired cognition, and depressive affect. The bedside mental status examination may reveal only mild cognitive impairments early in the course. In rapidly progressive or in advanced cases, disorganization and delirium may be evident. The cortical dementias, of which Alzheimer's disease may be said to be the prototype, cause more debilitating intellectual deficits, and the affected patients are more likely to show amnesia, agnosia, and aphasia. Motor abnormalities (dysarthria, ataxic gait, abnormal involuntary movements, and leg weakness) are more common with subcortical dementia.

Rapid deterioration is the rule. Progressive slowing of mentation brings on muteness and severe confusion, interfering with the accurate communication of needs. There may be periods of severe agitation if the patient becomes delirious; hallucinations and sensory illusions can occur. With advancement of the motor deficits, truncal ataxia can appear, as can spastic weakness, paraplegia, and quadriparesis.

The diagnosis of subcortical dementia is a clinical exercise; HIV dementia itself can be diagnosed definitively only at autopsy. The virus can be grown from the cerebrospinal fluid (CSF) of a fraction of the patients. The CSF is often normal, but may reveal a slight mononuclear pleocytosis and a mild elevation of protein. As mentioned earlier, the MRI and CT scans can be abnormal even before there are clinical manifestations of the dementia. Atrophy and ventricular enlargement can occur early in the course of the illness (Grant et al., 1987). Small white-matter lesions are better revealed by MRI than by CT scan. There are as yet no known scan features that are pathognomonic for HIV brain infection.

The previously discussed neuropsychiatric factors can undermine patients' capacity to modulate and manage their own affective states and adaptive responses to the news of the diagnosis and the evidence of illness progression. For example, delirious or demented patients may be relatively disinhibited and may be more likely to impulsively self-treat with alcohol or other drugs, further impairing their efforts at adapting appropriately to psychological insults. In vitro and in vivo evidence of immune suppression as a result of substance use, coupled with coexistent psychiatric illness, makes substance use especially destructive in patients with a lethal communicable disease (Flavin and Frances, 1987).

Psychological Aspects of AIDS

Early Phases

Even when free of HIV infection, members of groups at high risk for contracting AIDS face considerable anxiety and interpersonal tension because of the threat of the disease. Pressure, which at times can seem to these persons unreasonable and coercive, may be exerted by others in an attempt to change the lifestyles and sexual behavior of the members of the risk group. Persons at little risk for the disease also have psychological reactions to AIDS that powerfully determine their behavior, sometimes with phobias or unnecessary discrimination toward persons with AIDS. Other events with powerful meaning and serious impact include the inherent personal and vocational losses, debilitation, probability of isolation, sense of loss of control, and potential for loss of self-esteem seen in persons with AIDS (indeed, in most chronic, debilitating illnesses). Medical personnel need to be acutely aware of their attitudes about AIDS and the persons in the groups at highest risk in order to give the best medical care to affected patients.

The *psychological* reactions to the *meanings* of the illness form an important part of the clinical presentation. The psychological "malignancy" of the syndrome exerts powerful effects on the patient, caregivers, and family and other intimates in the patient's life (Wolcott, Fawzy, and Pasnau, 1986). Members of high-risk groups may respond to the risk of infection by changing their behavior (either toward reducing or increasing their risk), changing their mood and self-image, and altering their view of their lifestyle. Fear of the illness and its effects may be so intense that these feelings either are acted on destructively or are projected onto others, with resultant near-paranoia. Some persons who are not in high-risk groups can foster such projections by baiting and criticizing risk-group members, especially homosexual men. The fear of contracting an incurable illness that is associated with wasting, misery, and ostracism is a nightmare in itself. In a setting fueled by prejudicial fantasies and minimal factual information, irrational thought predominates. The crucial role of the physician as a provider of information, an educator, and a role model can help stem the destructive effects of phobic behavior and discrimination.

The Decision to Be Tested: A Painful Dilemma

Counseling for AIDS testing, for those persons who wish to know their serologic status, is described at length in an superb review (Perry and Markowitz, 1988). Pretest counseling involves giving information about the test, its usefulness, and its limitations and assessing the patient's strengths and psychological vulnerabilities. Making such an assessment allows the physician to figure the risk-benefit ratio for the test (as should be done for any medical procedure). The complexity of the decision to test, and its potential for adverse consequences, are well examined in the case illustrations of the paper mentioned.

The patient's ability to use his or her own coping capacities and outside support can best be assessed before the test results are given. The physician must systematically seek to understand why the patient wants the test now, what he or she expects the result to be, how he or she plans to react to positive or negative results, whom he or she plans to tell, and how he or she expects them to react. After this assessment, the patient usually can better tolerate the interviewer's questions about his or her current state of health, including specific questions about symptoms of HIV infection.

Lastly, recommendations can be made to patients about how to use the strengths and resources already available to them, regardless of the test results (Perry and Markowitz, 1988).

Posttest counseling includes reducing the stress of those who are seropositive and explaining methods to prevent transmission. This is also the time to arrange proper follow-up care.

The test results for HIV seropositivity are powerful information: the patient discovers whether he or she has a lethal illness. It comes as no surprise that such information could powerfully affect his or her risk-taking behavior. The prospect of a positive result can make some members of risk groups avoid obtaining test results: in one study of homosexual men who were offered the chance to be tested, only 67% elected to do so. Those found to be seronegative decreased risk-taking behavior by a significantly smaller margin than the seropositive patients did (Fox et al., 1987). In another study, over 2,000 homosexual men were tested for HIV, then asked by mail if they wanted their results. Among the responders, there was no difference between those who chose to learn the result and those who refused. However, there was a significant difference between those who responded and those who did not: the latter group tended to be younger, nonwhite, and less educated. The group that refused to learn the results said they declined because they felt the test was not predictive of the development of AIDS or they were concerned about the worry that a positive result would cause them (Lyter et al., 1987).

Most discussions on AIDS prevention emphasize that giving information, especially about modes of infection, is the way to modify the high-risk activities of certain groups. The nationwide mailing of the Department of Health and Human Services pamphlet "Understanding AIDS" in 1988 is an example of this kind of logic and intervention. Health-related behaviors have been shown to be related to possession of clear, consistent information. But other important factors impinge on such behavior. Peer group opinions and support also play a major role in maintaining or altering health-related behavior (Klein et al., 1987). When the risk behaviors of a group of homosexual male physicians and college students were studied, the authors concluded that such multifactorial determinants of behavior were at work, and that precise intervention was necessary if behaviors were to be changed. The authors suggested that programs for older, well-educated homosexual men should be designed so as to increase the sense of control over outcome (that is, to promote the notion that changing habits is *effective*). For young, well-educated men, programs aimed at appealing to peer-group norms were thought most likely to succeed (Klein et al., 1987).

This summary of the study is not meant to serve as a comprehensive list of interventions for groups at risk. For example, no mention is made here (nor was any made in the study) of intervention with drug users or prostitutes. The point is that in order to make a substantive change in the intended audience, the intervention will probably need to be tailored specifically to each group. Information, no matter how clearly presented, is usually not enough to change behavior.

Being in a high-risk group can itself be associated with severe psychological distress in the current setting of the AIDS epidemic. Symptoms are usually dominated by anxiety and can include panic attacks. Vigilant self-observation, when fostered by fear about a physical illness, can result in inordinate preoccupation with physical signs and symptoms. When these symptoms become severe enough, they can interfere with social and work functioning (Faulstich, 1987).

"Malignant" Progression of Psychological Symptoms

Once diagnosed, the psychological developments in AIDS patients closely resemble the sequence seen in terminal cancer patients. Many patients are filled with denial and disavowal at the news of their seropositivity or clinical immune deficiency. Anger, despair, and expressed or enacted hopelessness and helplessness are common. As mentioned before, an antecedent personality disorder, especially coupled with substance use, can render the patient prone to living out fantasized solutions to his or her situation or wishes for revenge and restitution. Some of the sense of being endangered and invaded (by the virus) is projected; caregivers are seen as the problem, or at least as inadequate. News reports that suggest slow progress with experimental treatments and minimal attention by the medical establishment to the concerns of affected persons and their associated high-risk groups promote these externalizations. The patient may feel and act overtly hostile to family members, physicians, and other intimates (Faulstich, 1987). If the patient acquired or suspects acquisition of the disease from a lover, that relationship can obviously come under the intense burdens of guilt, fault-finding, and desire for revenge. Other individuals find in the crisis an opportunity for increased emotional intimacy, and work together against a common enemy. Such a response is usually founded on the earlier presence of a solid and loving relationship.

Reports suggest that both homicidal and suicidal impulses can lead to sexually risky behavior among distressed infected persons. Alcohol, serving as an anxiolytic, may facilitate the living out of "love suicide" fantasies, in which the uninfected person tries to acquire HIV infection and the infected person tries to infect others. Intravenous drug users with the same conscious and unconscious wishes (to spread the infection or to commit suicide) may display the same kind of behavior by knowingly using and trading contaminated needles. Anecdotal reports suggest that similar behavior occurred in epidemics of polio, tuberculosis, and syphilis (Flavin, Franklin, and Frances, 1986).

Existential Issues

The existential issues of *worth*, *control*, and *lovability* are paramount in the psychological picture of this illness. Every attentive physician will be able to see the patient striving to regulate his or her feelings of being worthless, out of control, and unlovable. As the patient's ability to function at work or in other settings is eroded, he or she may become desperate to find a way to prove his or her worth or demand a show of being valued from others. This may take the form of seeming entitled and demanding with medical caregivers and others.

Chronic, debilitating physical illness is the prototype of an attack on control of one's life. AIDS patients lose their ability to control their bodies (even bowel and bladder function), their place of residence (through repeated hospitalizations), and their sensorium and level of awareness (because of delirium); usually, these relentlessly worsen. The patient's reactions to such loss of control can include what may appear to be a childish attempt to control others, or to fight medical care.

The illness severely strains the patient's sense of being lovable. As mentioned, the strain usually invades intimate relationships. The partners must struggle with questions of sexual intimacy and how to handle the new risk imposed by the disease. If one partner is uninfected and gives any evidence of withdrawal or unavailability in the relationship amidst the many medical and psychological crises that ensue, the patient will probably feel unloved. Family and friends who are frightened by the fear of easy contagion or who reject the patient's lifestyle (most often seen with male homosexual patients) may also withdraw. Usually, the patient is at some level aware of the feelings of these others, and major disruptions in the family can ensue. Feeling unloved, the angry and hurt patient may retaliate in an attempt to make others feel the same way. Such actions may serve only to further the avoidant and angry feelings and behavior of family and other loved ones. In other families, such intense evidence of feeling on both sides may provide the opportunity for reviewing the situation of the illness, and for allowing appropriate planning and support for the future. Such a scenario is uncommon in the early phases of the illness, where denial, disavowal, and projection of feelings dominate.

As with any patient faced with a virtually inevitable and fatal outcome, death and the meaning of ending one's life become issues with which to reckon. Most patients affected with AIDS are young men, usually healthy before the occurrence of the illness. For them especially, contemplating death is a horror, so out of alignment with "expectable" concerns at their stage in the lifecycle. After working through these issues to some extent, other fears often become apparent: many patients are less afraid of death per se than they are of suffocating, being alone as they die, or being left in agonizing pain. The latter is actually less common in the final stages of AIDS. But, as we have seen, *Pneumocystis carinii* pneumonia and interpersonal strife are real, and may lend extra credence to the chances of an isolated or suffocating death.

TREATMENT OF NEUROPSYCHIATRIC AND PSYCHOLOGICAL ASPECTS OF AIDS

In this section, treatment issues will be presented, dealing with the problems arising from neuropsychiatric sequelae (chiefly, delirium and dementia) and from psychological sequelae of AIDS. See Chapter 3 for a systematic overview of the treatment of delirium and dementia.

Treatment and Prevention of Delirium and Dementia

Specific medical treatment of the different infectious and metabolic complications of AIDS, the most common antecedents to delirium, is beyond the scope of this chapter, but details of a working approach will be presented. Preventive quarantine, in an effort to isolate the patient from potential carriers of superinfecting pathogens, is bound to fail; as mentioned before, most infections are reactivations of a previously acquired organism. Similarly, most AIDS patients with opportunistic infections do not represent an infectious threat to others. The only exceptions are infections due to *M. tuberculosis,* herpes, and perhaps salmonella (Glatt, Chirgwin, and Landesman, 1988). Thus, the delirium caused by infections and the accompanying fever, bacteremia, and viremia generally cannot be treated by prophylaxis, but rather requires specific treatment of the infection once clinically evident, and by supportive measures.

Persistence of the delirium in spite of what seems to be appropriate treatment should alert the physician to another cause of infection or a separate cause for the delirium, such as a medication, volume depletion, or an intracranial mass. An acute change in sensorium or the appearance of new neurologic signs should prompt the consideration of a complete system review and new physical examination. Rarely, CT and MRI scans might be useful when routine laboratory procedures or bedside examinations show no cause for the new delirium, but the scans are rarely diagnostic.

P. carinii pneumonia responds to appropriate antimicrobial treatment in 60 to 80% of the cases. The infection, and the potential for the associated delirium, recur in 65% of patients after 18 months. The efficacy of prophylactic antimicrobial medication is being investigated. Toxoplasmosis and cryptococcosis are also rarely cured; relapse is the rule. Thus, previous history of pulmonary or disseminated infection with either of these agents should prompt investigation for their presence in the setting of a new delirium.

M. avium-intracellulare infections are not cured in HIV patients by current methods. *M. tuberculosis* may be somewhat more likely to invade the central nervous system, and can do so despite appropriate therapy.

The other common causes of delirium are sometimes forestalled with meticulous maintenance and supportive care. Avoiding *medications* with psychotropic activity, especially sedative-hypnotics, anxiolytics, and drugs with high anticholinergic side effects, is an important cautionary step. If necessary, low starting doses (for example, half the dose for a young, otherwise healthy person) should be the rule. The nursing staff should be alerted to early signs of toxicity, such as sedation, confusion, or, in the case of anticholinergic drugs, dry mouth and urinary retention. However, central nervous system side effects can occur without these peripheral signs.

Vital signs can help track *volume status* and *oxygenation.* Patients with diarrhea who have impeded access to fluid replenishment, or who are too demented to ask for fluids, are at greatest risk for hypotension and accompanying cerebral dysfunction. Falls are also then more likely. Patients with pneumonia or antecedent lung disease might require arterial blood gases or saturation monitors to follow oxygenation status. Bedridden patients need close nursing attention to help avoid bedsores, another site for entry of infectious pathogens.

Those cases characterized by severe agitation or psychotic symptoms may require the addition of a high-potency neuroleptic, such as haloperidol, in low doses. The physician must remember that the AIDS patient has an increased susceptibility to extrapyramidal side effects and probably neuroleptic malignant syndrome because of the preexistent brain disease. (See also Chapter 18).

Many principles that apply to HIV-associated infections (Glatt, Chirgwin, and Landesman, 1988) are useful in the clinical management of delirium:

1. Most of the infections are incurable and require long-term suppressive therapy. Likewise, delirium may be chronic in many patients, requiring symptomatic, long-term treatment. A thorough search for reversible infectious, metabolic, and drug-induced causes can allow specific treatment of the delirium. The essential points here are the need for a high index of suspicion for the causes listed, careful elimination and treatment of the specific causes when possible, and judicious use of a neuroleptic in selected cases. The section on treatment will discuss the use of neuroleptics. (See also Chapter 3 for further details on the diagnosis and treatment of delirium.)

2. These patients rarely have just one infection. Similarly, the causes of delirium are often multiple. The physician's search for etiology should be thorough, and vigilance for changes in mental status should be maintained throughout the care of the patient. Clinical "failure" in the treatment of delirium may result not from clinical error, but from a second cause.

3. Certain infections occur at their observed frequency in AIDS patients because of the prevalence of asymptomatic infection in the local population (e.g., histoplasmosis and cryptococcosis). Likewise, behavior that antedates the HIV infection, seen in the groups at highest risk for AIDS, may play a role in the susceptibility of AIDS patients for delirium. Examples of such behaviors include habitual alcohol or drug use preceding the onset of AIDS. If these behaviors are repeated after the cerebral compromise (from whatever specific etiology) is present in a case of AIDS, the patient is much less likely to tolerate the CNS effects of such behavior than before the HIV infection began. In the setting of depression and hopelessness, self-destructive or suicidal behavior can then occur because of decreased impulse control (Flavin, Franklin, and Frances, 1986).

To the extent that dementia is caused, in any one patient, by factors that show up early as delirium and are reversible, dementia might be forestalled or prevented. If caused by HIV, there is no current treatment. Whatever the cause, dementia in AIDS is generally managed through supportive measures. Here again, nursing care and meticulous attention to metabolic parameters and medications is preeminent.

Treatment of the psychological problems associated with AIDS can rarely be divorced from the nonpsychological or purely physiologically oriented treatments, for several reasons. First, organic mental states can masquerade as functional psychiatric disorders. An approach that arbitrarily separates the patient into two camps, mind and body, will fail in managing the illness. Second, the psychological reactions, if not addressed, will affect the patient's ability to care for himself or herself and to participate in medical treatment. Third, the psychological effects of the illness extend to the caregivers. If physicians are unaware of or deny the ways they can be affected by working with these patients, appropriate care of the patient will be impossible.

The treatment of *depression* in the AIDS patient is complex and filled with pitfalls. First, the presentation is rarely that of a classic vegetative depression: anger, self-criticism, projection of self-hatred, and preoccupation with somatic symptoms are rather common. In addition, as with any chronic or wasting disease, the absolute diagnosis *or* exclusion of depression is often impossible. The clinician, however, must maintain a high index of suspicion for depression and must be ready to deal with this treatable illness. Treatment includes psychotherapy, mobilization of the family and other supports, and antidepressants with low (desipramine) or no (fluoxetine) anti-cholinergic effects. Antidepressants must be used carefully because of their anti-cholinergic, sedating, and hypotensive effects. Studies are in progress to system-atically evaluate these drugs in AIDS patients. A number of reports have advocated the use of psychostimulants such as methylphenidate 10 to 40 mg/day given in divided doses early in the day as a treatment of depression in AIDS patients.

TREATMENT DECISIONS IN IRREVERSIBLE ILLNESS

Early in the course of the illness, soon after diagnosis, involvement of the support system of the patient (family, lover, friends) can be helpful. If this seems impossible, *support groups,* most readily available for homosexual men, are valuable resources. The physician's willingness to discuss the need for referral and support is in itself a supportive act, and can help pave the way for a useful experience working with the referral agency or specialist. Since substance use has such an augmenting effect on destructive behavior in this population, the physician should try to help the patient pay special attention to such behavior and obtain appropriate *counseling* and per-haps *disulfiram treatment.*

Emphasis on legal needs is also an important aspect of the counseling at this point. Attention to putting the patient's affairs in order, such as drawing up a will, may be too much for the patient in the acute setting, but dealing with such issues should not be inordinately delayed. Other considerations include designating a close *friend* or *relative* who could serve as legal guardian. Establishing individualized, clear-cut criteria for the timing of need for *hospice care,* or decisions about remaining at home for treatment should be considered. Consultation with *social services* can help in making the appropriate referrals.

In making decisions about major treatment and resuscitative efforts, the physi-cian can be a help and guide for the distressed patient and family. Most patients want the physician to spare them the risk of unnecessary and potentially harmful pro-cedures and drugs. However, such wishes may be obscured by a more overtly ex-pressed and persistent fantasy about cure. If the physician has his or her own fantasies about "rescuing" the patient, the combination can yield a fruitless and futile zeal for treatment. At some point in the course of the illness, a frank discussion with the patient, and perhaps with family or lovers, should focus on these issues. A treatment approach aimed at aggressive palliation of discomfort and symptoms, rather than at unattainable symbols of "cure," is usually experienced as reassuring and supportive (Cassem, 1987; Wachter et al., 1988).

Physicians must be aware of their own and others' reactions to AIDS patients in order to render the best care. Many of these patients are young men who were healthy and active before they contracted the illness. Overidentifying with the patient can thus be a hazard and could contribute to rescue fantasies (which are doomed to fail in the context of AIDS). The intense investment of time and emotional energy by physicians and staff can make these caregivers vulnerable to repeated assaults on their self-esteem when the patients die.

In addition, AIDS patients may be frightening: they have a severe infectious disease, and even education about the level of risk of contagion may not stem associated fears in medical personnel. In addition, the patient may be hostile because of low self-esteem and fears of dying, and out of control because of delirium.

Most AIDS patients are male homosexuals, intravenous drug users, or prostitutes. If the physician is shocked, offended, or disgusted by such persons and is not in control of those feelings, many reactions could occur. In an attempt to disavow such feelings, the physician may adopt an intense therapeutic zeal, aimed at giving "the best" to a hated patient. This could result in "working everything up," a futile and destructive approach in the context of end-stage irreversible illness (see the earlier discussion). In a less subtle form, hostility toward the patient may take the form of unnecessary intramuscular injections, invasive procedures, or restraints. Among nursing staff, these reactions may appear in a nurse's slowness to respond to the patient's calls, restrictions on visitation, and "forgetting" to take vital signs. Being aware of one's attitudes toward these patients, informal discussions with colleagues, and in-service training sessions can be helpful.

ROLE OF THE PSYCHIATRIST

The *psychiatrist* can assist in the treatment in several ways: in those situations where the primary physician needs help constructing and implementing a differential diagnostic approach to delirium and dementia; when the patient manifests a major psychiatric illness, such as depression or psychotic delirium; as a referral source for psychotherapy for patients or family members; when psychiatric hospitalization is required for psychotic or suicidal patients; and to help manage the reactions of support staff in their dealings with AIDS patients.

Many patients experience referral to a psychiatrist as a rejection or as a criticism by the primary physician. They may feel the primary doctor is saying, "It's all in your head." An open discussion with the patient about the importance of the care for his or her psychological state can reduce these concerns. The primary physician's unbiased attitude toward psychiatric care is essential. One approach that may be used is to speak of the referral as being helpful *to the primary physician* in further helping the patient. It is important to arrange a follow-up visit with the primary physician soon after the psychiatric appointment. Sometimes the patient will refuse to see the psychiatrist. The primary physician may then elect to proceed with the consultation through personal discussions of the case with the psychiatrist.

CLINICAL PEARLS

- Neuropsychiatric complications of AIDS can be the *first* presentation of the illness. They can also masquerade as functional psychological problems. Persons in high-risk groups and those who appear to be depressed, confused, disoriented, psychotic, or merely easily fatigued should be evaluated for active HIV infection, dementia, and delirium, as well as functional psychological illness.
- Heterosexuals (outside the high-risk groups of drug users, prostitutes, and hemophiliacs) are at risk for HIV infection, albeit at an undetermined level. HIV testing, when otherwise clinically indicated, should not be deferred merely because the person is heterosexual. Careful counseling and informed consent is required for HIV testing.
- Vigilance in diagnostic and therapeutic zeal must be tempered at some point in the illness with a consideration for what fate awaits the patient after treatment of the acute problem. Physicians treating AIDS patients need to acquaint themselves thoroughly with various strategies for dealing with irreversible illness.
- Some reports suggest that depression in patients with HIV infection responds to psychostimulants such as methylphenidate.

ANNOTATED BIBLIOGRAPHY

Cassem NH: Treatment decisions in irreversible illness. In Hackett TP, Cassem NH (eds): Massachusetts General Hospital handbook of general hospital psychiatry, 2nd ed. Littleton, MA, PSG Publishing Co., 1987

> This is a useful and detailed exploration of the issues facing any physician treating a terminally ill patient.

Dickens BM: Legal limits of AIDS confidentiality. JAMA 259:3449–3451, 1988

> This article gives a sense of the legal complexities that any physician may encounter when treating an AIDS patient. Especially instructive is the introduction to the multiple layers of laws concerning confidentiality.

Emanuel EJ: Do physicians have an obligation to treat patients with AIDS? N Engl J Med 318:1686–1690, 1988

> This is a thought-provoking examination of a question for every physician.

Ruark JE, Raffin TA, the Stanford University Medical Center Committee on Ethics: Initiating and withdrawing life support. N Engl J Med 318:25–30, 1988

> This thoughtful, scholarly review presents Stanford's approach to the difficult problem of initiating and withdrawing life support.

Wolcott DL, Fawzy F, Pasnau RO: Acquired immune deficiency syndrome (AIDS) and consultation-liaison psychiatry. Gen Hosp Psychiatry 7:280–292, 1986

> The authors give a concise summary of the major neuropsychiatric and psychological issues.

REFERENCES

Beckett A, Summergrad P, Manschreck T, et al: Symptomatic HIV infection of the CNS in a patient without clinical evidence of immune deficiency. Am J Psychiatry 144:1342–1344, 1987

Cassem NH: Treatment decisions in irreversible illness. In Hackett TP, Cassem NH, eds. Massachusetts General Hospital handbook of general hospital psychiatry, 2nd ed. Littleton, Mass., PSG Publishing Co., 1987

Centers for Disease Control: Update, acquired immune deficiency syndrome (AIDS) worldwide. MMWR 34:286–295, 1988

Centers for Disease Control: Revision of the case definition of acquired immune deficiency syndrome. MMWR 36:1S–15S, 1987

Faulstich ME: Psychiatric aspects of AIDS. Am J Psychiatry 144:551–556, 1987

Flavin DK, Frances RJ: Risk-taking behavior, substance abuse disorders, and the acquired immune deficiency syndrome. Adv Alcohol Subst Abuse 6(3):23–32, 1987

Flavin DK, Franklin JE, Frances RJ: The acquired immune deficiency syndrome (AIDS) and suicidal behavior in alcohol-dependent homosexual men. Am J Psychiatry 143:1440–1442, 1986

Fox R, Odaka NJ, Brookmeyer R, et al.: Effect of HIV antibody disclosure on subsequent sexual activity in homosexual men. AIDS 1(4):241–246, 1987

Glatt AE, Chirgwin K, Landesman SH: Treatment of infections associated with human immunodeficiency virus. N Engl J Med 318:1439–1448, 1988

Goedert JJ, Biggar RJ, Weiss SH, et al.: Three-year incidence of AIDS in five cohorts of HTLV-III risk group members. Science 231:992–995, 1986

Grant I, Atkinson JH, Hesselink JR, et al.: Evidence for early central nervous system involvement in the acquired immune deficiency syndrome (AIDS) and other human immunodeficiency virus (HIV) infections. Studies with neuropsychologic testing and magnetic resonance imaging. Ann Intern Med 107(6):828–836, 1987

Hawkins CC, Gold JWM, Whimbey E et al.: *Mycobacterium avium* complex infections in patients with the acquired immunodeficiency syndrome. Ann Intern Med 105:184–188, 1986

Klein DE, Sullivan G, Wolcott DL, et al.: Changes in AIDS risk behaviors among homosexual male physicians and university students. Am J Psychiatry 144:742–747, 1987

Moran MG: Psychological and neuropsychiatric aspects of acquired immune deficiency syndrome. In Stoudemire A, Fogel BS (eds): Principles of medical psychiatry. Orlando, Fla., Grune & Stratton, 1987

Perry SW, Markowitz JC: Counseling for HIV testing. Hosp Commun Psychiatry 39(7):731–739, 1988

Pitchenik AE, Fischl MA, Walls KW: Evaluation of cerebral-mass lesions in acquired immunodeficiency syndrome. N Engl J Med 308:1099, 1983

Thomas CS, Szabadi E: Paranoid psychosis as the first presentation of a fulminating lethal case of AIDS. Br J Psychiatry 151:693–695, 1987

Wachter RM, Cooke M, Hopewell PC, et al.: Attitude of medical residents regarding intensive care for patients with the acquired immunodeficiency syndrome. Arch Intern Med 148(1):149–152, 1988

Wheelan MA, Kricheff II, Handler M, et al.: Acquired immunodeficiency syndrome: cerebral computed tomographic manifestations. Radiology 149:477–484, 1983

Wolcott DL, Fawzy F, Pasnau RO: Acquired immune deficiency syndrome (AIDS) and consultation-liaison psychiatry. Gen Hosp Psychiatry 7:280–292, 1986

21

Sleep Disorders

Quentin R. Regestein

This chapter addresses the assessment and treatment of disturbed sleep. The major group of sleep disorders consists of the dyssomnias (insomnia and hypersomnia) and parasomnias (automatisms occurring during sleep). Discussions of these disorders form the major sections of this chapter.

On epidemiological surveys, 20 to 30% of adults report that they have difficulty sleeping at least occasionally (Kales, Kales, 1984); about 7% use some pills to increase sleep; and about 1% use a prescription hypnotic 30 days or more per year (Balter, Bauer, 1975). Complaints of excessive sleepiness have varied from 0.02% to 1% of general populations surveyed. In a survey of physicians in the United States, insomnia was estimated for 17% of patients and hypersomnia for 3% (Bixler, Kales, Soldatos, 1979). Age and disease tend to increase the prevalence of disturbed sleep.

Sleep may be an outgrowth of the ecological niche of day-seeing humans who were at a survival disadvantage at night. All plants and animals, however, apparently have circadian (circa = about; dies = a day) rhythms that support physiological economy and efficiency. The sleep/wake cycle may signify perturbations in hormonal, temperature, and other circadian rhythms and a lack of the normal synchronization among them (Moore-Ede, Sulzman, Fuller, 1982).

SLEEP ARCHITECTURE AND ELECTROPHYSIOLOGY

Sleep is divided into nonrapid-eye-movement (NREM) sleep and REM sleep. NREM shows a continuous spectrum from light sleep, where it is characterized by low-voltage, fast electroencephalographic (EEG) activity, to deep sleep, with high-voltage slow waves (Figs. 21-1 through 21-6). "Deep sleep," i.e., Stages 3 and 4 sleep, occurs mostly at the beginning of the night and involves secretion of growth hormone (Fig. 21-7). During "light sleep," i.e., Stage 1, many patients will report that they are awake when asked. Adults spend about 50% of the night in medium sleep (Stage 2), 20 to 25% of the night in REM sleep, 15 to 20% of the night in deep sleep (Stages 3 and 4), and the rest in wakefulness and Stage 1 (Table 21-1).

REM and NREM sleep alternate with each other in a cycle that, in total, lasts from 70 to 100 minutes. There are usually four to six NREM–REM cycles in each sleep

EEG (L)

EEG (R)

EOG (L)

EOG (R)

EMG (chin)

EKG

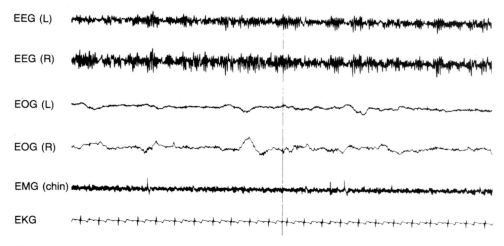

Figure 21–1. *Patient awake and calm. The top two lines show a very regular, easy-to-see, up-and-down trace of the pens about eight times per second. This is the "alpha" brain wave pattern, most often seen when a person has his eyes closed and is awake. Heart rate on the last line is 54 beats per minute. (Reprinted with permission from Regestein QR, Rechs JR: Sound Sleep, pp 31–33. New York, Simon & Schuster, 1980)*

EEG (L)

EEG (R)

EOG (L)

EOG (R)

EMG (chin)

EKG

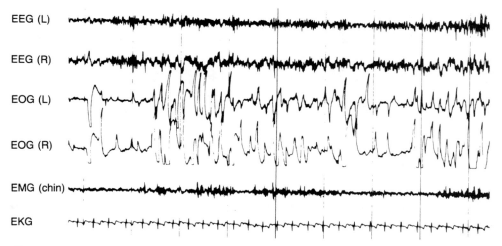

Figure 21–2. *Patient awake and talking. The top two lines show some alpha rhythm still present, but mostly interrupted by random, higher-frequency irregularities that obscure the alpha pattern. The third and fourth lines show lots of eye movements throughout the 30 seconds. On the fifth line, where the ink tracing widens, muscle activity under the chin increases when she is talking. Heart rate is 62 beats per minute. (Reprinted with permission from Regestein QR, Rechs JR: Sound Sleep, pp 31–33. New York, Simon & Schuster, 1980)*

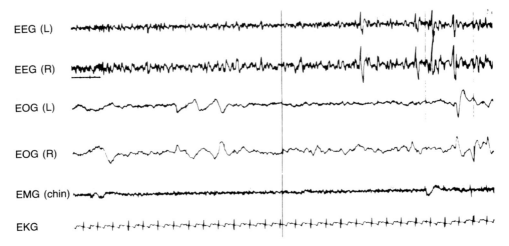

Figure 21–3. *Patient in Stage 1 sleep, the "drowsy" state. In the second line, the underlined section shows some ragged-looking alpha rhythm. Toward the right side of the record, about 20 seconds later, taller, lower-frequency brain-wave patterns are seen as the patient is falling asleep. The eye movement traces show some slow eye movements; the chin muscle activity has calmed down. (Reprinted with permission from Regestein QR, Rechs JR: Sound Sleep, pp 31–33. New York, Simon & Schuster, 1980)*

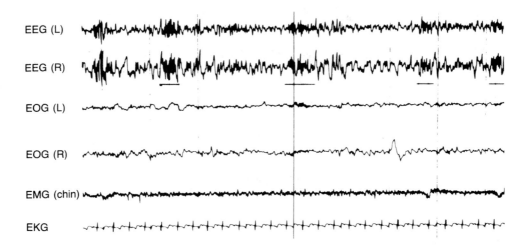

Figure 21–4. *Patient in Stage 2 or medium sleep. The underlined patterns are called sleep "spindles" even though these little bursts of electrical activity rarely look like actual spindles. They contain 14 to 16 pen deflections per second and signify Stage 2 sleep. (Reprinted with permission from Regestein QR, Rechs JR: Sound Sleep, pp 31–33. New York, Simon & Schuster, 1980)*

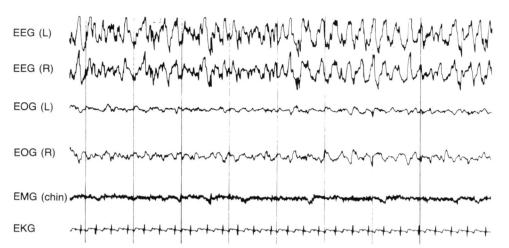

Figure 21–5. *Stage 4 sleep or slow-wave sleep. This deepest stage of sleep is marked by giant slow brain waves, as seen in the top two tracings, especially easy to pick out on the right side of the figure. This represents the slow ebb and flow of brain electrical activity as the brain idles in deep sleep. (Reprinted with permission from Regestein QR, Rechs JR: Sound Sleep, pp 31–33. New York, Simon & Schuster, 1980)*

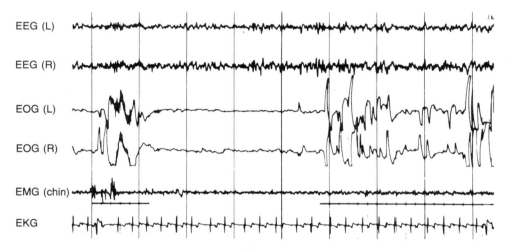

Figure 21–6. *Rapid Eye Movement or dreaming sleep. Here the top two lines resemble those seen in Stage 1 sleep, but the third and fourth lines look a bit like the Fig. 21-2 record which showed plenty of eye movements when the patient was awake and talking. The muscle line, however, is as thin as it gets, showing the least muscle activity level of the night. Where the muscle trace is underlined on the left, however, there is a burst of muscle activity, and you will notice some noisy widening of the lines tracing eye movements, especially of the left eye, third line from the top. These indicate a muscle twitch that involved areas under the chin and around the left eye. The patient awoke less than a minute later and said she had dreamed that it was hard to breathe. (Reprinted with permission from Regestein QR, Rechs JR: Sound Sleep, pp 31–33. New York, Simon & Schuster, 1980)*

period. While the first REM period is about 5 to 10 minutes, REM periods tend to become longer and closer together and show a greater density of rapid eye movements as the night proceeds.

The stages of sleep may be summarized as follows: Stage 0—a stage of wakefulness with the eyes closed. The waking EEG shows alpha waves (8 to 12 cycles per second [cps]) and/or low-voltage mixed frequency activity. Some eye movements may be observed, and the muscle tone is usually relatively high. Stage 1—characterized by relatively low-voltage beta (14 to 35 cps) and theta (4 to 7.5 cps) activity. There is a mixture of beta and theta activity on the EEG but without REM activity. Stage 2— characterized by irregular theta waves and two types of periodic phasic activity, sleep spindles and K-complexes. Sleep spindles are sinusoidal bursts of 12 to 14 cps seen primarily in the central region. K-complexes are high-amplitude negative waves followed by positive activity. High-amplitude delta waves (0.5 to 3.5 cps) can be found in Stage 2 but usually do not constitute more than 20% of the EEG activity in this stage. Stage 3—recognized by slow (0.5 to 3.5 cps), high-amplitude waves (delta or slow waves) that constitute 20 to 25% of Stage 3. Stage 4—predominantly (>50%) slow-wave sleep. Stages 3 and 4 sleep are usually collectively referred to as "deep sleep" (Karacan, Moore, 1985; Rechtschaffen, Kales, 1968).

REM sleep, accompanied by rapid eye movements and desynchronized, low-voltage fast activity, is also known as "desynchronized sleep." The first REM period appears on the average about 60–90 minutes into the sleep cycle and is preceded by an NREM period (Stages 1–4). REM periods tend to progressively increase as the night continues. REM sleep is associated with increased brain oxygen consumption, slight rise in body temperature, penile erections, markedly decreased skeletal muscle tone, and increased physiologic activity with marked variations in blood pressure and respirations. In contrast, in NREM sleep, heart rate and respiratory rates are more regular (Reynolds, Kupfer, 1988). REM sleep also is qualitatively different from NREM sleep. There is activation of brain stem nuclei associated with eye movements, well-defined dreams, sensations of movement, and secretion of 17-hydroxycorticosteroids.

Biochemically, *deep sleep* (Stages 3 and 4 sleep) is *lessened* by depletion of central nervous system (CNS) serotonin, whereas *REM sleep* is increased by depletion of CNS catecholamines (such as that caused by catecholamine-blocking drugs). Thus, central indolamine- and catecholamine-affecting drugs, such as certain antidepressants, stimulants, and antihypertensive agents, affect the sleep of many patients.

Table 21–1 **Distribution of Normal Sleep in Average Adults**

STAGE	PERCENT
NREM sleep	
Stage 1	5
Stage 2	50
Stage 3	15–20
Stage 4	15–20
REM sleep	20–25

Over the human life span, sleep gradually changes from the lengthy, solid, deep sleep of the newborn to the lighter, more disrupted sleep of old age. The normal 30-year-old, for instance, shows half the Stage 4 sleep and twice the wakefulness of the normal 20-year-old (Gaillard, 1978). There are progressive changes in sleep as we age. The percentage of sleep time spent in REM is about 80% in newborns and then declines and plateaus to about 25% by age 10 before declining slightly again in the 70s and 80s. The amount of time spent in deep (or delta) sleep decreases in later life, and Stage 4 sleep may be completely absent by the 60s. Advanced age is also associated with an increased number of awakenings. Hence, as we age, sleep becomes progressively more shallow and fragmented, leaving the elderly at particularly high risk for sleep disturbances. The number of apneic episodes per night tends to increase with age, as does the frequency of nocturnal myoclonus. Sleep problems tend to increase in parallel with this general trend toward deterioration of sleep quality with aging (see Fig. 21-7).

Adults average about 7.5 hours of sleep daily (Carskadon et al., 1982). Beyond the averages, however, people vary greatly in their total daily sleep. A small but "lucky" segment of the population appears to function well on 4 hours of sleep per night, while another small percentage is burdened with needing more than 9 hours of sleep (Jones

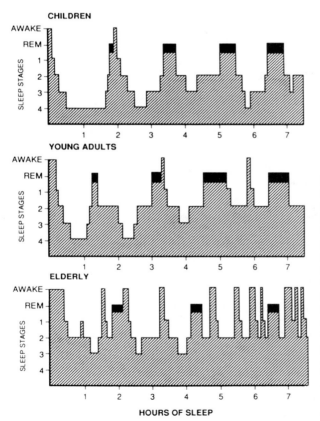

Figure 21–7. *Normal sleep cycles. REM sleep (darkened area) occurs cyclically throughout the night at intervals of approximately 90 minutes in all age groups. REM sleep shows little variation in the different age groups, whereas Stage 4 sleep decreases with age. In addition, the elderly have frequent awakenings and a marked increase in total wake time. (Reprinted with permission from Kales A, Kales JD: Sleep disorders: Recent findings in the diagnosis and treatment of disturbed sleep. N Engl J Med 290:487–499, 1974)*

and Oswald, 1968; Hartmann, 1974). Although variable sleep length has been described, sleep length seems determined, in part, by heredity, as indicated by twin studies.

The frenetic demands of an industrial culture may have induced briefer average sleep times. Experiments indicate that adults allowed ad-lib rather than usual sleep times are less sleepy the next day (Carskadon et al., 1982). When obligations compel abbreviated sleep hours, short sleepers tolerate it better.

Quality sleep normally requires good health, comfortable circumstances, and a lengthy daily period that is free of stressful obligations, along with freedom from the influence of stimulants and other drugs that negatively affect its structure. Thus, sleep may be easily disrupted.

INSOMNIA

Insomnia is defined as complaint of insufficient sleep to support good daytime functioning. Although about 15% of adults say they have insomnia on epidemiological surveys (Kales, Kales, 1984), only about 2% of them take any medication for it (Mellinger, Balter, Uhlenhuth, 1985). The majority of those taking hypnotic drugs use them less than 30 times a year. Thus, transient insomnia is relatively common, but *persistent* insomnia is rare. Sleep disorder clinics, for instance, see more hypersomniac than insomniac patients (Coleman et al., 1982).

General Treatment of Insomnia

There are common, nonspecific disruptions of sleep that precipitate and aggravate insomnia. Much can be done for patients by instituting good sleep habits or "sleep hygiene" when they first present with complaints of chronic insomnia. Table 21-2

Table 21-2 **Nonspecific Measures to Induce Sleep (Sleep Hygiene)**

1. Arise the same time daily.
2. Limit daily in-bed time to usual amount present prior to sleep disturbance.
3. Discontinue CNS-acting drugs (caffeine, nicotine, alcohol, stimulants).
4. Avoid daytime naps (except where sleep chart shows they induce better night sleep).
5. Establish physical fitness by means of graded program of vigorous exercise early in the day.
6. Avoid evening stimulation; substitute radio or relaxed reading for television.
7. Try very hot, 20-minute, body temperature–raising bath soaks near bedtime.
8. Eat at regular times daily; avoid large meals near bedtime.
9. Practice evening relaxation routines, such as progressive muscle relaxation or meditation.
10. Maintain comfortable sleeping conditions.

includes traditional "sleep hygiene" measures (Hauri, 1985) plus newer nonspecific treatments for insomnia.

Actual in-bed times and estimated sleep times should be charted daily in evaluating a person's sleep. The patient should be instructed to get up at the same time 7 days a week. This helps induce regular circadian rhythms, as may regularly scheduled daily meal times (see below). The patient should also withdraw from *CNS-acting drugs*. This is *especially* true for *caffeine*, which has a 12- to 20-hour duration of action (Hollingsworth, 1912). Caffeine also increases next-morning drowsiness (Goldstein, Kaizer, Whitby, 1969). *Alcohol* induces lighter sleep through rebound effects many hours after ingestion (Borg, Krande, Sedval, 1981). *Nicotine,* a long-acting stimulant, decreases sleep in addition to having other stimulant properties, such as appetite suppression and addiction (Soldatos et al., 1980; Henningfield, 1984). Total "in-bed times" should be *limited* (especially in older and unemployed patients), daytime naps *avoided,* and cardiovascular fitness gradually achieved through aerobic exercise performed earlier in the day. Large meals before bedtime should be avoided, as should stimulating television viewing (Saletu, Gruenberger, Anderer, 1983). Evening routines should be predictable and relaxing.

In instituting such a sleep hygiene program, the patient's interests and motivation should be considered. Some aspects of good sleep hygiene are difficult for almost all patients, especially quitting smoking. Other aspects, even if less arduous, such as getting up at regular times, may not always be possible. Caffeine withdrawal commonly causes *headaches* and a sluggishness that in some cases lasts months. Patients for whom daytime functioning is important, however, are more likely to invest considerable effort in obtaining good sleep.

Causes of Insomnia

Persistent insomnia that happens without apparent medical or psychiatric causes is called primary insomnia in DSM-III-R or "psychophysiological" insomnia in other classification systems. Patients with primary insomnia tend to be careful, scrupulous, detail-oriented, alert people by day, as distinguished from more relaxed, phlegmatic types. Those prone to insomnia may have arousal profiles different from those of others, as suggested by heart rate, body temperature, and evoked potential studies (Coursey, Buchsbaum, Frankel, 1975; Freedman, Sattler, 1982). Theories differ on the possible role of psychopathology in such insomnia. Although some consider psychopathological factors as contributors to the development of primary insomnia, others do not (Carskadon et al., 1976; Kales, Kales, 1984). Hyperaroused individuals may be prone to develop fears, feel anxiety more intensely, and ruminate longer than others, serving to disrupt their sleep. Hypervigilance, anxiety, neuroticism, introversion, and insomnia theoretically all derive from a common CNS profile of increased arousal (Gray, 1982).

Treatment of the primary insomnia patient is devoted to lessening arousal at bedtime. Relaxation procedures may be used, such as the relaxation response described by Benson et al. (1974). In one variation, patients lie relaxed with one eye closed and arms and legs uncrossed, silently saying "one" to themselves during both inspiration and expiration. This routine is continued for 10 to 20 minutes once or twice daily. Jacobsen's Progressive Muscle Relaxation involves the patient's successively focusing on muscle groups from feet to head and concentrating on relaxing them over a 20- to 30-minute period, but not tensing them as in some other methods. Soaks, in bath water hot enough to raise the body temperature a few degrees shortly prior to bedtime, induce relaxation as well as various discomforts in some patients. Despite the latter, sleep becomes deeper. Body temperature increases apparently underlie the deeper sleep induced by exercise (Horne, Moore, 1985). Tape recordings of directions for relaxing, guided imagery, soothing music, and forest or ocean sounds all have helped some patients.

Psychiatric Disorders and Insomnia

Patients and doctors alike are quick to attribute insomnia generally to psychological problems. But most patients with severe problems such as schizophrenia or antisocial personality disorder do not tend to be particularly plagued by insomnia. Specific psychiatric conditions, however, do predispose to insomnia, especially mood and anxiety disorders, as well as some dementias (Tan et al., 1984). Insomnia cannot be attributed to such conditions, however, until reasonably good sleep hygiene measures are in place. Many patients have spent fruitless years seeking dependable sleep through anxiety reduction and psychotherapy while working late, drinking coffee, and sleeping late on weekends!

Patients may complain bitterly of insomnia because it feels like the most debilitating, the most socially acceptable, or the most identifiable symptom from which they suffer. What the *depressed* patient complains of initially (e.g., depressed mood, diarrhea, weight loss, or insomnia) depends on a complex mixture of biopsychosocial factors. Thus, depressed patients may complain not of mood disturbance or crying spells but rather fatigue, pain, inability to work or concentrate, and so forth. Anxious patients who present with insomnia may seem intense or irritable. Posttraumatic stress syndrome patients who complain of insomnia may also be preoccupied with their painful surgery, physical abuse, war memories, or other traumas. Insomnia from such psychiatric causes tends to be chronic.

Both mood disorders and disruptions of the sleep/wake cycle are related through disturbance in the circadian timing system. In depression, the *circadian oscillator* that controls REM sleep, body temperature, and cortisol secretion rhythms, moves peaks out of their usual synchrony in these functions to earlier hours of the sleep/wake cycle (Goodwin, Wirz-Justice, Wehr, 1982). The earlier the advance, the more depressed the patient. The practical consequences of this phase advance in depression are that clinical relief and establishment of efficient, previously failed antidepressants can be induced by advancing the patient's sleep/wake schedule to earlier hours to synchronize with his or her body temperature schedule (Sack et al., 1985) (see also Chapter 6).

The phase advance of REM sleep in *depression* makes REM sleep appear abnormally soon after usual bedtime (e.g., in less than 60 minutes and in some cases much sooner, instead of the normal 90 minutes [shortened REM latency]) (Mendelson, 1987). Early onset of REM sleep also appears in other states, such as in patients treated with CNS catecholamine-blocking drugs. Early REM onset is also seen after traumatic experiences, in circadian desynchrony, and in narcolepsy. Depressed patients also take longer to fall asleep; have lighter, more fragmented sleep and a higher percentage of REM sleep; and awaken earlier.

Many patients will *ascribe their depression to insomnia*, rather than vice versa. Indeed, normal individuals may suffer depressed mood after significant sleep deprivation. Patients whose moods co-vary closely with their sleep hours may be promptly helped by sedative–hypnotic drugs; however, long-lasting relief of insomnia by means of hypnotics will be sustained only by a small minority of depressed patients. This probably accounts for the parsimonious use of hypnotics as indicated by epidemiological surveys.

Treatment of insomnia from a primary psychiatric disorder depends on relief of the underlying disorder itself. For instance, where insomnia is primarily due to depression, a sedating antidepressant such as doxepin or nortriptyline may be given at night.

Drugs, caffeine, nicotine, and *alcohol* so ubiquitously disrupt sleep that they should be discontinued in all insomnia patients. These affect arousal mechanisms, and thus the sleep/wake cycle, and therefore may cause insomnia. *Twelve to twenty-five percent* of insomnia patients in sleep disorder clinics reportedly have sleep problems caused or aggravated by drug abuse (Coleman et al., 1982; Tan et al., 1984).

Over-the-counter nasal decongestants may be quite stimulating and can disrupt sleep. Prescription drugs with CNS actions are commonly overlooked as causes for insomnia. These include catecholamine-blockers, antibronchospastic agents, stimulating antidepressants (fluoxetine, protriptyline), antiarrhythmic drugs, steroids, thyroid hormone, and methysergide. Diuretics may cause cramps in bed and also restless legs syndrome, which is characterized by the continual need to move one's legs, which disrupts sleep. *Even sleeping pills paradoxically may worsen sleep.* Shorter-acting ones such as triazolam or temazepam may induce agitated, amnestic episodes, early-morning awakening or next-day anxiety, and next-night rebound insomnia probably through a withdrawal syndrome associated with rapid drug washout (Kales, Kales, 1984). Chronic use of hypnotics may also diminish sleep quality.

Judiciously tapering or discontinuing CNS-acting drugs may restore sleep quality. Although stopping caffeine or methyldopa may restore solid sleep, discontinuation of some drugs often raises a dilemma. Asthmatic patients who need significant doses of beta-agonists, for example, will require adjustments in their drug regimen. Judicious use of counteracting sedatives and vigorous sleep hygiene may be required.

Sleep Schedule Disorders

Two circadian "oscillators" apparently control timing of the daily peaks and nadirs of all physiological functions. One of these oscillators times the propensity for *deep sleep* and the *sleep/wake rhythms* and *REM sleep.* The *light/dark cycle, social schedules,* and to some extent the *timing of meals* serve as pacemakers for the circadian oscillators. The oscillator for the temperature cycle is more inert and less changeable compared with the one for the sleep/wake cycle. However, maximal sleep quality, as well as optimal physiological integration in general, depends on synchronization of these two bodily timing systems. Thus, sleep normally begun during the downward-moving phase of the circadian temperature cycle will be much longer than shifted sleep begun against an upward-moving body temperature, as may happen in jet lag or shift work. When the body lacks timing information (e.g., under experimental conditions in a cave or in constant light), circadian oscillators show a sleep/wake cycle *longer* than 24 hours. A 25-hour cycle means that the subject would go to bed 1 hour later than usual each day. This underlying tendency toward later arising times manifests itself clinically in the delayed arising times commonly seen in those without regular morning obligations as well as in the delayed sleep phase syndrome. Sleep schedule disorders such as phase delay problems present with complaints of insomnia until late hours (e.g., 2:00 A.M. to 3:00 A.M. or later). Sleep then occurs, but at hours that will obviously conflict with morning obligations. Any attempt to move sleep hours earlier results in the patient lying awake in bed, increasing his or her frustration. Patients may reestablish desirable sleep hours after remaining up all night to promote falling asleep from exhaustion at an earlier bedtime. But *desychronization* between circadian oscillators *remains,* as does the delaying tendency, which manifests itself as a *lack* of appropriate sleepiness at a desirable bedtime and therefore increasingly late arising times. The progressively delayed sleep schedule again moves up later against morning obligations, and the cycle is repeated. Patients will often arrange multiple telephone calls at arising time and other maneuvers to get them up at a desirable time, but these efforts generally fail because motivation falters at early hours and because such ploys are usually neglected on weekends and holidays.

   Treatment for delayed sleep phase syndrome involves first standardizing the existing sleep schedule, then *progressively* shifting sleep hours in *small steps* toward a desirable schedule; then, and most important, a *fixed daily arising time* is set. The progressive shifts can be done by *delaying* sleep by 2- or 3-hour steps until desirable hours are established or by going to sleep earlier in exquisitely small steps (e.g., 10 minutes every other night). The former method (progressively delaying sleep) is more rapid and consistent with the natural tendencies of the circadian oscillators. The latter (moving sleep times up) is much slower but avoids having to sleep during daylight work hours. At the annual fall shift from daylight-saving time to standard time, patients with delayed sleep phase syndrome who have rigidly maintained their daily arising time can usually make their hours earlier in one or two steps (i.e., after arising an hour earlier). A newer approach to delayed sleep involves exposure to bright light during the second half of the sleep period, which induces a sleep phase advance (i.e., earlier bedtimes and wake times).

Shift Work

   There are those among the quarter of the country's work force who have evening or night hours who prefer this type of evening schedule and others who tolerate it quite poorly (Czeisler, Moore-Ede, Coleman, 1982). Some of these individuals have short sleep needs, prefer night work, and function well on the few hours of sleep they obtain between night shift and an active daytime. Others sleep poorly and feel chronically fatigued.

   Workers on rotating shifts suffer the most. The design of such shifts often does not consider the later-moving properties of the circadian oscillators. The shift rotations that are the most desirable are those which take place toward later hours, with changes in shifts occurring rarely (e.g., monthly rather than weekly). For example, when an industrial plant redesigned its work schedule according to these guidelines, production increased and personnel turnover diminished by 18% (Czeisler, Moore-Ede, Coleman, 1982). The individual intolerant to shifting work schedules, however, may suffer chronic fatigue or loss of work and probably should seek other types of employment. This may even mean a career change, because some unemployment fields (e.g., nursing, meteorology, the military) have obligatory shift changes at entry-level positions.

Irregular Hours

A person's sleep hours normally vary. Those with a tendency toward insomnia, however, may disrupt their sleep quality by late sleeping on weekends or other frequent changes in their arising times. Those without work hours to provide them with a steady pacemaker are at risk for a more haphazard sleep schedule, which risks poor sleep quality. The important timing information derived from arising at a predictable hour, the timing of the propensity to fall asleep, and the normal sequencing of sleep stages may all be lessened by irregular sleep hours.

Often patients are unaware of their irregular sleep schedules; they feel that the irregularities they have are exceptions, and they are surprised upon examination of a month's sleep chart at the wide range of arising times they keep.

Treatment of the sleep disturbance due to irregular scheduling depends primarily upon maintenance of regular arising times, because of their crucial role in regulating the circadian period, and also upon the avoidance of naps. Bedtimes will gradually stabilize according to the patient's sleep need.

MEDICAL PROBLEMS AND DISTURBED SLEEP

Disturbing symptoms of disease such as itching or pain raise the threshold for sleep. Symptoms such as dyspnea, nocturia, diarrhea, angina, or migraine may supervene to disrupt sleep. On the other hand, insomnia may be erroneously ascribed to chronic and mild medical symptoms without further appraisal of other possible causes. Frequently, sleep-disrupting medical symptoms occur within a matrix of other sleep-related factors (e.g., when a depressed patient, fearful of nocturnal angina, takes beta-blockers or when a patient with a nocturnal wheezing takes beta-agonists).

Inpatient hospital settings, with their constant activity, enforced positions, daytime inactivity, noises, and periodic crises hardly encourage adequate sleep. Against this problematic background, the specifics of the patient's illness and treatment may further worsen sleep. Intensive care unit patients averaged five interruptions per hour during the calmest night hours in one study (Dlin et al., 1971). Preoperatively, elective surgery patients had shortened sleep, while heart surgery patients were noted to have 1 to 4 hours' sleep the first postoperative day (Johns et al., 1974).

Any disease state that potentially disrupts sleep risks insomnia (Regestein, 1987). Pathological mechanisms vary from fear and worry in an inherently obsessional "neurotic" or hyperaroused individual to physical discomforts or features of the treatment situation (e.g., the schedule disruptions of chronic outpatient renal dialysis, the symptomatic aftermath of physiotherapy). Direct effects of disease upon sleep-regulating mechanisms commonly worsen sleep (e.g., altered neurotransmitter metabolism in liver disease or cortical dysfunction in primary dementia) (Reynolds et al., 1985). Of the various medical causes for insomnia, some are particularly common and will be discussed below.

Obstructive Sleep Apnea

The decreased ventilatory response and increased work of breathing in the asleep recumbent individual predispose to breathing problems. Constriction of the upper airway from any cause, such as partial or complete nasal blockage, impaired airway-widening reflexes during inspiration from nasal anesthesia or sedation, or enlargement of the soft palate or of pharyngeal structures (e.g., tonsils, uvula, tongue, or patulous mucosa, micrognathia, or the thickened tissues of acromegaly), in conjunction with the diminished ventilatory response during sleep and the recumbent position, increases the risk of obstructed breathing. Obesity further increases breathing impairment by rendering the diaphragm broad, flat, and thus inefficient, which further diminishes the ventilatory response. In such cases, the sleeper awakens briefly dozens or hundreds of unremembered times to take a breath. Thereafter, he feels groggy and sleepy the next day, without knowing why. Snoring in a sleepy person raises suspicions of breathing disorder, termed *sleep apnea*. Impairment of ventilatory control mechanisms may be present in states of hypoxia, hypercapnia, or slow circulation time, further predisposing to sleep apnea (Cherniak, 1984).

Cardiovascular Problems

The sleep of angina patients is worse than their nocturnal pain alone explains. Coronary artery disease patients seem predisposed to breathing impairment during sleep, again for unclear reasons (Olazebal et al., 1982).

Endocrine Problems

Increased metabolic rate induces deeper sleep. Mild hyperthyroidism causes *more* and hypothyroidism *less* deep sleep, although clinically this varies. Similarly, fever makes more sleep in some patients, less in others. Diabetes interferes with innervation of the pharyngeal airway and may increase the risk of sleep apnea. Menopause tends to be associated with insomnia because of vasomotor changes from fluctuating estrogen levels, which may be ameliorated by hormonal replacement (Campbell, 1976). The premenstrual state may provoke transient insomnia. Cushing's syndrome and exogenous steroid medications as well as Addison's disease all potentially lessen sleep quality.

Neurological Conditions

Cortical impairments often cause continuing poor-quality sleep, although even in severe cases sleep patterns vary a great deal among individuals. The same heterogeneity is seen in seizure disorders, although insomnia, sleepwalking, and night terrors are all increased. Mental retardation also tends to worsen sleep quality, but individual patterns vary according to the cause.

Sleep quality often suffers from the indirect effects of neurological impairments (e.g., enforced inactivity, failure to adhere to sleep hygiene measures of breathing problems associated with rigidity in parkinsonism).

Pregnancy

Third-trimester pregnancy often involves urinary frequency, movements of the unborn, and difficulty achieving a comfortable position, all of which lessen sleep quality.

Gastrointestinal Factors

Esophageal reflux increased by recumbency interferes with sleep, even in the absence of pain, as do large meals prior to bedtime. Nocturnal symptoms of irritable bowel syndrome also may disrupt sleep. Liver disease worsens sleep, possibly by interfering with uptake of normal precursors for sleep-regulating neurotransmitters. Peptic ulcer pain, however, rarely disrupts sleep.

Often a medical condition will provide several reasons for worse sleep. For instance, *chronic renal failure* patients with uremia show impaired sleep that is only partially remedied by hemodialysis. The scheduling and direct effects of hemodialysis, however, may worsen sleep. The alcoholic suffers the direct disruptive effects of alcohol on sleep, as well as withdrawal effects, but long-term negative effects on sleep quality have been observed even after sobriety has been maintained for years.

Frequently, a medical symptom is simply one of several disruptive factors present. Normally, with age, the return to sleep after awakening takes increasingly longer. Thus, an elderly patient who awakens frequently because movements during sleep irritated his arthritic pain or because of nocturia may have many prolonged waking periods during the night.

Poor sleep quality may cause either hypersomnia or insomnia. Both complaints derive from similar common causes (e.g., use of sedatives, sleep apnea, or major depression). Poor sleep quality of multiple causes may give rise to the complaint of hypersomnia, sleepiness, and obligatory naps when the patient fails to remember the frequent brief wakefulness episodes of unrefreshing light sleep.

Use of Sedatives

Use of sedatives to relieve insomnia is empirical and should be temporary. Long-term use of sedatives usually relieves sedative-withdrawal insomnia rather than some other insomnia problem. Of the 3% of adults who use prescription hypnotics, about

20% use them more than 120 days a year (Mellinger, Balter, Uhlenhuth, 1985). In one study, 22% of hypnotic-dependent patients had begun their habit on routine prescription drugs during hospitalization (Johnson, Clift, 1968). Such drugs are disproportionately used by older people, in whom they potentially aggravate cortical dysfunction and psychological regression.

Benzodiazepines are the sedatives of choice because they are safer in overdose and in rapid withdrawal and do not induce hepatic enzymes. They act at specific CNS postsynaptic receptor sites to enhance the action of γ-aminobutyric acid (GABA), a major inhibitory neurotransmitter (Mendelson, 1987) (see also Chapter 7).

The more lipid-soluble benzodiazepines readily enter the CNS, producing the rapid sedation preferred by most patients. These include diazepam and flurazepam, with an absorption half-life of 10 minutes, compared with oxazepam and clorazepate, with absorption half-lives of 18 and 35 minutes, respectively. Slowly excreted drugs include diazepam and flurazepam, with *elimination* half-lives of 20 to 50 and 40 to 280 hours, respectively. These may promote ease of sleep onset the following day and prolonged anxiety reduction. Compared with more rapidly excreted benzodiazepines, longer-acting drugs induce similar next-day levels of subjective sleepiness and psychometric test performance (Bliwise et al., 1984). They are theoretically less likely to provoke untoward reactions upon abrupt withdrawal, although this does not hold true for some patients. Practically, the difference between slowly and rapidly excreted benzodiazepines provides a precarious guide for the individual patient, given large differences in tolerance and sensitivity. In general, next-day performance is much more influenced by the dose of drug rather than its elimination half-life (Johnson, Cherniak, 1982).

The most rapidly excreted benzodiazepine is triazolam, with an elimination half-life of 1.5 to 5 hours. Oxazepam has an elimination half-life of 5 to 20 hours, and lorazepam, temazepam, alprazolam, and chlordiazepoxide have half-lives between approximately 10 and 30 hours, generally taking longer in the elderly. Triazolam may be useful where next-day sedation has occurred, but in some patients its rapid washout provokes rebound insomnia in the early morning, next-day anxiety, and anterograde amnesia (Kales, Kales, 1984).

The lack of active metabolites makes oxazepam preferred in liver disease. Lorazepam has a particular propensity for anterograde amnestic effects. Antacids and anticholinergic drugs decrease absorption of benzodiazepines, but cimetidine slows their metabolism to a minor degree.

The barbiturates have been largely replaced by the benzodiazepines because of their much narrower safety margins as well as their significant interactions with many common prescription drugs (Mendelson, 1980). However, they remain useful in some insomnia patients with seizure disorders or in those who are otherwise treatment resistant.

Chloral hydrate is cross-tolerant with alcohol, inexpensive, and available in syrup form for those who have difficulty swallowing pills. Ethchlorvynol is another alcohol but, compared with chloral hydrate, does not stimulate dicumarol metabolism, peaks later, and is excreted more slowly.

Glutethimide has a rapid onset of action, rapid metabolism, high mortality in overdose, and much abuse potential. Of over-the-counter agents, diphenhydramine is a histamine blocker and a mild sedative; methyprylon has a rapid onset of action and has verifiable sedative actions. *Methapyrilene* is anticholinergic. L-tryptophan (recently withdrawn from the market), which has mild sedative properties in higher doses, is an amino acid precursor to CNS serotonin production, has no side effects and reaches maximum benefit at doses of 2 gm.

Hypersomnia

Hypersomnia is a persistent need for excessive sleep. Any disease or drug state affecting the sleep/wake cycle can be responsible. The sleepiness of neurological, endocrine, or psychiatric problems will be accompanied by other stigmata of disease.

Sleepiness is typically provoked by prolonged monotony (e.g., television watching or attending meetings). Turnpike driving may be particularly dangerous. The conditions discussed below commonly present in the patient who feels otherwise healthy.

Idiopathic Hypersomnia

Idiopathic hypersomnia involves prolonged, polygraphically normal nocturnal sleep and continual daytime drowsiness. It commonly develops in adolescence where patients may be noticed to tolerate poorly any late-night activities with their friends. Dating the onset of idiopathic hypersomnia is often difficult because a change in work requirements or social obligations precipitates complaints in a patient who has previously coped with abnormally increased sleep. About one-half of patients manifest "sleep drunkenness," a period of incapacitating drowsiness upon first awakening, sometimes lasting for more than an hour. A nap or even two naps daily are commonly taken. These usually last an hour or more, unlike the shorter naps of narcolepsy. The large sleep requirement impedes fulfilling daytime obligations. Frequently, a family member also has a history that suggests idiopathic hypersomnia. Depression appears to be increased also among patients and family members. Laboratory tests show impaired daytime concentration and abnormally prolonged normal night sleep.

Treatment of *idiopathic hypersomnia* involves a systematic scheduling of sleep, stimulant drugs, recording of night sleep hours and naps, and progressive refinement, by trial and error, of the treatment regimen. Napping will be scheduled according to social demands. A mother with young children may nap when they do; workers may arrange abbreviated or split-up hours, but some work may be irreconcilable with a patient's sleep requirements. Stimulants are helpful adjuncts but must be used systematically. Stimulants work better to maintain rather than restore wakefulness. Pemoline, a longer-acting stimulant, comes in 18.75-mg pills. Two to six pills are commonly taken in divided doses in the morning. Dextroamphetamine and methylphenidate (which sometimes provokes relatively less motor stimulation than amphetamines) have shorter durations of action and must be taken in periodic divided doses, the first one upon arising or, in the presence of sleep drunkenness, prior to arising. Occasionally, stimulant cyclic antidepressants such as protriptyline or even monoamine oxidase (MAO) inhibitors may also be of value. The outcome of therapeutic drug trials is best judged against steady maintenance of the previously shaped optimal sleep/wake schedule.

Narcolepsy

Narcolepsy is present in one to two persons per thousand and has a genetic component. It seems to involve REM sleep-related features that suddenly and abnormally intrude on wakefulness during the day. The patient is seized with an irresistible urge to nap for 10 to 20 minutes. The paralysis of REM sleep appears as cataplexy attacks that are characterized by brief bilateral paresis brought on by laughter, anger, or surprise. Patients may be unable to talk or move their limbs. Frank falling down is rarer. Consciousness and thus memory for the event is preserved, thus distinguishing the episode from a seizure. "Sleep paralysis" (i.e., suddenly awakening and being transiently unable to move or talk) may also occur. Hypnogogic hallucinations are vivid dreamlike visual experiences at sleep onset and may be accompanied by apprehension that someone else is present in the room.

The above represents the classical "tetrad" of symptoms associated with narcolepsy. Paradoxically, wakeful periods may occur during night sleep, which are typically not seen in idiopathic hypersomnia. Troublesome dreams and depression are other features commonly seen. Narcolepsy, as well as other causes of sleepiness, also entails automatic behavior that is inefficient and repetitive so that no progress is made on a task. Social, familial, and occupational functioning is often impaired.

Laboratory tests reveal naps with onset averaging 5 minutes or less with rapid onset REM sleep. Almost all patients have a leukocyte antigen (DR-2), compared with about 20% of controls.

Treatment of narcolepsy is similar to that of idiopathic hypersomnia. Protriptyline and other antidepressants suppress REM sleep and therefore narcolepsy symptoms. Stimulants such as methylphenidate and pemoline may also be warranted. Mild cases may be managed by scheduled naps and small, measured doses of caffeine.

Sleep Apnea

This has become a generic term for breathing disorders during sleep, as discussed above. A common stereotypical clinical picture is found in an obese middle-aged or older man who frequently drinks alcohol, uses large amounts of caffeine, or smokes. There may be mild hypertension or cardiac arrhythmias present. The cardinal symptom is *loud snoring.* Where snoring is mild or absent, sleep apnea episodes may be due to Cheyne-Stokes breathing or "central" dysregulation of breathing, as distinguished from upper-airway "obstructive" mechanisms. Sleepiness may be mild or may be noticed more by others than by the patients themselves. Dry mouth and headache upon first arising are common. The sleep apnea occurring in asymptomatic individuals testifies to varying CNS tolerance for poor sleep quality. However, denial of the problem tends to be common in sleep apnea patients. Their condition, like sleepiness in general, may induce psychopathology of all types, including depression (Kales et al., 1985). Less typical patients, such as thin, young women who snore, often have some compromise in the dimensions or functions of the upper airway. Table 21-3 summarizes diagnostic distinctions of sleep disorder characterized by hypersomnia.

Table 21–3 **Diagnostic Distinctions in Hypersomnia**

	SLEEP APNEA	NARCOLEPSY	IDIOPATHIC HYPERSOMNIA	SLEEP DEPRIVATION
Begins	Middle age	Youth	Youth	Any time
Complaint	Often none	Irresistible naps	Constant sleepiness	Frequent sleepiness
Features	Snoring	Cataplexy, brief naps	Long sleep, sleep drunk, long naps	
Predispositions	Age, obesity, male	Heredity	?Heredity	Obsessionality
Associated features	Mild hypertension, headache	Bad dreams, broken night sleep	Depression	Improves after recovery sleep
Most awake time of day	Afternoon	Immediately after night sleep	Mid-morning	On awakening
Sleepiest time of day	Evening	Periodically during day	On awakening	Varies
Lab test results	Apnea during sleep	Sleep onset REM, sleeps within 5 min., leukocyte antibody DR-2	Prolonged normal sleep	Increased deep sleep, little intervening wakefulness

Parasomnias

Parasomnias are unwanted automatisms that occur during *deep* sleep. Often these occur during deep sleep when cortical suppression of fixed action patterns is lessened compared to other stages. Adult enuresis may be the most common type of parasomnia and is associated with urethral abnormalities, cystitis, diabetes, developmental immaturity, or frontal lobe impairments. Management of childhood enuresis is discussed in Chapter 15.

Sleepwalking is relatively rare during adulthood. A childhood or family history of sleepwalking is frequently found. Early-night sleepwalking occurs during deep sleep. Movements are slow, poorly coordinated, without integrated purpose, and unremembered. Patients rarely hurt themselves.

Other sleep automatisms include *bruxism* (teeth grinding) or repetitive movements of head or extremities. These differ from more complex behaviors associated with partial arousal and poorly remembered stereotypes, such as sitting or standing up, stroking the wall, saluting, or punching.

Night terrors (parvor nocturnus) rarely occur in adults. As opposed to "nightmares," which occur during REM sleep, night terrors arise during deep sleep. They also happen earlier in the night with sudden screaming, sweating, tachycardia, and apparent panic. This is unremembered, unlike nocturnal panic attacks, which commonly happen later in the night and may be associated with diurnal panic disorder or prolapsed mitral valve syndrome.

Nightmares are dreams involving floridly upsetting content (e.g., monsters, instinctual threats such as snakes or heights, death, being attacked, drowned, or overwhelmed). The patient may not awaken or may awaken with emotional arousal.

Table 21–4 **Sleep Disorders**

DISORDER	SLEEP-LABORATORY FINDINGS	PSYCHOLOGIC EVALUATION	MANAGEMENT & TREATMENT
Somnambulism	Incidents occur out of stage 4 sleep: critical skills & reactivity are impaired during the incident.	Psychiatric disturbances infrequent in children & frequent in adults	Prophylactic measures: children frequently outgrow disorders, so parents should be reassured: psychiatric evaluation for adults.
Enuresis	Occurs out of all sleep stages: misconception of dreaming as a frequent causal factor is explained.	Psychiatric disturbances infrequent with primary enuresis: psychologic evaluation often indicated for secondary enuresis.	Parental counseling & reassurance critical so that parental mishandling does not create psychiatric problems: pharmacologic treatment (imipramine) may be indicated in older children.
Night terrors	Occur out of stage 4 sleep: characterized by extreme vocalizations, motility & autonomic response; recall minimal or absent.	Psychiatric disturbances infrequent in children & frequent in adults	Parents reassured that children frequently outgrow the disorder: for adults, psychological evaluation often indicated; use of stage 4 suppressants under investigation.
Nightmares	Occur out of REM sleep; characterized by less motility & autonomic response: recall frequent & elaborate.	Frequent nightmares in children or adults may indicate psychopathology; rule out drug withdrawal as a possible cause of nightmares	Parents reassured that nightmares in children are often transient: if episodes are frequent in children or adults, psychologic evaluation is indicated.
Narcolepsy	Sleep attacks of narcolepsy may be accompanied by 3 auxiliary symptoms: cataplexy, sleep paralysis & hypnogogic hallucinations (cataplexy is accompanied by sleep-onset REM periods).	Sleep attacks may be misinterpreted for laziness, irresponsibility, or emotional instability	Establishing diagnosis critical: stimulants effective for sleep attacks: imipramine effective for auxiliary symptoms: danger in using imipramine & amphetamines simultaneously.
Hypersomnia	Sleep-stage patterns normal, but sleep is extended: associated with post dormital confusion & difficulty in awakening: autonomic variables are increased.	Often a symptom of psychologic disorder (e.g., depression).	Stimulant drugs effective: neurologic & psychologic evaluation important in establishing diagnosis.
Insomnia	Complaints of patients have been verified in the sleep laboratory; sleep is more aroused (i.e., heart rate & respiration are increased): most hypnotic drugs lose their effectiveness within 2 wk.	Insomnia most often symptom of psychologic disturbance & not a primary disorder; depression a common feature.	When insomnia is secondary to medical conditions, pharmacologic treatment may be useful: if psychologic factors are primary, pharmacologic therapy should be combined with psychotherapy.

(Reprinted with permission from Kales A, Kales JD: Sleep disorders: Recent findings in the diagnosis and treatment of disturbed sleep. N Engl J Med 290:487–499, 1974)

Nightmares may be provoked by REM sleep–increasing factors such as depression, trauma, catecholamine-blockers, and withdrawal from sedatives or stimulants. Table 21-4 summarizes key diagnostic and treatment issues of the clinical assessment of sleep disorders.

CLINICAL PEARLS

- The most commonly overlooked strategy in treating patients with insomnia is addressing their basic "sleep hygiene." Along these lines, perhaps the substance that physicians are *least likely* to inquire about is the use of caffeine.
- Depression in middle-aged and other individuals (especially the elderly) is almost always accompanied by fragmented sleep patterns, with the patient most typically awakening around 3 or 4 A.M. and being unable to go back to sleep.
- The most frequent error made by primary care physicians is to mistake the fragmented sleep caused by depression as "simple insomnia" and to treat the patient with benzodiazepines. This effectively serves to "mask" the sleep disturbance, which, as noted above, is a major symptom of depression.
- In patients who have a primary diagnosis of depression or who have chronic sleep difficulties associated with a tendency toward dysphoric mood and anxiety, low-dose sedating cyclic antidepressants, such as 25 to 50 mg of doxepin or nortriptyline at bedtime, may be effective alternatives to benzodiazepines.
- In general, unless a specialized sleep evaluation has been performed, no more than 10 to 15 benzodiazepine sleeping pills should be prescribed at any one time. Prescriptions for sleeping pills should generally not be refilled over the telephone. When sleeping pills are prescribed, the patient should be made aware that the pills are to be prescribed only for a short period of time.
- In patients who are persistent in demanding sleeping pills, be careful to look for concurrent alcohol dependence or other substance abuse disorder.
- When patients present with the chief complaint of difficulty sleeping, always rule out a core diagnosis of major depression first.
- In choosing a benzodiazepine, temazepam may have some advantages over both flurazepam and triazolam. Flurazepam has an extended half-life that may cause excessive daytime sedation. On the other hand, triazolam, although it may have the advantage of an ultrashort half-life, can also cause rebound insomnia later the same evening, rebound anxiety during the daytime, and rebound anxiety the next night. If triazolam is used, it should be used in doses of no more than 0.25 mg or less for a brief period of time. Temazepam is a good alternative to consider between the two because it has a relatively short half-life (12 to 16 hours) and its metabolism is not affected by age or liver disease.
- In evaluating patients for an obstructive sleep apnea syndrome, almost all of these patients have a history of predominantly noisy snoring, and many are also obese. Be sure to interview the patient's bed partner or other individuals in the household for a history of snoring.

ANNOTATED BIBLIOGRAPHY

Cherniak NS: Sleep apnea and its causes. J Clin Invest 73:1501–1505, 1984

Discusses sleep apnea as a final common expression of a number of pathophysiological mechanisms.

Czeisler CA, Moore-Ede MD, Coleman RM: Rotating shift work schedules that disrupt sleep are improved by applying circadian principles. Science 217:460–463, 1982

> Changes in work scheduling lessened personnel complaints and increased production.

Diagnostic and Statistical Manual of Mental Disorders, pp 297–313. American Psychiatric Association, Washington, D.C., 1987

> Gives diagnostic criteria for sleep disorders in a widely recognized classification.

Ekbom KA: Restless legs syndrome. Neurology 10:868–873, 1960

> Classical description of a movement disorder of many causes.

Goodwin FK, Wirz-Justice A, Wehr TA: Evidence that the pathophysiology of depression and the mechanism of action of antidepressant drugs both involve alterations in circadian rhythms. In Costa E, Racagni C (eds): Typical and Atypical Antidepressants: Clinical Practice, pp 1–11. New York, Raven Press, 1982

> Desynchrony between the REM cycle and the sleep/wake rhythm induces mood disorders. Sleep phase advances may relieve them.

Gray JA: The Neuropsychology of Anxiety. New York, Oxford University Press, 1982

> Discusses neurophysiological substrata of arousal and their psychological effects.

Guilleminault C, van den Hoed J, Mitler M: Clinical overview of the sleep apnea syndrome. In Guilleminault C, Dement WC (eds): Sleep Apnea Syndromes, pp 233–260. New York, Alan R Liss, 1978

> Summarizes clinical aspects of sleep apnea.

Hartmann EL: The Functions of Sleep. New Haven, Yale University Press, 1974

> A compact source of much basic information about sleep.

Hauri P: The Sleep Disorders. Kalamazoo, MI, Upjohn, 1982

> Succinctly covers the major sleep disorders, with basic information, case examples, and good illustrations.

Kales A, Kales JD: Evaluation and Treatment of Insomnia. New York, Oxford University Press, 1984

> A rich compendium of information about insomnia.

Kelly DD: Sleep and dreaming. In Kandel ER, Schwarz JH (eds): Principles of Neural Science, pp 648–657. New York, Elsevier, 1985

> A summary of neurophysiological observations related to sleep.

Mellinger GD, Balter MB, Uhlenhuth EH: Insomnia and its treatment. Arch Gen Psychiatry 42:225–232, 1985

> In the U.S., 6% of men and 8% of women take some type of medication to promote sleep. Only 3% of adults take sleeping pills, and most of those who do use them less than 30 times a year.

Mendelson WB: The Use and Misuse of Sleeping Pills. New York, Plenum Press, 1980

> Summarizes information about most agents, giving history and perspective in a readable format.

Mendelson WB: Human Sleep. New York, Plenum Press, 1987

> Summarizes much information about sleep in a detailed but readable manner.

Moore-Ede MC, Sulzman FM, Fuller CA: The Clocks That Time Us. Cambridge, MA, Harvard University Press, 1982

> Presents in readable fashion the basic principles of chronobiology. Profusely illustrated.

Pokorny AD: Sleep disturbances, alcohol and alcoholism: A review. In Williams RC, Karacan I (eds): Sleep Disorders: Diagnosis and Treatment, pp 233–260. New York, John Wiley & Sons, 1978

> A comprehensive review of alcohol-related sleep problems.

Prinz PN: Sleep patterns in the healthy aged: Relationship with intellectual function. J Gerontol 32:179–186, 1977

Several indices of cortical function, followed long-term in an aged population, correlated with sleep quality.

Regestein QR: Sleep disorders in the medically ill. In Stoudemire A, Fogel B (eds): Principles of Medical Psychiatry. Orlando, Grune & Stratton, 1987

Reviews disruptions of sleep quality caused by medical illness.

Roth B, Nevsimalova S, Rechtschaffen A: Hypersomnia and sleep drunkenness. Arch Gen Psychiatry 26:456–462, 1972

Describes idiopathic hypersomnia.

REFERENCES

Balter MB, Bauer ML: Patterns of prescribing and use of hypnotic drugs in the United States. In Clift AD (ed): Sleep Disturbances and Hypnotic Drug Dependence, pp 261–293. Amsterdam, Excerpta Medica, 1975

Benson H, Rosner BA, Margetta BR, Klemschuk H: Decreased blood pressure in pharmacologically-treated hypertensive patients who regularly elicited the relaxation response. Lancet 1:289–291, 1974

Bixler EO, Kales A, Soldatos CR: Sleep disorders encountered in medical practice: A national survey of physicians. Behav Med 6:13–21, 1979

Bliwise D, Seidel W, Greenblatt DJ, Dement W: Nighttime and daytime efficacy of fluroxepam and oxazepam in chronic insomnia. Am J Psychiatry 141:191–195, 1984

Borg S, Krande H, Sedval G: Central norepinephrine metabolism during alcohol intoxification in addicts and healthy volunteers. Science 213:1135–1137, 1981

Campbell S: Double blind psychometric studies on the effect of natural estrogens on post-menopausal women. In Campbell S (ed): The Management of Menopause and Post-menopausal Years, pp 149–158. London, University Park Press, 1976

Carskadon MA, Dement WC: Nocturnal determinants of daytime sleepiness. Sleep 5 (Supp2):73–82, 1982

Carskadon MA, Dement W, Mitler M, et al: Self-reports versus sleep laboratory findings in 122 drug-free subjects with complaints of chronic insomnia. Am J Psychiatry 133:1382–1388, 1976

Coleman RM, Roffwarg HP, Kennedy SJ, et al: Sleep-wake disorders based on a polysomnographic diagnosis. JAMA 247:997–1003, 1982

Coursey RD, Buchsbaum M, Frankel BL: Personality measures and evoked responses in chronic insomniacs. J Abnorm Psychol 91:380–389, 1975

Dlin BM, Rosen H, Dickstein K, et al: The problems of sleep and rest in the intensive care unit. Psychosomatics 12:155–163, 1971

Freedman RR, Sattler HL: Physiological and psychological factors in sleep-onset insomnia. J Abnorm Psychol 91:380–389, 1982

Gaillard JM: Chronic primary insomnia: Possible physiopathological involvement of slow wave sleep efficiency. Sleep 1:133–147, 1978

Goldstein A, Kaizer S, Whitby O: Psychotropic effects of caffeine in man. IV. Quantitative and qualitative differences associated with habituation to coffee. Clin Pharmacol Ther 10:489–497, 1969

Gray JA: The Neuropsychology of Anxiety. New York, Oxford University Press, 1982

Hauri P: What can insomniacs teach us about the function of sleep? In Druckers-Colin M, Shkiurowich MF, Sterman MB (eds): The Functions of Sleep, pp 251–277. New York, Academic Press, 1979

Hauri P: Primary sleep disorders and insomnia. In Riley TL (ed): Clinical Aspects of Sleep and Sleep Disturbance, pp 81–112. Boston, Butterworth & Co, 1985

Henningfield JE: Pharmacologic basis and treatment of cigarette smoking. J Clin Psychiatry 45(12 sec 2):24–34, 1984

Hollingsworth HL: The influence of caffeine on mental and motor efficiency. Arch Psychol (Frankf) 20:1–166, 1912

Horne JA, Moore VJ: Sleep EEG effects of exercise with and without additional body cooling. Electroencephalogr Clin Neurophysiol 60:33–38, 1985

Johns MW, Large AA, Masterton JP, et al: Sleep and delirium after open heart surgery. Br J Surg 61:377–381, 1974

Johnson J, Clift AD: Dependence on hypnotic drugs in general practice. Br Med J 4:613–616, 1968

Johnson LL, Cherniak DA: Sedative hypnotics and human performance. Psychopharmacology (Berlin) 76:101–113, 1982

Jones HS, Oswald I: Two cases of healthy insomnia. Electroencephalogr Clin Neurophysiol 24:378–380, 1968

Kales A, Caldwell AB, Cadieux RJ, et al: Severe obstructive sleep apnea. II: Associated psychopathology and psychosocial consequences. J Chronic Disorders 38:427–434, 1985

Karacan I, Moore C: Physiology and neurochemistry of sleep. Annu Rev Psychiatry 4:266–269, 1985

Kupfer DJ: REM latency: A psychobiological marker for primary depressive disease. Biol Psychiatry 11:159–174, 1976

Morgan K, Oswald I: Anxiety caused by a short-life hypnotic. Br Med J 284:942, 1982

Olazabal JR, Miller MJ, Cook WR, et al: Disordered breathing and hypoxia during sleep in coronary artery disease. Chest 82:548–551, 1982

Rechtschaffen A, Kales A: The manual of standardized terminology, techniques and scoring system for sleep stages of human objects. NIH Publication No. 204. Washington, DC, National Institutes of Health, 1968

Reynolds CF, Kupfer DJ: Sleep disorders. In Talbott JA, Hales RE, Yudofsky SC (eds): Textbook of Psychiatry, pp 737, 739. Washington, DC, American Psychiatric Press, 1988

Reynolds CF, Kupfer DJ, Taska LS, et al: EEG sleep in elderly depressed, demented and healthy subjects. Biol Psychiatry, 20:431–442, 1985

Sack DA, Nurnberger J, Rosenthal NE, et al: Potentiation of antidepressant medications by phase advance of the sleep-wake cycle. Am J Psychiatry 142:606–608, 1985

Saletu B, Gruenberger J, Anderer P: Evening television and sleep. Medizinliche Welt 34:866–870, 1983

Soldatos CR, Kales JD, Scharf MB, et al: Cigarette smoking associated with sleep difficulty. Science 207:551–553, 1980

Tan TL, Kales JD, Kales A, et al: Biopsychobehavioral correlates of insomnia. IV: Diagnosis based on DSM III. Am J Psychiatry 141:357–362, 1984

Tune GS: Sleep and wakefulness in normal human adults. Br Med J 2:269–271, 1968

Basic Principles of Pain Management

Richard J. Goldberg

The control of pain is a principal concern of both patients and physicians. While most pain management is successfully undertaken by the patient's primary physician, a number of problems in pain management may require multidisciplinary involvement, including input from such specialists as anesthesiologists, neurosurgeons, and psychiatrists. This chapter addresses principles of pain management that are practically useful to both general physicians and psychiatrists who are consultants in this area. Issues that are addressed include advocacy for proper medical diagnosis; the proper use of narcotic analgesics; psychosocial problems that complicate pain management; the role of anxiety and depression in pain; and the psychiatrist's role in chronic pain syndromes.

Pain is a private experience. There is no questionnaire, blood test, or technology that can quantify the amount of pain that someone feels. Pain is a complex product with contributions from personality, memory, fantasy, and cultural traditions in the context of neurophysiologic processes. Pain serves an important signaling function in the organism and often leads to recognition of some underlying disease that can be medically or surgically treated. However, despite the available technology, pain often remains inadequately treated, at times because of underlying patient or physician attitudes and sometimes because of medical or psychosocial misunderstandings.

ADVOCACY FOR PROPER DIAGNOSIS

Proper evaluation of the patient with pain includes a review of medical, diagnostic, and management issues pertinent to the pain complaint. For example, a careful review of history and physical examination in an elderly somatizing patient may lead to recognition of the need for evaluation of possible hip fracture. The history and physical examination of patients with low back pain syndromes must always be reviewed carefully with attention to the results of electromyography, nerve conduction studies, myelogram, and computerized tomography (CT) scan or magnetic resonance imaging (MRI) findings. Pain in patients with a history of malignancy should be carefully evaluated with a high index of suspicion that the pain complaint, presumed to require psychological management, is actually associated with cancer progression or cancer treatment (Foley, 1985b).

Patients with a known or presumed history of drug abuse are at special risk for having a medical basis for their pain overlooked, because the medical team often assumes that these patients' pain complaints are simply drug-seeking behaviors. Similarly, patients with chronic schizophrenia or mental retardation may not be able to communicate pain complaints in a way that leads to proper medical diagnostic evaluation, and the psychiatrist should be especially careful before taking a symptomatic treatment approach in these populations. The drug abuser who gets into a motor vehicle accident and is admitted to an orthopedic unit may have complaints of foot pain that are dismissed as drug-seeking behavior but that actually represent early symptoms of a compartment syndrome from an excessively tight cast.

Patients who are suspected of not having "real" pain are often given placebos (usually as saline injections) before the psychiatrist is consulted. A positive response to placebo is often misinterpreted as evidence that the pain has no physiologic basis. Such an interpretation is unwarranted, because 30 to 40% of the population are placebo responders, even in the presence of severe disease (Beecher, 1955). Therefore, rather than having any diagnostic value, placebo use itself is symptomatic of a problem in pain management that is more likely the result of inadequate diagnosis, inadequate use of analgesics, or some psychosocial management issue.

THE PROPER USE OF NARCOTIC ANALGESICS

Dose and Frequency

Nonnarcotic analgesics generally do not play a central role in the treatment of *severe* pain in the medically ill. In addition to their use in mild or moderate pain and their specific anti-inflammatory properties, they provide an important and often underutilized adjunctive role in treating severe pain (Moertel, 1980) (see Table 22-1).

The most common cause of problems in acute pain management is the underuse of narcotic analgesics (Marks, Sachar, 1973). In addition to inadequate doses, narcotics are often prescribed in time intervals that extend beyond the effective half-life of the drug. For example, it is not unusual to find patients on a schedule of meperidine given every *4 to 6 hours,* when this drug *actually requires administration every 3 to 4 hours.* When patients start to complain of severe pain at 3 hours after the last dose, they are often thought of as "addicted" to or excessively preoccupied with medication. In fact, such patients may only be expressing the fact that their pain has re-emerged because their dose time has gone beyond the effective duration of the narcotic. Table 22-2 lists usual dose ranges for commonly prescribed analgesics, and Table 22-3 lists the average duration of analgesic activity.

When dealing with an acute pain management problem, look first at the dose and frequency of delivered analgesic. It is important to look directly at the drug administration record, not at orders or progress notes, to confirm what has actually been given to the patient and on what schedule. Ask patients to rate on a scale of 0 to 10 (where 0

Table 22–1 **Commonly Prescribed Nonnarcotic Analgesics**

DRUG	USUAL ORAL DOSE (milligrams)	COMMENT
Aspirin	600 q3–4h	Gastric distress, GI bleeding
Acetaminophen	650 q3–4h	Useful with aspirin allergy, bleeding diathesis; overdose can cause severe hepatic toxicity; no significant anti-inflammatory effect
Ibuprofen	400 q4–6h; do not exceed 3200/d	Does affect bleeding time but probably less than aspirin; anti-inflammatory response similar to aspirin; gastric distress less than aspirin; useful in arthritides
Indomethacin	25 q8h; do not exceed 150–200/d	As analgesic, probably not superior to aspirin; useful in arthritides; can cause corneal deposits and retinal disturbance; may aggravate depression
Naproxen	250 q6–8h; do not exceed 1250/d	Similar to ibuprofen; may cause less GI upset
Sulindac	150 q12h; do not exceed 400/d	Similar to ibuprofen and naproxen; needs to be taken only two times a day
Piroxicam	20 qd	Long half-life, requires single daily dose

Note: Patients vary in their pharmacokinetic and pharmacodynamic responses to aspirin and the NSAIDs. Dosages should be individualized. In the case of aspirin, salicylate levels may aid in determining optimal dosage.
(Used with permission from Houpt JL: Chronic pain management. In Stoudemire A, Fogel BS (eds): Principles of Medical Psychiatry. Orlando, Grune & Stratton, 1987)

Table 22-2 **Usual Dose Ranges of Commonly Prescribed Narcotics***

AGENT	USUAL DOSE RANGE (miligrams)	COMMENT
Codeine	30–60 PO q.4–6 hr.	Usually combined with an NSAID
Oxycodone	5–10 PO q.4–6 hr.	Comes as tablets with 5 mg oxycodone plus aspirin or acetaminophen
Pentazocine	25–50 PO q.4–6 hr.	Mixed agonist-antagonist; may cause psychotic symptoms†
Butorphanol	1–4 IM q.3 hr.	Mixed agonist-antagonist; less respiratory depression
Meperidine	50–100 SC or IM q.2–3 hr. 50–100 PO q.3–4 hr.	Rapid onset of action; has a psychotoxic metabolite
Morphine	2–8 SC or IM q.4 hr. 5–30 PO q.4 .	Sedating; may lower blood pressure
Hydromorphone	1–2 SC or IM q.3 hr. 2–4 IV q.3 hr. 2–8 PO q.4 hr.	
Methadone	5–20 PO q.6–8 hr.	Long half-life; lower dose in renal failure

Note:
*Commonly used dose ranges are *not* equianalgesic (see Table 16–4). Higher or lower doses may be appropriate for particular patients, depending upon severity of pain, duration of treatment, tolerance, body weight, pharmacokinetics, drug interactions, and use of adjuncts.
†Mixed agonist-antagonists must not be given together with other narcotics.
(Used with permission from Goldberg RJ, Sokol MS, Cullen LO: Acute pain management. In Stoudemire A, Fogel BS (eds.): Principles of Medical Psychiatry. Orlando, Grune & Stratton, 1987)

represents no pain and 10 represents the most severe pain they have experienced) their level of pain within the first hour after their dose of narcotic and also at the time just before they are due to receive their next dose. If relief is inadequate in the first hour after their dose, the amount prescribed may be too low. If the first-hour pain relief is adequate but pain re-emerges before the next dose, then the duration between doses may be too long. Narcotics should be given on a schedule corresponding to their analgesic half-life. Regarding dose amount, there is no rule that a "typical" order such as 75 mg of meperidine is the correct dose for everyone having acute pain. Some patients may require 150 mg to achieve the same effect. Patients and providers are often fearful about creating addiction by providing regular narcotic doses. This fear is largely unwarranted. In a large review of over 11,000 Medicare inpatients who received narcotics, only four cases of iatrogenic narcotic addiction were documented (Porter, Jick, 1980).

Another issue in the timing of narcotic doses pertains to special procedures. It is important to note whether the patient's pain problem is the result of an intermittent procedure such as debridement, dressing changes, or physical therapy. In such instances, the most important intervention may be to ensure that the patient receives an adequate narcotic dose prior to such an intervention.

The use of narcotic doses that are higher than what is considered standard often raises concerns about respiratory depression, especially if the patient is also on benzodiazepines. Patients develop tolerance to the respiratory depressant effects of narcotics fairly rapidly and can tolerate huge doses if the drug is increased gradually. It is true that patients who have not had a chance to develop tolerance to the respiratory depressant effects of narcotics are at risk for acute respiratory depression, especially if parenteral narcotics are combined with parenteral benzodiazepines. Fortunately, respiratory depression can be reversed by naloxone. When it is necessary to use naloxone, it is best administered in a dilute solution (0.4 mg in 10 ml of saline)

Table 22–3 **Analgesic Duration (with Oral Dosing)**

ANALGESIC	DURATION OF ACTION
Morphine	4–7 hours
Meperidine	3–5 hours
Methadone	4–6 hours
Hydromorphone	4–6 hours
Pentazocine	4–7 hours
Codeine	4–7 hours
Propoxyphene	4–7 hours
Oxycodone	4–6 hours

(Used with permission from Goldberg RJ, Sokol MS, Cullen LO: Acute pain management. In Stoudemire A, Fogel BS (eds): Principles of Medical Psychiatry. Orlando, Grune & Stratton, 1987) slowly given intravenously, titrated against the patient's respiratory rate (Foley, 1985a). Patients receiving this treatment must be closely followed with frequent respiratory rate checks because naloxone has a short half-life, and patients may have to be redosed if taking the longer-acting narcotics such as methadone.

Constipation is an additional dose-dependent effect of narcotics. Uncomfortable and disturbing to patients, constipation can progress to functional ileus if not recognized and addressed by the proper use of diet and cathartics (Twycross, Lack, 1984).

Fixed Versus "As Needed" Dose Schedules

Acute pain management is often inadequate because of inconsistent scheduling of doses. Severe continuous pain is better treated on a fixed rather than "as needed" (p.r.n.) schedule for the following reasons (Goldberg, Tull, 1983): scheduled doses based on the half-life of the narcotic prevent the re-emergence of pain; the dose required to treat re-emergent pain is often larger than what is needed to prevent its recurrence on a fixed schedule; patients on a p.r.n. schedule are in a dependent position requiring them to ask for medication, which can create preoccupation with and delays in administration; and elderly and cognitively impaired patients may have difficulty in initiating appropriate requests for medication.

Route of Narcotic Administration

Oral analgesic administration is preferred when possible because it avoids the discomforts and potential complications of repeated injections and makes the patient less dependent on others for care. The use of parenteral narcotics is warranted when oral medications fail to provide adequate relief, when the patient is no longer able to swallow, or in the case of acute, severe pain requiring immediate relief, such as in trauma, burn, heart attack, or postoperative conditions.

The intravenous (IV) route is best reserved for acute situations, including trauma, burn, heart attack patients, severely cachectic patients who cannot tolerate intramuscular injections, or patients with bleeding disorders or low platelet counts for whom intramuscular injections are contraindicated. Unfortunately, the IV bolus route is associated with a short duration of analgesia because of rapid tissue uptake and elimination. As a result, larger and more frequent doses are needed to treat breakthrough pain, with the potential for a higher incidence of respiratory depression, sedation, nausea, and vomiting. Some of these disadvantages of IV bolus narcotic administration can be avoided by the use of a continuous opioid infusion. An intravenous narcotic drip may be rate controlled by medical and nursing staff or in some cases by patients themselves (White, 1988). Patient-controlled analgesia (PCA) provides improved titration of analgesic drugs, minimizing individual pharmacokinetic and pharmacodynamic differences. This method also decreases patient anxiety resulting from delays in receiving medication and the slow onset of action from oral or intramuscular routes. In settings in which patient-controlled analgesia is not considered appropriate or available, an intravenous morphine drip may be established (Portnoy, 1986; Goldberg, Sokol, Cullen, 1987). When an intravenous route is selected, morphine or Dilaudid seems to be tolerated better than meperidine, which is associated with delirium and psychosis after multiple IV doses because of the accumulation of toxic metabolites. One unfortunate drawback of continuous IV infusion of opiates is the relatively rapid development of tolerance.

Conversions Among Different Narcotics

Learning to convert to equianalgesic doses among narcotics is a fundamental skill for managing pain problems. To begin, there are several situations in which improper narcotic conversion creates the apparent need for psychiatric consultation. Typically, *this occurs when a patient is changed from a parenteral to an oral narcotic following surgery and is noted to have a dramatic increase in pain and agitation, which actually represent iatrogenic narcotic abstinence.* A successful switch from parenteral to oral narcotics must take into account differences in efficacy due to limited gastrointestinal absorption and first-pass hepatic metabolism. For example, for patients on regular scheduled morphine, the oral to parenteral ratio is approximately 3:1; in the case of meperidine, the oral to parenteral ratio is approximately 4:1. In practical terms, examples of equianalgesic conversions from inpatient parenteral narcotics to outpatient oral narcotics would be 75 mg meperidine IM q.3h. = 60 mg morphine PO q.3h. = approximately four Percocet tablets PO q.3h. (see Table 22-4).

In treating a patient who is having pain control problems, the clinician must always review the record and determine how much and which medications the patient has been receiving. Difficult pain problems often are associated with the use of multiple medications. It is not unusual to find a patient who is receiving injections of meperidine and oral acetominophen with codeine along with other "p.r.n." narcotics. In order to make sense of the total amount of narcotic that a patient is receiving, it is often helpful to convert all the various analgesics to a single standard. The concept of "oral morphine equivalents" (OME) is useful for this purpose (Goldberg et al., 1986) (see Table 22-4). However, there are some limitations in the data used to generate such conversions. Much of the information is derived from pain relief studies in cancer patients, whose acute pain needs and analgesic metabolism may be different from those of noncancer patients. In addition, figures are often derived from single-dose experiments that overlook the kinetic changes that take place following repeated dosing. Finally, standard conversions do not acknowledge probable differences in pain relief associated with age, sex, race, or quality of pain. Nevertheless, the use of a conversion table can be extremely helpful in the clinical setting in order to condense a variety of medication approaches into a single agent that can simplify treatment.

When evaluating the use of multiple narcotics, always be alert for the inappropriate combination of narcotic agonists and mixed narcotic agonist/antagonists. Specifically, pentazocine is a mixed narcotic agonist/antagonist that, if prescribed for a patient who is on narcotics, can precipitate symptoms of narcotic withdrawal.

The Phenomenon of Tolerance

Any patient who is exposed to continuous doses of narcotics for at least 5 to 7 days will develop tolerance. The tolerant patient is one who notices a shortened duration of analgesic effect and an eventual decrease in pain relief. Tolerance, of

Table 22–4 **Analgesic Equivalencies: Conversion to Oral Morphine Equivalents (OMEs)**

One mg of oral	Is equivalent to
Morphine	1 mg p.o. morphine
Meperidine	0.2 mg p.o. morphine
Methadone	3 mg p.o. morphine
Dilaudid	8 mg p.o. morphine
Pentazocine	1/3 mg p.o. morphine
Codeine	1/3 mg p.o. morphine
Propoxyphene	0.15 mg p.o. morphine
Oxycodone	2 mg p.o. morphine
One mg of i.m.	
Morphine	6 mg p.o. morphine
Meperidine	0.8 mg p.o. morphine
Methadone	6 mg p.o. morphine
Dilaudid	40 mg p.o. morphine
Pentazocine	1.5 mg p.o. morphine
One tab-cap oral	
Darvocet N 50	10 mg p.o. morphine
Darvocet N 100	20 mg p.o. morphine
Darvon cpd.	10 mg p.o. morphine
Percocet	15 mg p.o. morphine
Percodan	15 mg p.o. morphine
Tylox	18 mg p.o. morphine
Wygesic	20 mg p.o. morphine
Vicodin	13 mg p.o. morphine
ASA + 1.2 g codeine	15 mg p.o. morphine
ASA + 1 g codeine	25 mg p.o. morphine
APAP + 1.2 g codeine	15 mg p.o. morphine
APAP + 1 g codeine	25 mg p.o. morphine
One tab-cap oral	
ASA (325 mg)	5 mg p.o. morphine
APAP (325 mg)	5 mg p.o. morphine
Indocin (50 mg)	10 mg p.o. morphine
Mg. Salicylate (1000 mg)	10 mg p.o. morphine
Vistaril (25 mg)	2 mg p.o. morphine

(Used with permission from Goldberg RJ, Mor V, Wiemann M, et al: Analgesic use in terminal cancer patients: Report from The National Hospice Study. J Chronic Dis 39:37–45, 1986)

course, needs to be differentiated from loss of pain control due to new or advancing disease. Following these considerations, the clinician should determine whether the patient is developing tolerance. Nursing staffs often get anxious continuing narcotics for extended times, even in patients who are having repeated surgical procedures. As a result, there may be an attempt to decrease the dose for such patients just at the time when tolerance warrants an increase in dosage.

The need to adjust the narcotic dose upward because of associated tolerance is demonstrated clearly in the case of the narcotic-addicted patient who requires pain treatment. Patients on methadone maintenance or illicit narcotics may be under-treated because of a lack of understanding of tolerance, and such patients need to be treated with an analgesic dose 50% greater than normal. Generally, the physician or staff is reluctant to be seen as supporting the patient's "habit"; therefore, addicted patients are often given too little analgesic, whereas the pharmacology of addiction actually necessitates a greater dose.

In situations involving pain treatment in the narcotic addict, it is often helpful to keep the management of the addiction separate from the management of the pain. For example, the patient's underlying narcotic addiction can be managed with methadone. Most street addicts can be adequately managed on an oral dose of methadone between 20 and 40 mg/day (or an I.M. dose between 10 and 20 mg/day). With methadone used for maintenance of the underlying addiction, the pain can then be treated as a separate issue, using a different narcotic at doses 50% greater than normal.

Recognizing Narcotic Withdrawal

The recognition and management of narcotic withdrawal are two skills fundamental to solving some pain management problems. This is because unrecognized narcotic withdrawal may be mistaken for other psychiatric problems.

When narcotics are taken on a regular basis for approximately 3 to 4 weeks, physical dependence will develop. Physical dependence is a condition that is associated with withdrawal symptoms after an abrupt discontinuation or significant decrease in dosage. Withdrawal symptoms occur more rapidly and more intensively with drugs that have shorter half-lives. Withdrawal symptoms mostly represent noradrenergic hyperreactivity and include abdominal pain, diarrhea, muscle aching, yawning, rhinorrhea, and lacrimation.

Narcotic abstinence should always be considered in the evaluation of pain patients who show marked anxiety, agitation, or other autonomic symptoms. One problematic situation occurs when a pain patient with a previous narcotic addiction complains of withdrawal symptoms and requests increased narcotic medication. Clinicians must learn to sort out objectively a true abstinence syndrome. Street addicts will often complain of withdrawal symptoms as a way of obtaining more narcotics in the medical setting. Such claims are important to listen to but should be regarded skeptically. The naive clinician may inadvertently overdose the patient, because the actual narcotic amount the patient is taking is often much less than what is claimed. As a general rule, it is prudent never to treat a street addict's subjective complaints of withdrawal. Objective withdrawal symptoms should be used as a basis for providing narcotic coverage.

Managing Narcotic Withdrawal

There are several options available for decreasing or discontinuing narcotics in physically dependent patients:

1. Patients can be withdrawn from narcotics by weaning slowly to minimize the development of withdrawal symptoms. Bedtime doses should be decreased last in order to minimize sleep disruption. In general, decreasing the total daily dose between 10 and 25% each day can be attempted.

2. Another technique for narcotic withdrawal involves the use of methadone. With this technique, the narcotic-dependent patient is put on an equivalent dose of oral methadone (see Table 22-4). Because of the relatively long half-life of methadone, its withdrawal symptoms are less intense but more prolonged. With this technique, the withdrawal process may take up to 30 days, and many drug-dependent individuals require months before feeling free of abstinence symptoms.

3. The use of clonidine may allow for the most rapid narcotic withdrawal process. Clonidine is an alpha-2 adrenergic agonist that diminishes withdrawal symptoms by replacing opiate-mediated inhibition with alpha-2 adrenergic–mediated inhibition, primarily in the locus coeruleus. The disadvantage of using clonidine is the development of sedation and orthostatic hypertension. However, the technique of clonidine detoxification allows for the immediate discontinuation of all opiates. While the specifics of procedure are well described in more detail by Gold et al. (1980), a sample withdrawal regimen is shown in Table 22-5.

PSYCHOSOCIAL CONCERNS IN PAIN MANAGEMENT

When psychiatric consultation is requested to address a pain management problem, the consultant should always review the medical evaluation and the adequacy of the analgesic regimen. Many pain problems will be solved on this fairly

Table 22–5 **Example of Inpatient Clonidine Withdrawal Regimens for 70-kg Man**

I.	
Day 1:	0.4 mg P.O. test dose in morning. Repeat 0.4 mg P.O. at bedtime if no significant side effects
Day 2–10:	0.5 mg every morning 0.2 mg every afternoon 0.5 mg every evening
Day 11–14:	Taper dose on a daily basis by 50% of the previous dose. Stop on day 14.
II. For moderate to severe opioid dependence	
Day 1:	0.3 mg P.O. q.3h. when awake
2:	0.2 mg P.O. q.6h. when awake
3:	0.2 mg P.O. q.8h. when awake
4:	0.1 mg P.O. q.12h
5:	Discontinue medication

Hypotension, sedation, and dry mouth are the major side effects.

(Used with permission from Clonidine (Catapres) in detoxification. In Gelenberg AJ (ed): Biological Therapies in Psychiatry, Vol 8, pp 13, 16. Littleton, MA, PSG Publishing Co, Inc, 1985)

straightforward medical basis. However, it is often psychosocial issues that account for the inadequate treatment or unresolved pain.

The Role of Anxiety and Depression

Since pain is the product of an interaction between physical and psychosocial dimensions, as well as between peripheral and central neural systems, both significant anxiety and depression can adversely influence pain management (Ward et al., 1982). The consultant often confronts a situation involving the "chicken or the egg" dilemma in which it can be difficult to sort out whether the pain is the cause of the anxiety/depression or vice versa. It is usually not productive to try to definitively sort out this dilemma. Instead, the consultant should identify signs and symptoms of significant anxiety/depression and explain to the patient (and staff) that anxiety/depression and pain often coexist in a feedback loop in which they reinforce each other. The clinical strategy is to intervene in both areas. Treat the physical basis for the pain as aggressively as possible, and simultaneously address the anxiety/depression.

A thorough history of the anxiety/depression symptoms should reveal to what extent they may have antedated the pain problem. Obviously, there are patients who have pre-existing psychiatric conditions that may augment pain and interfere in management. The treatment of anxiety/depression symptoms in pain patients depends on how they are conceptualized and which of the following interventions the clinician is willing to consider.

Psychopharmacotherapy

Anxiolytics may be effective adjuncts in pain management. It is important to consider the potential augmentation of respiratory depression and additive sedative effects associated with benzodiazepines. The nonbenzodiazepine anxiolytic buspirone does not have these liabilities but takes at least a week to work (see Chapters 7 and 17).

Antidepressants are often useful adjuncts in pain management for several reasons. They have a physiologic effect on increasing pain threshold through serotonergic augmenting effects. In addition, they can provide symptomatic relief of symptoms that commonly accompany pain, such as insomnia, fatigue, or discouragement. No antidepressant seems to have an efficacy advantage in terms of analgesic properties. Whether or not one can actually diagnose a major mood disorder according to DSM-III-R criteria is not the issue (Goldberg, 1988). The use of psychiatric diagnostic criteria is problematic in medically ill patients because it is difficult to determine whether the patient's symptoms are due to psychiatric disorder or whether they are a direct effect of the patient's medical illness. Therefore, antidepressants are often used in pain patients on a "target symptom basis" (Goldberg, Cullen, 1986).

With the exception of methotrimeprazine, the neuroleptic medications have little specific analgesic activity and are mostly used for their antiemetic and anxiolytic properties in conjunction with narcotics (Foley, 1985a). (For further discussion of other agents used in analgesic augmentation, see Goldberg, Sokol, Cullen, 1987.)

Nondrug Treatments

Symptoms of pain, anxiety, and distress can often be addressed without additional medication use. Such approaches can be especially helpful to patients who are concerned about their use of medications and those who wish to play a more active role in their own management. Techniques to consider include relaxation therapy, self-hypnosis, and guided imagery (Goldberg, Tull, 1983). Such self-regulatory techniques are often overlooked because many clinicians are not trained in their use and because they take more time than prescribing medication.

Psychosocial Issues

Pain patients often feel that no one believes their pain is real, that people are not listening to them, that the staff sees them as drug addicts, and that some serious medical issues may have been overlooked. Patients also may feel that no one has addressed their fears, questions, and concerns about their illness and treatment. Therefore, engaging the trust of pain patients may be problematic because of their skepticism or outright hostility. They may begin the interview with a comment such as, "And what are you doing here?" or "Now, I suppose they think I'm crazy." Even if not greeted this way, the consultant needs to ask the patient, "What is your understanding about why I have been asked to see you?" Generally, starting with a review of the medical history is more effective than plunging into a review of psychiatric symptoms or history. During the course of the evaluation, the following issues generally should be covered:

1. What is the patient's understanding of the underlying medical disorder causing the pain? This question helps to elicit medical issues that the patient feels have been overlooked, as well as distortions in understanding that can lead to fears and exaggerated pain behaviors. Clarification is always important.
2. Are there any problems in the medical treatment system? Are there too many providers, all with different ideas about what needs to be done, writing contradictory or inconsistent orders? Are there issues involving the nursing staff causing delays in medication or biases against the patient, leading to a sense of isolation?
3. Is there a problem in the way the patient expresses pain? Individual, family, and cultural issues in pain behavior need to be taken into account (Fabrega, Tyma, 1976).
4. Are there family issues relevant to the pain problem? Do family members disagree with the management approach; are they undermining the program in some way? Is it necessary to meet with the patient and family together to get clues about what is going wrong? Are there new or ongoing stresses between the patient and family (or other close relationships) that may be leading to distress, thus augmenting the pain behaviors?
5. Are there legal issues pending or other issues of obvious secondary gain?

6. Are there significant psychological issues that may influence pain experience? For example, could the patient be "confusing" the situation with someone else's? It is not unusual for patients to assume that their experience will duplicate that of someone with similar symptoms. Does the patient have some morbid fear based on some private psychological associations? This material can be elicited by asking such questions as, "Do you know anyone else who has been through something like this?" Of course, this area can be difficult to uncover and address.

CHRONIC PAIN

This chapter has addressed issues typically encountered in acute pain management problems. Issues pertinent to chronic pain syndromes often require different strategies (Roy, Tunks, 1982; Wall, Melzack, 1984). In addressing a pain problem, the consultant should always try to determine, "Does this presumed acute pain management problem actually represent a chronic pain syndrome?" It is not unusual for a psychiatric consultation to be requested for a patient whose pain problem has exhausted other providers. Such situations are common with low back pain patients admitted for a myelogram that is read as questionable or negative, or with chronic abdominal pain patients with multiple surgeries and "million-dollar" work-ups. Medical patients and providers are used to thinking of pain in terms of an acute paradigm (i.e., "What can be done now?"). They often overlook the broader picture and can miss the fact that what they are dealing with is better conceptualized as a chronic pain syndrome. Instead of more diagnostic testing or battles over dose or drug, a shift in management philosophy is required.

The chronic pain management philosophy is multidimensional; it addresses diagnosis, of course, but also integrates physical rehabilitations, weight loss, exercise, and group or individual therapy with a focus on resuming more adaptive, normal behaviors. The treatment team does not reinforce maladaptive pain behaviors, including ongoing discussions of pain. The possibility of secondary gain should always be considered. Sometimes financial issues surrounding a lawsuit or disability claim complicate pain management. At other times, interventions with the family to change their view and their toleration of the patient's pain behaviors are necessary. The shift from an acute to a chronic paradigm is difficult but often extremely rewarding. Unfortunately, it usually requires the presence of a multidisciplinary chronic pain program, because it is difficult if not impossible to create and coordinate these resources independently. Finally, when evaluating patients with chronic pain, physicians should always be alert for concurrent or underlying psychiatric diagnoses (Katon, Egan, and Miller, 1985; Benjamin et al., 1988).

ANNOTATED BIBLIOGRAPHY

Bonica JJ, Ventafridda V (eds): Advances in Pain Research and Therapy, Vols 2–5. New York, Raven Press, 1979

Goldberg RJ, Sokol M, Cullen LC: Acute pain management. In Stoudemire A, Fogel BS (eds): Principles of Medical Psychiatry. Orlando, Grune & Stratton, 1987

> This chapter provides a comprehensive and thoroughly referenced review of acute pain management issues. Some of the supplementary topics include prevention and management of narcotic induced constipation, allergic and idiosyncratic reactions to narcotics, a more detailed review of the pharmacology of narcotics augmentation, as well as more details on the use of clonidine and narcotic withdrawal.

Goldberg RJ, Tull RM: Pain. In: The Psychosocial Dimensions of Cancer. New York, The Free Press, 1983

> This chapter focuses on the treatment of pain in cancer patients. Aside from an overview of the psychopharmacologic aspects of pain management treatment, the chapter addresses some of the psychosocial and attitudinal issues that often interfere with pain management. Other chapters in this volume would be of interest in relation to pain management, including Chapter 4 (Medical Disorders Masquerading as Psychiatric Symptoms) and Chapter 5 (Psychiatric Aspects of Medication). Since the experience of pain is a combination of psychological and physiological events, it also may be worth reviewing the key clinical issues that influence the patient's pain experience, presented in Chapters 1, 2, and 3 of this volume.

Graber RF: Easy-to-miss causes of pain. Patient Care 89–115, 1984

> This article reviews a number of treatable causes of pain that are frequently misdiagnosed: postherpetic neuralgia, atypical facial pain, reflex sympathetic dystrophy and causalgia, the myofascial syndrome, temporomandibular joint syndrome, and diabetic neuropathy.

Levine J: Pain and analgesia: The outlook for more rational treatment. Ann Intern Med 100:269–276, 1984

> This article reviews recent advances that have been made in research on the physiology of pain, especially research focusing on the primary afferent nociceptor and endogenous analgesia systems. These advances have shed new light on the mechanisms of action of some long-used methods of managing pain, have led to the development of several methods, and have suggested new lines of investigation that may lead to more rational treatment of pain.

Watkins LR, Mayer DJ: Organization of endogenous opiate and nonopiate control systems. Science 216:1185–1192, 1982

> This article presents data demonstrating that opiate and nonopiate analgesia systems can be selectively activated by different environmental manipulations and describes the neural circuitry involved. Both neural and hormonal pathways and both opiate and nonopiate substances play roles in the complex modulation of pain transmission. The existence and description of these modulatory mechanisms have important clinical implications for the treatment of pain.

REFERENCES

Beecher HK: The powerful placebo. JAMA 159:1602–1606, 1955

Benjamin S, Barnes D, Berger S, et al: The relationship of chronic pain, mental illness and organic disorders. Pain 32:185–195, 1988

Fabrega H, Tyma S: Language and cultural influences in the description of pain. Br J Med Psychol 49:349–371, 1976

Foley, KM: Non-narcotic and narcotic analgesics: Applications. In Foley KM (ed): Management of cancer pain, pp 135–148. Syllabus of postgraduate course. New York: Memorial Sloan Kettering Cancer Center, 1985a

Foley KM: The treatment of cancer pain. N Engl J Med 313:84–95, 1985b

Gold MS, Pottash AC, Sweeney DR, et al: Opiate withdrawal using clonidine. JAMA 243:343–346, 1980

Goldberg RJ: Depression in primary care: DSM-III diagnoses and other depressive syndromes. J Gen Intern Med 3:491–497, 1988

Goldberg RJ, Cullen LO: Use of psychotropics in cancer patients. Psychosomatics 27:687–700, 1986

Goldberg RJ, Sokol MS, Cullen LO: Acute pain management. In Stoudemire A, Fogel BS (eds): Principles of Medical Psychiatry, pp 365–388. Orlando, Grune & Stratton, 1987

Goldberg RJ, Tull RK: The Psychosocial Dimensions of Cancer. New York, Free Press, 1983

Hendler NH, Long DM, Wise NT: Diagnosis and Treatment of Chronic Pain. Littleton, MA, John Wright & Sons, 1982

Katon W, Egan K, Miller D: Chronic pain: Lifetime psychiatric diagnoses and family history. Am J Psychiatry 142:1156–1160, 1985

Marks RM, Sachar EJ: Undertreatment of medical inpatients with narcotic analgesics. Ann Intern Med 78:173–181, 1973

Moertel CG: Treatment of cancer pain with orally administered medications. JAMA 244:2448–2450, 1980

Porter J, Jick H: Addiction rare in patients treated with narcotics. N Engl J Med 302:123, 1980

Portnoy RK: Continuous infusion of opioid drugs in the treatment of cancer pain: Guidelines for use. J Pain Sympt Management 1:223–228, 1986

Roy R, Tunks E: Chronic Pain: Psychosocial Factors in Rehabilitation. Rehabilitation Medicine Library, Williams and Wilkins, Baltimore, 1982

Twycross RG, Lack SA: Therapeutics in Terminal Cancer. London, Pitman Publishing, 1984

Wall PD, Melzack R (eds): Textbook of Pain. Edinburgh, Churchill Livingstone, 1984

Ward NG, Bloom VL, Dworkin S, et al: Psychobiological markers in coexisting pain and depression: Toward a unified theory. J Clin Psychiatry 43:8, 32–39, 1982

White PF: Use of patient-controlled analgesia for management of acute pain. JAMA 259:243–247, 1988

23

Behavioral Medicine Strategies for Medical Patients

Michael G. Goldstein, Barrie J. Guise, Laurie Ruggiero, Michael A. Raciti, and David B. Abrams

It is now well established that lifestyle factors significantly contribute to more than half of the annual deaths in the United States (USDHEW, 1979A). Behavioral medicine is the interdisciplinary field concerned with the application of behavioral principles and strategies to the modification of lifestyle patterns for the prevention of disease and enhancement of health. Given that cardiovascular disease, chiefly coronary heart disease (CHD), is the major cause of death in American adults, the focus of this chapter is on the risk factors for CHD and behavioral medicine approaches to their modification.

It has become increasingly apparent that physicians have the opportunity to play a very important role in the area of prevention and health promotion, specifically in the reduction of risk factors for cardiovascular disease (Mullen 1985; Orleans et al., 1985). After providing an overview of the epidemiology of risk factors for CHD, we will define the physician's role in risk factor reduction, describe the barriers to physician involvement in this area, and provide a basic approach to cardiovascular risk factor reduction in the medical setting. Finally, we will use case histories of the assessment and treatment of obesity and smoking to illustrate the behavioral medicine approach.

CARDIOVASCULAR RISK FACTOR EPIDEMIOLOGY

The independent (primary) risk factors for CHD are cigarette smoking, hypercholesterolemia, and hypertension. These are known to directly affect risk for CHD. Other important factors associated with CHD are obesity, diabetes mellitus, sedentary lifestyle, and certain behavioral characteristics. It has been estimated that the three primary risk factors account for about 50% of the variance in CHD incidence and that psychosocial factors account for at least some of the remaining variance (Dorian, Taylor, 1984). Lifestyle modification aimed at reduction of these risk factors can significantly reduce coronary risk.

Cigarette Smoking

Cigarette smoking is thought to be the single most important of the known modifiable risk factors for CHD in the U.S. (USDHEW, 1979B; USDHHS, 1983). *If there is no significant change in the smoking habits of Americans, 24 million people (or 10% of all persons now living) will die prematurely of CHD due to smoking* (Abrams et al., 1987). Cigarette smoking is a powerful independent contributor to myocardial infarction, sudden death, peripheral vascular disease, and stroke (Kannel, 1981, 1987; USDHHS, 1983). The effect of cigarette smoking on CHD is dose related (Gordon et al., 1975; USDHHS, 1983), with heavier smokers at greater risk than light smokers. It is important to note that the effects of cigarette smoking on CHD are reversible. The Framingham study data indicate that CHD risk in smokers who have quit the habit returns to the risk level of nonsmokers within one year of quitting (Castelli, 1983). Studies have also demonstrated that, among patients who have already developed coronary disease, morbidity and mortality are significantly reduced after cessation of smoking compared with those who continue to smoke (USDHHS, 1983; Burling et al., 1984; Rosenberg et al., 1985). Therefore, smoking cessation must be placed as a high priority to improve coronary risk.

Hypercholesterolemia

There is convincing evidence that high levels of plasma total cholesterol are associated with increased risk of CHD (Neaton et al., 1984; Gordon et al., 1977). Epidemiologic data have yielded a continuum of relative risk. Specifically, in middle-aged adults, a cholesterol level below 200 mg/dl is associated with relatively low risk for CHD. In contrast, a level over 240 mg/dl nearly doubles the risk and accounts for the upper 20 to 25% of the adult population (Grundy et al., 1987). Dietary modification, both alone and in conjunction with lipid-lowering medications, improves lipid status and reduces coronary risk (Lipid Research Clinics, 1984).

Hypertension

Long-standing evidence indicates that hypertension is a significant risk factor for CHD. At least 35 million Americans fall within the hypertensive range (USDHEW, 1979A). Hypertensive individuals stand a twofold increased risk of sudden death, angina pectoris, and myocardial infarction over normotensives (blood pressure less than 140/90 mm Hg). Persons with borderline hypertension (blood pressure between 140/90 mm Hg and 160/95 mm Hg) are at 50% greater risk for CHD than normotensives (Castelli, 1983). Furthermore, hypertension is the major risk factor contributing to 80% of strokes and increases the likelihood of stroke sevenfold (Castelli, 1983). Studies have demonstrated that control of hypertension decreases the risk of CHD

(Kannel, 1983). Behavioral strategies such as dietary modification of sodium and fat intake, weight loss, and improved fitness are an important part of treatment, especially when mild to moderate hypertension is present (Kannel, 1983).

Other Risk Factors

Four additional risk factors for CHD are obesity, diabetes mellitus, sedentary lifestyle, and certain behavioral attributes. While of unequivocal significance, these risk factors are thought to influence the risk for CHD indirectly by worsening the primary risk factors. However, obesity (Hubert et al., 1983) and diabetes mellitus (O'Sullivan, 1982) may also independently affect coronary risk.

The estimated prevalence of obesity (20% or more over ideal body weight) in the American population ranges from 15 to 50%, depending upon the criteria used (Bray, 1976; VanItallie, 1979). Epidemiologic data have repeatedly shown that obesity is linked to amplified risk for CHD (Hubert et al., 1983). The relationship between diabetes and physical inactivity and increased risk for CHD has also been well established (O'Sullivan, 1982). It has also been found that increased physical activity lowers coronary risk. While it has generally been agreed that three weekly sessions of sustained, aerobic activity are needed for cardiac benefit, even modest amounts of exercise can be beneficial (Kannel and Sorlie, 1979; Kannel, 1987).

Mounting evidence suggests that certain behavioral characteristics (e.g., hostile elements of the coronary-prone behavior pattern or Type A) may be associated with increased risk of CHD (Jenkins, 1982). Coronary-prone behavior is characterized by a sense of impatience, aggressive competitiveness, ambitiousness, and hostility. The relationship between the Type A behavioral constellation and risk of CHD is controversial and unresolved (Ragland and Brand, 1988). At present, the "hostility" component of the Type A behavioral pattern is in vogue as the critical risk factor for the development of CHD (Dembroski and Costa, 1988).

Like cigarette smoking, hypercholesterolemia, and hypertension, obesity, diabetes mellitus, sedentary lifestyle, and coronary-prone behavior lend themselves to possible behavioral interventions to improve coronary risk.

Synergistic Effects of Cardiovascular Risk Factors and Their Modification

In addition to the independent roles that many of the risk factors play in CHD, there is a synergistic effect among them that further enhances coronary risk. For example, a 50-year-old man with a total plasma cholesterol of 310 mg/dl and hypertension has twice the risk for CHD as a same-aged male with this level of cholesterol alone. In comparison to his risk of CHD from hypercholesterolemia alone, the addition of diabetes mellitus to this picture increases his risk threefold, and smoking cigarettes quadruples his risk for CHD (Grundy et al., 1987). It is also notable that some of the risk factors for CHD act interdependently. Specifically, obesity is a powerful contributor to the expression of several other risk factors, such as hypercholesterolemia, hypertension, and diabetes mellitus.

In parallel, lifestyle modification targeting any one or more of the synergistic factors that may present in a given patient will improve his or her level of coronary risk. Likewise, weight loss is often accompanied by improved blood cholesterol, blood pressure, and blood glucose levels. It has also been demonstrated that quitting smoking can improve total cholesterol to lipoprotein ratios, and regular exercise helps control weight, cholesterol, and glucose levels (Hubert et al., 1983).

THE PHYSICIAN'S ROLE IN RISK FACTOR REDUCTION

Physicians have the potential to play a very important role in the reduction of risk factors for cardiovascular disease. Over 75% of the population contact a doctor at least once each year, and more than 95% contact a physician at least once every 5 years. Thus, physicians have the opportunity to intervene with the vast majority of individuals who are at risk for cardiovascular and other diseases.

Moreover, patients view their physicians as having considerable influence with respect to their preventive behavior. For example, smokers report that if they were asked by their physician to quit, 76% would give it a try (Louis Harris, 1978). Finally, physicians can be quite effective when they act to modify their patients' risk factors. Several smoking cessation strategies have been shown to be effective when used by physicians in the primary care setting (Kottke et al., 1988). *Studies have also demonstrated that physician-delivered patient education and counseling can lead to improvement in patients' adherence to treatment regimens* (Inui, Yourtee, Williamson, 1976; Mullen, Green, Persinger, 1985). Although a majority of physicians feel that they have an important role to play in health promotion, physicians are reluctant to engage in interventions to reduce risk factors for disease (Mullen, 1985; Orleans et al., 1985). Indeed, patient surveys indicate that only a relatively small percentage (27 to 50%) of smokers are advised to quit smoking by their physician (Anda et al., 1987), and only 10% of a sample of family physicians give advice about nutrition to more than 80% of their patients (Kottke et al., 1984). The barriers to physician involvement in risk factor reduction are discussed in the next section.

BARRIERS TO PHYSICIAN INVOLVEMENT IN RISK FACTOR REDUCTION

The barriers to physician involvement in counseling about risk factor reduction, listed in Table 23-1, fall within two domains: physician barriers and practice/organizational barriers. Although physicians are fairly well informed about the importance of health promotion and risk factor reduction, their *knowledge* of patient education and behavioral change interventions, materials, and resources is quite limited (Kottke et al., 1987; Orleans et al., 1985).

Lack of *skills* is a second important barrier to physician involvement in health promotion interventions (Kottke et al., 1987; Orleans et al., 1985). Skills required for effective health promotion and risk factor reduction include interviewing and assessment skills to enable the physician to make an accurate "diagnosis" of risk or educational need; patient education and counseling skills to enable the physician to intervene to help the patient reduce risk; and skills to help the patient maintain healthy behavior or prevent relapse.

Medical education has neglected training in patient education and counseling skills, although recently it has been recognized that training in such skills is needed (Preventive Health Care Committee, 1985). *Attitudes and beliefs* also play an important role in physicians' reluctance to provide health promotion interventions. Because of the deficits in knowledge and skills, physicians lack the confidence to successfully intervene with their patients to reduce or change risk factors (Kottke et al., 1987; Orleans et al., 1985). Physicians' self-perception of the ineffectiveness of such efforts is fueled by the low rates of successful behavior change among patients they try to help. An emphasis on final outcomes, such as smoking abstinence, leads to further frustration, because even the most effective physicians achieve 1-year abstinence rates of only 10 to 20% among their smoking patients.

The medical education process contributes to the development of attitudes that are not conducive to a preventive approach to patient care. Traditionally, physician training has emphasized a biomedical model, which is oriented toward diagnosis and treatment of diseases, rather than a systems model, which embraces prevention and health promotion (Engel, 1977; see also Chapters 1, 2, and 10). As a result, many physicians continue to view health promotion activities as outside their role or as unchallenging and uninteresting (Nutting, 1986). Moreover, traditional medical training promotes a paternalistic and directive style that is less likely to lead to change in patient behavior than a collaborative and patient-centered style that involves the patient in the process of change. The dearth of role models in academia and the community who espouse and practice health promotion reinforces the attitude that prevention and health are not as important as more traditional forms of medical intervention. These and other negative attitudes and beliefs listed in Table 23-1 contribute to a lack of commitment to become more involved in risk factor reduction and health promotion activities. The *organizational barriers* that interfere with physician involvement in risk factor reduction are also listed in Table 23-1. Deficits in primary care physicians' knowledge, skills, and attitudes about health promotion interventions and systems/organizational barriers interact to limit the effective use of counseling for risk factor reduction in primary care.

A MODEL FOR RISK FACTOR REDUCTION IN THE MEDICAL SETTING

In this section we will describe a model for risk factor reduction in the medical setting that is adapted from a model of patient education developed and described by Grueninger, Goldstein, and Duffy.* After describing the model, a practical step-by-step approach to risk factor assessment and intervention will be outlined.

---

* The authors who contributed to the development of the model of patient education described by Grueninger, Goldstein, and Duffy are too numerous to list here. Readers are referred to the work by Grueninger, Goldstein, and Duffy for a complete list of references and acknowledgments.

Table 23–1 **Barriers to Physician Involvement
in Risk Factor Reduction**

Physician Barriers
Knowledge deficit
Importance of risk factor reduction to health care
Effectiveness of physician intervention
Intervention methods
Resources for patients—materials and referrals

Skill deficit
Interviewing/assessment/diagnostic skills
Patient education skills
Behavioral counseling skills
Maintenance/relapse prevention skills

Beliefs and attitudes
Patients don't want to change or can't change
Perceived ineffectiveness in helping patients change
Lack of confidence in helping patients change
Emphasis on final outcomes
Disease-oriented biomedical approach
Paternalistic, directive style
Moralistic view of behavioral problems
Poor personal health habits
Dearth of role models practicing preventive care
Lack of commitment to risk factor reduction

Organizational Barriers
Limited use of reminder systems, tracking logs
Little or no reimbursement for preventive services
Poor coordination with self-help and behavioral treatment programs
Little or no involvement with treatment program staff

Grueninger and colleagues identify five levels of the patient education process (see Fig. 23-1): (1) cognitive (knowledge, concepts, and awareness about risks factors); (2) attitudinal (beliefs, intentions, and readiness for change); (3) instrumental (instrumental skills); (4) behavioral (coping behavior and skills); and (5) social (social support). At each level there is an opportunity for both assessment and intervention. *Assessment* involves gathering data to identify barriers and resources that may impede or facilitate patient education and behavior change. For example, assessment at the cognitive level might include asking the patient about his specific knowledge of risk factors and about his understanding of the relationship between risk factors and illness. *Intervention* involves providing the patient with the necessary information, skills, and support to help him overcome barriers and utilize resources. Thus, intervention at the cognitive level might include creating the individual's risk factors profile and informing the patient about his risk factors and what can be done to alter risk. This model also features a "patient-centered" approach to patient education and counseling, which emphasizes the importance of *tailoring the treatment plan* to each patient's specific needs. Presently, most physicians do not have the knowledge and skills to allow them to effectively assess and intervene at each of the levels,

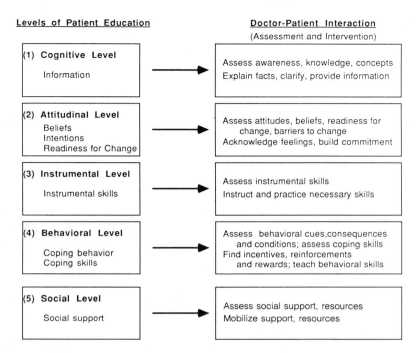

Figure 23–1. *Interactive Patient Education Model. (Adapted from Grueninger, Duffy, Goldstein. In press)*

especially the instrumental and behavioral levels. Although it may not be appropriate for the physician to intervene at each of these levels, knowledge of the assessment and intervention strategies used by others will help the physician to make appropriate referrals to those professionals who have these skills.

Identification of each patient's *stage of change,* a concept developed by Prochaska and DiClemente (1986), is an important element of patient assessment when counseling patients about lifestyle change. These investigators found that individuals making lifestyle changes, such as giving up smoking, move through predictable stages of change (see Fig. 23-2). The four stages are precontemplation, contemplation, action, and maintenance.

Precontemplation is a stage of unawareness or denial of the problem or condition. *Contemplation* is a stage of ambivalence, when pros and cons for change are weighed without definite commitment to taking action. Individuals who have reached the *action* phase have made a commitment to change and are actively attempting to change their behavior. *Maintenance* is the stage that is reached when the individual has successfully made a change but still needs to monitor behavior to prevent slips or relapses.

Prochaska and DiClemente (1986) found that individuals may take several years to move through the stages of change; moreover, they may cycle repeatedly through the last three stages. They also learned that individuals in a given stage respond best

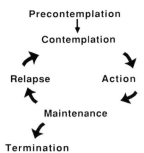

Precontemplation

Contemplation

Relapse   Action

Maintenance

Termination

Figure 23–2. *Self-Change Model. (Adapted from Prochaska, DiClemente, 1986)*

to specific change strategies. For example, consciousness-raising is most useful for individuals in the contemplation stage, while behavioral strategies are most effective when provided to individuals in the action stage. Knowledge of these findings might help physicians to feel less frustrated when their patients return without having made a recommended change in their behavior. It is unrealistic to expect precontemplators, who are not fully aware of the nature of their problem, to take definitive action. It is especially frustrating, and is not very useful, to provide precontemplators and contemplators with instructions to take action when they have not yet made a commitment to change.

An alternative to focusing exclusively on final outcomes is to focus on how to help individuals move more rapidly through the change process. Clinicians adopting this strategy can pick those interventions which are most likely to move the patient to the next stage. For example, for contemplators, helping the individual to recognize the benefits of change and offering personal support may facilitate movement to the action stage. Intermediary outcomes (i.e., movement to the next stage) become the goal of intervention. Further examples of the application of this patient-centered approach can be found in the sections on the management of smoking and obesity later in this chapter.

A PATIENT-CENTERED APPROACH TO RISK FACTOR INTERVENTION

The step-by-step strategy for risk factor intervention that follows is a modified version of the work of Grueninger, Goldstein, and Duffy (in press). This approach attempts to integrate aspects of the complex model of patient education described above with the Prochaska and DiClemente model of stages of change. The patient education and counseling process is transformed into a rather simple sequence of specific tasks. The five tasks fall into three domains: assessment, intervention, and follow-up, as listed in Table 23-2.

At the start of the assessment phase, the physician begins by giving specific information (e.g., diagnostic findings, information about risk). Then the physician involves the patient in the process by assessing his level of awareness of the risk and his readiness for change. If the physician determines that the patient is not close to the action stage, an attempt is made to increase the patient's awareness and build

Table 23-2 **A Patient-Centered Approach
to Risk Factor Intervention**

Assessment
1. Provide information about risk
2. Assess awareness and build commitment

Intervention
3. Give advice and instruction
4. Negotiate implementation plan

Follow-up
5. Arrange follow-up

commitment for change. If the patient is ready for action, the clinician moves into the intervention section. After providing specific advice and instruction, the next task is the negotiation of an intervention plan with the patient. During this phase, the patient's resources are used as much as possible, and potential implementation problems are solved.

Table 23-3 describes the approach in more detail, delineating specific "skills" for each of the five tasks. Sample physician statements are provided for initiating dialogue with the patient. Clearly, there is more to each of these skills than just asking these questions and making these statements. Information should be provided using language that is at the patient's level of comprehension, checking frequently to ensure that the information is understood. Clarification of the patient's knowledge, beliefs, and feelings requires skill in interviewing. The physician also needs to know how to manage feelings when they are expressed by the patient. Development of rapport and establishment of a trusting therapeutic relationship will facilitate the process of change, especially when the physician is attempting to increase the patient's commitment.

When negotiating an intervention plan to help the patient change his risk-related behavior, the physician can choose from a variety of options. These options range from simple advice and provision of educational materials to face-to-face counseling by the physician and referral to a formal behavioral medicine treatment program. How does one choose among the various options? Careful assessment of the patient can help to provide the answer to this question.

Patient characteristics that predict decreased likelihood of response to minimal interventions include poor motivation or readiness for change, repeated failures during previous attempts to change, high levels of psychological dependence on the targeted risk behavior, poor social support, and high levels of physical dependence on the targeted risk behavior when appropriate (e.g., nicotine dependence when smoking is the targeted risk factor). When one or several of these patient characteristics are present, it is likely that these patients will require a more intensive intervention or one that combines several modalities (e.g., behavioral, pharmacological, and social interventions). For other patients, a stepwise approach to treatment is reasonable, starting with a minimal intervention (e.g., provision of self-help materials) and moving to more intensive treatments if the minimal interventions are not effective.

Table 23-3 **A Patient-Centered Approach to Risk Factor Intervention (Expanded)**

Assessment

1. *Provide information about risk*
   Define problem
      "You have _____"
   Explain prognosis
      "This means _____"
   Describe treatment approaches
      "You can reduce your risk by _____"
   Offer support
      "I can help you by _____"
2. *Assess awareness and build commitment*
   Assess and clarify patient's knowledge, beliefs, and experience
      "What do you know about _____?"
   Assess and clarify patient's feelings
      "How do you feel about _____?"
   Assess and clarify patient's goals and readiness for change
      "What are you willing to do?"

Intervention

3. *Give advice and instruction*
   Provide unequivocal advice
      "I would advise you to _____"
   Describe treatment options
      "Here are the options _____"
4. *Negotiate implementation plan*
   Solve problems with commitment or implementation
      "What problems might arise _____?"
   Identify patient's skills and resources
      "What might help you _____?"
   Reaffirm plan
      "Now, what are you going to do?"

Follow-up

5. *Arrange follow-up*
   Arrange follow-up date and plan
      "I'd like to see you again on _____"

As noted in the section of this chapter on the barriers to physician involvement in patient behavior change, most physicians don't feel they have the skills to engage in effective counseling in the area of risk factor reduction. Thus, most physicians are unlikely to provide face-to-face counseling to patients themselves. However, skills can be taught in this area if sufficient time and faculty effort are allocated to training (Levenkron, Greenland, Bowley, 1987; Ockene et al., 1988). It must also be recognized that even minimal physician-delivered counseling interventions can be quite effective, especially in the area of smoking cessation (Kottke, Battista, DeFriesse, Brekke, 1988; Schwartz, 1987).

The previous discussion has described a generic patient-centered approach to risk factor intervention, which stressed the importance of developing an understanding of the patient's readiness to engage in behavior change and also the need to build commitment in patients who were not yet ready to take action. In the next section, we will describe some specific behavioral strategies that can be used to provide assistance to those patients who are ready to change their risk-associated behaviors. We will use case examples to illustrate the approach to obese patients and patients who smoke.

ASSESSMENT AND TREATMENT OF OBESITY

A CASE STUDY

A 46-year-old woman weighing 80% over ideal body weight presents to her physician because she is "feeling lousy" with fatigue and frequent headaches. The physician's examination reveals that she has a total cholesterol of 310 and a fasting blood sugar of 210. A dialogue that reflects a patient-centered approach to management follows.

Doctor: Mrs. Jones, your blood sugar is elevated. In addition, your total cholesterol is 310. Both your blood sugar level and your cholesterol level need to come down, or else you stand an increased risk of heart attack, stroke, and the many complications of diabetes. Your weight problem in all likelihood has a significant influence on your blood sugar and cholesterol. Therefore, the best way to reduce your risk is to lose weight and to eat fewer fatty foods. I can help you to select the best means of weight loss. What do you know about weight loss?

Mrs. Jones: Weight loss? I'm constantly on a diet. I know so much about weight loss I could write a book. I've been on everything. I've done Weight Watchers, the Scarsdale Diet, all-protein diets . . . ; you name it, I've done it.

Doctor: I'm glad you're interested in losing weight. How many times have you been on a medically supervised diet using such principles as behavior modification and calorie counting?

Mrs. Jones: Well, my previous doctor told me that I should try to lose weight by sticking to 1200 calories per day, but then I just went off. It didn't last much more than a week or two.

Doctor: So you've never really been closely supervised. I have some ideas that may help you, but they involve a significant commitment.

Mrs. Jones: If you recommend a program, then I'll do my best.

Doctor: Very well, then. Here is my advice. Number one, you need to lose weight—I would estimate that losing 25 pounds over the next 3 months is a reasonable goal. Number 2, because your cholesterol is high, you need to reduce your intake of fatty foods. Number 3, I recommend that you increase your activity level and even get into a formal exercise program. Given the extent of your weight problem and the amount of experience you have had at commercially available programs, I recommend that you go to a professionally led behavior modification program. They will do a thorough assessment of your problem and come up with a treatment program that is tailored for you. They will also be able to help you make dietary changes to reduce your intake of fats. In addition, I can give you this table, which lists foods high and low in fat content. Finally, I will let them know you are able to start an exercise program. You need to begin very modestly and gradually build up. If you like to walk or swim, either one would be fine for you. How do you feel about these options?

Mrs. Jones: Fine. I'm happy to give it a shot.

Doctor: What problems do you see that might arise with your attempt to follow through on this plan?

Mrs. Jones: The main thing, Doctor, is my work. This is a very busy time of year, and it's hard for me to get away from the office. If I can't get an appointment time at the clinic that's suitable, that might get in the way of my following through. Also, trying to exercise when you're real busy at work is just not realistic.

Doctor: I'm glad you are aware of the possible problems you might run into. What might help you to overcome these obstacles and stick to a lifestyle change program that is really essential for your health at this time?

Mrs. Jones: Well, I can ask my boss to let me come in a little earlier so that I can leave and make an afternoon appointment.

Doctor: That sounds like a good idea. Also, be sure to get in touch with me if you have any other questions or need clarification about this plan. So, once again, what exactly are you going to do?

Mrs. Jones: I'll give the behavioral medicine clinic a call to set up an appointment as soon as possible. Changing my dietary intake of fats shouldn't be that hard, at least not when I'm home. Exercise will be tougher, but I guess I could walk in the evening after I get home from the office, maybe a mile at first and build up from there.

Doctor: That sounds like an excellent plan. I'd like to see you again in 3 months and check how much you have improved your cholesterol and blood sugar level. Let's aim for a 25-pound weight loss by then.

In this case, the physician was quickly able to determine that the patient was at the action stage. The appropriate intervention for this type of patient, given the severity of her medical problems and her previous experience, was at the intermediate level. The levels of intervention using a step-care approach will be outlined in the next section.

Patient Assessment

In deciding when to intervene and at what level, several dimensions of patient characteristics are used to assess severity: (1) biological factors and medical risk status, (2) psychological factors related to motivation, abnormal eating patterns, and poor exercise habits, and (3) social factors, including potential support from family, friends, and the work environment (see also Fig. 23-1).

Biobehavioral factors must be evaluated to help determine which program might be best for a particular patient. A review of the patient's personal and familial weight history, eating habits, and previous attempts to lose weight (with a focus on what went wrong) can be helpful. Patients may report eating in response to psychological events (such as stress, depression, or social anxiety). They may reveal fatigue, dizziness, or cravings for protein, carbohydrates, or sugar that could reflect biochemical imbalances (e.g., hypoglycemia). They may have an underlying eating disorder such as bulimia.

Interpersonal and sociocultural factors should also be evaluated. The educational level, economic situation, and living environment of the patient may make it more difficult to change lifestyle. Social support (or lack of it) can also play a crucial role. Sometimes spouses, parents, or family are unaware of their power to support and sustain change; alternatively, they can unwittingly sabotage treatment efforts because of their own lifestyle habits or values. An assessment of the patient's environment often reveals a need to involve other members of the family in lifestyle change efforts.

Patients should be prepared for treatment by ensuring appropriate goals and expectations. One major barrier to successful weight loss is unrealistic expectations about speed and ease of weight loss. Patients should be discouraged from seeking rapid weight loss, or "fad diets." One drawback of all "fad diets" is that patients eventually feel deprived and must stop the diet. This is when they typically return to their prior eating habits and regain weight.

A Step-Care Model of Treatment

Brownell (1986) has proposed a step-care approach to weight loss that is perhaps the most rational and cost-effective way to proceed. The challenge to the physician is to determine which type of treatment is most appropriate for a particular patient (see Table 23-4). Since cost, risk, and invasiveness increase with each step, it should be recommended that the patient begin at the lowest step not yet given a fair test. More costly and risky procedures should be reserved for those patients who have not responded to basic strategies.

In general, mildly to moderately obese individuals should be encouraged to seek treatment in low-cost self-help or commercial programs. However, recent evidence suggests that repeated unsuccessful efforts to lose weight can be medically dangerous and can lead to even greater obesity, making each future attempt more difficult (Brownell, 1986). Therefore, those who have tried and failed to lose weight on several occasions by these methods and those who are moderately to morbidly obese should be strongly encouraged to seek an intermediate level of care, such as a hospital-based behavior modification program.

The basic philosophy of behavior modification is that in order to lose weight and keep it off, a person must gradually replace old maladaptive eating behaviors and exercise habits with new health-promoting ones that can be maintained for a lifetime. Components typically employed include self-monitoring of food intake, calorie-counting, goal-setting and self-reinforcement, and various stimulus-control procedures (e.g., restrictions on access to food, timing of meals, location of meals, and portion control). Patients typically are taught to slow down their eating, to use alternative

Table 23–4 **A Step-Care Model for the Treatment of Obesity**

I. Minimal interventions

Self-help programs
Commercial programs

II. Intermediate interventions

Professionally led programs
    Caloric restriction
    Formal exercise
    Nutritional counseling
    Behavior modification
        Self-monitoring of food intake
        Goal setting and self-reinforcement
        Stimulus control
        Coping skills
            Cognitive restructuring
            Assertiveness training
            Problem solving
            Relaxation training

III. Maximal interventions

Combined behavior modification/
   pharmacotherapy
Very-low-calorie diet (VLCD)
Surgery (e.g., gastroplasty)

skills in managing moods (e.g., relaxation training), to use social support (assertiveness), to apply problem-solving skills to increase activity level, and to change their ways of thinking about food (cognitive restructuring). (For more details about clinical techniques, see Abrams, 1984.)

Maintenance of weight loss is the key problem, because long-term results (more than 1 year) have demonstrated that as many as 75% regain the weight lost in programs (Jeffery, 1987). The inclusion of the patient's support system (usually spouse involvement) and much emphasis on exercise are two components of behavioral programs that show promise as aids to maintenance. Many experts now consider exercise to be one of the best strategies for the maintenance of weight loss and the improvement of health status (Donahoe et al., 1984). Education and ongoing support over many months or years may be necessary for success. The physician can play an important role in providing reinforcement and support for continued efforts.

Finally, the severely overweight patient and those who have failed with a variety of conventional treatments might be appropriate candidates for a very-low-calorie diet (VLCD) or gastroplasty surgery. These options are most appropriate when obesity poses a definite and sometimes imminent hazard to health, because maximal interventions also carry a significant degree of risk in the form of side effects and/or complications. Behavior modification programs are now being combined with VLCDs and with gastroplasty to increase adherence/compliance and to improve the maintenance of weight loss (Brownell, 1986; Wadden, Stunkard, 1986).

ASSESSMENT AND TREATMENT OF SMOKING

A CASE STUDY

Ms. Williams is a 37-year-old, hard-working lawyer with two small children. She visits her physician complaining of productive cough and fever for 3 days. After obtaining a history, performing a physical exam, and obtaining a chest x-ray, the physician returns to the examining room to tell the patient the chest X-ray is negative and that she has bronchitis. He also notices from her chart that she has been a chronic smoker. The dialogue that follows reflects a patient-centered approach to smoking cessation.

Doctor: Your chest x-ray looks normal. I think you have bronchitis. I will discuss the treatment of your bronchitis with you, but first I'd like to talk with you about smoking. Are you still smoking?

Ms. Williams: Yes, I'm ashamed to say.

Doctor: Have you thought about giving it up?

Ms. Williams: Yes, I'd like to quit, but smoking really helps me to relax and concentrate at work, and I have this big case coming up.

Doctor: Hmm, it seems like you depend on cigarettes to help you deal with work. Your work sounds pretty stressful right now. What reasons do you have for wanting to quit?

Ms. Williams: Well, I know it's not good for my health, especially since I keep getting bronchitis. Also, my father smoked and he died of a heart attack. My husband is not a smoker and he and the kids have been after me to quit, too.

Doctor: You've mentioned some good reasons for quitting. I think your infections would decrease if you quit, and your risk of developing heart disease will decrease dramatically when you quit. I know I've told you about the risks of passive smoke as well as the important influence you have on your kids as a role model. I'm glad you're willing to consider quitting, but it sounds like quitting now would be hard on you. I'd like to help you to quit when your case is over, though.

Ms. Williams: That would be fine. My case will be over in 2 months.

Doctor: Why don't you schedule an appointment with me in 2 months, then.

Ms. Williams: OK.

In this case, the physician (1) raised the issue of smoking and allowed the patient to express her ideas and feelings about quitting, (2) explored her reasons for quitting as well as her reasons for continuing to smoke, and (3) recognized that the patient was contemplating quitting, but also that she was not ready for action. Therefore, the physician elected to reinforce the patient's reasons for quitting, personalize her risk, offer to help her quit, and ask her to schedule a follow-up appointment after her court case was over. It is likely that the physician helped to accelerate the patient's movement from the contemplation stage to the action stage with these interventions.

If she returns in 2 months, or when she returns for any future visit, the physician can continue to build commitment, complete further assessment, and begin to suggest specific smoking cessation strategies.

Patient Assessment for Smoking Cessation

It is helpful to assess patient characteristics before deciding on the appropriate level of intervention. Five major characteristics need to be evaluated. These are: (1) readiness or motivation to change, (2) degree of biological addiction, (3) degree of psychological dependence (4) history of attempts to quit, and (5) degree of positive social support and negative support (e.g., another smoker in the household).

If the patient is not strongly motivated to change, then motivating him or her becomes the first priority before deciding on treatment options. Assuming an individual is ready for action, the rule of thumb is that smokers should receive a more intensive (maximal) treatment program if they: (1) are biologically addicted (smoke more than 25 cigarettes per day, usually smoke within 30 minutes of awakening during the morning, and will report smoking even during a cold or other minor respiratory illness), (2) are psychologically dependent (smoke as part of their "image," for stress management, or to help cope with social interactions), or (3) have tried to quit on their own and failed.

Smokers who report severe withdrawal symptoms may be candidates for nicotine chewing gum as an adjunct to comprehensive behavioral treatment. In contrast, first-time quitters and those individuals who are less biologically addicted and less psychosocially dependent are candidates for minimal levels of treatment, such as self-help or other brief interventions (Abrams, Wilson, 1986).

A review of the patient's previous attempts to quit can be revealing (Best, 1976). They may show, for example, that the patient was unable to quit even though he or she cut down (suggesting biological addiction), or that he or she quit for a period but slipped back into smoking when stressed, angry, or depressed (suggesting psychological dependence). If the patient relapsed in a social situation, then social anxiety or lack of assertiveness may be a problem that needs correcting before the next quit attempt.

A Step-Care Model of Treatment

By exploring the patient's status and history on biopsychosocial dimensions, one can decide on how to move him or her in a stepwise fashion through three possible levels of treatment: (1) minimal interventions (self-help, physician counseling, commercial programs, hypnosis), (2) intermediate interventions (behavior modification), and (3) maximal interventions (behavior modification plus pharmacological treatments).

Minimal Interventions

Several studies suggest the potential power of brief intervention in physicians' offices. Strategies that increase the likelihood of success include face-to-face interventions, the combination of physician and nonphysician counselors, multiple sessions, and multiple intervention modalities (Kottke et al., 1988). Studies have demonstrated that physician interventions are particularly effective in patients with smoking-related illnesses or in those "at risk" for smoking-related disease (Schwartz, 1987). Physician advice is improved when follow-up is provided (Wilson et al., 1982). Other simple strategies that physicians can use in the office are listed in Table 23-5. The use of nicotine resin complex will be described in the section on maximal interventions. In general, the resin complex is not very effective when dispensed in the medical setting unless it is combined with some other specific modality (Ockene, 1987).

Other minimal interventions are listed in Table 23-5. Generally, it is the lighter, less dependent smokers who are highly motivated to quit and who have excellent social support for quitting that are the preferred candidates for brief or minimal interventions.

Table 23–5 **A Step-Care Model for the Treatment of Smoking**

I. Minimal interventions
Self-help programs
Physician counseling
   Advice
   Provide quitting materials (e.g., self-help
      manuals)
   Contracts
   Set quit date
   Follow-up visits or calls
Commercial programs
Hypnosis/acupuncture

II. Intermediate interventions
Professionally led programs
   Nicotine fading
   Aversive techniques
   Behavior modification
      Self-monitoring of smoking behavior
      Goal setting and self-reinforcement
      Stimulus control
      Coping skills
         Cognitive restructuring
         Assertiveness training
         Problem solving
         Relaxation training
         Relapse-prevention training

III. Maximal interventions
Combined behavior modification/
pharmacotherapy
   Nicotine resin complex
   Clonidine
   Antidepressants
Inpatient treatment programs

Intermediate Interventions

If minimal interventions have been attempted without success, or if the individual is more biologically or psychologically dependent on cigarettes, then formal behavioral treatment programs of several weeks' duration should be considered. These programs teach skills for quitting, managing acute withdrawal, and maintenance/preventing relapse (Lichtenstein, 1982; Abrams, Wilson, 1986).

Behavioral approaches to quitting include nicotine fading, stimulus control, aversive techniques, cognitive approaches to deal with urges and craving, and relaxation training. Nicotine fading involves switching to a brand of cigarettes with lower nicotine and reducing the number of cigarettes smoked per day on a systematic basis over a period of 3 to 5 weeks (Foxx, Brown, 1979). Gradual reduction of nicotine is designed to minimize withdrawal symptoms. Stimulus control involves rearranging the environment and self to make smoking more and more difficult (remove all ashtrays, smoke only in one room of the house, buy packs instead of cartons). Although aversive strategies are unlikely to be widely accepted by consumers, they have yielded some of the most successful outcomes. Most current programs include a variety of techniques rather than one strategy. Reviews of the behavioral literature indicate that at a 1-year follow-up, the average participant in the typical behavioral program has a 20 to 40% chance of being abstinent.

Maximal Interventions

Programs that add nicotine resin complex or other pharmacologic procedures (e.g., clonidine) to behavior modification should be considered for the chronic and more "difficult to treat" heavy smoker who has tried to quit repeatedly without success (Fagerstrom, 1978). A pharmacological agent may help to alleviate withdrawal symptoms and facilitate cessation (Hughes, Miller, 1984). Once cessation has been achieved and maintained, gradual withdrawal from the agent can then be dealt with separately. Use of nicotine resin complex alone, without a behavioral treatment program that addresses psychosocial factors, may severely reduce efficacy (Abrams, Wilson, 1986), because simply using a pharmacological agent to reduce withdrawal is considered an incomplete treatment of a multifactorial habit.

Maintenance Strategies

Behavioral techniques for maintenance and prevention of relapse are of recent origin and hold much promise, because 60% of those who quit smoking will relapse within the first 3 months of quitting (Marlatt, Gordon, 1985). Techniques for relapse prevention include a detailed analysis of "high-risk situations." These are people, places, or emotional states that the smoker feels are most likely to precipitate a return to smoking. Individuals are taught how to cope with these situations using rehearsal and other techniques to resist temptation. If they should have a slip back into smoking (one or two cigarettes), then they are provided with techniques to prevent the slip from becoming a full-blown relapse. Additional support and follow-up (e.g., telephone hot lines) are usually provided during the critical 3 to 6 months after quitting, when people are most vulnerable to relapse.

In summary, even a small amount of physician time can have a large impact on helping patients become motivated for quitting smoking and then take action, quit, and resist relapse. A step-care plan can be adopted with every smoker in the office practice and in the hospital. More time and effort are placed on high-risk individuals and those who are willing to take action. Those who are not yet ready to quit are still targeted for systematic counseling, education, and follow-up. Beyond physician advice (which can be very effective), self-help and comprehensive formal programs can be used. Helping patients to quit smoking can have the largest impact on chronic disease and disability in the United States over the next decades. (Nicotine addiction is also discussed in Chapter 9.)

ANNOTATED BIBLIOGRAPHY

Abrams DB, Wilson GT: Habit disorders: Alcohol and tobacco dependence. In Frances AJ, Hales RE (eds): American Psychiatric Association, Annual Review, Vol. 5. Washington DC, American Psychiatric Press, Inc., 1986

> A review of the biobehavioral factors contributing to tobacco dependence and a summary of cessation treatments.

Coates TJ, Polonsky WH: Behavior therapy. In Michels R (ed): Psychiatry. Philadephia, J.B. Lippincott Co., 1986

> Provides a description of the principles and techniques used in behavior therapy with case examples.

Grueninger UJ, Duffy FD, Goldstein MG: Patient education in the medical encounter: An interactive approach. In Lipkin M Jr, Lazare A, Putnam S (eds): The Medical Interview. Boston, Springer-Verlag, in press

> Describes a comprehensive model for patient education and counseling in the medical setting as well as a practical patient-centered strategy for physician-delivered counseling.

Houpt JL: Introduction: Psychosomatic medicine, consultation-liaison psychiatry, and behavioral medicine. In Michels R, Cavenar JO (eds): Psychiatry. Philadelphia, J.B. Lippincott Co., 1986

> Defines basic terminology and describes the history of the fields of behavioral medicine, psychosomatic medicine, and consultation-liaison psychiatry.

Kaplan NM, Stamler J (eds): Prevention of coronary heart disease: Practical management of the risk factors. Philadelphia, W.B. Saunders Co., 1983

> A detailed disussion of the risk factors for cardiovascular disease and interventions to modify them.

Kristeller JL, Ockene JK: Assessment and treatment of smoking on a consultation service. In Michels R, Cavenar JO (eds): Psychiatry. Philadelphia, J.B. Lippincott Co., 1986

> A practical approach for providing smoking cessation interventions in the inpatient medical setting.

Prochaska JO, DiClemente CC: Towards a comprehensive model of change. In Miller WR, Heather N (eds): Treating Addictive Disorders: Processes of Change. New York, Plenum Press, 1986

> Description of a comprehensive model of behavioral change that includes an explanation of the stages and processes of change.

Russell ML: Behavioral Counseling in Medicine: Strategies for Modifying At-Risk Behavior. New York, Oxford University Press, 1986

> A practical primer for physicians in behavioral counseling techniques.

Sheridan DP, Winogrond IR (eds): The Preventive Approach to Patient Care. New York, Elsevier, 1987

> A text on the theory and practice of preventive medicine, using a life-cycle approach.

Stunkard AJ: Obesity. In Michels R, Cavenar JO (eds): Psychiatry. Philadelphia, J.B. Lippincott Co., 1986

> A concise but thorough discussion of definitions, epidemiology, clinical description, etiology, and treatment.

REFERENCES

Abrams DB: Current status and clinical developments in the behavioral treatment of obesity. In Franks CM (ed): New Developments in Behavior Therapy: From Research to Clinical Application. New York, Haworth Press, 1984

Abrams DB, Raciti MA, Ruggiero L, et al: Cardiovascular risk factor reduction in the medical setting. In Stoudemire A, Fogel BS (eds): Principles of Medical Psychiatry. Orlando, Grune & Stratton, 1987

Abrams DB, Wilson GT: Habit Disorders: Alcohol and Tobacco Dependence. Edited by Frances AJ and Hales RE. American Psychiatric Association, Annual Review. Washington, DC, American Psychiatric Press, Inc, 5:1986

Anda RF, Remington PL, Sienko DG, et al: Are physicians advising smokers to quit? The patient's perspective. JAMA 257:1916–1919, 1987

Best JA: Tailoring smoking withdrawal procedures to personality and motivational differences. J Consult Clin Psychol 4:1–8, 1976

Bray GA: The Obese Patient. Philadelphia, WB Saunders, 1976

Brownell KD: Public health approaches to obesity and its management. Annu Rev Public Health 7:521–533, 1986

Burling TA, Singleton EG, Bigelow GE, et al: Smoking following myocardial infarction: A critical review of the literature. Health Psychol 3:83–96, 1984

Castelli WP: Cardiovascular disease and multifactorial risk: Challenge of the 1980s. Am Heart J 106:1191–1200, 1983.

Dembroski TM, Costa PT: Assessment of coronary-prone behavior: A current overview. Ann Behav Med 10:60–63, 1988

Donahoe CP, Lin DH, Kirschenbaum DS, Keesey RE: Metabolic consequences of dieting and exercise in the treatment of obesity. J Consult Clin Psychol 52(5):827–836, 1984

Dorian B, Taylor CB: Stress factors in the development of coronary artery disease. J Occup Med 26:747–756, 1984

Engel GL: The need for a new medical model: A challenge for biomedicine. Science 196:129–136, 1977

Fagerstrom KO: Measuring degree of physical dependence to tobacco smoking with reference to individualization of treatment. Addict Behav 3:235–241, 1978

Foxx RM, Brown RA: Nicotine fading and self-monitoring for cigarette abstinence as controlled smoking. J Appl Behav Anal 12:111–125, 1979

Gordon T, Castelli WP, Hjortland MC, et al: Predicting coronary heart disease in middle-aged and older persons: The Framingham study. JAMA 238:497–499, 1977

Gordon T, Kannel WB, Dawber TR, et al: Changes associated with quitting cigarette smoking: The Framingham study. Am Heart J 90:322, 1975

Grueninger UJ, Duffy FD, Goldstein MG: Patient education in the medical encounter: An interactive approach. In Lipkin M Jr, Lazare A, Putnam S (eds): The Medical Interview. New York, Springer-Verlag (in press)

Grueninger UJ, Goldstein MG, Duffy FD: Patient education in hypertension: Five essential steps. J Hypertension 7(Suppl 3):593–598, 1989

Grundy SM, Greenland P, Herd A, et al: Cardiovascular and risk factor evaluation of healthy American adults. Circulation 75:1340A–1362A, 1987

Hubert HB, Feinleib M, McNamara PM, et al: Obesity as an independent risk factor for cardiovascular disease: A 26-year follow-up of participants in the Framingham Heart Study. Circulation 67:968–977, 1983

Hughes JR, Miller SA: Nicotine gum to help stop smoking. JAMA 20:2855–2858, 1984

Inui TS, Yourtee EL, Williamson JW: Improved outcome in hypertension after physician tutorials: A controlled trial. Ann Intern Med 84:646–651, 1976

Jeffrey RW: Behavioral treatment of obesity. Ann Behav Med 9(1):20–24, 1987

Jenkins CD: Psychosocial risk factors for coronary heart disease. Acta Med Scand 660(Suppl):123–136, 1982

Kannel WB: Update on the role of cigarette smoking in coronary artery disease. Am Heart J 101:319–328, 1981

Kannel WB: An overview of the risk factors for cardiovascular disease. In Kaplan NM, Stamler J (eds): Prevention of Coronary Heart Disease: Practical Management of the Risk Factors. Philadelphia, WB Saunders, 1983

Kannel WB: New perspectives on cardiovascular disease. Am Heart J 114:213–219, 1987

Kannel WB, Sorlie P: Some health benefits of physical activity: The Framingham Study. Arch Intern Med 139:857–861, 1979

Kottke TE, Battista RN, DeFriesse GH, Brekke ML: Attributes of successful smoking cessation interventions in medical practice: A meta-analysis of 39 controlled trials. JAMA 259:2882–2889, 1988

Kottke TE, Blackburn H, Brekke ML, Solberg LI: The systematic practice of preventive cardiology. Am J Cardiol 59:690–694, 1987

Kottke TE, Foels JK, Hill C, et al: Nutrition counseling in private practice: Attitudes and activities of family physicians. Prev Med 13:219–225, 1984

Levenkron JC, Greenland P, Bowley N: Using patient instructors to teach behavioral counseling skills. J Med Educ 65:665–672, 1987

Lichtenstein E: The smoking problem: A behavioral perspective. J Consult Clin Psychol 50:804–819, 1982

The Lipid Research Clinics coronary primary prevention trial results: I. Reduction in incidence of coronary heart disease. JAMA 251:351, 1984

Louis Harris and Associates, Inc: Health Maintenance. Pacific Mutual Life Insurance Co, Newport Beach, CA, 1978

Marlatt GA, Gordon JR: Relapse Prevention. New York, Guilford Press, 1985

Mullen PD, Katayama CK: Health promotion in private practice: An analysis. Fam Commun Health 8:79–87, 1985

Neaton JD, Kuller LH, Wentworth D, et al: Total and cardiovascular mortality in relation to cigarette smoking, serum cholesterol concentration, and diastolic blood pressure among black and white males followed up for five years (MRFIT). Am Heart J 108:759–769, 1984

Nutting PA: Health promotion in primary medical care: Problems and potential. Prev Med 15:537–548, 1986

Ockene JK: Physician-delivered intervention for smoking cessation: Strategies for increasing effectiveness. Prev Med 16:723–737, 1987

Ockene JK, Quirk ME, Goldberg RJ, et al: A residents training program for the development of smoking intervention skills. Arch Intern Med 148:1039–1045, 1988

Orleans CT, George LK, Houpt JL, Brodie KH: Health promotion in primary care: A survey of US family practitioners. Prev Med 14:636–647, 1985

O'Sullivan JB: The epidemiology of cardiovascular disease and diabetes mellitus in perspective. Mt Sinai J Med (NY) 49:163–168, 1982

Preventive Health Care Committee, Society for Research and Education in Primary Care Internal Medicine: Preventive medicine in general internal medicine residency training. Ann Intern Med 102:859–861, 1985

Prochaska JO, DiClemente, CC: Towards a comprehensive model of change. In Miller WR, Heather N (eds): Treating Addictive Disorders: Processes of Change. New York, Plenum Press, 1986

Ragland DR, Brand RJ: Type A behavior and mortality from coronary heart disease. N Engl J Med 318:65–67, 1988

Rosenberg L, Kaufman DW, Helmrich SP, et al: The risk of myocardial infarction in men under 55 years of age. N Engl J Med 310:951–954, 1985

Schwartz JL: Review and evaluation of smoking cessation methods. The United States and Canada, 1978–1985. US Department of Health and Human Services, Public Health Service, National Institute of Health, National Cancer Institute, Division of Cancer Prevention and Control. NIH Publication No. 87–2940, 1987

US Department of Health, Education and Welfare, Public Health Service: Healthy people: The Surgeon General's report on health promotion and disease prevention. Government Printing Office, 1979A

US Department of Health, Education and Welfare, Public Health Service: The health consequences of smoking: A report of the Surgeon General. Government Printing Office, 1979B

US Department of Health and Human Services: The health consequences of smoking: Cardiovascular disease: A report of the Surgeon General. Rockville, MD, US Department of Health and Human Services, Public Health Service, Office on Smoking and Health. DHHS Publication No. (PHS) 85–50204, 1983

VanItallie TB: Obesity: Adverse effects on health and longevity. J Clin Nutr 32:2723–2733, 1979

Wadden TA, Stunkard AJ: Controlled trial of very low calorie diet, behavior therapy, and their combination in the treatment of obesity. J Consult Clin Psychol 54:482–488, 1986

Wilson D, Wood G, Johnston N, et al: Randomized clinical trial of supportive follow-up for smokers in family practice. Can Med Assoc J 126:127–129, 1982

Appendix 1:
A Problem-Oriented Method for Teaching Clinical Psychiatry

Donald C. Fidler
and Mark G. Fuller

This section will briefly present a practical approach to developing a problem-oriented course in clinical psychiatry. Since the traditional lecture-based course has received extensive criticism (GPEP report, 1984; Resnick, 1987; Strayhorn, 1973), curricula that stimulate thinking and higher-order reasoning have been recommended by several sources (Wales, et al., 1987; Browne, 1989; Brinton, et al., 1988). One of the barriers to the more traditional approaches to problem-oriented learning, however, has been the large number of faculty members required to staff small group sessions. Our method requires little (if any) additional faculty commitment, yet stimulates students to become active participants in learning. Problem-oriented class sessions may be intermixed with periodic traditional didactic lectures. This overview presents the basic model we have implemented at the West Virginia University School of Medicine, which may be used in conjunction with this textbook.

METHODS

We have eliminated the use of lectures in our preclinical behavior science courses. In most cases, we believed that lectures simply repeated the material presented in the reading and did not promote the use of critical reasoning or problem solving. In the place of lectures, we have substituted textbook chapters, clinical problem-solving case discussions in the classroom setting, and other relevant material. The availability of the text in which this chapter appears has decreased the need for ancillary formal didactic lectures because pertinent background information can be derived during the students' reading time.

630

The purpose of the clinical problem-solving approach is to encourage students to actively apply didactic knowledge. We believe that simple memorization of facts does not adequately prepare students for the complexities of clinical medicine and the management of problematic behavior. The clinical problems should be designed so that certain aspects can be solved by applying information found in the assigned chapters. Other parts of the problems should require critical thinking and higher level judgments that exercise students' ethical, philosophical, and emotional reasoning. Ideally, the cases presented throughout the course also should be designed to interconnect so that students can learn about continuity and relationships in illness and health rather than be limited to learning about isolated cross-sectional concepts.

Preparing for this type of class format requires that students work alone or in groups before the lecture. The basic classroom experience can be divided into the following four sections:

1. The class beings with a student presenting the case, along with his or her understanding of it.
2. The presenting student is encouraged to call on colleagues to comment, agree, disagree, or question.
3. The teacher summarizes the discoveries and questions of the class. The teacher or an invited expert can then conclude discussion of the more straightforward aspects of the material and address any points of the case that were overlooked.
4. The students are challenged to explore more complex aspects of the case, which enhances the learning process.

The role of the teacher is crucial to the successful outcome of this method. It is essential that the instructor make the conceptual shift from deliverer of information to facilitator of learning. We recommend the use of a course coordinator, who is present at all class sessions. This provides a sense of continuity to the class and guidance to invited experts who may be present. These experts are usually faculty members who may formerly have served as guest lecturers on topics of special interest. In our program, with assistance from the course coordinator, all the experts found participating enjoyable, although many of them were apprehensive at first.

During the first two sections of the class, we recommend that the instructor be attentive and somewhat reserved while encouraging the students to explore the clinical problems. If there are too many comments from the instructor early on, the students may shift into a more passive "lecture mode" and it may be difficult to re-engaged them. The exception to this would be correcting students who present erroneous information, but even this may be handled best by questioning the student about the information or asking other students to express their opinion.

The third and fourth sections of a given class should be approached by the judicious use of questions (along the lines of the Socratic method). We recommend that students be challenged to examine the cases from various viewpoints and asked to support their reasoning. Questioning the students about the assigned readings as they apply to the cases may be useful in ascertaining if they have learned the information accurately and can apply it appropriately. Teachers should be reminded that multiple perspective solutions may exist and that the correct answer may be elusive.

Presenting a case to the class understandably may cause anxiety for some students. Instructors should try to be as helpful as possible in assisting students with this. Medical students and physicians are called on to answer questions about clinical material throughout their careers and this can be an excellent opportunity to practice. If students feel overwhelmed by this task, they should seek assistance from their instructors and be encouraged to work through their apprehensions. Teachers should be gentle but firm as they introduce this learning technique, which may be new to some students.

Our experience is that although students may be more comfortable initially with the traditional lecture and memorization format, given the opportunity, they are willing to explore alternative methods.

The Genogram

We have included a genogram of two fictional families used in developing clinical cases. Use of a genogram brings a sense of continuity to the course. Students also have the opportunity to see how an individual's problem can affect other family members; thus, the students' understanding of the interrelatedness of human behavior is supported. In our course, we designated several of the family members as physicians and one as a medical student. Their interactions with patients were the basis for the development of many educational situations. Various clinical situations and interrelationships between the family members in this genogram can be created as needed.

The Audiovisual Guide

Videotapes are used in our classes to enhance the students' appreciation of various concepts. Whether they are assigned as resource material to be viewed and interpreted before class or shown as a short segment during class, videotapes provide an alternative medium for illustrating some concepts further. In the audiovisual guide of this text, you will find a listing of tapes arranged by topic.

Evaluations

We use several methods to evaluate our students and enhance their learning. First, we evaluate the students on their participation in class. In larger classes, this may be problematic and should account for only a small part of the grade. In addition, we give four quizzes, evenly spaced throughout the semester. This encourages the students to stay up to date with their readings and provides them with regular feedback. At the suggestion of our students, we use questions modeled on the national boards to assess whether the students are acquiring the necessary factual material. This also allows the students to practice for their licensing exams. Our final exam is a comprehensive "take-home test" consisting of two essay questions that require a broad understanding of major course principles and how they interconnect. We believe this more closely simulates the type of problem-solving the students will be faced with in their clinical years and can be an excellent learning experience.

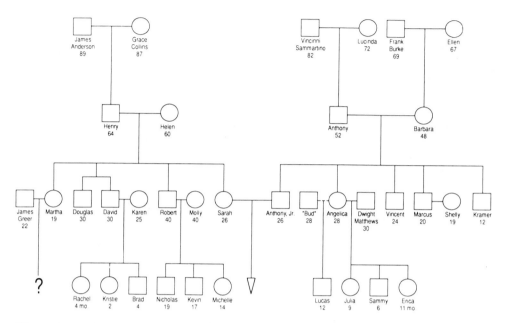

Figure A–1. *Sample genogram to be used with problem-solving oriented case discussion.*

CLINICAL CASES

The following case is an example of one of the clinical problems used in our courses. We encourage the use of this text, the genogram, and the audiovisual guide to develop a problem-solving-oriented course based on the didactic information contained in this text.

A CASE STUDY

Vince Sammartino (see genogram), a fourth-year medical student, is rotating through the emergency room service and presents a patient to you, his attending physician. He tells you that Ernest Simpson is 62 and has been widowed for 2 years. He was brought in by the police because he was violent and confused and tried to attack an apartment manager. Mr. Simpson claims he has had mild memory problems for several years, and is being treated by his local physician. Mr. Simpson was agitated and cursing in the emergency room and needed to be sedated with a low dose of haloperidol (an anti-psychotic medication). He yelled that he was "tired of people screwing him over." A social worker who recognized him informed you that Mr. Simpson's wife was killed 2 years ago when a police car engaged in a high-speed chase of drug dealers hit her as she sat on a park bench in front of their high-rise apartment building. The social worker also reported that the city is trying to condemn the apartment building to build a parking deck to accompany an already planned indoor sports arena. Many of Mr. Simpson's neighbors of 42 years have already moved out, and the majority of the building is now a haven for drug dealers and "shooting galleries." Most of Mr. Simpson's best friends have moved out recently. After Mrs. Simpson's death, and until several weeks ago, his friends used to have Mr. Simpson over for dinner and accompanied him on walks before the park was cleared for the sports arena. The apartment manager had come by to discuss Mr. Simpson's need to move when he noticed that the apartment was in disarray, there were several dogs and cats present, and there was very little food in the kitchen.

You ask Vincent about his evaluation. He tells you that the patient was oriented to person, place, and year but not the day of the week. "When I asked him what he was going to do he cursed at me. He refused to do serial sevens or any other calculations and just continued to yell at me. When I asked him about his wife, he was tearful but refused to discuss it." Vincent goes on to tell you that the patient has poor judgment and insight, but this can be attributed to his confusion. "In summary, I believe he is suffering from senile dementia and he needs a CT scan, EEG LP, and maybe a PET scan before he is transferred to a nursing home."

QUESTIONS

1. As Vincent's supervisor, do you agree with his assessment? Why or why not?

2. What model of patient care does Vincent Sammartino seem to be using? Describe it.

3. In developing a case formulation of Mr. Simpson, what are the relevant variables (biologic, psychologic, and social)?

4. In developing a plan of management of Mr. Simpson's problems, use the biopsychosocial model to explain how you would intervene.

5. Do psychological and behavioral factors predispose people to physical illness? Explain.

6. Do psychosocial factors affect the course and outcome of illness? Explain.

7. Is Mr. Simpson's case unique or do psychiatric and social problems show up in a general medical practice? Explain.

8. What is social epidemiology and how does it relate to Mr. Simpson?

9. What factors impact on the use of medical care in this case, or why did Mr. Simpson really come to the emergency room?

SUGGESTED READING

Dornhorst AC: Information overload: Why medical student education needs a shake-up. Lancet 2:513–514, 1981

Eichna L: Medical school education, 1975–1979: A student's perspective. N Engl J Med 303:727–734, 1980

West DA, Moore-West M: Problem-based learning of behavioral science in a traditional medical school curriculum. J Psych Ed 12:111–116, 1988

REFERENCES

Brinton DA, Jarvis JQ, Harris DL: A small group instruction experiment in medical education. J Med Ed 59:13–18, 1988

Browne MN: Necessary tensions in assignments that stimulate critical thinking. Connexions 2:1–2, 1989

GPEP report: Physicians for the Twenty-first Century. Report of the Panel on the General Professional Education of the Physician and College Preparation for Medicine. Washington, DC, Association of American Medical Colleges, 1984

Resnick LB: Education and Learning to Think. Washington, DC, The National Academy Press, 1987

Strayhorn J: Aspects of motivation in preclinical medical training: A student's viewpoint. J Med Ed 48:1104–1110, 1973

Wales CE, Nardi AH, Stager RA: Thinking Skills: Making a Choice. Morgantown, WV, Center for Guided Design, 1987

Appendix 2: *Audiovisual Guide*

Donald C. Fidler

The following notes are based on my reviews of videotapes for the American Psychiatric Association and the Association of Academic Psychiatry, and the experiences of myself and other psychiatric educators in using videotapes with medical students, psychiatry and internal medicine residents, nursing students, and audiences comprised of a variety of health professionals. Many of the videotapes are programs that I helped design and programs that my friends and colleagues, Ed Mason and Jim Lurie, helped design specifically for medical student education. I attempted to be as objective in reporting about our programs as I was with the other programs, having compiled data from other instructors as well as my own data about successes and failures.

I did not attempt to simplify my choices by considering programs to be "bad" or "good" in the fashion that many film and theater critics choose to review productions for entertainment value, but instead I attempted to approach the reviews with a knowledge of the great complexity of what makes teaching with a videotape a success or a failure. One must always ask the following questions and understand the multiple factors influencing the answers:

1. How large is the audience?
2. What is the philosophy of the instructor presenting the videotape? Does the instructor introduce the program with enthusiasm or disdain?
3. What is the admission philosophy of the school whose students form this particular audience? Did the school select students who enjoy learning about abstract issues such as emotions, ethics, and conflict, or did it select students who are fascinated only by hard data?
4. What are the developmental learning levels of the students? Are they just beginning to master a subject and therefore need simple, concrete facts? Are they further in their training and need emotional stimulation to encourage them to dwell more on the truths of how difficult decisions are made? Are they so far along in their development to be thinking about thinking itself?

5. How much time does the instructor have to cover the topic? Will the topic be covered in one teaching event? Will the instructor and students have the luxury of spreading the topic over multiple sessions with time to ponder the topic between sessions?

6. What ratio of media to discussion time will the instructor use? Most media need about a 3:1 ratio of discussion to viewing time.

7. How much exposure do the students get to videotape and film? Is this a new or overused format? Are the instructors and students "media-sophisticated" enough to attend to the content without being distracted by the technology? Do they suffer from media burnout and starve for real human interaction?

Occasionally in my notes I address the above questions, but more often I describe the tapes in a manner that will hopefully allow instructors and students to decide the usefulness of a particular tape by asking the above questions.

SPECIAL NOTES

Many of the reviews are followed by the word *Trigger.* This means that there is no didactic teaching in the production, and the tape can be used to enhance lecture material, much like a case presentation is a trigger that is then followed by a didactic presentation or discussion. Reviews that are not followed by this caption have narration or graphics that allow the tape to stand alone without supplementary reading or lectures.

It is my strong belief that it is best to use all tapes as triggers and unfailingly have teachers present to be involved with the audience and students. Assigning tapes for students to watch without arranging time for teachers to teach is not recommended.

Many of these productions use real patients and should be restricted to audiences of health professionals. Health professionals and health professional students should be cautioned to observe proper conduct of confidentiality. Patients and physicians were kind enough to consent to sharing themselves for our learning, and there have been horror stories of students and teachers not respecting videotapes of patients, leading to embarrassment, bad feelings, and mistrust. Please insist on confidentiality and respect.

Many of the productions are simulations, frequently using actors who are also trained in psychiatry or psychology. Often these are portrayals of actual case histories or re-creations of previously videotaped patient interviews but have changed names and localities to protect confidentiality. These tapes can thus be shared with non-professional audiences but should be used with the respect that was intended by the producers, that of furthering our knowledge and understanding of the thinking, behaviors, feelings, growth, and suffering of people. They should not be used for entertainment or for any exploitative reasons. Although these tapes are listed here as useful for medical students, they are often helpful in college and high school classes. Since many of the presentations are performed by health professionals, they, too, should be treated with respect and thanked for their contributions to education rather than ridiculed for their courage in performing the roles of people who are in pain or are in helplessly compromising circumstances.

When simulated videotapes are used, audiences and teachers require a certain "TV" or "film" sophistication. They must understand that one of the advantages of using scripted material is that we can make lengthy material into concise, summarizing material. Rather than watch 1 hour of material to focus on five specific events out of the hundreds of events, we can shorten the material to show only the five specific points. What would have required hours to watch may then be viewed in a matter of minutes or even seconds. This helps us to focus on what we learn, much like during medical rounds when we summarize our patients' histories, or in writing journal articles we summarize our patients by including only what we wish to focus upon, excluding much other material. This process is the same for scripting videotapes and for editing documentaries. The process of editing is enormously helpful, but helpful only as long as we understand it for what it is and remind ourselves frequently that we are seeing only a segment of truth rather than an all-encompassing truth. If we fail to remember this, then we start to believe that interviews can be brief, that every question or interpretation can be right on the mark, and that every patient can quickly reveal what we need to know. If we can rise above this kind of simplistic thinking, then simulated interviews, dramas, and edited documentaries can add enormous value to our learning.

I also include some commercial entertainment movies (noted "*") as suggestions for films that can be used with medical students outside of class, perhaps in psychiatry clubs or in electives, as triggers for further discussions about human growth or psychopathology. Although there are numerous films useful for this, I include only my favorites, which I have already used with students, and I include only those which are currently available on videotape format. Public viewing of such films may be restricted.

All programs are available in ¾-inch and VHS videotape formats, unless otherwise noted.

CHAPTERS 1 and 2: PSYCHIATRIC ASSESSMENT, DSM-III-R, AND DIFFERENTIAL DIAGNOSIS

Psychiatric Interviewing

Psychiatry Learning System: Psychiatric Evaluation (color, 41 min.). University of South Carolina, Producer; HSC, Distributor.

> *By using excerpts from several patient interviews with minimum narration and with many clarifying subtitles, this tape teaches how to begin and conduct a psychiatric interview.*

Interviews that Find and Interviews that Blind (color, 45 min.). UNC-CH, Producer; HSC, Distributor.

Useful with medical students because the same two actors (both are also really psychiatrists) perform four different interviews. Three are very short and bad, and one is lengthy and excellent. Students can compare what is good and bad among the four interviews because many of the variables do not vary. (Trigger)

Patton, M.D. (also incorrectly listed in some catalogues as "G. Patton, M.D.") (color, 7 min.). UNC-CH, Producer; HSC, Distributor.

No teaching of psychiatric interviewing is complete without a copy of this short tape. Dr. Patton, who is patterned after George C. Scott's portrayal of General Patton, stands in an attending, long white coat in front of a gargantuan American flag as he pounds his stick and welcomes medical students to the "real world of medicine." Prompts lots of laughter, lots of nervous gestures, and better, lots of discussion.

Maximizing the Interview (color, 12 min.). UNC-CH, Producer; Medical Interview Tapes, Distributor.

This brief tape with accompanying guide is useful with medical students because it focuses on interviewing techniques—not just with psychiatric patients, but with all patients. (Trigger)

Mental Status Examination

Psychiatry Learning System: Psychiatric Evaluation.

See description above, the second part of the tape.

Clinical Methods Learning System: Mental Status Examination (color, 18 min.). Emory University, Producer; Butterworth, Inc., Distributor.

Subtitles mark what is being tested or observed: appearance, orientation, memory, general intellectual function, attention span, judgment, abstraction, and questions to elicit information about delusions, hallucinations, and illusions. Clearly demonstrates that by performing the examination in a highly systematic fashion, nothing will be overlooked (including orientation to situation).

Overview of Psychopathology

Abnormal Behavior: Fact and Fiction. Also, Psychopathology: Causes and Correlates (color, 60 min. each; VHS or Beta II formats only). Wilfrid Laurier University, Producer; Beacon Films, Distributor.

Presents divergent opinions of leading U.S. and Canadian authorities in the field of psychopathology. (Not reviewed. Free previews available.)

CHAPTER 3: ORGANIC MENTAL DISORDERS

Someone I Once Knew (color, 30 min.). MTI Teleprograms.

Excellent production dealing with almost all aspects of Alzheimer's disease. Takes a NOVA-like approach as it uses superb graphics, brain models, and CT scans to demonstrate recent neurological research into dementia and normal brain aging.

Alzheimer's Disease (color, 10 min.). IMS, Faculty of Medicine, University of Toronto, and Medical Productions and Associates, Producers; The Altschul Group, Distributor.

A shorter and shallower treatment of Alzheimer's than "Someone I Once Knew" designed for the public and families of patients, but it is a brief introduction for beginning medical students, dealing with diagnosing and treatment, which is mostly the management of disposition.

Psychiatry Learning System: Organic Mental Disorders (color, 30 min.). University of South Carolina, Producer; HSC, Distributor.

The workbook discusses 30 cases. The videotape shows three cases of dementia: (1) a man with head injury, (2) a man with progressive degenerative dementia, and (3) a man with severe dementia secondary to alcohol abuse. The interviews well demonstrate difficulty with recent memory and inability to abstract while other abilities remain intact.

Recognition of Alzheimer's Dementia (color, 19 min.). Thomas Hacket, M.D., Producer; West Glen Communications, Distributor.

Shows actual patient cases in which dementia is assessed through a series of brief assessment tasks. Pharmacotherapy for symptomatic treatment is also discussed. (Not reviewed.)

CHAPTER 4: SCHIZOPHRENIA AND OTHER PSYCHOTIC DISORDERS

Schizophrenia: Family Understanding (color, 10 min.). IMS, Faculty of Medicine, University of Toronto, and Medicine Productions and Associates, Producers; The Altschul Group, Distributor.

Excellent brief introduction for beginning medical students and patient families, but does not show acute symptoms.

Psychiatry Learning System: Schizophrenic Disorders, Psychoses Not Elsewhere Classified, and Paranoid Disorders. Parts 1 and 2 (color, 33 min. each part). University of South Carolina, Producer; HSC, Distributor.

Part 1 is a superb introduction for medical students because it takes very short excerpts from interviews to illustrate the definitions and signs of psychoses. Part 2 shows two interviews.

Simulated Psychiatric Profiles: Psychoses (color, 21 min.). UNC-CH and Burroughs-Welcome, Producers; HSC, Distributor.

Two actors portray patients with psychoses.

The Change (color, 34 min.). UNC-CH, Producer; HSC, Distributor.

What does it feel like to slowly become psychotic? An actor plays a young man who slowly becomes confused, disoriented, and paranoid. (Trigger)

The Minotaur (color, 55 min.). UNC-CH, Producer; HSC, Distributor.

If the above tape is fun, this one is terrifying. Constantly rides on the edge of violence and perversity. Skilled teachers should guide students into realizing that psychotic people are rarely dangerous, but often they live in a world that feels tremendously dangerous.

*Taxi Driver (color, 112 min.).

A classic film that shows the internal evolution of a paranoid psychosis, starring Robert de Niro and Jody Foster.

Looking at the Brain: PET and the Pathophysiology of Schizophrenia (color, 21 min.). McNeil Pharmaceuticals.

Dr. Jonathan Brodie summarizes important findings of research groups about metabolic underactivity of the frontal lobes in schizophrenic patients.

CHAPTER 5: PERSONALITY DISORDERS

Personality Disorders: Simulated (color, 90 min.). WVU Department of Behavioral Medicine and Psychiatry.

Using actors who are also trained in psychiatry, the personality disorders are portrayed in interviews exactly as they should look according to DSM-III-R.

Psychiatry Learning Systems: Personality Disorders, Parts I and II (color, 33 min. each). University of South Carolina, Producer; HSC, Distributor.

Although the workbook discusses all personality disorders, the two tapes demonstrate only six of the categories: schizoid, histrionic (two examples), antisocial, borderline, compulsive, and passive–aggressive.

*Bonnie and Clyde (color, 111 min.).

Many people classify Bonnie and Clyde as psychotic killers of the 1920s, but I diagnose them as antisocial personality disorders.

*The Sterile Cuckoo (color, 107 min.) and Cabaret (color, 124 min.)

Do Liza Minelli's characters in these two movies have borderline personality disorders, histrionic personality disorders, or are they merely neurotic, as some people have suggested? She certainly is different.

*Fatal Attraction (color).

Glenn Close was nominated for an Academy Award for her portrayal of a woman with a borderline personality disorder in this frightening movie.

*Bad Boys (color, 123 min.).

Sean Penn gives an extremely realistic performance as an antisocial personality disorder in prison, so realistic that you feel his pain and the pain of people almost being able to help him.

*At Close Range (color, 111 min.).

This is a classic study of sociopathy. Sean Penn stars, but is not the sociopath!

CHAPTER 6: MOOD DISORDERS

Depression: Beating the Blues (color, 28 min.). Filmmakers Library.

An excellent overview and introduction to depression.

Depression: Signs and Symptoms (color, 10 min.). IMS, Faculty of Medicine, University of Toronto, and Medical Productions and Associates, Producers; The Altschul Group, Distributor.

Shorter and more superficial than the above, and useful for patients and their families as well as an introduction for medical students.

Simulated Psychiatric Profiles: Affective Disorders (color, 51 min.). UNC-CH and Burroughs-Wellcome, Producers; HSC, Distributor.

Six simulated interviews demonstrate bipolar illness, mania, and three varieties of major depression. (Trigger)

The Judgment (black and white, 15 min.). UNC-CH, Producer; HSC, Distributor.

After the above tapes are used for cognitive understanding and recognition of depression, this tape is excellent to raise empathy levels in students so they can better experience what it feels like to be depressed.

Four Lives (color, 60 min.). Fanlight Productions.

Four treated manic patients talk in a group about the way manic depressive illness has altered their lives, usually in devastating ways as they angered or frightened friends and family members to the point of losing them permanently.

'Night, Mother (color, 96 min.).

Film adaption of the Pulitzer Prize–winning Broadway play. Sissy Spacek plays the suicidal daughter who could be diagnosed as having dysthymia.

CHAPTER 7: ANXIETY DISORDERS

Attacking Anxiety (color, 28 min.). Rebecca Coffey, Veritas Programming.

Documentary on three patients with anxiety and their treatments.

Simulated Psychiatric Profiles: Anxiety Disorders, Parts I and II (color, 60 min.) UNC-CH and Burroughs-Wellcome, Producers; HSC, Distributor.

Five actors portray three patients with generalized anxiety, one with agoraphobia, and one with obsessive–compulsive anxiety. (Trigger)

Anxiety: Panic Disorder (color, 10 min.). IMS, Faculty of Medicine, University of Toronto, and Medical Productions and Associates, Producers; The Altschul Group, Distributor.

Very brief overview with interviews of patients and physicians describing symptoms and treatments, including behavioral modification and pharmacological and psychotherapy treatments.

CHAPTER 8: SOMATOFORM DISORDERS, FACTITIOUS DISORDERS, AND MALINGERING

Munchausen Syndrome (35 min.). Michael R. Louvain, M.D.

Shows a 30-year-old woman who spends most of her life in hospitals, up to 350 days in 1 year.

CHAPTER 9: ALCOHOLISM AND SUBSTANCE ABUSE

Angel Death (color, 33 min.). MTI Film & Video.

Paul Newman and Joanne Woodward narrate this Emmy Award–winning documentary about the impact of PCP on people. Shows research with animals.

Growing Up Stoned (color, 56 min.). Niemack/Hassett Productions, Inc.

HBO program for the award-winning "America Undercover" series. Interviews with three adolescents and their families—the teens live for being stoned or intoxicated.

Alcohol and Pregnancy (color, 17 min.). Edward A. Mason, M.D., Producer; Documentaries for Learning, Distributor.

Demonstrates techniques for taking a prenatal drinking history, counseling, and referring pregnant women who abuse alcohol. (Not reviewed, but recommended.)

Born with a Habit (color, 30 min.). Edward A. Mason, M.D., Producer; Documentaries for Learning, Distributor.

Covers problems of neonatal narcotic addiction, care of the mother, the great importance of prenatal care. Two addicted women talk about their experiences. (Not reviewed, but recommended.)

Cocaine: Beyond the Looking Glass (color, 30 min.). Hazeldon Foundation.

Documentary about cocaine addiction with interviews of several recovering addicts, including an anesthesiologist who has recovered and returned to practice.

The Case of the Frozen Addict (color, 60 min.). Cornet Film & Video.

A NOVA documentary. In 1982, a 42-year-old addict, George Carillo, took a bad batch of synthetic heroin, a designer drug, that unfortunately contained a chemical contaminant that did irreparable damage to his brain and left him with all of the symptoms of classic Parkinson's disease. Research on this contaminant, MPTP, has in turn yielded important clues as to the genesis of Parkinson's disease. Dramatically presents this scientific detective story.

Seniors and Alcohol Abuse (color, 23 min.). Joseph D. Peters, Producer; FMS Productions, Inc., Distributor.

A personal view of two recovering alcoholics. Their story and lives are interwoven with comments, insights, and advice from three noted experts in the field. A dream sequence, newsreel footage, and a montage were also used to illustrate various viewpoints. (Not reviewed, but recommended.)

Cocaine and the Student/Athlete, Part One (color, 20 min.). Creative Media and ESI Productions, Producer; Health Alert, Distributor.

A student talks about how he was once charged as a felon for using cocaine and how he can no longer vote, hunt, or feel free. Over 22 million Americans report using cocaine, with over 6 million claiming to use cocaine or crack daily. A brief history is given of cocaine and crack as they made their way from the natives in South America to the streets of the U.S.

Cocaine and the Student/Athlete, Part Two (color, 22 min., and on the same tape).

Addresses medical aspects of cocaine use: changing sleep patterns, loss of energy, irritability, forgetfulness, withdrawal, and nosebleeds.

*Days of Wine and Roses (117 min.).

A bit dated but still a classic.

*Clean and Sober

Michael Keaton in an excellent portrayal of the phenomenon of denial.

CHAPTER 10: PSYCHOLOGICAL FACTORS AFFECTING PHYSICAL CONDITION AND RESPONSE TO STRESS

Doctor? What's Wrong with Me? (color, 60 min.). UNC-CH, Producer; Doug Drossman, M.D., UNC Department of Medicine, Distributor.

Mrs. Byerly is depressed over her husband's death and living alone when her son moves far away, which is expressed as irritable bowel syndrome. (Trigger)

Simulated Psychiatric Profiles: Adjustment Disorders (color, 41 min., but first interview is only 20 min.). UNC-CH, Producer; HSC, Distributor.

Three young adults are interviewed in this docudrama as a group, each showing signs of stress following an accident in the insecticide research company where they work. The second simulated interview is a 12-year-old boy with adjustment disorder with suicidal thinking.

The Wall Within (color, 49 min.). CBS, Producer; Carousel Film & Video, Distributor.

Dan Rather reports on the 1 million Vietnam War U.S. veterans who suffer from posttraumatic stress disorder. Filmed in Washington State, where many of the veterans have settled to hide from society. Almost as many veterans have committed suicide as appear on the stone walls of the Vietnam War Veterans Memorial. Others abuse alcohol, drugs, or their families.

CHAPTER 11: EATING DISORDERS

The Enigma of Anorexia Nervosa, Part 1: Delusion and Discord (color, 18 min., 3/4-inch format). Carle Medical Communications.

Excellent overview of the thinking about eating disorders, present and past.

The Enigma of Anorexia Nervosa, Part 2: Clinical Intervention and Rehabilitation (color, 16 min., 3/4-inch format). Carle Medical Communications.

Although made with excellent technical quality, as was Part 1, it is disappointing in the dryness of the presentation. Part 2 may be better put to use as a nonemotional didactic presentation to patients.

The Enigma of Anorexia Nervosa, Part 3: The Battle of Wills (color, 26 min., 3/4-inch format). Carle Medical Communications.

Some may think this docudrama a bit melodramatic, but I would suggest they revisit adolescent units that treat patients with anorexia.

Anorexia is a Greek Word (Part II): Perception: The Personal Aspects of Therapy (color, 60 min.). Boston Family Institute.

Once in a while I view a tape or film that is not of very high video quality, but the content is overwhelming so as to forgive a little soft video focus. This is such a video. It is brilliant in content as Dr. Salvadore Minuchin interviews a family of seven whose 14-year-old daughter is anorexic.

Bulimia: The Binge–Purge Obsession (color, 25 min.). Carle Medical Communications.

Presented and narrated by Anita Siegman, Ph.D., with superb photography of food, restaurants, and patients worrying, exercising, and attending group therapy. In interviews or in narrations over video of themselves, patients talk about dieting, comparing themselves with peers, and feeling the need to binge.

CHAPTER 12: DISSOCIATIVE DISORDERS

Multiple Personality and Long-Term Psychotherapy (color, 30 min.). Kenneth Matthews, M.D., and Daniel Nelson, M.D., Producers; Kenneth Matthews, Distributor.

Illustrates various personalities of a 35-year-old woman with multiple personality disorder.

CHAPTER 13: PSYCHOSEXUAL DISORDERS

Sexual Problems (color, 50 min., VHS only). Sander J. Breiner, M.D.

A good lecture that covers genital compatibility, sexual attraction, sexual positions, sexual domination, forbidden sex, sex and sports, sexual frequency, sexual stimulants/aphrodisiacs, homosexual thoughts and feelings, mate selection, masturbation, dyspareunia, vaginismus, impotence, and sexual activity for the elderly. It has also been useful to educate patients with sexual symptoms.

Psychiatry Learning System: Psychosexual Disorders, Parts 1 and 2 (color and black and white, 30 min. and 48 min., respectively). University of South Carolina, Producer; HSC, Distributor.

Part 1 is a series of four interviews with one patient demonstrating the sexual identity disorder of transvestism.

CHAPTER 14: PARAPHILIAS

Men Who Molest (color). Rachael V. Lyon, Producer; Filmmaker's Library, Distributor.

As the extent of sexual abuse of children has become better known, the debate has increased over who should treat the abusers; what forms of treatment, if any, are effective; and what role the victim can play in terms of punishment and restitution in the whole process.

Psychiatry Learning Systems: Psychosexual Disorders. (See review above under Chapter 13.)

Part of this tape deals with voyeurism.

9½ Weeks

This film will be offensive to women, but exemplifies a degrading sadomasochistic sexual relationship.

CHAPTER 15: PSYCHIATRIC DISORDERS OF CHILDHOOD AND ADOLESCENCE

Attention-Deficit Disorder (and Disorders of Conduct)

Out of Control (color, 15 min.). ABC Video Enterprises, Producer; Film-makers Library, Inc., Distributor.

A "20/20" television show, somewhat outdated, about children with attention-deficit disorder frequently becoming criminals if not properly treated as children.

Boys in Conflict (color, 60 min.). Edward A. Mason, M.D., Producer; Documentaries for Learning, Distributor.

Shows a camp counselor's experiences with emotionally disturbed boys over an entire summer. Communicates a real sense of what it is like to deal with such children on a day-to-day basis. (Not reviewed, but recommended.)

Bruce (color, 26 min.). Edward A. Mason, M.D., Producer; Documentaries for Learning, Distributor.

Shows the struggles of a lonely, compulsive, angry, 13-year-old boy at a summer camp. He fights with everyone, threatens to run away, and explodes in a dramatic cabin group meeting. (Not reviewed, but recommended.)

Moonstones (color, 76 min.). UNC-CH, Producer; HSC, Distributor.

Docudrama of a 13-year-old boy admitted for raping a girl at knife point. Based on a true case study. (Trigger)

Psychiatry Learning System: Disorders of Infancy, Childhood, and Adolescence, Part 1 (color, 42 min.). University of South Carolina, Producer; HSC, Distributor.

The first 15 minutes show normal development. Remainder shows interviews of children or teenagers with psychiatric diagnoses.

Pervasive Developmental Disorders

Pervasive Developmental Disorders (color, 45 min.). Peter Goldfine, M.D.

Dr. Goldfine discusses the criteria for infantile autism and demonstrates this with videotaped patients.

Portrait of an Autistic Young Man (color, 49 min.). Daniel Hubert, M.D., and Addis Barnett, Ph.D., Producers; Behavioral Sciences Media Laboratory, Distributor.

Shows the peculiar symptomatology and lifestyle of a relatively functional, yet severely disabled, 24-year-old man in Huntington, West Virginia.

Rain Man

Oscar-winning movie of what could be construed as an autistic adult "idiot savant."

Anxiety Disorders and School Phobias

Medicine Playhouse: Play D (color, 20 min.). WVU Department of Behavioral Medicine and Psychiatry.

Simulated interview of a 9-year-old boy with school phobia.

Childhood Depression

Kids in Crisis (color, 56 min.). Niemack/Hassett Productions, Inc., Producer; International Film Bureau, Inc., Distributor.

This HBO tape was produced for the award-winning "America Undercover" series.

Medicine Playhouse: Play B (color, 35 min.). WVU Department of Behavioral Medicine and Psychiatry.

Diagnosing children is not easy because, like adults, they often do not fall neatly into one category. This is a play staged for television about an 11-year-old girl who probably has depression but covers it with misbehaving, suicidal attempts, arguing, and abusing drugs. (Trigger)

Mental Retardation

And Then Came John (color, 45 min.). Scott Andrews, Cultural and Educational Media and Telesis Productions International, Producers; Filmmakers Library, Distributor.

Old photographs of John, who has Down's syndrome, current videotapes of John, and interviews of John and his parents capture the pleasures and pains of being retarded and caring for someone who is retarded.

CHAPTER 16: THE PSYCHOTHERAPIES: BASIC THEORETICAL PRINCIPLES, TECHNIQUES, AND INDICATIONS

Psychoanalytic Psychotherapy

The Talking Cure: A Portrait of Psychoanalysis (color, 56 min.). AIMS Media.

Experimental approach combining images from patients' daily lives with their personal reflections to help explain what happens in psycho-analysis. (Not reviewed.)

Once Upon a Couch: Gretel (color, 105 min., or divided into ten segments averaging about 15 min. each). UNC-CH, Producer; HSC, Distributor.

For use by instructors who have great respect for psychoanalytic-based psychotherapy and who have the time to have fun with their students.

A Bad Baseball (color, 50 min.). UNC-CH, Producer; HSC, Distributor.

An actor faces the camera so the audience feels they are the therapist as this man is treated in six sessions excerpted from 36 psycho-analytically based psychotherapy sessions. (Trigger)

Three Approaches to Psychotherapy: I and II (black and white, 16-mm, six reels of 48 min. each). Psychological Films, Inc.

Three interviews in 1965 by Drs. Carl Rogers, Frederick Perls, and Albert Ellis demonstrating their methods of therapy with introductions and descriptions.

Equus

Pure culture Freudian drama, demonstrating a psychoanalytic treat-ment.

Behavioral Therapies

Mind Over Medicine (color, 55 min.). WCCO-TV, Producer; Indiana University Audio-Visual Center, Distributor.

Shows a number of physicians and patients working with techniques such as biofeedback, hypnosis, and acupuncture to deal with problems ranging from asthma to acute pain. (Not reviewed.)

Psychiatry Learning System: Behavioral Treatment, Parts I and II (color, 31 and 25 min., respectively). University of South Carolina, Producer; HSC, Distributor.

Part I demonstrates three behavioral therapies: (1) progressive relax-ation in individual therapy, (2) systematic desensitization with the same patient now that he's learned to relax, and (3) assertiveness training in group therapy, including use of role-playing techniques. Part II demonstrates cognitive therapy in a simulated interview with a "patient" anxious about speaking in crowds.

Hypnosis in Psychotherapy (color, 22 min.). UNC-CH, Producer; HSC, Distributor.

Each of the three vignettes on this tape presents a different patient situation and a different application of hypnosis: one motivated, one resistant, and another with a group. The program's goal is to give the user an understanding of the techniques and use of hypnosis as it may be applied in psychotherapy. (Trigger)

Time-mirror (color, 37 min.). James H. Lurie, M.D.

This award-winning teaching tape illustrates the office use of video replay with simple, inexpensive equipment. (Not reviewed, but recom-mended.)

Cognitive Therapies

Demonstration of the Cognitive Therapy of Depression: The First Inter-view (black and white, 40 min.). Center for Cognitive Therapy.

Aaron T. Beck conducts an interview with a simulated patient demon-strating preparation of the agenda, defining specific problems, and developing solutions.

Demonstration of the Cognitive Therapy of Depression: A Dramatiza-tion—Acute Exacerbation of Depression and Suicidal Wishes (black and white, 45 min.). Center for Cognitive Therapy.

Dr. Aaron T. Beck uses the same simulated patient from above to demonstrate cognitive therapy in a relapsed depressive patient. (Not reviewed, but recommended.)

Cognitive Therapy with Hopeless, Depressed Patients (black and white, 35 min.).

Produced and distributed by the same team in the two tapes above, but this is with an actual patient treated by Dr. Beck and requires special permission from him and the Center for Cognitive Therapy.

Group Therapy

An Adolescent Group: Social Springboard for Personal Growth (color, 33 min.). Edward A. Mason, M.D., Producer; Documentaries for Learning, Distributor.

Focuses on two boys and the changes they make in group therapy as they resolve conflicts and acquire new social skills and insight. (Not reviewed, but recommended.)

Collaborative Alliances (color, 50 min., but up to several hours in full version). Ian Alger, M.D., Producer; Family Studies Health, Distributor.

Designed to teach health professionals and staff how to develop psychoeducational programs for families and how to form and manage multiple-family groups.

Marital and Family Therapy

Family Therapy Consultation (color, 95 min.). H. James Lurie, M.D.

This two-part videotape highlights the work of Carl Whitaker. In the first tape, Dr. Whitaker joins the therapist and the family for a live consultation interview, shown in its entirety, and demonstrates the greater flexibility allowed a consultant as compared with the usual strategy used in a regular therapeutic session. (Not reviewed, but recommended.)

Marital Crisis (color, 60 min.). H. James Lurie, M.D.

Follows the course of a couple reenacting a brief nine-session therapy with Ian Alger, M.D., during which time there is a resolution of the acute crisis that threatened their marriage.

Sexual Dysfunction Therapy

Coping with Serious Illness: Sexuality (color, 30 min.). Time–Life Video, Producer; Time–Life Multimedia, Distributor.

Meryl Streep briefly introduces the topic and is not heard from again. Physicians, sex therapists, patients, and patients' spouses discuss the impact of disease upon sexuality.

Human Sexuality Videotape Series: Loving and Caring: Problem Solving (color, 15 min.). Sheldon Kule, D.O., and Med-Pro Productions, Producers; HSC, Distributor.

Dr. Kule briefly discusses sex therapy beginning with a warning that many states do not require a license for sex therapists, so it is imperative that patients question the qualifications of the therapists and contact medical schools or clinicians they trust to verify the respectability of their sex therapist.

CHAPTER 17: BIOLOGICAL THERAPIES FOR MENTAL DISORDERS

Psychopharmacology

Subjective Response to Psychoactive Drug Therapy (color, 16 min.). Theodore Van Putten, M.D., Producer; West Glen Communications, Distributor.

> *Shows the variety of responses that patients may have when they develop drug-induced extrapyramidal reactions. (Not reviewed.)*

Abnormal Involuntary Movement Scale in Acute EPS (color, 16 min.). Richard Borison, M.D., Ph.D., Producer; West Glen Communications, Distributor.

> *Shows patients who are on neuroleptics and have developed resultant acute movement disorders: tremors, dystonias, and akathisia. (Not reviewed.)*

Schizophrenia: Use and Side Effects of Medications (color, 10 min.). IMS, Faculty of Medicine, University of Toronto, and Medical Productions and Associates, Producers; The Altschul Group, Distributor.

> *Excellent artwork is first used as a metaphor in this concise overview of schizophrenia.*

Depression: Uses and Side Effects of Medications (color, 10 min.). IMS, Faculty of Medicine, University of Toronto, and Medical Productions and Associates, Producers; The Altschul Group, Distributor.

> *Good, brief overview of the tricyclics and monoamine oxidase inhibitors, including side effects, dosage, onset of action, precautions in changing from tricyclics to MAOIs, and precautions of MAOIs with diet (tyramine).*

Electroconvulsive Therapy

See Chapter 6 (Mood Disorders) for "Depression, Beating the Blues."

Electronic Textbook of Psychiatry: Electroshock Therapy in Depressive Illness (black and white, 30 min.). College of Physicians and Surgeons, Producer; Educational Research, Distributor.

> *A patient suffering from recurrent unipolar depression is interviewed before her course of electroshock therapy and discusses her symptoms and attitudes toward the treatment. She is then shown undergoing actual treatment. She is reinterviewed 6 months later and contrasts her behavior in the depressed and recovered states. (Not reviewed.)*

CHAPTER 18: PSYCHIATRIC EMERGENCIES: RECOGNITION AND MANAGEMENT

Suicidal Patients

Adolescent Depression and Suicide (color, 10 min.). IMS, Faculty of Medicine, University of Toronto, and Medical Productions and Associates, Producers; The Altschul Group, Distributor.

> *Brief and well-done interviews with a suicidal teenage boy who receives treatment. Treatment techniques of talking therapy, group therapy, and role-playing therapy are discussed.*

Simulated Psychiatric Profiles: Adjustment Disorders (color, 41 min.). UNC-CH, Producer; HSC, Distributor.

> *The first of two interviews is a nonemergency situation and is reviewed in Chapter 10. The second interview is a superb and moving simulated interview with a 12-year-old boy who threatened to shoot himself.*

Violent Patients

Management and Treatment of Violent Patients (color, 48 min.). Jim Lurie, M.D., Producer; University of Washington Instructional Media Services, Distributor.

> *Many simulated physician–patient violent and potentially violent interactions are presented. Viewers can stop the tape after each scene, discuss and assess, then continue the tape to see how the authors recommend handling the situations.*

The Art of Intervention (color, 24 min.). DMH.

> *Docudrama on violence prevention in institutions is quite realistic. Patient hurls a chair across the room, and the staff is shown handling his escalating behaviors in an incorrect manner and then in a proper manner.*

Why Did Johnny Kill? (color, 60 min.). Niemack/Hassett Productions, Inc.

> *HBO documentary from the Emmy Award–winning series "America Undercover" explores the lives of three teenage boys who are incarcerated for murder.*

Acute Psychosis

Management and Treatment of the Violent Patient. (See "Violent Patients.")

Case 2 of the many cases presented discusses well how to handle a potentially violent psychotic patient.

Child and Spouse Abuse

The Unquiet Death of Eli Creekmore (color, 55 min.). KCT Seattle 9, Producer; Filmakers Library, Distributor.

This grim documentary of a child brutally killed by his parents prompts discussion about child abuse, what we as health professionals can and should do about it, and the complex issues of how involved the state should be in protecting children from suspected family abuse versus keeping children at home at all costs.

Generations of Violence (color, 58 min.). Filmakers Library.

When one generation of children is treated violently, they treat the next generation of children violently.

Early Misgivings (color, 29 min., 3/4-inch format). Leonard Kurtz, Stanford University.

Superb introduction to child abuse.

Breaking Silence (color, 58 min.). Theresa Tollini, Producer; Distribution Center, Distributor.

Through the juxtaposition of interviews, photographs, and children's drawings, "Breaking Silence" reveals the dynamics of incest and child sexual abuse. (Not reviewed.)

Surviving Sexual Abuse (color, 27 min.). University of California Extension Media Center.

Two women and two men talk about their experiences of being sexually abused and how they survived. Shocking and deeply moving.

To a Safer Place (color, 58 min.). National Film Board of Canada.

The woman who produced this film was abused sexually by her father. She interviews the father and her sibs.

Sexual Abuse (color, 18 min.). National College of District Attorneys, and University of Texas Medical Branch at Galveston, Producers; HSC, Distributor.

Although the material is presented by a fairly stilted narrator, the close-up medical slides of the damaged genitals of abused children are disturbingly engaging. The narrator discusses sexual abuse and the legal responsibilities of notifying proper authorities, the emotional impact of sexual abuse upon families, and interventions such as legally removing children from abusive homes.

Response: Child Sexual Abuse, the Clinical Interview (color, 60 min.). United Way, Inc., and Children's Institute International.

An excellent blend of graphics, interviews with children, and narration.

Rape

Rapists: Can They Be Stopped? (color, 55 min.). John Zaritsky, Producer; Filmakers Library, Distributor.

Five male participants in the Oregon State Hospital are being rehabilitated for sexual offenses. They tell their hideous stories. They are treated with aversion therapy and negative reinforcement after being shown pornography, are forced to confront their victims, and are given drugs to lower male hormone levels. Most sex offenders drop out of the program, preferring prison. Those who stay in the program have high rehabilitation rates.

The Confrontation (color, 37 min.). Women Make Movies.

Docudrama portraying recent actions taken by women to deal with rape. After a woman has been raped, her friends and counselor try to seek justice through the legal system, all to no avail. They choose alternative action.

Forensic Issues in Emergency Psychiatry: Competency and Commitment

Commitment Evaluation (color, 20 min.). UNC-CH, Producer; HSC, Distributor.

Two actors (one is really a psychiatrist) re-create an almost verbatim interview of a psychiatrist evaluating a patient for commitment.

CHAPTER 19: PSYCHIATRIC ASPECTS OF MEDICAL PRACTICE

Managing Normal Grief and Identifying Pathological Grief Reactions: Dying Patients

In Our Sorrow: Hope (color). Eddy H. Pakes, M.D., Producer; Mt. Sinai Hospital, Distributor.

An interview with a group of women who have each lost a child. The women each participated in a self-help session led by other trained bereaved parents and supervised by a psychiatrist.

Some Babies Die (color, 54 min.). University of California Extension Media Center.

Australian documentary shows a counseling team helping grief-stricken families as they deal with depression and guilt after stillbirths and neonatal deaths.

Riding the Gale (color, 45 min.). Genni and Kim Batterham, Producers; Filmakers Library, Inc., Distributor.

Documentary about a New Zealand woman struggling with multiple sclerosis. Excellent at demonstrating grieving.

Julie and Bob: A 36-Year-Old Woman Dying of Cancer (color, 35 min.). Adult Program.

Covers the years from 1983 to 1986 in the life of a woman dying from cancer, up to 6 days before her death.

*Ordinary People (color, 123 min.).

A classic motion picture depicting an unresolved grief reaction in an adolescent boy over the death of his brother and how it affected both him and the family. Directed by Robert Redford.

CHAPTER 20: PSYCHIATRIC ASPECTS OF ACQUIRED IMMUNE DEFICIENCY SYNDROME (AIDS)

Chuck Solomon: Coming of Age (color, 58 min.). The Cinema Guild.

Many of the films and videotapes about AIDS are depressing throughout, but this moving and upbeat tape is a documentary showing how one AIDS victim and his San Francisco theater friends chose to celebrate his life while he was still alive rather than give in to the despair that is all too common with this tragic illness.

Too Little, Too Late (color, 48 min.). Fanlight Productions.

For every AIDS patient, the lives of at least eight family members and close friends are profoundly affected.

AIDS: All Involved Deserve Support (color, 50 min.). Dennis M. O'Connor, M.D., Producer; Department of Mental Health, State of California, Distributor.

Addresses couples dealing with AIDS and their need for support.

AIDS: A Priest's Testament (color, 52 min.). Strongbow Marketing.

Father Bernard Lynch, Irish-born U.S. priest, is a psychotherapist who set up an AIDS ministry in New York. He discusses the pressures of his work with AIDS patients.

*An Early Frost

AIDS comes home to the family.

CHAPTER 21: SLEEP DISORDERS

Regulating Sleep in the Elderly (color, 13 min.). Joel Posner, M.D., Producer; West Glen Communications, Distributor.

Shows the problems nursing staffs find in evaluating causes of sleep difficulty in the elderly.

CHAPTER 22: BASIC PRINCIPLES OF PAIN MANAGEMENT

Pain and Healing (color, 60 min., part of the nine-part series "The Mind"). WNET, New York, Producer; PBS Video, Distributor.

What is the mind's role in healing the body and controlling pain? Explores the ways in which attitudes affect patterns of disease and pain.

CHAPTER 23: BEHAVIORAL MEDICINE STRATEGIES FOR MEDICAL PATIENTS

Cigarette Smoking

Showdown on Tobacco Road (color, 60 min.). David Hoffman and Kirk Wolfinger, Varied Directions, Inc., Producers; PBS Video, Distributor.

Traces the history of tobacco use and interviews people on both sides of the smoking/no-smoking debate. Winner of Gold Award, John Muir Medical Film Festival.

Hugh McCabe: The Coach's Final Lesson (color, 18 min.). Herbert H. Rosen, Producer; American Lung Association, Distributor. (Free when available, otherwise available from Pyramid Film and Video.)

There is no better way to teach about nicotine addiction than by using this tape. Mr. McCabe was a high school teacher and football coach who

*was admired and loved by his students and community. He died in
1986 from lung cancer.*

Obesity

Heavy Load (color, 36 min.). Johnny Stevens Films, Inc.

Short narrative about a woman who suffers from the disease of compulsive overeating. Depicts how the family and friends are affected. Winner of CINE's Golden Eagle Award. (Not reviewed.)

Being a Fat Child (color, 15 min.). ABC News, Producer; MTI Film &
Video, Distributor.

*An ABC "20/20" segment dealing with adolescent obesity, one of the
most serious problems of childhood. Includes the problems these children face from social stigmata and includes how proper nutrition,
exercise, and behavior modification can control adolescent weight.*

Addresses:

United Way, Inc.
621 S. Virgil
Los Angeles, CA 90005

Health Sciences Consortium
201 Silver Cedar Court
Chapel Hill, NC 27514
919-942-8731

Media Guild
P.O. Box 88
Solana Beach, CA 92075
714-755-9195

The Altschul Group
930 Pitner Ave.
Evanston, IL 60202
312-328-6700

Butterworth Inc.
19 Cummings Park
Woburn, MA 01801

Health Alert
123 4th St., NW
Charlottesville, VA 22901

Carle Medical Communications
510 West Main St.
Urbana, IL 61801
217-384-4838

The Cinema Guild
1697 Broadway
Room 8102
New York, NY 10019

Mt. Sinai Hospital
Attn: Eddy H. Pakes, MD
600 University Ave.
Toronto, Ontario, Canada M5G 1X5

Fanlight Productions
47 Halifax St.
Boston, MA 02130

The Boston Family Institute
251 Harvard St.
Brookline, MA 02146

Coronet Films & Video
108 Wilmot Rd.
Deerfield, IL 60015
1-800-621-2131
(in Illinois or Alaska: 312-940-1260)

MTI Film & Video
108 Wilmot Rd.
Deerfield, IL 60015
(Same as Coronet)

Center for Cognitive Therapy
Department of Psychiatry
University of Pennsylvania
Room 602
133 South 36th St.
Philadelphia, PA 19104

American Medical Association
Medical School Section
535 North Dearborn St.
Chicago, IL 60610
312-645-5000

American Psychiatric Association
Office of Education
1400 K. St., N.W.
Washington, DC 20005

Documentaries for Learning
Massachusetts Mental Health Center
Harvard Medical School
74 Fenwood Rd.
Boston, MA 02115-6196
617-566-6793

Hazeldon Foundation
Box 176
Center City, Minnesota 55012-0176
1-800-328-0500

H. James Lurie, MD
Division of Community Psychiatry
University of Washington
School of Medicine
Seattle, WA 98195

Indiana University
Audio-Visual Center
Bloomington, IN 47405

FMS Productions, Inc.
520 East Montecito, Suite F
Santa Barbara, CA 93104

Filmakers Library, Inc.
124 E. 40th St.
New York, NY 10022
212-355-6545

Psychological Films, Inc.
Distribution Center
1215 East Chapman Ave.
Orange, CA 92669

Medical Interview Tapes
P.O. Box 3272
Chapel Hill, NC 27515-3272
919-966-3378 (Eric Jensen, M.D.)

Peter Goldfine, M.D.
Maine Medical Center
22 Bramhall St.
Portland, ME 04102

Doug Drossman, M.D.
Department of Medicine
Gastroenterology
UNC-CH School of Medicine
Chapel Hill, NC 27514
919-966-2511

Distribution Center
13500 NE 124th St., Suite 2
Kirkland, WA 98034

Kenneth Matthews, M.D.
UTHSC San Antonio
Department of Psychiatry
7703 Floyd Curl Dr.
San Antonio, TX 78284
512-567-5430

Veritas Programming
343 Seventh Ave.
New York, NY 10001

Niemack/Hassett Productions, Inc.
12001 Ventura Place
Suite 401
Studio City, CA 91604
818-508-8477

Phoenix Films & Video, Inc.
468 Park Ave. South
New York, NY 10016
212-684-5910

Sander J. Breiner, M.D.
7410 Franklin Rd.
Birmingham, MI 48010

AIMS Media
6901 Woodley Ave.
Van Nuys, CA 91406-4878
1-800-367-2467
(in California or Alaska: 818-785-4111)

Pierre Leichner, M.D.
Douglas Hospital
6875 Lasalle Blvd.
Verdun PQ
Canada H4H 1R3

McNeil Pharmaceutical
Haldol Product Manager
Springhouse, PA 19477

DMH
Atascadero State Hospital
P.O. Box 7001
Atascadero, CA 93423

International Film Bureau, Inc.
332 South Michigan Ave.
Chicago, IL 60604-4382
312-427-4545

Johnny Stevens Films, Inc.
4265 Brownsboro Rd.
Suite 168
Winston-Salem, NC 27106
919-721-0494

PBS Video
1320 Braddock Place
Alexandria, VA 22314-1698
1-800-344-3337

American Lung Association
1740 Broadway Ave.
New York, NY 10019

Michel R. Louvain, M.D.
300 N. State, Suite 5307
Chicago, IL 60610

WVU Department of Behavioral
  Medicine and Psychiatry
930 Chestnut Ridge Rd.
Morgantown, WV 26505
304-293-2411

National Film Board of Canada
1251 Ave. of the Americas
16th Floor
New York, NY 10020

Educational Research
New York State Psychiatric Institute
722 W. 168th St.
New York, NY 10032

Hubert Daniel, M.D.
14523 Hesby St.
Sherman Oaks, CA 91403

Carousel Film and Video
260 Fifth Ave.
New York, NY 10001
212-683-1660

Beacon Films
P.O. Box 575
Norwood, MA 02062
1-800-322-3307

University of California
Extension Media Center
2176 Shattuck Ave.
Berkeley, CA 94704
415-642-0460

Adult Program
Mt. Airy Psychiatric Center
4455 E. 12th Ave.
Denver, CO 80220

Family Studies Health Science Institute
1202 Lexington Ave.
Suite 226
New York, NY 10028

Department of Mental Health
State of California
1600 Ninth St.
Room 151
Sacramento, CA 95814

Strongbow Marketing
15 Sir John Togerson's Quay
Dublin 2
Ireland

Time–Life Multi-media
Women Make Movies, Inc.
225 Lafayette St., 211
New York, NY 10012
212-925-0606

West Glen Communications
1430 Broadway
New York, NY 10018
212-921-2800

(All productions in this review distributed by West Glen are also available on loan for free from: Film Department, Sandoz Pharmaceuticals, East Hanover, NJ 07936) Students, course directors, and instructors interested in obtaining an updated version of this annotated audiovisual bibliography may contact:

Donald C. Fidler, M.D.
Chestnut Ridge Hospital
930 Chestnut Ridge Road
Morgantown WV 26505
304-293-4000

Index

Page numbers followed by f indicate figures;
those followed by t indicate tabular material